Evolution and Behavior

GREG KRUKONIS • TRACY BARR •
TARA RODDEN ROBINSON

BIO 130
Henry Ford Community College

Wiley Custom Learning Solutions

ISBN 978-1-118-89546-7

10 9 8 7 6 5 4 3 2 1

Brief Contents

Taken from: *Genetics for Dummies*, Second Edition by Tara Rodden Robinson

Evolution FOR DUMMIES®

by Greg Krukonis, PhD, and Tracy Barr

WILEY

John Wiley & Sons, Inc.

Evolution For Dummies®

Published by
John Wiley & Sons, Inc.
111 River St.
Hoboken, NJ 07030-5774
www.wiley.com

WILEY

About the Authors

Dr. Greg Krukonis: Greg Kukonis has a Bachelor of Arts degree in Biology from the University of Pennsylvania and a PhD from the University of Arizona, Department of Ecology and Evolutionary Biology. He has been a postdoctoral researcher at Wesleyan University in Middletown, Connecticut, and Stanford University. He is currently an adjunct assistant professor of biology at Lewis and Clark College in Portland, Oregon.

Tracy Barr: Tracy Barr is a professional writer and editor who has authored or co-authored several other books for Wiley, including *Adoption For Dummies, Cast-Iron Cooking For Dummies, Yorkshire Terriers For Dummies,* and *Latin For Dummies.* She lives in Indianapolis with her husband and four children.

Dedication

From Greg: To my family, to Tarsah, and to the mentors, colleagues, and students who have shared their insights, their enthusiasm, and their friendship. And to everyone who's ever wondered what evolution really is and to anyone who's ever been struck by the beautiful and amazing diversity of life on Earth.

Acknowledgments

From Greg: I'd like to thank my friends and colleagues who were always telling me, "Greg, you should write more" and who encouraged me throughout the project. It turns out that I did have a book in me, but it definitely took a village to help me find my voice. To say that I got by with a little help from my friends doesn't begin to describe my gratitude for the both the general encouragement and the numerous specific helpful suggestions I was so fortunate to receive.

I would also like to give thanks for the limitless amount of patience that has been shown me in the face of an ever-changing and over extended schedule, late nights, canceled plans, and the various unexpected challenges inherent in such a project. A special thanks goes to Stacy Kennedy and the other folks at Wiley who were instrumental in bringing this book to life.

Finally I'd like to acknowledge the many conversations about evolution I've had with random strangers I've met on airplanes, in coffee shops, and at cocktail parties — everywhere from the top of a cold mountain in New Hampshire to a toasty warm pub in New Zealand. I learned a lot from those conversations about what people want to know about evolution and where things get confusing, and I've tried to address these areas in this book.

Publisher's Acknowledgments

We're proud of this book; please send us your comments through our Dummies online registration form located at www.dummies.com/register/.

Some of the people who helped bring this book to market include the following:

Acquisitions, Editorial, and Media Development

Acquisitions Editor: Stacy Kennedy

Copy Editor: Kathy Simpson

Technical Editor: Veronique Delesalle, Professor of Biology, Gettysburg College

Senior Editorial Manager: Jennifer Ehrlich

Editorial Supervisor and Reprint Editor: Carmen Krikorian

Editorial Assistants: Erin Calligan Mooney, Joe Niesen, Leeann Harney

Art Coordinator: Alicia South

Cover Photos: © Sally A. Morgan; Ecoscene/CORBIS

Cartoons: Rich Tennant (www.the5thwave.com)

Composition Services

Project Coordinator: Erin Smith

Layout and Graphics: Claudia Bell, Alissa D. Ellet, Joyce Haughey

Proofreaders: John Greenough, C.M. Jones

Indexer: Glassman Indexing Services

Publishing and Editorial for Consumer Dummies

Kathleen Nebenhaus, Vice President and Executive Publisher

Kristin Ferguson-Wagstaffe, Product Development Director

Ensley Eikenburg, Associate Publisher, Travel

Kelly Regan, Editorial Director, Travel

Publishing for Technology Dummies

Andy Cummings, Vice President and Publisher

Composition Services

Debbie Stailey, Director of Composition Services

Contents at a Glance

Table of Contents

Introduction

*E*volution is the process by which populations and species change over time. The principles of evolution explain why life on Earth is so varied and why organisms are the way they are. The study of evolution is not only interesting for its own sake, but it's also a fundamental part of the biological sciences. You can't understand (or combat) disease, can't understand the history of species (or the world, for that matter) — can't do a lot of things, in fact, without understanding evolution.

Simply put, evolution is *the* key scientific principle behind every substantive thing we know about biology, the study of living things. And its main points are remarkably easy to understand.

So why did I write a whole book about evolution? Because a lot of people are confused about exactly what evolution is, what it does, how it works, and why it's important. This book helps you sort everything out.

About This Book

You may have the sense that only the super-smart can understand any branch of science. If you didn't see the point of being able to identify the parts of a cell, or you didn't like memorizing the periodic table of elements, your experience confirms that sense. And you've probably figured out that you're no Einstein, but — here's a secret — most scientists (including yours truly) aren't Einsteins either.

In fact, the smart money says that Einstein was so smart that most of the rest of us aren't smart enough even to know how smart he was. A possible exception may be someone like Stephen Hawking, but none of us is smart enough to know how smart *he* is, either. But I digress. The point is that you don't have to be an Einstein or a Hawking to "get" science. As I'm fond of saying to my students, evolution isn't rocket science — and for that matter, rocket science isn't rocket science either.

I wrote this book to help you overcome whatever natural reluctance you may have about reading an evolution book and to clear away the confusion caused by all the bad info out there. To that end, I've divided each chapter into sections that contain information about some component of evolution or one of the many hot topics that evolutionary biology helps people understand, such as:

- ✔ What natural selection is and how it works
- ✔ How to trace the evolutionary history of organisms
- ✔ The evolutionary component of social systems
- ✔ Where modern man came from
- ✔ How diseases evolve, and what scientists are doing to fight them

If there's one thing I want you to take away from this book, it's this: The lion's share of science, if explained clearly, is accessible to everyone. Sure, you have to be an expert in the field to fully grasp the importance of the details. But the broad strokes should be accessible to everyone, and that is certainly the case for evolutionary biology.

Conventions Used in This Book

To help you navigate easily, this book uses a few standard conventions:

- ✔ *Italic* is used for emphasis and to highlight new words or terms that are defined.
- ✔ `Monofont` is used for Web addresses.
- ✔ You'll also see quite a bit of *we* in this book. Sometimes, *we* refers to me and other experts in the field of evolution. At other times, *we* refers to me and you. Just like you, I am constantly amazed by and in awe of the beauty of evolution.

What You're Not to Read

I love everything about evolution: the big points, the little points, the so-eso-teric-that-no-one-but-other-evolutionary-biologists-will-find-them-even-remotely-interesting points. I'd love to think that you're just as enamored of evolution as I am, but being a realist (and scientist), I have to face facts: You probably aren't. So to meet my need (to include as much information as possible) and yours (to get to the key points quickly), I've made it easy for you to identify material that you can safely skip:

   ✔ **Text in sidebars:** The sidebars are the shaded boxes that appear here and there. They aren't necessary reading.

   ✔ **Anything with a Technical Stuff icon attached:** This information is interesting but not critical to your understanding of evolution.

Foolish Assumptions

Every book is written with a particular reader in mind, and this one is no different. As I wrote this book, I made a few assumptions about you:

   ✔ You've heard about Charles Darwin but aren't quite clear about what he actually said or why it was so revolutionary.

   ✔ You're confused by all the contradictory claims you hear about evolution and want to know what the science actually says.

   ✔ You're curious about the evolution of species, both in general — where do they come from, for example — and more close to home, such as the evolution of our own species and the diseases that plague us and which seem to grow more dangerous with every new generation.

   ✔ You've seen the 1960 film *Inherit the Wind,* and beyond noting that Darrin Stephens is the defendant, you want to know the science behind the events depicted.

   ✔ Even though you know that 99.9999 percent of scientists accept the theory of evolution, you need proof that these 99.9999 percent aren't wrong.

How This Book Is Organized

To help you find information that you're looking for, this book is divided into five parts. Each part covers a particular aspect of evolution and contains chapters relating to that part.

Part 1: What Evolution Is

Look up the word *evolution* in a dictionary, and you'll come across a definition that says something about change or maybe change through time. That's good as far as it goes. But in the context of biology, evolution refers to specific changes — genetic changes — in a group of organisms through time. That concept isn't so hard to grasp, but you may be surprised by how revolutionary the idea of evolution was in the mid-1800s, when Darwin came up with his theory explaining what could cause such changes (natural selection).

Back then, the concept that species could change over time — even the concept of vast time spans — was foreign and frightening to most people. But facts are facts, evidence has a way of piling up, and the science of evolutionary biology has progressed in the century and a half since Darwin's major insight.

This part introduces the key principles of evolution by natural selection. And because to grasp the main idea, you need to know a bit about genetics, the part includes a brief discussion of that topic, too. If it makes you feel any better (and it should), reading this short discussion of genetics puts you in the position of knowing more about genetics and heredity than Darwin himself did.

Part II: How Evolution Works

Sometimes, evolution is the result of natural selection. Other times, it's the result of random factors (genetic drift). Populations have variability; not all the individuals are the same, and sometimes individuals with particular genetic traits leave more descendant than others. That's evolution in a nut shell: The next generation is genetically different from the last one because not everybody's genes made it! These changes can have big effects on populations. Sometimes they end up with altered proportions of different variants (more fast cheetahs than slow ones, for example). Sometimes, they lose genetic variation, and sometimes, just sometimes, populations speciate (that is, form a new species).

You can consider this part to be the nuts-and-bolts section of the book, because it explains that biological variation exists, where this variation comes from, and the different ways it can change through time. Plus this is the part where I explain how scientists can watch evolution happen both in laboratory experiments and in nature, as well as how they can use data about species today to come up with strong hypothesis about evolution in the past.

Part III: What Evolution Does

Evolution is no more complicated than genetic changes accumulating through time. Sounds almost boring, yet it's anything *but* boring. Because all those changes in the DNA, which you can't even see (outside a biology lab) influence all the things about living creatures that you cannot only see, but also be amazed by. Look out the window at nature's diversity: Evolution did that! Evolution has a pretty big impact on lots of things you can observe about life, such as:

- ✔ Physical characteristics (petal color, length of tail, eye color, and so on)
- ✔ Body shape (number of fins, fingers, limbs, and heads, for example)
- ✔ Sexual selection (who mates with whom, how, and why)
- ✔ Life histories (reproduction and life spans)
- ✔ Social behaviors (competitive, altruistic, and so on)

This part covers 'em all.

Part IV: Evolution and Your World

Two things hold folks' attention better than anything else: themselves and things that affect them. This part covers both topics, beginning with human evolution to explain where we came from (out of Africa), whether we're unique among all the animals in creation (it turns out that we aren't; quite a few other hominid species preceded us, and a couple even shared the Earth with us for a while), and how we continue to evolve.

The remainder of the part delves into antibiotic resistance and the evolution of two scourges: HIV and influenza. Why the shift from the exalted Us to the microbial Them? Because these buggers can and do wreak havoc on humans by evolving so quickly and in response to the very medications we use to fight them. Perhaps you've seen on the news that bacteria have "acquired" or "developed" antibiotic resistance. Those are just other ways of saying that these bacteria have evolved resistance to our antibiotics — a problem that we need to stay on top of.

Part V: The Part of Tens

Throughout the book, I spend a lot of time talking about the fossil record and adaptations, explaining what they are and why they're important to evolutionary study. But in this part, I list the fossils and adaptations that are particularly fun or revealing.

I also include the only response you're going to find to the challenges people throw at evolution. The purpose of these challenges isn't to clarify the science of evolution but to promote a particular theology. Unfortunately, the challengers do this by misstating scientific facts, which I clear up in this part.

Icons Used in This Book

The icons in this book help you find particular kinds of information that may be of use to you.

Sometimes, you can understand a scientific point by looking at it a little differently or comparing it to something similar, and this icon appears next to material that helps you do that.

This icon points out evolutionary principles that you want to remember because they're important to the topic at hand or because they're fundamental to understanding evolutionary biology.

This icon appears beside information that is interesting but not necessary to know. In fact, feel free to skip the info here, if you want. Doing so won't impair your understanding of evolution.

Sure, I could just tell you what evolutionary biologists say about evolution, but I prefer to show you how they know. This icon appears next to sections about scientific experiments designed to test evolutionary processes. And because the whole point of experiments is to test an idea, not to build up proof that the idea is right, some of these case studies end up revealing things that the researchers didn't necessarily expect.

Where to Go from Here

This book is organized so that you can go wherever you want to find complete information. Want to know about the role natural selection plays in evolution? Head to Chapter 5. If you're interested in the link between individual fitness and how certain social systems develop, go to Chapter 11. You can use the table of contents to find broad categories of information or the index to look up more specific things.

If you're just beginning to learn about evolution, I suggest that you start with Part I. It gives you all the basic information about evolutionary principles and points to places where you can find more detailed information.

Part I
What Evolution Is

The 5th Wave   By Rich Tennant

In this part . . .

Evolution is the process that explains how organisms change over time. It's really as simple — and as profound — as that. And in this part, I begin with the very basics: key evolutionary principles, from Darwin's day to today. You'll also find a very brief discussion of genetics. Why? Because the only changes that are important to evolutionary study are genetic ones.

Chapter 1

What Evolution Is and Why You Need to Know

In This Chapter

▶ Understanding what evolution is

▶ Introducing the scientific field of evolutionary biology

▶ Realizing why evolution is relevant

* *

*E*volution. You've no doubt heard about it, and you've probably seen a show or two about it on TV, but its significance likely escapes you. Watching a bunch of scientists on the Discovery Channel dig in the dirt with little toothbrushes and get really excited about some little bit of bone or a tooth may leave you thinking, "Well, yes, those do look like teeth, and they certainly do seem old, but . . ." A tooth, you say to yourself, is hardly reason to trade high fives and uncork champagne bottles. At times like these, evolution can seem pretty slippery. After all, there's got to be more to it than a stray fossilized tooth or bone fragment.

Well, there is. Evolution explains how we (and I'm using *we* collectively to mean all living organisms: you, me, and all other animals; moss, trees, and the roses in your garden; viruses, amoebas, bacteria, and all the other little critters) came to be in all our complexity and variation. The reason scientists get excited about fossilized teeth is because findings like these are consistent with what scientists understand about the evolution of life on Earth. That single tooth is just one piece of the evolutionary puzzle; thousands more pieces exist. All together, those pieces form a picture of our genetic past and a road map that leads from a common ancestor to who, and what, we are today. It's a journey over billions of years.

This chapter gives you an overview of evolution in all its glory: what it is, how it works, and what it does. By the end, you may begin to understand what the great evolutionary biologist Theodosius Dobzhansky meant when he wrote, "Nothing in biology makes sense except in the light of evolution."

Biological Evolution at a Glance

Evolution can be defined simply as change through time, and it can refer to anything that changes. Languages evolve; tastes evolve; cultures, art forms, and football offense strategy all evolve. This book isn't about evolution in general, though, but about biological evolution: the changes, over time, in organisms.

Biological evolution deals with a very specific type of change through time — changes in the frequencies of different genes — throughout an entire species, or within a single population of that species, from generation to generation. *Evolutionary biologists* — scientists who study evolution — just love that stuff. Their mission? To understand how evolution works (by figuring out what causes changes in gene frequencies) and what evolution does (by figuring out what sorts of things happen when gene frequencies change).

The following sections offer a general overview of how evolution works and what it does. Parts II and III delve into these topics in a great deal more detail.

Gene defined

Back in Charles Darwin's day, a *gene* was defined simply as the unit of heredity. People knew that specific traits, such as blue eyes or red hair, were passed from parent to child, but they didn't know exactly what a gene was or how the process worked. Today, we know a lot more:

- ✔ We know about DNA (*deoxyribonucleic acid*), which is what gets passed from parent to offspring.

- ✔ We know that DNA is a long molecule made up of a string of four *subunits* (four letters); that the order of these letters, commonly called the *DNA sequence,* stores genetic information; and that a gene is a particular sequence of a particular piece of an organism's DNA.

- ✔ We've developed the chemical techniques that allow researchers to determine the exact sequence of an organism's DNA. As a result of this ability to work with DNA, scientists have a much better handle on the details of the evolutionary process.

What this means — and why it's important enough to include here — is that by being able to identify the DNA sequence of a particular gene, scientists can measure exactly what genetic changes occur across generations. Being able to measure things, especially things like DNA strands, gets evolutionary biologists all goose-pimply. (For more information about genes and DNA, head to Chapter 3.)

What's the (gene) frequency, Kenneth?

Simply put, the *frequency* of a particular gene is how often it appears in a population. When researchers examine the DNA sequence at a particular location in a species' DNA in different individuals, they sometimes find that all the individuals have the same sequence. In this case, because only one gene (or one DNA sequence) exists at this location, its frequency is 100 percent. At other times, different sequences are present in different individuals. In this case, when more than one gene is present at this location, scientists speak of the frequencies of the different genes.

Suppose that you've discovered three different DNA sequences; call them genes A, B, and, C. If half the individuals you examine have gene A, one quarter have gene B, and one quarter have gene C, the frequencies of the three genes are 50 percent gene A, 25 percent gene B, and 25 percent gene C.

By identifying changes in the frequency of particular genes through the passing of generations, you can determine whether the organism has evolved. Using the example of genes A, B, and C from the preceding section, if you came back generations later to measure the frequency of these three genes again, and you found that the frequencies had changed, evolution has happened.

Here's an example: Suppose that you collect a bunch of a particular kind of bacteria and measure the frequency of the gene that makes the bacteria resistant to a new type of antibiotic. In your initial count, you find that the frequency of this gene is extremely low: Less than 1 percent of the bacteria have the gene that makes them antibiotic resistant. You come back in a few years. Your original bacteria are gone, but in their place are their great-great-great-great-etcetera grandkids, and you repeat the analysis. This time, you find that 30 percent of the bacteria have the antibiotic-resistant gene. Although you haven't actually witnessed evolution, you're looking at its result: the change in the frequency of particular genes over time. The antibiotic-resistant gene appeared in less than 1 percent of the original bacteria; it appears in 30 percent of the descendents. (Go to Chapter 17 for an in-depth discussion of the evolution of antibiotic resistance in bacteria.)

In a nutshell, biological evolution is simply a change in the frequency of one or more genes through time. Scientists collect this sort of data about the occurrence of evolution all the time — not only for bacteria, but also for all sorts of organisms, both simple and complex.

The timescales of evolution

Although the changes in gene frequencies happen gradually through time, the rate of evolution isn't constant. Gene frequencies can remain constant for long periods of time and then change in response to changes in the environment. The rate of change can increase or decrease, but the basic process — gene frequencies changing over time — continues. To differentiate between these time scales of the evolutionary process, scientists use the terms *microevolution* and *macroevolution:*

- **Microevolution** refers to the results of the evolutionary process over short time scales and small changes. An example is a bacterium in a laboratory beaker experiencing a mutation that creates a gene that confers higher growth and division rates relative to the other bacteria and beaker. Microevolution, because it happens on a time scale that we're able to observe, tends to be a bit easier for us to wrap our brains around than macroevolution.

- **Macroevolution** refers to the results of the evolutionary process typically among species (or above the species level; see Chapter 11) over long periods. Nothing is different about the process; nothing special is happening. Macroevolution simply refers to the larger changes researchers can observe when evolution has been going on for a longer time and involves processes such as extinction, which may have little to do with microevolution. *Speciation,* the process whereby one species gives rise to two, is an example of macroevolution. Speciation isn't all that complicated, and scientists are getting a pretty good idea about how it works; you can find out more in Chapter 8.

Other than the time frame, no difference exists between micro- and macroevolution. The process isn't any different from what scientists can observe in a test tube in the laboratory (an example of microevolution); there's just been a lot more of it.

Gene extremes: Mutation and extinction

Genes can go to extremes. At one extreme is the disappearing gene. Suppose that you measure the frequency of the three different genes at a particular site in a species' DNA and then return some years later to find that one of the genes is no longer present. That gene's frequency has dropped to zero. It's gone. It's extinct. When a gene goes extinct, the species that had the gene is still around, but at least at this particular location in its DNA, it's not as diverse.

At the other extreme, new genes can appear. The process by which the sequence of a parent's DNA is copied and passed on to the next generation is remarkably accurate. If it weren't, none of us would be here. But no process is perfect, and mistakes happen. These mistakes are called *mutations,* and they can result in a DNA sequence different from the original — in other words, a new, different gene. These new genes can affect the functioning of the organism in several ways:

- ✔ **They can have no effect at all.** Because there's a certain amount of redundancy in the code of the DNA sequence (go to Chapter 3 for the details), it's possible to change a letter here and there with no effect whatsoever. Even if the mutation does create a change, that change may not affect how the gene product functions. In both cases, the new genes don't have an impact — either positive or negative — on whether an organism survives.

- ✔ **They can result in a change that's harmful to the organism.** Most mutations that cause a change fall into this category. Even the simplest organisms are really quite complicated. If you change something randomly, most often the outcome is bad. Genes of this sort vanish as rapidly as they appear.

Occasionally, bad mutations — which typically are destined for a short run before becoming extinct — actually *increase* in frequency. Here's how it could happen: If a gene with negative effects is present in the same critter as a gene with positive effects, the frequency of the bad gene can increase as it rides the evolutionary coattails of the really great new gene. Suppose that two mutations occur simultaneously in different locations on an organism's DNA: one resulting in a gene that is slightly harmful and another resulting in a gene that is advantageous. The slightly harmful gene may increase in frequency simply because it's along for the ride.

- ✔ **They can result in a change that's advantageous to the organism.** This class of mutations is by far the rarest, but beneficial mutations do occur. These mutations, although rare, can increase in frequency. Ultimately, they're the source of all the variation upon which evolution by natural selection acts. (Skip to Chapter 4 for more detail about the role variation plays in evolution.)

All the different genes in all the organisms on earth started out as mutations that, though initially rare, ended up increasing in frequency. As the source of new genes, mutations are a key part of the evolutionary process. A gene can't increase or decrease in frequency until it first appears, and mutations are how that happens.

Darwin and His Big Ideas

You can't talk about evolution without talking about Charles Darwin (1809–1882), a would-be physician and theologian whose fascination with natural history and geography led him to accept a position as gentleman's companion to the captain of the *HMS Beagle,* a ship bound for South America with the purpose of mapping the area and sending plant, animal, and fossil specimens back to England. The voyage lasted five years, from 1831 to 1836.

Several things led Darwin to speculate about the changes that might occur in species over time: the diversity of life he observed on his voyage, the geographical patterns whereby different yet obviously related species were found in close proximity to one another, and the fossils he collected that made it clear present-day species weren't the ones that had been present in the past.

Darwin returned to England in 1836, already well known in the scientific community for the specimens and detailed notes that he had sent back. By 1838, Darwin had developed in more detail his theory of how gradual changes resulting from natural selection could result in changes in existing species as well as the formation of new ones. Over roughly the next 20 years, Darwin continued to develop and refine his ideas. In 1859, he published his seminal work, *On the Origin of Species,* which laid out the foundations of evolutionary theory. The following sections hit the highlights of Darwin's ideas. His other works include *The Descent of Man, and Selection in Relation to Sex* (1871) and *The Expression of the Emotions in Man and Animals* (1872).

Find the title *On the Origin of Species* a bit cryptic? Roll the full title around your mouth for a while: *On the Origin of Species by Means of Natural Selection, or the Preservation of Favoured Races in the Struggle for Life.* The shorter version may not be as descriptive, but it certainly is easier to remember — and say! You can read it (and all of Darwin's other works) at `http://darwin-online.org.uk/`.

Darwin didn't use the word *gene;* instead, in his work, he referred to *characters.* Yet because his ideas focused on *heritable* characters (that is, those that can be passed from parent to offspring), his "characters" are directly linked to genes.

Natural selection

One of Darwin's big ideas was what he called *natural selection,* the mechanism that he proposed to explain what he called "descent with modification" — that is, changes in an organism through subsequent generations. (Today, we'd say that natural selection explains how gene frequencies could change over generations.) This big idea, explained in depth in Chapter 5, is both remarkably insightful and remarkably simple, which explains why it's stood the test of time.

Basically, Darwin recognized that some characters get passed from one generation to the next and others don't. What he wanted to understand was *how* descent with modification could have occurred. What was the underlying driving force? He concluded that the driving force was the process of natural selection: Not all individuals in a given generation have an equal chance of contributing to the next generation. Some are selectively favored; some are selected against.

Darwin surmised that natural selection worked the same way as the process of artificial selection used in animal husbandry and agriculture:

- ✔ **Artificial selection:** Since before Darwin's time, people have been selectively breeding animals and plants: chickens that lay more eggs, cows that make more milk, pansies that are brighter and last longer . . . and the list goes on. Essentially, humans have been pretty apt hands at spurring evolution in agriculturally important plants and animals. *We* decide which genes are more likely to make into the next generation. The cows that produce more milk are the ones that we selectively breed to produce better dairy cows; the ones that make less milk, we eat. As a result of the choices we humans make as selecting agents, we can dramatically alter in a relatively short period the characteristics of the organisms we breed.

- ✔ **Natural selection:** Darwin realized that if humans, by the process of artificial selection, could create such major differences over the extremely short period of time, then the natural environment, acting over a much longer time scale, could have produced much larger changes. Darwin called his process *natural selection* because the natural environment, not humans, was the selecting agent.

In artificial selection, farmers and breeders determine which characters they like and work to propagate in their produce and livestock. In natural selection, the same type of selection occurs, but the selecting factor isn't man, but nature, or the environment in which the organism exists. To help you understand the difference between artificial and natural selection, consider the cow. In the barnyard, farmers selectively favor the cow that makes the most milk; in the wild, natural selection favors the cow that can make enough milk to feed its calf and still do all the other things the cow needs to do to survive on its own.

Whether natural selection favors an individual is a function of the individual's particular heritable characters. Some heritable characters increase the probability that the individuals containing them will contribute to the next generation; some characters decrease the probability that individuals will contribute to the next generation. What all this means is that organisms in the first category reproduce more than do the organisms in the second category. *That's* what makes one generation different from the next, the next different from the one that follows it, and the one that follows it different from the one that comes later . . . and so on and so forth, ad infinitum.

In case you're curious: Survival of the fittest

Although he didn't coin the phrase *survival of the fittest,* Darwin did make it a household term. Many people assume (erroneously) that it means the natural order mandates that the strong survive and the weak die away. But to Darwin and other evolutionists, *survival of the fittest* is simply synonymous with *natural selection.* In other words, those organisms that possess selectively favored heritable characters are the ones that pass their genes into the future with the most success.

This sidebar marks the first and the last time you'll see this phrase in this book. Why?

- ✔ **It's problematic.** The phrase doesn't clarify the concept Darwin was trying to explain (although he no doubt thought it did; otherwise, he wouldn't have used it). To express the concept more clearly, Darwin could

have used the term *survival and differential reproduction of the fittest,* but that's just not as sexy.

- ✔ **It doesn't make much sense semantically.** In beginning a study of evolution, students often say, "Well, if evolution is survival of the fittest, and the fittest are the ones that survive, that seems pretty circular." Indeed, it is.

- ✔ **Even evolutionary biologists never use it.** They use *natural selection* instead.

Don't let any of this get in the way of your developing an understanding of the term *fitness,* however; that word is crucially important to understanding evolution. Head to the section "How 'fitness' fits in with natural selection" for details.

Here's an example: Imagine a population of lions. Half the lions have the work-hard-run-fast-and-catch-lots-of-gazelles character. The other half have the sit-around-and-be-lazy character. It's tough in the Serengeti, and only the lions with the work-hard-run-fast character manage to store up enough energy to reproduce and raise offspring successfully. If you reanalyze this population after a few generations have passed and find fewer lions with the lazy character, that's evolution driven by natural selection!

Speciation

Darwin realized that because individuals differ in the characters they have, and because these differences affect their chances of survival and reproduction, some characters are more likely to get into the next generation than others. He also realized that as a result of this process, the frequency of characters changes over generations. Pass through enough generations, and the sum of all the little evolutionary changes may result in an organism that's evolved into an entirely different species.

Here's a quick example: Imagine you have two populations of the same animal. Each population lives in a different place, and the populations rarely interbreed. The selective forces in those two places — the combination of things we call the environment — is different. In one environment, it's good to have a long beak; in the other environment, a short beak is better. Other significant environmental differences exist as well. It's very wet on one side of the mountain range and very dry on the other, for example. In two such different environments, gene frequencies change in one way in the first location and another way in the second. Over a long period, the two populations become so different that they can no longer interbreed. They have become different species.

Today, scientists can identify all the stages of speciation in the natural world. They can find pairs of species that seem to have diverged from a single species very recently, and they can find pairs of populations that appear to be on the verge of becoming separate species. In some cases, the two populations are so close to becoming different species that all it would take is some minor habitat change to push them that last little bit and turn one species into two. For more detailed information about speciation, head to Chapter 8.

The idea of speciation got Darwin into a lot of hot water, and it's a hot-button issue today because it links organisms to common ancestors, which is all well and good for things like fish, oak trees, and invertebrates. But when you throw humans into the mix — whoa, Nelly. To read more about the conflict between evolutionary science and those who deny it, head to Chapter 22.

How "fitness" fits in with natural selection

The process of evolution by natural selection is driven by differences in *fitness,* or how successful an organism is at getting its genes (or characters) into the next generation. In short, fitness is all about how well an organism reproduces. Characters (or genes) that increase an individual's fitness are more likely to be passed to the next generation than genes that don't. This process is how the frequency of genes changes through time.

In the evolutionary process, fitness has nothing to do with how buff you are. It's purely a measure of the differential reproductive success among different individuals, which is a fancy way of saying that it refers to how successful an individual is at producing offspring. If one individual produces twice as many offspring as the next individual, all other things being equal, it's twice as fit.

Understanding adaptive characters

Some evolutionary changes are *adaptive,* meaning that a character has changed as a result of natural selection in a way that makes that character better suited to perform its function. Here's an example of the process of adaptation: Gazelles run away from cheetahs. The slow gazelles get eaten, leaving the faster gazelles to reproduce. In the next generation, the gazelles are faster on average than those in the past generation, because the run-away-from-cheetahs character has evolved. Being able to run really, really fast is an adaptation.

It's not always easy to tell whether a particular character is an adaptation because sometimes things that appear to be adaptive characters aren't. Suppose that you have a cat and decide to put its food outside. At some point, you notice that birds eat the cat food. Knowing a bit about evolution, you think that eating from the cat dish may well be good for the birds; they probably have more energy to sing songs, build nests, and raise baby birds. If you observe such successful foraging behavior in a different environment, you might conclude that the birds are foraging in your cat dish as the result of natural selection. But eating cat food isn't an adaptation (the birds haven't evolved to eat out of cat dishes); it's opportunistic. The food's available, and the cat . . . well, he's probably trapped behind a patio door. For more about adaptive characters, go to Chapter 5.

The Study of Evolution, Post-Darwin

Darwin had only a vague idea of what genes were and didn't know squat about DNA, but he hit the evolutionary nail on the head. Today, scientists know that the process of evolution by natural selection occurs pretty much the way Darwin first proposed it: Natural selection results in changes over time in any given population, and good genes (those that make the organism more fit — that is, more successful at surviving long enough to reproduce) become more frequent over time. Still, scientists' understanding of evolution has continued to evolve as they expand the theory of evolution to include some elements Darwin was unable to address:

- **Many DNA mutations are selectively neutral.** The DNA code contains a certain amount of redundancy, which means that many changes in the DNA don't result in a fitness advantage or a fitness cost. The extent to which these genes increase or decrease in a population has entirely to do with chance.

- **Chance can be an important factor contributing to the change in gene frequencies through time.** Imagine that half the deer in the forest have blue eyes, and half have brown eyes. Now suppose that a couple of trees fall over and accidentally crush a couple of deer with blue eyes. All other things being equal, the next generation will have a higher proportion of the brown-eyed gene than the previous generation. Evolution has happened, but *not* as a result of natural selection. (Yes, I know that deer don't have blue eyes; it's just an example.) For more information on how chance factors into the evolutionary process, head to Chapter 6.

  I can imagine what you must be thinking: Two deer more or less are hardly going to make much of a difference. In a large population, you'd be right, but in a small population, a few deer more or less can make a difference that would be noticed in the future. When the population is large, chance events aren't as important, but when the population is small, random events can have larger repercussions.

> ✔ **Not all the characteristics of any particular organism are positively correlated with fitness.** This idea stems from scientists' understanding that not all evolutionary change is the result of natural selection. Sometimes, it's the result of chance; sometimes, it's the result of bad genes hitching a ride into the future with the good genes that made the organism more fit.
>
> ✔ **The environment affects fitness.** Populations in different places experience different selective forces. A gene for being able to survive a long time without water, for example, may offer a fitness advantage in the desert, but it may have rather negative consequences in a rain forest. Interaction between the gene and its environment is important in determining whether a given gene increases or decreases fitness.

Sickle cell anemia is an example of how the environment determines whether a particular gene increases or decreases fitness. The gene that causes sickle cell anemia produces a slightly different form of hemoglobin. The most extreme case occurs when someone has two copies of the sickle cell gene: one from the mother and one from the father. But even having just *one* sickle cell gene causes illness. At first glance, it seems obvious that this gene wouldn't increase anyone's fitness, yet it's present in high frequencies in certain areas of Africa. By examining the system from an evolutionary perspective, scientists learned an interesting thing about the sickle cell gene: Having a copy of this gene helps protect against malaria, which is present in those areas of Africa where the gene occurs at high frequency. So yes, it's bad to have this gene in the current era in the United States. But in the days before antimalaria drugs, it was a good gene to have in parts of Africa.

Applying Evolution Today

Evolution is interesting purely for its own sake, but of course, I *would* think that, having devoted years to studying, teaching, and writing about it. But evolution is good for more than just student lectures and small talk in academic circles: Understanding what evolution is and how it works makes all sorts of things possible. The following sections give a small sampling of how scientists apply aspects of evolutionary biology. You can find many more examples throughout this book.

Conservation

Understanding evolution helps conservationists in their efforts to protect endangered species. When resources are limited, as they often are, scientists have to make choices about which natural areas to protect and which populations of species to focus on. Understanding evolution can help them decide where to devote resources.

For example, many people think that the key to protecting endangered species is to conserve the maximum number of individuals possible. But understanding evolutionary biology and the patterns of variation present in natural populations helps us recognize that the real key is conserving genetic variability. If two populations are genetically different, part of a viable conservation management plan is maintaining this diversity, for two reasons:

- ✔ This diversity is a characteristic of the species that the scientists are trying to protect.

- ✔ The naturally existing variation allows the species to respond to future changes in the environment.

Another thing that evolution teaches — specifically, evolution by random events — is that we can't allow endangered populations to reach critically low numbers. In small populations, the variations scientists are trying to conserve — the very essence of what makes a particular species unique — are at risk of being lost due to random events that would be insignificant in a larger population. (For more information on the role chance plays in small populations, go to Chapter 6.)

Agriculture

Although humans have been breeding plants and animals for thousands of years, recent understanding of the evolutionary process lets us attack this task in a more scientific fashion. Following are some highlights in the field of agriculture, courtesy of our understanding of the evolutionary process and principles:

- ✔ **Advancements in breeding:** Understanding the detail of the evolutionary process can help us devise new breeding strategies. Head to Chapter 11, which explores in detail a breeding program that successfully bred chickens that produced more eggs by selecting for chickens that got along well together in chicken coops — definitely not the normal situation and something that had been a serious problem in chicken farming before these developments.

- ✔ **Crop variation:** The presence of genetic variation allows populations to respond to environmental changes; in the absence of such variation, populations can be destroyed by a sudden environmental change. Plant genetically similar crops over wide areas, and you run the risk of an agricultural disaster. Case in point? The Irish potato famine. Across Ireland, genetically identical potato plants were cultivated; a disease that attacked one potato turned out to be able to destroy them all, with horrific results.

✔ **Crop history:** Evolutionary biology allows scientists to understand the history of crop plants. Corn, for example, was domesticated by Native Americans, but for the longest time, biologists had no idea what wild plant it was derived from. Now, detailed studies of the evolutionary relationships of plants allow scientists to identify the wild plant from which corn was artificially selected. Having found the parent plant, scientists can study the genetics of how this plant survives in the presence of insects and microbial pests, which can only help in the quest to develop even better corn.

Medicine

The field of evolutionary biology affects the medical profession in three key ways: figuring out what has happened, understanding what is happening now, and trying to predict what will happen in the future to human disease. All three help researchers devise strategies for prevention and treatment of health problems big and small.

One area of particular medical importance is the evolution of microbes — the viruses, bacteria, and other microscopic critters that cause infection — that are increasingly resistant to antibiotics. The more researchers know about how and why microbes evolve as they do, the better they'll be able to counteract the effect of those microbes. Consider, for example, the virus that causes AIDS. Reconstructing evolutionary history has allowed researchers to trace the spread of human immunodeficiency viruses (HIV) across the globe, as well as to determine the relationships among human viruses and the immunodeficiency viruses of other animals. From these studies, scientists know that these viruses don't always cause disease in their hosts. By studying related harmless viruses, researchers may be better able to understand exactly why HIV is so dangerous in humans.

The study of evolutionary biology also guides treatment of diseases. The highly successful triple drug therapy that's been amazingly beneficial to HIV-positive individuals is the direct result of scientists' knowledge of how antibiotic resistance works in microbes: Even though mutations in the HIV virus render it resistant to medications, it's more difficult for the virus to evolve resistance to all the drugs at the same time. Finally, by examining how HIV evolves resistance to medicines, scientists hope not only to design better medicines, but also to identify how best to design a vaccine.

Chapters 17, 18, and 19 are chock full of information about the role of evolutionary biology in the fight against disease.

One Final Point: Just How Evolved Are You?

Evolution isn't a race to some cosmic finish line. No species is more evolved than the next. Every living thing is descended from the same common ancestor. All the different lineages have been evolving for exactly the same length of time. True, humans are better than pine trees at doing the things humans do, but we can't stand outside in the sun and soak up energy — something that pine trees do very well. The reason life is so different is that different environments select for different outcomes.

Neither is evolution a climb to the top of some life-form ladder on which the "higher" orders take over the top rungs (we humans are at the tippy-tippy top) and the "lowlier" creatures hang around the base. In fact, not all evolution results in more complex life forms. This point may seem like a small one, but it's actually quite important and is easily lost when most people think of evolution in terms of the "monkey-to-man" graphic — the one that shows the evolution of man in a series of stages, from monkey to ape to caveman to investment banker. Although you can make an argument that the caveman gave way to the investment banker and therefore forms a valid time series, other primates are still around and are just as evolved as humans are.

Evolution *can* lead to greater complexity, but it doesn't always. Over the history of the earth, since the first single-celled life forms, there was really nowhere to go but up in terms of size and obvious physical complexity. But as soon as larger, more complex critters evolved, the possibility existed that some would evolve simpler forms. Parasites, for example, have lost many of the functions that they can scam off their hosts. The eyes of cave-dwelling organisms constitute another example. Absent the need for the complex structure of the eye, mutations that cause a reduction in the eye can pile up.

P.S: Just between you and me, I do sometimes think of myself as being a bit more evolved than a bacterium — but then I think of the incredible biochemical diversity that bacteria are capable of, and I realize the error of my ways.

Chapter 2

The Science — Past and Present — of Evolution

. . . .

In This Chapter

▶ Getting familiar with the language of science

▶ Digging into fossils and rocks

▶ Comparing Darwin's knowledge with ours

. . . .

*T*oday, scientists know a lot more about fossils than they did back in Charles Darwin's day. They understand the molecular mechanisms of genetics and heredity. They can conduct experiments in the laboratory that allow them actually to observe the evolutionary process. In essence, science has come a long way since Darwin, whose investigations focused primarily on the process of natural selection. As this book explains, there's more to evolution than just the process of natural selection, but evolution by natural selection is an extremely important evolutionary force.

When it comes to natural selection, Darwin got the basics right, even though he had to speculate about the things that researchers can just measure today. Scientists since Darwin, in test after test and experiment after experiment, haven't been able to refute Darwin's theory. In fact, their work has provided copious evidence that the evolutionary process works almost exactly the way Darwin speculated it did.

This chapter looks at the information Darwin had when he formulated his theory of evolution via natural selection and at the things scientists have learned since then. The chapter also helps you understand exactly what scientists mean when they say *fact* and when they say *theory,* which, believe it or not, isn't code for "pulled out of thin air."

Evolution: A Fact and a Theory

One of the most common sources of confusion for people trying to understand evolution is the question of whether it's a fact or a theory. Here's the answer: It's both. The *fact* of evolution refers to the things scientists can see and measure. The *theory* of evolution refers to the intellectual framework science has developed to explain the underlying processes that account for those facts.

To help you understand how evolution can be both a fact and a theory, I talk about another natural process that is both fact and theory: gravity. And because a key to understanding anything you hear or read about evolution requires being familiar with scientific principles, I also offer a short and sweet explanation of how scientists think.

Evolution and gravity: Two peas in a scientific pod

The fact of gravity is beyond dispute. When you drop something, it falls — a fact that most (dare I say all?) of us have personally established, either intentionally or accidentally. We not only know that things fall, but we also know a few details about the falling process. We know that whatever we drop falls toward the Earth, and we can measure the downward acceleration. We know that the pull of gravity is different away from Earth. On a smaller body such as the moon, things don't fall as fast. In deep space, far from the Earth and the moon, things don't fall at all; they just float. The strength of this *attractive force* (a fancy way of saying *gravity*) has to do with the mass of the attractive body and the other object's distance from it. The moon, for example, which is smaller than Earth, has less gravity.

Humans know all these things about gravity, but it turns out that we're not exactly sure what gravity is or how it works. Why, for example, does a dropped object go down rather than up? Scientists in the field of physics called gravitational theory are trying to figure these things out, and they continually fine-tune their theories as more information becomes available. But just because they can't say definitively what gravity is doesn't mean that gravity is any less real.

Just because you and I don't understand gravitational theory doesn't affect how we interact with gravity on a daily basis. We know it happens even if we don't know why, and we take it into consideration when we launch things into space, skateboard, land an airplane, or try to get that nine-iron shot onto the green. The same is true of evolution: We have the facts of evolution (the aspects of heritable changes in living organisms that we can see and measure), and we have the processes that evolutionary biologists theorize are responsible for these facts. As it turns out, compared with their theories about gravity, scientists have an excellent understanding of the basic process of evolution.

How to think like a scientist

Science is by definition a very conservative discipline, and scientists are extremely hesitant to say that they are certain about *anything*. In fact, one of the rules of science is that you must always allow for the possibility that additional data will force you to let go of an idea that you were really sure about and quite possibly very fond of. Scientists take this rule *very* seriously — so seriously, in fact, that before they get their diplomas and lab coats, they have to pinky-swear that they'll follow it.

Suppose that you want to know whether a particular coin is a fair coin, that is, as likely to come up heads as tails when you flip it. So you flip the coin a few times, and it always comes up heads. The fact that you got heads in your first few flips may lead you to suspect that the coin isn't fair, but because you flipped it only a few times, you can't say for sure. What you have is a suspicion. What you need is more information. So you proceed to flip the coin all day long, and the next couple thousand times you toss it, the coin always comes up heads. With a few thousand flips under your belt and a head coming up each time, you conclude that the coin isn't fair. This process seems straightforward, and the conclusion seems obvious — to anyone who isn't a scientist.

But a scientist in the exact same position and with the exact same data would not say that the coin isn't fair. She would cite a very, very, very low probability that it's a fair coin, or she'd say that she's 99.99999 percent sure that the coin isn't fair. The reason for the difference is the precision with which scientists state what they know. After all, it *is* possible that a fair coin could come up heads that many times in a row; that possibility just isn't very big.

To which the layperson may reasonably respond, "So you're not really sure!" What the scientist is really saying is that she *is* sure — within a reasonable doubt. (If that explanation's not good enough for you, consider the shaky ground on which it puts the entire American justice system, which also relies on the standard of reasonable doubt.)

You say toMAYto; I say toMAHto: The language of science

Do scientists ever seem as though they speak their own language? In a way, they do. You probably recognize some words as scientific terms — words like *nucleotide, paedomorphosis, heterozygosity,* and others, which seem to be little more than Latin and Greek roots randomly strung together. But other terms — ones that mean one thing to laypeople and something else to scientists — are a bit trickier. The subtle differences in the way scientists and nonscientists use the same words are often sources of confusion.

You won't find a better example of this situation than the word *theory*. In scientific terms, a *theory* is a hypothesis that has overwhelming support — in essence, an idea that's been proved. In layman's terms, *theory* typically means *best guess*. See the problem?

To help you understand the scientific meanings of science's three most important words (the fourth is *funding*), I offer these definitions:

- ✔ **Fact:** Something you can observe or measure.
- ✔ **Hypothesis:** A working idea or set of ideas resulting from observations and measurements. The hypothesis serves to guide future investigations. It gives scientists suggestions about what facts they should try to collect next.
- ✔ **Theory:** A conceptual framework, tested repeatedly but not rejected, that explains the facts, observations, and measurements, and makes accurate predictions of how the system will behave in the future.

The facts of evolution, as I show throughout this book, are clearly established. The current theories of how evolution functions are solidly supported as well. But the linguistic difficulties in communication are such that people continue to ask scientists, "But it's just a theory, right?"

Scientific investigation

Scientists don't start talking about something as a theory until it has overwhelming support. How do they get that support? Through scientific investigation. A coin toss is a good example of the process of scientific investigation:

1. **Start with some observations about the natural world.**

   In the example of the coin toss, you observe that the first few tosses always end up heads.

2. **Formulate a hypothesis.**

   Your hypothesis after flipping head after head? That the coin isn't fair.

   The hypothesis serves as the scientist's starting point; maybe it's right, and maybe it's wrong. They key is to do enough testing to find out.

3. **Gather additional data to test this hypothesis.**

   In the coin example, you gather additional data by tossing the coin several thousand more times.

   Repeating one type of test ad infinitum — exhaustively flipping a coin, for example — and getting a particular result isn't good enough. First, you have to address and eliminate any other factors that could affect the test results. Maybe the coin is fine, but something about the person flipping it isn't quite right. Or maybe the coin is fine, but some other factor — like an air vent blowing air over the researcher's head — keeps it from landing heads or tails half of the time. You need to have the coin flipped by a bunch of other researchers in other parts of the room to make sure they get the same result.

4. **As your data accumulates, it either supports your hypothesis, or it forces you to revise or abandon the hypothesis.**

    In the coin-toss example, heads continue to come up, thus lending support to the original hypothesis that the coin isn't fair.

5. **At the point where an overwhelming amount of information starts to accumulate in support of the hypothesis, the hypothesis is elevated to a theory.**

The hypothesis must get tested and tested to the best of everyone's ability before it arrives in the exalted land of theory. And even a theory is only one good experiment away from being rejected, which is one of the fundamental components of the scientific method: that the ideas scientists come up with must be *falsifiable*. That is, scientists must be able to imagine some set of results that would cause them to reject the theory; then they must see that over and over again, they never get the expected results. This process always sounds somewhat backward to nonscientists, but that's just the way scientists do things. We scientists never say that an idea is true; what we say is that, even after our best efforts, we've been unable to show that it is false. Then it's high fives all around, and we go grab a beer.

The Evidence of Evolution

Evolution is simply the change over time in the frequencies of different heritable traits (that is, the frequencies of different genes) in a group of organisms. One year, half the birds have blue eyes and the other half have brown. Some years later, two thirds of the birds have blue eyes. If eye color is a heritable trait, that is, one that is passed from parent to offspring, then that change is evolution.

Darwin's big idea was coming up with a process that could cause these changes. This theory of natural selection is simply a process in which heritable traits that help an organism survive in its current environment occur more frequently in subsequent generations. In other words, *genes* (the heritable traits) that are *favored* (help survival) increase over time. Evolution by natural selection really is that simple, regardless of what you may have heard to the contrary.

Darwin, the father of evolutionary theory (refer to Chapter 1), did a phenomenally good job of piecing this part of evolutionary process together, but he could only hypothesize about the underlying details of what he called *descent with modification*. What he didn't understand was the underlying genetic mechanism that was responsible.

Knowledge about DNA and genetics

Making out heritable traits just requires knowing a little bit about DNA, genes, and the genetic code — topics covered in more detail in Chapter 3. This knowledge of genetics allows researchers to measure gene frequencies. Today, scientists can do more than just observe that evolution has happened; instead, they can determine the specific genes involved and measure the rates at which the genes' frequencies change in populations where different selective forces are at play. Scientists' knowledge of exactly what is going on gives them a much richer understanding of the process and allows them to ask far more detailed questions than Darwin could.

Experimental evidence

Darwin saw evidence that the process of natural selection had occurred in nature, but he was unable to watch it happen. Scientists today, however, can actually observe the evolutionary process in action. Using organisms that reproduce rapidly and can be kept in laboratories in large numbers (such as fruit flies and bacteria), and employing modern tools and techniques (such as DNA sequencing), evolutionary biologists can conduct actual evolution experiments and watch the results.

Scientists don't pick fruit flies because anything about that species is special; they pick fruit flies for expediency. Experiments conducted with fruit flies go a lot faster than experiments with other organisms (such as dogs or sea turtles) because the generation time of the flies is much, much shorter. A fruit fly is born, reproduces, and dies within a couple of weeks. This short life span gives scientists more opportunity to examine changes in heritable traits.

Measurement of the rates of change

Scientists can measure the rates at which evolutionary changes happen. By measuring changes in the frequencies of existing genes and observing mutations, they can describe the evolutionary process exactly. They can see in the laboratory how selection can result in changes in gene frequencies.

Here's a favorite example of mine to show how witnessing evolution in action is possible: antibiotic resistance. Scientists can observe how the frequencies of genes that make a microbe resistant to antibiotics increase when the environment changes to include an antibiotic. They take a beaker full of microbes and add some antibiotics. Then — big drumroll here — they come back the next day and find that the frequency of genes conferring resistance to antibiotics is much higher than it was before the antibiotics were added. Why? Because all the bacteria that didn't have antibiotic-resistance genes died and the ones that did have antibiotic resistant genes reproduced a lot! Hence, the favored trait — resistance to antibiotics — increased over time. You can read more about antibiotic resistance in Chapter 17.

Mutations don't occur in *response* to environmental change. Instead, the mutations already exist and are favored in the new environment. Beakers full of bacteria tend to contain mutants that are resistant to antibiotics even when no antibiotics are around. Toss an antibiotic into the mix, and the mutation gets its chance to shine by enabling the bacteria to survive in the presence of the antibiotic.

The Scientific Foundation of Evolution by Natural Selection

Charles Darwin observed that the offspring of a particular parent, although they resembled the parent, tended to differ from the parent in various ways. That is, the offspring were *variable*. Based on his observations, Darwin hypothesized that, because of their inherent differences, some of the offspring would be better than others at doing whatever it is they needed to do to survive and reproduce. Further, he surmised that if the differences that resulted in increased survival and reproduction were *heritable* (that is, passed from parent to offspring), they would be passed disproportionately to the next generation, and through time, this process would lead to changes in the species.

Darwin didn't pull his ideas out of thin air. He developed his theory of evolution during the period when rapid advances were being made in a variety of fields, including geology, selective breeding in agriculture, and *biogeography* (the study of the locations of different species).

Not surprising, scientists have learned a fair bit more about the natural world in the hundred-plus years since Darwin proposed his theory of evolution by natural selection. What *is* surprising is how well most of what researchers have learned since Darwin has been in agreement with his hypothesis. As scientists have developed a more complex understanding of the details of the evolutionary process, their confidence has only increased that the mechanism Darwin first proposed is correct. This section outlines what Darwin knew and some of the things scientists have learned about the evolutionary process since Darwin.

Gradualism: Changes over time

Although people now take for granted the idea that gradual processes acting over long periods can have dramatic effects — think, for example, of the slow erosion by the Colorado River that led to the formation of the Grand Canyon — this idea was at odds with the prevailing view in the 1800s that the Earth was very young. Then along came the field of *stratigraphy,* which deals with the horizontal banding patterns that you can observe in the faces of cliffs or when a highway is cut through deep rock.

By Darwin's day, detailed geological mapping of Europe had revealed that a reproducible sequence of bands was spread across a large geographical area and that these bands contained fossils. Even in the absence of detailed information about the absolute ages of the different bands, scientists concluded that the ones on the bottom were typically older than the ones on the top. The very existence of these bands and the fossils that were found within them hinted at a process of gradual change.

If the new geological views about gradualism were correct — that is, that the Earth formed over long periods, as indicated by the banding patterns of different geological eras — scientists could imagine that the changes in the biological community were also the result of small changes occurring over a large period. Turns out that they were right on both counts.

The age of the Earth

Although earlier scientists didn't have the tools to date the age of the Earth as we do today, they understood that the lower bands (and the fossils in them) were older than the higher bands and their fossils. Still, Darwin had no idea how immensely old the Earth was or how long the evolutionary process had been going on. Even when people began to understand that the world was quite a bit older than previously thought, they couldn't give an exact age to it.

Dating the age of the Earth: Radioisotope dating

Scientists know that the Earth is about 4.5 billion years old by using radioisotope dating techniques. To understand how this process works, you need to know a little bit about atoms and isotopes. For those who need little refresher course on basic chemistry, think of water, or H_2O. The *H* and the *O* refer to hydrogen and oxygen, the two atoms that make up water. As the notation indicates, water consists of one molecule of oxygen and two molecules of hydrogen.

Often, any one atom has several different forms, which are referred to as *isotopes*. Atoms are made up of electrons, protons, and neutrons, and the number of electrons and protons determines the type of atom. Hydrogen, for example, has one electron and one proton. Sometimes, it also has a neutron. The term *heavy water* refers to water in which each hydrogen atom has a neutron. This isotope of hydrogen is also called *deuterium*.

Some isotopes, like deuterium, are *stable*, which means that they're perfectly happy with the number of electrons, protons, and neutrons they have. Other isotopes are *unstable* because the different number of neutrons interacts with the other atomic components in such a way that some of the bits go flying off and, over a period of time, the isotope changes into some other atom. When these unstable isotopes change to a different atom, they emit radioactivity. For that reason, they're called *radioisotopes*.

An important property of radioactive isotopes is that scientists can describe very accurately the average probability of the transition's happening and express that probability as a number called the *half-life* — the time it takes for half of the atoms to undergo this transition. In the first half-life, half of the atoms transition. In the second half-life, half of the remaining atoms transition, leaving one quarter of the original parent material. In the third half-life, half again transition, leaving one eighth, and so on. (**Remember:** Just because half the isotopes decay in the first half-life doesn't mean that the other half decay in the second half-life—you'd be surprised at the number of students who make this assumption. Only half decay every half-life.)

To determine the age of material, researchers compare the ratio of the parent and daughter products that were initially in the sample with the ratio of these products at the current time. By doing so, they can calculate how much time has passed. The atomic clock is a very accurate national timekeeping apparatus calibrated by the precise regularity of radioactive decay.

Numerous radioactive isotopes exist. One system that has been very successful in dating the ages of fossils is potassium-argon dating. Potassium is an extremely common element. Although most potassium isotopes aren't radioactive, one of them is, and one of its decay products is the gas argon.

Potassium–argon dating relies on the fact that although potassium is a solid, argon is a gas. When rock is melted (think lava), all the argon in the rock escapes, and when the rock solidifies again, only potassium is left. The melting of the rock and releasing of any argon present set the potassium–argon clock at zero. As time passes, argon accumulates in the rock as a result of radioactive potassium decay. When scientists analyze these rocks and compute the ratio of argon to potassium, they're able to determine how long it's been since the lava cooled. When scientists date rocks from our solar system this way, the oldest dates they find are 4.5 billion years.

No fossils are present in lava, obviously; anything that was there melted along with the rock. But by dating the lava flows above and below a fossil find, scientists can put exact boundaries on the maximum and minimum age of that fossil. In this case, the variation in possible ages of the fossil simply reflects the fact that the fossil exists between the dated lava flows.

Radioactive dating has been perfected to the extent that scientists can get within a few percentage points of the actual date. They know this because they're able to date lava flows that happened recently enough for their dates to be known historically. Potassium–argon dating has been used to date accurately the age of the eruption of Mount Vesuvius at Pompeii, for example. The scientists knew that the technique worked because the age their equipment indicated matched the age noted in historical Roman records.

Types of rocks and fossils

Geologists in Darwin's day were familiar with the diversity of types of rocks, but they were only beginning to appreciate the vast time scales over which geological events occurred. They had yet to understand the dynamic nature of the Earth's crust, and they lacked modern understanding of how these types of rocks formed:

✔ **Igneous:** Igneous rocks are of volcanic origin. They form when molten lava from volcanoes cools and solidifies. Basalt and obsidian are examples of igneous rocks.

✔ **Sedimentary:** Sedimentary rocks are formed by the gradual deposits of sediments. Sandstone is an example of sedimentary rock.

✔ **Metamorphic:** Metamorphic rocks are rocks of any origin that have been subjected to the extreme stresses and temperatures caused by the folding and crushing of the Earth's crust.

Understanding these rock types helps biologists understand the fossil record. Fossils are found only in sedimentary rocks. The molten lava that bubbles up from beneath the Earth's crust during a volcanic eruption doesn't contain any fossils (whatever had been there would have melted in the molten rock). Metamorphic rocks — even those of sedimentary-rock origin — don't contain fossils, because the extreme temperatures and pressures that converted the rock from sedimentary to metamorphic would have destroyed whatever fossils may have been there.

Today, scientists know quite a bit more. First, through radioactive dating, a painfully complex process whose details you don't need to worry about, they know that the Earth is about 4.5 billion years old. Scientists also know that life has existed on Earth for at least 3.5 billion years — a number that keeps changing as older and older fossils are found.

Although the age of the Earth may seem to be somewhat unrelated to evolution (rock, stone, and tectonic plates aren't living organisms and, therefore, don't "evolve"), it's actually very important to the theory of evolution because biological evolution needs time to happen. By knowing the actual age of the Earth and how long life has been present, scientists can ask whether enough time has passed for simple creatures such as the ones they see in the oldest rocks to evolve into more complex creatures, such as the ones that can write and edit books. The quick answer: Yes.

The fossil record

Fossils are the preserved remains of the bodies of dead organisms or the remains of the organism's actions — things such as footprints or burrows. The total of all fossils is called the *fossil record.* The fossil record informs scientists about evolution in several important ways:

- ✔ In the past, creatures that we don't find today lived on the planet.

- ✔ Not all creatures alive today are represented in the past.

- ✔ Through time, the physical complexity of organisms has increased. The earliest organisms that scientists can identify were single celled; now complex creatures exist.

- ✔ The earliest forms of life were aquatic; terrestrial forms appeared later.

The fossil record, incomplete though it may be, is a record of change through time. This record gives us clues to the progression of the development of life on Earth: Small single-celled organisms evolved into more complex ones; life started in the oceans and only later moved onto dry land. The fossil record provides a rough draft of the tree of life. (Head to Chapter 9 for a detailed explanation of the role that the tree of life — code word *phyolgenetics* — plays in evolution.)

A few things about the fossil record stymied Darwin and others in his day, however:

- ✔ They seemed to find a lot of older rock that had no fossils and newer rock that had complex life forms, making it seem as though complex life forms appeared suddenly.

- ✔ It wasn't clear why certain fossils were found in the locations where they were found — marine fossils on mountaintops, for example.

- ✔ Darwin was puzzled by the sudden changes from one type of fossil to the next, when there seemed to be very few, if any, transitional life forms.

The following sections explain what modern science says about these issues.

Conundrum 1: The seemingly sudden appearance of complex life forms

In studying the fossil record, scientists in Darwin's day were limited in a couple of ways that scientists today aren't:

- ✔ Their fossil record was even more incomplete than ours today. They didn't have any fossils older than 500 million years.

- ✔ They lacked the technology to find microscopic fossils. What Darwin and others perceived as gaps in the fossil record actually weren't gaps at all. Today, scientists have the advantage of a much more thorough search of the planet for older fossils and, more important, far more sophisticated techniques for identifying microscopic fossils in rocks.

The earliest fossils that scientists find are single-celled organisms, which Darwin lacked the ability to see physically. Today, scientists know that life has existed continuously on Earth for about the past 3.5 billion to 4 billion years, and they see the same increase in complexity through time that scientists observed in Darwin's day.

Fossils: Not just rock anymore

Back in Darwin's day, everyone knew that what was so cool about fossils was that biological material had been turned to stone through a process of mineralization. But today, people know something even cooler: Some of the biological material can survive this process and persist for a very long time. Scientists have been able to isolate DNA from organisms, like mammoths and cave bears, that died tens of thousands of years ago.

In retrospect, this feat is not as surprising as it first sounds. DNA is awfully tough stuff; your survival depends on it, after all. Also, techniques for isolating DNA are becoming more and more precise, allowing scientists to work with smaller and smaller quantities.

Even more amazing, scientists recently showed that soft tissue can survive for at least 68 million years inside fossilized *Tyrannosaurus rex* bone. It hasn't been possible (yet) to isolate DNA from such material, but it has been possible to determine the amino acid sequences of some of the remaining proteins. Tyrannosaurus rex proteins show considerable similarity to the proteins of modern birds — it turns out that *T. rex* might've tasted a lot like chicken — not surprising, given the close relationship suggested between dinosaurs and birds by the fossils of *Archaeopteryx* and other feathered dinosaurs. Now scientists have biochemical evidence supporting the same connection.

Conundrum 2: Marine fossils on mountaintops

Today, scientists understand the process of *plate tectonics* — the moving around of large chunks of the Earth's surface. The idea that the continents may not be fixed in place was greeted with skepticism as recently as 50 years ago, yet now we know that Earth's crust is composed of a series of plates that move relative to one another, fuse, and break apart, resulting in earthquakes and volcanoes.

What seemed like science fiction a little while ago is now something that science can routinely observe and measure. Submarines can dive to the depths of the ocean where plates are separating so researchers can measure the process. Very accurate markers can be placed in different locations across fault lines and their relative movements can be tracked with satellites and lasers. Scientists know, for example, the rate at which parts of California are moving apart and mountain ranges are pushing higher.

The fact that continents move explains why fossils turn up in the unlikeliest places: tropical fossils in Antarctica, for example (biologists have every reason to believe that Antarctica was once in the tropics), or seashell fossils on mountaintops (rocks that were once at sea level can be pushed upward over long periods to form mountain ranges). By understanding more about geological processes and time scales, the fossil record is more comprehensible.

Conundrum 3: The seeming lack of transitional forms

Darwin wondered where to find the transitional life forms (consider them the in-between-this-and-that forms). Although we've had more success in finding transitional life forms, today's scientists feel his pain. They are better at knowing where to look and they have more people looking, but they still struggle to find them.

Scientists hypothesize that evolution doesn't occur at a constant rate: It can occur in bursts separated by long periods when not much happens. If the transitional period was brief, the chance that such forms would have been fossilized is even more dicey.

When you think about it, it's really quite amazing that people find fossils at all because the events leading to the fossilization of those wonderfully complete skeletons you read about in the news are quite rare. Conditions have to be just right — leave something in your vegetable crisper for sixty million years, and it's not likely to be enough material to do any sort of analysis on! The organism not only has to die, but it also has to be buried intact and remain undisturbed in conditions hospitable to the mineralization process that preserves the remains. Then, possibly millions of years later, someone stumbles across it and calls in the news cameras.

Biogeographic patterns, or location, location, location

Darwin carefully studied the biogeographical patterns of existing species. (*Biogeography* is the study of the locations of different species through space.) Biogeography reveals that species that appear to be closely related tend to be geographically close as well, as though groups of species had a common origin at a particular geographic location and radiated out from there. Darwin was especially interested in the study of species on islands, and he observed that they seemed to be most closely related to species found on the nearest mainland. Darwin was interested in what, if anything, these biogeographical patterns revealed about evolutionary history.

In developing his ideas, Darwin focused on finches that lived on the Galapagos Islands, an archipelago in the Pacific Ocean off South America. Several species of finches live on the Galapagos, each species inhabiting a different island. The species seemed quite similar to one another *and* to a species on the mainland, leading Darwin to hypothesize that the different species of Galapagos finches were descended from individuals in the mainland species that had reached the islands sometime in the past. Because conditions on the islands differed from conditions on the mainland, the selective pressures acting on the finches also differed, resulting in new traits being favored in the new environment.

Archaeopteryx and Tiktaalik

Archaeopteryx is one of the few transitional life forms that was known in Darwin's time. This early birdlike creature had many characteristics in common with some dinosaurs, yet it also had wings and feathers. Most obvious to the casual observer, *Archaeopteryx* had jaws full of sharp teeth, rather than the beak structure of birds. *Archaeopteryx* was clearly more toward the bird end of the transition to flight. Recently, paleontologists have discovered feathered dinosaurs that did not have wings.

Another interesting creature, *Tiktaalik*, had a skeletal structure intermediate between fish and *tetrapods* (critters with four legs) and had both gills and lungs. This skeletal structure was sufficient to have allowed the organism to support itself, at least briefly, out of water. When the first creatures crawled onto the land, they might have looked like *Tiktaalik*. You can read more about these and other fossil finds in Chapter 20.

As a result of the different evolutionary tracks between the mainland finches and island finches, the gradual changes accumulated to the point where the island finches were different enough from the mainland finches to be considered a new species. The concept of *speciation,* in which one species gives rise to a new species, can seem a bit slippery at first, but it's really not. Head to Chapter 8 for the details.

This process occurred on the various Galapagos Islands, which are far enough apart that travel among them by finches is uncommon. After those rare events when finches *did* make it to a new island — perhaps as a result of being blown there by a storm — they evolved separately from the population on the island from which they came, in response to whatever novel environmental factors were present in their new home.

When Darwin proposed that the Galapagos Islands had become inhabited by so many different but apparently related species of finches through the process of evolution, he had only his observations of existing variation to rely on. Today's scientists, by analyzing DNA, have confirmed these relationships, and detailed studies support Darwin's hypotheses about the existence of different selective pressures on different islands.

Natural selection and speciation

As the preceding section explains, Darwin hypothesized that natural selection operating over a long period accumulates enough small changes in a population to make that population so different that it would be its own species, no longer able to interbreed with other populations of the species it had previously been a member of. Once again, Darwin turns out to have been right. Scientists have evidence that such small changes can have such large consequences over time.

What constitutes a species? The answer depends on the type of organisms you're talking about. Scientists have a reasonably good handle on what constitutes an animal species; determining what differentiates plant and microbial species (such as viruses and bacteria) is a bit slipperier. For animals, though, differentiating one species from another is fairly clear cut. A *species* is a group of organisms that can breed with one another but not with organisms in different species. In other words, reproductive isolation is the key to differentiating species.

Given the way evolution works (small changes over time produce enough changes to create a different species), researchers should be able to find all intermediate forms in nature. *Ring species,* species in which two populations of a particular species can't interbreed with each other (usually because of geographical distance) even though both can breed with other populations of that species, allow scientists to observe how the gradual changes can result in reproductive isolation. In addition to the ring species, scientists have numerous examples of intermediary species: those that have recently diverged and are very similar to one another yet unable to interbreed, and those that are in the process of diverging, in which case they've already differentiated to the point where reproduction is less successful or less common. You can find out more about these patterns in Chapter 8.

Origin of life

This book concerns itself with the evolution of organisms that are already present, not with the question — fascinating as it is — of where organisms came from in the first place. The question of how life arose on Earth really isn't a question for evolutionary biology. It's a question for chemistry, because in asking about the transition from nonliving to living systems, you must ask questions about the chemical environment that existed on Earth at the time when life appeared. Although no one has succeeded yet with an experiment that involves mixing a bunch of things in a beaker and waiting for something to crawl out, some very clever experiments have been conducted that show how complex biochemicals can arise spontaneously out of simple mixtures under conditions thought to be present on Earth more than 3 billion years ago.

Darwin imagined that such things might happen in a warm pond. Chemists Harold C. Urey (who won the Nobel Prize for discovering heavy water) and Stanley L. Miller actually made the pond. They combined water hydrogen, methane, and ammonia in a sterile glass system; heated the flask to produce a humid atmosphere; and then sent electrical shocks though the mixture to simulate lightning. They repeated this procedure for a week and then analyzed the contents of the flask. By using this simple procedure, they were able to produce DNA, RNA, amino acids, sugars, and lipids — all the building blocks of life from four very simple molecules.

Chapter 3

Getting into Your Genes: (Very) Basic Genetics

In This Chapter

▶ Defining genes and genomes

▶ Decoding the genetic code

▶ Going from genotype to phenotype

▶ Finding out about mutations

*T*he study of genetics is pretty fascinating, and the language of genetics is cropping up in a growing number of places. It's often in the news and even makes periodic appearances in movies and TV shows. You've probably heard references to DNA and genes; perhaps you've even heard of the Human Genome Project or of specific genes for human diseases. All this aside, you may be wondering why I've included a chapter on genetics in a book about evolution. The answer is simple. Evolution involves genetic changes over time, so to understand evolution, you need to know a little bit about genetics: what it is, how it works, and what parts are particularly important to the study of evolution.

What Is Genetics?

Genetics is the science of investigating the relationship between parental and offspring characteristics; in other words, it's the study of heredity. For most of human history, people have understood that offspring tend to resemble their parents. Only relatively recently, beginning in the late 1800s, have we begun to understand how the genetic process works.

An easy way to think about genetics is to think about it in terms of information. In every cell of your body is a complete instruction manual for making a person, and somehow, these instructions get passed on to your offspring. The instruction manual is your DNA — basically a repository for all the instructions that make you, you.

As our understanding of the underlying mechanisms of genetics has increased, the field of genetics has expanded to include several new areas:

✔ **Molecular genetics** is concerned with the biochemistry of DNA and genes, helping scientists understand exactly how DNA is replicated and transcribed. Molecular genetics is important to evolution because it helps clarify the process of *mutation* — that is, the errors that occur when something in the replication process goes awry. Most of these mutations are bad, but every so often, one of them results in something good. Mutations are the initial sources of the variations on which natural selection can act.

✔ **Genomics,** a new branch of genetics, is concerned with the properties and information content of whole genomes. Comparing the genomes of different organisms gives us a better idea of how, for example, humans can be so different from chimps when they have most of the same DNA sequences. Looking at major genome-wide differences between people can help us understand the health implications of these differences.

✔ **Population genetics** is the study of how the genetic variation that exists within groups of organisms changes over time. By studying large groups rather than individuals, scientists can observe the evolutionary process — some genes become more common, and others go extinct — to determine whether natural selection is involved.

Population geneticists can't use elephants or any other creature that has a long lifespan. Instead, they perform these studies with critters that don't live as long, such as bacteria. Sure, it takes some of the glamour out of the headlines, but the findings are still pretty amazing (to geneticists, anyway).

It's not always necessary to understand a process completely to make use of it. Although humans have only recently come to understand the details of how heredity works, we've been selectively breeding agriculturally important plant and animal types for thousands of years. For his part, Charles Darwin didn't understand exactly how it was that offspring resemble their parents; he just knew that they did. In the short span of this chapter, you'll discover more about genetics than Darwin ever knew! Because we now have a better understanding of the nuts and bolts of genetics and heredity, we are able to understand the evolutionary process in ways that Darwin could only dream of.

DNA: A Molecule for Storing Genetic Information

DNA, otherwise known as *deoxyribonucleic acid,* is the molecule that stores your genetic information. As you might imagine, the instruction manual for making you (or any other type of critter) can be very large, so it's not too surprising that a single molecule of DNA can be enormous — so big, in fact, that under the right circumstances you can see a DNA molecule with the naked eye. (To find out how, see the sidebar "A DNA cocktail: Extracting DNA at home.")

Chromosomes: Where your DNA is

An organism's DNA is found in a cellular structure called a *chromosome.* Some organisms have all their DNA on one chromosome, while other organisms have their DNA spread across several chromosomes. The DNA of sexually reproducing organisms, like animals and humans, is arranged on pairs of chromosomes. When these organisms make offspring, the offspring get one set of chromosomes from each parent. Humans, for example, have 23 pairs of chromosomes. Each of us got a set from each parent, meaning we each have half of Mom's genes and half of Dad's.

DNA isn't an abstract concept. It's an actual thing that appears in a particular place (the chromosomes) in each of your cells. And every cell has a copy of the chromosomes.

DNA's four-letter alphabet

Although DNA can be a huge molecule, it's actually a simple one. DNA is made up of just four different building blocks that are called *nucleotides,* or bases. The four nucleotides are

- ✔ Adenine, abbreviated as A
- ✔ Cytosine, abbreviated as C
- ✔ Thymine, abbreviated as T
- ✔ Guanine, abbreviated as G

The function of DNA is information storage, which is what's so cool about it. All the instructions needed to make you can be written with just four letters!

The structure of DNA is a double helix consisting of two strands winding around each other (see Figure 3-1). Each strand can contain up to thousands of the four nucleotides, and the two strands are joined in a very specific way:

- ✔ A always pairs with T.
- ✔ C always pairs with G.
- ✔ T always pairs with A.
- ✔ G always pairs with C.

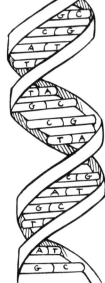

Figure 3-1:
The double-
helix
structure
of DNA.

One strand is an inverted version of the other, so if you know the sequence of one strand, you know the sequence of both strands. To give you an oversimplified example, if you have one strand of CATG, you know that the other strand is GTAC.

You may wonder how four nucleotides could possibly be the basis of all life in all its complexity. Well, you wouldn't be the first. What scientists discovered is that these four letters actually appear in groups of three, called *codons*. It turns out there are 64 codons. (You can read more about codons and the genetic code in the section "Protein-coding RNA and the genetic code" later in this chapter).

The double-helix structure of DNA has two properties that make it an excellent molecule for information storage:

- ✓ **It's an incredibly tough molecule.** DNA is so tough, in fact, that scientists have been able to isolate intact DNA from extinct mammoths found buried in Siberian ice and even, in some cases, from fossilized bones.

- ✓ **The double-stranded arrangement provides a very easy way to make accurate copies.** During DNA replication, the two strands of the double helix separate, and an *enzyme* (a protein that's involved in facilitating a chemical reaction) called *DNA polymerase* makes two new strands by using the original strands as guides. This produces two double helix molecules. Each is an exact copy of the original.

A DNA cocktail: Extracting DNA at home

DNA tends to strike people as being somewhat mysterious, but really, it's just a very long molecule. Although it's certainly amazing how organisms use DNA for information storage, it's not magic — just chemistry. If you want to *see* DNA rather than just read about it, the following recipe for a DNA cocktail shows you how to do so. The chemistry is simple.

Ingredients

8 strawberries

⅓ ounce blue Curaçao liqueur

⅔ ounce gin

2 ounces fresh pineapple juice

Instructions:

1. **Freeze the strawberries.**

2. **Chill the Curaçao, the gin, and a glass.**

   A tall narrow glass works best. A test tube would work too, but make sure it's a clean one!

3. **When the glass (or test tube) is cold, add the Curaçao.**

4. **Tilt the glass or tube with great care; then pour the chilled gin down the side to form a layer above the Curaçao.**

5. **Purée the frozen strawberries with the pineapple juice for 10 seconds.**

   Strawberries contain DNA. Blending them with pineapple juice allows the enzymatic activity in the juice to free the DNA from all the other bits of the strawberry that it hangs onto. The fresher the pineapple juice, the more enzymatic activity it will have, allowing the experiment to work even better.

6. **Layer the strawberry-pineapple mixture on top of the gin.**

   When the now-dissolved DNA comes into contact with the cold gin, it *precipitates out of solution* (that is, turns into a solid due to the chemical reaction), and you see little white wisps floating in the gin layer. Those white wisps are the actual DNA molecules, and they contain all the information that makes the strawberry plant what it is. The Curaçao doesn't serve any high-tech chemical function; it's just there to make the final product a nice red, white, and blue — and to make it taste nice!

Reading the Instructions: From DNA to RNA to Proteins

The four-letter alphabet of DNA is where an organism's instruction manual is stored, but when it comes time to actually make an organism, you need proteins. Proteins comprise most of the basic machinery that makes an organism work. Your muscles are made of proteins, your antibodies are proteins, your digestive enzymes are proteins — you just wouldn't be who you are without proteins.

To make proteins, you need RNA. RNA, or *ribonucleic acid,* is similar to DNA but has a couple of important differences:

- ✔ RNA is usually a single-stranded molecule, whereas DNA is a double-stranded molecule.

- ✔ Although both RNA and DNA are made of four nucleotides, RNA uses uracil instead of thymine. Specifically, RNA uses the nucleotides adenine, uracil, cytosine, and guanine, which are abbreviated A, U, C, and G.

Transcription: Producing RNA

The process in which a single-stranded RNA molecule is produced from a double-stranded DNA molecule is called *transcription.* The details of the transcription process aren't important for the purposes of this discussion (you can thank me later for sparing you), but the gist of it is that the double-stranded DNA molecule unwinds a bit, and a single-stranded RNA molecule is produced by copying one of the strands.

The four nucleotides that make up RNA line up to match the order of the DNA nucleotides, as follows:

- ✔ A (from RNA) lines up with T (from DNA).
- ✔ C (from RNA) lines up with G (from DNA).
- ✔ G (from RNA) lines up with C (from DNA).
- ✔ U (from RNA) lines up with A (from DNA).

In this way, the four-letter alphabet of DNA is transcribed into the four-letter alphabet of RNA.

 Different regions of DNA produce RNA transcripts with different functions. Some of the RNA transcripts code directly for the production of proteins, and other types of RNA transcripts don't code for proteins themselves, they just help the process along.

Protein-coding RNA and the genetic code

The RNA transcripts that code for the production of proteins are called *messenger RNA* (abbreviated mRNA). Messenger RNA's job is to transfer the information regarding what proteins need to be made from the DNA to the protein-producing machinery where proteins are assembled: the ribosomes (see the next section, "Non-protein-coding RNA").

RNA and DNA are each composed of four subunits (their four respective nucleotides). The DNA nucleotides appear in groups of three (the 64 codons, discussed in "DNA: A Molecule for Storing Genetic Information" earlier in this chapter). Proteins are composed of 20 subunits, called *amino acids.* The exact translation from codons to the amino acids is called the *genetic code.*

Back before anyone knew that DNA is the molecule where genetic information is stored, many people argued that DNA just wasn't complicated enough. They wondered how something with only four different letters could code for all the complexity of an organism. Thus, at one point, proteins were considered to be good candidates for the material used for information storage because they had 20 amino acids — or 20 different letters available in their alphabet. The breakthrough in understanding came when scientists determined that the 4 nucleotides were read in groups of 3, meaning that instead of containing 4 individual letters, DNA has an alphabet of 64 triplet letters, called codons. That discovery raised another question. Instead of wondering how to code for 20 amino acids with only 4 letters, people questioned how you would code for only 20 amino acids when you have 64 codons. The answer is that there is some redundancy in the translation of DNA into proteins.

Figure 3-2 shows all 64 codons of the genetic code. Most of the amino acids correspond to multiple codons, as you can see from the figure (the notations Phe, Leu, and so on). Some codons, though, don't code for amino acids at all; instead, they signal that protein synthesis should stop. These codons are called *stop codons.* They tell the protein-producing machinery to stop adding amino acids to a growing protein, and their presence indicates that the protein is finished.

Second Letter

		U	C	A	G	
First Letter	**U**	UUU UUC } Phe UUA UUG } Leu	UCU UCC UCA UCG } Ser	UAU UAC } Tyr UAA Stop UAG Stop	UGU UGC } Cys UGA Stop UGG Trp	U C A G
	C	CUU CUC CUA CUG } Leu	CCU CCC CCA CCG } Pro	CAU CAC } His CAA CAG } Gin	CGU CGC CGA CGG } Arg	U C A G
	A	AUU AUC } Ile AUA AUG Met	ACU ACC ACA ACG } Thr	AAU AAC } Asn AAA AAG } Lys	AGU AGC } Ser AGA AGG } Arg	U C A G
	G	GUU GUC GUA GUG } Val	GCU GCC GCA GCG } Ala	GAU GAC } Asp GAA GAG } Glu	GGU GGC GGA GGG } Gly	U C A G

Third Letter

Figure 3-2: The 64 codons of the genetic code.

Non-protein-coding RNA

In addition to the protein-coding transcripts, an organism's DNA produces other RNA transcripts that assist with the production of proteins. These other RNAs fall into several categories. For purposes of this book, I won't bore you by listing them. All you need to remember is that the most important category for evolution is ribosomal RNA.

Ribosomal RNA (abbreviated rRNA) is the class of RNA molecules that makes up the *ribosomes,* the cellular factories that produce proteins.

Ribosomal RNA is of special interest to evolutionary biologists because all organisms need ribosomes for protein production; therefore, ribosomal RNA can be used for a couple key evolutionary tasks:

- **Understanding relationships between different organisms:** Ribosomes provide a character that can be compared across all branches of life. Most characteristics aren't shared across all branches of life. Take eyes, for example. Few things have eyes. As a result, comparing a human with, say, a stalk of broccoli and a mushroom based on similarities and differences in the structure of the eye is impossible. But humans, mushrooms, and stalks of broccoli *do* all have ribosomal RNA. (In case you're curious, you and the mushroom are a fair bit more similar to each other at the ribosomal level than either of you is to the broccoli!)

- **Determining historical relationships between species:** Beyond explaining the level at which people and fungi share similarities, the really fascinating thing about ribosomal RNA is that evolutionists can use nucleotide sequences to determine the historical relationships among species. In other words, it can help clarify which branch of the tree of life an organism belongs to. You can read more about the tree of life in Chapter 9.

Ribosomal RNA isn't important just as a tool for evolutionary biology. It's also important to the proper functioning of the cell — so much so that 80 percent of the RNA in a given cell can be ribosomal RNA. The other categories of non-coding RNA are *transfer RNA* (abbreviated tRNA), which is involved in assembling the amino acids that make a protein, and a growing collection of small RNA molecules (we keep discovering new ones) that seem to be involved with the regulation of *gene expression* — a fancy way of referring to the process of deciding which genes get turned on and off in any given cell. (Think about it: All your cells have all your genes, but the genes needed to make your eyes aren't expressed in your fingers, or vice versa.)

Getting Specific about Genes

Oh, the poor gene. It has fallen mightily from its halcyon days of being defined as the fundamental unit of heredity. Back then, it was clear that somehow, some way, specific bits of information were passed from parent to offspring. No one had any idea exactly what these bits were, but it was clear that they existed, and we called them genes. Now that we understand genetic information is contained in an organism's DNA, we've booted . . . er, defined what we mean by *gene* more precisely.

Of alleles and loci

When most people think about heritable traits, they think about genes. Unfortunately, the term *gene* is a little too general for a discussion of evolution. Instead, you need to know a little more about how the DNA strand is put together. As I state earlier in this chapter, DNA is simply long strings of nucleotides, abbreviated A, C, T, and G. That's good for starters, but you need to know a bit more.

The word *gene* is commonly used in a couple of different but related ways:

- ✔ **To refer to a specific place in an organism's genome:** An organism's DNA contains a *lot* of information, including all the instructions for building and maintaining that particular life form. The different instructions for different genes are located in different places along the DNA sequence. A specific location of a gene in an organism's DNA is called a *locus* (plural *loci,* pronounced *low-sigh*).

- ✔ **To refer to the exact sequence of the DNA at a specific place (or locus) in the genome:** The sequence of nucleotides at a specific locus can differ among organisms. These different sequences are called *alleles.* Take the locus that stores the information to make the blood type protein. When scientists examine this locus in several individuals, they find variations; some alleles code for type O blood, some for type A blood, and so on. The exact sequence of the ACTG alphabet is different, and this is why people have different blood types.

Using the first, you might refer to a gene for "blood type," but using the second, you'd refer to a gene for "type O blood" — the specific DNA sequence that results in a particular blood type. Both definitions are workable as long as you keep track of which one you're using. In this book, when I talk about genes, I'm referring in most instances to the *loci.* And when I'm referring to alleles, I let you know.

At any given place *(locus)* on the DNA strand, the sequence of nucleotides (the alleles) that appears can be the same or different, with each particular sequence representing a different manifestation of a particular trait. At the locus where the eye-color trait resides, for example, you find alleles representing the different colors: blue, green, brown, and so on.

Imagine a single locus with two alleles, A and a, each representing a different manifestation of a particular trait. Because the locus has only two options, you can figure out pretty easily what individual combinations you may find in the population. In this case, some people would have AA (having received A from both parents), Aa (having received A from one parent and a from the other), and aa (having received a from both parents).

Here are a couple of other facts about alleles to keep in mind:

✔ As is the case with eye color (or blood type or a number of other traits, for that matter), you can have more than two alleles at a given locus *in the population,* but *any particular individual* can have at most only two alleles: one that came from the mother and one that came from the father.

✔ When two alleles at a particular locus are the same, they're said to be *homozygous.* When the alleles are different, they're *heterozygous.* I don't throw these terms in just for kicks. Whether the alleles are different or the same is an important factor in how, when, or even whether the heritable trait manifests itself, as the following sections explain.

Dominant, recessive, or passive-aggressive?

You probably won't be surprised that the genes you (or any other sexually reproducing organism) inherited from your parents can determine outward characteristics — hence the idiom "chip off the old block." The scientific way of stating this rather obvious point is "Genotype (genes) translates into phenotype (physical traits)." Here are the possibilities:

✔ **Each different genotype has different phenotypes.** Maybe AA makes red flowers, aa makes white flowers, and Aa makes pink flowers — an easy-to-understand example if you know that the A allele codes for a red-pigment protein, and the more of that protein the individual makes, the redder the pigment is.

✔ **The genes interact as dominant (represented by a capital letter) and recessive (represented by a small letter).** When a recessive allele is paired with a dominant allele, the phenotype is the same as for an individual with two dominant alleles. So in the AA, Aa, and aa example, AA and Aa have one phenotype, and aa has another.

To read more about genotype and phenotype — two key terms in evolutionary biology — go the later section "Genotype and phenotype."

Summing It All Up: Genomes

The sum of all the DNA in an organism is called the organism's *genome*. Studying the genome can reveal quite a bit. Scientists know, for example, that a gene exists for a trait like eye color. But sequence an entire genome, and they see that a lot of genes whose purpose isn't clear. They scratch their heads and say "I wonder what this one does?" or "Wow, the sequence of that gene looks a lot like a particular fish gene whose function we do know." Having a whole genome lets scientists asked questions about genes in a completely different way.

From an evolutionary point of view, the genome is intriguing because it presents evolutionary scientists with a bunch of deep questions to ponder like, if genome sizes are different for different organisms (and some in ways that make no obvious sense), then how did that happen? Or why does so much of the genome seem to be junk (and why is this the case in some species but not others)? Any why are similar genes in different places on the genomes of different species?

Size isn't everything: Sizing up the genome

Different organisms have radically different genome sizes, but not necessarily in the way you might expect. You have a much bigger genome than a bacterium or a mushroom does, and at first, that seems to make a lot of sense. After all, humans certainly appear to be more complex than bacteria or mushrooms. We have a lot more parts — arms, eyes, complicated nervous systems, and so on — so it seems reasonable that our genome would be bigger. Right? Well . . . maybe, and maybe not.

The range of genome sizes varies among several major groups of organisms. Your genome is much bigger than the genome of yeast or *Escherichia coli* (*E. coli*) bacteria, for example, yet many plants have more DNA that people do. And just in case your ego hasn't taken enough of a hit, you should be aware that some plants don't just have more DNA than we do, but more genes as well. Poplars, for example, have twice as many genes as people do.

For details about genome size and coding and non-coding DNA, head to Chapter 15.

Base pairs

The unit of genome size is the number of *base pairs* (abbreviated *bp*). Why base pairs? It's simple math, really — and understanding how the DNA sequence works. Think about the size of the human genome, which contains about 12 billion nucleotides. Because of the paired structure of DNA (A always pairs with T, C always pairs with G, and so on), when you know the 6 billion on one strand, you automatically know the 6 billion on the other strand. From an information standpoint, only 6 billion independent bits of information exist. As a result, scientists refer to the size of the human genome as 6 billion bp.

Junk DNA

Some DNA doesn't seem to contain much information; it's what scientists call *junk DNA*. Some junk DNA consists of long sections in which short sequences of nucleotides repeat over and over and over. Both plants and mammals have lots of junk DNA, but plants seem to have more (which explains why the fern hanging in your kitchen has more DNA than you do). That's quite a feat, considering that we humans have a lot of junk ourselves. And just how much junk do we have? As a matter of fact, it appears that more than 95 percent of human DNA doesn't contain any information about how to make a person! Researchers are still trying to figure out why so much of human DNA is junk — a problem that I discuss in Chapter 15.

Number of genes

Scientists have determined the DNA sequence of the entire human genome (a fact you may already know from the various news stories that accompanied the completion of the Human Genome Project). So it may come as a surprise that scientists still don't know exactly how many genes humans have. Are they lazy or just unmotivated? As it turns out, neither.

It's sometimes tricky to tell exactly when a sequence at some particular locus in human genome contains instructions used for making a person and when it contains junk. And because the human genome is more than 95 percent junk, small variations in how scientists go about deciding what is a gene and what isn't can make a big difference in the total number of genes they think humans have.

As researchers keep refining their techniques for identifying genes in this big sea of DNA, they end up revising their numbers progressively downward. Currently, they think they have a good handle on the situation and are reasonably certain that the human genome contains about 25,000 genes. Is that a lot? "A lot" is a relative thing. Common intestinal bacteria have about 5,000 genes; yeast has about 6,000; the common laboratory roundworm has around 18,000; and the fruit fly *Drosophila* has 14,000. And many plants seem to have as many genes as human do, and some have far more.

What's up with all this junk?

The human genome is not the only one that scientists have sequenced in its entirety. Initial genome sequencing projects concentrated on smaller creatures, such as bacteria, and it turns out that very little of those genomes is junk. Although researchers can't say with certainty why humans have so much junk DNA, it's not hard for them to come up with reasons why smaller, rapidly dividing organisms do not. For example:

✔ They're little, so all that junk DNA won't fit.

✔ They're in a hurry, because competing bacteria are sucking up nutrients and reproducing as fast as they can. They don't have time to replicate an enormous genome that's mostly junk without falling behind and being overrun by all the other bacteria.

Humans, however, are not in such a hurry all the time, and the energy it takes to copy human DNA is a very small part of our total energy budget.

When scientists look at a sequence of DNA and identify genes, they have techniques for determining that a particular piece of DNA makes something and can use the genetic code to determine the amino-acid sequence of the protein that piece of DNA makes. But they still don't have a very good way of looking at a protein sequence and figuring out what the protein actually *does*. If the protein looks like something else whose function scientists understand, they have some clues. But if the protein isn't similar to something scientists already know about, they're often in the dark about what particular genes do. Thus, researchers don't yet understand exactly why organisms have the numbers of genes that they have.

Genome organization: Nuclear, mitochondrial, or free floating?

Where in the world is your genome, anyway? In two different places within your cells: the nucleus and the mitochondria.

✔ **In the nucleus:** Your body is made of cells that have a structure in the middle called the *nucleus.* This is where most of your genetic material resides. The nucleus isn't just one long piece of DNA, but an arranged series of individual pieces called *chromosomes* (refer to the earlier section "Chromosomes: Where your DNA is" for information on what chromosomes do).

✔ **In the mitochondria:** Another structure in your cells contains DNA. This structure is called *mitochondria,* and each of your cells contains several dozens to hundreds of these structures. Mitochondria serve as the power plants of the cell; they're involved in metabolism and energy production.

Mitochondrial DNA doesn't contain many genes, but it's fascinating that mitochondria have any DNA at all. Why do these small things inside your cells have their own genome, and how did they get there? In later chapters, I get back to mitochondria, examining how they evolved and looking at what various studies of mitochondrial DNA tell scientists about human history. For now, just remember that you have some mitochondria and that your mitochondria have some DNA.

Not all organisms have cells with nuclei. In bacteria, the genetic material is happy to float around inside the cell, hanging out with everything else, and doesn't need its own special home. Furthermore, bacteria tend to keep their genome in one piece. It probably would be biochemically complicated for humans to have their entire genome in one segment, as the DNA would be extremely long. Bacteria can get away with keeping their genome together only because their genomes are much smaller. But small things don't necessarily have genomes that are just one piece; many viruses store their genomes in sections.

How many copies?

Some organisms have more copies of their genome than others do. At first, you may think it would be good to have extra copies of your own personal blueprints, just in case you lose one of the instructions. Although having an extra copy has obvious advantages, it also may have some costs, including the additional time it takes to replicate two copies of your genome before cell division. Biologists think that these costs must outweigh the benefits for most bacteria, which is why many bacteria have only a single copy of their genome.

Sometimes, when the benefits of having a backup copy outweigh the costs of growing more slowly, an organism has an extra copy of its genome. These cases include organisms that really need multiple spare genomes to fix errors. One such organism is the bacteria species *Deinococcus radiodurans.* This little critter has not one extra copy of its genome, but several copies, probably due to the fact that it lives in extremely harsh environments where DNA damage is more likely to occur from such factors as extreme drying. As a result of having these extra copies of its genetic material, *Deinococcus radiodurans* is the most radiation-resistant organism known. This little fellow can handle 500 times more radiation than you can.

Passing It On: Sexual Reproduction and the Genome

Diploid organisms — those with two sets of genetic information — don't have two copies of one genome. Instead, each locus on the genome is comprised of two sets of alleles.

When a sexually reproducing organism — such as a person — produces off-spring, it first must make gametes (in the case of a human, eggs or sperm). Each of the gametes gets one copy of the DNA segments. This gamete combines with a gamete from the organism's mate to produce an individual with two sets of DNA.

When one set comes from Mom and one set comes from Dad, the sets may be slightly different. This situation makes for some interesting genetic questions. One example: How do our bodies read the instructions if the two copies aren't the same? That depends on the particular alleles: what trait or characteristic they're coding for and whether either is dominant.

Dominating issues

Consider the snapdragons. Snapdragons are diploid, just like you are, though they make ovules and pollen rather than eggs or sperm. At a particular place in their genome is a locus that's responsible for flower color. Two possible alleles appear at this locus; call these alleles W and R. (Alleles are often referred to by letters.) Plants with two copies of the W allele are white; plants with two copies of the R allele are red. How about plants that have one copy of each allele? In the case of snapdragons, the plants with one W allele and one R allele are pink, which seems to make sense.

But it doesn't always work that way. Sometimes one of the alleles is *dominant*, explained in the earlier section "Dominant, recessive, or passive aggressive." If a plant has only one copy of that allele, that allele determines the organism's characteristics. In the pea plants that the famous geneticist Gregor Mendel worked with, there are two possible alleles at the locus responsible for flower color: one that codes for purple flowers (P) and one that codes for white flowers (w). In Mendel's peas, the purple allele is dominant (hence the capital rather than lowercase letter). If a plant has two alleles that code for purple, then it has purple flowers. If it has two alleles that code for white, then it has white flowers. But because the purple allele is dominant, a plant with one purple and one white allele turns out just as purple as a plant with two purple alleles.

In this case, knowing the color of the organism doesn't give you perfect information about the underlying genetics. If the pea flower is white, you know that it has two of white alleles (ww). But if the pea flower is purple, it may have two purple alleles (PP) or one purple allele and one white allele (Pw). This situation leads to the topic of genotype and phenotype, which very conveniently comes next.

Genotype and phenotype

Genotype refers to the alleles that a particular organism has — the actual sequences of DNA in its genome, such as a gene for growth hormone. *Phenotype* refers to the physical characteristics of the organism, such as the organism's height.

Genotype and phenotype are often connected, but the important thing to remember is that the connection is *not* always absolute. Organisms with the same phenotypes may have different genotypes; similarly, organizations with the same genotypes may have different phenotypes. What this means is that you can't always determine what DNA sequences are at play simply by identifying outward characteristics; neither can you always know whether an organism's characteristics are the result of genetics or of something else.

Different phenotypes, same genotype

An organism's phenotype — its physical characteristics — is not always determined by its genes alone. Grasping this concept is especially important when you think about evolution by natural selection. Environmental factors — like how much food we get or how big our pond is — interact with genotype to produce an organism's phenotype.

Imagine a pack of cheetahs chasing a gazelle across the African plains. One by one, the cheetahs get tired and give up. But one cheetah keeps at it and eventually catches the gazelle. It's a tough year out there in the Serengeti, and the mere difference of a single gazelle can determine whether a cheetah is able to reproduce.

Why this cheetah captured the gazelle while the others fell away, I have absolutely no idea. Are her genes especially good? Does she have different genes that make her go extra fast? Perhaps . . . but perhaps not. It could be that all the cheetahs have the same genes, but this particular cheetah was lucky enough to have been very well fed when she was a cub and, as a result, grew up to be faster and stronger. If that's the case, all these cheetahs have the same genotype, but the phenotype — in the successful cheetah's case, the strength and stamina to continue the chase — differs.

Same phenotype, different genotypes

Occasionally, organisms have the same phenotype (characteristics) but different genotypes (gene sequences). Consider the human blood-type alleles A, B, and O. Each of us has two of these alleles, receiving one from each parent. Six pairs of alleles are possible: AA, AO, BB, BO, AB, and OO. Yet only four blood types exist: A, B, AB, and O. How does that work?

Well, in one way, it's similar to the snapdragon with a red, white, and pink flower. Whether you have A, B, or AB blood depends on the genotype:

- The AA genotype (you got an A allele from each parent) gives you type A blood.
- The BB genotype (you got a B allele from each parent) gives you type B blood.
- The AB genotype (you got an A allele from one parent and a B from the other) gives you type AB blood.

To understand the others, you need to know that A and B are dominant over O, but neither is dominant over the other. Therefore:

- The AO genotype gives you type A blood.
- The BO genotype gives you type B blood.
- The OO genotype gives you type O blood.

Knowing the phenotype sometimes gives you complete information about the genotype, such as the phenotypes for type O blood and type AB blood. But in the cases of blood type A and blood type B, two possible genotypes could bring about each phenotype.

What this has to do with natural selection

Natural selection — the process by which organisms with favorable traits are more likely to reproduce and pass on their genes (see Chapter 5 for more in-depth info) — acts on phenotype, not genotype. Think about it. No matter how great an organism's genes are, they can be reproduced in subsequent generations only if that organism reproduces — and *that* depends on outward characteristics (phenotypes).

In the earlier cheetah example, you expect that faster cheetahs will leave more descendents in future generations than the slow ones that couldn't catch dinner. Some phenotypic variation existed in the cheetah population, and as a result, some cheetahs did better than others. That's natural selection. But is it evolution? Depends.

Selection results in evolution *only* if there are genetic differences between the cheetahs of different speeds. The difference in speed has to be a heritable one — one that can be passed on genetically from parent to offspring. If the faster cheetahs have different genes than the slower cheetahs, then the next generation will have a higher proportion of those genes because the cheetahs that had them eat more antelope and made more baby cheetahs. But if the faster cheetahs aren't any different genetically than the slower ones, then there won't be any evolutionary change from one generation to the next.

Part II
How Evolution Works

The 5th Wave   By Rich Tennant

"As you can see, the mutation exists across species, but specifically to those inhabiting the North Pole."

In this part . . .

*E*volution by natural selection requires mutations. Now, there aren't many times when you hear the word "mutation" and think it's a good thing. Even in evolutionary terms, most mutations are bad. But some mutations give an organism a fitness advantage resulting in its being able to survive and reproduce. The result? More of the genetically advantaged organisms in future populations.

But selection isn't the only evolutionary force. Genetic drift (a fancy way of saying random events) can affect gene frequencies, too. If a mudslide wipes out a large portion of a wildflower that just happens to bloom pink in a particular area, then there will be fewer pink-flowering plants in later generations.

This part tackles the mechanisms of evolutionary change (variation, mutation, selection — both natural and artificial — genetic drift, and so on); their results (loss of genetic variation, change in genetic variation, and speciation); and how to retrace past evolutionary events and see the relationships among species (through phylogenetic trees).

Chapter 4

Variation: A Key Requirement for Evolution

*E*volution can't happen without variation, but not just any type of variation will do. It must be *heritable* variation — that is, variation that gets passed genetically from parent to offspring. But some evolutionary forces, such as natural selection and genetic drift (covered in Chapters 5 and 6, respectively), actually cause a *reduction* in genetic variation over time. Fortunately, *mutations* — random errors in the genetic code — generate the very kind of variation that evolution needs. Despite the fact that most of the specific mutations aren't good for any organisms, mutations in general are absolutely necessary.

Variation and mutation go hand in hand, so this chapter examines both topics. And because it's always fun to see how the genes you get affect who you are, I also discuss how many of the traits you exhibit are determined by the genes you have.

Understanding Variation

In evolutionary terms, *variation* simply refers to the differences you see among individuals. In other words, individuals from any species aren't all the same. Look around a room full of people, and you notice that all of them look different. That's variation. You can see how heritable changes — hair color, eye color, facial structure, height, and so on — manifest themselves outwardly. But these changes also manifest themselves in ways that aren't so easy to see, such as propensity for certain illnesses or blood type. And if those differences are a result of genes, that's *heritable,* or *genetic, variation.*

Even though variation is a simple concept to grasp, it's a crucial component of evolution. Without heritable variation, evolution couldn't occur, because change couldn't occur from generation to generation. If every individual in one generation were the same, every individual in the next generation would be the same. Variation has to be present before natural selection occurs; you can't have the sorting-out process if nothing's available to sort.

You're most aware of small differences in things you spend a lot of time interacting with. Just because all hyenas (or wild dogs, ducks, or any other nonhuman organism) seem *to you* to look the same, act the same, and do the same things doesn't mean that those species lack variation.

Key concepts in variation

As stated previously, for evolution to occur, the variation has to be heritable. If all the individuals in a population are genetically identical, and they produce offspring that are genetically identical, evolution hasn't occurred, because the next generation is the same genetically as the current generation.

Variation exists in natural populations, and there's often a lot of it:

- **Variation within a species:** All species have variation. Just thinking of the variations within our own species is a good place to start. It would take at least 100 books this size to list all the ways that people are genetically different from one another. An important thing to remember, though, is that the variation within a species doesn't need to be uniformly distributed across all population in that species. The different populations will all have genetic variability, but they all won't always have the same genetic patterns. For example, a species may contain individuals of many different heights, but not all populations within that species will have individuals of all heights; some populations may be made up of, on average, taller individuals than others.

- **Variation within populations:** It's the variability within a population that allows the population to respond to natural selection. Take the finches in the Galapagos. Within one finch population that was studied, there was existing variation in beak size. When other birds arrived on the island and began eating the food these finches relied on, this existing variation allowed that species to evolve to better utilize a smaller seed resource.

- **Variations between populations:** It's the variation between populations that tells us that two populations have evolved in different ways. The populations are genetically different from one another, meaning that gene flow between the populations hasn't been able to overwhelm the different evolutionary forces they experience. That different alleles have increased or decreased in the different populations could be the result of natural selection (discussed in Chapter 5), random factors (the topic in Chapter 6), of both. If two populations continue to become genetically different, they can become too different to interbreed, a topic addressed in Chapter 8.

In evolution, the relevant variation occurs at the group or species level. You cannot talk about variation unless you have more than one individual. If you have variation in the genetic composition of the group or species, the next generation can be different. *That's* evolution.

A variety of mechanisms can cause the genetic makeup of the next generation to differ from the genetic makeup of the current generation. Natural selection (Chapter 5) and random factors (Chapter 6) are two immediate examples. These mechanisms change the genetic makeup of a population from one generation to the next: natural selection, because some genetic types have better reproductive success than others, and genetic drift, just because sometimes stuff happens — a fire kills many blue-eyed deer, leaving fewer blue-eyed deer to make more blue-eyed deer.

Two kinds of variation: Phenotypic and genotypic

The two kinds of variation are *phenotypic* (changes in outward physical traits) and *genotypic* (changes in the organism's underlying genetic makeup — basically, the DNA sequence of its genes).

Individuals with the same phenotype can have different genotypes, and individuals with the same genotype can have different phenotypes. Height, for example, has both a genetic component and an environmental component. You'd think that two people with identical genetic makeup (such as identical twins) would be the same height, but if only one received a healthy diet, the result could be two adults of different heights. In this example, two people with the same genotype have different phenotypes. Conversely, two people with different genetic make-ups can be the same height. In this case, the two individuals have different genotypes but the same phenotypes.

Keeping this distinction in mind is important when you think about how natural selection can cause evolutionary change. Because natural selection doesn't "see" the different genotypes, it acts only on the *phenotypes* — the physical features of the organism that can influence its survival and reproduction. But evolution can occur *only* if phenotypic differences are correlated with genotypic differences.

Imagine that being taller carries a selective advantage — that is, taller folks are better at surviving and reproducing. In the case of the identical twins with different heights, the taller of the two identical twins would be more likely to contribute genes to the next generation, but because the height difference was due to environmental factors and not genetic makeup, the genetic composition of the next generation doesn't change. In the case of the two unrelated people of the same height, the two individuals have different genotypes, but because natural selection acts only on phenotypes, both individuals are the same height, so they have an equal chance of contributing genes to the next generation.

Variation that's important to evolution

You can partition variation by whether it's heritable (or not) or has fitness consequences (or not):

- **Heritable variation:** This type of variation is genetic; these are the differences at the DNA level that are passed from parent to offspring.

- **Non-heritable variation:** This type of variation is the result of the environment factors, things like diet, amount of sunlight, and so on — not genes.

- **Variations that have fitness consequences:** These variations impact, for better or worse, how well an organism is able to survive and reproduce.

- **Variations that don't have fitness consequences:** These variations don't impact either positively or negatively an organism's ability to survive and reproduce.

The type of variation determines in what manner (or even whether) it has an impact on the genetic makeup of future generations:

- If a variation has a fitness consequences but the variation isn't heritable, it won't lead to evolution. For example, people with really cute tattoos may be more likely to pass along their genes, but there's no genetic component to getting a tattoo. Their genes are, on average, no different from anyone else's genes. *Remember:* Without heritable variation, there is no evolution (or evolution books, for that matter).

- If a variation is heritable but it doesn't cause any fitness differences, then the frequencies of these differences in a population will change only as a result of genetic drift, not natural selection.

- If variation is both heritable and has fitness consequences, well then, evolution by natural selection can occur.

Population structure and gene flow

Species are not uniformly mixed. All the people in the human population, for example, are completely capable of mating, but we're not totally genetically mixed, hence, the existence of regional heritable differences. The reason for this lack of mixing is remarkably simple: It's a matter of *gene flow,* which means the movement of genes in space.

The reason the genes within the human population (and the populations of many other species) aren't completely mixed is because we're more likely to mate with others who are nearby. Populations that are close together in space are more likely to exchange genes with each other than populations that are farther away.

Gene flow, the idea that genes can move from one population to another, is a key concept in evolution. You move to Sweden, find a nice, blue-eyed, blond spouse and raise a family. Your children are Swedish, but maybe they've got your eyes — that's gene flow.

Where Variation Comes From: Mutations

The process of evolution (via natural selection, drift, or both) eliminates heritable variation. If not all the alleles make it into the next generation — because some are selected against or disappear due to random forces — heritable variation eventually goes away. That scenario leads to the subject of mutation, which is the ultimate source of genetic variation.

Mutations are changes in an organism's DNA. If all the deer in the forest have only genes to produce normal noses and one deer is born with a blinking red nose (a heritable trait), a mutation must have occurred in one of the gametes (either the sperm or the egg) that led to that red-nosed baby deer.

DNA is an extremely stable molecule; that's what makes it so good for storing your genetic information. But mutations still occur:

- ✓ DNA is tough, but it's not indestructible. It can be damaged, and although your cells try to repair the damage, they don't always get it right, resulting in mutations. Agents that have this damaging effect are referred to as *mutagens.* Examples of mutagens include the ionizing radiation associated with nuclear material, ultraviolet radiation from the sun, and many chemicals.

- ✓ The process of DNA replication that occurs in all cell division — be it in the gametes (egg and sperm) or in *somatic tissue* (everything else) — is another source of mutations. DNA replication is an error-prone process — sometimes the copying isn't exact, and that also results in mutations. (To find out more about DNA replication, refer to Chapter 3.)

Mutations leading to cancer

When you hear the term *mutation,* the first thing that may spring to mind are mutations that cause diseases such as cancer. Stay out in the sun too long, and ultraviolet radiation bombards your skin cells. This radiation causes changes in your DNA that affect the regulation of cell division, and all of a sudden, one of your cells doesn't play nice with the rest of your body. These types of mutations certainly are important medically, but they don't affect the genetic composition of your offspring.

Cancer and other such mutations can be important in evolution if there are differences in the mutation rate between individuals, for example, with some individuals being much more likely to die of cancer than others and, therefore, less likely to have descendants in the next generation. In such a scenario, the characteristic of having a higher mutation rate would be the character under selection, not the cancer itself.

Sometimes, mutations are selectively advantageous. (Rudolph the Red-Nosed Reindeer did save Christmas, after all.) But most of the time, they're not. Mutations are either selectively neutral (they have no effect on fitness) or deleterious (they decrease fitness). Regardless, without mutation, there'd be no variation on which natural selection can act. Yet a number of forces can reduce variation from generation to generation. Variations that are selectively disadvantageous would be eliminated from the population over time, and the random forces of genetic drift (see Chapter 6) eventually would purge diversity from the population.

Important mutations

Mutations occur all the time, but only certain mutations are important for evolution: those that are heritable. For single-celled organisms like bacteria, all mutations are heritable. A bacterium reproduces by dividing, and any changes that occur in the organism's DNA before division are passed on to the daughter cells. That's not the case with animals. Most of the cells in the human body, for example, don't contribute directly to the next generation. Only the germ line (eggs and sperm) do, so only mutations in those tissues can be passed to offspring.

Which comes first — the mutant chicken or the selective agent?

Here's a major stumbling block many people have in understanding how mutations are involved in the process of evolution. Many people think that selectively advantageous mutations occur *in response to* environmental factors that make them advantageous. The thinking goes this way: All these short-necked creatures are running around on the plains in Africa; their main food supply is the vegetation on the ground, but they eat so much, not enough ground vegetation is left to feed the population. What do they do? They evolve to have longer necks so that they can eat the leaves off the trees. Voilà! Giraffes evolve, and the problem is solved. But this scenario is *absolutely not* how evolution works.

Mutations don't occur in response to environmental factors; they already exist in the population. In the presence of some new environmental factor that makes the mutation beneficial, the organism with that mutation is more likely to survive. In the example of the short-necked creatures in Africa, suppose that a few random mutations result in a few long-necked individuals. The long-necked ones and the short-necked ones still eat the rapidly diminishing grass supply, but the long-necked ones have an advantage because, in addition to grass, they can eat the leaves off trees. Being better fed, they are more likely to survive and reproduce.

This principle — that the mutation already exists in the population — is crystal clear when you witness evolution in progress, which is possible with organisms that have short generational time spans. Take a flask of bacteria, for example; put in some penicillin; and you're left with a flask that contains only a few surviving bacteria, all of which are penicillin resistant. What happened? Some of the bacteria in the flask already had slightly different DNA sequences that made them resistant to penicillin. Examples illustrating the evolution of antibiotic resistance come up several times in this book because they so beautifully illustrates how organisms — both simple and complex — evolve.

Variation needs to exist in a population *before* the evolutionary forces can select for it. Once the new selective force (climate change, new disease, and so on) appears, it's too late for any new mutations to be beneficial. Only individuals that already have characteristics that are beneficial in the presence of the new selective force will have an advantage.

Different kinds of mutations

A mutation is simply any change in the DNA sequence. As you can imagine, more than one type of change is possible. At each position in the DNA sequence, there are one of four possible nucleotides (A, C, T, and G). The simplest change to imagine is a change where the original nucleotide in a particular position is replaced by one of the other three possibilities. An A is changed to either G, T, or C, for example. Mutations of this type involving just a single point in the DNA sequence are called *point mutations.* More complicated changes are also possible. Whole sections of DNA can be removed, moved from one place to the next, or duplicated. The following sections explain these types of mutations in more detail (head to Chapter 15 for information on the significance of gene duplication).

DNA is a long string of four different nucleotides that thread off in groups of three. The different three-base sequences instruct the cell to assemble different amino acids into a protein. Some three-base sequences instruct the cell where to start along the DNA sequence and where to stop. Not all sections of an organism's DNA are used to code for proteins, but for the purposes of this discussion the important sections are those that do code for proteins. (Refer to Chapter 3 for more detail about how the sequence of the DNA is used to code for the specific amino acids needed to make a given protein and Chapter 15 if you want to know more about non-coding DNA.)

Point mutations

In a *point mutation,* a single nucleotide in the DNA is replaced by some other nucleotide, resulting in a particular three-letter sequence of DNA that's different. Because of the redundancy of the genetic code, point mutations don't always result in a change in the amino acid and, therefore, don't affect the organism's phenotype, making this particular mutation selectively neutral. There is no change in fitness between the original type and the mutant type.

Sometimes, though, a point mutation results in a different amino acid being used in the production of a protein. In this type of mutation, the protein may have a different structure and may behave differently. If the organism's phenotype is changed, this type of mutation may have fitness consequences. Or it may not — there are many examples where an amino acid change results in the production of a slightly different protein but one that works exactly as well. Changes of this sort may have fitness consequences, or they may be selectively neutral.

At other times, a point mutation could replace a three-letter sequence coding for an amino acid with a sequence that starts or stops protein production. Stopping production of a protein when only part of the amino acid sequence has been assembled is likely to result in a protein with a very different structure and is likely to have a negative affect an organism's phenotype. More often than not, making just half of a protein will be less advantageous than making the whole thing.

Insertion and deletion mutations

Larger changes also can occur in an organism's DNA. Sections of DNA can be lost or inserted into other sections. These sorts of changes are referred to as *deletions* and *insertions,* and although they don't always have a large effect, it's easy to see how they can.

Deleting a section of an organism's instructions set is not likely to be advantageous. Whatever information is eliminated may prove to be extremely important. Obviously the larger the deletion, the larger the potential problem, but even small deletions can cause major effect.

Preventing bad mutations

Mutations tend to be bad, so (not surprisingly) mechanisms exist within cells to reduce the probability of mutation. Biochemical mechanisms repair damaged DNA; proofreading mechanisms catch errors that occur during DNA replication. (Yes, each and every one of us has spell check built in!)

So if mutations can be fixed, why do they exist? For a few reasons.

Mistakes happen

No repair or proofreading system is perfect. I hope, for example, that this book has no typos; it's gone through several editing and proofreading checks. But every once in a while, you find a typo in a book; maybe you'll find one in this book. No matter how hard you try, being prefect isn't possible, and the same is true of cellular biochemistry.

Trade-offs

A trade-off may occur between speed of DNA replication and accuracy of DNA replication. Although mutations tend to be deleterious, slowing down reproduction is also bad for fitness. Genes responsible for a phenotype that reproduces slowly but accurately would be at a disadvantage against genes that generate a phenotype that reproduces more rapidly and is almost as accurate. Each of the individual descendants of the rapid (but sloppy) organism would be more likely to have a couple of extra deleterious mutations, but many more of them would be around, and the overall reproductive success of less error-prone individuals would be lower.

This argument suggests that the mutation rate itself is a character affected by natural selection. And it is. We know from laboratory experiments that mutation rate is a variable heritable character.

It's easy to see how too much mutation would be disadvantageous, so we know that natural selection will keep the mutation rate from getting too high. It's a bit harder to see how natural selection would *favor* any mutation rate, but there may be a couple of reasons: the short-term trade-offs such as the one described earlier between speed and accuracy, and long-term effects whereby lineages with low mutation rates are eventually eliminated by lineages with slightly higher mutation rates because the slightly higher mutation rate results in at least some favorable mutations. Perhaps the best mutation rate is not too much, but not too little. Consider this the Goldilocks principle: You don't want too many or too few mutations, but *just* the right amount:

- **Some mutations are advantageous.** Mutation is the ultimate source of the variation on which natural selection acts. Natural selection acts to eliminate deleterious mutations and increases the frequency of advantageous ones.

- **Maybe a too-low mutation rate is deleterious:** Some scientists speculate that over the long run, a very low mutation rate, while advantageous for individuals in the short-term (because most mutations are bad and you don't want to make mutated kids), may be disadvantageous for the species as a whole. Over long time periods, the selective forces acting on a species are likely to change (climate changes, species move to different habitats, and so on). Without sufficient variation, the species would be unable to respond evolutionarily to these challenges. Such a species could be outcompeted by a species with some higher level of mutation.

  This scenario is speculation and involves the tricky subject of selection acting a level other than that of the individual (a topic you can read more about in Chapter 11). Scientists lack a clear understanding of what sets a lower limit for mutation rate — maybe all the biochemistry involved in DNA replication eliminates the possibility of a zero mutation rate — still, the concept is an interesting one.

Bottom line: Mutations tend to be bad, and in the short term, *not* having any would be good relative to having some. Thinking that a mutation rate is a good thing because you could end up with descendants that are more fit is like thinking that sinking all your retirement funds into the lottery is a good idea because you could end up a millionaire. True, you could get that result, but chances are that you'll end up broke instead.

Gene Frequency and the Hardy-Weinberg Equilibrium

For asexually reproducing creatures (those with just one parent), reproduction is extremely simple: Make a copy of your DNA and divide. If no mutations occur, parent and offspring are identical.

For organisms that have two parents (called *diploid organisms*), reproduction is a bit more complicated. Each individual has two copies of DNA, one from each parent, and will pass on a single copy to each offspring (the other parent contributes the other copy). At each location in the genome, a diploid organism has two alleles, and one or the other will randomly end up in each gamete. When offspring are produced, the relative frequency of different genotypes produced will be a function of the frequency of the different alleles in the population.

Heritable variation is necessary for evolution by natural selection. The pattern of the existing variation (something that can be measured) can tell scientists about whether evolution is occurring.

To understand how allele and genotypic frequencies change under various evolutionary forces, scientists study what happens when none of these forces is at work. Under such conditions, the Hardy-Weinberg equilibrium states that allele frequencies don't change and predicts what the frequency of genotypes should be in a population. This equilibrium states that if you know the frequency of the alleles in a population, you can figure out the frequency of the genotypes in the next generation if (1) mating is random and (2) no evolutionary forces are changing the allele frequencies in the next generation.

To help you understand the Hardy-Weinberg equilibrium, the following information focuses on how allele frequencies correspond to genotype frequencies at a locus where, among all the individuals in the population, there are only two different alleles.

What's the big idea?

The Hardy-Weinberg equilibrium helps scientists determine when natural selection or genetic drift is at work. If the results deviate from the prediction, you know that one of the following situations has occurred, because any of them would cause a deviation:

- ✔ **Gene flow:** Gene flow is one of the factors that can lead to a deviation from the Hardy-Weinberg equilibrium. If one genotype rather than another moves into or out of a population, the genotype frequencies can't be predicted from the allele frequencies.

  Suppose that all the individuals with the aa genotype fly away. You're left with a population that consists only of AA and Aa individuals, and you can't predict the frequency of genotypes accurately from the frequency of the alleles. What's important is not just that movement of individuals into or out of the population is occurring, but that this movement is related to the genotypes of the individuals.

- ✔ **Selection:** Imagine that individuals with the aa allele die without reproducing (which would be the case with lethal recessive alleles). In such a case, only AA and Aa individuals would be left in the population. Again, the frequency of genotypes can't be accurately predicted by the frequency of the alleles. A deviation from expectations under Hardy-Weinberg indicates that some evolutionary force is at play.

Inbreeding: An example of nonrandom mating

Inbreeding, which is a special case of nonrandom mating, occurs when individuals mate with relatives. Because related individuals are more likely to have similar genes, they're also more likely to have similar deleterious recessive genes (which is why the offspring of close relatives tend to have reduced fitness). If these individuals mate, chances increase that two individuals with the recessive trait will get together and produce offspring that end up with two copies of the recessive genes and the condition that the recessive genes cause.

It's been estimated that the average human has perhaps a few lethal recessive alleles. But these alleles are rare in the population and express themselves only if a person happens to have children with someone who has the same lethal recessive gene.

✔ **Nonrandom mating:** The Hardy-Weinberg equilibrium assumes that individuals mate randomly. If that's not the case — if AA individuals prefer other AA individuals, for example — after one generation of such mating, the proportion of individuals that is heterozygous will decrease. (Only matings between heterozygous individuals can produce more heterozygous individuals, but not all their offspring will be heterozygotes; some will be AA and aa.) Matings between homozygous individuals always produce homozygous offspring.

✔ **Random events (that is, genetic drift):** When population sizes are small, random events can cause a deviation from Hardy-Weinberg. For example, while each allele in an individual has an equal chance of getting into a gamete, when only a small number of offspring are produced, just by chance one or another allele might be over (or under) represented, leading to yet another deviation from the expected genotype frequencies. Head to Chapter 6 for more information on genetic drift.

Using the Hardy-Weinberg equilibrium

Scientists use the Hardy-Weinberg equilibrium when they know the proportions of the different alleles in the population and want to predict the proportions of the different genotypes in the population. Here's a simple example using one locus with two alleles.

Suppose that you decide to measure the proportion of the alleles A and a in a population. Call these proportions p and q, where p is the proportion of A alleles and q is the proportion of a alleles. Because of the way proportions work (they represent portions of 100 percent), you know that p + q = 1. If 70 percent of the alleles are A, 30 percent are a, and p = 0.7 and q = 0.3.

So now you've got the proportion of A and a, and you want the proportion of AA, Aa, and aa. Here's how you do it:

$$p^2 + 2pq + q^2$$

Plug in the numbers you got for p and q, and you get

0.49 + 0.42 + 0.09

Translation: If 70 percent of the gametes are A, 49 percent of the offspring will be AA (0.7 x 0.7 = 0.49). If you don't find that result, you know that other forces are at play in this population.

Imagine that the a allele is a lethal recessive gene. Anyone unlucky enough to get two copies of this gene dies, which means that you won't find any individuals in the population that are aa. That result is a deviation from the Hardy-Weinberg equilibrium. In this particular example, this deviation is the result of natural selection selecting against people with the aa allele.

Chapter 5

Natural Selection and Adaptations in Action

*E*volution is nothing more — or less — than changes in the relative frequencies of heritable traits in a group of organisms (whether particular populations or whole species) over time. Simple enough.

But what causes traits to change over time? Often, it's *natural selection,* the process whereby some individuals, as a result of possessing specific traits (keener eyes, bigger leaves, etc.) leave more descendants than other individuals that lack these traits. If these advantageous traits are heritable (and thus are passed on to offspring), then over time, as some traits are favored and others are selected against, populations change — they evolve. Eyesight gets keener because the individuals with weaker eyes are not passing the genes for weaker eyes to future generations. Changes that are the result of natural selection are adaptations. In this example, keener eyes is an adaptation, as are bigger leaves.

Natural selection is not a difficult concept, but many people get all confused about it — particularly when it comes to differentiating between the process of selection (how it works) and the results of selection (the adaptations). This chapter helps you sort everything out.

Natural selection is only one of the mechanisms that cause evolution. Another mechanism — genetic drift — is the topic of the next chapter.

Natural versus Artificial Selection

As Darwin was formulating his theory of evolution by natural selection, he was influenced by the vast body of knowledge on the domestication of plants and animals. *Artificial selection* refers to the selective process when humans are acting as a selective agent. Darwin was aware of the power of artificial selection to affect genetic changes in domestic animals over a relatively short period of time. Imagine, he perhaps exclaimed, what sort of changes might occur over the history of life on Earth!

Charles Darwin wrote *On the Origin of Species by Means of Natural Selection, or the Preservation of Favoured Races in the Struggle for Life.* In this book, one of his key insights was to recognize that the struggle for life had winners and losers, and that it would result in changes in populations through time as the winners contributed their genes to the next generation but the losers didn't.

Darwin saw that the process of natural selection, where the environment in which a population lived could impact what genes made it into subsequent generations, was very similar the process used in animal breeding. The key difference is that in husbandry, humans — and not nature — decide who the winners and losers are.

When nature is the selective agent, the process is called *natural selection.* When humans are the selective agent, the process is called *artificial selection.* We can use artificial selection to examine the process of evolution in the laboratory, and we can observe natural selection occurring in the wild.

The process of artificial selection isn't exactly identical to what happens in the natural environment because humans can get pretty creative in their animal and plant breeding. A particular breeding endeavor, for example, could require a cocktail of approaches: perhaps a little directional selection, just a touch of genetic drift, and a dash of in-breeding followed by some more selection. The result is that allele frequencies of the domestic population change, but it's not strictly identical to the natural process.

Evolution by natural selection (or any other mechanism) is a property of groups, not individuals. Have you ever seen that cartoon of the fish that grew legs and crawled up onto the land? If that seemed confusing, it's because it is. No one fish grows legs. It lives and dies with the same fins it always had. But if, in a population of fish, there is heritable variation in fin structure (and remember, there is heritable variation for pretty much everything) and fish with stiffer, stubblier fins leave more offspring, then the population at some future time will have, on average, stiffer fins. If mutations that results in even *stiffer* fins are selectively favored, the process keeps going until you have fish that waddle around in the mud (such fish exist), and up up up we go from there.

The following sections tease apart in more detail some of the different ways that selection can act.

Directional selection

In *directional selection,* natural selection favors an extreme phenotype — for example, the fastest individuals. If selection for the extreme phenotype continues through time, the population will become faster and faster so long as sufficient heritable variation in speed is present on which natural selection can act.

Think about a cheetah and its prey. All other things being equal, faster is always better, so natural selection acts to increase the speed of both the predator and the prey from one generation to the next. (Some physical limits exist on how fast animals can run, of course, but this process has generated some very fast creatures on the plains of the Serengeti!)

Stabilizing selection

Stabilizing selection (also called *balancing selection*) favors the middle ground — that is, traits that aren't too hot or too cold, but just right, when *just right* means comfortably in the middle between two extremes. Think of this form as the Goldilocks of selection.

In stabilizing selection, the most-fit trait is intermediate with respect to whatever characteristic selection is acting on. An example is the birth weight of babies. Very small babies have a lower probability of survival, but very large babies are more likely to suffer complications during birth. Babies of intermediate size, however, are most likely to survive to reproduce.

Adaptation: Changes Resulting from Natural Selection

An *adaptation* is a trait that has resulted from evolution by natural selection. In the example of the cheetahs earlier in this chapter, the ability to run faster is an example of an adaptation. Antibiotic resistance (see Chapter 17) is another example of an adaptation. This trait appears in a bacterial population because of random mutations that made some bacteria better able to survive and reproduce in the presence of antibiotics.

Some folks quibble over whether the evolution of antibiotic resistance is truly the result of natural selection since people are hosing down the world with tons of antibiotics and thus exerting selective pressure of their own. Others say that it is natural rather than artificial selection because even though people altered the environment in this instance, the bacteria responded (naturally!) to that change. (Also, antibiotics occur naturally — lots of microbes make them — and bacteria evolve in response to those. Many microorganisms produce antibiotics to inhibit the growth of other microorganisms. Penicillin, for example, is a natural antibiotic that gets its name from the mold that produces it, *Penicillium chrysogenum*.)

If the whole concept of adaptation seems to be ridiculously straightforward, that's because overall it is. The following sections explain why recognizing an adaptation isn't not always easy though.

Is it an adaptation—or not?

Distinguishing adaptive from non-adaptive traits isn't easy. Identifying an adaptation and the selective force that caused it is pretty clear cut when it comes to something like antibiotic resistance because we've been around to observe the whole process. The situation gets a bit dicier when you talk about adaptations we haven't observed, because in nature, it's not always crystal clear whether a particular trait is an adaptation.

Acclimatization

Adaptation, the result of evolution by natural selection, works at the species level, not at the individual level. Acclimatization, on the other hand, occurs within individuals.

Suppose that you decide to visit Denver, which is a mile above sea level and has less oxygen than lower-lying areas of the country. On your first day in the city, you decide to go jogging and find the activity much more difficult than usual. After a few days, however, you begin to feel like your old self and can jog just as you used to. Why? Because your body reacted to the lower levels of oxygen by producing additional red blood cells. Although most people in this situation would say that they've adapted to the altitude, they'd be more accurate if they said that

they've acclimatized. This kind of distinction is exactly the idiosyncratic type of parsing that scientists (and English teachers) love.

While you won't be doing any adapting on your trip to Denver, there is evidence to suggest that human populations that have lived for long periods at high altitude show genetic changes that could be adaptations to the lower oxygen concentrations at altitude. When you acclimate in Denver, you make more red blood cells which are the same as the red blood cells you had before. The Sherpas living at high altitude in the Himalayas, however, have differences in blood chemistry that result in their red blood cells having higher affinity for oxygen than others.

There are limits

Some limits exist to what natural selection can accomplish. If natural selection always favors more-fit genes, all species would be on the road to super-organism — forever getting faster, glowier, taller, whatever. And there'd be no limit in numbers of limbs, eyes, hearts, tails, and fins, if having more of these things means being more fit. But that's not what happens.

- ✔ **Some things may just not be physically possible:** Mammals will never run at the speed of sound.

- ✔ **Others may not be biologically possible:** The mammal lineage seems limited to four limbs — variation in limb number is absent.

- ✔ **Some adaptations may preclude others:** A bird can have wings that function like a penguin or a hummingbird, but not both. This idea is explained in more detail in the later section "You can't get there from here: Constraints and trade-offs."

Exaptation: Selecting for one trait, ending up with another

An *exaptation* is a trait that resulted from selection for something other than the trait's current function. Think about feathers. Scientists know from the fossil record that the earliest creatures with feathers didn't fly. So what was the purpose of feathers on these early flightless animals? Maybe they served as insulation (as feathers today do), or maybe they served some other function. Regardless of their actual purpose, what scientists do know is that the feathers didn't have anything to do with flight — which they can tell from the skeletal structure of the fossils (these creatures didn't have wings!).

So although feathers subsequently evolved to be used in flight, the benefit of flight wasn't the selective force responsible for their origin. It just so happened that feathers — an adaptation selected by some fitness advantage unrelated to flight — subsequently became something that natural selection shaped into a wing.

Occasionally, you hear the term *preadaptation,* which means the same thing as *exaptation.* The problem with preadaptation is that folks tend to misinterpret the word, thinking that it implies premeditation in the process of selection. But selection isn't premeditated, of course, so the preferred term is *exaptation.* Truth to tell, however, most evolutionary biologists are likely to say *preadaptation* instead of *exaptation* when they're sitting around talking science over a few beers. But that's when happens when scientists get sloppy drunk.

One of the beauties of the evolutionary process is the way that existing structures are altered for new uses. For that reason, scientists always need to be cautious with any specific example in which they state that a particular trait evolved for a particular reason. Why? If you're trying to understand the process of natural selection, you need to make sure that the traits you're examining were actually the result of natural selection.

Chromosomes in action: Linkage and hitchhikers

The human genome (and the genomes of most sexually reproducing organisms) consists of several pieces of DNA called *chromosomes*. Parents make copies of their chromosomes and pass one copy of each chromosome to their off-spring (refer to Chapter 3 for more info on chromosomes). How the genome is put together sometimes has consequences for how natural selection results in changes in gene frequencies over generations.

Imagine that loci are on the same chromosome. One codes for hair color (its alleles are A and a); the other codes for eye color (its alleles are B and b). Suppose the parent has the AaBb genotype. This parent could have the allele combination Ab and aB (or the combination ab and AB) on each chromosome. Because the loci are linked, the transmission of one allele determines the transmission of the other.

If the hair color locus and the eye color locus are on different chromosomes, their alleles sort independently; if they're on the same chromosome, they *may* be transmitted together. Note that I say *may*. Here's where things get more complicated.

The chromosomes can break and rejoin, so even if two genes are on the same chromosome, they aren't necessarily inherited together. What that means is that

- ✔ Even if the parent had the AB and ab allele combinations on its chromosomes, there's still some possibility of producing aB and Ab gametes — and this possibility is greater the farther apart the two loci are on the chromosome.
- ✔ The closer two genes are, the more likely they are to be inherited together. If the eye color gene is right next to the hair color gene, it's more likely that when you passed on these traits to your children, they got whatever combination of alleles were found together on one of your chromosomes.

Now suppose that a beneficial mutation occurs at the eye color locus, and selection acts on that allele. Because the mutation is beneficial, the person who carries it will be more likely to leave descendants; hence, this particular allele will increase through time. As a result of the close link between the eye color gene and the hair color gene, whatever hair color allele happens to be next to it on the chromosome will also increase in frequency, even though it may not have any significance.

Why is this example important? Because if you don't know that a ho-hum allele can increase in frequency simply because it's next to a wham-bang allele, you may misinterpret the increasing frequency of the ho-hum allele as being evidence of strong selection for that allele. In this case, you may think that something about the hair color gene itself is important evolution-wise, when what really happened is that it hitchhiked a ride because of its proximity to the eye color.

In hitchhiking, changes through time in the allele frequencies at one locus can be caused by selection acting on a different locus.

But wait — not all traits are adaptations

Some traits are obviously adaptive, such as antibiotic resistance in bacteria. Because scientists understand the selective force — humans added the antibiotics — they know that the evolutionary change they observe is a response to that selection. The increase in frequency in the population of antibiotic-resistant bacteria is an adaptation to the presence of antibiotics.

Other traits are obviously not adaptations. An example is a change at the level of the DNA that doesn't result in a change in the way a gene works or is expressed. Traits of this type are *selectively neutral:* They don't change the fitness of the organisms that carry them, so their frequency increases or decreases based solely on random factors (see Chapter 6 for details). And any change caused by random factors rather than selection isn't an adaptation.

The spandrels of San Marco

Some traits that may seem to be adaptive aren't necessarily adaptations. Maybe the traits exist for reasons that we don't understand — developmental constraints, past events, whatever. The point is that although the traits appear to serve some purposeful function, that function had nothing to do with their evolution. In a paper written in 1979, Stephen Jay Gould and Richard C. Lewontin warn evolutionary biologists not to confuse current purpose with past adaptations. To make this point, they wrote about the spandrels of St. Mark's Cathedral in Venice.

A *spandrel* is a structure connecting the dome to the rest of the roof in a particular type of architecture. And in St. Mark's, the spandrels have been painted so amazingly, you'd think that they exist solely for the purpose of bearing the remarkable images. Wrong! The spandrels are just necessary consequences of how the rest of the structure is put together, meaning their purpose is solely architectural, not artistic. But that doesn't mean they didn't make a decent canvas for the artists who added the pictures later.

Unfortunately, the distinction between adaptive and non-adaptive traits isn't always obvious. Some traits appear to be adaptations but aren't. Why is knowing the difference important? Because you don't want to be fooled. Stating that things are adaptations that actually aren't can lead to errors in the way you interpret data.

You can't get there from here: Constraints and trade-offs

Constraints are problems that natural selection can't seem to solve. As a result of how an organism is put together, some types of variation just aren't expected to appear. All vertebrates, for example, have (at most) four limbs. Think about it: You never see mice with six legs. And based on human understanding of mammalian development, it's pretty unlikely that Pegasus, with his four legs and two wings, would ever evolve. Being a mammal and having six limbs is just not a variant you ever see. So even if having a few extra limbs conferred a fitness advantage, natural selection can't get there because there is no heritable variation for extra limbs.

Trade-offs, the balance between fitness benefits and fitness costs, represent another key concept in evolutionary biology. You can think of trade-offs as being the "jack of all trades, master of none" phenomenon. Consider all the different kinds of birds in nature. Why isn't there a superbird with the talons of an eagle, the webbed feet of a duck, and all the other avian parts you can think of rolled up into one bird? Well, you can start to see the problem right away: It would be hard for an eagle to sink its talons into a poor little bunny if the eagle had webbed feet. A pretty obvious trade-off exists between swimming feet and grasping feet. The evolution of life histories is rife with examples of trade-offs; head to Chapter 10 for details.

Run, Mouse, Run

Throughout this book, I occasionally bring up the cheetah's running speed as an example of an adaptation. I've always thought cheetahs were fascinating creatures and looked forward to seeing them on the Nature Channel. The nice story that I tell you is that there was variation for running speed, that cheetahs that ran faster left more descendents, and that, as a result, the cheetah population got really good at running. It's a good story, but science is more than just a good story.

The ghost of evolution past

When they're talking about adaptations, scientists have to be careful not to identify as an adaptation to current phenomena a trait that's really an adaptation to past phenomena that are no longer active.

Until fairly recently (not much more than 10,000 years ago), for example, North America and South America were home to a diverse group of large mammals such as gomphotheres (four-tusked, elephant-like creatures) that would have eaten a lot of the local vegetation and may have been potential seed-dispersers. As a result, these large herbivores would have been a key factor in the evolution of the local vegetation — that is, the plants would have evolved in concert with the herbivores that ate them and dispersed their seeds. Probably, the plants evolved defenses against herbivory (the eating of plants) and also evolved traits that led to increased seed dispersal. (This idea that two organisms evolve in response to each other is called *co-evolution*. You can read about it in Chapter 13.)

One of the main reasons plants produce fruit is to get their seeds dispersed. Animals eat the fruit; the seeds pass out of the animals' guts and land in new environments where they germinate and produce new plants (if the environment is suitable). One obvious benefit of such a system is that the seed ends up in a pile of fertilizer. A disadvantage is that the animal may eat the seed as well. So seeds need adaptations to prevent them from being digested on their journey through the digestive tract — hence, the hard coatings that many seeds have. Yet a coating hard enough to pass through an animal unscathed may actually make it more difficult for the seed to break through the shell and germinate. A seed with a coating that allows it to survive passage through an animal's gut may now need to go through the gut before it can germinate. And indeed, the Americas have plants that seem to require passage through a large herbivore for optimum germination.

Then humans arrived in the New World, spotted the giant herbivores, thought, "Dinner!" and gobbled them all up. (Well, not necessarily. Some controversy exists about the exact role that humans played in the extinction of these large animals. But the current thinking is that our species did play a significant role — and spent the next few centuries trying to come up with a suitable antacid.) Regardless of how the gomphotheres disappeared, disappear they did, leaving plants without the herbivores needed to facilitate germination of their seeds. In fact, some species of plants in the tropics may have been undergoing a gradual decline in population as a result of an absence of these seed-dispersal agents.

Then along came horses, which aren't native to the Americas. As it turned out, horses also serve as excellent seed dispersers for some American flora, and in some cases, they are the only animals able to facilitate the germination of native plants. But the plants didn't evolve in the presence of horses, which only just got to the New World a few hundred years ago.

Scientists can examine selection for increased running in the laboratory. Of course, it's tough to do experiments with big cats in the laboratory: You need a lot of room for them to run, feeding them is expensive, and if you're not careful, you could end up on the dinner menu. But cats are not the only things that run. Mice run, too. And they're a lot cheaper to keep and a lot less likely to turn on you. And the best part? They're happy to run in those little wheels, so with a minimum of analytical equipment, you can keep track of how far they're running.

Theodore Garland, Jr., and coworkers set up a long-term evolution study looking at the consequences of artificially selecting for mice that like to run. They got a bunch of mice, gave them all a chance to run, and then founded the next generation by selected the ones that just plain liked to run more. They've continued this selective regime for almost 15 years, continuing to selectively favor the mice than most like to run.

The results: Mice lineages selected for increased voluntary running now run everyday several times farther than the original mice, and they do it by running for just as long but several times faster. These fast running mice have undergone other changes as well as a result of this artificial selection:

- ✔ They have larger hearts.
- ✔ Their muscle fibers are different from the original unselected mice.
- ✔ Their hind limbs or more symmetrical.

There was plenty of variation for characters associated with running on which artificial selection could act. It didn't take long to produce evolved mice that like nothing more than to go to the gym for a workout.

Oh — one last thing: The hearts of the mice that ran farther aged better, so when you're done with this book, go take a walk or jog. It'll be good for you.

Darwin's and Grants' Finches

When Darwin was visiting the Galapagos Islands, he came across a strange assortment of birds which subsequent investigation revealed to be an assortment of different kinds of finches. These finches were so different from the finches found on the mainland that Darwin didn't even recognize them as finches and, while on the Galapagos Islands, didn't pay that much attention to them. It was only when he returned to England and shared his collection with fellow scientists that he realized what he'd missed. But it didn't take him long to realize the significance of the little beasties.

The finches on different islands have different morphological characteristics — things like the size and shape of the beak — that might reasonably be thought to have something to do with feeding. Darwin hypothesized that different selective pressures on the different islands had led the birds to diverge from each other morphologically. Specifically, he surmised that natural selection was at work (refer to Chapter 2).

Darwin hasn't been the only scientist interested in finches. Rosemary and Peter Grant of Princeton University are, too. And what's more, they set out to watch natural selection happen, and they've been doing it successfully for about thirty years.

In one particularly nice example, one of the larger finches which had not previously been present on the island where the Grants work took up residence there and began to compete for food with the smaller finch that was already there.

To grasp the significance of what happened next, you need to know a little bit about the structure of finches' beaks. A finch's beak structure determines what the bird can most efficiently eat: A bird can't crack large seeds with the tiny beak, and it can't pick up tiny seeds with a large beak. Both the larger and smaller finches had a preference for some large, yummy seeds found on the island. And both have bills of sufficient size to crack and eat these seeds.

Prior to the arrival of the larger finch on the island, the small finches had all the big nuts to themselves. When the larger finches arrived, they took over the prime feeding areas as a result of bigger beak size and hogged all the good food. This led to tough times for the smaller birds, especially during periods of low food availability; they weren't getting enough of the big seeds, and they couldn't easily forge on the smaller seeds. Tough times, and a lot of the smaller birds didn't make it, but some of the smaller birds had an easier time of it than others.

Which of the smaller birds were most successful? The ones with slightly smaller beaks. There was variation in beak size, and in the absence of the large seed food resource, the small finches with smaller beaks were able to get more food because they could more efficiently forage on smaller size seeds. As a result of this selective pressure, the big size of the smaller finch decreased. And that's natural selection in action!

Chapter 6

Random Evolution and Genetic Drift: Sometimes It's All about Chance

Charles Darwin (see Chapter 1) had natural selection nailed, even though he didn't have the tools to test his ideas that evolutionary biologists have today. A great deal of modern evolutionary biology has been about confirming and refining Darwin's hypotheses. Since Darwin, one of the most important advances has been the recognition of the role of genetic drift as an evolutionary force. *Genetic drift* refers to the power random events can have in influencing whether genes increase or decrease in future populations.

Here's the take-home message of this chapter: Genetic drift can result in evolution, even in the absence of natural selection. If two critters are equally well suited to their environment, only chance determines which one leaves more descendants. Genetic drift also can work in the presence of natural selection. Even when some individuals are potentially better than others, chance events still occur. If lightning strikes the fastest cheetah, it won't be contributing its genes to the next generation.

Genetic Drift Defined

A main principle of evolution by natural selection is that the environment favors traits that make individual organisms more fit (better able to get their genes into the next generation). More-fit parents produce offspring who, by virtue of having inherited traits from their parents, are more fit. The most fit of these offspring produce offspring who are even more fit than they, and so on and so forth until . . . well, you get the picture. These changes are not random. More-fit characteristics increase in frequency in subsequent generations at the expense of less fit characteristics.

Here's the rub: Natural selection isn't the only force that determines what genes get into the next generation. It can be doing its thing, stacking the cards in favor of certain characteristics, and then — *bam!* — a tree falls on the genetically favored organism. In the words of the philosopher Dylan, blame it on a simple twist of fate. If that tree happens to fall on a fast cheetah, there'll be just a few more gazelles for the slower cheetahs to eat and they may leave more descendents than they otherwise would have.

When random processes affect the probability of different traits being present in the next generation, you've got what evolutionary biologists call *genetic drift*. And it's one of the two major driving forces changing the frequencies of existing genes through time (natural selection being the other). As such, it can

- ✔ Affect whether the frequencies of different alleles increase or decrease in subsequent generations.

- ✔ Result in the frequencies of all but one allele at a given locus decreasing to the point that they are eliminated. When only a single allele is found at a given locus, that allele is *fixed;* its frequency has gone to a hundred percent and all the other alleles are gone. Until such time as a mutation happens to generate a new allele at this locus, all individuals in the population will be genetically identical at this point in their DNA. No further evolution is possible because, until such a mutation occurs, there is no variation.

The key to understanding genetic drift is to understand what could possibly be random in evolution (quite a bit, actually) and when these random events are evolutionarily significant (sometimes).

Natural selection and genetic drift aren't either/or processes. Think of the processes as happening simultaneously and the circumstances (such as population size or the neutrality of a mutation, as explained in later sections) determining which process holds more sway.

Wrapping Your Head Around Randomness

Random, as you no doubt are aware, means out of the blue, without rhyme or reason, hit or miss — in a word, arbitrary. Random events, by their very randomness, exhibit no discernible pattern, even if they look like a pattern; hint at a pattern; or, gosh darn it, *must* form a pattern if you could just figure out what the pattern is. That's precisely the part about randomness that trips us humans up: We're always looking for a pattern, and if we don't see one, we expect it to emerge eventually.

Well, randomness doesn't work that way. Random is random, and that means:

- ✔ The absence of a pattern or the unpredictability of an outcome
- ✔ No correlation between the outcome of one event and the outcome of another

A coin toss is an example of a random event. You toss a coin in the air (assume it's a fair coin), and it's going to come down either heads or tails. So say you toss this coin, and it lands heads. What's the chance that it'll land heads the next time you toss it? The right answer is 50 percent. But a fair number of people think (incorrectly) that it is more likely to land tails the second time because it landed heads the first time. This sort of thinking is the same kind that makes gambling so dangerous.

Imagine yourself, flush with coins, sitting at a slot machine and feeling lucky. You drop in your first coin, pull the lever, and . . . nothing happens. You put in the next coin. Again, nothing happens. And again. And again. Why do you keep playing? Probably at some level, you think that all these losses are leading up to a big win, even though you may be fully aware that a slot machine generates numbers or patterns randomly.

The important thing about the coin toss (or the slot machines) is that, as a random process, the previous outcomes don't have any bearing on the upcoming results. Just because a coin lands heads one time doesn't mean that it's less — or more — likely to land heads the next time.

Random is just plain slippery to think about so following are a couple of examples of how it can be important in biology.

At the level of the individual

Any environmental factor that affects an individual's ability to reproduce regardless of its genes can cause genetic drift. Consider a lightening strike: There's probably no genetic component that determines whether one deer or another is hit by lightning. But when a deer *is* hit by lightning, it won't be reproducing. Because that deer's genes won't be represented in the next generation, this random event changes the relative representation of genes in the later generation.

Essentially, these are cases of being in the wrong (or right) place at the wrong (or right) time. Examples would be a lumberjack who fells a tree on a Nobel laureate who's walking through the forest pondering his acceptance speech or the bug that crashes into your windshield. If you're not around to reproduce, or if you don't reproduce (because you prefer a neat house and travel to children, for example), natural selection can't be the driving force behind the increases or decreases in gene frequencies.

Random variations also occur in the number of offspring that different individuals have. For the minute, ignore the fact that there might be a genetic component to wanting fewer children because you prefer not stepping on those little plastic farm animals with the sharp ears. Random variation still occurs in the number of offspring that different people produce. A hundred couples all trying to have three children won't each end up with three children. On average, they'll end up with more children than couples who prefer not to have children (a matter of choice, not random factors), but they won't all end up having exactly three. That's where the random factors come in.

At the level of the gametes

As a diploid individual, you have two copies of DNA: one that you got from your father and one that you got from your mother (refer to Chapter 3). Your children will also have two copies of DNA: one copy that they got from you and one copy that they got from the other parent. That means that each of your offspring got only half of your genes and half of their other parent's genes. You're diploid, your partner is diploid, and the only way to make sure your offspring are diploid is for your gametes (the egg and sperm) to be haploid — that is, to contain only half of your DNA.

Which half? This is where genetic randomness kicks in. At some locations of your genome, both copies are the same. Or in science-speak, both alleles at that locus are identical. In this case each of your gametes (be that sperm or egg) will have the same allele at that locus; there's only one to choose from. But other times, you have two different alleles at that locus because the one you got from your mother and the one you got from your father weren't the same. Any given gamete you produce will get one or the other.

You've been successful: You've survived (you looked both ways before you crossed the street), you found food (maybe that was why you crossed the street), and now you're about to pass your genes on to the next generation, but it's a matter of chance which of the two different alleles you carry will make it into any particular gamete. On average, each allele will end up in half of your gametes. While you produce a huge number of gametes and the two alleles are equally represented, only a paltry number of offspring are likely to result from them.

Women have about 400,000 eggs; men produce even more sperm. But women don't have 400,000 offspring. For that reason, which particular genes your offspring have are up for grabs. In other words, the production of any one child involves an element of chance, and the kids you end up with are the result of random pairings, as it were.

Situations in Which Drift Is Important

Genetic drift is an important evolutionary force — some of the time. When? When populations are small, for example, or with the subset of genetic differences that don't result in fitness differences.

When a population is small

Genetic drift plays a bigger role in evolutionary change when a population is small. In larger populations, the forces of genetic drift are muted. In a population of 1 million, one extra fast cheetah more or less isn't going to make much difference in the grand scheme of gene frequencies. In a population of 20, however, that single cheetah *does* make a difference — at least in terms of her genes — if she does (or doesn't) reproduce.

Consider the coin toss again. If you throw up a bunch of coins — say, 400 — the outcome would be lots of heads and lots of tails — about half of each, in fact. Although you'd be willing to accept a few more or less than half either way, you know that only a very small chance exists that all 400 coins will end up falling on the same side. Now imagine that you're tossing a small handful of coins — say, four. The possible outcomes are fairly limited: You could get two of each, three of one and one of the other, or four of either heads or tails. Although you're not likely to see the coins come up four of a kind, that result is still within the realm of possibility. In fact, if you compute the actual probability, you realize that, on average, one of every eight times you throw four coins in the air, they'll end up on the same side.

The point? That even though a handful of coins will on average land half heads and half tails, that's just the average result. Individual tosses will vary randomly, and the smaller the handful, the more likely the chance that the results will be much different from 50-50.

Now think about allele frequencies rather than head-tail frequencies. A population may have two alleles in equal proportion, 50 percent each, at one point in time. And then, at some later point in time, the frequencies are drastically different. The smaller the population, the more likely that this change is simply the result of random factors affecting which individuals did and didn't leave more descendents.

When genetically different individuals have the same fitness

The degree to which a new mutation is neutral affects how important a role genetic drift plays in the evolutionary process. As Chapter 4 explains, mutations, which add genetic diversity to populations and come in three categories (advantageous, deleterious, and neutral), are always occurring.

For mutations that are advantageous or deleterious, and when population size is large, natural selection is the primary driving force that determines whether the frequency of particular alleles increase or decrease in subsequent generations. If mutations are deleterious, natural selection removes them; if they're advantageous, natural selection favors them, and they increase in frequency.

But if the particular new mutant is *neutral*, neither advantageous nor disadvantageous compared to the original, natural selection can't be responsible for changes in its frequency through time. In this case, genetic drift is the driving force.

Drift or selection? When it's hard to tell

Genetic drift is always occurring, even when an allele is advantageous or disadvantageous. Randomness is still at work — lightning is still hitting the occasional deer, for example — but these random events don't make much difference to the outcome. The slow deer will get eaten by wolves, and the fast deer will pass their genes on to the next generation. If a lightning bolt happens to hit one of the fast deer, the outcome won't change. But sometimes, it's not so clear cut when natural selection is the main force and when genetic drift is.

The effect of population size

In a small population, the weakly advantageous allele could be eliminated by random genetic drift before it could be fixed by natural selection, or a weakly deleterious allele could increase to fixation. For example, a cheetah with a mutation that made it just a tiny bit faster might be expected to catch a few more antelope and have a slightly better chance at leaving more descendents than its neighbor. This new mutant would tend to increase in frequency in the population through time, but it would increase very slowly because the difference between the mutant gene and the other cheetahs is miniscule.

It might also increase or decrease in the population purely as a result of chance events. It's possible that even though it's selectively advantageous (you get to catch a couple more antelope, just not very many more), it might be eliminated by chance events before it could sweep through the population.

Whether a particular neutral allele increases to fixation is a function of population size. In small populations, random factors can be of greater importance. But — and this is a big *but* — the probability that there will be a neutral mutation that will increase to fixation is *independent* of population size. The key is that larger populations have more individuals and, as a result, more errors in DNA replication (errors by the mutations). So although it's true that any particular mutation has a much lower chance of increasing to fixation in a large population, that population has proportionally more mutations. Mathematically, everything pretty much cancels out. The effect of large population size on slowing fixation as a result of genetic drift is balanced out by the fact that a large population also has more mutations.

Here's why this little tidbit is important: Knowing that the overall rate of accumulation of neutral mutations doesn't have anything to do with population size lets scientists estimate the time since two lineages diverged. Neutral mutations in particular genes sometimes accumulate at a relatively constant rate. Therefore, the differences between two lineages can be used to determine the time since their divergence — a subject covered in more detail in Chapter 15.

The strength of selection

Natural selection doesn't operate at the same strength at all times. Imagine a gene that allows an organism to survive extremely dry conditions. Natural selection will result in an increase in the frequency of this gene in environments with very dry conditions. Now imagine that those conditions occur only once every ten generations. During the other nine generations, changes in the frequency of that particular gene from generation to generation will be due entirely to drift.

If a new allele is neutral, random forces determine its future frequency. It may disappear, or it may increase in frequency. Consider the gene that determines which of your thumbs is on top when you interlace your fingers. As it turns out, you always put the same thumb on top. Try interlacing your fingers so that the other thumb is on top. Feels weird, doesn't it? Yep, a locus with two alleles actually determines your thumb preference.

Assuming that both alleles have always been identical with respect to fitness (scientists can't be certain, but neither can they think of the slightest reason why they wouldn't be), both alleles exist in the human population because of random events — an initial mutant increasing in frequency as a result of chance in the absence of any effects of natural selection. The relative frequency of the two genes is still subject to the process of genetic drift, but human populations are so large that both alleles will persist in the population for the foreseeable future.

Genetic Drift in Action: When Big Populations Get Little

Understanding the importance of population size is fundamental to understanding genetic drift (see the earlier section "Situations in which drift is important" for details). But population sizes don't remain constant; they fluctuate over time, sometimes growing larger and sometimes smaller. To understand how genetic drift is operating in nature, it helps to understand the factors that result in a small population. Here are a couple:

- **Fluctuations in population size:** The mere fact that a population is large today doesn't mean that it wasn't small at some other time or that it won't decrease someday. The populations of many organisms that need water may drop to low levels during a drought, for example. When a population is or becomes exceedingly small, the phenomenon is called a *population bottleneck* (discussed later in this chapter).

- **Founder effects:** Founder effects refers to those chance events that occur when a population is founded in a new location by a small number of individuals from a population somewhere else.

As a population shrinks (which can happen for a variety of reasons), it begins to feel the effects of genetic drift more acutely, mainly because while it's growing smaller, it's losing diversity. This loss is a bad thing, because diversity can protect a species or a group of individuals from the vagaries of fate. This discussion is important for a couple of reasons, one of which may appeal to folks in general (tree-huggers and animal-lovers in particular), and the other may appeal primarily to scientists (but is cool anyway):

- **It informs conservation efforts.** Numbers aren't enough when it comes to saving animals from extinction. Diversity in the endangered population is key, and genetic drift undermines diversity.

- **It lets scientists figure out when one group diverged from another.** I know — this reason lacks the pizzazz of saving cute little furry creatures, but it's still important.

The following sections go into more details.

Population bottlenecks

Population bottleneck simply refers to a period when the population of a particular organism grows smaller. If, as the population decreases, it also loses genetic variation through genetic drift, it doesn't get that variation back right away when (or if) it gets bigger again.

For an example of a population bottleneck, consider the plight of the northern elephant seal. This seal was hunted almost to extinction in the late 1800s. On a couple of occasions, folks thought that the species had actually gone extinct, but a few seals occasionally turned up on an island off Baja California. Most of these seals were killed as well (sometimes by biologists collecting them for museum specimens!). Obviously, things weren't going well for the northern elephant seal; at the species' low point, the population was estimated to be between 20 and 100 individuals.

In the early 1900s, the Mexican government made the seals' last breeding ground a protected area, and the species began to rebound. Today, the species numbers over 100,000, and elephant seals appear to be out of immediate danger of extinction. This example is a nice success story of species conservation in a world that has too many unhappy endings.

Before you get out the party hats, however, remember that genetic variation is necessary for evolution by natural selection. If the species we humans conserve are going to respond to future environmental changes, those species require genetic variability. The world may have 30,000 elephant seals now, but those 30,000 seals are descended from the few that survived hunting. That means they're very closely related to one other and, as a result, are genetically very similar, so they are still at risk from events such as diseases. In a genetically uniform population, a disease that can attack one of the individuals is likely to attack them all.

The southern elephant seal was also extensively hunted, but its population was not driven as low at that of the northern elephant seal. As a result, the southern species has more genetic diversity than the northern species.

The genetic diversity of a species is a fundamental part of what is unique about that species. Yet the forces of genetic drift can eliminate genetic diversity in small populations, and small populations are often characteristic of species that humans are trying to prevent from going extinct. Therefore, counteracting the effects of genetic drift — and not inadvertently creating more population bottlenecks by using too few individuals for breeding in captive breeding programs — is important in species-conservation efforts. Genetic diversity (heritable variation) is what allows species to respond to selective events (such as novel diseases or environmental change). Conservationists want not just to conserve a few individuals of a species but also to conserve the genetic variation that will allow the species to survive events it may encounter in the future.

Founder effects

Periodically, a few individuals decide to strike out on their own and set up a community away from kith and kin. The founders of this new community — be they rats, bats, bears, or humans — determine the genetic makeup of the new population. *Founder effects* refers to their influence in this regard. Understanding founder effects helps scientists understand how the genetic makeup of original members of the new community affects the gene frequencies in subsequent generations.

Every time a few individuals separate themselves from their original population and move to a novel environment, you can see how founder effects can be important in determining allele frequencies. Quite a bit of variation in human blood type occurs across different geographical regions, for example. Some areas have a preponderance of one blood type; other areas have a preponderance of another type. Founder effects, spurred by human migration patterns that often involve small groups founding new populations, can explain these differences, as the following sections explain.

Crossing the Bering Strait

Ten thousand years ago, a small group of humans crossed the Bering Strait and colonized North America (and subsequently South America). Genetic drift probably is the cause of the very low frequency of the type B blood allele in Native Americans (4 percent), even though it is much more frequent in people from Asia — the presumed source of the Native American colonists.

Amish immigration to America

The Amish population was founded by a small group of Europeans in the early 16th century. In the 18th century, the first Amish migrated to the Pennsylvania colony in the New World.

The Amish, who remain almost entirely reproductively isolated from the rest of America, have a distribution of blood types different from those in the rest of the United States or in Europe. Additionally one of the original couples carried the allele for polydactily (extra fingers or toes) which has increased in frequency in the small Amish population by chance; they just happen to have more than the average number of descendants.

Colonization of planet Beta

Okay, this example isn't for real. But if you've seen the 1950s-era sci-fi flick *When Worlds Collide,* you can imagine founder effects in action. In the film, Earth is doomed by the approach of a runaway planet. Humanity is saved when a group of scientists and engineers (including the requisite cynic-turned-true-believing hero, the brilliant-and-self-sacrificing old scientist, his beautiful-but-prone-to-melodramatic-emotional-displays daughter, and the steady-but-dull-as-dishwater-and-soon-to-be-spurned boyfriend) gets together to build a spaceship large enough to carry a few humans, a few head of livestock, a few plants, and one adorable dog to another planet to begin life again. Think of the genes this bunch has to work with! Their blood type — given that they left the riffraff on Earth to perish — definitely would be blue.

The Shifting-Balance Hypothesis: It's What's Wright

Sewell Wright (1889–1988) was a key founder of the science of population genetics, and his shifting-balance hypothesis is one of the coolest hypotheses about how evolution might work in certain circumstances. This hypothesis says natural selection and genetic drift can work together to allow populations to reach higher fitness.

To help visualize how this might work, you need to get cozy with an especially slippery concept called the *adaptive landscape* (or *fitness landscape*). It's slippery even for professional evolutionary biologists, but of course that's part of the fun!

The adaptive landscape: A 3-D fitness map

In any giving species, there are a huge number of different possible genotypes, and we can't possibly know the fitness of each different genotype — we just know that each genotype has a fitness. In order to think about all that information, scientists use the *adaptive landscape.* The adaptive landscape is a three-dimensional imaginary structure that gives us a way of talking and thinking about how differences in genotype affect fitness. Figure 6-1 is an example of a fitness landscape. The letter A represents a mutation that's beneficial (moving the species up the hill to greater fitness); the letter B represents a mutation that decreases a species' fitness.

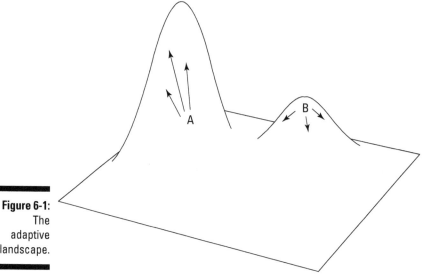

Figure 6-1:
The
adaptive
landscape.

This landscape is like a 3-D relief map that you can set down on your coffee table. A relief map indicates, through the height of the bumps, the altitude of any region — such a map of the U.S. would show the Rockies and the Sierra Nevadas, the Midwestern plains, the small mountains of Appalachia, and so on. The adaptive landscape has the same bumps, but here, the bumps don't show altitude; instead, they correspond to increased fitness.

Here are some things to know about the adaptive landscape:

- **Each location on the adaptive landscape can be though of as a genotype.** Neighboring points are very similar genetically, distant point less so.

- **The adaptive landscape deals with one species at a time and in one set of conditions.** Imagine the adaptive landscape for chickens on an island in the Pacific, for example. For this particular population, some genotypes confer greater fitness and other genotypes confer lower fitness.

- **The top of each bump on the adaptive landscape represents a genotype more fit than those just a little different from it.** The different heights of these bumps indicate relative fitness. Higher bumps equal higher fitness levels; lower bumps equal lower fitness levels.

Any particular adaptive landscape represents the fitness of a single species in a particular set of conditions. Move to a different island and the fitness landscape might change. Genotypes that were great on the first island might be hopeless on the next, and therefore, the peaks and valleys would be in different places.

It's impossible to measure the fitness of every genotype of the species being studied. But you can think about how mutations change fitness. A mutation that switches an amino acid from one kind to another, for example, nudges you a little bit on the adaptive landscape. Maybe the protein works better (you move up the hill); maybe it doesn't work as well (you move down the hill); or maybe it works exactly the same way (you move sideways on the hill, meaning that you're in a different place — you have a different genotype — but you have the same fitness. Your genome could change in millions of ways as a result of mutation; it's a big genome. Each of those changes moves you around somewhere in the fitness landscape.

Being the best you can be — on your own peak

You expect that natural selection will favor the genotypes that make an organism more fit and select against those that make it less fit. For example, plants with better roots get more water and make more seeds, and natural selection drives the population to have better roots from one generation to the next. But maybe there are different ways to make a good root (or anything else in the biological world).

The adaptive landscape is a way of thinking about the fact that several peaks of high fitness may exist, each peak corresponding to a different genotype. Natural selection will drive a population to the top of whatever peak it's already on, whether or not that peak is the highest one in the adaptive landscape.

What natural selection *won't* do is move the population to an even higher peak if that move means crossing a valley of lower fitness. Why? Because natural selection won't backtrack by favoring individuals with lower reproductive success. Individuals with lower fitness arise all the time (remember that most mutations are bad), but they don't increase in frequency as a result of selection.

You just can't get there from here

Sewell Wright's key insight (one of his many key insights — he's one of the hot shots of post-Darwinian evolutionary biology) was suggesting that genetic drift is the mechanism that lets a population move from one fitness peak (one really great genotype) to another because, unlike natural selection, genetic drift lets populations wander around low-fitness parts of the adaptive space. In his hypothesis, a small population could descend (genetically speaking) into an adaptive valley (an area of low fitness) and then climb a different, higher, adaptive peak as a result of natural selection. Essentially, a small population has a chance of hitting the genetic jackpot and ending up on a high adaptive peak.

Genetic drift is like a lottery; no guarantee exists that genetic drift is going to make it possible for a species to wander over to another peak. Wright's argument is just that it can do so *some of the time.* The low part of the fitness landscape means that those are genotypes that have a lower chance of leaving descendants. But they might get lucky once in a while.

When a small population does hit the genetic jackpot and gets to the slope of a higher peak, natural selection will kick in again and the population will climb up the new higher peak.

With a really fit combination of alleles, the population can spread through the *actual* physical landscape. Because the individuals have higher fitness (they're at the top of a really high fitness peak), they increase in frequency and can migrate in the physical landscape, spreading their selectively advantageous genetic combination far and wide. In other words, one small population hits the fitness jackpot; then these individuals sow their oats in other populations.

Chapter 7

Quantitative Genetics: When Many Genes Act at Once

. . . .

In This Chapter

▶ Teasing apart phenotypic variation into genetic and environmental components

▶ Making sense of broad- and narrow-sense heritability

▶ Measuring the response to selection on quantitative traits

. . . .

*M*any of the traits scientists are interested in aren't the result of a single gene, but of multiple genes. As discussed in previous chapters, some traits are controlled by one gene (or by a known few genes). In contrast, *quantitative* (or *multigenetic*) *traits* are determined by multiple (more than two) genes.

When multiple genes and environmental factors, which can have a big impact on how traits are expressed, both play significant roles in the phenotype, how much of the phenotype depends on the genes (and therefore is heritable), and how much depends on the environment (and is not heritable)?

If you expect that the next question is "Why in the world would anyone care?" remember that in evolution, only heritable variation is important. Many of the traits scientists, agriculturalists, and medical professionals care about turn out to be quantitative traits. The field of quantitative genetics deals with determining what proportion of the variation is due to genetic factors when multiple genes and the environment play a role.

Geneticists in this field use all sorts of mathematical formulas and statistical techniques to figure out all this information, none of which you need to know. So this chapter skips the math and focuses on the key principles instead. Here, I paint with a broad brush but give you the foundation you need to understand this topic — just in case you run across it in the science section of the newspaper.

Why Quantitative Genetics Is Important

Quantitative genetics is relevant to evolution because it has to do with heredity and understanding how heredity works. Darwin didn't understand how heredity worked; he just knew that it did — sort of. Back in those days, folks understood that the heritability of some traits was more predictable than others. For some things, such as hemophilia, researchers could trace the ailment back to a single factor that they could map onto a family tree. (Today, scientists know that this factor is a particular DNA sequence.)

Other traits, such as how much milk a cow made, weren't so clear cut. True, researchers in Darwin's day knew that things like how much milk a cow made had a heritable component, but figuring out what that heritable component was wasn't as simple as determining the heritable component of eye color or a disease like hemophilia.

Fast-forward several generations. Scientists now can explain some of the things Darwin and his contemporaries could only wonder about. We now know that a character is often the result of several genes rather than a single gene.

Interacting genes

When a whole bunch of genes affect a particular trait, these genes can interact in different ways. The effect of the different genes can be additive, though some genes might be more important than others in determining the final phenotype. Imagine a lot of genes for milk production where, at each locus (location on the DNA strand), some alleles result in more milk and some result in less. The heritable part of milk production will be determined by the sum of the effects at all the involved loci.

Different loci can also interact in non-additive ways. In some cases, the non-additive interaction of the different genes is important. Imagine that a particular locus may influence milk production, for example, but only when a specific allele occurs at some particular other locus. Without that allele at the second locus, the first locus doesn't have anything to do with how much milk a cow makes. This process is called *epistasis*.

Epistatic interactions are those in which the fitness of a particular allele at one locus depends on alleles at another locus.

Imagine epistatic interactions that affect the A locus, in which the relative fitness of the aa and AA individuals depends on the alleles at a second locus, which I'll call B. If that second locus has one combination of alleles, AA individuals will have higher fitness than aa individuals. But if the B locus has a different combination of alleles, aa individuals will have higher fitness than AA individuals.

I made up the milk example for illustrative purposes, but one actual case of epistasis that you might be familiar with concerns those colored squash that you see around Halloween and Thanksgiving. In one genetic system, the colors white, green, and yellow are controlled by two genes, each of which have two alleles (of the dominant/recessive type; refer to Chapter 3).

When at least one of the genes at the white locus is the dominant form, the squash is white and the other locus has no effect on color. But when both alleles at the white locus are of the recessive form, then the color of the squash (green or yellow) is determined by the alleles at the green/yellow locus. You can see that it starts to get complicated even with only two loci involved — there can be many more.

These examples have consequences for the way selection operates. In both cases, the extent to which selection increases the frequency of the alleles at the one locus depends on the frequency of the alleles at other locus.

Multigenetic traits in medicine and agriculture

Being able to figure out the correlation between heritable genes and phenotype when the genetics is more complicated and environment plays a role has several benefits. Multigenetic traits are important to the fields of medicine and agriculture, for example.

In agriculture

Most of the characteristics that farmers breed for are quantitative traits, such as the amount of milk a cow produces or how many ears of corn a corn plant produces. To help farmers breed better cows and better corn plants, researchers need to understand what's involved when they start thinking about traits controlled by many genes.

In medicine

Understanding genetic interactions can help scientists sort out the genetics of human disease. For many diseases, the heritable component is not absolute. People say that a disease or condition tends to "run in families" or that you're more likely to have the condition if your recent ancestors had it. Both expressions indicate that you may be predisposed to a particular condition that has a genetic component, but you won't definitely get it. Maybe the ailment appears only under certain environment conditions or only when certain genes interact in a particular way.

Understanding Quantitative Traits

Although all quantitative traits are multigenic traits, not all multigenic traits are quantitative traits. Strictly speaking, a multigenic trait is any trait controlled by more than one gene, yet when only a couple of loci are involved, researchers can sort out all the different combinations of outcomes and understand the phenotypes, as in the squash color example in the earlier section. As the number of genes gets larger, doing that isn't so easy, so scientists have to use the mathematics of quantitative genetics.

Continuous and non-continuous traits

Quantitative traits fall into two camps: those that vary continuously and those that don't:

- **Continuous quantitative characters:** Quantitative traits often are continuously variable across some range. An example is adult height. Although you may consider yourself to be either tall or short, heights vary smoothly from the tallest to shortest.

- **Non-continuous quantitative characters:** Although many multigenetic traits are continuous, some aren't — at least, not in the same way that continuous characters are. Take bristles on fruit flies, for example. Fruit flies have a discrete number of bristles that varies from some bristles to more bristles, but they don't have half a bristle. Your weight can vary by any fraction of a pound (or gram or stone), but a bristle or a pound is either "on" or "off." Some diseases or conditions (those that have two states: sick or not sick) are also non-continuous characters.

The environment has a big impact on many quantitative traits. Taller parents, for example, tend to have taller children, but environmental factors, such as nutrition, also affect adult height.

Crossing a threshold

For a non-continuous quantitative trait to be expressed, some threshold combination — of genetic interactions alone or of genetic interactions combined with environmental factors — has to occur.

Take mental illness, which scientists are still trying to understand. Researchers hypothesize that disorders such as schizophrenia are controlled by multiple loci and that the condition manifests in people who have a certain number of specific alleles at specific loci (and perhaps in certain environments), but whether the condition manifests itself depends on more than the genetic component.

The case of hemophilia

In the case of hemophilia, several different loci code for different clotting factors, and different forms of hemophilia result from alleles (that code for bad clotting factors) at several of these loci. But hemophilia isn't a multigenetic character, even though several genes can be responsible for it. Why? In each case of hemophilia, a single locus is responsible for the trait. Which one you just happen to have been unlucky enough to inherit determines the type of hemophilia you have.

Here are a couple of other interesting tidbits about hemophilia:

✔ It's an X-linked recessive character, which means that two copies are necessary for a woman to have hemophilia, but only one copy is necessary for a man to have it.

✔ As a result of modern medicine, hemophilia has gone from a trait associated with very low fitness to one with greatly reduced fitness consequences. Having hemophilia is never good, but it's not as bad as it used to be because today medications can replace the lost clotting ability. This situation is yet another example of how the fitness consequences of a particular gene are a function of the environment.

Schizophrenia, for example, definitely has a genetic component. If one of your parents has schizophrenia, you're at higher risk of developing schizophrenia than someone in the general population; if both your parents are schizophrenic, your changes are even greater. This situation makes sense, given that you share some, but not all, of your parents' genes. But here's a particularly interesting point that reveals that genetics isn't the only factor: If your *identical* twin is schizophrenic, you have about a 50 percent change of developing the disease yourself, even though you share 100 percent of your twin's genes.

Although the genetic component is significant, something beyond genetics is going on. Maybe environmental factors are the key. In the case of relatives other than identical twins, perhaps different combinations of genes and their interactions are important as well. These questions are what schizophrenia researchers are trying to sort out.

QTL mapping: Identifying what genes matter

When you're dealing with multigenetic traits, figuring out what genes are responsible for a particular trait is harder but not impossible. The strategy for identifying the relevant genes in the genome of a particular organism involves *quantitative trait loci mapping* (*QTL mapping*, for short). With QTL mapping, you cross lots of individuals and keep track of how particular genetic markers in the offspring correlate with the character you're interested in. These markers aren't themselves the genes responsible for the quantitative trait, but because they're correlated with the phenotype, they can be used to identify the location on the chromosomes where the genes reside.

A *marker gene* is any gene that's easy to recognize because its location on the genome is known. Imagine, for example, that people with green eyes are on average taller. We know that tallness is a function of many genes, but now we know that one of these genes is near the gene that controls green eye color. The two genes are in close proximity. They are closely *linked* — they tend to be inherited together. (Go to Chapter 5 or more details on linkage.)

Here's how QTL mapping works: Scientists know where the marker gene is, and now they know that some gene near it is responsible in part for a multigenetic trait. The mathematics of how this works is beyond the scope of this book, but what's important is that it does work. (And it works even better for species for which we have a lot of gene sequences where we can go in and see exactly which genes are near the marker loci!)

By using the markers as signposts, scientists can

1. Figure out approximately how many genes underlie a given multigenetic trait

2. Tease apart the details of gene interactions

3. Understand the relative importance of different genes to see which genes have stronger effects than others

4. Voila! Actually have a good idea where to look in the genome for the relevant genes.

Analyzing the Heritability of Quantitative Traits

As stated earlier in this chapter, quantitative traits are traits that result from complex interactions between multiple genes and that may be influenced by environmental factors. To understand how these traits evolve, evolutionary biologists analyze the heritability of quantitative traits.

As you can imagine, the first task is to determine what proportion of the trait (or phenotype) is due to genetic factors (the heritable bits) and what portion is due to the environment (the non-heritable bits). As tough as that job is, the analysis is made even more complicated by the fact that any given gene, or allele, may impact the resulting phenotype in an additive or non-additive way.

Additive or non-additive?

The concept of additivity can be a little slippery. To understand it better, think about a single gene with two alleles: for example, wrinkled or smooth peas. In this case, the smooth form (A) is dominant over the wrinkled form (a). An individual with a single allele for the smooth form (Aa) would express the smooth phenotype. Having two copies of the smooth form (AA) produces the same smooth phenotype. In the first case (Aa), the single recessive allele is non-additive, as is the second dominant allele in the second case (AA). Neither allele affects the final expression of the trait. (For details on dominant and recessive genes, see Chapter 3.)

This situation, wherein the combinations of different alleles can result in some alleles not having an effect on the phenotype, can happen across different loci. A gene may have the potential to influence a particular phenotype, but it may not influence the phenotype in an additive way. In other words, when the conditions are right (a certain combination of alleles across loci or a particular interaction with other alleles), the gene may influence the phenotype. At other times, this same gene may not affect the phenotype, because the necessary combination or interaction didn't occur.

A hot subtopic of quantitative genetics is sorting through the non-additive nature of multiple genes to figure out whether some of them are especially important (or especially important some of the time). Given that some ailments certainly have a genetic component that's controlled by multiple genes, it would be nice if researchers could identify genes that have large effects and then figure out what they do. This is crucially important for understanding the genetics of some human diseases.

Determining phenotypic variation

Evolution requires that variation exist and that this variation be heritable. The upshot of environmental effects and of the non-additive genetic variation is to *decrease* heritability and, as a result, decrease the power of selection to transform populations. To determine the strength of selection, scientists separate the variation in a population into the differences due to genetics (both additive and non-additive) and the differences due to environment.

Variation is a property of *groups* of individuals or populations, not individuals alone, no matter how fickle, unpredictable, or changeable those individuals are. All the analysis performed to determine variation relates to groups of individuals.

To understand all the components of an analysis of the heritability of quantitative traits, consider a simple hypothetical example: height. (Why height? No particular reason. You could use any quantitative trait.)

The phenotype — in this example, whether you're tall or short — is a function of the genotype and the environment. Height has a heritable component: Tall parents tend to have taller offspring. It also has an environmental component: Absent a proper diet, you won't get very tall.

You can further partition the genetic component of the phenotype into additive and non-additive parts. How strong selection is for this trait is determined by the additive component of genetic variation.

Here's the math: The phenotypic variation within a population is the sum of additive genetic variation plus the non-additive genetic variation plus the environmental variation. If you like formulas, here's what this one looks like:

> phenotypic variation = additive genetic variation + non-additive genetic variation + environmental variation

Broad- and narrow-sense heritability

Environmental variation isn't heritable. Imagine two people who have a similar genetic makeup, one of whom is taller due only to a better diet. Because the variation between these two individuals isn't due to genetic factors, the taller person won't have taller offspring. But variation that is a function of genetics and not of the environment is heritable.

For the purposes of understanding natural selection, it's helpful to think of heritability as being either the broad-sense or the narrow-sense type:

- **Broad-sense heritability:** The total of all of the genetic factors, be they additive or non-additive
- **Narrow-sense heritability:** The subset of the genetic component that is additive.

Heritability is measured as a number from 0 to 1, indicating the degree of correlation between the parental phenotype and the offspring phenotype:

- If the offspring phenotype is predicted by the phenotype of the parents, heritability is 1.
- If the offspring phenotype is *not* predicted by the phenotype of the parents, heritability is 0.

In the height example, in which the difference between the height of two people was due simply to diet, the phenotype of the offspring of the tall parent would not be any different from the phenotype of the offspring of the short parent, and heritability would be close to zero.

Think back to the example of the smooth and wrinkly peas. Imagine two pea plants, both of which are heterozygous for the smooth character — that is, each plant has both a dominant smooth allele and a recessive wrinkled allele. Because of the dominant interaction between these two genes, all the peas are smooth. Now suppose that you cross these two pea plants. On average, one quarter of the offspring will have wrinkly seeds. In this very simple case, you can see that although the phenotype of the offspring was a direct result of the genes they inherited from their parents (broad-sense heritability), the phenotype of the parents was an inexact predictor of the phenotype of the offspring. Heritability in the narrow sense was less than 1.

In evolution, narrow-sense heritability is the important form of heritability. Imagine that for some reason, being a pea plant with smooth seeds is advantageous. Natural selection will result in the pea plants with smooth seeds being the ones to leave more descendents, and as a result, the next generation will have fewer plants with wrinkly seeds — but not as many fewer as you would expect based just on the relative selective advantage of having smooth seeds. Why? Some of the plants with smooth seeds will have wrinkly offspring. That phenomenon is the non-additive part of the genetic variation.

Measuring the Strength of Selection

Evolution by natural selection relies on heritable variation and the strength of selection. For that reason, examining those two different factors is important. Scientists can easily measure how phenotypes vary in a population. What they don't know as easily is how much of this variation is heritable. But they can find out.

Figure 7-1 shows the variation of a particular quantitative continuous phenotypic trait in a population — in this case, height. The measured heights fall along the x-axis. Individuals on the left are shorter than individuals on the right. The y-axis shows the frequency in the population of different phenotypes. In this particular example, most of the individuals cluster in the middle range; some of them are very short, and some of them are very tall, but most of them are in between.

To find out how heritable height is in this population, you can selectively breed the tallest (or the shortest) individuals and then examine the frequency distribution of their offspring's height. Figure 7-2 is the same frequency distribution as Figure 7-1, highlighting the subset of the original population you plan to use to create the next generation in your experimental population. In this case, assume that you picked the tall ones.

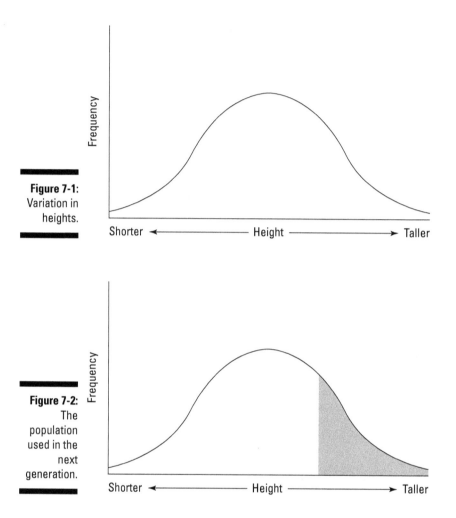

Frequency

Shorter ← — — — — Height — — — → Taller

Frequency

Shorter ← — — — — Height — — — → Taller

So what will the offspring population look like? Specifically, what will be the frequency distribution of phenotypes of this quantitative trait? Figure 7-3 and Figure 7-4 show two of many possibilities. Each figure shows two frequency distributions. The first is the frequency distribution of the phenotypes of the original population, and the second is the distribution of the offspring population resulting from breeding only the tallest individuals. In both cases, the average height of the population has been shifted to the right. In both cases, on average the offspring population is taller. But in Figure 7-4, the population has shifted much farther to the right, meaning that the offspring population is significantly taller.

A result such as the one in Figure 7-4 tells you that the trait (in this case, height) is much more heritable in that experiment than it was for the case in Figure 7-3. The difference between the two figures can't be due to the strength of selection, because that was the same in both cases. (Remember, you were the selective agent because you picked which ones would have offspring.) Given that the strength of selection was the same, the difference in the response to selection was purely a function of the difference in heritability between these two populations.

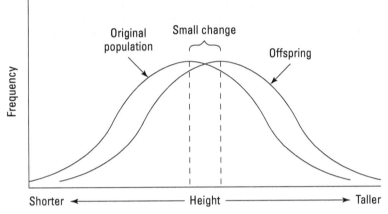

Figure 7-3:
Phenotypes
of offspring
from the
original
population.

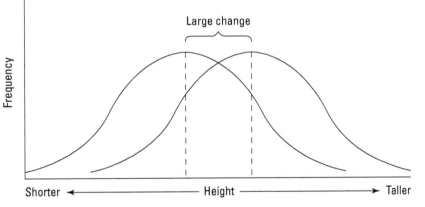

Figure 7-4:
Height
distribution
of the
offspring of
the tallest
people.

If you increase the strength of selection, you would expect an even greater increase in the change in average height in the offspring population, which is exactly what Figure 7-5 illustrates. Here, the new population was founded with a much smaller subset of the original population, comprising only the tallest of the tall (compare the shaded area here with the shaded area in Figure 7-2). The result is a greater shift toward an even taller offspring population.

All of this — QTL mapping, continuous/non-continuous and additive/non-additive traits, broad- and narrow-sense heritability — is pretty academic, and you probably need to be a scientist (or a very devoted reader) to grasp the fine and not-so-fine points of the topic. But anyone can appreciate the advantages that the study of quantitative genetics can bring to fields that touch us all. The closer we get to figuring out where all the genes are on the genome, how they interact, and what they actually do, the closer we get to treating diseases that confound us now.

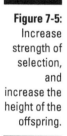

Figure 7-5:
Increase strength of selection, and increase the height of the offspring.

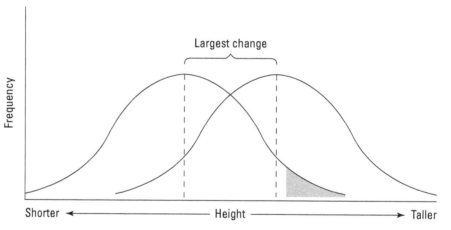

Chapter 8

Species and Speciation

*E*volution is nothing more than changes in gene frequencies in a group of organisms through time. Accumulate enough of these genetic changes in one population of a particular species, and that population could evolve into a new species. This process, whereby members of one species become another species, is called *speciation,* and it's one of the most fascinating areas of evolutionary biology.

As you can imagine, speciation can take a very long time — at least compared with the human life span. For that reason, scientists can't perform a single experiment in a laboratory that allows them to start with one species and watch a new one evolve. What they can do instead is observe the process in nature and study the individual parts of the process in the laboratory and in the natural environment.

Evolution doesn't need to lead to speciation. A species can evolve through time without splitting to create a second species. The study of speciation is the study of what factors are responsible for causing one species split into two species.

Species and Speciation at a Glance

Speciation is simply the process whereby a single lineage splits into two lineages. In other words, new species arise from existing species.

But what constitutes a species and how does speciation occur? The following sections explain.

The biological-species concept

Scientists have a pretty good handle on what constitutes a species for sexually reproducing animals: the *biological-species concept.* According to this concept, a species is a group of organisms that can interbreed and produce viable and fertile offspring.

Individuals can mate and reproduce with members of their own species but not with members of other species. The defining characteristic separating one species from another is that they are reproductively isolated from each other. When a speciation event occurs — when evolution results in members of one species developing into another species — that group of individuals can no longer interbreed with members of the original species.

The biological-species concept best applies to sexually reproducing animals. It doesn't adequately define what bacterial species are. In fact, defining the term *species* in other cases is an active area of evolutionary biology. For more on bacterial species, head to the later section "A Species Concept for Bacteria."

When one species becomes two

When new species arise from existing species, you have speciation. Here's how it works: Two different populations of the same species evolve in different ways. They become progressively more different until they are so different that they are no longer able to interbreed. That's all there is to it.

You've heard about speciation, and it might be one of the major reasons you bought this book. Can it be that such a thing really happens? It's clear that some people don't even like the idea of it. How do we know that the whole idea of speciation wasn't just something that Darwin concocted with after one too many beers? Because of ring species, which are explained in the next section. At this point, suffice it to say that by studying ring species, scientists know that a gradual accumulation of small differences is sufficient to cause two populations of the same species to become reproductively isolated.

Of course, ring species aren't the only interesting thing in this chapter. I hope you read the rest of the chapter, too, because speciation is a fascinating topic and one that evolutionary biologists think about a lot. But even if you read no more than the next section, you'll see how scientists — and now you — know that speciation can indeed happen.

Going in Circles: Ring Species

Through the existence of ring species, scientists can say with 100 percent certainty that small differences can accumulate in nature to the point that two populations of the same species can become reproductively isolated. They can actually go out and see it.

Subspecies, races, and breeds

Variation exists among different populations of the same species. The following terms are used to describe the different types of variation:

- **Subspecies:** A group within a particular species that shares genetic characters with other group members that it doesn't share with members of the larger species. Subspecies may interbreed quite freely or may be partially reproductively isolated — that is, they can interbreed but don't do it as well, or produce offspring as viable, as when they mate within their own subspecies group. Subspecies can range from ever-so-slightly-different groups within a species to groups that are on the verge of speciating.

- **Race:** Used most often to describe variation within the human species. Human races are differentiated primarily by skin color, but even though the genes responsible for skin color are noticeable, the actual genetic differences among races are slight. In fact, skin color doesn't accurately reflect the genetic differences among humans. Two people of African descent could easily be more genetically different from each other than a person of European descent may be from a person of Asian descent. Bottom line: Races have slight differences, and these differences are no where near the level they'd have to be to decrease gene exchange.

- **Breed:** Domestic animals (such as dogs and cows) whose characteristics are artificially selected and maintained by humans through animal husbandry are divided into breeds. The goal of selective breeding is to create animals that differ from their wild counterparts and possess relatively predictable traits. Take dogs, for example. Humans have been breeding dogs for only a relatively short period, and over that time, starting with wolves, we've managed to produce everything from Chihuahuas to Great Danes. All breeds of dogs are the same species. They can all interbreed, although admittedly, interbreeding is easier for some pairs than for others. **Note:** Standard convention gives species names to products of animal husbandry. That doesn't mean, however, that dogs and wolves are different species (in fact they share the same species name: *canis domesticus*). Dogs and wolves can still interbreed, even though a "happily ever after" probably wouldn't be in the cards for the Big Bad Wolf and your Pomeranian.

Ring species are species with these specific features:

- ✔ **Their habitat surrounds an area of hostile environment that they can't cross.** Think about a bird species living in the lower elevations around the Himalayan mountain plateau. Or a little salamander living around the edges of California Central Valley. Or a bird that lives on the land masses surrounding the Arctic ice cap. They can move around the edges, but they can't cross over the middle, where they wouldn't be able to survive. Figure 8-1 shows a habitat for a ring species.

- ✔ **Neighboring subpopulations around the circle, or ring, are slightly genetically different from each other.** These genetic differences can be measured. Maybe there's been selection for different alleles in different places; maybe the genetic differences are the result of drift; maybe both.

- ✔ **Most neighboring populations can interbreed with each other.** The populations near one another are a little different genetically, but they are still the same species and can therefore mate and produce viable offspring.

- ✔ **At one place around the ring — the ends — the neighboring populations can't interbreed with each other.** Each population can breed with its neighbors (because neighboring populations are just a little bit different), yet all those differences add up as you go from one end of the ring to the other. The result is that, by the time you've gone all the way around from the beginning of the circle to the end, the two populations on the ends are too different to interbreed. If it wasn't for all the populations in the middle, the two end populations would be different species.

Think of the ring as a horse shoe with the ends bent together so they touch. The two populations at the ends of the horse shoe are just too different to interbreed.

San Joaquin Valley, CA

Figure 8-1:
The range for a ring species.

You can still think of populations comprising a ring species as being part of the same species because they share a common gene pool, and their genes can be combined via the intermediate populations (so they're not completely reproductively isolated), but obviously, this is a gray area because the populations at the ends of the range can't interbreed.

It wouldn't take much for a ring species to become two separate species. Nothing evolutionary has to happen (that's happened already): All you need is for something to wipe out some of the middle populations and break the ring. What could cause the elimination of the middle populations? Take your pick:

- ✔ Any event, natural or manmade, leading to a fractured habitat that literally separates the range (such as an erupting volcano or earthquake)

- ✔ Any event that wipes out the populations in the middle (such as an epidemic or uncontrolled hunting).

The Components of Speciation

Speciation usually doesn't happen overnight. It's a gradual process that involves these 3 components:

- ✔ **Reduction in *gene flow* (the exchange of genes between adjacent, or nearby populations):** The mating and reproduction that go on within a species does a pretty effective job of keeping all the genes between populations mixed and, therefore, keeping these populations genetically homogenous. As long as the genes can be easily exchanged between populations, the two populations can't diverge genetically. Mating keeps mixing the genes back together. For speciation to occur there needs to be a reduction in gene flow.

- ✔ **A decrease in the genetic similarities among populations within a species:** Once populations aren't being mixed together, they can become more dissimilar as a consequence of the different evolutionary trajectories experienced by the two populations.

- ✔ **The development of reproductive isolation between the two populations:** Reproductive isolation can happen via two mechanisms.

  - • The accumulation of differences can, by itself, lead to a reduction in the ability to interbreed. The different populations are just too different.

  - • When the populations have diverged to the extent that the offspring of such matings are less fit, natural selection acts to prevent mating between individuals of the two populations. If individuals from the two populations can still interbreed but with reduced success, natural selection will favor individuals that say, "I'm just not that into you." Matings that won't produce quality offspring aren't good for fitness — alleles for avoiding such mistakes will increase as a result of selection.

Numerous events can bring about reduction in gene flow, decrease in similarities among populations, and their eventual reproductive isolation. Sometimes, these events are physical barriers; other times, they're not.

How little changes add up: Local adaptations

As Chapter 4 explains, genetic variation occurs among members of the same species — hardly an earth-shattering piece of information. Just look around. All people are humans, but identical twins aside, all of us look different. (Even identical twins aren't exactly identical, of course, because of environmental factors that affect their phenotypes; refer to Chapter 4.)

By studying naturally occurring variation, scientists have discovered that some of this variation can be accounted for by organisms having adapted to their local environment. Think about it: Some species have ranges that extend over areas so large that environmental factors differ from place to place within the species' range. A species of flowering plant, for example, can have a range that extends from Texas to Minnesota, and given the very different conditions in the two areas, it shouldn't come as a surprise that plants in Texas and Minnesota would flower at different times. These differences often have a genetic basis; natural selection has favored alleles for flowering earlier in Texas and later in Minnesota.

If you're a flowering plant, you want to flower at the same time that your neighbors are flowering, because mating is hard if your flowers are the only ones that are open. For that reason, flowering time, which is crucial to a plant's fitness, is under strong selection. A plant that flowers too early may lose its flowers to a late frost; one that flowers too late may lack sufficient time to produce seeds before winter comes.

A fair number of plants self-pollinate — information that is of absolutely no value in this discussion except as a little bit of trivia. Mull it over at your leisure.

One of the tricks plants use to make sure that they flower at the right time is to assess day length — a perfect predictor of the time of year regardless of where you are. The "right" day-night cycle for flowering, though, depends on where the plant grows. By taking sample plants of a species from different places across the entire species range and growing them under controlled conditions in a greenhouse where day length can be varied, scientists have found that the various populations of plants have adapted to respond to the different day-night cycles of their respective original locations, even though they all belong to the same species.

Although plants with different light-dark cycles can interbreed, they generally don't, for the simple reason that the plants that are most different are likely to be ones that are farthest away, and Minnesota pollen has little chance of landing on a Texas flower. Because *gene flow,* gene exchange between adjacent populations, is low to non-existent over such long distances, plants in different parts of this large area can evolve different combinations of genes. By growing the plants from different locations in a controlled environment, scientists were able to show that some populations in the same species are adapted to the local conditions where they were found.

Reproductive isolation: The final step of speciation

Speciation occurs when the separate populations become reproductively isolated, losing their ability to produce live or fertile offspring. The mechanisms responsible for reproductive incompatibility fall into two categories: prezygotic isolating mechanisms and postzygotic isolating mechanisms.

- **Prezygotic isolating mechanisms:** Specifically, *prezygotic* refers to those things that occur before the egg is fertilized. Basically, this type of isolating mechanism stops sperm and egg from getting together.

- **Postzygotic isolating mechanisms:** Postzygotic isolating mechanisms are those that occur after the egg is fertilized. They don't stop mating, but they stop the offspring from being viable or able to reproduce.

The following sections go into more detail.

Prezygotic isolating mechanisms

Anything that could prevent the sperm and egg from coming together is considered to be a prezygotic isolating mechanism, such as the following:

- **Reproductive timing differences:** Hey, when the time isn't right, what can you do?

- **Spatial separation:** If one population is always on hawthorn trees, and the other is on apple trees, never the twain shall meet.

- **Mate-choice specificity:** Basically, this situation is the evolution of being picky.

- **Physical incompatibilities between the two sexes:** This mechanism is common among insects. Have you ever seen *Drosophila* genitalia? Let me just say this: If the pieces don't fit, you really must quit.

- **Inability of the sperm and egg to fuse:** No fusing means no offspring.

Postzygotic isolating mechanisms

Postzygotic isolating mechanisms are those that come into play even though individuals from the two diverging groups do mate. As a result of different evolutionary trajectories, the parents are different enough that they don't produce fertile offspring (or any offspring, perhaps). Postzygotic isolating mechanisms include

- ✔ **Spontaneous abortion of hybrid embryos:** The offspring are never born.
- ✔ **Low offspring viability:** The offspring die, often before reproducing.
- ✔ **Offspring sterility:** The offspring themselves can't reproduce. (As far as one's fitness goes, producing sterile offspring is exactly the same as producing no offspring at all.)

Postzygotic isolating mechanisms drive the evolution of prezygotic isolating mechanisms. Why? Because mating with someone you can't produce viable offspring with is a bad idea, and natural selection favors genes connected with correct mate choice.

Types of Speciation

The ring species example is all we need to be sure that the process of speciation can happen. There's nothing magical about: Little differences add up until you get a big difference. But most species don't have a ring-shaped distributions, so while ring species provide an excellent example of the nuts and bolts of the process, that's not how we usually imagine the speciation happening.

Allopatric speciation: There IS a mountain high enough

In *allopatric* speciation, a physical barrier separates the populations and limits or eliminates gene flow between them. Any physical barrier that reduces gene flow will do: a mountain range, a patch of unsuitable habitat that's difficult to cross, or an ocean.

Allopatric speciation is considered to be the most important speciation mechanism — lots of examples occur in nature — and also the easiest to understand. It just stands to reason that a reduction in gene flow will occur when populations are physically separated, and you can easily see how species can become separated: continents drift apart; mountain ranges rise; climates change and alter the availability of suitable habitat.

Although scientists can't experimentally witness the process of speciation from beginning to end because of the long time periods involved for full speciation to occur, they can find pairs of populations at every stage of the process, from recently physically separated and not very divergent all the way through very divergent and not very able to reproduce.

Allopatric speciation by founder effect: Getting carried away

Allopatric speciation by founder effect, like allopatric speciation (explained in the preceding section), requires that the two populations be isolated physically. The difference is that in founder effect speciation, the second population originates from a small group of individuals separating from the main group, such as a flock of birds being blown to an island.

Common locations for allopatric speciation by founder effect are islands, which tend to be colonized initially by small numbers of individuals. Scientists find that isolated populations on islands often are very different from the larger mainland population. The farther an island is from the mainland, for example, the less likely it is that large numbers of individuals will be blowing or drifting there. Hence, the differences between the mainland and island populations can be attributed to either (or both) of the following situations:

- ✔ **Genetic drift**: The founding population already starts off a little differently genetically and thus by chance may have gene combinations that predispose it to a different evolutionary future. This process may be helped by genetic drift in the small initial population. For the details on genetic drift, go to Chapter 6.

- ✔ **Natural selection:** When a population is in a novel environment, genetic differences accumulate as a result of natural selection. Differences in predators, prey, or other food resources could drive natural selection in different directions compared with the mainland population.

Parapatric speciation: I just can't live in your world

In *parapatric* speciation, the two populations aren't physically separated; instead, they abut each other. Because they're within mating distance, something other than a physical barrier must be causing the reduction in gene flow between these populations. That impediment? Natural selection.

Suppose that a species' range encompasses two adjacent environments with conditions different enough that genes advantageous on one side aren't advantageous on the other. As a consequence, natural selection favors particular traits on one side that it doesn't favor on the other side. If an individual from one side meanders over to the other side for a little procreation, his offspring with his genes from the "bad" side will be selected against. As a result, the usual homogenizing effect of mating between individuals of two habitats will be reduced or eliminated, and the two populations will become more divergent.

A classic example of the first stages of parapatric population divergence is the evolution of plants in areas contaminated with mine waste such as heavy metals. These areas aren't ideal places to set up house, but some plants can. In these hostile environments, natural selection favors genes that allow plants to survive high concentrations of lead and other metals. In the absence of this contamination, these genes aren't necessarily favored.

These plants haven't speciated yet; some interbreeding still occurs. Interestingly, the hybrid plants — those that form as a result of matings between the mine-waste plants and the native plants — do less well in both the mine-waste environment and the native environment. Therefore, selection favors genes that reduce the likelihood of matings between plants on either side of the line, and as a result, the plants living on the mine waste have changed in a couple of interesting ways:

- ✔ **They have evolved different flowering times from the original population.** Different flowering times prevent gene flow across the mine waste. The difference in flowering times is most pronounced at the border between the two environments, because plants that are farther from the mine waste are less likely to receive pollen from mine-waste plants and, therefore, are less likely to experience a selective force favoring different flowering time.

- ✔ **They have evolved to have a higher rate of self-fertilization.** Self-fertilization could be selectively advantageous for two reasons:

    - It prevents the production of offspring with low fitness by preventing matings with plants from uncontaminated soil.

    - It comes in handy if getting pollen from another compatible plant is difficult.

In parapatric speciation, selection is strong enough to reduce the likelihood that genes from one environment will make it in the gene pool of a population living in a different environment. Further evolution of reproductive characters (like different flowering times, for example) decreases gene flow between populations even more. In the mine-waste example, the two populations are adjacent, and pollen blows back and forth, yet the offspring that result from matings between the two populations are not likely to contribute their genes to the next generation. Different selective regimes in the two environments have resulted in a reduction in gene flow between the two populations, which will only increase the degree to which the two populations diverge.

Sympatric speciation: Let's just be friends

Sympatric speciation occurs without the organisms in the two populations being physically separated at all. No physical barrier prevents gene flow (as in allopatric or allopatric speciation by founder effect speciation), and no spatial discontinuity exists (as in parapatric speciation). In sympatric speciation, it is some detail of the environment that results in a reduction of gene flow between the two populations.

Suppose that one particular combination of genes makes some individuals better at foraging at night, and another combination generates individuals that are better at foraging during the day. If some of the individuals are active only at night and others are active only during the day, the night-active critters are more likely to breed with other night-active critters, simply because those are the creatures they interact with.

Although researchers suspect that sympatric speciation is unlikely to be a very common speciation mechanism, evidence suggests that the process can be important occasionally. A possible example is the case of the apple maggot worm — a pest of apples in the United States.

Apples aren't native to the United States; they were introduced by European settlers. The apple maggot worm, on the other hand, is native to the United States. Before the introduction of apples, it fed on hawthorns, and many maggot worms still feed on hawthorns. Hawthorns and apples can grow in similar locations. The apple worms that infest apple trees have ample opportunity to mate with worms from hawthorns and produce offspring, but when scientists examine them, they see that the apple worms infesting one type of tree are genetically different from those feeding on the other type of tree.

Something's preventing gene flow between these two types of worms. Even though apples and hawthorns exist in the same environment, for some reason the flies that lay eggs on one species avoid laying eggs on the other. One possible answer involves ripening times. Apples ripen earlier than hawthorn fruits, and the flies living on the different species reproduce at slightly different times.

More interesting, the flies seem to have developed a preference for either apples or hawthorns. The flies laying eggs on apples have a preference for apples, whereas the flies laying eggs on hawthorns have a preference for hawthorns — preferences that must have evolved after the introduction of apples to the United States, arising in a location where apples and hawthorns coexist. It's this feeding preference that's driving the flies' divergence.

Speciation hasn't occurred for the apple maggot flies yet. The two populations can still reproduce (even though doing so would be the entomological equivalent of a Capulet-Montague pairing), but they're beginning to diverge genetically even though they live in exactly the same place, as close to each other as neighboring trees.

Diverging on the fly

As two populations diverge, they can become reproductively isolated. Populations living in different environments experience different selective pressures. As a result, they become genetically different and less able to reproduce. In this case, reproductive isolation is a by-product of selection. Alternatively, reproductive isolation can be selected for when two populations have diverged to the point where hybrids have lower fitness. In that case, any mutations that result in the organisms' wanting to avoid "interbreeding" will increase in frequency.

Diane Dodd designed an experiment in which several generations of fruit flies were raised on different kinds of food: either a starch-based food or a sugar maltose-based food. Starting with a single population of flies, the researchers produced different fly lineages. The initial flies were the same, and the experiment was set up in such a way that the only selective pressure was the food type. Flies that did well on maltose (or starch) were more likely to leave more descendants and hence their genes were more likely to end up in the next maltose (or starch) generation. After 8 generations, Dodd conducted experiments to investigate the mating preferences of the evolved flies.

To conduct these experiments, Dodd introduced male and female flies from the different populations into a cage and kept track of which flies got together. When the flies came from different populations that had been fed the same food, they didn't exhibit a preference for mating with flies from their own population. A fly raised on starch was just as likely to mate with a fly raised on starch from a different population as it was to mate with a fly raised on starch from its own population. The same results held for flies raised on maltose: They didn't exhibit a preference for their own population compared with others raised on similar food.

When the experiment involved flies that had been fed different food types, however, the situation changed. In this case, the flies exhibited a distinct preference for mating with flies that had been raised on the same food they had.

What's important about this experiment is that in producing the flies, Dodd didn't select for reproductive preferences; she selected for increased fitness on one type of fly food or another. But as a result of evolutionary changes for increased fitness, the flies also developed changes in mating preference! This experiment clearly indicates that selection for fitness in different environments may result in reduced ability to interbreed.

Islands: Good Places to Vacation and Speciate

Some places are just plain better for speciating and studying speciation than others — islands, for example. As stated earlier, islands are just tailor-made for allopatric speciation via founder events.

Islands can be hot spots for speciation. Hawaii is a good example. So are the Galapagos Islands, where Darwin got his first insights into the process of speciation by natural selection. Two factors combine to make islands areas that can facilitate speciation:

- ✔ **Isolation:** Islands are by definition places where populations are isolated from the rest of the species. As gene flow is low, opportunities for genetic diversification increase.

- ✔ **Potential for subsequent speciation:** After a species has evolved on one island in a chain, some of its members can blow or drift to another island, where they may diverge further. In the future, some of them may be blown back to the first island — where, if they're different enough, they may diverge from the population on the original island to produce a second new species.

Islands aren't populated solely by species that just happen to wash up on their shores or get dumped there by a wayward breeze. If an archipelago is far enough from the mainland to make colonization from mainland organisms unlikely, the island is often populated by the species that are unique to the island. You can safely assume that these species arose via speciation on the island. Hawaii, for example, has several native species (like ukulele players) that don't exist anywhere else. They arose in the Hawaiian archipelago.

A Species Concept for Bacteria

The biological-species concept, explained in an earlier section, classifies species based on their ability to mate and reproduce. That system is all well and good for organisms that mate and reproduce, but it leaves lots of other organisms out in the cold.

Bacteria are perhaps the best examples of organisms that reproduce without mating. They simply divide into two daughter bacteria, each of which goes happily on its way, dividing further. Mutations can occur in this process, just as in any other DNA-replication process; hence, bacteria evolve.

Bacteria categories

When microbiologists go out to the environment (such as some exotic foreign location the likes of which you see on the Discovery Channel or the back of your throat), they find that they can group the microbes they collect into different categories such as:

- ✔ *Escherichia coli (E. coli):* Common gut bacteria
- ✔ *Staphylococcus aureus:* microbes that can cause staph infections
- ✔ *Neisseria meningitides:* One of the many organisms that can cause meningitis

Because scientists can group bacteria into separate, recognizable categories, they give those groups names like *E. coli* and call them species. But the bacterial species doesn't mean the same thing as it does for animals, plants, and other sexually reproducing organisms.

E. coli isn't a species because all *E. coli* mate with one another and not with *Neisseria.* It's a "species" for some other reason. The key is determining what cohesive force differentiates one species of bacteria from another. What keeps the groups separate?

Periodic selection and selective sweeps

One possible cohesive force that could be responsible for the existence of groups of nonsexually reproducing but similar organisms is periodic selection. In *periodic selection,* natural selection favors a mutation that confers high fitness, which leads to a purging of genetic diversity within a group of nonsexual organisms.

The process works this way. Think about our friend *E. coli.* As one *E. coli* bacterium divides, different mutations begin to accumulate, and the population of *E. coli* bacteria gets more and more variable. Now imagine that a mutation arises that is especially beneficial for an *E. coli* bacterium, enabling it to out-compete all the other *E. coli.* It's more fit, and as it takes over, all the other *E. coli* bacteria are eliminated; as a consequence, genetic diversity within the species is reduced.

This process, called a *selective sweep,* may be the reason why scientists can identify species of bacteria and name them based on their overall similarity — something called *phenetic species* or *ecological species.* In this type of system, natural selection periodically reduces the variation found in a species and keeps, for example, all *E. coli* bacteria looking pretty much the same.

Chapter 9

Phylogenetics: Reconstructing the Tree of Life

*E*volution can lead to *speciation,* in which two species arise from a single parent species (refer to Chapter 8). Starting with one life form a long, long time ago, the process of evolution has generated the diversity of life forms we see all around us. This process, all by itself, is just ridiculously cool!

Over time, the sum of these speciation events generates what scientists refer to as the *tree of life.* The neat thing about trees of life (scientific name: *phylogenetic trees*) is that they enable us to trace the history of species in much the same way that genealogical trees let people trace their family histories. In a nutshell, phylogenetics lets biologists figure out the actual history of branching (speciation) for a given set of species.

This chapter introduces you to phylogenetic trees, describing what they are and how they're made. Although knowing the history of species is pretty darned amazing in and of itself, these trees can provide a wealth of other information, too — and you also find that info in this chapter.

Understanding the Importance of Phylogenetic Classification

Scientists in general like to classify things, and they've been doing it for centuries. Why? Not because it makes them feel good (although it does), but because it helps keep things neat while at the same time providing a wealth of information. The simple process of sorting reveals patterns and relationships, and gives clues to past events — revelations that are absolutely fundamental to the study of evolution. This information is so important to evolutionary biologists, in fact, that they've come up with a way to show how related organisms are, evolution-wise, and to classify them accordingly. This method is called *phylogenetic classification*.

The advantage of a phylogenetic classification is that it shows the underlying biological processes that are responsible for the diversity of organisms. Through phylogenetics, scientists have been able to trace the genetic history of different species and, in doing so, have proved that the process of speciation — whereby ancestral species gives rise to descendent species — is real. (For more information on speciation, head to Chapter 8.) In fact, they've shown, as far as available data allows, that all species existing today descended from a single common ancestor.

Other classification systems, courtesy of Aristotle and Linneaus

The field of biological classification began with Aristotle (384–322 BCE). He concerned himself primarily with the classification of animals and recognized two major groups: those with blood and those without blood. In the "with blood" group, Aristotle recognized five subgroups: birds, things with four legs that lay eggs, things with legs that don't lay eggs, fish, and whales. The things-with-legs-that-lay-eggs group included animals such as crocodiles, lizards, frogs. The things-with-legs-that-don't-lay-eggs group corresponded mostly with what we now call mammals, except that Aristotle's group didn't include whales. (He recognized that whales are different from fish but didn't realize that they're mammals.) The main thing to know about Aristotle's system is that it used nested groups; he divided organisms into two main groups and then created subdivisions within those groups. This structure set the standard for later classification systems.

Carolus Linnaeus (1707–1778) developed Aristotle's idea of a nested classification scheme more completely. He divided all of life into two kingdoms: animal and vegetable. Then he subdivided those kingdoms into classes, divided classes into orders, divided orders into *genera* (singular: *genus*), and divided genera into species. Linnaeus brought a huge amount of order to the study of biology. The diversity of life is far more manageable if it can be broken down into smaller groups, and Linnaeus was the guy who really got the ball rolling on that front.

Today, scientists have modified the Linnean classification system to incorporate new discoveries and understanding. Instead of Linnaeus's two kingdoms (plants and animals), scientists have proposed additional kingdoms corresponding to such things as single-celled organisms and fungi, and even "grab bag" kingdoms for organisms that don't fit into one of the other kingdoms. The modern version of the Linnean classification system, which scientists use today and is probably the one you learned in high school, looks like this:

- Domain
- Kingdom
- Phylum
- Class
- Order
- Family
- Genus
- Species

Classify humans according to this system and you get

- **Domain:** Eukarya (organisms with one or more cells with a nucleus)
- **Kingdom:** Animalia (other kingdoms are plants and fungi)
- **Phylum:** Chordata (animals having a dorsal nerve tube, like the one that runs down your spine)
- **Class:** Mammalia (animals that have hair, nurse their young, and so on.)
- **Order:** Primates (yes, you're a primate — so are orangutans, apes, chimps, and others)
- **Family:** Hominidae (modern man and extinct ancestors of man)
- **Genus:** Homo (species of humans, both extinct and currently living)
- **Species:** sapien (wise — proving scientists do have senses of humor)

Here's a little tip: A fun way to remember each level of this system in order is to use the mnemonic "<u>D</u>id <u>K</u>ing <u>P</u>hillip <u>C</u>ome <u>O</u>ver <u>F</u>or <u>G</u>ood <u>S</u>ex?" And if you leave out Domain, which some systems do, the mnemonic changes only slightly: "<u>K</u>ing <u>P</u>hillip <u>C</u>ame <u>O</u>ver <u>F</u>or <u>G</u>ood <u>S</u>ex."

The evidence that all life descends from a single common ancestor includes such things as the unity of the genetic code. Organisms use a simple code to determine how to make proteins from DNA sequences, and all organisms use the same code (although some minor exceptions exist; go to Chapter 15 for details.) To find out more about the genetic code and its importance to evolution, refer to Chapter 3.

Beyond enabling scientists to trace genetic connections back through time, phylogenetics lets scientists better predict what's to come. Being able to anticipate future mutations is an especially important function in areas like health care; virologists and epidemiologists use info gleaned from phylogenetics to stay one step ahead of the bugs that are trying to stay one step ahead of the human immune system. (You can read more about viruses and the race for vaccines in Chapter 19.)

Drawing the Tree of Life: Branching Patterns and Speciation

Scientists show phylogenetic relationships by drawing phylogenetic trees. If you trace the process of speciation on paper, you end up with a branching pattern that's referred to as the tree of life. Each branch in the tree represents a speciation event, when one species evolved into another.

A simple tree

The easiest way to explain phylogenetic trees is to start with the simplest tree possible: one with three species, which I'll call species A, B, and C.

Imagine that you know that species B and C are more closely related to each other than either of them is to species A. More specifically, species B and C have a common ancestor that they don't share with species A. All three species also have a common ancestor that dates from a time before the common ancestor of species B and C. A phylogenetic tree for these species would look like the one shown on the left in Figure 9-1. Plug in species names, and you have the tree shown on the right.

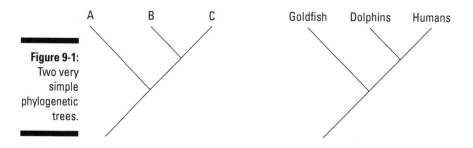

Figure 9-1:
Two very simple phylogenetic trees.

A more complex tree

Most phylogenetic trees are not as simple as the one in Figure 9-1, of course. A more realistic (and complex) tree appears in Figure 9-2. This tree shows the relationships among some of the major vertebrate groups. Located at the tips of the branches are the names of the groups (lampreys, sharks, sturgeons, mammals, birds, and so on).

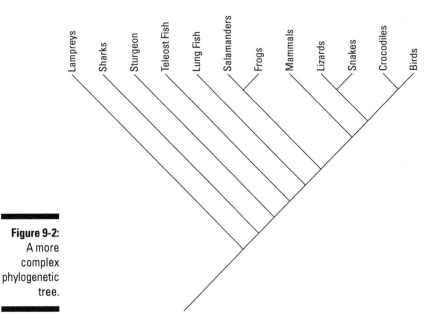

Figure 9-2:
A more
complex
phylogenetic
tree.

As stated earlier, Figure 9-2 shows the phylogeny, or evolutionary relatedness, among some of the major vertebrate groups. Strictly speaking, however, the scientific convention would be to refer to this diagram as a *phylogenetic hypothesis* rather than a phylogeny. Not having been around that many millions of years ago when these relationships were forming, modern scientists can only infer how these things evolved; they can't state it directly.

Reading Trees

Phylogenetic trees convey quite a bit of information. To figure out what that information is, you have to be able to read the tree — that is, to understand the relationships that the tree illustrates. This section explains what you need to know.

Knowing your nodes

A phylogenetic tree is comprised of branches and *nodes* — places where branches connect — that represent ancestral species (species that give rise to the species at the tips of the branches). Figure 9-3 shows the same tree as does Figure 9-2, except that the nodes are circled. Note that, among the many connections, you can see that crocodiles and birds share a common ancestor. Go a bit farther back in time, and you can see another ancestral species that they share with lizards and snakes.

Scientists refer to nodes as *taxa*. All the organisms that appear at the tips of the tree (in Figure 9-3, the birds, crocodiles, lizards, snakes, mammals, etc.) are *terminal taxa*.

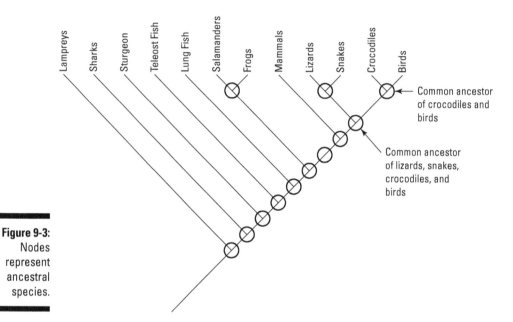

Figure 9-3:
Nodes
represent
ancestral
species.

Getting oriented: Up, down, or round and round

As you read phylogenetic trees, keep in mind that the important thing is the positions of the groups relative to one another. Changes in how the diagram is drawn that don't change these relative positions are unimportant. Exactly the same information is conveyed either way.

Figure 9-4 shows the simple human-dolphin-goldfish tree from Figure 9-1 drawn four different ways, but — and this part is the important part — all four diagrams in this figure represent exactly the same relationships among these organisms. In each diagram, dolphins and humans have a common ancestor more recent than the ancestor they share with goldfish. The differences among the four trees can be described as the results of rotating the branches around the nodes.

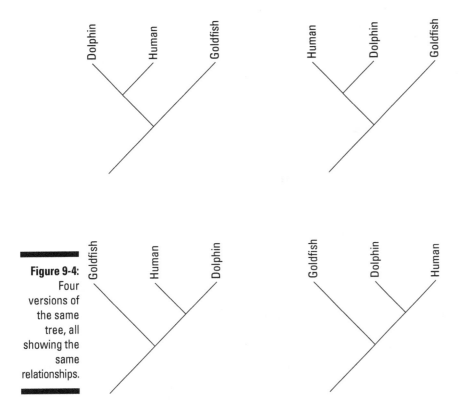

Figure 9-4:
Four
versions of
the same
tree, all
showing the
same
relationships.

From each of the diagrams in this figure, you can see that at some point in the past, a speciation event led to the goldfish lineage and to the lineage that subsequently diverged into dolphins and humans. Note that the dolphin and human (both of which are mammals and have a fair bit in common) share a most recent common ancestor that neither shares with the goldfish. But all three species have more distant common ancestor: All three are vertebrates.

The left-to-right order of the diagram conveys *absolutely no information.* You can draw exactly the same tree with humans in the left position or the middle position. The branching pattern relative to the nodes is what's important.

Figure 9-5 shows another, more complex tree with a section that's been rotated. Again, the branches for a particular node can be rotated around a node without changing the information in the tree. Both sections convey exactly the same evolutionary relationships: Lizards and sharks are just as related to each other as they were before, and the combined group of mammals/lizards/sharks/crocodiles/birds is in exactly the same position relative to the other branches of the tree as it was before the rotation. The horizontal order of the tips of the tree is different, but the positions of the groups relative to one another haven't changed.

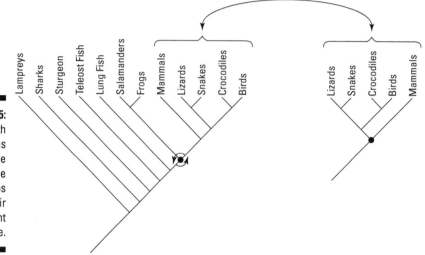

Figure 9-5:
Both
diagrams
show the
same
relationships
despite their
different
appearance.

Understanding groups

When you look at a tree, one of the key things you notice is that the branching pattern creates groupings of species. This section explains the two types of groups: monophyletic and paraphyletic:

- ✔ **Monophyletic groups** represent all the descendants of a common ancestor.

- ✔ **Paraphyletic groups** also represent shared ancestry, but of only part of the group.

Why do we even care about these groups? Because they're "real" — they indicate an actual past connection. Mammals are a monophyletic group, for example, and so are bats. The members may have diverged in different ways, but they all started the same.

Monophyletic group

A *monophyletic group* is a group of species that (1) has a common ancestor and (2) includes all the descendants of that ancestor. Figure 9-6, for example, includes three monophyletic groups:

- ✔ All the *vertebrates* in Figure 9-6 have a common ancestor, indicated by the number 1.

- ✔ All the *mammals* comprise a monophyletic group (the bigger box) that includes all the descendants of the common ancestor indicated by the number 2.

- ✔ Dolphins and chimps comprise a monophyletic group (the smaller box) descended from the ancestor indicated by the number 3.

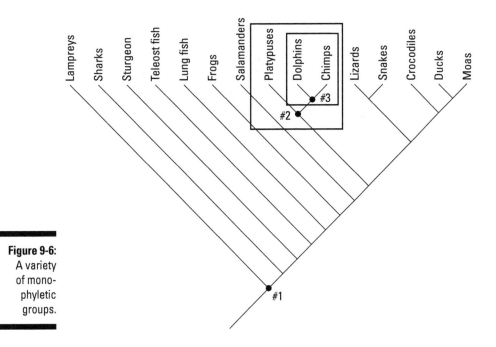

Figure 9-6:
A variety
of mono-
phyletic
groups.

A monophyletic group is also referred to as a *clade,* as in "Aren't you clade a monophyletic group has another, equally hard-to-remember name?"

Monophyletic groups are important in a phylogenetic classification system because they're based on the evolutionary process, not on some arbitrarily selected character.

Paraphyletic group

A group of organisms that has a common ancestor but doesn't include all the descendents of that ancestor is called a *paraphyletic group.* Figure 9-7 shows two paraphyletic groups, the first of which is fish. Although the figure includes several monophyletic groups of fish (sturgeon, lungfish, and teleost), fish as a whole don't make up a monophyletic group. The common ancestor of the fish, indicated by the number 1, gave rise to many other vertebrate groups.

Another paraphyletic group in the vertebrates is the group commonly referred to as the reptiles, represented in Figure 9-7 by the snake, lizard, and crocodile. The reptiles are a paraphyletic group rather than a monophyletic group because the common ancestor of snakes, lizards, and crocodiles also gave rise to birds.

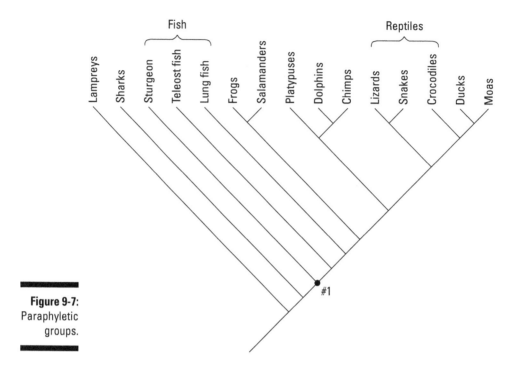

Figure 9-7:
Paraphyletic
groups.

Reconstructing Trees: A How To Guide

Reconstructing a phylogenetic tree involves searching for the clues that tell you about the relationships among different species and then applying rigorous, and often quite complicated, analytical techniques to turn your pile of clues into your best hypothesis about the actual tree.

This process boils down to essentially three steps:

1. **Identify and analyze characters shared by the species for which you're constructing the tree.**

2. **Use outgroup analysis to determine whether each character state is either ancestral or derived.**

3. **Group the species based on your analysis.**

The following sections explain these steps in more detail.

Finding clues (aka characters)

So what are these clues that you use to make the trees? Well, evolution involves change, and in tree reconstruction, you use these changes to map out the history of evolution. The clues to look for are *changes in the states of characters*. Gathering clues involves

- ✔ **Identifying the characters:** *Character* simply refers to an organism's specific, measurable traits. A character can be just about anything — hair, eye color, ability to digest milk, and resistance to antibiotics, for example.

- ✔ **Determining the different states the characters have:** The character states could be hair present and hair absent.

- ✔ **Polarizing the characters:** *Polarizing* characters refers to determining the direction of evolution with respect to each particular change. When you take all your clues and put them together into a tree, it helps to know which of the character states is the *ancestral state* (the one before the evolutionary event) and which is the *derived state* (the one after the evolutionary event).

Imagine three species — turtle, platypus, and rabbit — for which you want to reconstruct the evolutionary history. First, you find some clues — things about these organisms that allow you to group them based on their ancestry. You decide to start with just two clues:

- ✔ Both the platypus and the rabbit have hair.
- ✔ Both the platypus and the turtle lay eggs.

You know that both characters (hair and egg-laying) have two states: present and absent, as in "has hair/doesn't have hair" and "lays eggs/doesn't lay eggs."

When scientists decide to reconstruct a phylogenetic tree, they have to decide what characters, or traits, to use. These characters can be either morphological (visible physical characters) or molecular (genetic). In this section, I limit the discussion to morphological characters, such as wings, flippers, and eggs. Before scientists knew about DNA and DNA sequencing, they were limited to these types of characters as well. Today, the ever-increasing amount of information available about DNA sequences gives scientists the opportunity to use the organism's nucleotide sequence (basically, its genes; refer to Chapter 3) as a character.

Using outgroup analysis to determine derived and ancestral states

Now you need to determine which character state is ancestral and which is derived. To do that, you use *outgroup analysis.* Collectively, the species you're trying to make a tree for — in this example, the platypus, turtle, and rabbit — are called the *in group.* The *outgroup* includes species that don't belong in the in group. In this example, they'd be things like clams, bumblebees, and mushrooms — things without backbones and four legs and stuff like that.

Although clams, bumblebees, and mushrooms share a common ancestor with rabbits, turtles, and platypuses, that ancestor is pretty far back in the tree. So you can use the character states of these other organisms to assess character polarity, which refers to which character state is the derived one and which is ancestral. Mushrooms aren't much help in this case; they're just too far out. But you can learn some things from other animals:

- ✔ Almost all the animals in the outgroup lay eggs. From this character, you can conclude that live birth is the derived character state and that laying eggs is ancestral.
- ✔ None of the organisms in the outgroup has hair. From this character, you can conclude that hair is a derived state.

After you've polarized the characters, you're able to conclude that the split between the platypus and the rabbit occurred *after* the split between the lineage that led to the turtle and the lineage that led to the ancestor of the platypus and the rabbit.

Grouping species

Based on analyzing the outgroups, you know that "laying eggs" is the ancestral state and "live birth" is the derived state. You also know that "no hair" is the ancestral state and "hair" is the derived state.

From this analysis, you know that in the past, farther down the tree of life, critters laid eggs but didn't have hair. Under this scenario, the change from egg-laying to live birth doesn't help you group any two species as having the most recent common ancestor. Only one of the species — the rabbit — has this derived character state. Because only one species has the derived state, you can't use it to form a group.

The situation is different for hair. Two species — the platypus and the rabbit — have the derived character state, which allows you to group these two species as having a more recent common ancestor than the common ancestor of all three species. You envision that the platypus and the bunny have a hairy ancestor, so they both have hair.

To reconstruct evolutionary history successfully, you need *shared derived characters* — evolutionary events that enable you to differentiate among different groups of organisms. In Figure 9-6, shown earlier in this chapter, the monophyletic-group mammals can be distinguished based on the presence of several novel traits, such as hair and the production of milk. The dolphin and the chimpanzee can be further classified as a monophyletic group based on the derived character of live birth. The platypus retains the ancestral condition of laying eggs.

Understanding homologous traits

When comparing character states among different species, you have to make certain that you're comparing two different states of the *same* character rather than two completely different characters.

Take the case of forelimbs. Humans have forelimbs; earthworms and bacteria don't. A scan through the diversity of life suggests that having forelimbs is a derived character state. Because the forelimbs in vertebrates share a common evolutionary origin, they are said to be *homologous*.

Homology, which is similarity as a result of common descent, helps scientists reconstruct the history of evolution and determine the best estimate of the tree of life. Although forelimbs themselves are homologous, they can evolve in several directions: into wings in birds and bats, flippers in dolphins, arms in humans, front legs in horses, and so on.

Looking at homoplasies

Traits that are similar for reasons *other* than common history are called *homoplasies.* Homoplasies can have several evolutionary origins, most easily categorized as convergence, parallelism, and reversal:

- ✔ **Convergence:** Different structures in two different organisms evolve to appear similar. The streamlined shape and fins of dolphins appear similar to those of sharks and fish, but closer analysis reveals that the structures are quite different — an example of convergence. Dolphins and sharks don't share fins because their common ancestor had fins; they share fins because fins evolved independently in the dolphin lineage.

✔ **Reversal:** A structure that previously evolved is subsequently lost. The moa is an example of a reversal. Moas, like most of the other vertebrates, don't fly; they're similar to chimpanzees in this regard. But the similarity is not the result of descent from a common ancestor that didn't fly (though it's true that the most recent common ancestor of the moa and chimp didn't have wings). Numerous structural characteristics of the moa skeleton place the moa firmly within the group of birds, and its ancestors had wings, but these wings were lost during the course of evolution to larger body size.

✔ **Parallelism:** Two organisms evolve to acquire the same trait, *but* — and this point is key — they don't share this trait because of a common ancestor. Rather, they share the trait because it evolved independently in both lineages. As the preceding section explains, the presence of forelimbs in birds and bats is the result of homology; both species descended from an ancestor that had front limbs. The fact that the front limbs of bats and birds now function as wings is a *homoplasy* because wings evolved independently in the two different lineages. Most mammals don't fly; the evolution of flight in bats happened independently of the evolution of flight in birds.

The fact that dolphins and sharks evolved fins independently doesn't mean that their common ancestor didn't have fins. Fins are the ancestral condition in vertebrates in the lineage, but they were lost in the lineage leading to the tetrapods and subsequently re-evolved in the lineage leading to the dolphins. (If you feel like your head is going to explode, take heart. Cranial explosion is neither a derived nor an ancestral trait in any known organism.)

The presence of homoplasy throws a wrench into the works, limiting your ability to reconstruct the tree accurately, because it's not always simple to tell when a character similarity is due to homology or homoplasy.

Testing phylogenetic trees

So how do you know that the phylogenetic trees you can create represent evolutionary relationships accurately? The answer is the way you know anything: Someone did an experiment and checked.

David Hillis and co-researchers set out to determine how well different methods of phylogenetic reconstruction worked at reconstructing the history of evolution. To do this, they needed to know the history of evolution, and they came up with a very clever method.

Taking advantage of the fact that viruses have extremely short generation times, they produced the tree of viral lineages in the laboratory. They started with one virus, from which they collected different mutants. Then they grew these slightly different viruses, collecting mutants from these viruses in turn. In this way they were able to generate a branching tree for which they knew the exact pattern of the branches, because they knew which viruses came out of which flasks.

The different strains of viruses didn't become different species over the course of the experiment (and as Chapter 8 explains, scientists aren't completely clear on what constitutes a species in viruses). But the descendant viruses were different enough from the parent virus to allow Hillis and his co-workers to construct an evolutionary tree.

Viruses don't have a lot of characters like eggs and hair, so the researchers determined what changes had occurred in the viral DNA. They were able to demonstrate that it's possible to measure the traits of the terminal taxa and accurately reconstruct their evolutionary history. In addition, they were able to use the character states of the terminal taxa to make good predictions about the character states of the ancestral taxa at the nodes of the tree. Because they had kept all these ancestral taxa in little vials in a freezer, they were able to show that their predictions were accurate.

Reconstructing Trees: An Example

One way to reconstruct phylogenetic trees is to use *maximum parsimony analysis.* In this method, you determine the minimum amount of evolution required to explain a particular character set. The tree with the minimum number of evolutionary events is called the *most parsimonious, or shortest,* tree.

You can reconstruct a phylogenetic tree in other ways, such as maximum likelihood, Bayesian analysis, and UPGMA (Unweighted Pair Group Method with Arithmetic mean). Each method has its advantages and disadvantages, but I'm not going to explain them all. I cover parsimony because it involves the smallest amount of mathematics. (Google *maximum likelihood,* and you'll see that you're getting off easy!)

The following sections take you through a simple example of tree construction.

Identifying characters

Suppose you want to reconstruct a phylogenetic tree for Species A, B, and C, using seven different character states (1 through 7). For this example, what the characters are doesn't matter; the characters could be eggs present or absent, hair present or absent, and so on.

This example is uncomplicated by homoplasies (refer to the earlier section "Looking at homoplasies" for info), but phylogenetic reconstruction can get very complicated very quickly. Fortunately, for the purposes of this book, you don't need to know how to reconstruct complex trees. I just want you to understand the basic process and to realize that reconstructing these trees isn't magic.

Assigning polarity

Through comparison with the outgroup species (X), which has the ancestral character state for all seven characters under consideration, you assign a character polarity to each one. The number 1 represents the derived character state, and the number 0 represents the ancestral character state.

Looking at the characters for the other three species, suppose that you find the following:

- ✔ For characters 1 and 2, all three species have the derived condition, making species A, B, and C different from species X (the outgroup).

- ✔ For characters 3 and 4, only species B and C have the derived characteristics.

- ✔ For characters 5, 6, and 7, only species C has the derived characters.

Grouping species

Because species A, B, and C have the derived character for characters 1 and 2, you know that they are a monophyletic group that doesn't include species X. On the phylogenetic tree, you indicate characters 1 and 2 with two slash marks — one labeled with the number 1 and another labeled with the number 2 — at a point below the common ancestor of A, B, and C (see Figure 9-8). It's most parsimonious to assume that these two evolutionary events happened only one time.

Because only species B and C have the derived character states of characters 3 and 4, you separate these two species as a monophyletic group and indicate the characters 3 and 4 with slash marks below the point of *their* common ancestor (see Figure 9-9).

In the case of characters 5, 6, and 7, only species C has the derived characters. Because these derived traits aren't shared with any other species, they don't give you any information about the topology of the tree. (Remember, to group species within a tree, you must have shared characters.)

Placing these characters on the tree adds to the total *tree length,* which is defined as the total number of changes required to explain the data matrix, which in this case is seven (see Figure 9-10).

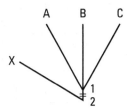

Figure 9-8: Character states for different species.

Characters

Taxon	1	2	3	4	5	6	7
X (outgroup)	0	0	0	0	0	0	0
A	1	1	0	0	0	0	0
B	1	1	1	1	0	0	0
C	1	1	1	1	1	1	1

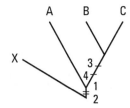

Figure 9-9: Species A, B, and C comprise one monophyletic group; species B and C another.

Characters

Taxon	1	2	3	4	5	6	7
X (outgroup)	0	0	0	0	0	0	0
A	1	1	0	0	0	0	0
B	1	1	1	1	0	0	0
C	1	1	1	1	1	1	1

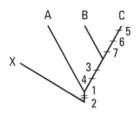

		Characters					
Taxon	**1**	**2**	**3**	**4**	**5**	**6**	**7**
X (outgroup)	0	0	0	0	0	0	0
A	1	1	0	0	0	0	0
B	1	1	1	1	0	0	0
C	1	1	1	1	1	1	1

Figure 9-10: Only species C has derived characters 5, 6, and 7.

A word about more complicated trees

The preceding example includes only homologous characters — those that appear as a result of sharing a common ancestor. When homoplasies are involved (similar characters that don't indicate a common ancestor), things get more complicated.

If you assume that sharing similar characteristics means that species belong in monophyletic groups and plot the species accordingly, you end up in with a tree that doesn't make sense: A species may appear in different groups, for example, indicating that they evolved more than once.

To avoid such a scenario, you need to remember that similar characters can evolve independently, or they can appear, disappear in subsequent evolutionary changes, and then reappear. When multiple scenarios are possible, the one(s) you support end up being those that have the fewest (or most parsimonious) evolutionary steps.

Seeing Phylogenetic Trees in Action

As this chapter shows, it's possible to reconstruct the history of evolution through phylogenetic trees. Now the question is how scientists can use these trees. The answer is that they can use trees for all sorts of purposes, like these:

- ✔ Reconstructing the history of human migration patterns
- ✔ Quantifying the process of co-evolution

✔ Tracing the spread of the human immunodeficiency virus (HIV) epidemic

✔ Designing a better flu vaccine

The following paragraphs offer several examples that involve the HIV virus. The other items are covered in detail in other chapters.

Example 1: The Florida dentist

In the early 1990s, a large number of patients of a particular Florida dentist contracted HIV. The research question at the time was whether they could have contracted the HIV virus from the dentist. Specifically, given that many strains of the HIV virus were circulating in the community, was it possible to connect the HIV strains found in the infected patients with the virus found in their dentist?

By constructing a phylogenetic tree that included the dentist's HIV strain, the six patients' HIV strains, and a selection of HIV strains from the broader community, investigators showed that the patient strains had a recent common ancestor with the dentist's strain, not with the strains sampled from the community.

The take-home message is that even though researchers don't know exactly how these viruses got from the dentist to the patients, they know that the patients did indeed contract HIV from the dentist.

Example 2: General exposure to HIV

In this example, the question is how did the human species become exposed to HIV? Phylogenetic analysis can address this question by reconstructing an evolutionary tree of not just HIV, but of other species' immunodeficiency viruses as well.

The two major types of human immunodeficiency virus are HIV-1 and HIV-2. Reconstructing the tree of immunodeficiency viruses reveals that HIV-1 strains are most closely related to the simian immunodeficiency virus found in chimpanzees, whereas HIV-2 strains are more closely related to the simian immunodeficiency virus found in sooty mangabeys.

The fact that each human virus is related to a different simian virus indicates that the human viruses are the result of two separate events in which a simian immunodeficiency virus jumped to a human host. The phylogenetic analysis that produced this information also directs researchers' attention to the specific simian viruses that are implicated as the parent of the human infection.

You can read more about the origins of HIV in Chapter 18.

Example 3: Legal cases

The science of phylogenetics has made its way into the legal world, where it has been used to prove both guilt and innocence. In the first case, a doctor was convicted of attempted murder after infecting his former girlfriend with an HIV strain from one of his patients. This case was the first instance in which phylogenetic evidence was admitted in a U.S. court. Phylogenetic analysis of HIV sequences from the infected woman and the patient, as well as analysis of additional sequences from the community, revealed that the infected woman's HIV strain was most closely related to the strain from the patient. Her strain even had resistance genes against the HIV medications with which the patient was being treated.

The second case involved six foreign health workers in Libya accused of intentionally spreading the HIV virus to hospital patients. An analysis of the HIV strains infecting those patients revealed such a diversity of strains that the parent strain from which the strains evolved would have to have been present in Libya before any of the foreign health workers arrived. Initially sentenced to death despite the scientific evidence supporting their innocence, the sentence was later commuted to life imprisonment. Jailed since 1999, the workers were finally able to leave Libya in the summer of 2007 following diplomatic negotiations.

Part III
What Evolution Does

The 5th Wave   By Rich Tennant

THE FIRST HOMO ERECTUS

"Is this so difficult? Just bend at the waist and lift with your legs."

In this part . . .

An organism's genetic make up has a huge impact on more than just its physical characteristics, like how many limbs it has or how fast it can run. It can also affect sex selection (how an organism picks a mate), social behaviors (how — and how well — an organism gets along with others), and life histories (life spans and age of reproductive viability). See the connection? If genes impact everything, and evolution impacts genes, then there's an evolutionary component in not only how we look, but also how we behave and interact. This part explains it all.

Chapter 10

The Evolution of Life History

*T*he specific details of an organism's life cycle and reproductive strategy are its *life history,* which includes longevity, age at reproductive maturity, how often the organism reproduces, and how many offspring are produced. Life histories are fascinating to evolutionary biologists because so many of them exist and can be so different. Of course, all this information is interesting at the individual level, but evolutionary scientists look at life histories at the species level.

An oak tree will make thousands of acorns over its life, but it's not likely you're going to make more than one minivan full of children. The human life history is very different from the oak tree life history, yet both strategies have been very good at getting offspring into the next generation. There are lots of people and lots of oak trees, but from a life history perspective, these two species go about it in different ways.

This chapter introduces you to the current theories concerning life-history evolution, theories that seek to answer questions such as these:

✔ Why is it best sometimes to make lots of eggs once, but at other times it's best to make one egg lots of times?

✔ Why do some animals live for weeks and others for decades?

✔ Why do we grow old, and why do we die when we do?

Evolution and the Diversity of Life Histories

Life histories — the specific details of an organism's life cycle and reproductive strategy — differ greatly among species. To get a glimpse of this diversity, consider the differences between a penguin and a salmon.

A salmon swims up a river to spawn, struggling against the current, jumping waterfalls, and dodging hungry bears. After years of living in the ocean chasing prey, avoiding predators, and storing up enough energy, it makes this final trip to the place of its birth. When it arrives, it produces thousands of eggs and dies soon after.

An emperor penguin — the only terrestrial vertebrate (other than a few scientists) to winter in Antarctica — can live more than 20 years. Each year, it makes a perilous trip to its inland breeding grounds, walking almost 100 miles in tiny steps, only to produce a single egg.

Both of these species have been shaped by evolution, but in very different ways. What it takes to be a fit salmon is obviously very different from what it takes to be a fit penguin. And before you say well, sure, one's a fish and the other's a bird, remember that not all fish die after reproducing once, and not all birds lay one egg a year for 20 years. Life histories vary significantly even among the same types of animals.

Scientists understand enough of the underlying genetics to know that life-history characteristics are heritable and that, over time, they change, or evolve. The fact of life-history evolution is that like evolution of other traits, it happens. What evolutionary biologists want to understand is why. How does selection drive this process? And how can so many different life-history strategies exist?

Scientists have a theoretical framework that explains the facts they observe, and they can test these ideas both in the lab and in nature. Concepts that at first seemed confusing (such as death and aging) make sense now, in light of an understanding of the evolutionary process.

Organisms don't live in a vacuum. The selective pressures they experience are a combination of their *biotic* and *abiotic* environment — that is, the organisms they interact with and the physical factors (temperature and such) they contend with. These factors are different for each organism, and the variations are responsible for the corresponding diversity of life-history patterns. In other words, no single life-history strategy is best because no one pattern could be best across all the different environments. Fortunately, scientists have a good understanding of how specific environmental differences influence the evolution of life histories.

'Til Death Do Us Part: The Evolution of Life Span

Evolution via natural selection acts to maximize fitness, and fitness is all about making sure that your genes are around in the future. That being the case, dying just doesn't seem like an especially good idea. After all, death doesn't seem to bode well for the "Get your genes to last forever" imperative of natural selection.

You may think that the simplest way to get your genes into the future is for *you* to exist into the future. After all, you've got all your genes; if you live into the future, your genes live into the future, too. Voilà — fitness without the rather depressing and (often) messy process of dying. But organisms don't get their genes into the future by living forever, even though they may live for a very long time. All this leaves evolutionary biologists, and not just older ones, puzzling over why things eventually (or not so eventually) die.

Evolution has led to many types of life spans. Giant sequoias, for example, live for thousands of years, but most plants have much shorter life spans. Your pet guinea pig, with the best food and care, might live as long as 8 years, but humans live longer than that, and other animals live much longer than we do.

Why die? Trade-offs and risks

It's not hard to think of genes that definitely should increase in frequency. Imagine an animal that lived forever; reproduced early and often; and had huge numbers of offspring, all of which survived. Talk about fit! Those are some fantastic genes. But these genes don't occur in nature. Why not? Two reasons:

- **Trade-offs:** Often, one thing happens only at the expense of another.
- **Risks:** The longer you're around, the more likely it is that something bad will happen to you.

Farewell, sweet Harriet

Biologists were much saddened in 2006 by the passing of Harriet, age 176 (approximate). Before you run out to get whatever vitamins she must have been taking, I should mention that Harriet was a giant tortoise Charles Darwin collected from the Galapagos Islands.

Tortoise or not, Harriet showed us via her longevity that an animal can live to be 176 years old. The heart can beat that long, brain cells can think that long — it's biologically possible. But most animals (sadly, humans included) just don't bother.

A common misconception is that dying is an adaptation to make room for younger, more vigorous individuals — the idea that organisms die for the good of the species. Although this theory may sound good at first, remember that selection acts most strongly at the level of individuals. In a population in which some individuals have a gene for graciously dying to make room for everybody else and other individuals don't, it wouldn't take long for the "die graciously" gene to go extinct.

Even if such a gene were good for the species as a whole, it would be bad for the individuals that had it because they'd be more likely to die, making them *less* likely to pass this gene on to the next generation. As a result, the gene would decrease in frequency over time and vanish from the population, along with any individuals who were dying for the good of the population. Not surprising, nature shows no evidence of a "die graciously" gene.

Trade-offs: Evolutionary cost-benefit analysis

The different life-history components involve trade-offs. Because an organism has only a finite number of resources available, it doesn't have the energy to do everything. Energy spent on reproducing, for example, is energy that can't be spent on surviving. Reproducing early and often may mean not having enough energy left to stay alive.

In this scenario, allocating lots of resource for reproducing even though it makes you die sooner would be adaptive if, by trading longer life for more offspring, the organism increases its ability to pass on its genes. The crucial point here is that the organism is getting more copies of its *own* genes into the next generation, not just making room for somebody else's.

Risky business

Living longer can be risky. The longer an organism lives, the greater the chance that it will become ill or get eaten by a predator. As the risk of death increases, so does the advantage of earlier reproduction, even if this early reproduction results in a shorter life span.

Think of the salmon, which jumps waterfalls and dodges bears to make it all the way upstream: She puts every last calorie into reproducing because the chance of making it up that river twice is too small to make reproducing fewer eggs the first time worth the risk. When the risk of death is higher, natural selection favors genes for earlier reproduction.

Methuselah flies: The evolution of life span in the laboratory

Laboratory experiments have shown that life-history traits — specifically, life span and metabolic trade-offs — do evolve as scientists expect. This section

Test tubes and teacups

Peter Brian Medawar was the first person to articulate the idea that allocating resources to survival instead of reproduction increased exposure to risk. Where'd he get this idea? By imagining a population of test tubes. Test tubes don't reproduce, but neither do they grow old and die. So why do you ever have to buy more test tubes? The answer, of course, is that test tubes experience accidental death: They get dropped or knocked over, shattering into pieces so that they're no longer usable.

You can say the same thing about teacups. Even though teacups have been made for thousands of years, you've probably had to buy some yourself, because they didn't all survive.

Medawar's key insight was recognizing that an organism whose strategy for making sure its genes were around in the future consisted of devoting all its energy to surviving instead of reproducing would eventually run out of luck. Even if it's possible to avoid aging, in the end the risk of death remains by means other than old age. You could get eaten, for example, or you could be crushed by a falling tree.

As an interesting aside, Medawar spent only part of his time thinking about evolutionary issues and shopping for test tubes. His primary research involved the immune system — work for which he received the Nobel Prize in Physiology or Medicine in 1960.

looks at one experiment conducted on fruit flies by evolutionary biologist Michael Rose and company. With their fruit flies, these scientists conducted two experiments that tested the following:

- **Whether aging could be postponed by strengthening the force of selection at later ages.** If so, this result would provide evidence that a contributing factor of aging is that selection doesn't remove mutations that are only harmful late in life, after you're done reproducing. The mutations aren't neutral from an individual fly's health perspective, but they are *selectively neutral* because, by the time they rear their ugly heads, they've already been passed on to the next generation. An experiment that increases the strength of selection at later ages changes these mutations (assuming they exist) from neutral (because there isn't any selection at later ages) to deleterious (because the researchers have added selection at later ages).

- **Whether metabolic trade-offs may be involved in life-history evolution.** If so, this result would show that the trade-offs are real. It makes sense that energy spent doing one thing can't be spent doing something else. The scientists hypothesized that spending all your energy on reproduction means you have less energy to devote to survival because of these trade-offs.

The art of testing evolutionary theories

Biologists often perform experiments to test evolutionary theories. People often wonder how this is possible, because they think that evolution is supposed to take a really long time. The answer is evolution can take a long time, but it doesn't have to. The trick is picking the right organisms — ones that live fast and die soon. Insects, for example, can be good experimental subjects, but elephants — not so good.

You need organisms with very short life spans so that you can squeeze in as many generations as possible. These organisms should also be small, so that it's easy to keep large numbers of them, and they should be easy to raise in a laboratory.

Fruit flies (often, the species *Drosophila melanogaster*) meet these criteria nicely.

Laboratory experiments replace natural selection with *artificial selection,* which means that the experimenter — not nature — decides what traits will increase an organism's chance of contributing to the next generation. This replacement is done for many generations, and the researchers track how the organisms change in response to the laboratory selection regime.

Humans have actually been using artificial selection for thousands of years. It's how we make different breeds of dogs, cows that give more milk, and roses that are more resistant to pests.

Experimental selection for increased life span

To test the hypothesis that aging can be postponed by strengthening the force of selection at later ages, Rose set up 10 replicate populations of fruit flies in his laboratory. For each population, he allowed the flies to feed, mate, and lay eggs; then he transferred a sample of eggs to a new container with fresh food. These eggs hatched; the flies matured, mated, and laid eggs; and the process was repeated with each new generation of flies.

The flies Rose used had been living in the laboratory for 5 years before he started his experiment, and for those 5 years, the eggs used to start the next generation of flies had always been the ones produced on the 14th day after transfer. Females from this laboratory population lived on average about 33 days, and a fit fly was one that made lots of eggs at age 14 days. But that situation was about to change.

In 5 of his 10 populations, Rose changed nothing. New generations continued to be founded with eggs produced on the 14th day. These populations were the control populations. In the other 5 populations, Rose progressively increased the age at which the eggs used to start the next generation were collected; instead of gathering the eggs on the 14th day, Rose began collecting them on the 15th day, the 16th day, and so on. These populations were the ones experiencing Rose's artificial selection. All of a sudden, a fly wasn't very fit unless it could produce eggs at an older age; it didn't matter how many eggs a fly produced on Day 14, because none of those offspring were going to make it into the next generation.

After just 15 generations (15 transfers of eggs to new containers), Rose measured the life span of flies from the 10 populations and found that the flies from the populations selected for later reproduction lived an average of 20 percent longer than flies transferred every 14 days! By increasing the importance of events later in life, Rose had increased the strength of selection at later ages; as a result, the flies evolved to live longer.

Selection experiments always compare a control group of organisms with an experimental group. The experimental group experiences the artificial selection regimen, and the control group doesn't. In all other ways, both sets of organisms are treated exactly the same; they are kept in the same lab environment, handled by the same people, and so on. This technique eliminates doubt that any interesting results are caused by the artificial selection, not by some random factor (such as how hot the lab was that summer). As a further precaution, the same experiment with the same control treatments are performed many times. In experimental science, unless something happens several times, it doesn't really happen at all.

Testing for metabolic trade-offs

With the two different groups of flies that he created in his life-span experiment, Rose tested the theory that metabolic trade-offs are involved in life-history evolution. Rose and his co-workers set out to look for evidence of these trade-offs in their selected flies. Here's what they found:

- ✔ The longer-lived flies had increased storage reserves of fats and carbohydrates compared with the control flies.

- ✔ The longer-lived flies had lower *fecundity* (lifetime reproductive potential) and devoted less energy to the production of eggs than the control flies did.

Bottom line: Rose's experiment produced evidence of the predicted life-history trade-offs: The longer-lived flies spent more energy on living and less on reproducing.

The Trade-Off between Survival and Reproduction

From a fitness perspective, the best (that is, most "fit") reproductive scenario is one in which the organism begins to reproduce early and often, and all the offspring survive. But that's not the way it happens in nature, mainly because of the trade-offs between survival and reproduction. The resources required for survival are resources that aren't available for reproduction, and the resources necessary for reproduction aren't available for survival. So when and how often an organism reproduces, and how many offspring it produces, are the results of trade-offs that give that organism the best chance for sending its genes into the future.

You find various life histories in nature. Some organisms produce over and over again; some produce a few times throughout their lives; and some produce a single time and then die (perhaps the most extreme case of putting all your eggs in one basket!). Each species evolved in a way that allowed it to persist in its physical environment.

It's good to reproduce often, except when it's not

Organisms that reproduce several times — humans, birds, and numerous other creatures — are called *iteroparous*. Organisms that reproduce only once are called *semelparous*. Semelparity is the most extreme example of the trade-off between survival and reproduction. The salmon is one example of a semelparous organism. After swimming back to the spawning ground where it was born, a salmon devotes every last ounce of its energy to reproduction; then it dies.

Two classes of environmental conditions lead to selection favoring the "reproduce once and die" genes:

✔ When getting a second chance to reproduce is pretty much impossible

✔ When some particular condition of the environment makes the reproductive payoff for reproducing once and then dying much greater than the payoff for reproducing over several years

The following sections examine these scenarios.

One chance to make good

Reproducing just once before dying is the fittest thing to do when the odds of making it to the next reproductive season are very low.

After dodging all those bears and jumping all those waterfalls on the way to the spawning grounds, the friendly salmon is pretty lucky to have made it at all. If a gene appeared that made the salmon produce fewer offspring, with the expectation that it would swim back out to sea to feed again so it could reproduce more the following year, the fish would leave some descendents, but the odds of its leaving any more are fairly low. Instead, it might die as it tried to make it to the spawning grounds a second time. For this reason, this particular "produce less now so you can produce more later" gene isn't very likely to increase through time. In fact, from what scientists know about the risks facing the salmon, it makes sense that they don't see salmon with this strategy. Salmon are wonderful examples of the "reproduce once and die" strategy, but they aren't the only ones.

Lots of different organisms have a pretty low chance of making it from one reproductive season to the next. For many of these organisms, the culprit isn't anything nearly as picturesque as cascading waterfalls and hungry predators; it's the rather mundane reality of living in a seasonal world.

Imagine some tiny plant in the desert that's managed to germinate and grow during the wettest part of the year. If that plant is to have any chance of leaving descendents, it has to do it fast, while it still has enough water to survive. Because the adult plants can't make it to the hottest part of the year, they devote all their energy to reproduction, producing seeds that can withstand drought and soaring temperatures and that will germinate during the next rainy season.

Big payoff for a one-shot deal

Most semelparous organisms — those annual desert plants, for example — are relatively short lived. They gather the resources they need to reproduce and get on with it. Other very long-lived semelparous species could reproduce earlier but don't; they just hang out, continuing to grow and acquire resources, all the while taking the chance that they'll die before they get around to reproducing. You can see the potential down side of this strategy. So what's the advantage?

Although the details vary from case to case, the bottom line is that peculiarities in the ecology of a particular species result in a disproportionate benefit to having a big bang in reproduction that outweigh the risks. The risk is big, but the payoff is also big, big enough that the genes for hanging back and stocking up are favored.

One of the best-known examples of this pattern is the blue agave *(Agave tequilana)*, the plant from which we distill tequila. The blue agave has a very high rate of year-to-year survival yet exhibits a life-history pattern of semelparous reproduction. (Although most agaves behave in a similar fashion, iteroparous agaves exist as well, but they're rare.)

When the blue agave finally decides to reproduce, it reallocates all its energy to reproduction and then dies. The selective pressures on this agave are different in nature from the pressures on the small annual desert plants growing all around. The little plants have to reproduce once because they can't survive the heat of the summer. The agave, on the other hand, can survive just fine in the summer, but it still has a greater chance of getting its genes into the next generation if it devotes all its energy to reproducing just one time.

The reason has to do with a peculiarity of agave reproduction. The agave needs something that's in short supply: *pollinators,* which are animals that move pollen to and from other agaves so that the plant can make seeds. When an agave reproduces, it makes a flower stalk. These stalks can be huge, reaching 25 feet in height. The agave uses every last bit of energy it has to make the largest, most visible floral display possible — a good plan, given that pollinators preferentially go to the most visible spike. If your spike is only half as big as another, you get fewer than half as many pollinators.

An agave with a gene that produced the trait of making a smaller spike and surviving until next year to make another smaller spike eventually would be eliminated from the population. Although that particular agave would keep surviving, it wouldn't make as many seeds because it wouldn't be as attractive to the animals that pollinate agaves.

Early vs. later reproduction: Why wait?

An important component of an organism's life history is the way that the life span is divided between the pre-reproductive and the reproductive periods — or, in more common terms, between the time spent as a juvenile and the time spent as an adult. When scientists look at nature, they see a huge variation in the ages at which different organisms mature and become reproductive. Some organisms reproduce at very young ages; others wait until they are much older. Once again, organisms can do the same thing in many ways — in this case, producing offspring.

As I mention earlier in this chapter, you may think that the best strategy for promulgating genes would be reproducing early, making a lot of offspring, and doing all that for a very long time. But studies of the natural environment show that it's not possible to do everything well.

When it comes to reproduction and getting your genes into the next generation, it's not just how soon you can make the first offspring, but the total offspring you can produce throughout your lifetime. An organism that waits a little bit longer to get started but makes many more offspring than an organism that started earlier will have a greater effect on the genetic makeup of the next generation — that is, a higher proportion of organisms in the next generation will carry its genes.

The following list outlines the advantages and disadvantages of both strategies:

 ✔ **Reproducing early:** The benefits of early reproduction seem obvious. Genes involved in early reproduction will make it into the next generation that much faster. All other things being equal, earlier reduction would always be better than later reproduction. But early reproduction creates problems, the main one being that producing early saps the energy an organism needs for survival and growth.

✔ **Reproducing later:** An organism that delays reproduction has more resources to devote to survival than an organism that reproduces early. In addition, large organisms are often much better at making offspring than smaller organisms; they can produce more or healthier offspring. So it seems that some types of organisms get a real payoff from devoting energy to growth early in life and waiting until it's more efficient to begin reproducing.

In comparing the two strategies, it certainly appears that the better reproductive strategy is to wait until the organism is large enough to make many more offspring. In turn, these offspring should overwhelm the descendents of the individuals that reproduce early, which are wasting precious energy to maximize their reproductive output. But one pesky problem occurs: During the time that an organism is devoting energy to growth rather than reproduction, it could die, leaving no descendents. So which strategy is better: early or later reproduction? The answer is that it depends.

Scientists' understanding of evolution by natural selection suggests that as the risk of mortality increases, organisms evolve to reproduce earlier. Genes connected with early reproduction are favored and are more likely to make it to the next generation. Organisms with genes that result in later reproduction have a good chance of dying before they reproduce; as a result, these genes are not favored.

Proving the point with guppies

David Resnick and co-workers set up an experiment in a natural environment to examine how altering the likelihood of surviving at different life stages could lead to evolutionary change in life-history parameters, such as when to start reproducing. Resnick conducted his experiments with naturally occurring guppies in a series of streams on the island of Trinidad. The goal of the experiment was to see whether changing the relative importance of mortality for juveniles and adults would lead to changes in the guppies' life history. Specifically, Resnick wanted to see whether guppies' reproductive patterns, such as age at maturity, would change if their risk of death changed.

The setup

The basic structure of the experiment was to figure out some way in nature to tinker with the survival chances of the fish. Resnick made use of a few things he knew about guppies in Trinidadian streams:

✔ **The major cause of mortality for guppies is getting eaten by two other types of fish.** For simplicity's sake, I'll call these species *the big predator* and *the little predator*. Although both species eat guppies, they prefer different sizes: The little predator likes to eat little guppies, and the big predator likes to eat big guppies.

✔ **Different places in streams have different assortments of fish.** Some guppies live in areas of a stream that have a large predator; other guppies live in areas that have a little predator; and some places in streams don't have any guppies. In other words, the distribution of fish is uneven. Some guppies live in a low-predation environment where the adult guppies are less threatened because only the little predator lives there. Other guppies live in a high-predation environment with a big predator that's very fond of eating adult guppies.

The reason for these variations is that in Trinidad, many streams run down hills steep enough to produce waterfalls. Because fish can't get up waterfalls easily, the waterfalls effectively keep them from moving from one place to the next.

✔ **The guppies in the different habitats had different characteristics.** Resnick noticed that guppies living in the low-predation environments have different life-history characteristics from guppies living in high-predation environments:

- In the low-predation environment, guppies reproduced at a later age, when they were larger. They were able to invest energy in growth and survival that ultimately delayed reproduction — a successful strategy in the absence of a big predator. When these guppies made it to adult size, they had a reduced chance of being eaten.

- In the high-predation environments, the guppies reproduced earlier, when they were smaller. This strategy could be the result of predation pressure from the large fish. Delaying reproduction to a later date, when you're a bigger fish, isn't advantageous if you have a good likelihood of being eaten before you make any offspring. As the chance of being eaten increases, so does the selective pressure for early reproduction.

What Resnick saw was consistent with scientists' understanding of life-history evolution. As the chance of not making it to an older age increases, so does the advantage of reproducing earlier. Even better, not only were the results consistent with hypotheses about the evolution of reproductive life history, but this natural system was ready-made to test these ideas in nature.

The experiment

Resnick found places in the streams that had little predators but neither big predators nor guppies. He proceeded to move guppies that had been coexisting with big predators into this new environment, where they had to contend with only a little predator. (To be sure that other fish wouldn't swim into his experimental areas, Resnick chose study locations in parts of the stream separated by waterfalls.)

Natural settings vs. labs

The advantage of conducting artificial selection experiments in the laboratory is that it's possible to control all the variables of the experiment. The experimenters can change just one thing, hold everything else constant, and then see what the result of changing that one thing was. The goal of any experiment is to change as few things as possible so that when it's time to analyze the results, a lot of confusing questions won't be asked, such as exactly what caused those results. Another advantage of the laboratory is that it is easy to repeat the experiment to make sure of getting the same result a second time. The disadvantage, of course, is that laboratory experiments are always open to criticism that whatever happened in the laboratory doesn't really happen in nature. (For an example of a laboratory experiment, refer to "Methuselah flies: The evolution of life span in the laboratory" earlier in this chapter.)

Experiments conducted in nature overcome this problem. Any effects that are measured are obviously the result of natural processes. For this reason, they are important for developing scientists' understanding of how evolution functions in the wild. It's exciting to see that over a relatively short period, natural selection can lead to changes in populations. But this advantage comes at a cost: Changing just one thing is rarely possible. Controlling for all the variables is impossible, so natural experiments will always be open to criticism that the results were caused not by whatever the experimenter was manipulating but by something else.

Which type of experiment is better? Actually, neither. Researchers need laboratory experiments in which they can alter just a few things at a time, but they also need experiments in the field, where they can make some manipulations, let nature take its course, and see what happens.

After moving the fish, he waited to see how the guppies would evolve. If the pattern of early reproduction he observed among guppies in the presence of the big predator was due to increased predation pressure, moving the guppies to the different environment might result in the evolution of later reproduction.

After 4 years in one experiment and 11 years in another, here's what he found: The populations that were moved from a high-predation environment evolved their life-history characteristics in the expected direction. That is, the fish devoted more energy early in life to growth and less to reproduction. As a result, they were larger when they first reproduced.

Determining whether the changes were heritable

To determine whether the changes were heritable — that is, genetic and therefore capable of being passed from one generation to the next — and not the result of some environmental factor, such as different food or different water chemicals in the various streams, Resnick took back to his laboratory some guppies from the old population that was living with the large predatory fish and some guppies from the experimental population that had been living with just the little predators. In the lab, he grew the guppies separately for several generations in identical fish tanks, to eliminate any effects due to the environment rather than the fishes' genes.

What Resnick found was that the fish really were genetically different. The fish from the low-predation experiment really *had* become different genetically from the original population. They spent more energy growing and reproduced later than the original population. The fish had indeed evolved.

One fish, two fish, small fish, adieu fish: The evolution of overfishing

Understanding life-history evolution can help researchers understand some of the changes in major fisheries, where commercial fishing has made humans the major predator.

Different kinds of fish grow to different sizes, based on what's most advantageous in their environment: Tuna get really big; trout so big. A fish's life history involves growing for a while and then spending energy on reproduction. Natural selection favors variants that get the details right: Reproduce at too early or too late an age, and you won't be as successful as the fish that reproduces at just the right time. So the basic strategy is to grow, grow, grow until the point when it's better to start reproducing rather than growing some more. Bottom line: Fish in nature grow to some particular size because that's a good size to be as far as getting your genes into the next population.

Now along comes the fisherman, who sets out some fishing nets to catch fish. These nets aren't designed to catch just any fish, but bigger fish, and they're so effective that that they often cause a noticeable decline in the numbers of fish in the ocean. The fish numbers become so depleted that the fisheries stop or reduce their operations, with the intent of giving the fish stocks a chance to recover. Sounds all well and good, but guess what? The stocks don't recover as quickly as expected. Even after a lull, the big fish that the nets catch just aren't there.

Why not? What's happened is that a new selective force has been added to the environment. All of a sudden, being a fish of the size that gets caught in those nets is bad. What used to be a good size for getting your genes into the next-generation is now a good size for getting your genes grilled and covered with a nice lemon dill sauce.

Scientists and conservationists hypothesize that, in the past, before commercial fishing, genes for reaching adulthood at a smaller size hadn't been favored. To best survive a life in the ocean, fish evolved to grow to a sufficient size and then reproduce. Commercial fishing add a new selective pressure that makes it better to be a smaller fish. Their nets don't just physically remove the big fish from the population, but they also remove the genetic variants that result in larger fish, leaving only those that don't grow so big. Although being smaller may not be great as far as life in the ocean is concerned, it's the best thing going. Fish that don't grow big enough to get caught in the nets will pass more genes to the next generation. The result is a population of fish that just doesn't get so big. They reach adulthood at a smaller size and start devoting energy to reproduction. Just because we stop fishing doesn't mean that all the little fish that are left will grow up to be bigger fish; they've already grown up. And this is an explanation for why fisheries stocks don't rebound when we reduce the fishing pressure.

Evidence from natural fisheries suggests that the fish humans harvest have indeed shifted to earlier reproduction and smaller adult size. Northern cod populations, for example, exhibited a decline in the size at which females became reproductive before the collapse of the fishery.

To test the hypothesis that fish will evolve to be smaller if mortality at large sizes is increased, Matthew Walsh and coworkers conducted an experiment using laboratory populations of Atlantic silverside. They set up three different treatments and harvested fish differently in each one. From the control tanks they took a random sample of fish, from the other tanks they took large individuals — a protocol that mimics fishing. (To find out about the third treatment, read the sidebar "Fishin' for a small one.")

All the populations started out exactly the same — a bunch of wild fish in tanks. Over five generations, the fish populations responded to the new selective pressure. The results were exactly what the researchers had predicted. When large fish are more likely to be harvested from a population, the advantage of alleles that cause fish to grow large decreases. These alleles are less likely to make it into the next-generation while alleles that result in smaller size now have higher fitness. These changes will cause the fish to be smaller, and that's exactly what happened. Selection favoring small fish over large ones resulted in fish that just don't grow as big. These changes included differences in metabolic efficiency, foraging, and even the number of vertebrae.

Fishin' for a small one

Walsh and his coworkers also had a treatment from which they removed the smallest fish, which is not something any fisherman—commercial or otherwise—ever does when actually fishing for food, but it's a nice experiment anyway because the prediction is that removing the smaller individuals would cause the fish to spend less of their lives at the smaller size. Alleles that caused the fish to grow really fast would be favored because they'd be less likely to be removed from the tank by the experimenters. It's bad to be a small fish, and the only way to not be a small fish is to grow. The result of this treatment was bigger fish.

Figure 10-1 shows the result of Walsh's experiment. The fish on the right came from the population from which the largest fish were harvested. In the center are fish from the control tank. On the left are fish that came from the population from which small fish were harvested (see the sidebar "Fishin' for a small one for details on this part of the experiment).

Figure 10-1:
The results
of Walsh's
experiments.

The take-home message is two-fold:

✔ Over-fishing is bad for all the reasons we used to think it was, plus it's bad because the study of the evolution of fish suggests that fish stocks won't bounce back to include a large individuals as fast as we'd like them to if we stop fishing. We used to think that if we stopped fishing, the little fish we hadn't caught would grow up to be big fish. Now we have the added worry that we've selected for fish that don't grow up to be big.

✔ The remaining fish may not be as well adapted to their environment as they would have been had they not had to respond to fishing pressure. Fish that reach maturity at the smaller size are favored when there are lots of nets, but that may be the only thing good about a smaller size. The smaller size wasn't favored before fishing, and it may just not be a very good size with respect to doing all the things fish have to do to survive in the ocean.

The trade-off between size and number of offspring

Just as a huge variation exists in life span and reproductive timing among organisms, a huge variation exists in fecundity and in *clutch size,* the number of offspring an organism produces at any one time. Trade-offs come into play here as well.

For any given amount of resources devoted to reproduction, the pie can be divided in many ways. (For fun, call this division *resource partitioning* among offspring.) It comes down to the question of whether a species produces lots of little offspring or fewer bigger ones. Human clutch size, for example, tends to be one, despite rare cases of twins or triplets, and total lifetime fecundity rarely exceeds ten. But a sturgeon — the kind of fish from which we get caviar — can easily make 60,000 eggs at a time. That figure makes humans look pretty pathetic in comparison until you consider that the human pattern seems to be successful; an awful lot of humans are around, and our numbers just keep going up.

What explains the huge differences in fecundity, and why haven't sturgeon taken over the world? The number of offspring produced is important, but so is the probability that these offspring survive to reproduce themselves. Any gene that results in the production of a huge number of offspring, but none of which ended up making any offspring of its own, wouldn't last very long. The gene's frequency would increase for an instant, but by the time of the grand-child generation, it would be gone.

As always, organisms go about producing fit offspring in many ways, favoring different strategies in different environments. Specific conditions favor different clutch sizes. Parental care — or the lack thereof — also has an impact, as the following sections explain.

Without parental care

Not all organisms have a reproductive strategy that includes parental care. Sturgeons, for example, don't care for their young. After they release their eggs, they hit the road, leaving the eggs to fend for themselves. For these organisms, the question becomes how best to use the available resources for egg production to maximize the number of successful offspring. The organism can make a few large eggs or many small eggs. Whether big eggs or little eggs are best (or the most *fit,* in evolution-speak) depends on the environment the eggs will face.

At minimum, the egg needs to have sufficient resources to develop into a juvenile. Although an individual offspring's survival is increased if more than the minimum resources are provided, the parents' fitness depends on producing the maximum number of surviving offspring. Bottom line: How hostile or welcoming the environment is affects how much energy the parents invest in each individual offspring. Some environments result in a little extra provisioning of fewer eggs, but when the environment is hostile enough to make it unlikely for any particular offspring to reach maturity, the parents are better off spreading the risk among many eggs rather than investing a great deal of energy in each individual egg. The result? Smaller but more plentiful eggs.

This pattern occurs in sturgeons (60,000 eggs at a time, remember?) and in the plants commonly referred to as weeds, which tend to make large numbers of very small seeds that disperse through the environment. Where the seeds end up — whether in your freshly turned garden or in the middle of the highway — is anyone's guess. The point is they're scattered in the wind and have a low probability of survival.

Oak trees employ a different strategy. Although an individual tree makes lots of seeds, these seeds are quite large by plant standards. An oak tree doesn't make the maximum number of very small seeds; instead, it prepares the seeds — acorns — with a larger number of maternal resources. Acorns don't disperse very far from their mother plant. Instead, they tend to fall on the forest floor under a tree's canopy, and they need enough energy to sprout. With a little luck, they'll have a chance of getting big enough to gather enough light to survive. If the oak tree made just very small seeds, none would survive, because they would never have the energy to get big enough in the dark canopy of the oak forest. Thus, the environment facing the offspring of the oak tree favors genes for larger seeds, whereas the environment facing the weed seeds favors small seeds.

With parental care

In the cases where natural selection favors organisms that provide parental care, it doesn't make any sense to produce more offspring than the parents can care for at any one time, because the parents continue to provide resources to the offspring after birth or hatching.

A fair number of studies have been conducted on why birds lay the number of eggs they do. The naturally occurring variation in the number of eggs produced gives scientists a sense of the optimal number for any particular species.

Ideally, the birds would produce exactly the number of offspring that they could feed well enough so that the offspring would survive and reproduce, passing the parents' genes into the future. What researchers find when they look at natural patterns, however, is a point in the number of eggs produced at which laying more eggs results in fewer surviving baby birds. The number of eggs that birds lay seems to cluster around this ideal number.

For an interesting case of how parental care can limit clutch size, think back to the emperor penguin. Penguin parents care for their single egg in a unique way: Dad balances the egg on his feet to keep it off the ice while Mom goes off to catch fish. Maybe the daddy penguin could balance a bigger egg or a smaller one, but it's not clear how he could balance two at the same time. Because no nest-building materials are available in Antarctica, an emperor penguin can't have more than one egg at a time.

Why Age?

Organisms often seem to undergo a gradual breakdown before death — a process referred to as *aging*. Because aging, like death, seems to be a bad idea, you may think that natural selection would favor individuals that age less. Unfortunately (for humans), it doesn't.

The process of aging turns out to be consistent with scientists' understanding of how evolution works. You may think natural selection would eliminate genes that make people age, but natural selection won't eliminate certain classes of genes that cause aging, either because the detrimental effects of these genes don't show up until later or because the gene that causes aging offers some benefit earlier:

- **Bad genes that act later in life:** Selection acts less strongly on traits that are expressed late in life. Natural selection certainly won't favor any genes that cause the aches and pains of old age, but it can't select against them either. Long before the traits appear and can be noticed by selection, the genes that control them have already been passed to the next generation.

- **Genes that are bad later in life but good when you're younger:** Natural selection favors genes that have beneficial effects when the organism is younger, even if these same genes are responsible for old age. The reason? Selection is stronger earlier in life. It doesn't matter what the genes do when you're old, because by then, you've already passed them to your children.

The two classes of genes are not mutually exclusive, and evidence exists that both types of genes are involved in the process of aging. Yippee.

TECHNICAL STUFF

Conducting a thought experiment

If you're finding it a bit tricky to keep track of all these hypothetical classes of genes, try considering more specific examples. Conduct a thought experiment: Imagine a specific gene, and then try to figure out whether natural selection will favor it, select against it, or remain neutral. If you want to try to understand aging, for example, imagine the fate of a series of genes that does exactly the same thing, but at different times in the organism's life. In this way, you can get a better handle on how the frequencies of genes that act at different ages change in response to natural selection. Start with an easy one — say a gene the causes spontaneous combustion — and let your mind play with the ideas from there:

- Imagine a gene that causes people to spontaneously combust at age 10. What happens to people with this gene? It's safe to say that they won't be making a lot of offspring, so extremely strong selection will be against this gene. Because this gene causes death before reproductive age, it will be eliminated from the population as fast as new mutations make it appear. In other words, the genetic lifeguard says, "You're out of the gene pool!"

- How about a gene that makes people spontaneously combust at age 150? In this case, natural selection will never see the trait. None of us makes it to 150, so no one would ever go up in flames. This gene is completely neutral, and if it appeared in one of your children, you'd never even know it. Whether or not it increases in frequency depends only on whether your child has more or fewer children. Because the "combust at 150" gene has no effect on fitness, it's selectively neutral — just along for the ride.

- How about spontaneous combustion at 60? This, you'd notice. Would it make you less fit? Not really. By the time you're 60, you've

pretty much finished passing on your genes. This gene wouldn't help you reproduce more, but it wouldn't hurt you, either — unless you happen to be one of the occasional people who burst into flames. Hence, the "combust at 60" mutation is also selectively neutral.

- How about a gene that made you spontaneously combust at age 60 but *also* made you much more likely to have lots of children? This gene increases your fitness because it increases your contribution to the next generation. Natural selection causes this gene to increase in frequency.

These last two categories of genes are the kinds of genes that would be responsible for the phenomena of aging. The negative effects of these genes occur only late in life, after they've already been passed to the next generation. In the last example, selection will cause the gene to increase in the population because it's advantageous early, even though it's really bad later.

Now step back from the example of spontaneous combustion, and think about some of the more real examples of things associated with aging. Nothing about your eyes failing or your knees getting creaky is at odds with the mechanism of evolution by natural selection. By the time those phenomena start to occur, you're probably finished reproducing. There may be better ways to build an eye or a knee, but natural selection won't favor those methods unless they have value earlier in life.

One last important note: Zero evidence exists that spontaneous human combustion really happens. It's in the same category as ESP and Roswell aliens. But just coincidentally, most of the people who are said to have spontaneously combusted were older than 60.

Chapter 11

Units of Selection and the Evolution of Social Behavior

In This Chapter
- Making fitness inclusive
- Benefiting your own kin
- Being selective individually and in groups
- Evolving altruism

*T*hroughout this book, I emphasize the importance of evolution acting on individuals. Why? Because the individual is far and away the most important unit on which selection acts. But natural selection doesn't act *only* on individuals. Sometimes selection acts at other levels. This chapter explores levels of selection: the power of natural selection to act on genes and groups.

Understanding the levels of selection is important in trying to fathom some of the behavior you see in nature. Some organisms, for example, don't reproduce. Others delay reproduction. Some behave altruistically toward others (giving up their own stores of food, for example, to prevent another organism from starving). In these systems, something besides individual selection is probably going on.

Inclusive Fitness and Kin Selection

Evolutionary fitness is a measure of how good an organism is at getting its genes into future generations. One way for an organism to get its genes into future generations is to make lots of offspring, which go out and make lots of offspring themselves, and so on and so forth. But another way for an organism to get its genes into the next generation is to help its relatives get *their* genes into the next generation — which is the main idea behind inclusive fitness and kin selection.

Your fitness + your relatives' fitness = inclusive fitness

Inclusive fitness is simply the sum of an individual's fitness *plus* the additional benefits accrued through increasing the fitness of related individuals. In English: You're more fit not only if you reproduce, but also if relatives who share your genes reproduce, too.

Here's a simple example of inclusive fitness in action: Helping your identical twin sister have a baby that she would not have been able to have without your help is just as good a way to pass on your genes to the next generation as having a baby of your own. Most humans aren't one half of an identical pair, of course. To understand how inclusive fitness works in more common situations, you need to understand a concept called *degree of relatedness,* which simply means how many of your genes you share with others.

For sexually reproducing organisms (such as humans, antelope, or titmice), the degree of relatedness is as follows:

- **Between parents and offspring:** One half of an individual's genes come from its mother and half come from its father. The degree of relatedness between parent (mother or father) and offspring is one half (or 0.5).

- **To full siblings (individuals that have the same mother and father):** Full siblings, on average, have half their genes in common. The degree of relatedness is 0.5.

- **To half siblings (individuals that have either the same mother or the same father):** Half siblings, on average, have one quarter of their genes in common. The degree of relatedness is 0.25.

- **To your siblings' children:** The degree of relatedness between you and any of your nieces and nephews is on average one quarter (0.25), because you share one half of your genes with your sibling, and that sibling shares half of his or her genes with his or her offspring.

So how many offspring do you have to help your siblings make to equal one of your own offspring? If you're an identical twin (that is, you and your twin have a degree of relatedness of 1.0 because you have exactly the same genes), helping her (or him) make an additional baby is just as good as making one of your own as far as your fitness is concerned. But if you're helping a non-identical full sibling reproduce at the expense of your own reproduction, to come out even you'd have to help produce at least *two* nieces or nephews for every one son or daughter you could have created yourself.

Not reproducing to help your family: Kin selection

Nearly everything about evolution by natural selection involves some sort of cost-benefit analysis. Is the cost of the mutation offset by its benefit? Does having an elaborate tail help you more than hurt you? Natural selection favors the trait that confers the most benefit from a fitness perspective, meaning that traits that enhance your ability to get your genes into the next generation increase in frequency in subsequent generations.

The situation is no different for reproduction. If, for some reason, you were unable to produce any offspring of your own, helping produce even one extra niece or nephew would still enable you to get some of your genes into the next generation. Or if by forgoing producing a single offspring of your own, you were able to help produce three nieces or nephews who would not otherwise have existed, you come out ahead, evolutionarily speaking.

Because the cost (the single offspring that you did not produce who would have shared half of your genes) is less than the benefit (the three nieces or nephews who each share one quarter of your genes), natural selection will favor helping your sibling reproduce. For this reason, genes that are responsible for behaviors that help relatives reproduce can increase in frequency even if they decrease individual fitness as long as they increase inclusive fitness. This type of selective force is called *kin selection*.

The concept of kin selection explains many of the altruistic behaviors that Charles Darwin found confusing. For Darwin, who lacked modern knowledge of genetics, it wasn't as obvious how helping a related individual could be advantageous to the helper.

CASE STUDY

It's a salamander-eat-salamander world

David Pfennig raised tiger salamander larvae in groups with and without siblings. Tiger salamanders are cannibalistic. For a tiger salamander, eating one of your own kind is good if it increases your chance of getting your genes into the next generation — but not as good if the one you eat has your genes.

In the study, Pfennig raised his salamanders in groups of full siblings, half siblings, and unre-
lated individuals. The results: Full siblings were least likely to cannibalize their neighbors, and unrelated individuals were most likely. Half-sibling groups were in between.

The result makes sense from the standpoint of inclusive fitness and kin selection. Genes that allow a salamander to tell kin from stranger (and to avoid eating the kin) appear to have been selectively favored.

Levels of Selection

In individual selection, some individuals survive to reproduce, and some don't. If the differences in survival and reproduction are the result of particular genes, these genes will increase in frequency in the next generation. *Group selection* theory adds another evolutionary layer to this tidy little setup. The idea is that in addition to selection at the individual level, selection can also occur at the group level. (You can even think of kin selection as an example of group selection where the group is the family.)

Evolutionary scientists have also become aware that selection can act at the level of the gene, beyond the forces of individual or group selection. Essentially, this theory recognizes that occasionally, certain genes increase in frequency simply because they've got a better-than-average chance of getting into the gamete during reproduction, regardless of the negative effect they may have on the offspring.

Group selection

According to group selection theory, some genes have an effect at the level of the group. Genes that act at the group level affect survival and reproduction between groups in such a way that some groups leave descendants and other groups don't. Think about a gene for getting along nicely with other people, for example. If selection acts at the group level, a get-along-with-others gene may increase in frequency if groups of people who have this gene are more successful than groups of people who don't have this gene.

As you wrap your brain around group selection, keep these points in mind:

- Group selection, when it occurs, acts *in addition to* selection at the level of the individual. Selection still occurs at the level of the individual.

- Selection at the level of the individual could act in the same direction as selection at the level of the group or in a different direction. For evolutionary biologists, the most intriguing cases are those where different levels of selection conflict and as a result are of considerable interest.

- Group selection can be important when the population structure of the species involves interacting groups.

Flour beetles: A group selection example

Michael Wade set up a laboratory experiment to investigate group selection with the goal of showing that it occurs. In his experiment, Wade used flour beetles — little insects that are happy to grow and reproduce in a vial of flour. They eat flour, but they're also cannibalistic: Adult beetles eat larvae and eggs, and the larvae eat eggs.

Wade set up four experimental treatments, each consisting of 48 populations of beetles. For each population, he allowed 16 individual beetles to grow and reproduce for 37 days. Then he took 16 individuals from each of these populations, put them in new vials of flour, and allowed *them* to grow for 37 days. He continued in this way until he had the number of populations he needed. What differed between the populations in the various treatments was the factor that Wade selected for. For his experiment, he decided that population size — a group rather than an individual characteristic — would be the favored characteristic:

- ✔ **Treatment 1 (the control treatment).** In this treatment, individual selection was the key. For the control group, Wade randomly picked 16 beetles from a population to start the next flask. As a result, individual beetles that were more successful at reproducing were more likely to have offspring — and, hence, their genes — in the next generation. (If you make twice as many offspring as the next beetle, you have twice the chance of getting some children into the next generation.)

  Individual selection is always happening, so scientists can study group selection only by keeping track of individual selection at the same time and then comparing the results from the group selection treatments to the individual selection control treatment. The control group is the one in which selection acts at the individual level.

- ✔ **Treatment 2 (a group selection treatment selected for large population size).** Wade created his new populations by using beetles from only the biggest populations.

- ✔ **Treatment 3 (a group selection treatment selected for a low population size).** Wade used only individuals from the smallest populations to found new populations.

  Treatments 2 and 3 represent group selection, because not all beetles in all vials contribute to the next generation — only those that meet the selection criteria (in the experiment, either large or small group size). You could be a really fit beetle in your particular vial (that is, a disproportionate number of the offspring are yours), but if you exist in a population that isn't large (or small) enough to be used, none of your genes get into the next generation.

Here's what Wade found: The original beetle stock used in this experiment generated population sizes of about 200 beetles after 37 days. But after nine generations, population size decreased in all his treatments. Population dropped in the control treatment (individual selection); it decreased more in the group selection treatment for small populations and less in the group selection treatment for large populations. The following sections explain why.

In the control treatment (Treatment 1)

In this case, selection was acting at the level of the individual. Whatever heritable traits increased the chance of a beetle's having descendents in the next generation increased in frequency. It just so happened that as a result of this selection on individuals, population size decreased from about 200 beetles in the stock population to 50 beetles after 9 generations. Although that result may seem odd, keep in mind what these beetles like to eat: flour and baby beetles (those in the larval and egg stages). Essentially, this treatment selected for beetles that were more voracious cannibals.

In Treatment 2 (group selection favoring large population size)

In this treatment, population size had decreased after nine generations, but not as much as in Treatment 1 (the individual selection control). Selection at the level of the group for larger population size had an effect in the opposite direction of selection at the level of the individual.

Selection at different levels can act in the same direction or in a different direction. If selection acts in the same direction, it compounds the effect; if it acts in a different direction, it mitigates the effect.

In Treatment 3 (selection favoring groups with small populations size)

In this treatment, population size decreased even more than in the control population. Selection at the level of the individual and selection at the level of the group each had an effect on population size, and these effects were in the same direction. After 9 generations of selection, the population had decreased from 200 beetles to 19.

Selecting for nicer chickens: Applications of group selection

Although group selection can seem awfully technical, it has practical applications. Take, for example, egg production. A great deal of effort has gone into producing chickens that lay lots of eggs. Historically, farmers have tackled the problem at the level of the individual chicken. The chicken breeder would found the next population with the descendents of the most prodigious egg-layers. The strategy was successful: Chickens can lay 100 eggs a year.

Here's a little bit of detail that you should know about chickens. They don't live isolated lives on the farm. They are raised in group pens, where interaction among chickens can be downright nasty — so much so that chickens often have their beaks removed to prevent them from pecking one another. If the best egg-layer lays many more eggs than the other chickens because she takes resources away from them, you can easily see why the other chickens in the pen won't produce as many eggs as the individual egg-laying champ. What the egg farmer wants, however, is to maximize the total number of eggs produced. Because chickens are raised in pens, the important number isn't eggs produced by any particular chicken, but eggs produced per pen.

William Muir and coworkers wanted to see whether it was possible to increase the number of eggs that the chickens laid as a group rather than merely increasing the number of eggs laid by individuals. So they expanded on the farmer's breeding practices, which favored the chickens that laid the most eggs, by introducing selection at the group level.

Muir selected for the largest number of eggs per pen. Chickens from pens that produced a large number of eggs were used to found the pens for the next generation. The best-producing pens of that generation were the source of individuals for the subsequent generation. After five generations, Muir was able to produce chickens that got along so nicely with the other chickens in the pen that removing the beaks was no longer necessary. Just as significantly, egg production increased by 100 percent, to 200 eggs per year per chicken.

Selection at the level of the gene

Selection can also work at the gene level. When a *diploid individual* (one that has two copies of its genome) produces *haploid gametes* (sperm cells or eggs, which have only one copy of the genome), each parental gene has a 50-50 chance of ending up in the gamete population — usually. Sometimes, though, for reasons that are poorly understood, one gene is better than another at making it into the gametes. This phenomenon is selection at the gene level, or *meiotic drive*.

Meiotic drive occurs when a particular gene has better than a 50 percent chance of making it into the gamete pool and from there to the offspring. Although on its face, selection at the gene level seems to be at odds with how you expect evolution to work, by taking a closer look at meiotic drive, you can see that the same evolutionary forces are at play.

Increases in subsequent populations

In nearly all the other discussions in this book, the probability of a gene's ending up in the next generation depends on whether that particular gene increases the survival and/or reproduction of the individual. The gene that makes a cheetah run fast, for example, is more likely to make it into the next generation than the gene that makes a cheetah run slowly.

Meiotic drive is different. The frequency of a gene increases because it ends up in a disproportionate number of offspring — not because it necessarily increases the organism's fitness. Even a gene that has a negative effect on the survival and reproduction of the organism could increase in frequency if the degree to which it disables the individual is compensated for by its increased representation in the offspring. In other words, individuals carrying this gene may be less fit, but there are more of them than individuals carrying the gene left behind by meiotic drive.

Any gene that's better at ending up in the offspring will increase in frequency, even if ending up in more offspring is the only thing it's better at doing and even if it has fitness costs for the individual carrying it.

When selection levels collide

If the gene that increases in frequency has a high fitness cost to the individual, the direction of selection can be different at different levels. Suppose that a gene that reduces the speed at which cheetahs can run is one that, through meiotic drive, has a better than 50 percent chance of ending up in the gamete population. Selection at the level of the individual will act to remove such a costly gene, because cheetahs with this gene will be slower and will produce fewer offspring.

Because the fitness of a particular gene can be at odds with the fitness of the individual that carries it, selection at the level of the individual acts to combat the deleterious driver gene. Take, for example, fruit flies.

A particular species of fruit fly has an X-linked driver gene. This driver gene causes males to have only female offspring. Because producing both male and female offspring is the most successful strategy for getting genes into the subsequent generations, female flies are at a disadvantage if they mate with the male flies carrying this driver gene.

Interestingly, the female fruit flies choose mates that have long eye stalks. The connection? The driver gene is associated with a gene for short eye stalk. The female preference for the long eye stalk evolved because the length of the eye stalk correlates to the quality of the mate. Mate with a short-eye-stalk fruit fly, and you end up with only daughters and decreased fitness. But avoid short-eye-stalk fellas, and you get both male and female offspring and increased fitness. (For a down-and-dirty explanation of sex selection, head to Chapter 12.)

Selection at the individual level operates to oppose selection at the level of the driver gene. Females with a preference for males with long eye stalks are less likely to mate with males carrying the driver gene. So even though the gene is in twice as many gametes (males containing the driver gene make only gametes that carry this gene), it doesn't have twice the chance of making it into the next generation because the male fly isn't as likely to be chosen as a mate.

The Evolution of Altruistic Social Systems

As I explain throughout this book, evolution by natural selection means that nature selects or favors heritable traits (or characteristics) that increase an organism's fitness — how successful it is at getting its genes into future generations. Yet some organisms actually postpone reproduction or forgo it.

At first glance, such actions seem to be absolutely out of step with the core concepts of evolution until you realize that in some cases, such as those highlighted in the following sections, delaying or abandoning reproduction can actually make an organism *more* fit. Which brings me to the evolution of altruism and how doing good for others can be good for you.

Cooperative breeding

Although not common (only about 300 out of approximately 10,000 bird species have cooperative breeding), cooperative breeding does happen. Birds with helpers, regardless of whether the helpers are related or not, typically raise more offspring — sometimes twice as many — than birds without helpers.

There are two kinds of cooperative breeding among birds:

- **Non-reproductive individuals helping other birds to reproduce:** In some cases, the helpers are related; in other cases, they're not. Helpers who are related benefit because doing so increases their inclusive fitness (refer to the earlier section "Your fitness + your relatives' fitness = inclusive fitness" for details on inclusive fitness). Unrelated helpers benefit because if male dies they have the inside track on widow: wife and home all packaged together.

- **Groups of reproductive individuals getting together and helping each other (often with some non-reproducing individuals, too):** An example of this type of system is found with the groove-billed ani, as explained in the section "Other cooperative breeding behaviors."

Helpers at the nest: When the helpers are related

Helpers at the nest refers to a situation in which offspring don't leave the parental environment immediately to raise offspring of their own, but remain with the parents for some period of time and assist the parents in raising additional broods.

Waiting to reproduce may be beneficial for birds whose probability of reproductive success is low. Suppose, for example, that reproductive success is limited by the number of available territories in which pairs of birds can breed. A younger, less-experienced bird may not be able to get and hold any territory;

therefore, on his own, he won't have much opportunity for reproduction. If he stays at the parental nest and helps care for his younger siblings, however, he can boost his inclusive fitness.

The reason bird studies tend to focus on the behavior of males rather than females is because it's usually males that defend territories and females that disperse to find mates — you know, the male bird sits and sings and hopes a female flies by. When territories are scarce, extra males pile up around home. In addition, the fact that the females are on the move can also mean increased female mortality, which skews the sex ratio of males to females.

Sometimes, no evidence exists that the helpers at the nest increase the number of offspring the parents are able to raise. In these cases, selection favors helping for different reasons:

- **To gain experience:** A wealth of evidence shows that inexperienced pairs of birds are much less successful at raising offspring than are experienced birds. By sticking around to help, the young birds gain experience in parenting.

- **To inherit the territory:** In an environment where territories are both limited *and* needed to successfully raise offspring, staying in the parents' territory may result in a better chance of inheriting the territory when the parents die. (Consider this the suck-up principle.)

- **To wait out tough times:** Environments fluctuate, and sometimes there just isn't enough food or enough available mates. In this case, hanging around in a bad year may increase your chance of surviving to breed in a good one later. Got a 30-year-old child living at home? Then you're intimately familiar with this scenario.

The young bird isn't sticking around just to be helpful; he's looking out for himself. The fact that his parents or siblings may benefit from his presence is beside the point. For that matter, the parents aren't acting altruistically either. Even if having the young bird around doesn't increase their own number of offspring, the parents still benefit if, by delaying leaving home, the young bird can increase his own reproductive success.

When the helper isn't related

In some species, the male bird that helps out the mother bird isn't one of her sons or related to her at all. How can helping a complete stranger make more offspring be selectively advantageous?

In these species, mortality can be quite high. If the breeding male dies while the unrelated male is hanging around being oh-so-helpful, who do you think the female will turn to as a new mate? You've got it: Mr. Helpful himself, who, by assisting her, has given himself the inside track on the job!

Other cooperative breeding behaviors

The groove-billed ani is a kind of cuckoo that lives primarily in Central and South America. These birds live in small groups (between one and five pairs) within a single nest. They all help defend territory, provide food, sit on the eggs, and feed the young. But this isn't an avian utopia. Before they lay their own eggs, the females make room for their own eggs by kicking others' eggs out.

The ani engages in cooperative breeding, but it isn't an example of kin selection because the helpers are other reproducing birds; they don't forgo or delay their own reproduction to help the others. Even with the problems of this system (the danger of your eggs getting tossed by another female, for example), each reproducing pair produces more offspring than it otherwise would have.

One good turn deserves another: Reciprocal altruism

An individual can increase its own fitness through *reciprocal altruism,* the situation in which altruistic acts are repaid. Forgot your lunch? No problem. I'll give you half of mine. But at some point in the future, I'll expect you to return the favor. Unlike kin selection (described in the earlier section), in which the good-deed-doer gets an immediate benefit, in reciprocal altruism, the benefit comes at some future time. In addition, reciprocal altruism can occur whether the individuals are genetically related or not.

When it's more likely to occur

Natural selection favors traits for reciprocal altruism (doing a good deed today in the hope of being repaid at some point in the future) under certain conditions:

- ✔ The individual that benefits from the altruistic behavior will be around in the future to do a good deed in return.
- ✔ The benefit you accrue from doing a good deed is greater than the cost of doing the good deed in the first place.
- ✔ Individuals are able to identify cheaters — individuals who accept altruism but never pay anyone back.

Because these conditions occur rarely in nature, instances of reciprocal altruism are rare as well. Still, examples of reciprocal altruism exist in nature. One naturally altruistic creature is — believe it or not — the female vampire bat, as shown in an experiment performed by Gerald Wilkinson.

Reciprocal altruism in action

Female vampire bats live in colonies made up of unrelated females and their offspring, and they feed exclusively on blood. At feeding time, these bats leave the roost, find a mammal (usually, a nice juicy cow), bite it without being detected, and lap up the blood. On a good night, they can consume almost one third of their body weight in blood before they head back to the roost — which is like a 150-pound person having a 50-pound dinner.

But if a bat can't find food (sometimes, no cows are to be had), it's in big trouble. If it goes more than two nights without eating, it starves. In fact, studies have shown that vampire bats fail to find food often enough that, left on their own, most would be dead within a year. Yet vampire bats tend to live a long time. Why? Vampire bats share the wealth.

Back at the roost, the bats who were successful share some of the blood they collected with the bats that are starving. Then, when they themselves are on death's doorstep, they get a sip of blood in return. This exchange among the bats meets the conditions necessary for altruistic reciprocity:

- ✔ **The colonies are long-term communities of the same individuals who have many opportunities to share blood as needed.** In one case, the same pair of bats lived together for more than 10 years. Familiar bats — those with which the donor has a longer association — are more likely to receive a donation of blood, because they're the ones most likely to be around to reciprocate in the future.

  Gerald Wilkinson removed a sample of bats from a colony and held them without food until they reached the weight at which they would solicit food from other bats. Then he compared how the bats remaining in the colony responded to their returning (hungry) compatriots and how they responded to hungry bats from a different colony. He found that the full bats were likely to feed the hungry bats with which they had previous associations and were much less likely to feed the bats that were strangers.

- ✔ **The altruistic act is more beneficial to the recipient than harmful to the giver.** When a bat is close to starvation, a little bit of blood can buy a fair bit of time. But that same amount of blood isn't as big a loss to the donating bat that's flush from a successful feeding trip.

- ✔ **Vampire bats seem to have mechanisms in place to make sure that other bats can't cheat:**

  - They're able to recognize and remember other individual bats.

  - Before a hungry bat solicits food from one of its roostmates, it grooms that bat's belly. Given that full bats are noticeably more rotund than starving bats, the hungry bat probably has a good sense of who has food to share.

  - The bat that's being asked for food can assess the condition of the bat that's asking. Roostmates that are close to starvation are much more likely to be fed than roostmates that are only a little hungry.

Going to extremes: Eusociality

Eusociality is a social system characterized by reproductive specialization. One or some individuals in the colony bear all the offspring, and non-reproductive individuals assist in caring for the offspring. This system sounds nice and tidy, but evolutionary biologists had to work long and hard to figure out why eusociality works or what benefits it confers to the workers to make them want to hang around rather than flit off to start their own colonies.

The biggest question is why a non-reproductive worker class exists at all. These individuals aren't postponing reproduction until sometime in the future (as is the case for birds helping at the nest). They're forgoing reproduction entirely. Their genes will make it into future generations only to the extent that they are able to help related individuals reproduce and their offspring survive.

For some eusocial species, like ants, bees, and wasps (all *Hymenoptera* species), kin selection and inclusive fitness explain why a nonreproductive worker class can develop, and it all goes back to a reproductive system that makes individuals more related to their siblings than to their own offspring. For the other organisms, researchers suspect that other forces are at play.

Kin selection in bees, ants, and wasps

Bees, wasps, and ants live in highly structured colonies, with each individual performing particular tasks. Each colony, for example, contains a single reproducing female and many non-reproducing females that gather food, feed the young, and defend the nest but don't lay eggs of their own. So how does helping the group help (that is, increase the fitness of) the individuals, especially those that forgo reproduction themselves?

You could say that all these insects are working toward the good of the colony (and every animated ant or bee film ever made offers this explanation), but you'd be wrong. Evolution rarely works at the group level; it is more likely to work at the individual level. Each ant, wasp, or bee is really working toward its own benefit — not the colony's.

In these species, non-reproductive females (the workers) increase their own fitness more if they help the queen reproduce than if they reproduce themselves. It's a numbers game. Of all the relationships (parent to offspring, sister to sister, sister to brother), females in these systems share more genes with their sisters than they do with either parent, their brothers, or their own offspring. More sisters mean more fitness. The following sections explain.

Degree of relatedness in Hymenoptera species

In *Hymenoptera* reproduction, fertilized eggs become females; unfertilized eggs become males. Because they result from fertilized eggs, females are diploid. A female, being diploid, gets half of its genetic material from each of its parents, just as humans do. What's different is that the daughters receive exactly the same genes from the father, because the males, having arisen from unfertilized eggs, have only a single copy of the genetic material to pass on to their children.

The upshot of this strange sex-determination mechanism is that females in this reproductive system are three times as closely related to their sisters as they are to their brothers, and mothers are more closely related to their sisters (three quarters) than they are to their offspring (one half). In terms of kin selection, being more related to your sisters than to your own offspring means that a female can increase her fitness more efficiently by helping her mother make another reproductive daughter than to make a daughter herself.

And guess what? That's exactly what happens in many *Hymenoptera* species. That beehive, anthill, or wasp's nest in your backyard usually contains one reproducing female and many non-reproducing daughters that take care of the nest and the babies but don't reproduce themselves.

Intrigue in the queen's court

The mere fact that non-reproductive workers aren't laying eggs on their own doesn't mean that they're not affecting the reproductive decisions of the hive. Consider bees as an example.

The queen bee controls which eggs get fertilized, using sperm she stored from her maiden mating flight. Because her sons and daughters each share half of her genes, she would just as soon make half of each. It's all the same to her. But regardless of the sex ratio of the eggs laid by the queen, the ratio of reproductive bees produced by a hive often has a three-to-one bias in favor of females. So if half of the Queen's offspring are males and half are females, how does the hive end up with many times more females than males?

The answer? Her daughters, the worker bees. For their own fitness (being three times more related to their sisters than to their brothers), they prefer that the queen make more daughters. And because the worker bees control the feeding of the larvae, they control how many fertilized eggs will become reproductive females and how many unfertilized eggs (males) will survive.

Genes that result in worker bees producing more sisters are selectively favored because the sisters are likely to have those genes. A gene that favors producing more brothers is not as likely to get passed to future generations, because the brother bee is not as likely to share that gene (or any particular gene) with the sister.

Other eusocial organisms

Not all eusocial organisms have the same reproductive system that *Hymenoptera* species do. Termites, for example, live in colonies with a reproductive pair (one female and one male) and sterile female workers, but the workers aren't more closely related to their siblings than they are to their own offspring (were they to have any). For them and other such creatures, kin selection isn't what compels them to remain in the colony.

In trying to understand these other eusocial systems, biologists suspect that eusociality may have been the result of a dynamic between selection at the level of the individual (which favors the fitness of the individual and therefore tends to prevent the formation of such systems) and selection at the level of the group (which favors groups of organisms over individual ones).

If playing a minor role in a larger group makes an individual more fit than playing a solitary role, natural selection could favor genes for remaining in the group. Think of the dancers in a chorus line. They may never be the headliners that draw in the audiences, but the show can't go on without them — and they're dancing on Broadway.

So how do roles get assigned in such species? What mechanism dictates whether a budding young organism is the star or a background player? Genes. Specifically, genes for *plasticity* — those that allow individuals to develop into reproductive individuals or non-reproductive workers. If such genes led to increased efficiency in the division of labor within the colony, they would be selectively favored.

One is the loneliest number: Multicellularity

The fossil record makes it clear that organisms started out as single-celled entities and developed into multicelled organisms as time passed. It's not hard to imagine the evolutionary pathway that led from one condition to the other:

1. A single-celled organism divided into two daughter cells.

2. Each daughter cell divided into two daughter cells.

3. Each of those daughter cells divided, and so on and so forth, until a whole bunch of single-celled organisms were going happily about their business.

4. One day, a mutation occurred, resulting in two daughter cells remaining attached instead of separating after cell division.

   These two still-attached cells had a couple of advantages over individual cells — maybe they were harder to eat (because they were bigger), and maybe they had more access to food sources — so this particular mutation increased in frequency in the population.

This example seems fairly simple, but making a multicelled organism isn't as easy as assembling a collection of identical cells. In larger organisms, different cells have to become specialized to perform different functions. The cells in your own body, for example, are remarkably good at sharing resources, yet few of them do any of the reproducing; that task is left entirely to the tissues that produce eggs and sperm. Yet the specialization that makes complex functioning possible can also lead to conflicts between different cell lineages.

Cells can be selfish in a couple of ways:

✔ **By not performing their appropriate functions:** If all the cells want to be gonads, and none of them wants to be a thighbone, the community (the multicelled organism) breaks down. The only chance that one of your nose-hair cells has of getting its genes into the next generation is to play nice, do its job, and not suck up any more resources than necessary.

✔ **By trying to hog all the resources:** Every once in a while, a mutation in a cell can result in that cell's breaking ranks and going all out for the resources. Need a recognizable word for this phenomenon? Try *cancer.*

Part of the evolution of multicellularity — organisms growing from 4 cells to 8 cells to 16 cells to 32 to eventually billions of cells — seems to be the natural selection of traits that keep selfish cells in check. For the most part, things have gone swimmingly. Organisms have evolved from single-celled creatures to multicelled creatures of amazing complexity and variety that can, for example, write or read a book about evolution.

Chapter 12

Evolution and Sex

· ·

In This Chapter

▶ Understanding why sex is poorly understood

▶ Balancing the costs and benefits of sex

▶ Fighting for (or preening for) a mate

▶ Recognizing potential conflicts between the sexes

· ·

*E*volutionary biologists spend a fair bit of time thinking about sex, and in this chapter, you find out what it is, exactly, that they're thinking about. The evolutionary biology of sex encompasses several areas that can be conveniently broken down into the following major topics:

✔ How does the added complication of mating affect the process of evolution in sexual species?

✔ Why have two sexes, and what's the optimum male-to-female ratio?

✔ Why have sex at all?

Just as this chapter covers a range of topics, it also illustrates a range in scientists' understanding of these topics. The evolution of sex is a hot area of research, and knowledge is growing rapidly. In some cases, researchers are confident that they understand what they see in nature; in other cases, they're not. In this chapter, I tell you what scientists know and what they're not yet sure of. As always, I continue to introduce you to the data and experiments that shape current understanding.

Sex Terms You Probably Thought You Knew

The term *sex* can mean several things. Ask a seventh-grader straight out of health class, and you're likely to get one definition (with a few sniggers thrown in). Ask a parent of a brood of children, and you're likely to get another. Often, these definitions equate sex with sexual reproduction. But ask an evolutionary biologist to define *sex* and *sexual reproduction,* and you get definitions that are beautifully precise, even if they do suck all the fun and innuendo out of the terms.

For evolutionary biologists, *sex* is not mating but the combining of genetic material from different individuals, and *reproduction* simply means making offspring; reproduction, in other words, doesn't have to include sex:

- ✔ **Sexual reproduction:** *Sexual reproduction* is the system in which two individuals mate and produce offspring whose genes are a combination of some of the genes from each parent. Sexually reproducing organisms produce offspring that have only half of each parent's genes.

- ✔ **Asexual reproduction:** *Asexual* organisms produce offspring without mating, and these offspring contain only the single parent's genes.

For some species (like humans), reproduction *always* relies on sex. Other species (like rotifers and a few kinds of lizards) never have sex at all and still manage to reproduce. Still other species can reproduce with *or* without sex, proving that sexual reproduction isn't necessarily an all-or-nothing proposition.

As mentioned in numerous places throughout this book, *fitness* is all about passing on your genes to the next generation. The more successful you are at that task, the more fit you are. All other things being equal, an organism that makes twice as many offspring is twice as fit. (Go to Chapter 2 for a more in-depth discussion of fitness from an evolutionary perspective.) But in reproduction, the quality of the offspring's reproductive success also impacts an individual's fitness. If two individuals each produce four offspring, but the four offspring of one individual die before getting a chance to reproduce, the two individuals aren't equally fit.

Sexual Selection: The Art of Picking a Mate

For sexually reproducing species, it's not enough just to find food and dodge predators. You also have to get a mate, because the prime directive, evolutionarily speaking, is to pass on your genes. How you go about choosing the best candidate to help you do just that is the topic of sexual selection.

Sexual selection refers to choosing certain characteristics over others when looking for a mate, and it's a subcategory of natural selection — the process by which heritable traits that promote survival become more common.

Sexual selection can lead to the evolution of some traits that, on the face of it, don't make much sense. It may favor a trait that increases an individual's ability to find a mate but decreases its ability to survive, for example. Although this arrangement seems strange at first, it's perfectly reasonable if the trade-off is a good one — that is, if the fitness increase from increased mating is greater than the fitness loss from earlier death.

Sexual selection has two components: choice and competition. For the vast majority of cases, this means female choice and male-male competition. These are not mutually exclusive; you can see both in the same species and sometimes you even see the reverse (male choice and female-female competition). Also remember that sexual selection is found in lots of animal species from insects to mammals.

Some evolutionary biologists argue that sexual selection should be considered separately from natural selection, as the evolutionary changes produced are of a slightly different nature (flashy feathers as opposed to anything that's actually helpful for surviving, finding food, and so on.) But for our purposes here, I treat sexual selection as a subcategory of natural selection.

The Peacock's Tail: Sexual Selection and Female Choice

One kind of sexual selection system is one in which females choose their partners based on some outward characteristic. In these cases, the females' choice results in the males having some increasingly elaborate trait, even when that trait doesn't offer an obvious advantage in the male's survival. At face value, it's the classic example of choosing style over substance. This phenomenon has been puzzling evolutionary biologists since Darwin, because although it's obvious that females choose showy males, it's not entirely clear why.

In these species, evolutionary biologists figure that something else must be at play — something that makes it advantageous for the male (with the showy trait that serves no other purpose) and the female (whose choice of mate means that her offspring will end up with a trait that may actually be a disadvantage) to get together.

To understand this system, consider peacocks. If you've had the opportunity to see a peacock, you've no doubt been impressed by the size and beauty of his tail. The huge fan of iridescent green and blue feathers, which he displays so proudly, is unquestionably one of the most magnificent displays in the bird family.

That said, from a survival point of view, the fancy tail doesn't appear to have a lot of advantages. In fact, the tail seems to increase the chance that the peacock will be caught and eaten by predators. Peacocks don't fly especially gracefully, and the tail certainly makes it hard to hide. In addition, although the tail can't possibly make finding food any easier, the energy required to produce such an elaborate tail means that the peacock needs to find more.

In short, a showy tail doesn't seem to have any obvious fitness advantages, but it turns out that there is one, and it's a big one: Peahens like it! In fact, peahens like flashy tails so much that they preferentially choose to mate with males that have showier tails. Therefore, males with showier tails are much more likely to pass on their genes to the next generation than are males with less-showy tales. So having a fancy tail does indeed make a peacock more fit.

But what about the peahen? How does mating with the showy male increase her fitness? After all, she's deliberately choosing to mate with a very showy but otherwise less capable male. Although she's passing on her genes to the next generation (good from a fitness perspective), she's combining them with some genes that appear to make it more likely that her offspring will get eaten or starve (bad from a fitness perspective).

Two major ideas explain the curious choices that the females seem to make (and shallowness isn't one of them): the runaway-selection hypothesis and the good-genes hypothesis. The different mechanisms may be important in different systems.

It's not always the females that do the choosing. In some cases, the females display, and the males choose the females. These examples are very rare, however, so throughout this section, I concentrate on examples in which the female does the choosing. Just remember that in some cases, exactly the same phenomenon occurs, but with the roles of the sexes reversed.

It's not how you feel, it's how you look: Runaway-selection hypothesis

The runaway-selection hypothesis says that, if females choose mates based on some random showy character simply because they're attracted to that character, that character becomes more pronounced in each successive generation *until* the disadvantages of the having the trait (it makes you less likely to survive) outweigh the advantages (it makes the ladies like you).

Here's how runaway-selection works: Females choose males with, for example, bigger tails for no other reason than that they like big tails. Because the biggest-tailed birds father the most offspring, the average male in the next generation will have a slightly bigger tail. When the next generation's females choose among these males, they select for even longer tails. In this way, male tail length increases until it reaches the point where the increased risk of predation, starvation, or some other unfortunate outcome of having an enormous tail outweighs any additional attractiveness to the females.

Two questions come to mind in considering this model: How does it benefit the females to mate with showy males, and what makes them prefer one particular trait over others? The next sections provide the answers.

The runaway-selection hypothesis seems as though it shouldn't be right simply because . . . well, evolution shouldn't work in such a strange way. But it's important to remember that our emotional reaction to any particular hypothesis rarely has anything to do with whether it's correct.

Like father, like son: The sexy-sons hypothesis

Beyond looking good as a couple, how does picking a male with a showy tail increase the female's fitness, particularly if the showy tail makes survival more difficult? You'd think that if she wants to get her genes into the future, the female would be better off choosing males with less-showy tails so that her offspring have a better chance of survival.

As it turns out, that's not quite how it works. Instead, specific cases have been found in which female fitness is *reduced* when females mate with less-showy males because the mating success of their sons is lower. In other words, having a sexy son can provide a fitness advantage for a female who chooses to mate with an elaborate male.

Imagine a mutation that makes a female less likely to choose a male with a big tail. Now consider how that choice may affect her fitness. True, her sons wouldn't be hobbled with enormous tails, *but* they wouldn't be prime mating material either. If these poor sons can't get mates, they can't pass on their (and their mom's) genes.

To see whether this hypothesis were true, evolutionary biologists came up with a testable prediction: The sons of less-flashy fathers should have lower mating success than the sons of more-flashy fathers. After identifying species in the wild for which they could measure the attractiveness of males, who mates with whom, and the mating success of the sons of more- and less-flashy fathers, scientists discovered that less-flashy sons actually do have less success in the mating department — and that decreases both their fitness and their mothers'.

The case for pre-existing preferences

The brain, as you may have noticed, can be a strange thing. It allows us to do a lot of things that are obviously adaptive: find food, avoid bears, and so on. At the same time, it is responsible for traits that don't have obvious advantages, such as dreaming or a propensity to enjoy skydiving. As Chapter 5 explains, not all traits are adaptive. Some traits that aren't adaptive can get dragged along by the traits that are. Pre-existing preferences could fall into this category: in this scenario. females have a pre-existing preference for the trait. Something about how the female brain is wired leads them to favor the trait just because.

Scientists have tested ideas about pre-existing preferences in the laboratory, using fish closely related to swordtails. Swordtails are small freshwater fish common in home aquariums. Males have a long pointed tail — hence, the name *swordtail*. Females, as you've probably guessed, have a mating preference for males with long tails.

The fish used in the studies, although otherwise very similar to the swordtails, differed from them in a couple of key ways: The males lack the long pointed tails, and the females obviously don't choose mates based on tail length, because none of the males has a long tail. To find out what would happen if the males *did* have long tails, researchers attached fake long pointed tails to the male fish. And what did the females do? They preferred to mate with the males wearing the fake tails.

This experiment was important because scientists were able to demonstrate that pre-existing preferences exist. These preferences — in combination with the data showing that the reproductive success of sons is decreased if their fathers were less flashy — suggests that the runaway-selection model is a very real possibility even if the showy trait never had any ecological advantage.

Or maybe it IS how you feel: The good-genes hypothesis

The good-genes hypothesis proposes that females select mates with elaborate traits because the presence of these traits provides reliable indicators of overall male quality. Under this model, peahens prefer the peacocks with the most elaborate tails because the presence of a large tail indicates that the male has other qualities that would be beneficial for the female's offspring.

For evidence that the good-genes hypothesis sometimes explains female choice, consider a study using a particularly species of stickleback, a small freshwater fish. Males of this species have bright red bellies, and the females preferentially choose to mate with the males with the reddest bellies.

Iain Barber and coworkers measured the resistance to parasitic worms of the offspring of males who differed in how red their bellies were. What they found was that the males with the reddest bellies fathered offspring that were more resistant to parasites. In this case, the redness of a male's belly was a true indicator of his genetic quality with respect to offspring parasite resistance. Females choosing to mate with the reddest males produced fitter offspring than females that selected duller males. The good-genes hypothesis provides a good explanation for female choice in this fish.

The handicap hypothesis

The handicap hypothesis is a special variation of the good-genes hypothesis. Under the handicap hypothesis, the elaborate male trait indicates the presence of other good genes, specifically because the male trait is so costly that only males with especially good genes could produce the elaborate trait and still survive. According to this hypothesis, a peacock that can survive with an enormous tail must have some other really good genes to balance out the obviously bad tail. Maybe it's especially good at evading predators and at finding food, for example, if it can manage to do both while still dragging around that beautiful but cumbersome tail.

An important component of the handicap hypothesis is that the elaborate male trait must actually be a handicap. In the example of the peacock, researchers have been taking for granted that the peacock's enormous tail hinders its ability to do all the sorts of things that birds need to do to survive.

No studies have been done with actual peacocks (mainly because they don't make good laboratory critters — they're big, they're expensive, and they bite) — but studies of other birds have provided evidence that elaborate tails are a handicap. For their study, Andres Moller and Florentino de Lope used barn swallows. Male barn swallows have long tails, and the females preferentially mate with the males that have the longest tails.

Moller and de Lope artificially increased or decreased the length of male barn swallows' tails and then measured the effects of different tail lengths on feeding ability and mating success. They found that giving males longer tails increased their attractiveness to females and at the same time decreased their efficiency in catching food. These experimental results show that in this bird species, the elaborate trait that is attractive to females is indeed a handicap for the male birds.

Sexual Selection and Male-Male Competition

As explained in the preceding section, female choice is one type of sexual section. The other type is male-male competition, when males compete with each other for access to females. Competition among males for access to females can take several forms. In each case, natural selection favors characters that increase success in those contests.

In the case of male-male competition, as in female choice, selection favors characters that increase male mating success, which can lead to physical differences between the two sexes. Unlike the case of female choice, however, in which the differences result in males having some increasingly elaborate attractive trait, selection resulting from male-male competition favor traits that facilitate winning contests with other males.

Finally, there may be cases when female choice and male-male competition both operate. For example, male deer use their antlers in contests with other males. Yet it is also possible that large antlers could be appealing to female deer. Female preference could drive the evolution of antler size past the optimum needed to bash other male deer. Or visa versa. Remember that in either case, selection for being able to do all the other more mundane things that deer do (like find food and run away from predators) will place some upper limit on antler size.

The largest deer antlers on record are from the extinct Giant Deer which had antlers 12 feet across! Sexual selection has been suggested as a reason for the evolution of these impressive antlers, but we can't know for sure. If you've heard about this beast, you might have also heard the idea that the reason they went extinct was that their antlers got too big for their own good. But of course, evolution doesn't work that way. Any deer with antlers that were simply too big to allow him to survive wouldn't be passing those super duper antler genes to the next generation.

Direct male-male contests

The most obvious example of male-male competition for females is the case in which males actually fight one another, and the winners are the ones that get to mate. The stakes are high, because the losers won't be passing their genes on to the next generation (at least during this particular mating season), and sometimes the contests are quite violent. Common examples of animals that engage in male-male contests are elephant seals and lions. In both cases, selection has led to increased size in males because larger males are more successful fighters.

Run away! Run away!

Individuals typically don't engage in contests that they don't stand some chance of winning. For that reason, many contests in the animal kingdom are preceded by a period of posturing in which the two combatants check each other out to judge relative size and strength. After this initial period, a weaker individual chooses to withdraw rather than risk death in a contest he probably can't win. The same logic applies when, part of the way through a fight, one individual realizes that he's beaten and withdraws. This situation is also quite common in nature.

This phenomenon is responsible for male elephant seals being the largest members of the carnivore family. Although female elephant seals are generally between 1,000 and 2,000 pounds, males routinely weigh between 3,000 and 5,000 pounds, with the record weight being more than 7,000 pounds.

Studies have shown that the larger males do indeed father most of the young in elephant seals and some other species. But living the life of a giant warrior-lover isn't all peaches and cream.

Natural selection favors genes that increase size and fighting ability, but not genes for increased longevity. Although enormous size is necessary to fight for a mate, the violent contests and huge energy costs associated with it seem to take their toll. Male elephant-seals live much shorter lives than females — about 14 years as opposed to about 20. Because of how mating is structured in this species, being an older male has no advantage; being a bigger, stronger male does. Death is definitely a bad idea and certainly something to be avoided. But if the only way to get access to females is at the cost of a reduced lifespan, natural selection will favor the bigger-and-stronger genes over the lifespan genes.

From an evolutionary point of view, not reproducing — that is, not passing your genes on to the next generation — is the same as dying. Either way, your genes aren't in the next generation, and your fitness is effectively zero.

Indirect competition

Competition between males isn't always direct face-to-face conflict. Males also compete in indirect ways. In these cases, selection doesn't favor increased male fighting ability; it favors whatever traits are required to gain access to females.

One obvious example of indirect competition is competition to find females. In many species of butterflies, females mate with the first male that finds them, so finding a female fast is a big advantage. Females often produce chemicals called pheromones that the males can smell. As a result, males have evolved to be incredibly sensitive to these pheromones. Some butterfly males can detect a female more than five miles away!

This type of male-male competition is called *scramble competition* because rather than fighting, the males are scrambling to find the females as fast as they can.

Sperm competition

In some species, females mate with multiple males, which provides an additional battleground for male-male competition: the battle among the sperm. Natural selection has produced a variety of male adaptations designed to fight this battle, including:

- ✔ **More sperm:** Males of non-monogamous species produce more sperm than males of monogamous species.

- ✔ **Seminal plugs:** Most common in insects, but also seen in some vertebrates, is the production of seminal fluid that solidifies into a plug to prevent subsequent males from mating — a strange but predictable adaptation to the problem of competition from other males' sperm.

- ✔ **Toxic seminal fluid:** Fruit flies are one species that employs this strategy. Their sperm contains toxic compounds that inhibit the sperm of subsequent males. Unfortunately, poison semen isn't too good for the female; head to the later section "The Battle of the Sexes: Male-Female Conflict" to find out more about what happens when what the male wants is at odds with what the female wants.

Being sneaky: Alternative male strategies

In the evolutionary process, there is often more than one way to accomplish the same task. As biologists continue to study systems in which mating success seems to be determined by the outcome of male-male competition, they're discovering some interesting alternative male strategies. One example is the *sneaky strategy*. Scientists speculate that the sneaky strategy is a way for younger males to have some chance of reproductive success before they get old enough to bark with the big dogs.

Males that use the sneaky strategy avoid direct conflict and try to mate with females while the other males are busy bashing their horns together or otherwise carrying on. It's not clear how common this phenomenon is, but it's been seen in several species, including frogs and red deer. It's also not clear how successful this strategy is compared with the strategy of the dominant male. For males that would be unable to win physical contests, however, it provides the only chance to contribute genes to the next generation.

The Battle of the Sexes: Male-Female Conflict

In a monogamous species in which males and females enter into long-term reproductive relationships, parents will have an interest in each other's survival because only through the survival of their partners will they be able to produce any offspring. The situation is much different for species with short-lived or no pair bonds. In this case, selection can favor traits of one individual in the pair even if they decrease the partner's fitness.

A sneaky sperm competition

Several adaptations seem to facilitate the sneaky strategy. One good example occurs in Atlantic salmon. In this species, larger, dominant males guard females and then fertilize their eggs externally as soon as the eggs are laid. The dominant male chases away smaller males that attempt to approach the female he's guarding. The smaller males can't get as close to the female as the dominant male can, but they have an interesting characteristic that may serve to increase their chances of fertilizing at least some of the female's eggs.

Matthew Gage and coworkers found that smaller males' sperm swim faster and can survive longer in the water than those of larger males. Smaller males also produce sperm with different characteristics from those of the dominant males, and these sperm may have a better chance of reaching the female's eggs.

Parents have an interest in providing for the survival of their offspring. From a strictly evolutionary point of view, they don't necessarily have any interest in each other's survival. Why? Because from a fitness perspective, it's better for a male if his partner makes only a few offspring, all of which are his, than if she makes very many offspring that aren't his. The female's fitness is increased by adaptations that favor her reproductive output over that of her mate's. The result of the conflicting goals is an evolutionary version of the battle of the sexes.

The following sections discuss some of the ways this conflict manifests itself in the animal kingdom.

Infanticide

When male lions take over a pride of female lions, they kill or attempt to kill the cubs. They don't indiscriminately kill baby lions, however. They leave their own offspring alone but kill cubs fathered by the previous dominant male. Killing the cubs sired by the previous dominant male increases the new male's fitness, because it gives him a better shot of producing his own offspring before he gets dethroned by some other male lion.

The violent male-male competition to control a pride of females results in frequent changes in the dominant male. When a new male takes over, he must reproduce as rapidly as possible, as the risk exists that he too will soon be displaced. Because female lions with cubs are not reproductively receptive while they're caring for existing young, the fastest way for the male to gain reproductive access to females is to kill their offspring, which he does as soon as he takes over the pride. The females are then soon ready to mate with him and have his offspring, passing along his genes.

CASE STUDY

Should I stay or should I go?

In monogamous species, males and females have either a short or a long-term interest in the fitness of their partners. Non-monogamous species don't have the same concerns. But how would they evolve if they did? Brett Holland and William Rice designed an experiment with fruit flies to investigate this question. They separated the flies into two groups:

✔ For one group of flies, they continued to grow the flies together in large groups in which multiple non-monogamous matings would occur. In this case, an individual fly's fitness is maximized by producing as many offspring as it can, regardless of the consequences for its partners.

✔ In the other group, they raised the flies in monogamous pairs. In this treatment, the fitness of the two flies is interconnected. Flies whose behaviors maximize their partner's fitness also maximize their own fitness.

The researchers raised flies in these two treatments for 47 generations; at the end of the experiment, they measured female fitness characteristics such as life span and reproductive output. Here's what they found:

✔ The male flies in the monogamous pairs had evolved to be less harmful to the female flies. The original male flies were rough; the evolved monogamous ones more gentlemanly.

✔ The female flies had evolved to be less resistant to the male flies. The original female flies watched their backs; the monogamous evolved ones relax and let their hair down.

Their experiment shows that changing the mating system such that the interests of the sexes were no longer in conflict led to rapid evolution that decreased the strength of traits associated with male-female conflict.

In this scenario, the male's fitness increases at the expense of the female's fitness. She's invested time and energy in her litter, which is now lost. Because the new dominant male is so much larger and stronger than the female, she isn't able to protect her young after the new dominant male takes over.

Before then, the females aren't completely powerless, however. Groups of female lions often attempt to chase away solitary male lions that approach the pride. How much — or whether — these actions decrease the probability of the dominant male's being replaced isn't known, but the actions are certainly consistent with the view that the females are trying to prevent the deaths of their cubs.

Poison semen

Because of the promiscuous mating system of fruit flies, each fly will mate with many other flies over its lifetime. Neither partner has any interest in increasing the fitness of any particular mate, only in increasing its own fitness:

✔ Male fruit flies have toxic chemicals in their seminal fluid that inhibit the sperm of other males (this is an example of sperm competition, explained in the earlier section "Sperm competition" in this chapter). This trait is advantageous for the male because it increases the chance that his sperm will be the ones that fertilize the female's eggs. But the same trait is bad for the female because the semen is toxic to her; she's being poisoned.

✔ The very act of mating seems to decrease the survival of female flies, because repeated mating with males is physically damaging — a situation the female fly tries to avoid.

Sex: It's Expensive, So Why Bother?

Lots of organisms reproduce sexually, but plenty don't. Many organisms reproduce *asexually,* without sex. Given that sex is expensive and some organisms reproduce just fine without it, why do it? Evolutionary biologists ponder this question because at first glance, sex doesn't seem like a very fit thing to do:

✔ **A sexual organism is effectively throwing away half its genes when it reproduces.** When an organism reproduces sexually, only half its genes get passed to its offspring; the other half come from the other parent. Asexual organisms, on the other hand, pass on *all* their genes. So from a fitness perspective, it would seem that asexual reproduction is better (read, more fit), hands down.

✔ **All other things being equal, the sexual individuals will soon be over-run, and sexual reproduction will be eliminated.** For sex, you need males. Asexual females don't have to make any males, so they produce all daughters, which in turn produce all granddaughters, which produce great-granddaughters, and so on. A sexual female that produces the same number of offspring will make only half as many daughters as the asexual female. She spends the other half of her energy making sons. Because her daughters will, on average, make only half as many daughters as the daughters of the asexual female, the original sexual female will end up with only one quarter as many grandchildren as the asexual female, one eighth as many great-grandchildren, and so on.

But sexual reproduction *hasn't* been eliminated, of course, which means that reproducing sexually must have one or more fitness advantages. So what are these advantages? Well, the truth is that evolutionary biologists just aren't sure. Many ideas have been suggested, and probably more that we haven't thought of yet will be suggested. The following sections look at the current ideas.

The ideas outlined in the following sections are not intended to be mutually exclusive; they could be working together simultaneously to maintain sexual reproduction. The question "Why have sex?" may well have many answers.

Why males don't count

Males don't contribute to population growth; they are needed so that the females can reproduce, but they are otherwise a waste of resources, and that's why they don't get counted. Suppose that two sexual females each make one daughter and one son. The daughter of one mates with the son of the other, and vice versa. Each sexual female ends up with four grandchildren, but that doesn't mean there are eight grandchildren; there are still only four total, and only two of these are female. The population has gone from two females to two females. That's why the males don't get counted.

Idea 1: Sex produces parasite-resistant offspring

Sex produces parasite-resistant offspring, making sexual organisms better able to adapt to changing parasitic environment than asexual organisms are.

Sexual reproduction produces *variable offspring* (offspring that are not genetically identical to their parents), whereas asexual reproduction doesn't. Asexual females produce daughters, granddaughters, and so on that are genetically identical to Mom.

Asexual reproduction is also called *clonal reproduction,* and all the resulting descendants of a single asexual female are referred to collectively as a clone. All the members of a clone are identical except for possible rare random mutations that may have occurred in DNA during the reproductive process. Sexual females, although they produce only half as many daughters, produce daughters that aren't identical to Mom or to one another.

Evolutionary biologists since Darwin have pondered the possible advantages of producing variable offspring. The first argument — that because natural selection requires variation on which to act, having variable offspring makes it more likely that your descendants will evolve faster than the other critters — seems like a no-brainer until you consider the following:

- ✔ The parent sexual organism clearly has a very fit combination of genes already. It's survived, found food, dodged predators, and found a mate; now it's reproducing.

- ✔ Sexual reproduction is dicey — you're more likely to break up a perfectly good set of genes with a proven track record in the current environment than hit on an even more fit combination.

So why take the gamble?

The key words here are *current environment*. In the current environment, this sexual organism does just fine. But what happens when the environment changes? This year's very fit gene combinations won't necessarily be very fit next year. The evolutionary interaction between parasites and their hosts can lead to such year-to-year changes in the hosts' environment.

The parasites experience selection pressure to infect their hosts better, whereas the hosts experience selection pressures to better resist infection by their parasites. In this sort of system, the genes of last year's really fit host won't be really fit next year, because the parasites will have evolved to infect it better.

With parasites evolving to better infect their hosts, an asexual host will be in trouble, because all its offspring will be exact copies of itself, but they will have to fend off better-adapted parasites. A sexual host, on the other hand, produces variable offspring with gene combinations the parasite population has not yet had a chance to adapt to. For this reason, the offspring of sexually reproducing organisms are less susceptible to attack by the parasites. So although the parent organism may not fare too well with new or better-adapted parasites, its offspring will.

Idea 2: Sex speeds up adaptation by combining rare beneficial mutations

Most mutations are bad. After all, randomly changing some piece of an organism's DNA is far more likely to mess up something that was working just fine than it is to improve upon something that wasn't. Every once in a while, however, some random change is actually beneficial and makes an organism better at doing whatever it is that particular organism does. One possible benefit of sexual reproduction is the ability to combine these rare but beneficial mutations more rapidly.

Imagine a couple of beneficial mutations; call them mutation A and mutation B. Both are rare, but they do occasionally occur. Either of the mutations makes the organisms more fit than the organisms without the mutations, but having both is better still.

Sex makes it easier for the two mutations to end up in the same organism. If an individual with mutation B mates with an individual with mutation A, some of the offspring should end up with both beneficial mutations. If this population were an asexual one, each individual would be reproducing in a clonal fashion, and the only way a lineage with mutation A would end up with mutation B (or vice-versa) would be if that mutation occurred in that lineage.

Studying snails and worms

Curt Lively and coworkers tested the theory that sex produces parasite-resistant offspring by using a freshwater snail that lives in New Zealand and is parasitized by a trematode worm. Through their investigation, the researchers provide strong support for the theory that sexual reproduction is advantageous in the presence of parasites.

Lively chose this particular snail because the species has both sexual and asexual forms. The species can reproduce sexually, with a female mating with a male to produce sexual female and male snails. Sometimes, however, offspring have an extra set of chromosomes and are *triploid* instead of *diploid,* which means that they have three sets of chromosomes instead of just two sets. The triploid snails appear to be similar to the diploid snails in every respect except one: They don't need to mate to reproduce. That means that all the triploid snails are females that reproduce asexually, creating identical triploid daughters.

In any given lake, both sexual and asexual snails coexist. The researchers used genetic techniques to determine that many different clones often coexisted in the same location. Each of these clones was the result of a separate instance of sexual reproduction between two diploid snails that resulted in a triploid offspring. Because the different clones have different genes, it's reasonable to assume that one or more of these clones would be better at doing all the things that snails do. The better, more fit clones may outcompete all the others in the short run, but they clearly have not eliminated all the other clones nor the sexual snails.

Lively and company were ready to test some of the specific predictions of the theory that the presence of the parasite was responsible for maintaining sexual reproduction in this system.

Prediction 1: Sexual individuals should be more common in locations that have more parasites

Measuring the density of parasites and the frequency of sexual reproduction at many lakes throughout New Zealand, Lively and company found that as the density of parasites increased the frequency of sexual reproduction increased as well. They also measured the frequency of sexually reproducing snails in both shallow and deep areas within individual lakes and found the same thing: As the density of parasites increased, the proportion of snails that reproduced sexually increased.

Prediction 2: If parasites are adapting to infect their hosts better, parasites should be better at infecting the host snails from their own lake rather than the snails from other lakes

The researchers performed two sets of experiments to test this prediction. They collected parasites and snails from two lakes on opposite sides of the southern New Zealand Alps and brought them back to the laboratory. (The distance between the lakes made it unlikely that the snails or their parasites had ever encountered each other in nature.) Then they measured the degree to which the parasites from each lake were able to infect snails from the two lakes. They found that for each lake, the parasites were better able to infect the coexisting snails than the snails from the other side of the mountains.

Next, they chose three lakes that were much closer to each other — close enough that ducks could easily fly between them, transporting the parasitic worms from one lake to the next. They again collected worms and snails from the lakes and brought them back to the laboratory to measure the ability of the parasites to infect snails from their own lake as well as the other two. In all three cases, they found that the parasites were better able to infect the snails from their own lake, and the effect was strong enough that it was not overwhelmed by the genetic mixing that could be occurring among the three lakes.

Prediction 3: The genotypes that were most common in the past should be most susceptible to the current parasites

In testing this prediction, the researchers focused on the clonal, asexual snails. For their test subjects, they selected clones that possessed the clonal genotypes most common in previous years. Using these clones, they performed two sets of experiments.

They tested the susceptibility of clones from the recent past to the parasitic worms presently inhabiting the lakes from which the clones were collected. What they found was that the clones that had been common in the past were more readily attacked than the clones that had been rare.

If you're a worm, you're well served by having characteristics (naturally selected, of course) that make you better able to overcome the defenses of the most common clone genotypes. A parasite better able to attack these clones would leave more descendents (because there are more of these "common" snails than the others) and therefore would increase faster than those of parasites attacking snails with rare types.

Idea 3: Sex is beneficial because it can eliminate bad mutations

One of the problems faced by asexual organisms is that, after they have a bad mutation, all their descendents will have the same bad mutation. Then, when a second bad mutation occurs in one of these descendents, all its descendents will have two bad mutations, and so on. This suggestion was first made by Hermann Joseph Muller (1890–1967), and the process is referred to as Muller's Ratchet because the increasing number of bad mutations ratchets down the organism's fitness.

This problem would be especially pronounced in small populations, in which random events might more readily result in the fixation of bad mutations (refer to Chapter 6 for info about how random events impact small populations). Sex provides a solution to this problem. Two sexual organisms, each of which had a different bad mutation, could mate and produce offspring that had neither mutation. Problem solved!

Using a virus that attacks bacteria, called phi-6, Lin Chao and coworkers tested the theory that sex can eliminate harmful mutations.

 Unlike most organisms that have genomes made of DNA, the phi-6 virus has a genome made of RNA. RNA replication is much more likely to result in errors than DNA replication, and as a result, organisms with RNA genomes have much higher mutation rates. This situation makes phi-6 an excellent subject for a study involving mutations, because many mutations occur over a reasonably short experiment.

Step 1: Producing viruses with decreased fitness

First, Chao established that he could actually observe the phenomenon of Muller's ratchet in the laboratory. He produced viruses that had decreased fitness due to the accumulation of harmful mutations. He did this by making sure that his laboratory population sizes would become quite low periodically. When population sizes are low, evolution via genetic drift can lead to fixation of deleterious mutations, which was what Chao observed. (Refer to Chapter 6 for information about genetic drift.)

Then Chao randomly plucked a few viruses out of one flask to populate the next flask, creating the next generation. (Whereas in a large population, the process of natural selection would weed out less-fit genotypes, Chao increased the chances that a harmful mutation would make it to the next generation by randomly choosing a *few* individuals. In small populations, a virus that's a little less fit still would do fine because it wouldn't have the more-fit strains breathing down its neck.) By repeating this process numerous times, Chao ended up with a population of less-fit viruses on which he could test his idea that sexual reproduction can increase fitness.

Step 2: Testing whether viral sex leads to increased fitness

With his low-fitness viruses, Chao collaborated with Thutrang Tran and Crystal Matthews in designing experiments to test whether viral sex leads to an increase in fitness. The scientists grew different pairs of the debilitated viruses together with their host bacteria, and they controlled how much sex was going on by altering the ratio of bacteria to viruses. When they put in far fewer bacteria than viruses, they ensured that multiple viruses would be infecting the same host bacterium. As they increased the likelihood of producing viral progeny that had genetic material from two parent viruses, they found that they were more likely to find progeny with increased fitness.

Here's why: An asexually reproducing virus will pass on all its harmful mutations to each of its descendants, but if the descendants have genetic material from two parents, they can end up with the best parts of both. Imagine that one virus has a deleterious mutation on segment 1, and the other one has a deleterious mutation on segment 2. If the viruses are reproducing in the same bacterium, out can pop a virus with neither bad segment.

Evolution of Separate Sexes and the 50-50 Sex Ratio

Why do humans — and a lot of other species — have different sexes? Why are some individuals males and others females? Evolutionary biologists have offered a couple of suggestions to answer these questions.

Viral sex

Sex in viruses is quite a bit different from what we commonly think of as sex. In fact, viruses typically reproduce asexually. In phi-6, sex works like this:

1. The virus injects its genome, consisting of three segments, into an unlucky bacterium.

2. The virus hijacks the cell's biochemical machinery to make more copies of itself.

3. Out pop progeny viruses, each of which has copies of the three parental genome segments.

Nothing about this process requires a second virus. Viruses don't need mates and are perfectly able to reproduce asexually. Sometimes, though, two viruses simultaneously infect the same host cell, and all the various replicating bits get mixed together. Now when the new viruses pop out, they can have genome segments from both of the original viruses (that is, one segment from one virus, and the other two segments from the other virus).

These new viruses have two "parents" instead of just one. This process is what scientists are referring to when they talk about viral sex.

Given that two sexes *do* exist, the next question for evolutionary theory is how many offspring of each sex an individual should make. And how is it that species with separate sexes end up with a 50-50 sex ratio: 50 boys for every 50 girls? It turns out that 50-50 sex ratio is something that is perfectly and easily explained by natural selection.

Sometimes, it's good to be discrete

"Why have males and females?" is a question that often strikes people as surprising, because we humans are so used to having two separate sexes. It doesn't always have to be that way, however. In fact, in many species, the male and female reproductive roles are combined in the same individual! These organisms are called *hermaphrodites,* and if you take a moment to look out the window, you can see that they're just about everywhere.

Most trees are hermaphrodites, containing both male and female functions in the same individual. Each individual apple tree, for example, makes both ovules and pollen. Its pollen is carried to other apple trees to fertilize their ovules while it awaits pollen from other trees to fertilize its own ovules. In the end, all the apple trees produce fruit.

The same is true for most of the fruits you encounter in the orchard or the fruit section of your local supermarket, but not for all of them. Persimmon trees, for example, have distinct sexes. Some persimmon trees are male and make just pollen; others are female and make just the ovules that become the persimmons you buy at the store.

Evolutionary biologists are still trying to figure out the exact mechanisms that led to the evolution of separate sexes. A good place to start is to imagine that increased specialization toward one sex or the other resulted in increased efficiency:

- ✓ A hermaphrodite has to produce both types of sexual organs, whereas a single-sex individual needs to produce only one set of reproductive organs and can devote the saved resources to additional reproduction.

- ✓ A single-sex individual can specialize in one particular task, such as finding resources to produce eggs, whereas the other sex can specialize in finding mates.

One girl for every boy

Because one male is able to fertilize many females, the species will reproduce faster if a higher proportion of females is produced. So the obvious question is "Why not make fewer males?" The reason is one of the key principles of evolution.

Evolution acts most strongly at the level of the individual. The individual isn't concerned with the fate of the population's genes; it's concerned with the fate of its own genes.

An individual's genes are passed down through the generations in this way:

- ✓ First, the individual makes children.
- ✓ Then these children make grandchildren.

The 50-50 sex ratio makes sense when you think about the grandchild generation in the following way. Each grandchild has exactly one mother and one father. When the sex ratio of the children is exactly 50-50, the two sexes have identical fitness. If the sex ratio of the children changes, the fitness of the two sexes is no longer balanced.

Imagine a mutation that changes the sex ratio of the children in favor of the production of females. Now more of the children are female than male. As a consequence, the smaller number of males will average more grandchildren than will the more numerous females. Due to the shortage of males, these males end up producing offspring with multiple females. By producing more children, the male offspring has greater fitness. Because of the bias in the sex ratio, they're in a better position to get their genes into the next generation. If there is a mutation that favors producing more males, it will increase until the sex ratio is again 50-50 and the two sexes have identical fitness.

Changing sexes: Sequential hermaphrodites

An interesting example of the trade-offs inherent in being different sexes is the special case of *sequential hermaphrodites:* species that began life as one sex but then changed into the other sex. In some species, these organisms start out as females and change to males; in other species, they start out as males and change to females. This lifestyle appears in several fish species.

In the case of female-to-male, these species have mating systems whereby males compete for access to females. Large males are more successful than small males and, perhaps as a result of this selection, have favored a system in which small fish avoid being males. All the fish are born females. They mature, mate with the larger males, and reproduce. When they become large enough to compete for mates as males, they simply change sex. Voilà! They grow male sex organs (female organs get reabsorbed) and begin battling to fertilize eggs.

Whenever the sex ratio deviates from 50-50, the rare sex has a fitness advantage, and selection responds by favoring individuals that produce more of the rare sex until the numbers balance out again. As a result, the sex ratio never strays very far from 50-50.

'Sex' in Bacteria

To spice things up a bit, I decided to end this chapter with a brief section on sex in bacteria. In this case, I'm talking about sex in the sense of genetic reassortment — that is, the combining of genetic material from different individuals.

Bacteria don't need sex to reproduce. For the most part, they reproduce by dividing in half. One bacterium makes two bacteria; then these two make four, and so on. But occasionally, a bacterium acquires DNA from other bacteria and combines that DNA with its genome; henceforth, all its descendents have this new combination of genes.

Here are a few interesting tidbits about the product of bacterial sex:

✔ **Bacteria don't seem to be very picky about which bacteria they get the new genes from.** Some bacteria even absorb free DNA from the environment and incorporate these genes into their own genomes. This phenomenon is especially puzzling from a fitness perspective, because the free DNA has most likely come from bacteria that died and ruptured, releasing their genetic material into the environment. Because these particular bacteria died, it's not clear why other bacteria would want their genes.

✔ **Bacteria occasionally incorporate large numbers of genes from distantly related bacteria.** A trick like this wouldn't even be possible for most organisms, because even if they had a way to transfer some of the genes — from a pine tree to a duck, for example — the resulting combination wouldn't actually be functional. Most organisms have tightly interconnected sets of genes, and it's not possible to just splice into a genome a bunch of genes from some other organism and expect the resulting combination to work. You probably wouldn't end up with a functional organism.

Although scientists don't completely understand the selective forces that favor bacteria's ability to incorporate foreign genes, they have the tools to see its results. With the increase in the use of DNA sequencing — the technique that determines the specific sequence of an organism's DNA — scientists have discovered that the new genes the bacteria acquire often confer new function.

Take the common intestinal bacteria *E. coli.* You have some of it living in you right now. It keeps to itself and doesn't do you any harm. It's even possible that by taking up space, this particular strain of *E. coli* keeps more harmful bacteria from taking over your intestines.

But some strains of *E. coli* don't just sit quietly in your gut; they disrupt the intestinal walls and cause illness. *E. coli* O157:H7, commonly known as Jack in the Box *E. coli,* is one such strain, and it's an especially nasty one. The reason this particular *E. coli* strain causes illness is that it has picked up a variety of toxin-producing genes from other bacteria, including a large cluster from the bacterial species Shigella, which causes dysentery in humans and animals.

E. coli O157:H7 was first noticed in 1982, and the Centers for Disease Control and Prevention estimates that it causes approximately 73,000 cases of illness and 61 deaths in the United States each year.

Scientists don't have a clear understanding of what regulates bacterial sex. But at least in the case of E. coli O157:H6, the new combination of genes seems pretty good from the bacteria's perspective. O157:H7 has been extremely successful. Today, it can be found in most cattle farms and most petting zoos. So remember to wash your hands regularly!

Chapter 13

Co-evolution: The Evolution of Interacting Species

*C*o-evolution is what happens when a change in one species selects for a change in another species, and it's ridiculously cool because it makes for a lot of fascinating species interactions. When two species are evolving reciprocally, they end up with some really beautiful patterns and neat adaptations. I mean, think about it — cheetahs run ridiculously fast. Why? Because the antelope that they chase run really fast too. The existence of cheetahs selects for faster antelope, and those faster antelope select for faster cheetahs.

The cheetah-antelope scenario is an example of an *antagonist interaction,* in which one species is looking to eat the other one. Possibly even more beautiful are complicated examples of *mutualism,* in which, for example, plants with long curved flowers are pollinated by hummingbirds with long curved beaks — beaks that are curved to match the curved flowers exactly!

But even beyond how amazing all these interactions are, co-evolution serves as a nice reminder that evolution is always about your own fitness, not somebody else's.

Co-evolution Defined

Co-evolution is what happens when interacting species evolve together. A change in species A selects for a change in species B, which then selects for another change in species A, which in turn selects for another change in species B . . . and so on and so forth, ad infinitum.

For co-evolution to occur, the interacting species must affect each other's survival and reproduction — in other words, their fitness. The antelope affects the cheetah when it avoids being eaten; the cheetah affects the antelope when it eats it. By running away, antelope affect which cheetah genes end up in the next population (hint: the fast ones). Cheetahs affect which antelope genes end up in the next population (yep, the genes for fastness).

Having said that, I ask you to keep in mind that the strength of these interactions doesn't have to be equal. A cheetah that just misses an antelope misses lunch; it might get one tomorrow. An antelope that just misses getting away *is* lunch; it has no tomorrows. Hence, the selection on antelope by cheetahs may be a little stronger than the selection on cheetahs by antelope.

The following sections explain the types of interactions that co-evolving species can have and the outcomes that co-evolution can result in. The remaining sections of this chapter offer examples of co-evolution in nature and in the laboratory.

Co-evolution and species interactions

Co-evolution requires that two or more species interact such that they evolve in response to each other. Sometimes, these interactions are beneficial to both parties, sometimes they're beneficial to just one and bad for the other, and sometimes they're bad for both.

The following sections explain the main categories of species' interactions.

Although these discussions focus on pairs of species, co-evolution can involve interactions among more than two species. The relationship categories remain the same, regardless of how many organisms are co-evolving, even though any one species may be interacting with other species in a variety of different ways (like trying to eat some and not get eaten by others).

Mutualism: You scratch my back; I'll scratch yours

In a mutualistic interaction, the presence of each species has a positive effect on the other. Bees and flowers, for example, can co-evolve mutualistically. Another example is the sea anemone and the clown fish. The clown fish hangs out (and even lays its eggs) around the poisonous tentacles of the anemone, but doesn't get stung. Why? Because of a combination of the clown fish's sting resistant mucus and the fact that the anemone doesn't mind it being there.

Every once in awhile the clown fish will leave the safety of the stinging tentacles and venture off into the surrounding waters where its bright colors make it visible to predatory fish. When the predatory fish attacks, the clown fish

Commensalism

For co-evolution to occur, both species have to be affected. For that reason, commensalism — in which the interaction affects only one of the partners, not both — isn't really an example of co-evolution, but it's still interesting.

In *commensal* interactions, one species receives a benefit, while the other remains unaffected. Little organisms that hitch rides on bigger ones or use them as places to live are examples.

No evidence exists that a turtle cares whether a little bit of algae grows on it, but the turtle gives the algae a nice place to live. But if being on a turtle is an important part of algal ecology, there might be selection favoring algae that better stick to turtles.

heads back into the anemone, the predator pursues, and the anemone eats the predator, leaving the scraps for the clown fish! Clown fish that lure prey into the anemone tentacles get more food for themselves while anemones that provide a safe haven for clown fish get more food, too. The participants are in it for themselves, but the result is a beautiful mutualistic interaction.

Here's a key point to keep in mind: The connotation of the term *mutualism* and the fact that both of the co-evolving species benefit may lead you to think that the species *intend* to help each other out. That is absolutely not the case. Each organism does what it does for its own benefit. The fact that it's also benefiting the other organism is irrelevant.

Competition: Unrest in the forest

In a competitive interaction, each species has a negative effect on the other. Take trees, for example. Why are trees tall, and why do they have trunks? The energy that trees convert from sunlight needs to travel all the way down to the roots, and the water from the roots needs to travel all the way up to the leaves, but the trunk is expensive to make and not the most efficient conveyor of nutrients or energy. It certainly seems that a more-efficient arrangement would be to have the leaves close to the water supply instead of many feet off the ground.

The answer is that trees have to fight for light — a key ingredient in their fitness. A tree can survive only if it's tall enough not to be overshadowed by the tree next to it. When you have to grow tall, a stem just won't cut it. You need something a bit more substantive — hence, the trunk. The next thing you know, all the trees have to make trunks; otherwise, they're overshadowed by the trunky trees next to them.

There's a limit to how tall a tree can grow, of course. This limit is determined by the amount of light that hits the forest where that particular tree grows, the amount of rain, and the soil condition and type. These factors limit how much energy a tree can devote to making trunks. Another limiting factor is wind, which may blow a tree down when the tree is too tall.

Predation and parasitism: I'm a giver; you're a taker

In both predation and parasitism, one species has a positive effect on the second species, but the second species has a negative effect on the first. Examples are predators and parasites. Antelope are good for cheetahs, but cheetahs are bad for antelope. Ditto a dog and its fleas.

The antelope-cheetah interaction is an example of predation. The dog-flea interaction is an example of parasitism. Whether the system is one or the other depends on whether the parasitic organism wants to eat all of you or some of you. In some parasitic interactions — such as deadly parasitic diseases, to which you succumb in the end — there's not much fitness difference being eaten by a cheetah or wasting away from a disease. You're dead either way. You can read about co-evolving disease organisms in "Diseased Systems: Parasitic Co-evolution," later in this chapter.

When the interactions change

As you think about co-evolution, keep in mind that these interactions aren't always completely fixed in nature. The type of co-evolution between species can change over time. Bees, for example, need nectar; flowers need pollinators. The two species co-evolve in a mutualism: Their interaction is mutually beneficial because when the bee takes the nectar, the flower gets pollinated.

Now imagine a mutation in bees that results in their boring holes in the side of flowers and sucking up the nectar. The system has gone from being mutually beneficial to being parasitic: One species benefits to the detriment of the

The pronghorn antelope

Evolution has an endless number of fascinating stories, and here's another one for your reading pleasure. The fastest land mammal in North America is the pronghorn antelope, which can outrun by a substantial margin absolutely everything that it might ever come across. Why on earth does it run so fast? How could natural selection have caused that speed if nothing is chasing this antelope?

Well, as it turns out, even though no cheetahs exist in North America today, plenty of cheetah fossils turn up on the continent. I can't say for sure that those fossil cheetahs used to chase pronghorns, but they did chase something, and they ran very fast (info gleaned from their bone structure being similar to that of modern cheetahs in Africa).

other. The flowers' nectar is gone, and no pollination has taken place because the bees aren't coming anywhere near where the pollen is or needs to be.

In response, natural selection will favor plants that keep the bees from getting the nectar. Selection may make the flower harder to chew through, in which case plants that happen to have thicker flowers are going to leave more descendents because they still have some nectar left in them to attract other pollinators. The process is still co-evolution, but a transition from one type of interaction to another has occurred.

Outcomes of co-evolution

In co-evolution, one organism evolves to its own benefit in response to the other organism. As one changes, the other changes. So what's the endpoint for all this change?

In antagonistic interactions, the end point could be that one organism eliminates the other. In mutualisms, the end point would be when there's no further selection for a tighter association. In the example of the long-flowered orchid and the long-tongued moth, unless something changes to make the association less or more beneficial for either organism, the flower's length and the moth's tongue are plenty long enough. Other times, the end point is just that an organism has reached the limits of how tall or fast or whatever it can be.

The Red Queen

One possible outcome is a scenario referred to as the Red Queen hypothesis. The expression comes from *Alice in Wonderland,* in which the queen runs in place but doesn't get anywhere.

In the Red Queen scenario, species that co-evolve essentially run in place. You can find lots of examples in the co-evolution of plants and insects. When a plant evolves a novel chemical defense mechanism, for example, it drives the insects to evolve a novel detoxification mechanism. You can also see the Red Queen scenario in the fossil record. Fossil evidence shows steady advances in characteristics such as shell thickness and brain size in predators and prey.

You can think of co-evolution acting this way if you imagine it in the context of an arms race. To give itself an edge, each side evolves new or better adaptations, which the other side counteracts as it adapts in response. At the start of WWI, for example, pilots shot at each other from the cockpit with pistols. Frightfully fearsome — until somebody strapped a whole machine gun to the front of a plane. Reciprocal adaptations of this sort took aircraft from the wood-and-fabric aeroplanes that the Red Baron flew over the fields of France to the carbon-fiber-and-titanium jets that fighter pilots "strap on" today. Where does that leave the respective air forces? Traveling faster than the speed of sound but not really much ahead of the other guy.

Extinction

Another possible outcome of co-evolution is that one of the participants can't keep up and goes extinct. Obviously, scientists don't see these systems, because one of the participants no longer exists, but they know from the fossil record that extinction is a common phenomenon. Lots of organisms that used to be around just couldn't keep up.

A little stability

Yet another possible outcome is that the process leads to some, at least temporarily, stable end point. An example would be cheetahs and antelope whizzing across the plains of Africa at 65 miles an hour. Given the physics of the mammalian body plan, animals are unlikely to evolve to run at the speed of sound. The cheetah is at the current upper limit of animal land mammal speed. (Scientists don't know how much faster an animal could run, but they know that some upper limit must exist.)

Interactions between Plants and Animals

Some of the best examples of co-evolution involve interactions among plants, animals, and insects. These interactions revolve around:

- ✔ **Sex (more specifically, reproduction through pollination or seed dispersal):** Plant reproduction relies on getting pollinated or sowing seeds. The flowers of some plants, for example, require particular pollinators; not just any animal or insect will do. In this case, the co-evolutionary pair — the plant and the specific pollinator — evolve to maximize their own fitness, each trying to get more of what's good for it from the other.

  Other plants don't require a specific pollinator; they share pollinators with other plants. In these cases, the plant species have to compete, so natural selection favors traits that make each species better than the other at attracting pollinators.

- ✔ **Protection in exchange for room and board:** In some systems, plants provide food and shelter to insects in return for the protection that the insects provide.

Although these instances certainly aren't the only examples of co-evolution, they offer a good glimpse of the way interactions among species can influence the characteristics that the species evolve. Also, they let me write about a moth that has a 10-inch-long tongue.

Pollination wars

Pollination involves plants and often insects. (Forget pollination by other animals — such as birds and bats — and wind for now; those situations aren't important in this discussion.) Each species has a vested interest in getting what it needs. The plant, for example, is trying to get its pollen to (or get pollen from) another plant of the same species. To do that, the plant needs to spend effort and resources on attracting pollinators. It has absolutely no interest in helping its pollinator unless, by doing so, it helps itself. For its part, the insect (or pollinator) cares nothing about whether the plant gets pollinated; it's after the reward offered, or promised, by the plant.

Ideally, plants want a pollinator that's very *species-specific* — that is, attracted only to plants of the same species. After all, what good is a pollinator that dumps your pollen on incompatible plants? With a species-specific pollinator, the plant would be assured that its pollen would go to an individual of the same species.

Consider the orchid species that has nectar 10 inches down in a very long, thin flower. Based on his study of this orchid, Charles Darwin predicted that the pollinator would be a moth with a 10-inch tongue. At the time, no one had ever seen a moth with a tongue that long, and people considered his idea to be pretty ridiculous. But 40 years after Darwin's prediction, exactly such a moth was found — and whaddya know, it turned out to be the pollinator of this particular orchid. In honor of Darwin's prediction, the moth was named *Xanthopan morgani subspecies praedicta,* just barely beating out *Darwin-He's-the-Man Moth.*

The example of the moth with the long tongue shows the benefits of a tight association between the two mutualists. The orchid gets its pollen delivered only to its own species while the moth gets access to resources that the shorter tongued moths can't reach. But there are also potential downsides to being involved in such a tight interaction:

- ✔ If one of the partners is absent, then the other is out of luck. And if one species should go extinct, the other one might not be far behind.

- ✔ It reduces the probability of dispersal to new environments. Imagine an orchid seed carried on the wind to a remote island. The soil's just right, the temperature is perfect, and lots of other plants are doing just fine. But that orchid had better hope that some of those moths get blown over to the island too! Because if none do, then that wandering orchid is doomed.

The evolution of pollination by animals

How animal pollination evolved in the first place is fun to think about. Pollination by animals has been an incredibly successful strategy for plants. Not that wind pollination doesn't work, but it has its disadvantages, first of which is the fact that the plant has to make a huge amount of pollen, because most of it isn't going to get anywhere near the target.

An interesting feature of wind pollination is that the plant needs to be able to snatch the pollen from the air. Toward this end, some plants have developed sticky fluids that assist in pollen capture. Some scientists envision that animal pollination arose when insects or other animals fed on these plant secretions and, as a result, moved pollen from one plant to another.

Figs and wasps: I couldn't live without you, baby

One of the classic examples of a mutualistic interaction is that between figs and the wasps that pollinate them.

The fig's reproductive structure is complicated. The flowering portion of the fig is a hollow structure with male flowers on the outside and female flowers, which produce seeds, on the inside (which is called the *syconium,* but I'm guessing that you don't care!). Here's what happens:

1. A female wasp arrives at one of these structures and gathers pollen. She then enters and deposits pollen on the female flowers within and also deposits an egg in each of the ovules that she can reach. Then she dies.

2. The eggs hatch; the larvae feed on the developing seeds; the larvae pupate; and adult wasps emerge.

3. The males mate with females and chew a hole through which the females depart. The male promptly dies; lacking wings, he wasn't going anywhere anyway.

So how is it good for the plant to have eggs dumped inside it, its developing seeds eaten, and a hole chewed through it? As it turns out, the female flowers on the inside are different lengths. Some are too long for the wasp to reach down and deposit an egg on. As a result, some seeds escape predation by the developing wasps. So the wasp gets food for her offspring, and the fig gets a very reliable pollinator.

Even though in this case the plant and the insect are completely reliant on each other for survival, each species is acting in its own interests. The fig wasps don't pollinate the fig tree because they care about the fig; they do it because their offspring will feast on the developing seeds. And successful fig trees are the ones that produce seeds above and beyond the ones that get eaten. The wasp uses the fig; the fig uses the wasp; and the species are so tightly co-evolved that each would go extinct without the other (what scientists term an *obligate mutualism*) because each species of wasp pollinates only a single species of fig, and vice versa. But they're still not pals!

Oh, and if you've been keeping track of the dead wasps, you've noted that every time you eat a fig, you're eating a few dead wasps, too. Don't worry, though; they're very tiny — small enough to fit through the eye of a needle.

Your cheatin' heart: Non-mutualism pollinators

Some plants don't play fair. They cheat to get what they want and leave the poor, gullible insects no better off for their trouble. Basically, the plant tricks the pollinator into visiting the flower with the promise of a good time or a good meal and then doesn't pay up. As you can imagine, the interactions between these plants and their unsuspecting pollinators are not mutualistic; one of the partners is coming out behind. In these cases, co-evolution acts to make the plant better at deceiving the pollinator and the pollinator better at not being deceived.

A couple of examples:

- ✔ Some plants have flowers that smell like rotting meat. These flowers are pollinated by flies and beetles that arrive expecting to find a carcass. Instead, they end up getting a dusting of the flower's pollen, which they deposit the next time they make the same mistake.

- ✔ Several species of orchids have evolved the ability to attract male insects by mimicking the sex pheromones, and sometimes the shape, of the female insect. Imagining what happens in this case is easy: The male insect pounces on the orchid and makes a really good attempt at mating with the flower, getting covered with pollen in the process. In the end, he gives up because the process just isn't going very well and flies off to find a different female. But he may end up on another orchid and transfer the pollen that he picked up on the first orchid.

  Don't blame the poor male insects for being clueless. The compounds that the female insects use to attract males are actually very similar chemically to the waxy substances that the orchid uses to avoid drying out. You can easily imagine how at some point, one or a few mutations resulted in an orchid that smelled good in a whole different way.

Parasitic non-pollinators

Just as some plants avoid giving a reward, some animals take the reward but don't provide any pollination services. Think back to the 10-inch-long flower. Many flowers have deep (though not quite so extreme) nectar sources, which make them inaccessible to insects with short proboscises.

Some insects have developed a clever solution to this problem: They just hold the base of the flower, chew a hole, and slurp out the nectar, never getting anywhere near the pollen. In this case, the insect is a parasite of the flower. As the species co-evolve, the plant species is selected to have less-chewable flowers, and the insect is selected to be better able to chew its way to the nectar.

Sharing pollinators

Plants that share pollinators have to compete to attract them. This competition among plants introduces another place for selection to operate. Plants that rely on the same pollinators, for example, will be selected to flower at different times.

By flowering in a narrow window of time, a plant increases the chance that its pollen will go to an individual of the same species. Similarly, a species of plant that flowers at a time when other species don't has better access to pollinators and, as a result, is more likely to leave descendents.

Seed dispersal

If seeds are light and small, they can be dispersed by wind. The problem with this system is that the plant has to make a lot of seeds, because most of them end up in the wrong place.

Having an animal disperse your seeds can solve this problem, though it may introduce others (the animal might eat your seeds). Animals can move larger seeds, and they provide a bit more specificity in where the seeds end up. If a particular bird is eating a particular fruit, that bird is known to visit places where that particular kind of plant can grow and may end up depositing the seeds in a similar habitat. This system is how mistletoe seeds get dispersed. Mistletoe is a parasitic plant that grows on other plants. Mistletoe fruit is eaten and the seeds dispersed by perching birds, which conveniently deposit the seeds right onto another potential host plant. The fruit is the lure that gets the birds to eat the seed.

Not all relationships that result in seed dispersal are mutualisms, of course. Some plants are very good at getting animals to disperse their seeds without giving any reward. If you've ever had to pull seeds out of your socks or off your dog after a hike, you know exactly what I'm talking about. Some plants have evolved quite clever mechanisms that allow their seeds to be attached to animals.

Not all seed or fruit eaters disperse the seeds; some just digest those as well, setting up another co-evolutionary interaction that has resulted in plants producing seeds with toxins and animals developing the ability to cope with these toxins.

Trading food and shelter for defense

This mutualism is my favorite one, occurring between the bullthorn acacia (*Acacia cornigera*) and the ant *Pseudomyrmex ferrugiea*.

The bullthorn acacia has large hollow thorns where ants live, and it produces nectar (not associated with flowers) and protein-rich structures that the ants eat. The ants patrol the plant and sting anything that tries to nibble or land on it, and they clear the ground under and around the plant, killing any plants that might compete with the host acacia.

Not such a big deal, right? Wrong. The bullthorn acacia is unusual. Other acacias don't produce extrafloral nectaries; they don't produce the protein structures, which have no known function other than to feed the ants; and they're poisonous, producing chemicals to defend against herbivores. The bullthorn acacia doesn't have these characteristics because it doesn't need them; it has the ants instead.

And let me tell you, these ants really hurt when they sting. I know because I checked — personally. And I'm not the only person who thinks so. The Schmidt Sting Pain Index — yes, there really is one; you can see for yourself by going to `http://scientiaestpotentia.blogspot.com/2006/06/schmidt-sting-pain-index.html` — rates them at 1.8 (a bald-faced hornet gets a 2) and describes the pain as "A rare, piercing, elevated sort of pain. Someone has fired a staple into your cheek." Someone there must have been stung, too, which just goes to prove the lengths to which scientists will go to collect data.

Disease Systems: Parasitic Co-evolution

In host-parasite systems — specifically, disease systems — one member of the co-evolving pair preys on the other. In such a system, scientists expect the host to evolve increased resistance to the parasite. All things being equal, being resistant must always be better.

So how should scientists expect the disease organism to evolve? A common misconception is that selection will cause the disease organism to evolve in a way that's less harmful to its host. The rationale: Because the disease organism needs the host, it should be nice (i.e., less virulent) to it. (*Virulence* refers to the fitness decrease that results from infection with a particular disease. A disease that kills you right away has a high virulence; if it just gives you the sniffles, and you can still make it to the office, it has a low virulence.)

But that's not the way it works. To a disease organism, maximum fitness isn't just about surviving; it's also about spreading to other hosts. Therefore, evolution selects for whatever virulence level makes the disease more effectively transmitted. A disease will become highly virulent, for example, when high virulence increases its fitness even as it decreases its host's fitness.

The specific virulence that maximizes fitness varies from organism to organism, based on how the disease is transmitted. This point is key. No one "right" level of virulence exists. The common cold won't be more fit if it kills me before I can make it to school, but when I'm at school, it's more fit if it makes me cough on someone else.

Bunnies in the Outback

Australia didn't have any native rabbits. A few were introduced in the mid-1800s, and by the mid-1900s, Australia had half a billion. That's a lot of rabbits. In 1950, the myxoma virus was introduced to control the rabbit population. The virus, which had an extremely high fatality rate, was very effective. But soon after it was introduced, the virus evolved to be less virulent.

Here's why: The virus was spread from rabbit to rabbit via mosquitoes, which bit infected rabbits and transferred the virus to uninfected rabbits. It just so happened that if the host rabbits had survived longer, a greater chance existed that a mosquito would bite an infected rabbit and transfer the virus to a new host.

That being the case, you'd think that the virus would eventually evolve extremely low virulence to maximize the opportunity for transmission. But this didn't happen either, because mosquito transmission is maximized if the rabbit is covered with virus-filled lesions on which mosquitoes can feed. (If that situation sounds like it's bad for the rabbit, that's because it is.)

The myxoma virus needs a certain level of virulence to be transmitted to a new host. It's not good for the virus to kill its host immediately or to float around in the bloodstream relatively harmlessly. But it *is* good for the virus if the host is covered with lesions.

The rabbit population wasn't taking this virus lying down; it was evolving to be more resistant to the virus. As the rabbit population became more resistant, the virus population evolved increased virulence to maintain maximum mosquito transmissibility.

Scientists know all these things because the original rabbits (from places other than Australia that had never been exposed to the myxoma virus) and the original virus were still available for study. Using the original virus, scientists showed that the rabbits living in Australia evolved increased resistance. Using the original rabbit population, scientists showed that the virulence of the virus in the Australian rabbit population first decreased but then increased in concert with the increased resistance of the host rabbit population. So there you have it — a classic example of host-disease co-evolution in a natural setting.

Disease-host interaction in the lab

In trying to understand disease-host interaction, Sharon Messenger, Ian Molineux, and J.J. Bull conducted an experiment to examine how different viral transfer mechanisms affect the relative advantage of different levels of viral virulence. The two basic types of transfer mechanisms are

- ✔ **Vertical:** Transmission from parent to descendent (essentially, transmission through time)
- ✔ **Horizontal:** Transmission from one individual to the next in the current time

What they discovered is that when many hosts are available, a virus that harms its host but increases the chance that its progeny will infect new hosts is favored. But when few hosts are available (that is, a reduced chance of horizontal transfer exists), selection favors a virus that's less harmful to its host, because only through the host's survival and reproduction can the virus survive and reproduce.

The experiment used bacteria and a virus that infects the bacteria. The experiment first selected for different varieties of the virus that had a range of effects on host growth rate. More-benevolent strains had a small effect on host growth rate but couldn't be transmitted horizontally, and less-benevolent strains had a larger effect on host growth rate and could be transmitted horizontally. This part of the experiment generated a variable virus population. After the experimenters had variation of exactly the sort that interested them in their virus population, they were able to set up different experimental scenarios to see when the different viral variants would have higher fitness.

Taking a 50-50 mixture of bacteria infected with the two viral types, the scientists grew them in the presence or absence of additional bacteria that either were or weren't susceptible to infection. After allowing time for viral and bacterial reproduction, they assessed the relative proportion of the two viral types at the end of the experiment. As predicted, in the absence of an opportunity for horizontal transfer, lower virulence was selectively favored. In the presence of available susceptible host bacteria, the less-benevolent viral strain was favored even though it was more harmful to its host.

Chapter 14

Evo-Devo: The Evolution of Development

A species with one particular form can give rise to a species with another form. Take humans and fruit flies, for example. They have a common ancestor somewhere in the distant past. This common ancestor gave rise to two very different organisms. The question is how. What process is at work that results in such different creatures?

The answer has to do with the interplay between evolution and development, which is one of the hottest areas of current evolutionary research and one in which today's scientists are able to learn lots of things that people back in Charles Darwin's time didn't have a clue about.

This chapter talks primarily about the development of animals because animal development is for the most part *deterministic* — that is, all the members of the species end up looking pretty much identical, at least structurally. Humans have two arms, two legs, one heart, one head, and so on, and all these parts need to be in the right places. Compare this structure with that of a maple tree; branches can go every which way, and their reproductive structures (flowers) can be all over the place. Lop off one of the branches, and another one may grow and produce its own flowers — definitely not the way that human structures work! All this doesn't mean that plants don't have development; they're just a little bit more free-form about it.

Defining Development: From Embryo to Adult

Development, in evolutionary terms, refers to the process by which a fertilized egg develops into the adult form.

By *adult form,* I don't mean that the organism has reached the age of majority and is heading off to college — or, for that matter, has reached sexual maturity and is getting ready to set up its own pride on the Serengeti. In evolutionary terms, development ends when the organism has all its parts, that is, when it has its final shape. In this context, *adult* doesn't mean *grown up.*

The time frame for development differs for each organism, but the process starts with a single cell, which develops as a result of

- *✔* **Cell division:** The process whereby one cell splits into two, two into four, four into eight, and so on.

- *✔* **Differentiation:** The process whereby one lineage of cells gives rise to different types of cells of another lineage, such as a skin cell or a heart-muscle cell, or any number of other types of cells.

The *embryo stage* starts with the first cell division and goes until the organism has all its adult parts. This stage doesn't end at birth (most animals aren't born, but develop from eggs outside the mother) but at some time before birth, when all the parts that will be recognizable in the adult organism have formed. The organism has legs, eyes, all the various internal organ systems, and so on. As you can imagine in complex organisms such as mammals, pinning down exactly when the embryo stage ends is difficult. The key is that you know it when you see it: The developing embryo looks like a little version of the adult organism.

Humans have a lot more names for various stages of development. In human reproduction, you hear the terms *zygote* (to refer to the fertilized egg), *embryo* (to mean any stage of development before birth or the particular early stage of development), *fetus* (to refer to later developmental stages), and *pain in the keister* (to refer to the teenage years). Don't let these alternative uses confuse you. In this chapter, the term *embryo* refers to the developmental stage from the first cell division to the formation of all the adult parts.

Under construction: The development process in action

Starting from a single cell, the embryo divides and grows. As this growth progresses, different lineages of cells become specialized to perform different tasks. All the cells in the organism contain the same DNA — the same instructions, but the instructions are expressed differently in the different cells. In this way, the various structures of the organism develop.

From initial populations of cells that haven't yet specialized (called *pluripotent cells*) and that can transition into any cell type, specific cell lineages are derived. These pluripotent cells are called *embryonic stem cells.* Some will give rise to skin cells, others to bone cells, and so on.

After cells have transitioned to specific cell types, the lineage's future appears to be fixed. Skin cells divide to produce other skin cells, for example; they can't make other types of cells. Liver cells grow, divide, and go on to form the liver; they don't go popping up in other parts of the body.

Scientists have made great strides in understanding how this process works, and I go into some of the details in the next sections. But for now, keep two things in mind:

- ✔ Starting from cells with exactly the same DNA, it's possible to obtain cells of very many types. One component of the development process is the mechanism by which this differentiation occurs.

- ✔ To make an organism, the different cell types have to develop in the correct place. The spatial patterning within the developing embryo is a key to creating a viable organism. (The liver needs to develop in the abdomen, for example, not in the skull!)

The effect of environment

An organism's *phenotype* (physical characteristics) is a result of the interaction between its *genotype* (genetic makeup) and the environment. A person with the genetic potential to be 7 feet tall won't achieve that height in the absence of proper diet, for example. A malnourished person will be stunted compared with a genetically identical individual who was well fed. The impact of the environment on the developing organism is called *environmental effects,* and one way that the environment can affect phenotype is by affecting development. (You can read more about what affects phenotype in Chapters 4 and 7.)

The following sections highlight examples of environmental effects. Here's the take-home message: Small changes in the regulation of development in genetically similar individuals can have major effects.

The development of queen vs. worker bees

A beehive consists of at least one queen bee who lays the eggs, a larger number of worker bees who tend the eggs, and developing larvae. The queen and worker bees look very different. The most noticeable difference is the size of the queen: she's much larger than the workers. Yet the size difference isn't the result of different genes.

Whether an egg develops into a queen or into a worker bee depends on its environment within the hive, specifically whether it's fed exclusively royal jelly for the first days of its life. Royal jelly is a substance produced by special glands of worker bees and fed to all larvae. An all-royal-jelly diet equals a new queen.

The existence of different castes in bees (and in other social *hymenoptera* — a class of insects that includes ants and wasps) offers a nice example of how changes in the path of development can result in organisms with different body forms. We know that any female bee can become a worker or a queen — the final form isn't based on differences at the DNA sequence level but instead on differences in how those genes are expressed.

Researchers can look at patterns of gene expression in developing bees and figure out exactly which genes are regulated differently in queens versus workers. Queens develop from eggs that experience an increase in the production of metabolic enzymes and that regulate the genes associated with hormonal activity differently.

The Thrifty Phenotype hypothesis: Genes for flexibility

For mammals, the embryo develops within the mother; therefore, the maternal environment influences development. Because one major component of the maternal environment is how well nourished Mom is, embryonic development may respond to changes in maternal nutrition — a position that medical evidence seems to support.

Medical evidence indicates that a fetus deprived of nutrition during key parts of development will develop into a baby with a greater degree of *metabolic thriftiness,* a group of characteristics that reduce caloric requirements (smaller size and lower metabolism, for example).

Some scientists postulate that these fetal changes may be the result of natural selection; genes that allow a developing human embryo to better prepare for existence outside the mother will be selectively favored. This hypothesis is called the *Thrifty Phenotype hypothesis,* and it goes something like this: Some of the fetal developmental changes observed in low-birth-weight babies may have been adaptive early in human history. If the mother's condition predicted low food availability when the baby was born (for example, she was deprived of food during pregnancy), genes that allowed for developmental flexibility — like growing slowly, but more efficiently, when food is scarce — may be selectively advantageous.

From an evolutionary viewpoint, what the fetus would be responding to is unclear. The condition of the mother could correlate with any of the following:

- ✔ The environment in which the mother was living
- ✔ The mother's ability to provide resources
- ✔ The environment in which the adult offspring would find itself as predicted by the mother's environment (in those situations in which the environment changes slowly over a time scale longer than the organism's generation time)

But the jury's still out on whether natural selection had anything to do with the fact that human embryos may develop differently when maternal resources are scarce. At this point, the Thrifty Phenotype hypothesis is pure speculation (often the first part of scientific inquiry). What's not speculation is that embryonic developmental changes do occur, which unfortunately are related to other medical problems, such as diabetes and obesity, so being able to identify the cause and the mechanism by which the development pathway is altered is medically important.

The thrifty phenotype hypothesis postulates genes for *plasticity,* genes that allow the developing fetus to develop to be more or less thrifty based on the maternal environment. This hypothesis is different from the *thrifty genotype hypothesis,* which states that natural selection for particular genes in some human populations makes these individuals more metabolically efficient. This theory has been implicated in diseases among Native Americans who are now subjected to the modern American diet.

Little changes mean a lot

Given that environmental factors can alter developmental trajectories (think queen bee), it's not surprising that changes in the DNA sequence of developmental genes will do so as well. In fact, as you probably can guess, small changes in developmental genes can have tremendous impact on the adult organism. Take flies that have grown legs where their eyes should be (see Figure 14-1). This example is a little bit Frankenstein-like (and not too good for the poor fly that happened to have this mutation), but it's a wonderful example of a small change in development that has a big change in morphology.

Figure 14-1:
A mutant fly.

What the fly example shows is how small mutational changes in regulatory systems can influence the diversification of multi-cellular organisms. Scientists had been struggling to reconcile how the small mutations we see all the time — a DNA letter or two changed here, a few bases deleted there — could result in major changes in body plan. Now scientists know from laboratory evidence that tiny changes in DNA sequence can have major implications.

With the fly, scientists noticed the mutation and tried to figure out what had happened. What they discovered was that a single mutation in a gene that acts early in flies' larval development results in antennae where eyes should be. In other words, while this fly was still just an innocent little maggot, the pattern of development that resulted in the adult fly had already been determined.

A small change in a single gene involved in development can cause a large change in the final phenotype.

Key Ideas about Evo-Devo

As I'm fond of mentioning throughout this book, biology has come a long way since Darwin's day, and the field of developmental biology is another good example. Today, scientists are busy trying to figure out exactly how genes work; in Darwin's time, they were struggling just to understand what genes might be. Absent all the molecular techniques available today, it's no surprise that the study of embryology in the mid-1800s involved primarily the examination of embryos from different stages of development.

The following sections look at what early embryologists found — or, more accurately, what they *thought* they found — and explains what scientists know today.

Developmental stages = Evolutionary stages

According to biologist Ernst Haeckel (1834–1919), the developmental stages that an embryo passes through reveal the evolutionary history of the species. In other words — and brace yourself; it's a mouthful — the *ontogeny* (the developmental process) *recapitulates* (summarizes) *phylogeny* (the evolutionary history).

Haeckel saw in the various stages of mammalian development what he described as stages of development corresponding to specific ancestral species. At one point in their development, for example, human embryos have a tail-like structure, which was thought to signify tailed ancestors. Earlier developmental stages included pharyngeal arches, which were thought to resemble gill slits. This feature was taken to indicate that the developing human embryo passes through a fishlike stage.

Haeckel's investigations were conducted during a period when Darwin's theory of evolution by natural selection and the concept of the common ancestry of all life were stimulating a fair amount of research. The proposition that ontogeny recapitulates phylogeny was seen as being consistent with Darwinian theory, though it was difficult to understand why such a pattern would occur.

Today, scientists understand that the different stages a developing embryo goes through are in no way the equivalents of other species in the tree of life. There is no fish stage in mammalian development, for example. But humans do have structures that are *homologous to* (share the same ancestor with) structures that a fish has, and some of these structures are most evident at early embryological stages.

Two traits that are homologous have a common ancestor. The wings of birds, for example, are all homologous. All birds are descended from an initial bird ancestor. Go back farther, and you can see that the front limbs of all *tetrapods* (four-footed animals and the things descended from them — so whales and snakes are called tetrapods, too, as are humans) are homologous. Your arms, the wings of all birds, the front legs of crocodiles, and the front flippers of dolphins all trace back to the first tetrapod. Homologous characters can be similar in appearance, but they don't have to be. Contrast that with *analogous.* The wings of birds and the wings of butterflies are analogous. They have similar functions, but not as a result of having a common evolutionary ancestor. Insect wings are derived from very different parts than are the front limbs of ducks, for example.

Although Haeckel's idea that ontogeny recapitulates phylogeny turns out not to be true, he was right in thinking that embryology can tell scientists something about evolution. Today, 150 years later, scientists have a much better handle on what that something is.

Earlier vs. later stages

For related species, earlier stages of development are usually more similar than later stages. In the early stages of human and chimpanzee development, the fetuses are very similar, but as development proceeds, the developmental pathways diverge.

For a more detailed example, take crustaceans. Crustaceans include critters you've heard of, such as crabs, lobsters, and shrimp. But the group also contains some members that aren't immediately recognizable as being related to crabs and lobsters. Perhaps the best example is the barnacle. Barnacles, believe it or not, are really quite like lobsters. Although an adult lobster (mmm, mmm, good) is quite a bit different from an adult barnacle (not delicious at all), the early larval stages are extremely similar.

In the early stages of development, the different members of a group are extremely similar, but as development proceeds, the specific adult features of each group are expressed. From this fact, researchers discovered that much of the diversification in body structure within the crustacean group results from developmental shifts later in development.

It's all in the timing

Haeckel was a clever guy, and although he didn't quite hit the nail on the head with ontogeny recapitulating phylogeny, he did recognize the importance of developmental timing in differences among species. Developmental timing is also important within the same species, with small changes during the embryonic level having dramatic effects at the adult level.

The fancy word for a change in developmental timing is *heterochrony,* which includes any of the following:

✔ A change in the start or end of a developmental stage

✔ A change in the rate of a process

✔ The loss of the developmental stage

Human babies

If you like watching nature shows on TV, you've probably seen films of animals being born. The newborn tiger/wildebeest/whatever shakes itself off, stumbles to its feet, and trots along after Mom. If you've had children of your own, you probably noticed that your newborn didn't do that, even though the newborns of all our closest relatives — chimpanzees, gorillas, and so on — are reasonably mobile from day one. Humans are the branch of the primate family tree in which something changed.

To make a long story short, human babies are born before their heads are finished developing. (If you've had a baby pass through your birth canal, you might realize that a malleable skull made delivery easier; if it still didn't seem like a stroll through the park, remember that evolution often involves compromises!) The human child's head and brain continue to develop and grow after birth. This process of juvenile traits persisting later in development is called *neoteny*.

The Mexican salamander

In a more-extreme form of neoteny, development doesn't progress past the larval stage. One example is the Mexican salamander *Ambystoma mexicanum*, a species that's currently endangered because it lives in a single Mexican lake that's been heavily affected by human activities.

Salamanders typically progress from an aquatic larval stage to a terrestrial stage, but the Mexican salamander doesn't pass beyond the aquatic stage. The gonads mature, but the rest of the body keeps its larval form. It appears that this form originated through mutation in a thyroid hormone, and individuals can be made to change into a form more typical of adult salamanders if you give them hormone injections. A small mutation results in a dramatic shift in development — in the case of this particular salamander species, resulting in an adult that is entirely aquatic.

These salamanders have a couple of interesting features:

✔ **They have enhanced regenerative abilities.** They're able to manufacture replacement body parts to a degree much greater than that of salamanders that reach the terrestrial stage. In fact, if they're forced to metamorphose to the typical adult form via thyroid hormone injections, they lose this regenerative ability. It's the typical "Do I want great power or good looks?" dilemma. Unfortunately, these little critters don't get to decide for themselves. Why? Read on.

✔ **They're not uncommon pets in America.** You'd be surprised at the number of parents who let their kids have creatures with fully mature gonads in a larval body that's able to regenerate larval parts as necessary.

The Caribbean tree frog

You'd think that mutations that prevent development from progressing to the next stage or that eliminate a stage are not good. Interestingly enough, the resulting mutants sometimes survive. In the case of one Caribbean tree frog, they do very well indeed.

When you think of the developmental stages of frogs, you probably think of tadpoles. Well, the Caribbean tree frog *Eleutherodactylus coqui* is a frog with no tadpoles; its developmental pathway has lost the tadpole stage. Eggs develop directly into very tiny frogs.

As a result of this developmental shift, the species is able to live in areas without bodies of water, which tadpoles require for development. These frogs can live in trees, and they colonize mountainous regions where ponds are rare.

Here's an interesting tidbit about these frogs: They've unfortunately and accidentally been introduced into Hawaii, where they're doing extremely well. Hawaii has so many Caribbean tree frogs, in fact, and their calls are so loud that people are reportedly being kept awake! (People who finally do get to sleep are generally awakened again by the thousands of introduced wild chickens — which, on the island of Kauai, have no natural predators, but that's a story for another day.)

Why any of this is important

The evolution of development is still a young area of evolutionary biology, but it's already extremely important. Understanding the interaction between evolution and development can help scientists figure out the following:

✔ **How specific developmental processes affect the outcome of natural selection.** When researchers know how processes work, they can understand the kinds of changes expected to result from random mutations.

✔ **How the developmental process itself evolves.** The genes that are responsible for determining body pattern, called the *Hox genes* (see the later section "Genes Responsible for Development: Hox Genes"), are slightly different from one class of organism to another. Hox genes of mammals differ from the Hox genes of insects, indicating that the machinery itself is evolving.

✔ **How the great diversity of animals on Earth could have evolved from a common ancestor.** DNA sequence data has allowed researchers to refine the picture of the tree of life and the details of the branching process, but DNA sequence information by itself does not explain how so many varied body plans can have arisen from a common ancestor. Knowledge of developmental controls, as well as laboratory experiments showing how small changes in developmental genes result in large changes in animal body plan (think multi-headed jellyfish), are giving scientists this understanding.

Genes Responsible for Development: Hox Genes

Certain genes are responsible for some major aspects of animal development. One of the most important discoveries in developmental biology (or in evolutionary biology, biology in general, and medicine, for that matter) is a set of genes called the *Hox genes*. These genes are responsible for the determination of body pattern — a sort of design plan for items such as where the legs go and where the head should be. Pretty important stuff! In effect, these genes control the process whereby the embryo is divided into segments, and then they determine the specific fates of different segments.

The initial research on Hox genes involved a fruit fly, *Drosophila*. Like other arthropods (invertebrates such as spiders, crustaceans, and insects), the fruit fly is made up of a series of segments, some that are the same and some that are different.

If you know what a millipede looks like, you're familiar with an arthropod with a lot of segments that are all pretty much the same. After the head each segment has two pairs of legs — a very simple design and the fossil record tells us that millipedes are a very ancient group of land animals.

Now consider a fly or other insect. The segments are more differentiated:

✔ **Head segments:** This is where . . . well, where the head is. What can I say?

✔ **Thoracic segments:** The thoracic segment includes the internal organs. It's also where the legs are.

✔ **Abdominal segments:** No legs, but this is where the reproductive structures are.

For an up-close-and-personal look at sections, treat yourself by performing a tasty and very informative dissection of a lobster. Find the head and thoracic segments, and then the repeating segments of the tail/abdomen, which are delectable! Note that seeing the segments in the thorax is easier if you take it apart a little bit — externally the thoracic segments are fused together. Not much *in* the lobster thorax is edible (although some people swear that the liver is a delicacy), but it offers a lot of good biology. Lobsters aren't cheap, of course, so it's important that you get the most for your dollar. Education is priceless!

You may be thinking, "Whoa! How can the mammalian body plan be organized by the same family of genes that organized the arthropod body plan, especially when the human body lacks all those repeating segments?" Consider your backbone. It's a structure of repeating segments (all those vertebrae). And at particular points along your spinal column, you have other structures, such as arms and legs.

Keeping it in the family

As stated previously, Hox genes are the family of genes that control development of body plan. They determine how different areas of the developing embryo become different body parts: where does the head go, where do the legs go — that sort of thing.

The Hox genes are responsible for body patterning in most animals. Even though different animals look completely different, the underlying genes are clearly related. You have them, a mouse has them, a fly has them. Although humans are extremely different from fruit flies, the genes responsible for body patterning are identifiable in both species. The copies in mammals are different from the ones in flies, but not so different in DNA sequence that scientists can't see their common origin in a distant ancestor.

A fly and a mouse have similar Hox genes, for example, but they don't have exactly the same collection of these genes; the exact sequences are different. Also, Hox genes can become duplicated just as can other genes in the imperfect DNA replication process, so different animals have different numbers of Hox genes. Looking across different animals, scientists see cases where some animals have several copies a very similar Hox genes — evidence of past gene duplications — while others will have a different number of copies of related genes.

The fact that the genes for body patterning would be recognizably similar across such different animals was quite a revelation — and a major breakthrough in the evo-devo field. It gives scientists deep insights into how changes at the level of the DNA can result in changes in animal body plan.

Here's the big take-home message: Developmentally you're not all that different from a fly. Understanding Hox genes takes us a long way toward understanding how small changes at the level of the DNA, besides the things we actually know to happen, could result in large differences in animal form.

Of mice and men and . . . jellyfish!

The preceding discussion focuses on *bilaterally symmetrical animals* — those with a right and left side, a head, and a tail end. Most animals are bilaterally symmetrical: you, your dog, your goldfish, your hamster, and your houseflies.

But a few animals aren't symmetrical — jellyfish, for example. As it turns out, jellyfish also have genes related to the Hox cluster. They're much different from the genes that humans share with mice or even flies, which makes sense, because the hypothesized common ancestor of the bilateral animals and the jellyfish lived millions and millions (and millions) of years ago.

Now, a jellyfish doesn't have a head in the sense that humans do, but it does have a place where the mouth is, which is probably as close to a head as you can imagine. Jellyfish have an oral side and an *aboral* side — in plain English, a mouth side and a side opposite the mouth side. Genes related to the Hox genes in bilateral animals are responsible for this oral-aboral patterning, and in honor of the group that jellyfish find themselves in — the Cnidarians — these genes are called Cnox, instead of Hox, genes. (The C is silent; it's just there to mess with you.)

Cnox genes are similar to the ones involved in head formation in bilateral animals. Scientists can investigate the function of these genes in jellyfish by altering them genetically. One such experiment resulted in a jellyfish with multiple heads and multiple functional mouths!

Chapter 15

Molecular Evolution

- -

In This Chapter

▶ Understanding what genomes do (and don't do)

▶ Deciphering genomes

▶ Distinguishing between coding and non-coding DNA

▶ Discovering neutral mutations

▶ Telling time with the molecular clock

- -

*E*volution is all about heritable changes, and DNA is the material that's inherited. Other chapters in this book don't go into a lot of detail about the various sorts of changes that can occur at the DNA level. Instead, they focus mostly on examples involving changes in alleles at particular loci, like changes in some bit of bacterial machinery that renders the bacteria antibiotic resistant. This simple process, whereby one of the nucleotides (A, C, T, or G) in a bacterium's genome was incorrectly copied and thus changed the bacterium's phenotype, is an example of a change at a locus from one allele to another and an example of how a new allele appears in a population.

But there are other evolutionary questions we can ask about an organism's DNA. For example, how many genes are there? It turns out organisms don't have the same number of genes. Since all organisms share a common ancestor, where did the new genes come from? What sort of evolutionary changes can result in new instructions in the organism's instruction manual? Another question is how much DNA is there, and is all of it genes? Scientists have discovered that the number varies a fair bit between organisms and not always in a way you'd expect. In some organisms, most of the DNA doesn't correspond to different genes, and in other organisms, such as ourselves, lots of the DNA doesn't seem to do very much.

The field of molecular evolution seeks to understand how these changes come about, how evolution works at the DNA level, and what understanding the details of the process can tell us about how evolution might proceed.

My Genome's Bigger than Your Genome!

As discussed in Chapter 3, every organism has a genome made up of DNA, which is the instruction manual for making the organism, spelled out in a four-letter alphabet: A, C, T, and G. These letters are called *nucleotides,* or bases. The size of the genome is the total number of DNA bases used to spell out the instructions. (OK, not every organism has a genome made up of DNA; some types of viruses have genomes made of RNA instead of DNA. But that exception's not important here.)

Genome sizes at a glance

Haploid organisms have only one copy of their DNA; diploid organisms have two copies. Humans are diploid: A person's genome consists of two DNA copies, one from Mom and one from Dad. Both copies contain the same type of genes (eye-color genes, for example), whose "specifics" (blue eyes versus brown eyes, for example) may or may not be different.

To standardize across all organisms, when scientists talk about genome size, they talk about the size of a haploid genome. For diploid organisms, genome size corresponds to the amount of DNA in a non-fertilized egg or in a sperm cell. Table 15-1 lists the haploid genome sizes and the number of genes for many organisms. It also identifies what branch of the tree of life the organism occupies.

Table 15-1		Genome Sizes		
Organism	*Branch of Tree of Life*	*Estimated Size (Mb= million bases)*	*Estimated Number of Genes*	*Average Gene Density**
Humans	Eukaryote	2900 Mb	30,000	1 gene per 100,000 bases
Mice	Eukaryote	2500 Mb	30,000	1 gene per 100,000 bases
Fruit flies	Eukaryote	180 Mb	13,600	1 gene per 9,000 bases
Arabidopsis thaliana (a little flowering plant)	Eukaryote	125 Mb	25,500	1 gene per 4,000 bases
Round worm	Eukaryote	97 Mb	19,100	1 gene per 5,000 bases

Organism	Branch of Tree of Life	Estimated Size (Mb= million bases)	Estimated Number of Genes	Average Gene Density*
Yeast	Eukaryote	12 Mb	6,300	1 gene per 2,000 bases
E. coli	Eubacteria	4.7 Mb	3,200	1 gene per 1,400 bases
H. influenzae (can cause blood poisoning and meningitis)	Eubacteria	1.8 Mb	1,700	1 gene per 1,000 bases
Rice	Eukaryote	430 Mb	32,000–56,000	1 gene per 10,000 bases
Entamoeba histolytica (a single-celled amoeba)	Eukaryote	24 Mb	10,000	1 gene per 4,000 bases

*Average gene density refers to how many bases of DNA there are for each gene.

Note: The reason the numbers in Table 15-1 differ between "Estimated Size" and "Estimated Number of Genes" is that the "Estimated Size" includes both coding and non-coding DNA (explained in the section "Distinguishing between genes and non-coding DNA"), whereas the "Estimated Number of Genes" entries include only the coding DNA.

The tree of life (refer to Chapter 9) has three main branches:

- **The Eubacteria:** These are all the bacteria you've heard of, including *E. coli,* staph, strep, and other such critters

- **The Archea:** These are the other group of single-celled things without a nucleus. These look pretty similar to the Eubacteria under a microscope but turn out to be very different when scientists are able to figure out their DNA sequences.

- **The Eukaryotes:** These include all the organisms whose cells have a nucleus — yeast, pine trees, you, and so on — basically anything big enough to see as well as most of the biggest things that are still too small to see.

The C value and the C-value paradox

When scientists began to measure the genome sizes of different organisms, two things became apparent: Within a species, genome sizes are the same, but across species they differ quite a bit and not necessarily in the way you'd expect. The following sections explain.

Genome sizes consistent within a species

Within a species, every organism has the same size of genome. This finding makes perfect sense. The instruction manual to make one person should be the same length as the instruction manual to make somebody else, although the details vary from person to person. Both people need the instructions to make eyes, for example, but the exact details — the color and shape of the eyes — may vary from person to person.

What's true for people is true for other species as well: The instruction manual is the same length, even if some of the instructions are slightly different. There are some exceptions to this, however, such as with E. coli, whose genome size can vary, as explained in the later section, "Getting genes from other lines: Lateral gene transfer."

Because the size of the genome is constant across all individuals in a species, a species' genome size is referred to as its *C value,* with *C* standing for *constant.*

Genome sizes vary between species

Between species, genome size varies greatly — a fact that is extremely puzzling, because although it makes sense that different organisms require different-size instruction manuals, no obvious connection exists between the size of the species' genome and that species' complexity. For that reason, scientists call the discrepancy between complexity and genome size the *C-value paradox* (or the *C-value enigma*).

Distinguishing between genes and non-coding DNA

An organism's genome can roughly be divided into two parts:

- ✔ **Genes (coding DNA):** These sequences of DNA are transcribed and are the genes that determine phenotype.

  During transcription, DNA sequences are copied to RNA. During another process called *translation,* the RNA is copied to amino acids, chains of which are called *proteins.* Not all the transcribed RNAs are translated into proteins; they have some other jobs. Chapter 3 has the details on these processes.

✔ **Non-coding DNA.** These areas of DNA aren't transcribed. In other words, they don't seem to do anything.

Number of genes

If you take a close look at the numbers in Table 15-1, you may notice that some of the differences make sense. You'd probably expect single-celled organisms to have fewer genes than multicelled organisms, and that's what you find in some instances. Humans, for example, have about 20,000 genes, whereas *E. coli,* a species of Eubacteria (beneficial bacteria) that inhabits the human gut, has slightly more than 4,000 genes.

But in other instances, the numbers aren't what you'd expect. Although humans have twice as many genes as fruit flies, rice plants have almost twice as many genes as we do. At first pass, rice isn't obviously twice as complex as humans are. Because scientists don't know what most of the rice genes do, they don't really understand why rice has so many genes, but they do know that having this many genes isn't a universal property of plants. The small weed *Arabidopsis* has about the same number of genes as humans but far fewer than the rice plant has.

While it's true that the littlest critters — viruses, eubacteria, and archea — have the smallest genomes and the smallest numbers of genes, there are other single-celled creatures, like certain amoebas, that have enormous genomes and the same number of genes as some (but not all) multicellular organisms. The single celled amoeba *Entamoeba histolytica* has almost 10,000 genes, not that many fewer than a fly!

Amount of non-coding DNA

Another thing you may notice in Table 15-1 is that different organisms have different amounts of non-coding DNA, represented in the "Average Gene Density" column. The more bases there are for each gene indicates more non-coding DNA. So humans, who have only one gene for every 100,000 bases, have quite a bit of "wasted" space, or non-coding DNA. *H. influenzae,* on the other hand, has one gene per thousand bases, meaning it has virtually no non-coding DNA.

Clear patterns appear between the major groups of organisms:

✔ Eubacteria and Archea have almost no non-coding DNA.

✔ Eukaryotes have non-coding DNA, but the amount of non-coding DNA varies widely among them. Some ferns have 100 times as much non-coding DNA as humans do.

✔ Viruses don't have non-coding DNA, but they don't fit neatly on the tree of life. In fact, viruses probably are not a single group. They have such small genomes that very little information is available to group them with other organisms.

No one knows exactly why organisms on the different branches of the tree of life have different amounts of non-coding DNA, although scientists can make educated guesses:

- ✔ **Size of the organism:** It seems reasonable that the smallest organisms simply don't have room for extra stuff. You can't fit a gallon of milk into a quart container. The same constraints wouldn't exist for eukaryotic cells. Your genome has a lot of non-coding DNA, but the nucleus is still only a small part of the cell; it seems to have room to spare.

- ✔ **Rapid cell division:** For organisms such as viruses and bacteria, for which rapid division is a key component of fitness, the extra time that replicating a larger genome takes is too much of a selective disadvantage, so non-coding DNA doesn't accumulate.

- ✔ **Population size:** Maybe non-coding DNA can accumulate more easily in eukaryotic organisms because they have smaller population sizes, on which genetic drift (random events) can be a more influential evolutionary force. (Head to Chapter 6 for info on genetic drift.)

The Whys and Wherefores of Non-coding DNA

Imagine being the person who took the first gander ever at a genome, the instruction manual for life. Pretty amazing stuff. Now imagine ferreting out which bits do what and discovering that quite a lot of what you're looking at doesn't seem to do anything. It's just there, cluttering things up. In a word, it's junk. Quite a bit of the genomes of eukaryotic organisms is junk — non-coding DNA. Why is it there? No one really knows, but several explanations have been proposed, as the following sections explain.

It performs a function

Maybe non-coding DNA plays some role in controlling how other DNA sections are transcribed, even though it isn't transcribed itself. In this case, the non-coding DNA is advantageous to the organism (it performs a necessary job), so natural selection maintains it. Some evidence exists that this situation actually occurs; even so, it's not enough to account for the huge amounts of non-coding DNA.

Alternatively, the non-coding DNA may serve a structural function during cell division or the production of *gametes* (sperm and egg). Replicating the eukaryotic genome, which is packaged in a series of chromosomes (refer to Chapter 3 for info on chromosomes), is a pretty complex process. The non-coding DNA could be involved in putting the chromosome together — pairing things up and partitioning the copied chromosome in the daughter cells, for example.

It serves no function but isn't harmful

Some scientists hypothesize that the non-coding DNA serves no function, but because it's not especially harmful, natural selection doesn't select against it. If a certain amount of non-coding DNA doesn't have any negative fitness costs, it could just pile up in the genome and persist because it keeps getting dragged along to future generations by nearby advantageous genes. (Head to Chapter 4 for more on hitchhiking DNA.)

It's parasitic!

Much of the non-coding DNA may be parasitic DNA — the result of replicating elements in the eukaryotic genome reproducing themselves. As you can imagine, anything that's a parasite can't be good for the host organism, and selection would act to favor individuals with less of this parasitic DNA.

So why is it still there? Because parasitic DNA elements that are best able to reproduce themselves in the eukaryotic genome are selectively favored, even though selection is also acting to favor organisms in which they are less able to replicate. Lots of evidence exists that a large amount of your genome is really taken up by the selfish elements.

Retroelements

All kinds of selfish, non-coding DNA are around, but one very important kind is the retroelements. To understand the retroelements, think about retroviruses, the most famous of which is HIV (explained in detail in Chapter 18). Retroviruses are viruses that alternate between an RNA genome and a DNA genome. They start with an RNA genome, infect their host, make a DNA copy to integrate into the host, and then replicate an RNA copy so that they can spread.

A retroelement does essentially the same thing that a retrovirus does, except that it lacks the genes that enable it to package the RNA copy into a particle that spreads. (When scientists sequence retroelements, they find that they are closely related to retroviruses but have a reduced set of genes.)

Amazingly, 95 percent of the human genome is made up of retroelement-like sequences. What's their purpose? Like everything else in evolutionary biology, their purpose is simply to make more of themselves. They replicate in your genome, and you pass them along to your kids.

Harmless — until they mess things up

For the most part, retroelements don't seem to do you any harm — until they do. Retroelements can move around in your genome and mess things up. They can insert into a new location right in the middle of an existing gene.

An example of a retroelement in action is the blue merle pattern in some breeds of dog. This coloring pattern is caused by a particular retroelement popping in and out of the pigment genes during embryonic development. At a certain point, the retroelement stops jumping around, but the dog still ends up with splotches of different colors in different places. Another, more harmful effect of retroelements may be cancer, where certain retroelements move around more actively.

Bottom line: Retroelements don't do anything beneficial, take up space, can be harmful, and may be parasitic. You'd be better off if they weren't there, but they just keep reproducing.

Transposable elements in general (pieces of DNA which pop around from one place to the next in the genome) and retroelements in particular (a subclass of transposable elements whose replication involves a reverse transcription step — that is a transcription from RNA back to DNA) are a big part of your genome, but they don't do anything of value. Why oh why are they there? That's the sixty four million dollar question of genome size.

Coding DNA: Changing the Number of Genes an Organism Has

Although the largest differences in the amount of DNA between different species are the result non-coding DNA (see the preceding section), differences also occur in the number of genes between different organisms.

Think back to the branching tree of life (refer to Chapter 9) and the evolution of more complex organisms such as humans from less-complex organisms. You can appreciate why the number of genes has increased. In this section, I explain how the number of genes an organism has can change. New genes can appear in a variety of ways.

Getting genes from other lines: Lateral gene transfer

Lateral gene transfer is the process by which one evolving lineage acquires genes from other lineages. This mechanism isn't thought to be especially important for eukaryotes such as humans, but it's quite common among non-eukaryotes, the Eubacteria and Archea.

A good example of lateral gene transfer is the vastly different number of genes between the beneficial *E. coli* strain that all humans have in their guts and the disease-causing *E. coli* 0157:H7. The human-gut *E. coli* has about 4,300 genes, whereas the pathogenic strain has 5,400 — a huge difference. It's not clear where all these extra genes came from, but some of them clearly are related to genes from the bacteria species *Shigella dysenteriae,* whose name probably makes clear why these genes can turn a good *E. coli* bad.

Shuffling exons: Alternative gene splicing

DNA sequences are transcribed into RNA sequences. A subset of these RNA sequences, termed *messenger RNA* (or mRNA for short), are then translated into sequences of amino acids, called proteins.

The most sensible way for an organism to make proteins would be to have just enough DNA to code for the length and type of protein being made. And often that's what we find, especially in things like bacteria. But many times, the sequence of DNA, and thus mRNA, is much longer than necessary to make the desired protein.

In this too-long sequence, some sections of the RNA nucleotides are translated to amino acids (they're called *exons*), and others aren't (they're called *introns*). To make the amino acid, the mRNA is "processed" — the introns get spliced out, leaving just the exons all strung together. This new, shorter piece of mRNA codes for the amino acids that make the protein, and everything's hunky-dory.

Yet when scientists look at the details of this process, they find that sometimes there's more that one way to process the same mRNA.

  ✔ Sometimes all the exons get strung together

  ✔ Other times just some of the exons get strung together.

In the second case, when the exons are sewn back together to make the final piece of RNA, some of them get left out, and the result is that different proteins are made from a single gene. This is important, because using different combinations of exons from the same sequence of DNA can result in cells with different functions. This process is called *alternative splicing* or, more informally, *exon shuffling.*

In exon shuffling, a gene with four exons, for example, might be spliced differently to create several different types of mRNA. One obvious one would be an mRNA made up of all 4 exons. But mRNAs could also be made from just a subset of the exons — say exons 1, 2, and 4 in one case, and exons 1, 3, and 4 in another. In each of these cases, the protein produced from this mRNA could have a different function. In mammals, for example, the calcitonin gene produces a hormone in one cell type and a neurotransmitter in another cell type, due to alternative splicing.

Alternative splicing suggests one way that new functions can arise. A mutation that resulted in exons being spliced one way sometime and another way another time would create two protein products from the same DNA. In short, through exon shuffling, it would be possible to gain a new protein while still being able to make the original one. If the new protein were selectively advantageous, then the new mutant would increase in future generations.

Duplicating genes: A gene is born

Errors in DNA replication can lead to duplications of sections of DNA or, as in the creation of polyploids, duplication of the entire genome (see Chapter 4). It's akin to going to Kinko's for a single copy and ending up with two: the copy you needed and an extra you're not quite sure what to do with. The same thing goes for the DNA. What's an extra gene good for?

If a mutation knocks out a duplicate copy, the organism is pretty much back where it started: It still has the original copy and an extra. This situation is the spare-tire gene duplication theory. (Just kidding.) The extra copy may or may not be functional:

- **When the second copy is nonfunctional:** These nonfunctional genes are called *pseudo-genes.* Pseudo-genes look like the original genes, but they're a little, or a lot, broken, and they tend to accumulate more and more mutations over time. The more mutations occur, the harder it is to recognize that these genes are related to existing genes. But since they're already nonfunctional, there's no fitness cost to a few more mutations.

- **When the second copy is functional:** If the second copy mutates such that it is able to perform an additional function that's selectively advantageous, individuals with this mutation increase in frequency, resulting in two different yet related functional genes where one originally was. Many examples exist of families of genes that appear to have a common ancestor.

When you know about the possibility of gene duplications, you understand that natural selection could result in a change of function of one copy without having to worry about losing the function of the other copy. When you have two copies, you have room to move. Because most mutations are deleterious, these duplicated genes usually end up losing their original function without acquiring any new function. But sometimes beneficial mutations occur in the second copy, and a new gene is born.

The Neutral Theory of Molecular Evolution

The neutral theory of molecular evolution says that genetic drift — random events that affect evolutionary change (see Chapter 6) — accounts for much of the change in DNA. This is the case because most mutations are selectively neutral. In fact, much more variation is neutral than scientists once thought. The variation exists in the DNA, but either it doesn't result in a change at the level of the protein or, if it does result in changes in proteins, these changes don't change the protein's function.

The chance that a mutation will have no effect can vary between different genes. Some proteins, for example, are very tightly constrained in the shapes that they can adopt and still be functional. For these proteins, relatively few mutations are selectively neutral. When scientists examine the mutation rates of different proteins within the same organism, they find that some evolve faster than others.

As stated previously, neutral mutations are neither good nor bad, and when a mutation is neutral, natural selection doesn't act on it. (Why should it? A neutral mutation doesn't help the organism, which would cause an increase in frequency in subsequent generations. Neither does it hurt the organism, which would cause a decrease in frequency.) Therefore, the evolutionary force that acts on these genes is genetic drift. Over enough time, a selectively neutral mutation can reach a frequency of 100 percent in a population just by chance — a situation called *fixation*. (You can read more about fixation and genetic drift in Chapter 6.)

Many mutations are almost, but not quite, neutral. A slightly deleterious mutation, for example, might still increase in frequency as a result of genetic drift in a small population. Remember that for any given mutation, the chance of fixation (that is, the chance of reaching a frequency of 100 percent) is a function of population size. If population size fluctuates (as it often does), a particular gene may be changing in frequency primarily as a result of natural selection at one time and primarily due to genetic drift at another time.

Two evolutionary forces are at work: natural selection and genetic drift. If a mutation isn't neutral, both natural selection and genetic drift can be the cause of evolution. If a mutation *is* neutral, only genetic drift can result in a change in the frequency of the gene over time. (This discovery — that random events are evolutionary forces in and of themselves — has been the most important addition to the theory of evolution since Darwin.)

Telling Time with Genes: The Molecular Clock

The *molecular clock* refers to the idea that if mutations are often neutral, all other things being equal, they might be expected to accumulate at a constant rate. If this idea is true, it should be possible to measure the genetic differences between two species and determine how long ago the two lineages diverged. Sounds, good, but telling time with the molecular clock is tricky; sometimes you can, and sometimes you can't.

When you can't

Using the molecular clock to determine when lineages diverged requires that the neutral mutations accumulate at a constant rate. Which doesn't happen, for several reasons:

- **Differences between genes:** There is no reason to think that the proportion of neutral mutations should be constant across genes with different functions. One protein may function only if it's exactly the right shape or configuration to do its job; another protein may do its job pretty well even in spite of a few changes. At the very least, comparisons should be made only between the same gene in different species. But even then, scientists can't be sure that a gene shared across two species performs the same function. The function of the gene may have changed as the species evolved to a different environment, for example.

- **Population size and generation time:** The rate at which neutral mutations become fixed in a population is a function of population size and generation time, both of which may vary between lineages after they diverge. In small populations with short generation times, neutral mutations rise to fixation more rapidly.

- **Strength of selection:** The strength of natural selection may vary between species over time, thus changing the ratio of neutral to non-neutral mutations that rise to fixation.

When you can

Despite all the reasons why you shouldn't get too excited about the idea of the molecular clock (see the preceding section), in some cases, scientists can show that the accumulation of mutations is an excellent predictor of the time since two species diverged.

The key to using the molecular clock effectively is calibrating it. To do that, you must know the time at which some lineages diverged so that you can translate the amount of divergence between different lineages into time. Then you can use this information to estimate the divergence times of additional species.

Performing experiments in the lab

For organisms that have generation times short enough to create divergent lineages in the laboratory, you can ask how fast mutations accumulate in these microorganisms over time. Then you can look at sequence variation that you know to be neutral — changes in the DNA that don't result in any changes in the protein. These changes pile up over time, based on the mutation rate. You measure how fast they pile up, and then you know the mutation rate — simple as that! (This strategy doesn't work for organisms that are much longer lived, of course.)

Looking at ancient DNA and the fossil record

As researchers' biochemical techniques become more sophisticated, they've been able to retrieve DNA sequences from the distant (but quantifiable) past. By studying these ancient sequences, they've been able to put bounds on the rates of mutation accumulation between the date of the old sequence and the current time.

The fossil record also allows scientists to generate estimates of when different lineages diverged by noting the geological era in which the fossil was found. Then they can use these divergence times to calculate the rate at which mutations have accumulated in the lineages since the divergence.

Imagine you have three species: species 1, species 2, and species 3. You sequence all three, generate a phylogeny, and find that species 2 and 3 seem most closely related, and they're both related to species 1. Just by digging and finding fossils at different ages, you have a pretty good idea of when species 1 and 2 split. But you have absolutely no fossils telling you anything about the history of species 3, and you want know when species 3 split off from species 2.

By knowing when species 1 and 2 diverged, you can correlate the number of DNA differences between these two species and the amount of time since they diverged. You can then take this estimate and use it to translate the number of DNA differences between species 2 and 3 into the time since they diverged, even in the absence of any fossil record for species 3. And that's the molecular clock!

From the fossil record, scientists know the approximate times when many lineages arose. Date the rocks that a fossil is found in, and you pretty effectively date the fossil. Scientists know, for example, about when the mammal lineage split off from the rest of the tetrapods (four-limbed creatures, such as lizards, turtles, and birds). On a finer scale, they have a pretty good idea about when the hominid lineage diverged from the chimpanzee lineage.

Scientists can use the fossil record to generate divergence times for lineages for which there is a good fossil record, and then they can use the molecular clock to estimate divergence times for species for which a good fossil record isn't available.

Examining biogeographic patterns

Biogeographic patterns can also generate estimates of divergence times. Take, for example, the fruit fly species *(Drosophila)* that lives in the Hawaiian islands. Because geologists have an excellent understanding of how the Hawaiian islands formed, they can date the islands accurately.

The Earth's crust has a thin spot, and as the Pacific plate moves across this hot spot, periodic eruptions have generated the chain of the Hawaiian islands. Because geologists can date exactly the age at which lava solidifies, they can figure out when the islands were formed.

In addition, the Hawaiian islands are extremely distant from other land masses. As a result, much of the biological diversity on the islands is a result of speciation events that happened in Hawaii. Most of the fruit fly species in Hawaii occurs nowhere else, for example. Hawaii is so far from anywhere else that the rate at which fruit fly speciation occurs on the islands far exceeds the rate at which non-Hawaiian fruit fly species could arrive. So although some fruit flies got to Hawaii initially from elsewhere, the original colonists have radiated into many of the species you find there today.

As new islands appear in the chain, flies from the neighboring island colonize them and, over time, diverge to become separate species. As explained in Chapter 8, this divergence is a consequence of the very reduced rates of genetic exchange between the islands. A fruit fly occasionally gets from one island to another, but this migration doesn't happen often enough to overwhelm the gradual divergence between the separated populations and their subsequent speciation.

Phylogenetic analysis (refer to Chapter 9) of the Hawaiian fruit fly yields a tree that matches geologists' understanding of the geological formation of the islands — and sure enough, the fly species on different islands each share a most recent common ancestor with the species on the next island over.

Usually, we don't know when in the past two lineages became geographically separated, but with the Hawaiian islands, we know exactly when the new islands popped up out of the ocean. We can combine the data about how genetically different two species are (which we get from the sequence of their DNA) with the length of time they've been separate species.

Not surprisingly, the longer two species have been separated, the more genetically different they will be, simply because changes add up over time. But what's most important about these Hawaiian flies is that, because we know the dates the islands appeared, we can tell that the amount of genetic difference is exactly correlated with the length of time since the species diverged. If one pair of species diverged twice as long ago as another pair, it has twice the amount of genetic differences.

This information tells us that the molecular clock can tick at a constant rate for long periods of time. Proving that (through studying the phylogeny of Hawaiian fruit flies and knowing the dates when the islands formed) makes us more comfortable with assuming that the rate of molecular evolution may be constant in other species as well.

Part IV
Evolution and
Your World

The 5th Wave   By Rich Tennant

WHILE VISITING THE ISLAND OF MAURITIUS, JAN AND IRV PLOTKIN COME ACROSS THE LAST REMAING NATURE SIGN FOR THE NOW EXTINCT DODO.

Get all of it, Irv.

THE DODO

"Ooo! This would make a wonderful souvenir."

In this part . . .

Although many of us like to tell ourselves that we're different from other organisms in some fundamental ways, we're all subject to evolutionary processes. So evolution doesn't pertain only to animals, plants, bacteria, etc. It pertains to humans as well. As this part explains, we have our own evolutionary history as a species and an evolutionary future, as well.

Ironically, the other species that poses the biggest challenge — and threat — to us and therefore deserves attention in this part is the one we can't even see (without help): the microbes, like bacteria and viruses, organisms that evolve amazingly quickly and in response to the medicines we use to fight them.

Chapter 16

Human Evolution

. . . .

. . . .

Most people are very interested in human evolution and know something about it but still find the topic perplexing. They have an inkling, for example, that humans evolved from apes (actually, apelike creatures) but think that evolution works differently for humans than it does for other organisms. It doesn't. The same evolutionary principles that apply to every living organism apply to human beings: speciation, genetic drift, coalescence, you name it.

This chapter explains both the evolutionary origin of our species and subsequent evolution within the species *Homo sapiens*. In a way, this chapter answers two questions: "Where did we come from?" and "Where are we going?"

The Origin of Homo Sapiens: Where We Came From

When you think about human evolution, you may think immediately about the fossil record. Although fossils are extremely important parts of the evidence we humans have for understanding our own origins, other vital lines of evidence exist as well:

> ✔ **Phylogenetic reconstructions:** A *phylogenetic reconstruction* is essentially a visual representation of the genealogy of a group of species (refer to Chapter 9 for more details). This image can provide insight into where humans fit in the tree of life.

> ✔ **Human DNA studies:** By looking at our DNA, researchers can get intriguing information about the patterns of migration of *Homo sapiens* (humans) that help them sort out different hypotheses about where humans originated. They can't get this info just by looking at fossils, which aren't always clear.

> ✔ **Neanderthal DNA studies:** It's possible now to obtain DNA from one of our closest relatives: the Neanderthals. By comparing modern human DNA with Neanderthal DNA, scientists gain a better understanding of our relationship to this extinct species of hominid.

Phylogenetic evidence: Hangin' round on the Tree of Life

As I explain in Chapter 9, phylogenetics takes data about existing species and reconstructs the evolutionary branching pattern that led to those species. Not surprisingly, no small amount of effort has been devoted to reconstructing the parts of the tree of life where humans reside. Our particular branch includes the apes: gibbons, orangutans, gorillas, the two types of chimpanzees (the standard one that you're familiar with and the bonobo, which used to be called the pygmy chimp but which turns out to be a species of its own), and us!

When biologists started wondering where all these creatures should reside on our branch of the tree, they imagined one sub-branch leading to us and another sub-branch leading to all those charming, furry creatures who seem so different from us. Researchers could tell that, of all the animals, humans are most like apes, but in the past, they tended to think of the apes as belonging on the other twig of our shared branch of the tree.

Enter the amazing resource of DNA. Now that scientists have been able to sequence human DNA as well as good samples of DNA from the other apes (in the case of the chimpanzees, the entire genome), they've discovered that humans and chimps aren't very distant at all. The current best hypothesis about the relationships between humans and the rest of the great apes is shown in Figure 16-1.

In Figure 16-1, you can see that the two chimpanzee species (chimps and bonobos) have a most recent common ancestor. These species are a lot more like each other than they are like anything else. But — surprise! — humans have a most common ancestor with the chimpanzee lineage that we don't share with the other great apes. To find the most common ancestor of gorillas, humans, and chimpanzees, you have to go back a bit farther — and farther yet to find the most recent common ancestor of orangutans, gorillas, humans, and chimpanzees.

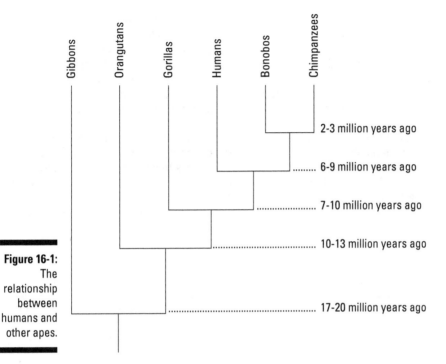

Figure 16-1:
The relationship between humans and other apes.

Figure 16-1 shows a point that I want to drive home: *Humans didn't evolve from chimps!* Instead, chimps and humans arose from the same common, apelike ancestor.

Kissing cousins

Humans turn out to be a lot more similar to chimpanzees than biologists first thought. Human DNA is about 95 percent the same as chimpanzee DNA. A lot of active research is going on in this area, and some studies put the number at 97 percent or 98 percent. Whatever the precise percentage, however, the bottom line is that humans are very similar to chimps.

Why do the different percentages exist? Because it's no easy task to figure out which bits in the DNA sequence are genes, which bits *might* be genes, and which bits are just junk. (Yes, believe it or not, humans, chimps, all other mammals, and most multicellular creatures have a lot of junk DNA; refer to Chapter 15 to find out more about non-coding DNA.) As a consequence, different researchers come up with different estimates regarding which parts are genes and which parts aren't, and thus different estimates of similarity between species.

By combining the information about the relative differences in the genomes of chimpanzees and humans with what we know about the rate of DNA substitutions in specific genes in these two organisms, researchers can tell that, approximately 5 million to 7 million years ago, the lineage leading to modern humans split from the lineage leading to modern chimps. (For information on how to use DNA as a molecular clock to determine the time in the past when two lineages split from a common ancestor, head to Chapter 15.)

If the DNA sequence of humans is so close to that of the chimpanzee, why do the two species look so different? They certainly don't seem to be only 5 percent different (at least, that's what we humans like to think!). The answer is that small changes in regions of the DNA that have a regulatory function can have major effects, as explained in Chapter 14, including examples of genes that may be important in the different developmental trajectories of chimps and humans.

You say hominid; I say hominian

Biologists commonly name every group; everything that has a common ancestor gets a name. And because humans (the species *Homo sapiens*) are the ones who do the naming, we've made sure that every higher group that includes us also starts with the letters *hom* — *hominid; hominine; hominin* (yes, it means something different from *hominine*); *hominian;* and, of course, *human.*

These names come up a lot in the published studies of human evolution, and they certainly do sound awfully scientific. My opinion? They're nothing but trouble. So in this book, I don't use any of these terms except *hominid,* which refers to all the creatures on the branch of life starting at the common ancestor of chimps and humans, and leading up in time along the human branch. If you need a more precise definition, try this one on for size:

> HOMINID: Modern humans and their extinct relatives, going back to the most common recent ancestor with the chimpanzee lineage.

Carved in stone: The fossils

As you can probably guess from the excitement with which paleontologists greet each new fossil find, hominid fossils are few and far between. This fact isn't especially surprising, given that great apes tend to have relatively low population densities (and our earliest ancestors probably did, too). That scientists have been able to find fossils of many early hominids at all is a cork-popping event.

The human species found in fossils

Paleontologists have found fossils for a large number of hominid species, including prehuman primates and human primates. In fact, various hominid species have been identified from fossil remains, as Table 16-1 shows.

Note: The *A* or *H* in the species' names is scientific shorthand. Instead of writing *Australopithecus*, for example, scientists simply write *A*. The term *Australopithecus* speaks to the origin of the fossil: southern Africa. *H*, of course, stands for *Homo*, which means *wise*. The name *Homo sapiens* means *wise man*.

Table 16-1	Hominid Species
Name	*Years on Earth (Based on Fossil Finds)*
A. anamensis	4.2 to 3.9 million years ago
A. afarensis (Lucy)	3.6 to 2.9 million years ago
A. africanus	3 to 2 million years ago
A. aethiopicus	2.7 to 2.3 million years ago
A. boisei	2.3 to 1.4 million years ago
A. robustus	1.8 to 1.5 million years ago
H. rudolphensis	2.4 to 1.8 million years ago
H. habilis	2.3 to 1.6 million years ago
H. ergaster	1.9 to 1.4 million years ago
H. erectus	1.9 to 0.3 million years ago (and possible 50,000 years ago)
H. heielbergensis	600,000 to 100,000 years ago
H. neanderthalensis	250,000 to 30,000 years ago
H. sapiens	100,000 years ago to today

As you can see, for most of the past 3 million or so years, multiple species of hominids have existed at any one time — a situation that persisted until about 25,000 years ago. In short, in the not-too-distant past, we shared Earth with human species other than our own.

The dates in Table 16-1 indicate the years from which fossil specimens of each species have been recovered. (For a review of how scientists determine the dates of fossils, see Chapter 2.) But — and this point is important — the lack of fossil evidence doesn't necessarily mean that a species wasn't around longer than the time periods indicated, only that scientists haven't found it. So even though the current dates indicate that a H. habilis, for example, lived from 2.3 to 1.6 million years ago, if H. habilis fossils dating from 1 million years ago are found, the dates would change. (It's also why you see the range for H. erectus and a note that this species also may have existed up to 50,000 years ago.)

The tricky task of separating one species from another

As Chapter 8 explains, a very useful way for determining whether two individuals are of the same or different species is to determine whether they can interbreed. If the answer is yes, the individuals are of the same species; a no answer means, they are different species. Obviously, this information isn't available for any of our fossil ancestors, so in this case, species names are simply a function of *morphology,* or body structure. All the fossils that look the same are assigned to the same species.

This arrangement sounds easy enough until you consider that the fossil record is sparse and fossil remains of hominids usually are extremely incomplete —part of the leg bone here, half a jaw there, part of the cranium somewhere else. Complicating matters even more is the expectation of finding both juvenile and adult individuals, as well as males and females which may vary in size. As a result, there's a fair bit of argument about whether a new find should be considered a new species or merely another representative of an existing species.

Using skull size and shape, jaw muscles, and limb length can help researchers distinguish between one hominid species and another, as follows:

- **Ratio of forelimb to hind-limb length:** Humans' arms are proportionally much shorter than the arms of chimpanzees, and scientists find different fossil hominids with different arm-length ratios.

  As *bipedal locomotion* (walking upright) developed, forelimb length shortened. (If you want to get persnickety, as scientists tend to do, you can say that forelimbs aren't really arms until the organism is walking on its hind legs — hence, the use of the term *forelimbs.*) Forelimb length is a good way to evaluate which group a fossil belongs to because it's relatively constant for individuals of different ages. The absolute lengths of forelimbs and hind-limbs change as the individual grows, but the ratio of the lengths is consistent over a range of individual sizes.

- **Skull shape:** Humans have proportionally much larger brains than do the other apes.

This just in

Don't you just love it when science keeps discovering things? Every time anthropologists dig up a new skull, humans' view of the fossil record and what it says about human evolution can change. After a recent bit of digging, researchers now know that *Homo habilis* and *Homo erectus* lived at the same time.

This bit of info changes nothing in the chapter; it just reconfirms that in the past, more than one type of hominid was around at the same time. But it does provide a clearer picture of whether one hominid gave rise to another (as opposed to both having descended from a common ancestor). Some paleontologists thought that perhaps *H. erectus* evolved from *H. habilis*. The new fossil find shows that both species were around together, meaning that (1) they both evolved from something else or (2) *H. erectus* could still have evolved from an offshoot of *H. habilis* (you know — some *habilis* got lost on the way to the office, ended up in a place with different selective pressures, and so on).

> ✔ **The form and arrangement of teeth (*dentition*):** Humans have markedly different dentition from other apes. We do a lot of our food processing with our hands rather than with our teeth, and we lack the powerful jaw muscles and large teeth that are characteristic of the rest of the primates (a group including the apes and other things like monkeys).

We humans have forelimbs, which just happen to be arms, but because we don't need them to reach to the ground when we walk, they can be shorter. Chimps can walk around on hind legs for a little bit, but soon resort to using their (longer) forelimbs again. Watch a chimp walk next time you're at the zoo; then try it with your comparatively short, little arms — you'll fall on your head! Why the difference? Because humans started to adopt a more upright posture that was selectively favored. The move to upright posture and the decrease in the importance of front limbs for locomotion would have happened at the same time.

Reconstructing the history of hominid evolution

With all these hominid species, scientists are still trying to figure out which species may have given rise to which other species along the lineage that led to humans. Because no one can say with certainty that a fossil represents a common ancestor of two other species (the fossil may represent a closely related dead end, for example), this task is fairly challenging.

Figure 16-2 shows a hypothetical evolutionary pathway from an ancestral species similar to the extant apes and leading to modern humans. It includes a sequence of intermediate species with increasingly large brains, reduced jaw musculature and dentition, and the evolution of *bipedalism* (walking on just two feet). I've thrown in stone tools and fire just for fun.

The actual intermediate species may not be the ones scientists have already found, or they may be; knowing for sure is impossible. What scientists *do* know is that we can reconstruct the evolutionary events that led from an ape-like ancestor to a modern human through the series of fossil species that have already been found. The following sections describe some of the major players; consider this a sort of hits list of the hominid fossil record.

Lucy in the sky with diamonds: Australopithecus afarensis

This famous fossil, called *Australopithecus afarensis* (*A. afarensis,* for short) is commonly known as Lucy. Named for Lucy in the Beatles song "Lucy in the Sky with Diamonds," which was playing at the time, Lucy was such an important find because a large part of her skeleton was found together, which gave paleontologists a fair bit of confidence in describing the species.

Lucy was found in 1974, but her species lived from about 2.9 million to 3.6 million years ago. She was about 3½ feet tall and weighed 60 pounds. She was bipedal. At the time of her discovery, Lucy was the earliest bipedal hominid that had been discovered. The relative length of her forelimbs is intermediate between that of apes and people.

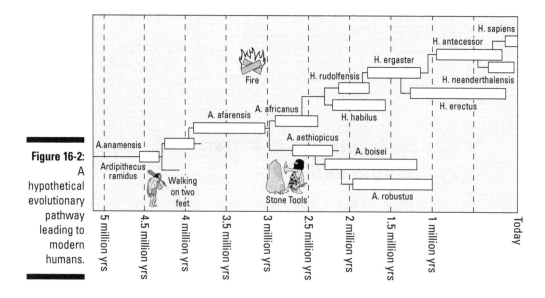

Figure 16-2: A hypothetical evolutionary pathway leading to modern humans.

Before Lucy's discovery, many researchers believed that the driving force behind the evolution of the large brain in the human lineage was that once the hands were free (due to the development of bipedalism) to use the tools, smarter individuals (those who were better toolmakers) would have an advantage. This idea is interesting, but it turns out that Lucy's brain was no bigger than a chimpanzee's — about one third the size of a human brain.

What this fossil species (and others since) have made clear is that the evolution of bipedal locomotion occurred *before* the evolution of a large brain. A long part of the human family tree is populated with ancient hominids that walked upright but had small brains. This is a nice example of a case in which the evidence provided by a fossil find allows scientists to reject one potential hypothesis about the pathway of human evolution. So it's back to the drawing board to come up with hypotheses that explain why a big brain was all of a sudden favored by natural selection.

The fossil record shows that after *A. afarensis,* the hominid lineage split into two branches. One branch eventually led to humans; the other branch led to a group referred to as the *robust Australopithecines: A. boisei* and *A. robustus.* These species had very strong jaws (perhaps for eating plant material). This lineage, which also includes *A. aethiopicus,* persisted from about 2.7 million to 1 million years ago and then became extinct.

I'm a traveling man: Homo erectus

Another important branching event in the hominid family tree is the one that separated *H. erectus* from the lineage leading to *H. sapiens. H. erectus* originated around 1.9 million years ago and went extinct almost everywhere 300,000 years ago, though one subspecies may have persisted on the island of Java perhaps as recently as 50,000 years ago.

H. erectus had a substantially larger brain than the *Australopithecines,* made and used tools, and may have been able to control fire. But the species' greatest claim to fame was being the first hominid species to leave Africa, which it did around 1.5 million years ago. By 1.2 million years ago, it had reached China and Southeast Asia.

H. erectus had a brain about two thirds the size of the human brain, but analysis of the internal structure of the *H. erectus* skull suggests that the area of the brain involved with speech wasn't developed to the extent that it is in later hominids. Meaning? Language came later.

Homo sapiens and Homo neanderthalensis

The last two species on the hominid tree are *Homo sapiens* and *Homo nean-derthalensis.* Both species originated in Africa — *H. neanderthalensis* about 250,000 years ago and *H. sapiens* about 100,000 years ago — and both moved out of Africa. *H. neanderthalensis* colonized Europe and parts of Central Asia, whereas *H. sapiens* went on to colonize the whole world. *H. neanderthalensis* coexisted with *H. sapiens* for a long time and went extinct only about 30,000 years ago, but anthropologists don't know why.

H. neanderthalensis was more robustly built than *H. sapiens,* possibly as an adaptation to the cold, but the two species' brains were the same size. Evidence has been found that *H. neanderthalensis* had advanced cultures: They modified their environment for shelter; they had art; and they buried their dead (the reason why a good fossil record for the species exists).

Many drawings of *H. neanderthalensis* incorrectly portray the species as having a hunched posture. The reason for the mistake? An early specimen had extreme arthritis. Analysis of many additional specimens reveals an upright posture like that of humans. If you were to pass a specimen of *H. neanderthalensis* on the sidewalk, you might notice the stockier build and facial features (such as a more pronounced brow and perhaps a larger nose), but if he was wearing a nicely tailored suit, you might not give him more than a second glance.

Hobbit Man: Homo floresienses

An incredible and still somewhat controversial fossil find, *Homo floresienses,* discovered on the Indonesian island of Flores in 2004, was possibly a dwarf species of the genus *Homo.* Nicknamed "Hobbit Man" after the character in J. R. R. Tolkien's *The Lord of the Rings,* the first skeleton found was a female approximately 3 feet tall, weighing perhaps 50 pounds, and estimated to be approximately 30 years old at the time of her death. The fossil evidence suggests that the species inhabited the island as recently as 13,000 years ago. (*Homo Neanderthalensis* went extinct approximately 25,000 years ago.) Because of the limited fossil record (so far, only one fossil has been found with an intact skull), no one knows exactly where *H. floresienses* fits in, but here are some suggestions:

- It's a dwarf form of *Homo erectus.*

- It's a *Homo sapiens* afflicted with *microcephaly,* a condition characterized by an unusually small head and mental impairments (This idea gained traction based on the fact that the *H. floresienses'* brain case is so small).

- It's a new species that lived into modern times — an interesting conjecture that's not supported by any physical fossil evidence but that has traction because people native to the island have legends of small furry people who lived in caves and had a different language. Sightings of such creatures were mentioned as recently as the 1800s and continue to this day on the island of Sumatra.

Did H. sapiens and H. neanderthalensis interbreed?

The fossil record seems to indicate that *Homo sapiens* and *Homo neanderthalensis* had far more similarities than differences. That being the case, was *H. neanderthalensis* truly a separate species? Maybe, as some researchers have suggested, it was simply another subspecies of *H. sapiens*, and possibly — just possibly — during the many years that the species overlapped in range, they interbred. This possibility is interesting, but you can't find clues in the fossil record. Instead, you have to turn to DNA.

Luckily, DNA is tough stuff, and advanced retrieval techniques have made it possible to obtain sequences of nuclear DNA from *H. neanderthalensis* specimens almost 40,000 years old.

The human and neanderthal DNA sequences are very similar, but there's about one half of a percent (0.5) difference. This is enough to identify specific DNA sequences that are specific to one or the other species.

Here's what DNA testing has revealed: The *H. neanderthalensis* genome is clearly distinct. Had any significant amount of mixing occurred, this result would be less clear. So DNA evidence clearly weighs in against the idea that the two groups interbred. Scientists can't rule out the possibility of any mating between the two species, but they *can* rule out the possibility that any significant genetic mixing occurred.

Out of Africa: Hominid migration patterns

Human beings originated in Africa. The evidence: Most hominid fossils are found only in Africa, and for those species with a wider distribution, the oldest specimens are always found in Africa. In addition, humans' most closely related living relative (both genetically and as placed on the tree of life; refer to Figure 16-1), the chimpanzee, lives in Africa. Not enough to convince you? The existing genetic variation in the human population provides another line of evidence.

Coalescence: Sharing a single ancestor

According to the concept of *coalescence*, all the genes in a given population have a single common ancestor — some individual in the past from whom they are all descended. Coalescence is the result of random processes whereby some individuals leave descendents and others don't (refer to Chapter 6).

Think of families in which different members have had different numbers of children. Perhaps one sibling has no children, and another sibling has many. In this way, random forces pile up through time. After enough time has passed, with some members having children and others not, eventually all the existing individuals will be descended from one ancestor. Scientists have discovered that this is essentially what happened, and they dubbed this common ancestor, because she is the one woman from whom all humans descended, "Mitochondrial Eve."

Coalescence doesn't mean that if you go back far enough, you find only one individual who started the whole population ball rolling. What it means is that only one individual, out of however many existed initially, has any descendents left.

Figure 16-3 shows a graphical representation of this process. Time progresses horizontally, from left to right. At the left are eight initial lineages, but as you go forward in time, more and more of these lineages die out due to random events until, in the end, all the current individuals are descendents of just one of the initial eight. Looking backward in time, you can see how the final lineages coalesce to a single ancestor in the past.

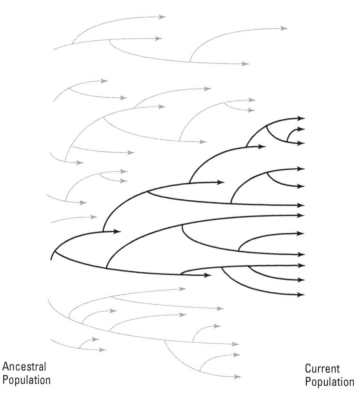

Figure 16-3:
As lineages
die out,
individuals
become
descendents
of one
individual.

Ancestral
Population

Current
Population

We're all descended from Mitochondrial Eve, but we're not all the same. Plenty of variation has been added to the population by mutation over the long period of time between the common ancestor and us. Eve's family tree has lots of branches, and there have been lots of mutation, selection, and genetic drift acting all that time. (Head to Part II for info on the key evolutionary processes.)

First Africa, then the world!

By sequencing information from the mitochondrial DNA and the Y-chromosomes (see the nearby sidebar "Of mitochondrial DNA and Y-chromosomes" for details on why these bits were used), scientists know the following:

- Humans probably originated in and spread through Africa first, with a small group leaving Africa and colonizing the rest of the world, although some scientists disagree about whether a single group left Africa and colonized the rest of the world or whether two different periods of emigration from Africa occurred. Figure 16-4 shows a map of the Earth with arrows indicating the patterns of human migration.

- The mitochondria of all living humans descend from one woman who lived in Africa perhaps 200,000 years ago. Because this one woman has been named "Mitochondrial Eve," many people misunderstand the findings, thinking that the name means that only one woman existed in the beginning — essentially, the Biblical Eve. What the name really means, however, is that only one out of however many women were alive at that time gave rise to all living humans. (This situation is the key point of coalescence, as explained in the preceding section.)

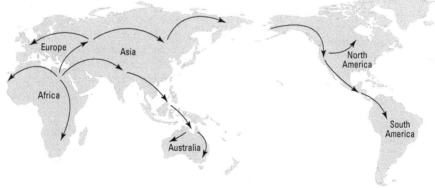

Figure 16-4:
Patterns of
human
migration.

Of mitochondrial DNA and Y-chromosomes

The name "Mitochondrial Eve" was never meant to be provocative, but unfortunately, most people focus on the "Eve" part (which is merely an allusion to the biblical Eve and *not* meant to imply that there was only a single woman on the planet) and completely skip over the "Mitochondrial" part, which is really the most important part of the name. Mitochondrial DNA, which remains intact through the female line, makes it possible to identify ancestors all the way back through time. The same is true for the Y- chromosome, which remains intact through the male line.

To understand mitochondrial DNA and Y-chromosomes, start by thinking about how you'd create a genealogy of your ancestors. You'd get a piece of paper, write your name down, then draw a couple of lines from you to your parents, draw a couple of lines from each parent to their parents (your grandparents), and so on and so forth until you went as far back as you could go.

Now think about your DNA. You got half of your DNA from each of your parents, who each gave you one set out the two sets of chromosomes you have. So they each gave you half of their own DNA, but because chromosomes break and rejoin during the process of gamete formation, the DNA you got from each parent was a mixture of the DNA *they* got from each of *their* parents. Which is why one quarter of your DNA came from each grandparent, one eighth came from each great grandparent, and so on and so forth.

Now from the genealogical point of view for any given bit of DNA in your genome, it's not really possible to tell which of your great-great-great-grandparents that bit of your DNA came from — with two exceptions: your mitochondrial DNA and, if you're male, your Y-chromosome DNA as well. That's because these two kinds of DNA don't get scrambled every generation. You got your mitochondrial DNA from your mother; she got it from her mother, who got it from her mother, and so on all the way back down the line.

All of a sudden, you (or scientists who trace lineages through mitochondrial DNA) can go back in time from one mother to the next. Through mitochondrial DNA, a lineage can be traced through the maternal line.

The same thing is true of the Y-chromosome. Because in males it pairs up with the X-chromosome and they're different, it doesn't do any recombining. (X-chromosomes do recombine when they're in women, because women have two of them; men only have one). In males, the Y-chromosome never has a partner for recombination. If you're a man, you got your Y-chromosome from your father, who got it from his father, and so on and so forth. Scientists can trace the Y-chromosome back through the male lineage.

And that's why these are the bits of ancestral information we can get from our DNA.

Recombination doesn't happen with mitochondrial DNA or Y-chromosomes, but mutations can happen, and these accumulate through time — most are probably neutral because good mutations are rare and bad ones get weeded out — in different lineages. By studying these mutations, scientists can say which of us are more closely related. If you and I had a nearly identical mitochondrial genome, we would've had a most recent common great-great-great-great-etc. grandmother more recently than someone who's mitochondrial DNA was a little bit more different than ours.

Apply this bit of knowledge to all the people on earth. The more mitochondrial DNA diversity we have, the more we've all been diverging from a common mother (called Mitochondrial Eve) — and that's the information we use to figure out how long ago that woman existed. The deep branches of the tree suggests that our most common recent female ancestor lived in Africa a couple of hundred thousand years ago.

Evolution within Homo Sapiens

Although the primary focus of this chapter is the evolutionary origin of the human species, human evolution didn't stop at the moment of speciation. Humans are still evolving. The following sections discuss some of the evolutionary events that have happened since the origin of our species.

Natural selection: Still acting on humans

Because humans can alter the environment to suit ourselves, we sometimes assume that we've stopped evolving, but we haven't. Natural selection has continued to act, increasing the frequency of advantageous genes. In fact, the very changes we make can select for evolutionary changes. For some examples, read on.

Of lice and men

If you always suspected that humans were special in some way, here's another bit of evidence to prove that you're absolutely right: Although most species of mammals have at most one kind of louse, the human species has three! This fact actually says quite a bit about human development.

Humans have head lice, adapted to hanging onto hair; body lice, adapted to hanging onto clothing; and pubic lice which like the nether regions. An analysis of the amount of genetic difference between the head lice and the body lice suggests that they diverged approximately 100,000 years ago, which gives scientists an approximate date of origin for tight-fitting fabric clothing — the sort body lice adapted to attach to. In the absence of clothing, lice were confined to hair, but when humans began to wear clothes, lice were able to spread to other regions of the body. Because the selective forces were different in each environment — head versus body — speciation between head and body lice eventually occurred.

So what about the third type of human lice: pubic lice? As it turns out, human pubic lice are closely related to gorilla body lice. They're divergent enough from gorilla lice, however, for scientists to be able to say that the transfer from gorillas to humans predated the evolution of body lice (and, therefore, the development of clothing). This finding suggests that humans lost their body hair (and, hence, had separate head and pubic-hair regions that different species of lice could colonize) long before they developed clothing.

Bottom line? Lice tell a story. If you have hair all over your body, you have only one kind of lice. Separate the hair into patches, and you can get lice adapted to each different patch. Cover some of the hairless area with a substance like clothing, and you can get diversification and speciation as one of the lice species (it just happened to be the one on the human head) radiates into this new habitat.

Oh, and by the way, lice are continuing to evolve. If you've ever had to deal with head lice and couldn't get rid of the buggers, you already know that many of them are now resistant to the chemicals we use to eradicate them.

The evolution of lactose digestion

None of our primate relatives can digest *lactose* — the sugar found in milk — as adults. Infant mammals need to be able to digest milk, but historically, they haven't needed this ability after weaning. By domesticating dairy animals, however, humans altered the environment in a way that selected for evolution of lactose-digesting ability in adults.

Human lineages that are associated with dairy farming have a much lower level of lactose intolerance than do lineages that aren't. In Africa, for example, the Nigerian Yoruba, an ethnic group in Nigeria, are 99 percent lactose intolerant, whereas cattle herders in the southern Sudan are less than 20 percent lactose intolerant.

Human disease and population density

The evolution of human disease is strongly affected by human population size. And large human populations became possible with advances in food production, namely the advent of farming. As human population density increased, human pests and parasites thrived, and humans evolved increased resistance to them. So in large populations, humans have developed built-in protection against the organisms that would do them harm.

But not all humans developed this resistance — just the ones living in high-density environments. Human populations living in low-density environments are relatively free of virulent pathogens. Small populations can't sustain infection, because everyone can be infected at the same time, and survivors of the disease become immune. The result? The pathogen goes extinct. If no one in the small group survives (in small groups, less chance exists that resistant individuals are present), the pathogen still goes extinct. As a result of the lack of constant exposure, small populations don't evolve resistance to disease. In a large population, on the other hand, new sensitive individuals are always being born.

When humans from large populations come into contact with humans who have traditionally lived in small groups, those from the large populations pass along diseases that can be far more serious for the people in the small populations. Tragic examples are the debilitating effects of disease on native populations in the Americas after contact with European explorers. The risk continues to this day when people from large populations come into contact with small groups in the Brazilian rain forest and other isolated locations.

Think about smallpox. Back in the day when smallpox was rampant, somebody always had it. (If at any instant no one was sick with smallpox, the virus would've gone extinct.) In a large population, new susceptible individuals were always being born, so the virus always had a refuge of new people to infect. Although smallpox was a dreaded disease, people in Europe, Asia, and

Africa were relatively resistant to it. Only 25 percent of people who contracted it died — a big number, true, but 75 percent of infected people survived. Compare that outcome with the experience of smaller populations, particularly in the New World.

The Americas were colonized via the Bering land bridge at a time preceding the development of agriculture and large population sizes. Movement to the New World would have been in small groups of hunter-gatherers — groups too small to maintain infectious diseases such as smallpox. As a result of the relative freedom from European diseases in the New World (an accident of history), human populations in the Americas didn't evolve resistance to these diseases and were devastated by them upon coming into contact with European explorers and colonists.

Relaxation of selection

Allele frequencies can change in response to natural selection or in response to a reduction in selection pressures. As some of the selective forces that have acted on humans in the past are eliminated — humans no longer need to run away from big, fierce, hungry animals, for example — other alleles can increase in frequency as a result of genetic drift (random events; refer to Chapter 6).

In an environment in which running fast doesn't confer any particular benefit, *not* being able to run fast doesn't mean that humans are in any way less fit. As long as no tigers are around, our slow alleles don't have a lower probability of being passed on to the next generation. So we may get slower, but we don't get less fit. (Note that there isn't selection for slower running; there just isn't selection either way.)

Cultural evolution

Cultural evolution isn't a biological phenomenon, but it's an interesting topic that can help you understand how humans are able to alter the environment rapidly and outcompete all the other species.

In biological evolution, genes get transmitted directly from parent to offspring, and they increase in the population as a result of either random forces or positive selection. Either way, the process can take some time. In cultural evolution, advancements (such as bright ideas or better ways of doing things) aren't limited to this vertical pathway of parent to offspring. If I figure out how to make a better spear, for example, I don't pass the information to my children genetically; I just show them how to do it. Then I show everybody else in the tribe how to do it, too.

Because cultural evolution can change behaviors or traits much faster than genetic evolution does, animals whose sole adaptive ability relies on genetic evolution are at a disadvantage. Rapid selection will occur to cause tigers to keep their distance from large groups of people armed with spears, for example, but changes in human hunting ability occur so suddenly that the tigers might still go extinct. Humans are still evolving biologically, but we're evolving culturally as well, which gives us an edge that other species can't match.

Chapter 17

The Evolution of Antibiotic Resistance

- -

In This Chapter

▶ Appreciating the power of antibiotics

▶ Understanding the evolutionary pressure that causes antibiotic resistance

▶ Figuring out what to do next

- -

*H*ere's an interesting tidbit to throw out at your next dinner party: Our
bodies have been colonized by all manner of bacteria. Yes, that's right;
you are your own big blue marble. Fortunately, many of the bacteria that
have set up housekeeping in your body are *commensal bacteria:* They colonize your skin or your gastrointestinal tract and are rarely of any concern.
Others, however, such as *Staphylococcus aureus,* aren't such good citizens.
They hang around on your skin and in your nasal (and other) passages, looking for ways to stir up trouble.

So why aren't you sick all the time? Because your immune system does a
pretty good job of keeping potentially harmful bacteria at bay. And when
your immune system has trouble, *antibiotics* — compounds designed to kill
or neutralize infectious agents — can help. There's one hitch, though:
Bacteria evolve in ways that make them better at overcoming our bodies'
defenses and more resistant to the antibiotics we use to get rid of them.

In this chapter, I explain the evolution of antibiotic resistance in bacteria and
show that the way humans use (and overuse) antibiotics is directly related to
how bacteria evolve.

Antibiotics and Antibiotic Resistance in a Nutshell

In this chapter, I use the term *antibiotic* to refer to any chemical that kills bacteria or inhibits bacterial growth. I'd stop there, but because the term *antibiotic* is often in the news and used interchangeably with terms like *antimicrobial* and *antiviral*, a little more explanation is in order — especially when these terms tend to appear in rather alarming news stories about infections running amok. To help you avoid confusion and gain a little perspective, I offer the following sections.

Splitting microbial hairs: Defining antibiotics

Microbes are a diverse collection of organisms, many of which have almost nothing in common except that they are extremely little. They fall into three major categories — bacteria, viruses, and eukaryotes, which include fungi (which have some important disease organisms) — as well as a bunch of other critters, like Giardia and other protozoan parasites, that cause diseases like diarrhea and malaria. Humans tend to lump them all together because, as a group, they're responsible for infectious diseases.

Antimicrobials, as you may cleverly guess, are compounds that are active against microbes. Each antimicrobial has a name that indicates which microbe it's active against:

- **Antivirals:** Antimicrobial compounds that target viruses.
- **Antifungals:** Compounds active against fungi.
- **Antimalarials and other compounds:** These are active against specific kinds of eukaryotic diseases (see the nearby sidebar "Eukaryotes for you and me"). (*Note:* Antimicrobials that are active against these types of infections tend to be named more specifically.)
- **Antibacterials:** Compounds that are active against bacteria.

Here's where matters get confusing: Antibacterials are often referred to as *antibiotics,* a term that is also occasionally used interchangeably with the term *antimicrobial.*

 Antibiotic can be used generally to refer to *all* disease-fighting compounds and specifically to mean *only* those compounds that are effective against bacterial agents. This dual-purpose use of the term leads to one of the biggest misunderstandings about what antibiotics can and can't do. You may have heard that antibiotics aren't effective against viral infections. That's true, when the term *antibiotics* is used specifically to mean *antibacterial,* which by definition means active only against bacteria, not against other microbes.

Technically, antibiotics are chemicals that kill or inhibit the growth of *biotic* (biological, or living) things, as opposed to abiotic things (like rocks). Rat poison is an antibiotic; so is Round Up. But when scientists use the term *antibiotic,* they're almost always referring to antibacterial agents — things that kill or inhibit the growth of bacteria — because the original antibiotic compounds, such as penicillin, were active against bacteria.

A brief history of antibiotic resistance

In the days before antibiotics were widely available and widely used, people knew the dangers of infection. Even minor injuries like cuts and scrapes were taken far more seriously; just ask your grandparents. That's because an ounce of prevention is worth a pound of cure — all the more so when there isn't any cure.

Fast-forward to today. People tend not to view cuts and scrapes as being potentially serious medical conditions. Prevention seems less important, because we have a pound of cure — pounds and pounds and pounds, in fact. In 2007, people in the United States used millions of pounds of antibiotics. Therein lies the problem. With each passing year, antibiotics become less effective as bacterial populations evolve to be resistant to them.

Although recent news stories warning people about antibiotic-resistant strains of bacteria may lead you to believe that the phenomenon is relatively recent, it's actually as old as the use of antibiotics. Penicillin, the first widely used antibiotic, dates to the end of World War II. Within four years after its introduction, scientists observed resistant bacteria, and the incidence of resistance has increased steadily to the present day.

You'd think that having identified the fact that bacteria began to evolve almost immediately in response to penicillin would have encouraged people to be a bit more careful about the use of antibiotics. But we weren't, partly because it's hard to *not* use a medication that's so effective (many people considered penicillin to be a miracle drug) and partly because at the time, new antibiotic compounds were being discovered regularly. When one compound was no longer effective, doctors simply switched to a different compound. The scenario is very different today.

In recent years, bacteria have been gaining on us: The rate at which researchers have discovered new medically useful antibiotics has slowed, but the steady march of the evolution of resistance continues unchecked.

TECHNICAL STUFF

Antibacterials, antifungals, antivirals, and you

Most of the antimicrobial compounds at humans' disposal are compounds that are active against bacteria rather than against other microorganisms, such as fungi and viruses. Why? Because developing compounds that are active against viruses and fungi is far harder. To be medically useful, a compound has to be able to stop the invading microorganisms without hurting the person taking the compound.

At the biochemical level, bacteria are quite different from people, making it possible to target specific details of the bacterial physiology without overly affecting human physiology. The same isn't true of viruses and fungi:

✔ Viruses replicate primarily by harnessing *human* cellular machinery. For that reason,

harming the virus without harming ourselves is very difficult.

✔ Fungi are quite a bit more similar to humans at the biochemical level than we might like to imagine; therefore, the substances that hurt fungi also hurt us (which is why it's so hard to cure a fungal infection like athlete's foot). Although chemicals are available that can harm the fungus pretty efficiently, the same chemicals tend to harm us, too.

This isn't to say that antibacterial compounds are without side effects. Many compounds do have side effects, which can be severe, but the medical risks of these side effects are balanced against the obvious benefits of curing the infection.

Again, the evolution of resistance isn't new. In every case, scientists have noted the existence of antibiotic-resistant bacteria shortly after the antibiotic was introduced.

Today, we humans now find ourselves facing bacteria that are resistant to many — and, in some cases, all — available antibiotics. Examples include staph, tuberculosis, syphilis, and gonorrhea. The most frightening thing we can observe from this information is that in the end, all of our antibacterial compounds end up being defeated.

Becoming Resistant to Antibiotics: A How-to Guide

Try as scientists might to develop new and better antibiotics, bacteria are gaining on them, evolving resistance against every compound science can throw their way. Bacteria, in other words, are pretty good at this evolution thing, and here's why:

> ✔ They reproduce extremely rapidly, and lots of them exist.
>
> ✔ They've been at it a long time. Antibiotics are common in nature. Penicillin, the first antibiotic in wide use, comes from a fungus, *Pennicillium chrysogenum*.
>
> ✔ They are the weapons bacteria and other organisms sometimes use in fighting each other.

Bacteria can gain antibiotic resistance in a couple of ways: by mutations and by gene transfers. The following sections give the details.

Evolution via mutation

As I explain in Chapter 5, evolution by natural selection requires the existence of a variation on which selection can act. The initial source of all variation is the random mutations in an organism's DNA. These mutations occur during the processes of DNA replication (when copies are made) or repair. Basically, whenever an organism is doing something with its DNA, a chance exists that a mistake will occur, resulting in DNA with a slightly different sequence.

Because bacteria reproduce rapidly (sometimes as fast as every 15 minutes), and because so many of them are around, many opportunities are available for these changes in DNA sequence to occur. Put a billion bacteria in a beaker, and come back 15 minutes later; you could find 2 billion bacteria. In the course of duplicating those 1 billion genomes, a substantial number of errors will have occurred. Bacteria's fast, high-density lifestyle gives them an evolutionary edge.

You can observe this phenomenon in the laboratory very easily. An experimenter takes a single bacterium that's known to be sensitive to a particular antibiotic, drops the bacterium into a nice cozy beaker, and lets the bacterium divide. Pretty soon the beaker contains two bacteria, then four, and then eight. By the next day, the beaker contains millions and millions of bacteria, all descendents of the same antibiotic-sensitive parent. Now the experimenter takes these millions of bacteria and exposes them all to the antibiotic. Often, he finds that the beaker now contains resistant bacteria. Mutations have appeared in these bacteria as a result of DNA replication errors, and these mutations confer resistance to the antibiotic. When the remaining bacteria reproduce to fill the flask again, the experimenter ends up with a flask full of antibiotic-resistant bacteria.

Scientists would really like to develop an antibiotic to which bacteria can't evolve resistance, but so far, they haven't had any luck. The process of evolution is so powerful that when scientists change the bacteria's environment by adding antibiotics, they always manage to select for resistant bacteria. In our new antibiotic-drenched world, any bacterium that's a little bit better at surviving in the presence of antibiotics is going to be the one that leaves the most descendents.

A common misconception is that the addition of the antibiotic leads to the genetic changes that result in antibiotic resistance. But evolution requires that the variation *already be present*. The addition of the antibiotic didn't cause the bacteria in the beaker to become antibiotic resistant; it just killed all the antibiotic-sensitive bacteria, leaving behind only the bacteria that happened to be antibiotic resistant already.

Evolution via gene transfer

An interesting characteristic of bacteria is that occasionally they acquire genes from bacteria of other species. Yes, that phenomenon is as weird as it sounds. Bacterial reproduction usually involves just dividing in two; no other bacteria is required, and both of the resulting bacteria are (excepting the occasional mutation) genetically identical. Every once in a while, however, a bacterium acquires genes from somewhere else. When it does, it's not too picky about which genes it gets.

An example of this kind of acquisition of new genes is the pathogenic *E. coli* 0157:H7 (see Chapter 15). *E. coli* 0157:H7 first came to light after an outbreak at a fast-food establishment; as of late, it's been found in a large number of domestic cattle operations, as well as in the occasional bag of spinach. This nasty version of *E. coli* started out as plain old, relatively harmless *E. coli,* but it picked up a whole bunch of genes that *E. coli* usually don't have, some of them quite nasty.

Gene transfer between bacteria can greatly speed the rate at which an antibiotic-resistant gene spreads. Rather than having to evolve separately in each individual bacterial species, antibiotic resistance can, after having evolved once, be transferred to different species.

This type of gene acquisition by bacteria (called *horizontal transfer* to differentiate it from *vertical transfer,* in which the trait is passed down through descendents), occurs via three mechanisms:

✔ **Transformation:** The process whereby a bacterial cell picks up DNA from its environment and incorporates it into its own genome.

✔ **Transduction:** The process whereby genes are carried from one bacterium to another in a bacterial virus. Occasionally, before leaving the host cell, a virus particle that's being assembled accidentally gets filled with bacterial DNA instead of viral DNA. When that virus particle latches onto a new bacterium, it injects that bacterium with the foreign bacterial DNA, which may then be incorporated into the bacterium's genome.

✔ **Conjugation:** The process in which two bacteria join and DNA is passed from one to the next. This process is controlled by a small circle of DNA living within the bacterium, called a *plasmid.*

Plasmids, which are much bigger than the pieces of DNA usually involved in transformation and transduction, are especially important in the spread of antibiotic resistance. Through a single plasmid, a bacterium can become resistant to numerous antibiotics in one fell swoop, sometimes with tragic results: An outbreak of Shigella dysentery containing a plasmid coding for resistance to four antibiotics was responsible for over 10,000 deaths in Guatemala during the late 1960s.

Resistance at the cellular and biochemical levels

In the preceding sections, I talk about antibiotic resistance in general terms: how bacteria can evolve through mutations and through gene transfer. Whether resistance is conferred by mutations in DNA or by gene transfers, something goes on at the cellular and biochemical levels that changes the bacteria from being antibiotic sensitive to being antibiotic resistant. Basically, the resistance comes in one of three forms:

✔ Mutations that reduce the amount of antibiotic entering the bacterial cell, such as changes in the cell membrane that make it more difficult for the antibiotic to get in or that pump out the antibiotic as soon as it gets in.

✔ Mutations that enable the bacteria to produce enzymes that destroy the antibiotic.

✔ Mutations that change what the antibiotic targets. These changes can range from changing the shape of proteins so that the antibiotic no longer recognizes them to reorganizing biochemical pathways to eliminate the stages that the antibiotic targets.

Mercy, mercy me! MRSA

Methicillin-resistant *Staphylococcus aureus* (MRSA) is a staph infection that can be very hard to treat because it's resistant to a lot of antibiotics including, no surprises here, methicillin, which otherwise would be wonderfully effective. According to the U.S. Centers for Disease Control and Prevention, MRSA infections (discovered in the early 1960s) accounted for 2 percent of staph infections in 1974. Thirty years later (by 2004), MRSA accounted for 63 percent.

MRSA is alarming for these reasons:

✔ Although MRSA staph infections can still be treated with other drugs, these drugs are more expensive, have greater side effects, and act more slowly than the drugs that were effective against it in the past. MRSA can often be treated with the antibiotic Vancomycin, for example. Unfortunately, we now have to worry about a new version of staph infection called, you guessed it, VRSA.

✔ MRSA infections cause thousands of deaths every year, but the most frightening ones, the ones that make for the most sensational news, are the cases of "flesh eating staph." Deep bacterial infections can cause massive tissue damage. While many kinds of bacteria have been implicated in such infections, MRSA is becoming an increasingly common cause. Because of the speed with which these deep infections can progress, treatment becomes a race against time. Even with the best medical care, fatality rates can be high, and having to use suboptimal antibiotics (because bacteria have grown resistant to the better ones) only makes the situation worse.

✔ Most MRSA infections (about 85 percent) are acquired in healthcare settings, but in the 1990s, MRSA began showing up in the broader community and are called CA-MRSA (for community associated MRSA).

Evolving a bit at a time: Partial resistance

Bacteria may evolve complete immunity to the particular antibiotic by first passing through a stage of partial immunity. Partially resistant bacteria can survive a concentration of the antibiotic sufficient to kill susceptible bacteria but will succumb to a greater concentration.

Imagine a scenario in which no single mutation can render the bacteria completely immune to a particular antibiotic, but some mutations convey partial resistance. These mutations are favored only when antibiotic concentrations are low; such conditions lead to a population of partially resistant bacteria. Then another single mutation could result in the partially resistant bacteria becoming either more or completely resistant to the antibiotic.

Partial resistance is the reason why doctors tell you to finish a course of antibiotics — even if you're feeling better and even if you've decided that the last couple of pills are unnecessary. The initial pulse of antibiotics kills all the sensitive bacteria (which is why you feel better), but some of the remaining bacteria may be partially resistant to the antibiotic. Rather than let the partially resistant bacteria off the hook, don't give them a chance to get a leg up on the antibiotic. After all, they're the ones you really want to control. Stop them while you still can!

The Battle against Antibiotic Resistance

Science is fighting a battle against antibiotic resistance — and losing because of how quickly microbes evolve. A big part of the problem is that we humans are the major selective force driving the evolution of antibiotic resistance in those critters that infect us. Every time scientists throw a new antibiotic at a microbe, they end up selecting for more resistant microbes. Science needs to change its strategy, and evolutionary biology can help:

- ✔ **Making new drugs:** If researchers understand exactly how the bacteria evolve resistance, they may be able to design better drugs.

- ✔ **Testing and refining theories about what happens if humans use antibiotics less:** The science of evolutionary biology, complete with all the beautiful experiments outlined in later sections of this chapter, is how scientists generate and modify their expectations. Unfortunately, much of what they learn from these experiments is bleak, but at least they learn something, and what they learn is important to understanding how microbial populations respond to changes in the way humans use antibiotics.

- ✔ **Not screwing up the drugs we already have:** By being careful about how and when we use antibiotic medications, humans can slow the development of antibiotic resistance.

New and improved! Making new drugs

By understanding the mechanisms that make a particular microorganism antibiotic resistant, scientists can tailor new antibiotics to undermine that mechanism. If a bacterium is antibiotic resistant because it can pump antibiotics out of its cell, doctors can change the way the antibiotic is administered: Instead of giving the antibiotic alone, they can give it along with a second compound that disrupts each bacterium's pumping ability. *Voilà* — an effective solution. Similarly, by understanding exactly how bacterial enzymes destroy an antibiotic, scientists can design new, slightly different antibiotics that aren't as readily degraded.

Turning back the clock to bacterial sensitivity

Some scientists have suggested that if humans temporarily cease using antibiotics, bacterial populations will lose their resistance in one of two ways — by evolving back to being susceptible to antibiotics or by being out competed by the remaining sensitive bacteria that are no longer at a disadvantage — at which point humans could resume using antibiotics with much greater effect.

Evolving back

The thinking goes like this: Removing the antibiotic would result in the evolution of sensitive bacteria *only if* the sensitive bacteria have an advantage over the resistant bacteria. The most commonly envisioned advantage? That antibiotic resistance has a cost. Maybe the changes that make bacteria resistant (changes in bacterial membranes, for example, or DNA replication) also make them less able to perform other bacterial functions. By removing the antibiotic from the environment, mutations back to the original bacterial physiology would be favored, because sensitive bacteria are better than resistant bacteria at doing all the things bacteria have to do in the absence of antibiotics.

This hypothesis is great, but would it work? Several experiments have been conducted regarding this question, and they show, unfortunately, that the solution isn't as simple as instituting a moratorium on antibiotic use. Why? For the reasons explained in the following sections.

Bacteria continue to evolve

Although bacteria resistance comes at a cost (they tend to grow more slowly in the presence of antibiotics than the original sensitive bacteria do), the process of *amelioration* — secondary mutations decreasing the debilitating effect of the initial mutation — is favored by selection. If the initial antibiotic-resistant mutant had a high fitness cost, subsequent evolution selects for additional mutations that increase the fitness of the antibiotic-resistant strain. As time goes by, the antibiotic-resistant bacteria don't have as low a fitness compared with the original bacteria (in the absence of antibiotics) as scientists would wish them to have. Thus, removing the antibiotics won't have as much of an effect as we would all want.

Starting with a wild sensitive bacterial strain, Stephanie Schrag and coworkers grew the strain until they could find and isolate an antibiotic-resistant bacterial mutant whose fitness was lower because of its mutation (the old DNA sequence was better than the new DNA sequence for some key bacterial function). They then grew this antibiotic-resistant bacteria for many generations in the lab and let evolution happen. As the antibiotic-resistant bacteria evolved, their fitness improved because of *compensatory mutations,* additional mutations that returned their fitness to about the level of the original antibiotic-sensitive strain.

Think back to that antibiotic-resistant bacterium that's not so good at DNA replication. Because it has the resistant allele, it manages to spread to the environment after all the sensitive bacteria have expired; now it lives in a sea of bacteria that are all resistant to the antibiotic but that all have a little trouble replicating their DNA. In this population, mutations that restore the ability to replicate DNA easily will be favored, and after selection has proceeded for some time, the antibiotic-resistant bacteria gain back much of the function they initially lost.

Compensatory and back mutations aren't what they're cut out to be

So you have a strain of antibiotic-resistant bacteria that are now just as fit as the original antibiotic-sensitive strain. Now imagine what would happen if you take away all the antibiotics. Mutations still occur, and eventually one will appear that undoes what the original resistance mutation did (replaces the new sequence with the old sequence again), making this strain sensitive again. Will this new antibiotic sensitive strain take over so we can start using antibiotics again? Unfortunately no, because the old DNA sequence *is not* better than the new DNA sequence in the presence of the subsequent, post resistance, DNA changes. It was in the original strain, but not any more.

To determine that compensatory mutations could actually *lower* the probability that the resistant bacteria would evolve back toward sensitivity to antibiotics if antibiotics were removed, Schrag and coworkers conducted a second study. Using genetic engineering, they replaced the DNA responsible for antibiotic resistance with the DNA sequence of the sensitive strain while leaving the compensatory mutations unchanged. In effect, they created the bacteria that would exist if the antibiotic-resistant strain mutated back to being antibiotic sensitive.

The surprising result was that the antibiotic-sensitive bacteria they'd created in the laboratory grew more slowly than the resistant strain in the absence of antibiotics. What this result means is that all the compensatory mutations that piled up in the antibiotic-resistant bacteria were advantageous only in the presence of the antibiotic-resistant gene; they were deleterious in the presence of the original sensitive gene.

After an antibiotic-resistant gene has appeared and compensatory mutations of the sort that Schrag and coworkers found in their laboratory have arisen, the antibiotic-resistant gene can be more fit than the antibiotic-sensitive gene, even in the absence of antibiotics. Why? Because a *back mutation* (a mutation that undoes exactly what the first mutation did) rendering one of these antibiotic-resistant bacteria susceptible could have lower fitness even in the absence of antibiotics. That situation is troubling because when all the bacteria become resistant, they stay resistant even if the antibiotic is stopped for a while. While we don't know exactly how common this sort of result would be, it's not good news.

Mutations aren't necessarily as costly as you'd think

Although most antibiotic-resistant mutations have associated costs, some of them have very small costs, and some even have no cost. An awful lot of bacteria are around, and if even a few of them are capable of acquiring antibiotic-resistant mutations with no deleterious effects, this small class of mutations will be able to beat out the much larger number of antibiotic-resistant mutations that result in less healthy resistant bacteria. In a battle between the debilitated bacteria and the undamaged bacteria, the debilitated ones won't last long.

Just as genetic differences exist between different humans, genetic differences exist between different bacteria within a species. This situation raises the question of how important these different genetic backgrounds are in determining the associated costs of resistance. Fred Cohan and coworkers found that the genetic background in which an antibiotic mutation appeared was an important factor in the associated costs of that mutation. They determined that in some cases, acquiring resistance to an antibiotic was associated with few or no costs in other areas of bacterial physiology.

Cohan and his coworkers performed an experiment using the common soil bacteria *Bacillus subtilis*, which can take up DNA from the environment and incorporate it into its own genetic material. The researchers isolated a strain of *Bacillus subtilis* that was resistant to the antibiotic rifampin, made many copies of the gene that made the bacteria antibiotic resistant, and then introduced this gene into a collection of wild *Bacillus subtilis* strains simply by exposing samples of the different bacteria to the DNA responsible for antibiotic resistance. As they expected, the sample bacteria took up this gene.

For each of the wild bacteria, they compared the growth rate of the strain before the introduction of the antibiotic-resistant gene with the growth rate of the strain after the introduction of antibiotic resistance. In most, but not all, cases, they found a substantial decrease in growth rate with the introduction of the antibiotic-resistant gene.

Their conclusion? Antibiotic resistance indeed had a cost — but not always. Costs differed greatly among the different genetic backgrounds, and in a small number of cases, the antibiotic-resistant bacteria weren't significantly debilitated compared with the original sensitive strain.

Antibiotic resistance and tuberculosis

To determine the clinical importance of antibiotic mutants with different fitness effects, Sebastien Gagneux, Clara Davis, Brendan Bohannan, and others conducted a series of experiments with the strain of bacteria that causes tuberculosis. They found that the mutations they could identify in the laboratory as having the lowest fitness costs were the same antibiotic-resistant mutations that were responsible for the resistant strains of tuberculosis present in clinical settings.

The researchers conducted laboratory experiments to measure the fitness costs of a series of antibiotic-resistant mutations. They examined a variety of mutations and found that some tended to have low fitness costs and that others tended to have high fitness costs. Then they examined the mutations present in clinical settings.

What they found was that antibiotic-resistant tuberculosis strains isolated from patients were very likely to contain antibiotic-resistance genes that had been shown in their laboratory experiments to have low fitness costs. They never found, in their patients, antibiotic-resistant tuberculosis strains with resistance alleles that had been shown to have high fitness costs. Both types of mutations occur, but the types with high fitness costs don't increase to the point where they are detectable. Furthermore, some of the clinical strains harboring the lowest-cost antibiotic-resistance mutation exhibited no decrease in fitness relative to the sensitive strain.

This is a finding of major importance, and unfortunately it's bad news. It had been suggested (and hoped) that if we reduced our use of antibiotics, the antibiotic-resistant bacteria would decline because they were supposed to be less fit than the original strains in the absence of antibiotics. They would just get overwhelmed by the few remaining resistant bacteria. Turns out that while many possible mutants are less fit, the ones that take over are the ones that aren't.

Changing the way antibiotics are used

The results of the experiments outlined in the preceding section suggest that we humans had better think seriously about battling antibiotic resistance by trying to slow its progression rather than hoping we'll be able to deal with it after it occurs. To do that, we have to make real changes in how we use antibiotics — such as taking all our medicine. Taking only some of the antibiotics can create partially resistant bacteria, which may acquire subsequent mutations that make them even more resistant.

Here's just a little personal (and public) health note: Once you've knocked the infection down with the first half of the bottle, you've selected for the most resistant bacteria. The only way to kill those off is to finish the course of pills.

Another change is that people can use antibiotics less, which will decrease the selective pressure on the remaining sensitive bacteria. With fewer antibiotics around, sensitive bacteria would be less likely to be outcompeted by resistant bacteria. The idea is that, although humans can't stop using antibiotics to cure diseases, maybe we can stop hosing down the entire agricultural world with the same compounds we rely on to survive those diseases.

Antibiotics and agriculture

Of the millions of pounds of antibiotics used annually in the United States, less than half are used to treat human diseases. The majority of antibiotics are used in agriculture and not primarily for treating sick animals:

✔ Low doses of antibiotics are used as a food additive to increase animal growth rate. The mechanism by which low doses of antibiotics increase animal growth rate is unclear, but what *is* clear is that farms and feedlots are growing reservoirs of antibiotic-resistance genes.

✔ Antibiotics are sprayed on fruit trees, resulting in a continuum of antibiotic concentrations starting from high at the center of the orchard and gradually fading to nothing at the edges of the antibiotic mist cloud. These continuous low doses of antibiotics in agricultural settings provide exactly the right situation for the evolution of fully resistant bacterial types.

Of the fraction of antibiotics in the United States that are used to treat human disease, evidence exists that many prescriptions are unnecessary. Patients want antibiotics even when they have no reason to think that their illness will respond to antibiotics — when they have the flu, for example — and the U.S. Centers for Disease Control and Prevention reports that more than 90 percent of physicians report feeling pressure to prescribe antibiotics that they know are unnecessary. So give your doctor a break!

For the past 60 years, antibiotics have allowed humans to live without fear of bacterial disease. With proper stewardship of this great resource, we can continue to enjoy the protections that antibiotics offer, but the point where we must take action to ensure the future efficacy of antibiotics is rapidly approaching. Scientists know with absolute certainty that bacteria will continue to evolve antibiotic resistance in response to human use of antibiotics. What is uncertain is whether we humans will make this evolution hard for them.

Chapter 18

HIV: The Origin and Evolution of a Virus

Smallpox. Influenza. Cholera. Syphilis. Yellow fever. Measles. Typhus. Plague. Malaria. Every age — and region — has its scourge, and some have more than their fair share. You may think that some these diseases are of the past (or of undeveloped countries) and that they don't really affect you. But when it comes to viral infections, no society or region is off the hook. Case in point: the appearance in the early 1980s of a new disease: *acquired immunodeficiency syndrome, or AIDS.*

AIDS scared the bejesus out of people. It was deadly. It was painful. And in the beginning at least, no one knew where it had come from or how it was spread. Fast-forward nearly 30 years. Scientists know quite a bit more about AIDS now than they did then. They know what causes it (the *human immunodeficiency virus, or HIV*), where it came from (other primates), and the path that the disease takes when it enters a human body.

How do they know all this stuff? By knowing how viruses work and by studying the evolution of the human immunodeficiency virus itself. Evolution is important in understanding HIV at many levels — from the origin of the virus to the disease process within a single patient to the development of effective treatment options.

What Viruses Are

Given that this chapter and the one on influenza that follows both deal with viruses, knowing exactly what a virus is and how it functions is probably a good idea. To that end, viruses are

- ✔ **Microscopic entities:** The smallest microorganisms are viruses, even if not all viruses are smaller than all other organisms.

    Viruses used to be considered the smallest of all microorganisms (the smallest things are still viruses) until scientists found a really big one — so big, in fact, that you can see it under a light microscope. This Baby Huey of viruses is bigger than a lot of bacteria, and it infects amoebas.

- ✔ **Obligate intercellular parasites:** This is a fancy phrase that means viruses can survive and multiply only in living cells. Whose living cells? Why the hosts', of course.

A virus is an extremely simple organism. It consists of the viral genome (which can be made up of DNA *or* RNA) and any other molecules that the virus needs to get going after it's invaded the host cell. All this stuff is enclosed in an outer coat made of proteins or, in some cases, of proteins and *lipids,* which is a fancy word for *fat.*

Are viruses alive? We say "Yes!"

Viruses are odd — so odd that no consensus exists on whether they're actually living things. Some people say yes; some people say no (and some people say sort of, but I'm not going to worry about the fence-sitters here).

One way to classify things as living or not living is to come up with a list of things that we think living things should have and then ask if our test object — in this case, viruses — has those things. Consider these examples of things that living organisms share:

- ✔ **Cells:** With the discovery of the microscope, which predated the discovery of viruses, scientists saw that all the living things they looked at had cells, so the definition of a living thing came to include having cells. Then scientists discovered viruses, which don't have cells. So under the "all living things have cells" definition, a virus, which doesn't have cells, can't be a living thing.

✔ **A genome made up of nucleic acid:** Viruses have a *genome,* the instruction set for making the organism, and when it's time to reproduce, they make new copies of the genome and package them into progeny viruses. The viral genome also codes for proteins, just as the human genome does, but because viruses are parasites, they don't need to make all the proteins — just the ones that the host doesn't already make. If having a nucleic-acid genome that codes for the production of proteins is the definition of life, viruses are alive.

If you say that, to be considered living things, viruses must have certain characteristics, then they are (or aren't) living organisms based on the characteristics you select. But this is a very nebulous way of defining what's alive and what isn't. If you say, for example, that having hair is a defining characteristic of a living organism, then you'd be alive, but a fish wouldn't. This example is silly, of course, but it shows how definitions have no foundations other than the ones humans give them.

A more helpful way to determine whether something is alive is to think about fundamental processes associated with life. Living things reproduce, for example. They also evolve. The process of copying the genome isn't error free, and mutations occur; mutations that are advantageous may increase in frequency. Being able to evolve is what fundamentally separates the living from the not living. A fire spreading through a forest reproduces itself, and a few flames lead to more flames, but fire itself doesn't evolve.

Viruses are independently evolving entities. They reproduce. They contain within themselves the instruction set for their own reproduction: the genome. And that genome changes through time: it evolves. If you use the life processes of reproduction and evolution as the fundamental characteristics of living organisms, viruses are alive.

The fact that viruses evolve is important not only for understanding where they come from and how they work, but also for addressing the threat that they pose and providing treatment. To treat a patient who's been poisoned, you just need to know how to counteract that particular poison. Treating a patient whose illness is the result of *an organism that can evolve* requires anticipating and responding to the adaptations that the organism can make. In the case of HIV, by the time a patient experiences symptoms, the virus has evolved and behaves differently from the original virus that infected the patient.

Whether you want to consider viruses living or not is entirely up to you. Regardless of which side of the debate you land on, all the information in this chapter still applies. Alive or not alive, viruses evolve, and *that's* the important thing.

Viral reproduction: DNA, RNA, or retro?

The only way a virus can reproduce is to infect a host cell, hijack the cell's machinery to make copies of itself, and then move on to infect other cells. But not all viruses do things the same way, and these differences can have consequences for everything from viral evolution to treatment.

Different viruses use different nucleic acids (DNA or RNA) as the genetic material. Some, like herpes, use DNA. Some, like the flu, use RNA. And some (like HIV) use both, alternating back and forth. This third type of virus is called a *retrovirus*. Retroviruses use the enzyme reverse-transcriptase to make RNA from DNA (refer to Figure 18-1).

Different viruses have different mutation rates, and viruses that use RNA (either all or some of the time) can have very high mutation rates. HIV is one such virus. Its reverse transcriptase makes a lot of mistakes, leading to many slightly different viral types.

Some viruses replicate in the host cell and then the progeny go on to find another cell to infect. But others, including HIV, will also sometimes slip their DNA into the host chromosome. When the HIV genome is present as DNA, it can integrate into the host chromosome and hide there. It's just a string of A, C, T, and G bases and the immune system can't find it. Neither can current antiviral drugs. Hopefully, drugs that can find the virus can be developed. HIV researchers know what sequence to target; it's just a matter of figuring out how.

What Is HIV?

HIV stands for *human immunodeficiency virus.* HIV attacks and impairs the cells in your immune system. HIV itself doesn't kill you; you die of any of the infections that your body usually would be able to fight off.

Several HIV viruses exist, and they can be divided into two major groups: HIV-1 and HIV-2. Both groups of viruses behave in a similar fashion, but the global HIV epidemic is primarily the result of HIV-1, and HIV-2 is confined mostly to one region of Africa.

The reason I say *groups* or *types* of viruses rather than *species* of virus is that scientists really have no idea what constitutes a viral species. Head to Chapter 8 for a discussion of what defines a species and why categorizing viral or bacterial organisms is so difficult.

Understanding the replication process that HIV uses is key to understanding why it's such a hard-to-treat disease. As the preceding section explains, HIV is a retrovirus; as such, it copies its RNA genome to DNA and then back to RNA. This replication process is important for two reasons, as explained in the following sections.

Sneaking around in your chromosome

HIV does this really sneaky thing: When it copies its RNA genome into DNA, it integrates that DNA into the host chromosome (your chromosome). Now looking like just a few more nucleotides in the genome, it can hide there.

Your immune system can't find it as long as it's dormant and not doing anything. This phenomenon is also a big problem for HIV treatments that might be able to target the viruses — if it could find them.

Attacking T cells

HIV targets cells of the immune system. Most important, it targets the *T cells* — white blood cells that fight infections either directly or indirectly. The type of T cell that is most susceptible to HIV infection is called the *helper T cell*. Helper T cells don't attack infection themselves, but they produce compounds that are involved in mediating the response of other T cells to the infection.

To do its dirty work, the virus looks around for something it can attach to, called a *receptor*. It finds the CD4 molecule on the T cell's surface and attaches to that.

Although the virus uses the CD4 molecule as a receptor, the molecule actually has some other purpose. Just as viruses hijack cells for their own purposes, HIV hijacks the CD4 molecule and uses it as an attachment point.

After attaching to the CD4 receptor, HIV attaches to a second receptor, called a *co-receptor*. HIV can use several co-receptors, but two are especially important in understanding the disease's progression:

- **CCR5:** This receptor is important in the early stages of infection. The form of HIV that attaches to the CCR5 receptor is called R5 HIV.

- **CXCR4:** This receptor is important later in the progression of the disease. The form of HIV that attaches to the CXCR4 receptor is called X4 HIV.

Mutating like crazy

HIV is prone to mutations. Reverse transcriptase, which enables the virus to copy RNA back into DNA, is very error prone. This means that HIV has a high mutation rate, but because the virus is small, it can survive with such a high mutation rate.

The shorter the genome, the greater the probability that a sloppy copying process will be able to generate a copy without too many errors. (If you're a bad typist, you're more likely to correctly spell a short word than a long one, just because you have more chances to get something wrong in a long word.)

And even though most mutations are deleterious, so many HIV particles exist that an advantageous mutation (one that makes the virus resistant to a drug, for example) is likely to occur by chance.

The History of the HIV Epidemic

Despite what some preachers said at the time, AIDS didn't drop out of the sky to plague the sinful or humble the proud. Instead, it was caused by a virus that simply did what viruses do. (Refer to the preceding section if you're unfamiliar with the general behavior of viruses.)

One thing that's so interesting about HIV viruses is that they're very similar to viruses that infect primates. Until this simian virus infected some unlucky person, AIDS didn't exist in the human population. Once in the human population, the previously simian virus was exposed to a new selective environment — namely us.

We don't know how often such cross-species transfers happen, but we do know (unfortunately) that sometimes the introduced virus heads down an evolutionary path that results in viruses that eat the new host for breakfast. In the case of AIDS, the primate virus can sometimes get a toehold in a human, and then selection sorts through all the various viral mutants, favoring those that are even better at infecting humans. Before such an event happened, AIDS wasn't a human epidemic; now it is.

Another interesting thing is that the primate-to-human transmission of the virus may have happened a whole lot earlier than people tend to think, given that most people think of AIDS and HIV as being "born" in the last decades of the 20th century. One of the reasons we noticed AIDS later may have been that people move around more nowadays. In the old days, you had to walk to the next village to spread whatever germs you might be carrying, and if people occasionally fell sick here and there due to an odd illness, not many people beyond their doctors or families knew about it. But today, with airplanes that can move people and viruses long distances in little time, a disease can get all the way around the world in a day, and many more people can be exposed in a very short period of time.

Where it came from

Many species of primates harbor viruses that are closely related to HIV. These viruses, called *SIV* for *simian immunodeficiency virus,* occur in 26 African primate species. Both major groups of HIV — HIV-1 and HIV-2 — arose when the simian virus transferred from primates to humans. Scientists have been able to pinpoint which primate-to-human transfers resulted in both HIV-1 and HIV-2:

  ✔ **HIV-1 jumped to humans from chimpanzees, which harbor SIVcpz.** In at least three different events, SIVcpz jumped to humans, resulting in the three major groups of HIV-1. Each group represents an independent origin for the virus.

  ✔ **HIV-2 jumped to humans from sooty mangabeys, which harbor SIVsm.** At least half a dozen independent origins of HIV-2 from sooty mangabeys exist.

The naming conventions of the simian viruses indicate the species of primate that harbors the particular virus: SIVcpz stands for the chimpanzee simian virus, SIMsm for the sooty-mangabey simian virus, and so on. If your eyes tend to glaze over when you see what appears to be a random string of uppercase and lowercase letters, you may not have figured this convention out already.

When a virus goes from one species to another

Sometimes, a virus in one species transfers to another species. In the case of HIV, a simian virus transferred to a human host, where it mutated into HIV. The phenomenon is fascinating and terrifying. People's fears about the bird flu — that after it's in a human host, it could mutate into a human version that's transmittable from human to human — have in essence already been realized with HIV viruses.

When people had no idea where HIV came from, they assumed a single origin. But when scientists started sequencing a bunch of simian immunodeficiency viruses, they realized that HIV (both 1 and 2) had leaped from primates to humans multiple times. Although scientists don't understand all that's involved in such a transfer, you shouldn't be too surprised. Given that humans are not all that different from primates (refer to Chapter 16), if we're going to catch a virus, getting it from other species of primates is as good a place as any.

The evidence of primate-to-human transfer

How can scientists be so sure that the human immunodeficiency virus originated in simian populations? First, they know that humans can catch primate retroviruses. In at least one case, an animal handler acquired a simian immunodeficiency virus from a rhesus macaque (SIVmac), and cases of acquisition of other retroviruses have occurred.

Also, a strong correlation exists in Africa between the distribution of HIV types and the distribution of primates. The center of HIV-2 infection is the same part of Africa where sooty mangabeys live. And although HIV-1 has spread throughout Africa and the world, the origin of that virus appears to be the region inhabited by the subspecies of chimpanzees that harbors a related virus. These regions also provide ample opportunity for human-primate contact. Both chimps and sooty mangabeys are hunted for food, and young ones are occasionally kept as pets.

Other evidence includes

- ✔ **Gene sequencing:** The HIV and SIV viruses have been sequenced and compared, and the human viruses are remarkably similar to the simian virus that's considered to be its parent.

- ✔ **An HIV phylogenetic tree:** In reconstructing the tree (refer to Chapter 9), researchers discovered that instead of the HIV-1 strains appearing off to one side on their own little branch (which would indicate a single origin from one chimpanzee virus), the HIV strains are interspersed with the SIVcpz strains, indicating that HIV originated from three different simian strains.

  The same is true for HIV-2. Phylogenetic analysis doesn't show all the HIV-2 strains on their own branch of the viral tree, but instead several branches pop out of the sooty mangabeys viral tree.

A timeline

HIV is a relatively new human disease. The U.S. Centers for Disease Control and Prevention (CDC) first reported on what we know now was the beginning of the AIDS epidemic in 1981. It wasn't until 1983 that the virus causing the disease, HIV, was identified.

Yet even though the disease was first recognized in 1981, it obviously was present before that time. Virologists decided to review old medical records and tissue samples to see whether anybody had suffered from the condition in the past.

People in the medical field often keep tissue samples in cases in which diagnosis proved to be difficult and an unknown disease seemed to be the culprit. Using modern molecular techniques in a process that can be thought of as a hunt for viral fossils, researchers were able to examine these historical samples for the presence of the human immunodeficiency virus.

You may be surprised to know just how early AIDS reared its head:

- The earliest known case of AIDS dates from a British sailor who developed AIDS-like symptoms in the late 1950s.

- The earliest known case of acquired immune deficiency in the United States (that is, the earliest date for which molecular evidence exists) occurred in 1968, involving a teenage male who reported that he'd been symptomatic for at least two years. Because he had never traveled outside the country, he must have caught the virus in the United States sometime before then.

- A survey of preserved blood samples has revealed antibodies to HIV dating back to the late 1950s.

- The degree of divergence between HIV and the suggested SIV source suggests that HIV mutated from SIV between 50 and 100 years ago.

So HIV was around possibly up to a century ago. A little more than 50 years ago, it presented itself in isolated cases. In the early 1980s, many people began to fall ill. What scientists don't know is whether the virus persisted at low levels until the later outbreak was noticed or whether it had gone extinct in the United States and then was reintroduced. What they do know is that by the end of the 1980s, AIDS was terrorizing the world.

The Path and Evolution of HIV in the Patient

Every person infected with HIV has his or her own story, and the disease takes a dramatically different course in different people. Yet when you take all the sufferers in total, you get a picture — albeit a general one — of what HIV does when it enters the body.

Basically, right after infection, the levels of HIV in the blood increase rapidly, but then the body's immune system kicks in and is successful in reducing the amount of HIV virus present. Yet over time, the amount of HIV in the blood increases as the number of T cells decrease. Eventually, HIV destroys the immune system, eliminating T cells until almost none are left. At this point, the patient succumbs to infections that the immune system is no longer able to battle.

A key component of understanding the progression of HIV infection is understanding how the viral population evolves in the patient. The following sections explain these different evolutionary stages of HIV in the human body.

During the course of HIV infection the viral population evolves, first in response to the host immune system, then in the absence of immune response. Viral types unlike those in the initial infection arise during the course of the infection and are associated with later stages of disease progression.

Increasing and growing more divergent

Right after infection, the levels of HIV in the blood increase very rapidly, yet the immune system is strong enough to fight back. As it suppresses the initial outbreak, the infected person's immune system also exerts a powerful selective force on the HIV virus.

The infected person's immune system recognizes HIV as a foreign invader and attacks it. But HIV has a high mutation rate, and not all of the individual viruses produced in the infection are exactly same, so some are able to avoid being targeted. So now the immune system has to go after these slightly different viruses and, in doing so, selects for viruses that are even more different. This cycle—in which the attacks launched by the immune system attacks select for slightly different viruses—goes on, back and forth for quite some time. The immune system puts up a valiant fight, often for years. During this period the HIV population evolves in two ways.

The viral population becomes progressively different from the original strain

The viral population evolves to be progressively more different from the original infecting strain. Initially, the person's immune system is pretty good at battling the virus. So although HIV increases immediately after infection, it drops back down when the immune system fights back.

But as the disease progresses, the HIV population in the person evolves. Mutant virus progeny that are less susceptible to the immune system increase in frequency. Over time, the virus population becomes more and more different from the original infecting particles. The viral population is evolving in response to the immune system — the immune system is fighting hard and only new viral mutants can avoid it.

The virus population grows increasingly diverse

The virus population as a whole becomes increasingly diverse — that is, there are progressively more different HIV types within the patient as the disease advances. The most fit HIV viruses will be the ones that are different from those that the immune system has responded to, but there are many ways to be different so viral diversity goes up.

Reaching a plateau

HIV destroys one of the key components of the immune system, a type of T cell. When enough of these cells have been destroyed, the immune system can no longer contain the virus, and the HIV population starts to evolve in a new way.

As T cells are destroyed, the crippled immune system no longer acts as an agent of selection on the HIV viruses. At this point, selection no longer favors viruses simply because they are different — they don't have to escape the immune system, which is worn out and can fight no more. The difference from the original strain reaches a plateau. Mutations still occur during HIV replication, but now if a particular strain is especially good at growing in the host, there's no immune system to knock it back down.

Destroying T-cells in a different way

HIV disease progression can vary dramatically from patient to patient, and evolution does not occur along exactly the same trajectory in each case. But one major event which is observed repeatedly is the evolution of viruses later in infection that attack the immune system in a different way. These viral variants (called X4 variants) are able to attach to a different part of the surface of immune cells (a cellular feature called the CXCR4 receptor) and destroy the T cells in a different way.

The X4 type begins to increase in frequency around the time that the overall genetic diversity of the viral population is decreasing, and the peak of the X4 virus type is associated with period proceeding transition to full blown AIDS symptoms.

Researchers don't completely understand how theses X4 viruses influence the disease or whether the X4 variants evolve in every patient. What they do know is that the X4 variants cause T cell death differently from the original variants.

Other Interesting Facts about HIV

HIV is as interesting as it is scary. Consider this to be the section of other cool things about the human immunodeficiency virus — if you can use the word *cool* when talking about a deadly pathogen. If you can't, consider this to be the section of noteworthy-but-not-vitally-important information for serious-minded readers.

Some people may be resistant

During the initial infection, the virus binds to a CCR5 co-receptor (refer to "Attacking T cells," earlier in this chapter). As it turns out, not everyone has that same molecule. Some people have a mutation that makes a slightly different CCR5 molecule. People who have one mutated copy of the CCR5 locus show delayed progression toward full-blown AIDS. And people who have two mutated copies appear to be resistant to HIV infection.

Interestingly, this mutation is found primarily in Europe, and its prevalence is correlated with the degree to which a particular location experienced plagues in the past. It's been hypothesized that this mutation may have made people more resistant to certain other disease organisms and that as a result the mutation increased in frequency in places that once experienced plague. Just by coincidence, the same mutation confers resistance to HIV infection.

Scientists aren't sure that the bubonic plague was caused by black-plague bacteria. Instead, it may have been caused by a viral hemorrhagic fever.

HIV evolves in a new host

Evolution within the patient selects for a more divergent virus, and that viral diversity increases through time in the individual (refer to the earlier section "HIV Evolution within the Patient"). When you compare the virus present during the initial period of infection across different people, however, you find less divergence among people than you see over time within one person.

Think about this for a minute: If the virus is diverging in one person, and that person infects a second person, you'd expect that the second person would start out with a more divergent population of the initially infecting virus. But that's not the case.

Here's why: After infection, strong selection for the ancestral viral type occurs, so the virus evolves back toward this condition. This selection may happen for at least a couple of reasons:

> ✔ The viral forms present in a person late in the infection may not be well suited to living in the environment present in a newly infected person. Hence, selection favors going back to an initial viral form.

> ✔ Although the diverse viral population may be perfectly capable of surviving in a newly infected host, this population may be outcompeted by viral variants that have mutations resurrecting the ancestral type.

HIV has a high recombination rate

One way that the HIV population generates all that diversity is via a huge amount of recombination among viruses. In *recombination,* a DNA or RNA sequence (whichever the critter uses for genomic information) is produced that's a combination of two original sequences. For most organisms, *recombination* is generally believed to happen far less frequently than mutation. But in HIV, the recombination rate may approach the rate of mutation.

Scientists know about the recombination rate by making and analyzing phylogenetic trees for a group of viruses with different genes. For organisms with low rates of recombination, phylogenies constructed from different genes should have trees that match. The extent to which they don't match allows scientists to determine the frequency of recombination.

When you take a bunch of HIV viruses, determine the sequence of several genes, and then make phylogenetic trees from these different genes, the resulting trees don't always match. This shows that, rather than being a rare event, recombination is a major source of the diversity in the HIV population within a patient.

Using Evolution to Fight HIV

The major problem we face in coming up with a vaccine for HIV is that the virus mutates so rapidly that it ends up being different enough from the strain used to make the vaccine that the vaccine doesn't confer immunity. Scientists can use the techniques of phylogenetic analysis to study the evolution of HIV and identity which parts of the HIV virus are more or less likely to change, and it might, and I stress *might,* be possible to use this information in our hunt for an effective vaccine.

Morgane Rolland, David Nickle, and James Mullins at the University of Washington have been working on just this problem: how to design a vaccine that essentially sneaks up on the virus when it's not looking. They hypothesize that the trick might be to eliminate all the info from the parts of the HIV genome that are mutating most rapidly and focus on the parts that aren't. The key is to figure out what parts of the HIV virus have been outwitting the immune system and then design a vaccine that targets parts of the virus that can't evolve.

By understanding how the virus evolves, we may be able to get a few steps ahead of it and make a vaccine that's harder for the virus to evade. This would be a remarkably cool application of evolutionary biology to a real-world problem.

Chapter 19

Influenza: One Flu, Two Flu, Your Flu, Bird Flu

*I*nfluenza. Before the mid-20th century, people gave this disease the respect it deserved. Now we call it the flu; act fairly cavalier about the symptoms unless we need a break from work; and poo-poo the vaccine unless we're in a high-risk group populated by babies, octogenarians, and hypochondriacs. Periodically, though, we get reminded that the flu can be serious business — a fact that epidemiologists and virologists have been trying to beat into our thick skulls forever — and then we fly into a panic.

Well, here's news for you, some good, some bad:

✔ Many strains of influenza exist, and courtesy of evolution, even more are on the way. Their rapid rate of evolution makes them a constant problem, and every so often, an especially nasty strain catches scientists by surprise.

✔ Although some of us may succumb, we aren't completely helpless. Scientists have been fighting back, even using the process of evolution to turn the tables on these pesky viruses. Thanks to techniques for vaccine design, scientists are getting closer to being prepared for these new and improved strains as well.

This chapter has the details on all the bad things the flu can do and all the reasons by you don't need to panic — at least not yet.

The Flu and Your Immune System

Most likely, your immune system has already been introduced to the flu. You got sick, felt lousy for a while, and eventually got better. Why? Because your body has an immune system. To understand the rather eventful history of influenza in the human population, you need to know how the flu virus infects humans and how the human immune system fights back. Consider it a play in three acts.

Act 1: The virus attacks and spreads

The influenza virus, which causes the illness commonly referred to as the flu, is most often transmitted from one person to the next in small droplets drifting through the air — possibly the result of somebody's sneeze or cough.

One day, you're unlucky enough to inhale one of these droplets, and a flu-virus particle attaches to one of your cells. Once inside the cell, the particle takes over the machinery necessary to make more copies of itself. Then your cell bursts and releases all these copies, which go looking for more cells to infect. At this point, you're sick, and you'll probably help the virus get to new cells in other people when you start coughing. End Act 1.

Act 2: The body fights back

You're sick, but you don't stay sick. Instead, your body responds to the invading flu, fights back, and overcomes the infection. How? Keep reading.

Your body has numerous, quite complicated systems for fighting off microscopic foreign invaders such as the flu virus. Combined, these various mechanisms make up your *immune system.* I won't get into the details here except to note that your body has two general classes of response:

- **Nonspecific responses:** Nonspecific responses are reactions, such as tissue inflammation and fever, that are generally bad for all invading microbes. When your body senses the presence of invading microbes, it sometimes turns up the heat in its fight against them. Indeed, having a fever may make you feel bad, but it makes the invading microbes feel even worse.

- **Specific responses:** *Specific responses* include such things as *antibodies,* which are special proteins that seek out and destroy invaders. When your body becomes aware of the flu, the first thing it notices is that the flu virus is foreign. It's not part of you and, as far as your body is concerned, doesn't belong in you. That's why as soon as the flu has been identified as "not self," your body begins to produce antibodies that specifically target this strain of flu.

As your body responds to the invader in both nonspecific and specific ways, it starts winning the battle against the flu. After a week of two, all the flu particles in your body have been killed, and you're on the road to recovery.

Act 3: Building up the guard

Your immune system has a very special property called *memory.* Although it takes a little time for your body to produce enough antibodies to beat back this strain of flu, memory means that after your body has responded once, it's immediately ready to respond again.

That's great news for you, because the flu strain you just recovered from can no longer invade your body; now you are immune to it. And since your body's antibodies are able to attach to different but similar flu strains, you also have resistance to those as well.

Which leads to a sequel: The return of the flu

The evolution of influenza is strongly affected by the immune system's response. The strain of flu from which you recovered was clearly quite good at being the flu. It managed to get not only from some other person into you, but quite possibly into a third person as well. In fact, it's possible that the strain of the flu you got also spread through your workplace, your kid's school, your town, the rest of the country, and even the world. Indeed, flu strains do this all the time. But after everyone who had a particular strain of flu gets better, all of them are immune to that strain. Thus, the next time you get the flu, it will be a genetically different flu strain.

The Three Types of Influenza: A, B, C

Three different strains of flu infect humans. These strains are conveniently named influenza A, influenza B, and influenza C. They all have genomes that use RNA instead of DNA as the genetic material:

- ✔ **Influenza A:** This flu sweeps through the human population each flu season. It evolves so fast that strains are sufficiently different to avoid existing antibodies every year. Influenza A occurs in humans and a variety of other animals, which makes the evolution of influenza A somewhat more complicated, as well as more interesting for this discussion. The remainder of this chapter concentrates mostly on influenza A.

✔ **Influenza B:** Influenza B is just like influenza A, except that influenza B exists only in humans. Beyond this single difference, you just need to remember that influenza B evolves similarly to influenza A.

✔ **Influenza C:** Because most people are immune to influenza C, this strain of flu is not characterized by epidemics that periodically sweep through the human population. Instead, it is primarily a disease of the young, because it has a chance to reproduce only in children who have not yet developed an immunity to this generally mild flu. I mention it here in case you're curious, but it really isn't important to the discussion in this chapter.

Unlike influenza A and B, influenza C evolves very slowly. We don't understand exactly why it evolves so slowly, but as result of this slower evolution, all influenza C strains are basically the same. About 97 percent of Americans have antibodies to influenza C, which means it's likely that at some point in your life, you were infected with it and developed a resistance to it. Now you are immune to the strain that infected you, and as a result of the high level of similarity among strains, you are also immune to all other influenza C viruses.

The Evolution of Influenza A

Influenza A is a very small virus with a genome made of RNA instead of DNA. Its genome is comprised of eight different RNA segments, and it has only ten genes. (For comparison, consider that people have over 25,000 genes.) Influenza A is a remarkably compact organism, and these ten genes enable it to do everything it needs to do to infect you and reproduce.

Mechanisms of evolution: Mutation, recombination, or reassortment

The influenza A virus (and the influenza B and C viruses too, for that matter) can evolve in three ways:

✔ **Mutations:** Influenza is a virus with an RNA genome, and RNA replication has a high error rate. For this reason, the virus mutates rapidly. That's why this year's flu is different from last year's flu. The strains may be similar enough for the immunity you developed to last year's flu to protect you (or at least partially protect you) but don't count on it.

✔ **Reassortment:** Because influenza has a genome divided into segments, new variants can also arise via *genetic reassortment,* the process whereby two different viruses infect the same cell, and the progeny have segments that are a combination of these two strains. (For an explanation of how viruses can reproduce this way, refer to Chapter 12.)

When reassortment involves the segments that code for the H or N proteins that cover the outside of the flu virus, the new strains (or the strains produced) can be so different from the parent strains that no host has even partial immunity. As a result, these strains can sweep rapidly through entire populations.

✔ **Recombination:** In *recombination,* one of the existing influenza genes is incorrectly replicated and ends up with a new section of RNA spliced into it. This sequence could come from another influenza strain or even from a host cell's RNA. Although such events are almost always likely to be harmful to the virus, every once in a while a new sequence with foreign RNA spliced into just the right part of one of the surface proteins may make the new flu strain resistant to existing host antibodies.

Genes to know

For the purposes of this discussion, you need to pay attention to only four genes: three on the outside and one that determines which species a particular strain can infect.

The three genes on the outside are

✔ Hemagglutinin (abbreviated H)

✔ Neuraminidase (abbreviated N)

✔ Matrix

The fourth is the Nucleoprotein gene (also called *Nucleocapsid*) and is abbreviated NP.

Hemagglutinin, neuraminidase, and matrix code for proteins that are on the surface of the influenza particle. These surface proteins are important because when the flu enters your body, these proteins are the ones that your immune system can potentially see — and guard against.

The Nucleoprotein gene is important is determining the *host-specificity* of a particular flu strain — a fancy way of saying which critters that particular strain can infect.

The importance of H and N

As noted in the preceding section, hemagglutinin and neuraminidase are abbreviated H and N, respectively. If you've been reading about the flu or hearing about it on TV, you may have heard a particular strain described in terms of H and N and some numbers — for example, avian influenza H5N1.

There are 16 different hemagglutinin proteins and 9 different neuraminidase proteins, but each individual influenza A virus has only 1 type of each protein. The numbers in a strain's name (H**5**N**1**, for example) indicate which neurominidase and hemagglutinin proteins that particular strain has.

All the H and N types occur in waterfowl, but only some of them occur in humans. At this time, two types of influenza A are circulating in the human population: H3N2 and H1N1. Ideally, avian strain H5N1 — the *bird flu* you occasionally hear about in the news — won't mutate to easily infect humans and be transmittable between them, and make it three. Right now we can catch this strain from handling infected birds, but we don't seem to pass it to other humans, so it can't spread in the human population. At least not yet.

NP: The host-specificity gene

From the earlier section as well as the reports in the newspapers these days, you know that humans aren't the only ones plagued by the flu. Birds get the flu, too, specifically waterfowl like ducks and geese. But people and birds don't usually get the same strain of the flu because flu strains tend to be species-specific. A human cell is different from a goose cell, and the flu strains that replicate in geese don't usually infect humans. In short, flu strains tend to be specific to a particular groups of animals. The gene that controls (in large part) which species of animal a flu strain can best infect is the NP gene.

The H and N types determine how readily your immune system can see the flu. If a particular strain is an H-N type that your body has seen before, then you've got a jump on it. If it's one your body hasn't seen before, then the flu has the jump on you. The NP gene determines whether the flu can see you, that is, whether it can reproduce in your body. The worst possible combination is an NP gene that lets the flu chow down on you wrapped in surface proteins that take your immune system by surprise.

Who gets the flu and from where

There are five major groups of Influenza A strains. In addition to the strains that infect humans and waterfowl (ducks and geese), there is a group of flu strains that infects horses, one that infects pigs, and one that infects seagulls (which, contrary to what you may reasonably assume, are *not* waterfowl).

By taking a closer look at the genetic sequences of the NP gene (the one that determines which species a flu strain can best infect), scientists find that it's usually easy to tell the human flu strains from the waterfowl flu strains from horse flu strains and so on because flu strains are species specific. Seagulls tend to get seagull flu, horses tend to get horse flu, pigs tend to get pig flu, and so on. But not always.

One of the most interesting conclusions that can be drawn from an analysis of the sequences of Influenza A is that, much as we tend to think of this little beast as a human virus, its home base appears to be waterfowl. It seems that every so often, a flu strain jumps from waterfowl to some other susceptible species where it persists for a while and then goes extinct and/or is replaced by another strain. All the seagull, human, pig, and horse influenza A strains currently in circulation were probably acquired from waterfowl within the last 100 years. Understanding what causes these events is particularly important today, when public health officials and governmental agencies are coping with the very real possibility of another devastating flu pandemic.

The evolutionary history and relatedness of different flu strains

The RNA sequence information allows scientists to reconstruct the family tree of the flu and figure out how the five major groups of the flu are related to each other. Humans, for example, have influenza strains similar to those in pigs; in fact, it's not unheard of for pigs to catch the flu from people, and vice versa. (The Swine flu scare of 1976 is one example).

In addition to helping scientists formulate hypotheses about the relationship between the different flu groups, surveying the RNA sequence variation for a collection of flu strains allows them to measure the amount of variation in the different groups of the flu. This information can provide information about underlying evolutionary processes.

An important finding is that not all groups have the same amount of variation in the host-specificity protein. A collection of human flu strains has quite a lot of variation, as do the flu strains that attack horses, pigs, and seagulls. But the flu strains infecting waterfowl are much more uniform at the protein level. The waterfowl strains have the greatest diversity of surface proteins — all the different H and N molecule types — but when it comes to the proteins important for actually chowing down on ducks and geese, most of the different waterfowl flu strains are about the same. There just isn't very much variation at the protein level, even though there's variation at the RNA level. (Remember that there could be changes at the nucleotide level that don't affect what protein is made.)

Scientists know that mutations are common in RNA replication, but when they look at the host specificity gene of the flu strain that infects waterfowl, they find that most of the variation is neutral; it doesn't affect proteins. Mutations that affect protein structure are certainly always appearing, but in the waterfowl population, it seems these mutations don't increase in frequency. We know they happen, but we don't see them. From this, we can speculate that the flu strains that are infecting waterfowl have, at least for now, gotten to be about as good as they can be.

Duck, duck, goose: How waterfowl flu spreads

Interestingly, the waterfowl flu strain doesn't usually tend to make waterfowl very sick, and it doesn't have to be spread from one duck or goose to the next. Waterfowl are really good at making bird droppings (if geese or ducks have ever taken up residence at your local park, you know what I'm talking about), and these droppings contain huge amounts of flu virus. The flu in ducks lives in the gastrointestinal tract, not the lungs, and those droppings spread the flu virus through the entire pond where it can easily infect many other ducks.

Every once in awhile, some other organism comes into contact with some of the waterfowl flu — easy to see how that can happen when you think of a pond full of influenza infected droppings. When this happens, the chance exists for the waterfowl flu to infect a different kind of animal. Scientists have evidence of several different cross-species transfers from ducks to a variety of mammals.

Which strains are evolving faster

Because of differences between neutral and non-neutral sequence variation, scientists can tell that the flu strains in waterfowl are evolving differently than the flu strains in the other groups. Although all five groups have variation at the nucleotide level, the waterfowl group doesn't have any significant variation at the protein level. The flu in waterfowl seems to be at an evolutionarily stable point, evidence that selection is acting differently in different groups of flu.

Take-home message: The host-specificity protein in waterfowl has evolved to some optimum level. Think of it as a peak on the adaptive landscape. (If you don't know what the adaptive landscape is, refer to Chapter 6.) Mutations that occur that change the protein are just as rapidly eliminated from the population, so we don't see them. What we do see are changes in the RNA that don't affect the protein.

Jumping from one species to another

Because different species tend to be infected with flu viruses specific to their species, scientists who collect flu strains simply have to know which organism it came from to make a pretty good prediction about which strain it is. Take a strain from a horse, for example, and analyze its genetic sequence, and chances are, it'll be recognizable as a horse flu. Sometimes, however, scientists find a sick animal, collect the specimen, do the analysis, and find an unexpected flu strain.

When an animal has been infected with a flu strain different from the one expected, scientists use phylogenetic analysis again, because in making the tree of the five groups they can spot when a particular strain is out of place. If they find that a horse is sick with the flu, for example, they only have to check the flu sequence to discover whether it's the strain they'd expect (one specific to horses) or one they didn't expect (a strain that horses don't typically get). They can also tell in what ways it's different: that it's way different from the horse flu, for example, and just like the bird flu.

Such sequence analysis tells scientists that sometimes flu from waterfowl can infect other groups. Its been shown to move to horses and pigs, as well as other animals not usually associated with the flu, such as whales, seals, and mink. Now of course we're finding these flu strains in unlucky people in Asia as well.

That waterfowl flu can be transferred to other species is significant because the waterfowl population contains the highest diversity of surface proteins. Were a change to occur in a waterfowl flu that would allow it to reproduce in human cells, for example, it could take our immune system by surprise. The strain wouldn't look like any of the other flu strains that your immune system has responded to before. Although your immune system would respond to the infection, it'd be starting from scratch. If the flu strain is particularly virulent, you might not have that much time.

Bottom line: The waterfowl flu population is a source of cross species infection, and it's implicated as a source of new variants that have infected the human population in the past, a process we may be seeing the early stages of with the H5N1 avian flu.

Learning from the Past: Flu Pandemics

The term *pandemic* refers to an epidemic of an infectious disease that occurs over a large area, such as a continent or even the entire world. The black plague that swept from Asia through Europe in the mid-1300s is a good example of a pandemic. Flu pandemics can occur when a flu strain that appears in the human population is so different from the circulating strains that the worldwide population is completely susceptible. As a result, this new flu is able to sweep rapidly through the entire world. Often, influenza pandemics are given names related to the regions where the virus first appeared.

In an average year, the Centers for Disease Control and Prevention estimates that influenza kills more than 20,000 Americans. The global total is harder to estimate accurately, but the World Health Organization places it at somewhere between 250,000 and 500,000 deaths per year. Pandemic years see a much, *much* higher death rate — sometimes into the millions.

Scientists have information on flu pandemics dating from the pandemic of 1889 to the more recent 1977 pandemic. By studying the genome sequences of the more recent strains and the antibodies of the victims in the more distant strains, researchers have been able to piece together the origin of these pandemic strains. The following sections take you on a little stroll through the pandemic flus of the last hundred years.

Pandemics of 1889 and 1900

Because sequence information isn't available, scientists have to rely on *seroarchaeology* — the search for antibodies in preserved tissue samples — for these pandemics. The antibodies in these tissue samples can't tell researchers about all the genes in the flu strains responsible for the pandemics, but they *can* identify the H and N proteins, because these proteins are the external parts of the flu virus that the body's immune system produces antibodies against. So we know that the 1889 and 1900 pandemics were caused by an H2N2 and an H3N8 strain, respectively.

The Spanish flu (1918)

This influenza pandemic strain is the first one for which researchers have complete sequence information. Sequence analysis of the genes from this strain suggests that it was the result of an H1N1 avian influenza virus entering the human population. This finding is important, particularly in light of recent concerns about the possibility that the rare but often fatal H5N1 avian flu will change to a form that can be easily spread between humans. The Spanish flu is an example of a flu strain from one host (waterfowl) infecting a new host (us).

The Asian flu (1957)

The Asian flu strain (H2N2) contained 5 gene segments from the circulating 1918 strain and 3 new ones — the different versions of the H and N genes, as well as a gene involved in RNA replication. These changes were almost certainly the result of a reassortment event with an avian strain of influenza A, and the new strain replaced the H1N1 strain from which it was derived.

The Asian flu pandemic was the result of a reassortment event between the original H1N1 strain and an avian strain that contributed the 3 new genes. These two strains ended up in the same host, the various segments got mixed up during the flu's replication, and out popped something new.

The last great pandemic

The 1918 Spanish-flu pandemic killed more people than any other disease outbreak in human history. It is estimated that between 20 million and 40 million people died of the flu during the 1918–1919 flu season. Furthermore, although influenza is usually most fatal among the very young and the very old, the 1918 flu had very high mortality across all ages.

It was not until very recently that scientists learned the complete genome sequence of the 1918 flu. No samples suitable for genome sequencing were known before that. However, in 2005, viral nucleic acids were isolated from the bodies of victims who died in Alaska during the epidemic. Their bodies had been buried in the Alaskan permafrost and had remained frozen until the present. These frozen samples were sufficiently preserved that scientists could isolate the viral genetic material (RNA) from them.

Before the rediscovery of the 1918 flu, scientists thought that the 1918 pandemic originated in a fashion similar to the 1957 and 1968 pandemics — that is, via the acquisition of several new genome segments from a reassortment event with an avian strain. Scientists now know, however, that all eight segments of the 1918 strain are very similar to avian strains, and the current hypothesis is that the 1918 pandemic was the result of an avian strain entering the human population.

The Hong Kong flu (1968)

When the Asian flu strain (H2N2; see the preceding section) went through a second reassortment with a different avian influenza strain, the H3N2 strain was born. This strain had the same N gene but had acquired 2 new genes, including a new H gene.

This is another example of a reassortment event between a human strain and an avian flu strain. This H3N2 strain replaced the H2N2 strain in the human population.

The Russian flu (1977)

In 1977, the H1N1 flu last seen in humans in 1950 reappeared. Because most people older than about 20 had been exposed to H1N1 flu, the resulting epidemic was not severe enough to be labeled a true pandemic, but it was certainly a significant event.

Scientists don't know exactly where this strain came from, but it has been suggested that it escaped from a laboratory somewhere. Support for this hypothesis is not just the strain's sudden reappearance, surprising though that is. More convincing is that the 1977 H1N1 was almost identical to the 1950 H1N1 — in all those years, this strain hadn't been evolving.

Remember that this year's flu isn't quite the same as last year's flu, and next year's flu won't be the same as the flu that follows it. The point? Twenty-seven years without change is hard to explain — hence the suggestion that maybe those 27 years were spent in a test tube in a freezer!

Since this event in 1977, two influenza A lineages have been circulating simultaneously in the human population: H3N2 and H1N1.

Fighting Back: The Art and Science of Making Flu Vaccines

Vaccines work because of immune-system memory, which essentially prepares your immune system to defend you immediately when it senses that a previous invader — or one like it — has returned for a repeat performance. (Refer to "Act 3: Building up the guard," earlier in this chapter, for details.) By combining their knowledge of how immune-system memory works and how flu strains evolve, scientists were able to come up with a strategy for vaccination.

A *vaccine* is a substance introduced into your body to trick it into bringing forth an immune response. This response creates antibodies, which can then protect you from the microorganism the vaccine is designed to imitate. Typically, the vaccine is developed in some way from the organism from which immunity is desired. The vaccine can be made from the whole organism or from some of the external parts, because those are the parts that your immune system recognizes. Moreover, vaccines can consist of live or dead organisms.

When you get vaccinated against the flu, you're actually receiving three different vaccines at the same time. That's because three major lineages of the flu are currently in circulation in the human population: two different types of influenza A and one influenza B strain. Because these three kinds of viruses are different enough that no single vaccine can protect against all of them, one strain from each of the three viral groups is chosen for vaccine production.

Dead vaccines

Initially, a dead vaccine appears to be the better vaccination option, if you consider that the vaccine consists of disease agents that you're going to be introducing into your body. But producing a dead flu-virus vaccine has a major disadvantage: You need to make a lot more of it than you do of a vaccine based on a living virus.

The problem doesn't sound so critical; surely manufacturers can just make more. But in fact, the production of the annual flu virus is a major undertaking. The viruses created for vaccine production are grown in chicken eggs, where the flu happily multiplies. But think about all the eggs you need to grow enough flu vaccine for all the people who need to be inoculated. In the United States alone, you need more than one quarter of a billion eggs. In addition to requiring a lot of eggs, this process takes a lot of time. It's approximately half a year between the time when flu-vaccine production starts and when the first doses are delivered for distribution.

Further complicating this long period of production is the fact that the decision about which three influenza strains should be used to make the vaccine has to be made months before the beginning of the flu season. Because the flu is always evolving, the earlier the decision is made, the less likely it is to be correct. Thus, as you may have noticed, flu shots work better in some years than in others.

Cell-based flu vaccines are newest thing in the manufacturing of flu vaccines. Rather than incubate the virus in eggs, the cell-based techniques grow vaccines in laboratory cell cultures. One of the main advantages of this technique is that, by not being dependent on a huge supply of eggs, the makers don't have the same quantity limitations or contamination challenges.

Live vaccines

The advantage of using a live flu virus in a vaccine is that a little goes a long way. The virus replicates in a person's body; the immune system ramps up to defeat the infection; and the result is immunity against further infection. Unfortunately, one of the risks is that the live virus is going to reproduce in your body before your immune system knocks it out. That situation complicates the vaccine-production process, because vaccine designers have to create a strain of the virus that won't make you sick but is still similar enough to the more virulent virus to kick your immune system into action.

Using evolution to create less harmful viruses for vaccines

The flu's ability to exchange genome segments with other influenza viruses has been nothing but trouble for humans. But scientists have turned the tables, using this mechanism to fight back. They've discovered a clever way to create new virus strains that are disguised on the outside with all the bits of the virus humans want to be immune to, but filled on the inside with a collection of different alleles (slightly different forms of the flu genes) that aren't that good at making people sick. Voilà! This "cream-filled" virus reproduces in the body well enough to cause the immune system to attack it, but not so well that the person actually gets ill.

The live-vaccine virus will begin evolving to attack you more efficiently as soon as it starts reproducing in your body. The plan, of course, is that long before enough time has gone by for the virus to develop greater efficiency at reproducing in you, your immune system will have had a chance to defeat it. That's the plan, anyway.

Using evolution to keep vaccines safe

The fly in the live-virus vaccine ointment is evolution, of course. Even though the live virus used for vaccine production has been constructed so that it's weak and can't reproduce rapidly in the human body, it may not stay that way. As the weakened live virus reproduces, it will produce offspring with random mutations, some of which may improve their ability to live in a person. These progeny in turn will produce offspring, and some of them may be even better at beating the body's defenses. If enough time goes by, a reasonably harmless virus designed for use as a vaccine could end up as one that's much better at eating human cells for lunch.

So can scientists do anything to reduce the chance that evolving viruses will get the best of us? Short answer: Yes, by using the evolutionary process to our advantage.

The influenza that makes you sick is happiest at your normal body temperature. That shouldn't be too surprising, because it lives in the human body, and selection has had a lot of time to tune the flu for 98.6 degrees Fahrenheit. That's one of the reasons your body turns up the heat when you get sick: It's trying to burn the virus out.

Scientists have used this bit of knowledge to their (and your) advantage: They decided to turn down the heat in the laboratory. By growing the flu in colder temperatures in the laboratory, they evolved a flu strain that reproduces well at lower temperatures. These new, cold-adapted flu strains aren't very good at growing at human body temperature.

Why did scientists want this cold-adapted flu strain? Some very clever vaccine designers realized that it's colder in your nose than it is in your lungs. Your lungs are deep inside your toasty-warm body, but your nose is right up there on the edge, breathing air that's generally below 98.6 degrees — especially during the flu season.

By creating a vaccine virus that can reproduce at temperatures slightly *below* your body temperature but not very well *at* your body temperature, the designers developed a very nifty live vaccine indeed. You can spritz a little bit of it in your nose, and although it will reproduce and stimulate your immune system to respond, it can't get from your nose into your lower respiratory system, where it's just too hot. (That's why when you get the live flu virus, the nurse spritzes it into your nose.)

The power of evolution is such that, given enough time, even this virus can get out of your nose. With each round of replication, variants that are a little bit better at growing in high-temperature cells may be produced by mutation. For this reason, people with weakened immune systems, including very young children and elderly individuals, should not get the live-virus vaccine.

Predicting the future to make next year's vaccine

It's a shame that each year, designers have to redesign the flu vaccine to account for recent flu evolution. It's even more of a shame that getting the vaccine right is so hard. The health officials who make these predictions use a variety of information concerning past patterns of flu outbreaks, as well as which strains are sweeping through different parts of the world. Given the rapid evolution and incredible variation of the flu population at any given time, it's amazing that vaccine designers do as good a job as they do.

Understanding the details of flu evolution can help scientists predict what flu strain may be coming next. We don't know what's going to happen next year (that flu isn't here yet), but we do know what has happened in the past (samples of those flu viruses are in the freezer, and their genetic sequences are known). Scientists can use this information about past years' flu strains to reconstruct the history of flu evolution. Phylogenetic analysis lets them make a family tree for the past years flu strains (refer to Chapter 9 for information on how to construct these trees). This tree is scientists' and virologists' best estimate of what begat what in the never ending progression of new flu strains.

Robin Bush, Walter Fitch, and colleagues used the sequence of the H gene to create such a tree for the H3N2 group of influenza A currently infecting humans. They used data from 1984 through 1996, and they were able to identify which flu lineages in each year gave rise to the flu strains that made people sick the next year.

They then set out to figure out what was it about those strains that predisposed them to being the ancestors of the next big wave of infection. There are lots of little branches of the flu family tree around at any one time — what we want to know is from which of those little branches will the strain that's going to sweep through your school district arise. We want to make a vaccine against that particular sort of flu strain. The trick is figuring out which strain it is.

By figuring our how the flu is evolving in response to our immune system, we learn clues that might help us predict what next years will look like and fine tune vaccine design in advance.

Making and testing predictions

With 12 years of data in this study, Bush and the others had 11 separate pairs of data sets to test different predictions. First, they looked really hard at the flu RNA sequences for 1985 and asked what they could measure about the 1985 flu strains that could be used to predict the major 1986 flu strain. They then went back to the 1986 records to check to see whether their predictions were right. Then they did the same thing ten more times to test their ideas further. The following section explains what they discovered.

Anticipating next year's flu: The clues

Possible factors indicating that a particular flu strain is likely to give rise to next year's outbreak include the changeability of a particular strain (maybe the strain that changes the most is the one that spawns the following year's flu) and the changeability at a particular region of the virus (maybe a virus that changes in a particular way is the culprit responsible for next year's flu).

What Bush and colleagues discovered is that the first one wasn't the key, but the second one was:

The degree of general change in a particular strain.

Maybe the best candidate is the flu strain that's changing the most overall. Because this strain is changing at a faster rate, maybe it will be the one that gets around your immunity to last year's flu.

Sounds good, but this predictor didn't turn out to be an especially accurate one. Having lots of random mutations is no guarantee that those mutations result in genes that are better at fooling our immune system.

The degree of change at particular regions.

Maybe the flu strain most likely to cause next winter's problems is the strain that's changing in some particular way — changing the most at just the regions where the H protein is interacting with the human immune system, for example. This strain would be more likely to catch your immune system napping!

Turns out we don't know the exact details about which parts of the flu are the most important in interacting with our immune system. But by studying the flu's evolution we can find out! By looking at the flu stains that had been successful in the past the researches were able to identify specific sites in the H gene where changes were associated with this success.

Bush and coworkers discovered that the more mutations that occurred in a particular isolate at just these key locations, the more likely that isolate was to spawn the next year's flu. These are the flu strains that seem to be rolling with the punches of the human immune system, and they're ones we need to be prepared for in the future.

Making a more universal influenza A vaccine

Because the H and N proteins that cover the surface of the flu are so variable, designers have to reassess which particular strains they should use as models for each year's vaccine (refer to the preceding section). It's a shame that the surface of the flu is so variable from one viral strain to the next; things would be a lot more convenient if they were all the same.

Fortunately, one part of the surface of influenza A is very uniform across many isolates: the Matrix, or M, protein. When your immune system finds the flu in your body, it doesn't seem to pay much attention to the M protein, as H and N proteins are much more obvious targets. But that protein is there, and it's possible to make your immune system see it, too.

Walter Fiers and colleagues set out to do just that. They manufactured virus-sized particles covered with the M protein. Once Fiers and company had the little M-protein-covered particles, they tested them on mice to see whether they could stimulate an immune response that would protect the mice from influenza A. They found that even though the mice still got sick, they got much less sick than the mice that had not been vaccinated with these particles.

The fact that it is possible to make the immune system respond to the M protein raises a question: How would evolution of the influenza A M protein be affected by the presence of many such vaccinated individuals? The M protein is very uniform among different influenza A strains right now. If many people had antibodies that attached to the M protein, however, that might select for increased variation in the M protein. All the influenza A viruses make their M proteins in about the same way, but that doesn't mean they have to. Perhaps the viruses can make the M protein in many ways.

Walter Gerhard and colleagues set up an experiment to see how influenza A viruses evolved in the presence of antibodies that targeted the M protein. They took mice with weakened immune systems and gave them antibodies against the M protein. They infected the mice with an influenza A strain, and after several weeks, they examined the descendents of the original viruses to look for changes in the M protein.

Because these mice had weakened systems, they were not able to eliminate the flu virus rapidly. Because the flu virus was replicating in the mice, random mutations were occurring, and it turned out that some of these mutations did result in changes in the M protein. The scientists found only two new variants of the M protein, however, rather than the huge number of variants that would occur in the H protein in the same sort of experiment.

These experiments are encouraging, because the results suggest that the influenza particle may have only a limited number of ways to make a functional M protein. With any luck, it might be possible to vaccinate against all influenza A viruses at the same time using a vaccine based on M protein.

This type of experiment shows the potential of incorporating evolutionary information in drug design. By trying to target a part of the flu that seems more evolutionarily constrained, it may be possible to create a more universal vaccine for use in the event of a dangerous outbreak. In the case of an extremely pathogenic flu, a vaccine that offered only partial protection would be much better than no protection at all. A vaccine like this could provide one line of defense against the threat of the H5N1 avian influenza.

In fact, British and American researchers have recently tested such a vaccine (one based on the M protein), and the results are very encouraging. They indicate that the vaccine could provide universal protection against the Influenza A virus.

Part V
The Part of Tens

The 5th Wave   By Rich Tennant

Part V

The Art of Tens

In this part . . .

C'mon. You can't possibly expect to get through a book on evolution without at least a little information on fossils. So this part has a list of ten of my own personal favorites, as well as a list of adaptations that I'm particularly fond of.

And let's be honest; you were probably also expecting a little bit of information about what the evolution naysayers have to say (beyond "nay"), as well as some discussion on what intelligent design is all about. As hesitant as I am to include non-science-parading-as-science in this book, I have included a list of ten arguments you'll hear against evolution. And then I explain why those arguments don't hold water.

Chapter 20

Ten Fascinating Fossil Finds

In This Chapter
▶ Sizing up fossils from the smallest to the biggest
▶ Finding strange things on islands
▶ Seeing how fossils can tell us about the past and help us in the present

*Y*ou can't talk about evolutionary biology without talking about fossils. They're the only physical evidence of plant, animal, and microbial forms that existed long before the first primordial human.

In this chapter, I offer ten fossil finds. I chose these fossils because they reveal information not only about specific organisms (such as miniature mammoths), but also about evolution and the world. I didn't organize this chapter in any particular order, but really, how can you begin a discussion of fossils and not begin with dinosaurs? You can't. So I start there.

Dinosaurs

Since the early 1800s, when the first dinosaur fossil was discovered (and recognized for what it was), people's imaginations have been fired by dinosaurs — not only because of their size (they included some of the largest animals the world has known), but also because they seem so unlike animals today.

What does the fossil record say about these beasts? Quite a bit, actually, but not nearly as much as you'd think, despite the attributes given to them by movie directors and novelists:

 ✔ They lived from approximately 230 million to 65 million years ago — a period long enough for them to see some species go extinct and other species arise.

 ✔ They were not lizards, even though the word *dinosaur* comes from the Greek, meaning "terrible lizard" and they have a common ancestor with lizards. The skeletal differences between lizards and dinosaurs are pronounced enough that dinosaurs get their own branch of the tree of life.

Dinosaurs' legs, for example, were directly under the body rather than off to the side, as is the case with lizards and crocodilians.

✔ They didn't live at the same time as humans. Modern humans have been here for only a few hundred thousand years, and the dinosaurs went extinct (mostly) 65 million years ago.

✔ No one can claim to know what color dinosaurs were (the fossil record doesn't give information about color), though it's reasonable to assume that, like every other group of animals, they came in a variety of colors.

✔ The largest dinosaurs may have weighed 100 tons or more. Why the uncertainty? Many dinosaur fossils are incomplete. It's reasonably straightforward to come up with a good estimate of an animal's weight based just on its skeleton — if you have a complete skeleton. The largest dinosaur species for which scientists have found all the various bits is Brachiosaurus, which weighed in at about 30 to 40 tons, but bones from much larger species have been found. Unfortunately, without all the bones, paleontologists can't be sure exactly what those dinosaurs looked like.

✔ Some species had social behavior. Fossilized tracks indicate that large groups of dinosaurs traveled together. Nesting areas where several dinosaurs made nests together have also been found. Evidence even exists that baby dinosaurs remained in the nest and were cared for by the parents (because fossils of young but not newly hatched dinosaurs have been found in nests).

✔ No one knows for sure what caused the dinosaurs to go extinct. One theory is that a large meteor smashed into the Earth, raising a cloud of dust big enough to alter sunlight and weather around the globe. As it turns out, scientists have found evidence that a large meteor struck the Earth around the time when the dinosaurs went extinct. The geological boundary corresponding to the time when the dinosaurs disappeared contains a layer of iridium — an element that is rare on Earth's surface but plentiful in some meteors; it would have settled on the Earth as dust from the sky after a meteor impact.

✔ One group of dinosaurs is still around today. You know this group as birds. The bird lineage has its origin within the dinosaur branch of the tree of life — an initially controversial idea that's now widely accepted.

The first "scientific" discovery of dinosaur fossils occurred in the early 1800s, but it's surmised that ancient peoples (such as the Romans and Chinese) discovered dinosaur fossils earlier. Those fossils could be the source of myths about dragons and other fantastical beasts that crop up in lore and literature from ancient times.

Archaeopteryx

Archaeopteryx (see Figure 20-1) is an example of what is often referred to as a missing link. Except of course that it isn't missing anymore because we found some! Archaeopteryx is a species of bird-like dinosaur that has many of the characteristics of modern birds — feathers, wings, flying — stuff like that. But it also has characteristics typical of the dinosaur lineage from which it arose: most obviously its toothy grin!

Archaeopteryx was discovered only a couple of years after Darwin published his book *On the Origin of Species.* As he said in his 4th edition:

> Until quite recently these authors might have maintained, and some have maintained, that the whole class of birds came suddenly into existence during the eocene period; but now we know, on the authority of Professor Owen, that a bird certainly lived during the deposition of the upper greensand; and still more recently, that strange bird, the Archeopteryx, with a long lizard-like tail, bearing a pair of feathers on each joint, and with its wings furnished with two free claws, has been discovered in the oolitic slates of Solenhofen. Hardly any recent discovery shows more forcibly than this how little we as yet know of the former inhabitants of the world.

Figure 20-1:
Archae-
opteryx.

As you can imagine, this discovery caused quite a stir for such a small creature. Archaeopteryx was about a foot and a half from nose to tail, hardly what we think about when we think about dinosaurs, but — ignoring the distraction of wings and feathers for a minute — many of its structures are clearly related to the dinosaurs. So it turns out the dinosaur branch of the family tree did not entirely die out. One small branch, the birds, remains with us still.

That birds might be a surviving lineage of the dinosaur branch of the tree of life was originally proposed by one of Darwin's contemporaries, Thomas Huxley, but the idea never really caught on. It wasn't until the 1970s and the developments of phylogenetic analysis that the question was revisited and found to have overwhelming support.

Wrangle Island Mammoths

Woolly mammoths lived at the same time as early humans but went extinct about 10,000 years ago. At least scientists thought so until the late 20th century discovery of fossils on Wrangle Island, off the coast of Siberia. Mammoths were living on this island as recently as 4,000 years ago — the same period when the Egyptians were building the pyramids.

These island mammoths are especially cool not because they survived to historical times (though that fact is fascinating), but because they were miniature mammoths, only about 7 feet tall — the Shetland ponies of the mammoth family. Why would pint-size mammoths have evolved? Possibly because there was no advantage to being huge on islands.

One of the major advantages of being a very large animal is that you're just too big for any predators to attack. When an elephant — or a mammoth, I suppose — reaches a certain size, nothing is going to eat it. But being large also has costs. An African elephant needs to eat around 300 pounds of food and drink 50 gallons of water every day. The evolution of smaller mammoths could have been selectively advantageous if the species had no predators on the island. Smaller mammoths that could survive on less food would be less likely to starve.

Pterosaurs (Pterodactyls)

The largest living flying bird in the world is the Andean condor, which can have a wingspan of more than 10 feet. Go back in time, and you can find fossils of an extinct bird with a wingspan twice as big — a creature that would make Big Bird look small. To find the largest animal that ever flew, you need to go back even farther — 65 million years back, in fact, to the time of the pterosaurs (or pterodactyls, as they are often called).

Pterosaurs were flying reptiles related to dinosaurs. Although some of them were quite small, the largest had a wingspan that reached almost 40 feet. Perch a pterosaur atop a school bus, and its wings would stretch the entire length of the bus. (Hang on to your children!)

Evolutionists like pterosaurs not just because the group includes the largest creature that ever flew, but also because it's represents yet another independent origin of the ability to fly. Pterosaurs' wings were structured differently from those of other vertebrate lineages that have taken to the air: birds and bats (which also differ from each other). In bats, for example, the wing is supported by the elongated digits of the forelimbs, but in pterosaurs, the wing was supported by an elongated third finger with the other digits being much reduced. Both mechanisms work to make a wing, but the random process of mutation and differences in initial structures nudged these lineages down different pathways.

Trilobites

If you ever owned an animal fossil, chances are that it was a trilobite — one of the most common types of animal fossils (see Figure 20-2). Trilobites were arthropods (things like lobsters, spiders, and bumblebees) that lived in the ocean. They appeared in the fossil record more than 540 million years ago and went extinct 250 million years ago.

The fossil record of trilobites is especially rich because aquatic sediments provide the perfect environment for fossilization. In addition to the trilobite fossils themselves, scientists have found fossils showing the organisms' burrows and tracks. Here's what these fossils tell researchers:

- ✓ Different trilobite species evolved different body shapes. Some were smooth; others were extremely spiny. They ranged in size from a few millimeters to a couple of feet.

- ✓ Some lineages had the ability to dig burrows; others were able to roll up in balls, like pillbugs and hedgehogs; and some evolved the ability to swim.

- ✓ They inhabited shallow waters as well as deep waters, though they have not been found in any freshwater environments.

Figure 20-2:
A trilobite.

Just as important as the trilobite-specific information that these fossils offer is what they show about the time frame of evolutionary transitions in lineages with a plentiful fossil record. We have so few human fossils, for example, that it's reasonable to assume we will miss transitional forms because the hominid fossil record is poor.

Even though trilobite fossils are numerous, we still see sudden (in geological time) transitions and the rapid appearance of new forms in this lineage. Where speciation events occur in a small, localized area, the probability of finding intermediate forms decreases, and the fossil record appears to contain more sudden transitions as species appear and go extinct. Head to Chapter 8 for info on speciation.

Tiktaalik Rosea

Perhaps you've seen cartoons depicting the transition of vertebrates from water to land animals. Usually, these drawings show some sort of fish with stubby little legs, which isn't too far off the truth. Scientists recently found a fossil quite similar to the type that's famous from all those evolution cartoons: Tiktaalik rosea.

Tiktaalik has a lot of fishlike structures, such as fins, scales, and gills. But its "fins" have a leg-like structure with wrists and parts like a hand or fingers (see Figure 20-3). This critter could do pushups! It's not clear to what extent Tiktaalik left the water, if it did at all. Some scientists hypothesize that this new fin structure would have been advantageous for maintaining position in fast-flowing shallow water.

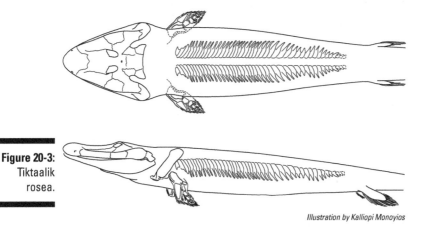

Figure 20-3:
Tiktaalik
rosea.

Illustration by Kalliopi Monoyios

Other interesting characteristics of this fossil are its neck and the eyes on top of its head — more like a crocodile than a salmon. What scientists have discovered from this fossil is that the anatomical modifications associated with the transition to land may have evolved first in the water.

Hallucigenia and the Burgess Shale

The Burgess Shale is a concentration of fossils in the Canadian Rockies containing large numbers of morphologically distinct species that at first glance don't seem much like the organisms that are around today.

The fossils found in this shale are cool for two reasons:

✔ Their excellent degree of preservation often reveals intricate structures of the softer body parts.

✔ The large diversity of forms that were new to science raises interesting questions about the evolutionary history of life on Earth.

For the most part with fossils, it's possible to identify the major group to which the organism belongs. For example, you might know that a particular fossil is a clam, perhaps not like any clam we have today, but a clam nevertheless. Before the discovery of the Burgess shale, scientists could identify fossil animals as earlier members of particular branches of the tree of life. Trilobites (see the preceding section), for example, were recognizable as members of the arthropods branch.

But when the animals in the Burgess Shale were examined, it wasn't clear immediately what groups many organisms belonged to, and in some cases, such as the organism hallucigenia, it wasn't even immediately clear which end was up (see Figure 20-4). Creatures like hallucigenia make one think that perhaps many such interesting and unusual creatures have evolved and subsequently gone extinct.

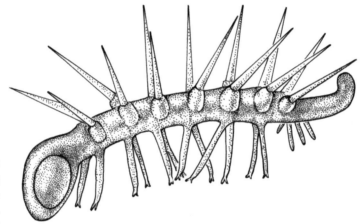

Figure 20-4: Halluci-genia.

Drawing by Mary Parrish. Courtesy of Smithsonian Institution

On subsequent analysis, and with the passing of considerable time and effort, scientists have been able to assign many of the fossils found in the Burgess Shale to existing groups. But some fossils still defy placement and may indeed be examples of unique body plans that turned out to be evolutionary dead ends.

Stromatolites

Stromatolite fossils dating back more than 3 billion years are among the oldest fossilized evidence of life on Earth. Stromatolites are pillars formed by layer upon layer of microorganisms, such as cyanobacteria (see "Micro-fossils," later in this chapter). These layers trap sediments that become incorporated into the structure, or in some cases, the organisms themselves are responsible for producing calcium carbonate, which becomes a component of a structure. Either way, when the structure is fossilized, the layers are visible as bands in the columnar structure.

Stromatolites are common in the fossil record; however, it wasn't until the discovery of living stromatolites that we could be sure that these structures were the result of biological activity. While there certainly seem to have been a fair number of stromatolites formed billions of years ago, they are a lot less frequent now. Living stromatolite structures are currently found only in areas where there are no predators to feed on the layers of microorganisms. In the days before anything else had evolved to eat them, being eaten wasn't a problem. Today, they're just out of luck in most places.

Microfossils

Microfossils are simply fossils too small to study with the naked eye. Micro-fossils are grouped based solely on their size and don't correspond to a particular branch of the tree of life. Following are a few examples:

- **Cyanobacteria:** The earliest cyanobacterial fossils date from approximately 3.6 billion years ago, and for the longest time, such single-cell organisms were the only life on the planet. Interestingly, the earliest fossils of these microorganisms are extremely similar to those that exist today.

- **Foraminifera:** Organisms typically about a millimeter in size that produce hard shells, with each species being unique. Because the species present at any given time vary (as a result of extinction and speciation), scientists can use the species to date different geological strata. If they find the same collection of foraminifera species in two samples, they know that the samples date from the same time.

  That info may seem rather useless, but it's pretty handy for marine oil exploration. Suppose that you find oil in strata of a particular age. Naturally, you want to explore the strata in a nearby location. But because of geological activity, the strata may be at a different depth in the second location. By analyzing the various species of foraminifera across the two locations, you can match strata of similar ages.

- **Spores and pollen:** Researchers can use changes in the composition of plant reproductive structures over time to glean information about how communities change through time. Scientists can use pollen samples to make inferences about climate change over shorter time scales, observing how pollen from plants characteristic of one set of environmental conditions is replaced in subsequent strata by pollen from plants characteristic of a different set of environmental conditions.

Amber

Amber is fossilized tree sap. It's quite commonly used in jewelry and has a beautiful golden color. As nice as the sap itself is, the really interesting thing about amber is that organisms — plant parts (such as leaves, seeds, and flowers), small mushrooms (representing fungi), insects, snails, spiders, and even frogs — can become trapped in it. These trapped organisms retain incredibly fine detail. Flowers, for example, can appear perfectly preserved. For groups that are poorly represented in other forms of fossils, amber provides the best clues about the timing of various evolutionary events.

Spiders, for example, are quite rare in the fossil record because they don't have hard exoskeletons, but these creatures, and even their fossilized webs, turn up in amber. Data from amber allows researchers to date the evolution of spider webs to more than 100 million years ago. A 130-million-year-old spider-web fossil has been preserved with enough detail that you can see the individual droplets of glue the spider placed on the web!

Chapter 21

Ten Amazing Adaptations

In This Chapter

▷ Adaptations that you see over and over again

▷ Big adaptations resulting from a series of small steps

▷ Weird adaptations

*A*daptations are evolutionary changes resulting from natural selection. The environment in which a species lives exerts selective pressures on species such that they change over time.

This chapter lists ten adaptations I particularly like because they represent the types of adaptations that are possible. Some are no-brainers. Want to live in the ocean, and you're a mammal? You'd better be streamlined and insulated. Others are breakthroughs. Photosynthesis, for example, changed the chemistry of the entire world because of all the oxygen it produced. And some are — almost — out of this world, such as the creatures that have evolved to live in the deep-sea thermal vents that you see on the National Geographic Channel.

Different Kinds of Teeth

You have different kinds of teeth, but have you ever thought about how helpful those differences are? According to the fossil record, the ancestral condition in reptiles and the reptilian lineage that led to mammals is to have teeth that are all the same. Think about a crocodile; it has lots of teeth, but they're all the same. The same goes for the dinosaurs.

But then things changed. The Dimetredon, a dinosaur-like creature that had a sail on its back, had two kinds of teeth. Having two kinds of teeth allows for the possibility of division of labor. The teeth in the rear can be used for processing food — for grinding in grazing mammals or for slicing up chunks of flesh in your house cat — and the teeth in the front can specialize in food acquisition or other functions: snipping plants in herbivores, subduing prey in carnivores, or other functions such as defense.

What's interesting about the evolution of teeth shape is that the lower jaw has to match the upper jaw. As a consequence, changes to both jaws have to occur at the same time. For this reason, teeth change very slowly. Things get a little more complicated for humans. We've taken to capturing and processing most of our food outside our mouths. We cook it (ever try to eat raw rice?) and use knives and forks to cut it (ever ripped raw meat apart with your teeth?). As a result, our dentition is much reduced.

Evolution has also gone in the other direction: an ancestor with different kinds of teeth evolving into a species with uniform teeth. Example are animals that don't need to process their food because they swallow it whole — like dolphins and some other marine mammals. These creatures are descended from ancestors with non-uniform teeth, but they evolved dentition with one kind of tooth designed for grabbing small, slippery prey, which they then swallow whole.

Sight: The Evolution of the Eye

Eyes are beautifully complex structures, and their evolution was a source of some mystery to Charles Darwin. The idea that the eye could not have arisen from the process of natural selection is a common misconception even today and is rooted in the idea of *irreproducible complexity* (see Chapter 22), which states that complex structures could not have arisen as a result of a gradual evolutionary process because humans can't imagine how intermediate forms would be advantageous. You often see this argument stated this way: "What good is half an eye?"

Darwin never suggested that natural selection couldn't produce the eye, of course; he just admitted that he didn't know exactly how the process unfolded. He imagined that many intermediate steps had to occur, leading from a very simple light-sensing structure to the structures you're using to read this page; he just didn't know what they were. Fast-forward to today, when scientists know that many of the intermediate stages exist in other animals. From this fact, they can imagine the series of small steps that would lead from the simplest light-sensitive cell to a more complex eye. For example:

- ✔ **Step 1: Start with the simplest light-sensitive cells.** A patch of these cells can determine the presence or absence of light but not much else.

- ✔ **Step 2: The cells are set slightly into the body in a little pit or cup.** After the cells reside in a depression in the surface of the organism, the light-sensing apparatus becomes capable of determining the direction from which the light is coming.

- ✔ **Step 3: The edges of the pit grow together so that light enters the pit through a very small opening.** This arrangement is the principle behind a pinhole camera. Even though the camera has no lens, restricting light to traveling through a small hole results in a crisper image.

The principle behind the pinhole camera is simple physics, and you can test it yourself. If you have to hold a book at a distance to focus (you young folks wait a few years), poke a tiny hole in a piece of paper and peer through it. You can read the text without having to move the book away (or so far away).

✔ **Step 4: A lens is added to the opening of the light-sensitive cells.** You don't have to imagine the lens evolving all at once as a lens; you can easily imagine that a layer of translucent cells over the opening of the pinhole had a protective function. And we have plenty of examples of see-through cells in the animal kingdom. When that layer was in place, any changes that resulted in a crisper image would be selectively advantageous.

Imagining such intermediate steps goes a long way toward helping you see how a series of small changes can lead to complex structures like the eye.

Cave Blindness

A common pattern that's repeated across a large number of animals in different locations is the evolution of *cave blindness* — the evolution of sightlessness in lineages that have come to inhabit caves. Cave blindness is an excellent example of convergent evolution, in which the same trait evolves independently in different organisms (refer to Chapter 9).

The ancestors of most cave-dwelling organisms came from non-cave environments that had light. In fact, you can go to any big cave with its own ecosystem full of cave critters, and you'll find blind cave animals whose closest relatives (in the tree of life) can see.

You can easily see why the selective pressures on organisms existing in darkness would be different from those existing in light: Perhaps the energy required to produce those structures was needed for other functions — it's wasted making eyes in the dark and is better spend it some other way. Perhaps rewiring the sensory system — cave critters often have a good sense of smell, extra-sensitive tactile feelers and antenna, or other stuff that's good to have in the dark — requires minimizing the eyes.

A common theme in evolutionary biology is that things can happen over and over. If something is good once, maybe it's good twice. Cave blindness is an example; over and over, organisms that move into caves lose their sight. Flight (discussed in "Vertebrate Flight," later in this chapter) is another good example; it evolved in insects, mammals, birds, and even the extinct lineage pterosaurs (which you can read about in Chapter 20).

Finally, as discussed in Chapter 5, we always need to be cautious about assuming that an evolutionary change is an adaptation. Once it's dark, mutations that degrade the eye are no longer bad; they just don't matter. So over enough time, genetic drift might be expected to result in the loss of eyes even if the change isn't adaptive — in which case cave blindness is an example of evolution but not adaptation.

Back to the Sea

Eons ago, the first vertebrates crawled out of the ocean and onto land. It seemed like a good idea at the time. But since then, a few species have headed back to sea. Some have gone back completely; others return to the land to reproduce. Sea snakes, penguins, seals, whales, manatees, and sea otters are examples of animals that evolved independently back to sea animals from terrestrial ancestors.

Through phylogenetic analysis (see Chapter 9), scientists can tell that vertebrates have returned to the sea on several occasions; that in each case, the aquatic group is nested within a larger terrestrial group; and that the common ancestor of all the individuals in the group was terrestrial. DNA-sequence evidence has been especially helpful in confirming relationships. The skeletal structures of whales and hippos, for example, provide evidence that they're related, even though they don't look all that similar. Through DNA evidence, scientists also know that the seal group is nested within the carnivores.

Living in the ocean selects for several suites of characters:

- **With the exception of the sea snakes, which live in warm tropical waters, all these groups have made adaptations to keep warm.** Penguins have an insulating layer of blubber, as do all the mammals that live in the ocean, except for sea otters, who have water-resistant coats that trap insulating air layers.

- **All ocean-dwelling species are reasonably streamlined to facilitate faster motion in water.** The manatee group is the least streamlined and, not surprisingly, the slowest. But then, manatees are also vegetarians, and plants don't run very fast.

- **Their appendages have become modified for locomotion in water:** flippers in the case of many of the mammals; wings that act like flippers and webbed feet in the case of the penguins. Sea snakes have a flattened body, especially in the tail region, allowing them to swim with an eel-like motion.

- **All have characteristics that indicate their descent from land animals.** They all breathe air, for example, which can be very inconvenient when you live in the water, but each has evolved a rather impressive capability for holding its breath. (Sperm whales can routinely hold their breath for an hour!) They also have vestigial structures indicative of terrestrial ancestors. One of the best examples is the hind leg bones of whales. These small bones are completely within the body (whales don't have hind limbs) but correspond to the rear leg bones of terrestrial quadrupeds.

And Back to the Land Again

Current research suggests that the elephant may have an aquatic ancestor. Keep in mind, though, that the jury's still out on this particular hypothesis. But I decided to share it with you nonetheless because it's a good story. Think of it as a trip to the cutting edge of science but remember: There's not a lot of room on the edge, so sometimes we fall off!

The evidence that the elephant evolved from an aquatic ancestor is threefold:

- **Elephants' closest living relatives are manatees.** The fossil record for the evolutionary transition of the manatee lineage to the aquatic environment is reasonably complete. Fossil manatees with the vestigial legs have been found, and in Jamaica recently, scientists discovered a fossil manatee with functional legs that could support the weight of the animal yet still showed adaptation to an aquatic lifestyle. The aquatic ancestor of elephants would have been similar to such a creature, but the elephant lineage returned to the land rather than transition to a fully aquatic lifestyle, as the manatee lineage did. What we know from the fossil record and the structure of existing manatees and whales is consistent with the hypothesis that the most recent common ancestor of these beasts already had its feet in the water. One branch of the family tree kept going, while the other headed back to shore.

- **Elephants are surprisingly good swimmers.** Although they can't raise their heads out of the water while swimming, they can use their trunks as snorkels. If you've ever breathed through a snorkel while standing in water (rather than floating on the top of the water), you know that this feat is difficult because of the pressure of the water. Well, snorkeling is even harder for elephants because of the length of their trunks, but they do it relatively easily because they don't have a *pleural cavity* (a membrane surrounding the lungs that's unique to mammals). The absence of this cavity prevents the pressure difference from damaging the lungs.

- **Elephants have traits that are common to mammals that have returned to the ocean.** Chief among these traits is internal testes — a characteristic found in no other land mammal but in all aquatic mammals.

Photosynthesis

Photosynthetic organisms convert light energy from the sun to chemical energy, which they use to power their bodies. Photosynthesis is responsible for almost all the energy used by organisms on this planet. Either directly, as a result of internal photosynthesis, or indirectly, by eating something that photosynthesizes itself (or that ate something that did), most species run on photosynthetic energy. Because oil is ancient fossilized plant matter, your car is running indirectly on photosynthetic energy, too.

When you think of photosynthesis, plants are probably the first (and likely the only) organisms that come to mind, but they aren't the only organisms that use photosynthesis. Some bacteria do, too. Figuring out the origin and evolution of the various chemical mechanisms by which bacteria photosynthesize is a source of active research. As with so many things, biologists are still learning about the evolutionary diversity of photosynthetic mechanisms. In the summer of 2007, a new type of photosynthetic bacteria with different chemical pathways was discovered in a hot spring in Yellowstone National Park.

Deep-Sea Thermal-Vent Organisms

Photosynthesis may be responsible for most of the energy that organisms use, but a group of organisms that live deep in the ocean use another source of energy. Down at the ocean bottom, in regions of sub-oceanic volcanic activity, are thermal vents that spew out hot, mineral-rich streams of water from within the Earth. These mineral-rich streams of water, which were unknown before the 1970s, can be used to generate energy in much the same way that photosynthesis does.

Specifically, some bacteria can generate energy by oxidizing the hydrogen sulfide (the substance that makes rotten eggs smell rotten) that is present in the hot vent water. So these organisms derive energy not from photosynthesis, but from *chemosynthesis.* The energy that forms the base of the food chain in these deep thermal vents is not the energy of the sun, but the energy at the core of the Earth.

Just as plants form the basis of an entire community on the surface of the earth, these bacteria form the basis of a whole community on the ocean floor. And what a community it is! Creatures found nowhere else live near these thermal vents. The sulfur-oxidizing bacteria live within large worms that have no digestive systems but derive their energy solely from the bacteria, which in turn get a secure location anchored right near the stream of hydrogen sulfide.

Finally, these deep thermal vents have a very dim glow, so additional photosynthetic bacteria may be lurking there somewhere. Things are always more complicated than they seem at first!

Endosymbiosis

One of the most amazing evolutionary events is called *endosymbiosis.* According to this theory, some of the structures in eukaryotic cells — such as mitochondria and chloroplasts — once were free-living bacteria that became engulfed in ancestral eukaryotic cells, and a symbiotic relationship evolved. Somehow, and we don't completely understand how, two ancient critters joined up and eventually became so tightly interdependent that they effectively became a single organism. Remember that we're eukaryotes so that means that we are derived from two different lineages that came together deep in the distant past to make the eukaryotic cell. That's why your mitochondria have their own genome — their distant ancestors used to fly solo.

Here are the details supporting this theory: Mitochondria and chloroplasts bear a strong resemblance to bacteria. When the eukaryotic cells divide, the organelles divide too, and the division process of these organelles is reminiscent of the division of bacteria. Most importantly, these organelles have their own DNA, and analysis of the DNA sequences shows that the organelles are closely related to some free-living species of bacteria.

As you can imagine, this hypothesis was quite controversial initially. Think about it: Descendents of ancient bacteria are living in all your cells. But the DNA evidence seems to be beyond doubt. Your mitochondria have their own genome, albeit much reduced, and it's a lot more similar to a bacteria genome than it is to anything in your nuclear genome. Luckily, we eukaryotes are all living happily ever after, and we've been doing so for at least 2 billion years.

Vertebrate Flight

Flight is another trait that has evolved several times in several lineages. Birds, bats, pterodactyls — all evolved true flight, and a couple of others have rudimentary gliding ability. Flight is a remarkably successful trait. Groups that are capable of flying radiate extensively. Bats account for one quarter of all mammal species, for example. And pterodactyls, though extinct, survived for 150 million years and encompassed many species, including the largest creatures ever to take to the air.

Theories about the evolution of flight can be divided into two groups: up from the ground and down from the trees. The second group is easier to visualize, because species living today, such as flying squirrels (which don't really fly, by the way), have structures that allow them to glide from tree to tree. Current thinking is that bats arose from an arboreal ancestor, so the gliding hypothesis may apply to them, too. Pterodactyls, on the other hand, don't seem to have descended from arboreal ancestors, so maybe both mechanisms are possible.

What scientists do know is that bats, pterodactyls, and birds evolved flight structures in different ways. In bats, the wing is constructed of a membrane stretched between what for humans would be the fingers of the hand. In the case of the pterodactyls, the wing is supported by just one elongated digit. In birds, the wing is comprised of feathers all along the arm. And that list covers just the vertebrates; flight has also evolved in the insect lineage. Bottom line: Several different mutational pathways generated wings.

Trap-jaw Ants

Trap-jaw ants are species of ants in which the mandibles (the jaw-like things that they grab prey or bite you with) are locked open and have a trigger that allows them to spring shut with great force. In one case, the jaws snap shut at speeds reaching up to almost 150 miles an hour. The principle is something like an archer drawing a bow: You pull and pull to load the bow, and when you suddenly release the bowstring, the energy is transferred to the arrow. This adaptation is cool on several levels:

- ✔ The jaw speed — 150 miles per hour — is the fastest attack motion in the animal kingdom.

- ✔ This trait has evolved at least four times in four different groups of ants. And although the final outcome is the same in all cases, the exact pathway by which the trait was obtained varies from one species to the next. Specifically, different parts have been modified to serve as the trigger in different ant species.

- ✔ At least one species uses the great force generated by the snapping jaws for functions other than biting — for example, as a means of escape from predators. To escape, the ant points its head at the ground, releases its jaws, and is propelled rapidly away from whatever it's trying to escape.

Chapter 22

Ten Arguments against Evolution and Why They're Wrong

In This Chapter

▷ Common misconceptions about evolution

▷ What the intelligent-design camp has to say

▷ Why science in general and evolution in particular aren't anti-religion

*F*or an idea that's almost beautifully simple, evolution certainly has gar-nered a lot of bad press. To hear some people talk, you'd think Darwin himself was the devil incarnate; evolutionary biologists are his handmaids; and people who teach evolution in the classroom are corrupting the minds of children across the land. Can we get a little perspective, people?

I wrote this chapter specifically to provide a little perspective — and facts to arguments that tend to lack them. Here I present the arguments some people make against evolution and then explain why these arguments are wrong.

It's Only a Theory

Yes. Evolution is a theory, but not in the way the naysayers mean. When they say it's only a theory, they mean it's only an idea—a guess, if you will. But as Chapter 2 explains in quite a bit of detail, a scientific theory is not merely a best guess. It's a hypothesis that — through experiment after experiment, study after study, analysis after analysis — has yet to be refuted.

Having said that, evolution is not *only* a theory; it's also a fact. The key to understanding evolution is to recognize how it can be both:

✔ **As a fact:** Evolution is simply genetic changes occurring through time in a group of individuals (a population, a species, and so on). Scientists *know* that these changes occur. They can see the changes; measure them; and, in many instances, figure out when they happened.

✔ **As a theory:** Evolutionary theory seeks to explain what's responsible for the evolutionary process — in other words, what causes these changes. What scientists know today is that natural selection (Chapter 5) and genetic drift (Chapter 6) are two key forces driving these changes.

It Violates the Second Law of Thermodynamics

The second law of thermodynamics states that *entropy* — essentially, randomness — increases (or stays constant) in a closed, or isolated, system; it cannot decrease. In other words, left on their own, isolated systems become more uniform, not less. The differences smooth out until one common state exists. Think about a glass of ice water. After the ice goes in, the water gets a little colder, and then the ice melts: The entropy has increased in the glass. According to the second law of thermodynamics, the whole universe is doing the same thing: Increasing entropy is "smoothing out" the world. Rather than having hot regions and cold regions, for example, the world would have all its parts the same temperature.

So what does this law have to do with evolution? Diversification of life on Earth has involved very complex organisms evolving from simple forms that were present a few billion years ago — a fact that seems to fly in the face of the second law, because on Earth entropy is decreasing, not increasing. And there's the key. Earth is *not* a closed system. It gets loads of energy from the sun, and that energy is what powers the increase in complexity.

It's Been Proved Wrong (by Scientists!)

I love this one! This argument stems from the fact that in the hundred-plus years since Darwin's death, scientists have contributed to his original thoughts and refined their understanding of evolutionary events and principles. The spin you see in lots of articles, though, implies that a particular piece of research is at odds with what Darwin thought and, therefore, is proof that Darwin got things wrong.

The best example is the importance of random factors — genetic drift (see Chapter 6), which is one of the key insights modern evolutionary biologists have added to our current understanding of evolution. What scientists know today that they didn't know during Darwin's time is that random events, as well as natural selection, can be evolutionary forces; that random events can be evolutionarily important is an example of a major change in theory of evolution, but it doesn't negate in any way Darwin's theory of evolution by natural selection. It simply makes his ideas more broadly applicable.

It's Completely Random

How long would it take a million monkeys hammering away on a million typewriters to produce *Moby-Dick?* Who knows? (How long did it take one monkey hammering away on one typewriter to come up with the premise for "Who Wants to Marry a Millionaire?") The point? That a complex work — whether it's a Shakespearean sonnet or a book about evolution — can't possibly be the result of random processes.

The problem is that people who make this argument are confusing the fact that some of the evolutionary process of natural selection involves random events with the idea that the whole process is random. True, the mutations produced are random (that is, not directed toward a goal), but natural selection sorts through these mutations in a nonrandom fashion, selecting for those that increase fitness.

A major stumbling block that prevents many religious people from accepting what science has learned about the evolutionary process is the idea that evolution is connected to a random process, the one whereby DNA sequences are passed inexactly from one generation to the next — in other words, the process of mutation. Yet the very process of replicating the DNA is error prone. Scientists can measure the rate at which errors occur in DNA replication just as they can measure the rate of radioisotope decay, but whether an error occurs in one location or another is random.

The random aspect is unsettling for many people. Although we *know* that, given the amount of time available, the process of natural selection acting on randomly produced mutations is more than sufficient to generate our own species, this viewpoint is at odds with some people's view of humanity's place in God's universe. To reconcile the role of randomness with the religious beliefs that things happen for a reason or with purpose, some people suggest that nothing is truly random — that perhaps God set into motion the series of events that caused exactly the particular sequence of mutations that resulted in *Homo sapiens*. Maybe. But no way exists to scientifically measure whether God is or isn't directing these mutations. So these possibilities are outside the realm of science.

It Can't Result in Big Changes

According to this argument, some changes (namely, the small ones, a mutated nucleotide here or there) can be the result of the evolutionary process, but others (namely, the big ones) can't be. The key areas of dissention are

- **Speciation:** The argument goes like this: Although evolution can lead to changes within a lineage, it can't lead to lineages splitting or speciating. *Au contraire.* Gradual changes can lead to reproductive isolation (and the key characteristic differentiating one species from another is the inability to interbreed). The best examples for understanding speciation involve ring species, species where some but not all subpopulations can interbreed. The geographically adjacent populations are different enough from each other such that reproductive isolation occurs in some but not all cases. Moreover, we can select for the start of reproductive isolation in the laboratory. For more on when, how, and why speciation occurs, and for a more complete explanation of ring species, go to Chapter 8.

- **Evolution of new characteristics:** Some folks insist that mutations can affect existing structures or traits but can't be responsible for new ones. Except that they can. As Chapter 15 explains, the process of gene duplication can result in multiple copies of a gene, and these copies can evolve along different trajectories. Changes in one copy that would have been deleterious in the absence of the other copy now *are not* deleterious (because you've got a spare copy) and *are* potentially advantageous. Through this process, the number of genes present in the organism can increase and diversify in function.

- **Big changes in physical characteristics:** If I'm starting to sound like a broken record, it's because the same goes for big changes in body structures: Small changes can produce big results. See Chapter 14 for more details on the evolution of development.

No Missing Link Means No Proof

In the period immediately after Darwin published *On the Origin of Species*, there was a lot of talk about missing links. If humans and apes were relatives, where was the fossil evidence? There wasn't a good answer back then, but fast forward to today and the answer is easy: in museums all over the world!

We've found a wealth of fossils, everything from recent relatives like Neanderthals, to more distant relations whose two-legged stance puts them clearly in our part of the tree of life but whose tiny brains suggest that *we* wonder about their lives a fair bit more than they probably did. Every few months a story appears in the news about some new fossil discovery. Modern paleontologists have gotten really good at finding these things! And this in spite of the fact that

- ✔ **Fossils generally are rare and hard to find.** If, as scientists suspect, speciation occurs more often in small, isolated populations (refer to Chapter 8), finding such fossils would be much harder. But just because a certain fossil hasn't been found doesn't mean that it doesn't exist. Just that we need to keep looking — and look we do.

- ✔ **As scientists get better at fossil-hunting, they've found more and more fossils, some of which definitely qualify as transitional life forms.** Although scientists haven't found all missing links, they have found series of fossils that document transitions for many cases. Any of the following creatures discovered in the fossil record could be considered missing links, for example:

  - The fish with legs

  - The whale with legs

  - The series of feathered dinosaurs leading up to flight

Who knows what we'll see on tomorrow's news!

It Can't Account for Everything: Enter the Intelligent Designer

There are almost as many descriptions of intelligent design (ID) as there are proponents of the theory, and some even allow a limited role for evolution via natural selection. But all the versions of ID have one thing in common: the belief that some things in the biological world could not have come about without a "designer."

Proponents of ID argue that some structures (or systems, processes, or whatever) in the biological world clearly show that they were produced by an intelligent designer. This designer may be a divine entity but doesn't need to be. Leading proponents of ID, testifying in a court of law, have suggested that the designer could be a space alien or a time-traveling biologist.

ID proponents identify complex biological structures and then state that these structures could not have been the product of natural selection and, therefore, are evidence of the designer. Yet they don't produce any testable hypotheses. Their arguments aren't scientific — regardless of the scientific terms and language they use — but theological, aliens and time travelers notwithstanding. They can't say, exactly, what it is that allows them to conclude that one structure shows the hand of the designer and another one doesn't. They just seem to know it when they see it. Many books are written on the subject of ID, but none of them share the methodology that would allow a student of ID to learn how these decisions are reached.

In this book, I don't attempt to address in detail the intricacies of religious beliefs. Religion can be a powerful force for good, but it is no more appropriate for a religious viewpoint to try to interject itself into the scientific process than it would be for the scientific view point to claim special knowledge of the mysteries of religion.

It Can't Create Complex Structures

Irreducible complexity is the key component of most of the arguments put forth by the ID camp. Proponents of ID argue that extremely complicated structures, such as the eye, could not have evolved through a series of small steps because an eye is so complicated that it won't work without all its parts. When something can't work without all its parts, they conclude that it could not have been assembled one part at a time.

To bolster their argument, ID proponents quote Darwin himself, claiming that his very words support their argument against evolution. Well, here's what Darwin actually said about the structure of the eye, an organ he considered "of extreme perfection complication" *(Note:* The italics are mine and they highlight the part of this quote that ID proponents don't share):

> To suppose that the eye, with all its inimitable contrivances for adjusting the focus to different distances, for admitting different amounts of light, and for the correction of spherical and chromatic aberration, could have been formed by natural selection, seems, I freely confess, absurd in the highest possible degree. *Yet reason tells me that if numerous gradations from a perfect and complex eye to one very imperfect and simple, each grade being useful to its possessor, can be shown to exist; if further, the eye does vary ever so slightly, and the variations be inherited, which is certainly*

the case; and if any variation or modification in the organ be ever useful to an animal under changing conditions of life, then the difficulty of believing that a perfect and complex eye could be formed by natural selection, though insuperable by our imagination, can hardly be considered real.

Time and again, for pretty much whatever the ID camp claims couldn't have evolved incrementally, evolutionary biologists have identified the intermediate steps that led to the complex structure. Two classic examples of highly complex structures that evolved precisely through intermediate steps are the eye and blood-clotting factors.

Just because a system is made up of a series of parts doesn't mean that those parts evolved to perform the functions they now perform. Take, for example, bacteria that have evolved to break down polychlorinated biphenyls (PCBs), which are new to the environment. Until humans made them, these very nasty chemicals didn't exist. But some bacteria have evolved very complicated biochemical mechanisms for breaking down these compounds. As it turns out, the biochemistry that allows these bacteria to degrade PCBs is kludged together from a series of other biochemical pathways that serve other functions. Such PCB-busting biochemical mechanisms seem irreducibly complex, but the individual parts are advantageous in ways that are not related to PCB degradation.

It Should Be Taught with ID in Science Class

ID proponents argue that the theory of evolution isn't the only theory explaining how life on Earth came to be; therefore, in the interest of fairness and balance, ID should be taught along with evolution in the science classroom.

The issue isn't what should be included in the school curriculum, but what should be included in a *science* class. This statement may sound like hair-splitting, but science instruction isn't about a simple accumulation of facts and data (even though facts and data are accumulated in the process of doing science).

Science is a way of asking questions by coming up with ideas and then trying hard to shoot them down. The ideas that scientists can't shoot down even after lots of trying become theories about how things work. And if at some point, other scientists come up with evidence that refutes these theories, they shoot the theories down.

Although the ID argument is compelling to many people, it *isn't* science. In fact, it turns the entire scientific process on its head. Instead of trying to shoot down their own premise that a designer is responsible for the complexity of the universe, ID proponents use the very complexity that they claim requires a designer to prove the existence of the designer. This reasoning is circular (and an error in logic); it's not science.

The ID argument relies on a particular world view that demands a designer. In essence, it promotes the religious viewpoint that something beyond natural processes created the world and the creatures in it. Evolution, on the other hand, is a scientific discipline; it doesn't concern itself with anything beyond what can be seen or observed in the natural world. That one deals with the supernatural and the other with the natural is the key difference between science and religion and why they don't have to be at odds.

It's a Fringe Topic

Evolution is a central part of modern biology. In fact, making sense of most of biology concepts in the absence of an evolutionary perspective is difficult. One of the most important things that an understanding of the evolutionary process provides to the study of biology is a way to understand the effect of history.

This historical perspective is important for fields as diverse as agriculture, conservation biology, and medicine. Doctors, for example, don't worry about removing an appendix, because they have a framework in which to understand that it's a vestigial organ — that is, it may have served a purpose once, but that purpose is long gone, even though the organ isn't. And understanding how organisms evolve continues to be vital in the fight against infectious diseases (see Chapters 18 and 19 to find out why).

Conservationists seeking to save species also need to preserve biological diversity. Without genetic diversity, endangered species — even those that are making headway in the numbers game — remain vulnerable to extinction. By understanding natural variation in the evolutionary process, conservationists better understand what their conservation goals should be and how to meet them. It's probably better to save a few spotted owls from a bunch of different forests than all the spotted owls from one isolated forest, for example.

It's at Odds with Biblical Creation

Quite a few people see discrepancies between the biblical creation story as they understand it and the idea of evolution. Young Earth creationism, for example, states that the Earth is only a few thousand years old and that all living organisms were created by God exactly as you see them today. Right there, you can see the areas of disagreement. This theory's creation date is at odds with most of what humans know from other fields of science — specifically, from physics and astronomy, which indicate that the Earth is about 4 billion years old. If the Earth were only a few thousand years old, the evolutionary process as scientists understand it wouldn't have had sufficient time to generate the diversity of the planet.

Old Earth creationism differs from Young Earth creationism in that it accepts that the Earth is as old as physicists and astronomers say, but it disagrees that any evolutionary processes would have occurred over that time. According to this theory, species were formed by God and did not change subsequently.

Other groups make other distinctions:

- ✔ Some allow for the possibility of small evolutionary changes that may have happened within a species over time but not for the origin of new species.

- ✔ Others allow for the possibility that speciation could have occurred within specific groups but say that larger taxonomic groups could not have arisen.

- ✔ Still others, recognizing that the Ark was only so big, have come up with a clever workaround that melds both biblical and evolutionary theory: Noah loaded the Ark with all the animals that existed on Earth at the time. Then somehow, in the few short years that followed the grounding of the Ark, the species diversified to produce the variety we see today.

In all these regards, evolution *is* at odds with a literal interpretation of biblical creation story. There's just no way around it. Many denominations of Christianity (as well as other religions), of course, have no problem with the theory of evolution or with the age of the Earth being a little over 4 billion years. Maybe, they say, that's just the way God did things.

Evolution is a fact that scientists can measure and test. As we further our understanding of the underlying processes responsible for evolution, we refine our theories about the details. If these theories ever seem at odds with particular aspects of religious belief, be assured that that was merely a consequence of following the data and never an intentional goal. The process of science has no mechanisms for addressing questions of a spiritual nature; it concerns itself solely with the natural world.

Index

• *G* •

• Q •

• R •

• S •

• W •

• Y •

• Z •

BUSINESS, CAREERS & PERSONAL FINANCE

0-7645-9847-3

0-7645-2431-3

Also available:
- Business Plans Kit For Dummies
  0-7645-9794-9
- Economics For Dummies
  0-7645-5726-2
- Grant Writing For Dummies
  0-7645-8416-2
- Home Buying For Dummies
  0-7645-5331-3
- Managing For Dummies
  0-7645-1771-6
- Marketing For Dummies
  0-7645-5600-2

- Personal Finance For Dummies
  0-7645-2590-5*
- Resumes For Dummies
  0-7645-5471-9
- Selling For Dummies
  0-7645-5363-1
- Six Sigma For Dummies
  0-7645-6798-5
- Small Business Kit For Dummies
  0-7645-5984-2
- Starting an eBay Business For Dummies
  0-7645-6924-4
- Your Dream Career For Dummies
  0-7645-9795-7

HOME & BUSINESS COMPUTER BASICS

0-470-05432-8

0-471-75421-8

Also available:
- Cleaning Windows Vista For Dummies
  0-471-78293-9
- Excel 2007 For Dummies
  0-470-03737-7
- Mac OS X Tiger For Dummies
  0-7645-7675-5
- MacBook For Dummies
  0-470-04859-X
- Macs For Dummies
  0-470-04849-2
- Office 2007 For Dummies
  0-470-00923-3

- Outlook 2007 For Dummies
  0-470-03830-6
- PCs For Dummies
  0-7645-8958-X
- Salesforce.com For Dummies
  0-470-04893-X
- Upgrading & Fixing Laptops For Dummies
  0-7645-8959-8
- Word 2007 For Dummies
  0-470-03658-3
- Quicken 2007 For Dummies
  0-470-04600-7

FOOD, HOME, GARDEN, HOBBIES, MUSIC & PETS

0-7645-8404-9

0-7645-9904-6

Also available:
- Candy Making For Dummies
  0-7645-9734-5
- Card Games For Dummies
  0-7645-9910-0
- Crocheting For Dummies
  0-7645-4151-X
- Dog Training For Dummies
  0-7645-8418-9
- Healthy Carb Cookbook For Dummies
  0-7645-8476-6
- Home Maintenance For Dummies
  0-7645-5215-5

- Horses For Dummies
  0-7645-9797-3
- Jewelry Making & Beading For Dummies
  0-7645-2571-9
- Orchids For Dummies
  0-7645-6759-4
- Puppies For Dummies
  0-7645-5255-4
- Rock Guitar For Dummies
  0-7645-5356-9
- Sewing For Dummies
  0-7645-6847-7
- Singing For Dummies
  0-7645-2475-5

INTERNET & DIGITAL MEDIA

0-470-04529-9

0-470-04894-8

Also available:
- Blogging For Dummies
  0-471-77084-1
- Digital Photography For Dummies
  0-7645-9802-3
- Digital Photography All-in-One Desk Reference For Dummies
  0-470-03743-1
- Digital SLR Cameras and Photography For Dummies
  0-7645-9803-1
- eBay Business All-in-One Desk Reference For Dummies
  0-7645-8438-3
- HDTV For Dummies
  0-470-09673-X

- Home Entertainment PCs For Dummies
  0-470-05523-5
- MySpace For Dummies
  0-470-09529-6
- Search Engine Optimization For Dummies
  0-471-97998-8
- Skype For Dummies
  0-470-04891-3
- The Internet For Dummies
  0-7645-8996-2
- Wiring Your Digital Home For Dummies
  0-471-91830-X

* Separate Canadian edition also available
† Separate U.K. edition also available

 WILEY

SPORTS, FITNESS, PARENTING, RELIGION & SPIRITUALITY

0-471-76871-5

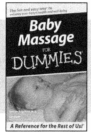
0-7645-7841-3

Also available:
- Catholicism For Dummies
  0-7645-5391-7
- Exercise Balls For Dummies
  0-7645-5623-1
- Fitness For Dummies
  0-7645-7851-0
- Football For Dummies
  0-7645-3936-1
- Judaism For Dummies
  0-7645-5299-6
- Potty Training For Dummies
  0-7645-5417-4
- Buddhism For Dummies
  0-7645-5359-3

- Pregnancy For Dummies
  0-7645-4483-7 †
- Ten Minute Tone-Ups For Dummies
  0-7645-7207-5
- NASCAR For Dummies
  0-7645-7681-X
- Religion For Dummies
  0-7645-5264-3
- Soccer For Dummies
  0-7645-5229-5
- Women in the Bible For Dummies
  0-7645-8475-8

TRAVEL

0-7645-7749-2

0-7645-6945-7

Also available:
- Alaska For Dummies
  0-7645-7746-8
- Cruise Vacations For Dummies
  0-7645-6941-4
- England For Dummies
  0-7645-4276-1
- Europe For Dummies
  0-7645-7529-5
- Germany For Dummies
  0-7645-7823-5
- Hawaii For Dummies
  0-7645-7402-7

- Italy For Dummies
  0-7645-7386-1
- Las Vegas For Dummies
  0-7645-7382-9
- London For Dummies
  0-7645-4277-X
- Paris For Dummies
  0-7645-7630-5
- RV Vacations For Dummies
  0-7645-4442-X
- Walt Disney World & Orlando
  For Dummies
  0-7645-9660-8

GRAPHICS, DESIGN & WEB DEVELOPMENT

0-7645-8815-X

0-7645-9571-7

Also available:
- 3D Game Animation For Dummies
  0-7645-8789-7
- AutoCAD 2006 For Dummies
  0-7645-8925-3
- Building a Web Site For Dummies
  0-7645-7144-3
- Creating Web Pages For Dummies
  0-470-08030-2
- Creating Web Pages All-in-One Desk
  Reference For Dummies
  0-7645-4345-8
- Dreamweaver 8 For Dummies
  0-7645-9649-7

- InDesign CS2 For Dummies
  0-7645-9572-5
- Macromedia Flash 8 For Dummies
  0-7645-9691-8
- Photoshop CS2 and Digital
  Photography For Dummies
  0-7645-9580-6
- Photoshop Elements 4 For Dummies
  0-471-77483-9
- Syndicating Web Sites with RSS Feeds
  For Dummies
  0-7645-8848-6
- Yahoo! SiteBuilder For Dummies
  0-7645-9800-7

NETWORKING, SECURITY, PROGRAMMING & DATABASES

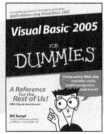
0-7645-7728-X

0-471-74940-0

Also available:
- Access 2007 For Dummies
  0-470-04612-0
- ASP.NET 2 For Dummies
  0-7645-7907-X
- C# 2005 For Dummies
  0-7645-9704-3
- Hacking For Dummies
  0-470-05235-X
- Hacking Wireless Networks
  For Dummies
  0-7645-9730-2
- Java For Dummies
  0-470-08716-1

- Microsoft SQL Server 2005 For Dummies
  0-7645-7755-7
- Networking All-in-One Desk Reference
  For Dummies
  0-7645-9939-9
- Preventing Identity Theft For Dummies
  0-7645-7336-5
- Telecom For Dummies
  0-471-77085-X
- Visual Studio 2005 All-in-One Desk
  Reference For Dummies
  0-7645-9775-2
- XML For Dummies
  0-7645-8845-1

HEALTH & SELF-HELP

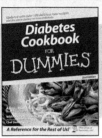

0-7645-8450-2

0-7645-4149-8

Also available:

- Bipolar Disorder For Dummies
  0-7645-8451-0
- Chemotherapy and Radiation
  For Dummies
  0-7645-7832-4
- Controlling Cholesterol For Dummies
  0-7645-5440-9
- Diabetes For Dummies
  0-7645-6820-5* †
- Divorce For Dummies
  0-7645-8417-0 †

- Fibromyalgia For Dummies
  0-7645-5441-7
- Low-Calorie Dieting For Dummies
  0-7645-9905-4
- Meditation For Dummies
  0-471-77774-9
- Osteoporosis For Dummies
  0-7645-7621-6
- Overcoming Anxiety For Dummies
  0-7645-5447-6
- Reiki For Dummies
  0-7645-9907-0
- Stress Management For Dummies
  0-7645-5144-2

EDUCATION, HISTORY, REFERENCE & TEST PREPARATION

0-7645-8381-6

0-7645-9554-7

Also available:

- The ACT For Dummies
  0-7645-9652-7
- Algebra For Dummies
  0-7645-5325-9
- Algebra Workbook For Dummies
  0-7645-8467-7
- Astronomy For Dummies
  0-7645-8465-0
- Calculus For Dummies
  0-7645-2498-4
- Chemistry For Dummies
  0-7645-5430-1
- Forensics For Dummies
  0-7645-5580-4

- Freemasons For Dummies
  0-7645-9796-5
- French For Dummies
  0-7645-5193-0
- Geometry For Dummies
  0-7645-5324-0
- Organic Chemistry I For Dummies
  0-7645-6902-3
- The SAT I For Dummies
  0-7645-7193-1
- Spanish For Dummies
  0-7645-5194-9
- Statistics For Dummies
  0-7645-5423-9

Get smart @ dummies.com®

- **Find a full list of Dummies titles**
- **Look into loads of FREE on-site articles**
- **Sign up for FREE eTips e-mailed to you weekly**
- **See what other products carry the Dummies name**
- **Shop directly from the Dummies bookstore**
- **Enter to win new prizes every month!**

* Separate Canadian edition also available
† Separate U.K. edition also available

Available wherever books are sold. For more information or to order direct: U.S. customers visit www.dummies.com or call 1-877-762-2974.
U.K. customers visit www.wileyeurope.com or call 0800 243407. Canadian customers visit www.wiley.ca or call 1-800-567-4797.

Evolution For Dummies®

Cheat Sheet

Scientific Process at a Glance

The thing that makes a science a science is the adherence to the scientific process:

1. **Make observations about the natural world.**
2. **Formulate a hypothesis.**

   The hypothesis serves as the scientist's starting point; maybe it's right, and maybe it's wrong. They key is to do enough testing to find out.

3. **Gather additional data to test this hypothesis.**

   As your data accumulates, it either supports your hypothesis, or it forces you to revise or abandon the hypothesis.

   Remember: The hypothesis scientists come up with must be *falsifiable*. That is, scientists must be able to imagine some set of results that would cause them to reject the theory, and then they must test those ideas out.

4. **Continue testing (if the data from Step 3 supports your hypothesis) or revise your hypothesis and test again.**

   After an overwhelming amount of information accumulates in support of the hypothesis, you elevate the hypothesis to a theory.

5. **If, at anytime in the future, new data arises that causes you to revise or reject your theory, then you revise or reject it and start again at Step 1.**

   Real scientists *never* ignore facts or observations in order to protect a hypothesis or theory, even one that they're particularly fond of.

The Hominid Family Tree

Your family tree holds more than Uncle Joe and Great-grandma Myrtle. Take a look these distant and not-so-distant relations:

Species*	Where Found	Lived (mya= million years ago)	Interesting Characteristics
A. anamensis	Kenya	4.2 to 3.9 mya	Probably walked upright
A. afarensis	Ethiopia, Kenya	3.6 to 2.9 mya	Walked upright. Most famous member (to us anyway) is Lucy, the nearly complete fossil found in 1974
A. africanus	South Africa	3 to 2 mya	Teeth more human-like than ape-like, probably bipedal
A. aethiopicus	Ethiopia	2.7 to 2.3 mya	Considered a transitional species between A. afarensis and A. boisei
A. garhi	Ethiopia	2.5 mya	Possibly the earliest tool user
A. boisei	Tanzania, Ethiopia	2.3 to 1.4 mya	Formerly considered to be a direct human ancestor until H. habilis was discovered
A. robustus	South Africa	1.8 to 1.5 mya	May have used tools to dig up edible roots
H. rudolfensis	Kenya, Tanzania	2.4 to 1.8 mya	Bipedal with a large brain
H. habilis	Kenya	2.3 to 1.6 mya	"Handy man"; used tools, brain larger and more human-shaped, possibly capable of rudimentary speech
H. ergaster	Eastern and Southern Africa	1.9 to 1.4 mya	Made some nice tools, had smaller teeth
H. erectus	Republic of Georgia, Kenya, China, Indonesia, Europe	1.9 to 0.3 mya (and possibly 50,000 years ago)	Definitely used tools, probably discovered fire, and may have lived at same time as modern humans
H. heielbergensis	Africa, Europe	600,000 to 100,000 years ago	Brain size equal to modern humans, found with tools sharp enough to slice through animal hides, almost certainly used fire
H. neanderthalensis	Europe, Middle East	250,000 to 30,000 years ago	Lived mostly in cold climates, shared the earth with H. sapiens, may have had a complex social system that included care for the elderly and burial rituals
H. sapiens	Worldwide	100,000 years ago to today	Large brains (not always used) and ability to manipulate tools, situations, and the emotions of other H. sapiens

*A = Australopithecus, H = Homo

Evolution For Dummies®

Interpreting Evolution Articles

Ever found yourself scratching your head at some of the terms used in the science section of the newspaper or a science article in a magazine? These definitions might come in handy. Keep them next to your morning coffee.

Adaptations: Changes resulting from natural selection.

Allele (plural *alleles*): The specific DNA sequence found at a given locus in an individual. A haploid individual has one allele at every locus while a diploid individual has two alleles at each locus (one on each set of chromosomes), which can be the same or different.

Artificial selection: The process of selection when people control which characters are favored—for example selectively breeding cows that make the most milk to produce the next generation of dairy cows.

Chromosome: The cellular structures that contain DNA. Humans, a diploid organism, have 23 pairs of chromosomes.

Diploid genome: The genome of an organism that has of two sets of chromosomes. In sexually reproducing organisms, diploid parents each contribute one set of chromosomes to the offspring, producing a new diploid individual whose genome is a combination of some of the DNA from each parent. Examples of diploid organisms include mammals, birds, many plants, and so on.

DNA (deoxyribonucleic acid): A long molecule made up of four different subunits (or nucleotides, which you can think of as a four-letter alphabet). The sequence of the four different nucleotides govern the specific details of traits. While almost all organisms have DNA as the genetic material, a few (some viruses) use a slightly different molecule (RNA, ribonucleic acid) but the process is otherwise the same.

DNA sequence: The exact arrangement of the four nucleotides in a specific individual. The sequence information can be for the entire genome or just some location of interest.

Evolution: A change in the percentage of inherited (heritable) traits in a group of organisms over time. For evolution, time is measured in generations (which is one of the reasons that bacteria evolve faster than elephants).

Evolutionary theory: The field of scientific investigation that works to understand what processes are responsible for the evolutionary changes we observe and what the consequences of those changes are.

Fitness: A measure of an organism's ability to contribute offspring to the next generation.

Gene: The classic unit of heredity that governs the traits that are passed from parent to offspring. The term predates an understanding of how the process of heredity actually works, which involves DNA. Therefore, in science articles, *gene* primarily serves as an easy-to-understand, if not exactly precise, stand in for *locus* and *allele*, which more precisely identify the exact units of heredity.

Genetic drift: Random factors—volcanoes erupting, trees falling, or airplanes crashing, for example—that impact the gene frequency in subsequent populations.

Genome: The sum total of all of an organism's DNA.

Genotype: The specific combination of alleles that an individual organism has. Genotype does not map directly to phenotype (or physical traits) because of the effect of environmental factors.

Haploid genome: The genome of an organism with a single set of chromosomes. Examples of haploid organisms include bacteria and fungi which produce asexually (new individuals simply divide from existing ones). *Note:* Diploid individuals produce haploid gametes (sperm and egg).

Locus (plural *loci*): A particular location in an organism's genome where the information for a particular trait resides. The eye color locus, for example, is the place in an individual organism's genome that has the DNA sequence controlling eye color.

Mutations: Changes in the DNA sequence caused by errors in DNA replication or such factors (like radiation) that can cause DNA damage.

Natural selection: The process of selection when the natural environment is the selective force.

Neutral evolution: Evolution as the result of genetic drift. When two different alleles are selectively neutral—that is, they don't differ in fitness—changes in their relative frequencies can only be caused by random events.

Phenotype: The physical traits that the organism has, including things like body structure, wing span, running speed, and so on. Phenotype is a product of both the genotype and the effects of the environment.

Selection: When a particular character is favored such that organisms that possess that character are more likely to contribute offspring to the next generation. If the character under selection is heritable, then the frequency of that character in future generations increases. Selection acts on phenotypes rather than genotypes.

Speciation: When a group of individuals in a species evolves differently from the rest of the species, leading to the accumulation of enough genetic differences to prevent the two groups from interbreeding.

For Dummies: Bestselling Book Series for Beginners

Taken from:
Genetics for Dummies: Second Edition by
Tara Rodden Robinson

Genetics

FOR

DUMMIES®

2ND EDITION

by Tara Rodden Robinson

WILEY

Wiley Publishing, Inc.

Genetics For Dummies®, 2nd Edition

Published by
Wiley Publishing, Inc.
111 River St.
Hoboken, NJ 07030-5774
www.wiley.com

WILEY

About the Author

Tara Rodden Robinson, RN, BSN, PhD, is a native of Monroe, Louisiana, where she graduated from Ouachita Parish High School. She earned her degree in nursing at the University of Southern Mississippi and worked as a registered nurse for nearly six years (mostly in surgery) before running away from home to study birds in the Costa Rican rain forest. From the rain forests, Tara traveled to the cornfields of the Midwest to earn her PhD in biology at the University of Illinois, Urbana-Champaign. She conducted her dissertation work in the Republic of Panama, where she examined the social lives of song wrens. She received her postdoctoral training in genetics with Dr. Colin Hughes (then at the University of Miami) and through a postdoctoral fellowship at Auburn University. Dr. Robinson received a teaching award for her genetics course at Auburn and was twice included in *Who's Who Among America's Teachers* (2002 and 2005).

Currently, Tara teaches genetics via distance education on behalf of the biology program at Oregon State University. On the research side, Dr. Robinson has conducted research on birds in locations all over the map, including Oregon, Michigan, Yap (part of the Federated States of Micronesia), and the Republic of Panama. Examples of her work include using paternity analysis to uncover the mysteries of birds' social lives, examining the population genetics of endangered salmon, and using DNA to find out which species of salmon that seagoing birds like to eat.

When not traveling to exotic places with her husband, ornithologist W. Douglas Robinson, Tara enjoys hiking the Coast Range of Oregon with her two dogs in training for the Susan G. Komen 3-Day for the Cure. You can find out more about her at www.thegeneticsprofessor.com.

Dedication

For Douglas: You are my Vitamin D.

Author's Acknowledgments

I extend thanks to my wonderful editors at Wiley: Elizabeth Rea, Chad Sievers, Todd Lothery, Stacy Kennedy, Lisa J. Cushman, and Mike Baker (first edition). Many other people at Wiley worked hard to make both editions of this book a reality; special thanks go to Melisa Duffy, Lindsay MacGregor, Abbie Enneking, Grace Davis, and David Hobson.

Many colleagues and friends provided help. I enjoyed lively discussions with and gained much insight into the nature of the epigenome from Jonathan Weitzman. I thank Doug P. Lyle, MD, Walter D. Smith, Benoit Leclair, Maddy Delone, and Jen Dolan of the Innocence Project; and Jorge Berreno (Applied Biosystems, Inc.), Paul Farber (Oregon State University), Iris Sandler (University of Washington), Robert J. Robbins (Fred Hutchinson Cancer Research Center), and Garland E. Allen (Washington University in St. Louis) for assistance in preparing the first edition. I am indebted to Peter and Rosemary Grant for figure-use permission. I also want to thank my post-doctoral mentor, Colin Hughes (now of Florida Atlantic University). I send a hearty "War Eagle!" to my friends, former students, and colleagues from Auburn University, especially Mike and Marie Wooten, Sharon Roberts, and Shreekumar Pulai.

My deepest gratitude goes to my husband, Douglas, who hikes with me, makes me laugh, and keeps my perspective balanced. Finally, I thank my mom and dad for love, support, prayers, and gumbo.

Publisher's Acknowledgments

We're proud of this book; please send us your comments at `http://dummies.custhelp.com`. For other comments, please contact our Customer Care Department within the U.S. at 877-762-2974, outside the U.S. at 317-572-3993, or fax 317-572-4002.

Some of the people who helped bring this book to market include the following:

Acquisitions, Editorial, and Media Development

Project Editor: Elizabeth Rea
(Previous Edition: Mike Baker)

Acquisitions Editor: Michael Lewis
(Previous Edition: Stacy Kennedy)

Copy Editor: Todd Lothery
(Previous Edition: Elizabeth Rea)

Assistant Editor: Erin Calligan Mooney

Senior Editorial Assistant: David Lutton

Technical Editor: Lisa J. Cushman

Editorial Manager: Michelle Hacker

Editorial Assistant: Jennette ElNaggar

Cover Photos: iStock

Cartoons: Rich Tennant
(`www.the5thwave.com`)

Composition Services

Project Coordinator: Katherine Crocker

Layout and Graphics: Ashley Chamberlain, Joyce Haughey

Proofreaders: Melissa Cossell, Leeann Harney

Indexer: Slivoskey Indexing Services

Publishing and Editorial for Consumer Dummies

Diane Graves Steele, Vice President and Publisher, Consumer Dummies

Kristin Ferguson-Wagstaffe, Product Development Director, Consumer Dummies

Ensley Eikenburg, Associate Publisher, Travel

Kelly Regan, Editorial Director, Travel

Publishing for Technology Dummies

Andy Cummings, Vice President and Publisher, Dummies Technology/General User

Composition Services

Debbie Stailey, Director of Composition Services

Contents at a Glance

Table of Contents

Introduction

· ·

*G*enetics affects all living things. Although sometimes complicated and always diverse, all genetics comes down to basic principles of *heredity* — how traits are passed from one generation to the next — and how DNA is put together. As a science, genetics is a fast growing field because of its untapped potential — for good and for bad. Despite its complexity, genetics can be surprisingly accessible. Genetics is a bit like peeking behind a movie's special effects to find a deceptively simple and elegant system running the whole show.

About This Book

Genetics For Dummies, 2nd Edition, is an overview of the entire field of genetics. My goal is to explain every topic so that anyone, even someone without any genetics background at all, can follow the subject and understand how it works. As in the first edition, I include many examples from the frontiers of research. I also make sure that the book has detailed coverage of some of the hottest topics that you hear about in the news: cloning, gene therapy, and forensics. And I address the practical side of genetics: how it affects your health and the world around you. In short, this book is designed to be a solid introduction to genetics basics and to provide some details on the subject.

Genetics is a fast-paced field; new discoveries are coming out all the time. You can use this book to help you get through your genetics course or for self-guided study. *Genetics For Dummies,* 2nd Edition, provides enough information for you to get a handle on the latest press coverage, understand the genetics jargon that mystery writers like to toss around, and translate information imparted to you by medical professionals. The book is filled with stories of key discoveries and "wow" developments. Although I try to keep things light and inject some humor when possible, at the same time, I make every effort to be sensitive to whatever your circumstances may be.

This book is a great guide if you know nothing at all about genetics. If you already have some background, then you're set to dive into the details of the subject and expand your horizons.

Conventions Used in This Book

I teach genetics in a university. It would be very easy for me to use specialized language that you'd need a translator to understand, but what fun would that be? Throughout this book, I avoid jargon as much as possible, but at the same time, I use and carefully define terms that scientists actually use. After all, it may be important for you to understand some of these multisyllabic jawbreakers in the course of your studies or your, or a loved one's, medical treatment.

To help you navigate through this book, I also use the following typographical conventions:

- I use *italic* for emphasis and to highlight new words or terms that I define in the text.
- I use **boldface** to indicate keywords in bulleted lists or the action parts of numbered steps.
- I use `monofont` for Web sites and e-mail addresses. Note that some Web addresses may break across two lines of text. In such cases, I haven't inserted any hyphens to indicate a break. So if you type exactly what you see — pretending that the line break doesn't exist — you can get to your Web destination.

What You're Not to Read

Anytime you see a Technical Stuff icon (see "Icons Used in This Book" later in this introduction), you can cruise past the information it's attached to without missing a key explanation. For the serious reader (or a student intent on earning a high score), the technical bits add depth and detail to the book. You also have permission to skip the shaded gray boxes known as sidebars. Doing so doesn't affect your understanding of the subject at hand, but I pull together lots of amazing details in these boxes — from how aging affects your DNA (and vice versa) to how genetics affects your food — so I'm guessing (or at least hoping!) that the sidebars will grab your attention more often than not.

Foolish Assumptions

It's a privilege to be your guide into the amazing world of genetics. Given this responsibility, you were in my thoughts often while I was writing this book. Here's how I imagine you, my reader:

✔ You're a student in a genetics or biology class.

✔ You're curious to understand more about the science you hear reported in the news.

✔ You're an expectant or new parent or a family member who's struggling to come to terms with what doctors have told you.

✔ You're affected by cancer or some hereditary disease, wondering what it means for you and your family.

If any of these descriptions fit, you've come to the right place.

How This Book Is Organized

I designed this book to cover background material in the first two parts and then all the applications in the rest of the book. I think you'll find it quite accessible.

Part I: The Lowdown on Genetics: Just the Basics

This part explains how trait inheritance works. The first chapter gives you a handle on how genetic information gets divvied up during cell division; these events provide the foundation for just about everything else that has to do with genetics. From there, I explain simple inheritance of one gene and then move on to more complex forms of inheritance. This part ends with an explanation of how sex works — that is, how genetics determines maleness or femaleness and how sex affects how your genes work. (If you're wondering how sex *really* works, check out *Sex For Dummies,* coauthored by Dr. Ruth.)

Part II: DNA: The Genetic Material

This part covers what's sometimes called *molecular genetics.* But don't let the word "molecular" scare you off. It's the nitty-gritty details all right, but broken down so that you can easily follow along. I track the progress of how your genes work from start to finish: how your DNA is put together, how it gets copied, and how the building plans for your body are encoded in the double helix. To help you understand how scientists explore the secrets stored in your DNA, I cover how DNA is sequenced. In the process, I relate the fascinating story behind the Human Genome Project.

Part III: Genetics and Your Health

Part III is intended to help you see how genetics affects your health and well-being. I cover the subjects of genetic counseling, inherited diseases, genetics and cancer, and chromosome disorders such as Down syndrome. I also include a chapter on gene therapy, a practice that may hold the key to cures or treatments for many of the disorders I describe in this part of the book.

Part IV: Genetics and Your World

This part explains the broader impact of genetics and covers some hot topics that are often in the news. I explain how various technologies work and highlight both the possibilities and the perils of each. I delve into population genetics (of both humans, past and present, and endangered animal species), evolution, DNA and forensics, genetically modified plants and animals, cloning, and the issue of ethics, which is raised on a daily basis as scientists push the boundaries of the possible with cutting-edge technology.

Part V: The Part of Tens

In Part V, you get my lists of ten milestone events and important people that have shaped genetics history, ten of the next big things in the field, and ten "believe it or not" stories that can provide you with more insights on the issues found elsewhere in the book that interest you.

Icons Used in This Book

All *For Dummies* books use icons to help readers keep track of what's what. Here's a rundown of the icons I use in this book and what they all mean.

This icon flags information that's critical to your understanding or that's particularly important to keep in mind.

Points in the text where I provide added insight on how to get a better handle on a concept are found here. I draw on my teaching experience for these tips and alert you to other sources of information you can check out.

These details are useful but not necessary to know. If you're a student, though, these sections may be especially important to you.

This icon points out stories about the people behind the science and accounts of how discoveries came about.

This fine piece of art alerts you to recent applications of genetics in the field or in the lab.

Where to Go from Here

With *Genetics For Dummies,* 2nd Edition, you can start anywhere, in any chapter, and get a handle on what you're interested in right away. I make generous use of cross-references throughout the book to help you get background details that you may have skipped earlier. The table of contents and index can point you to specific topics in a hurry, or you can just start at the beginning and work your way straight through. If you read the book from front to back, you'll get a short course in genetics in the style and order that it's often taught in colleges and universities — Mendel first and DNA second.

Part I
The Lowdown on Genetics: Just the Basics

"The results of our genetic testing have come in, and it appears you may share some DNA with the people of—get this—Easter Island."

In this part . . .

First and foremost, genetics is concerned with how traits are inherited. The process of cell division is central to how chromosomes are divvyed up among offspring. When genes are passed on, some are assertive and dominant while others are shy and recessive. The study of how different traits are inherited and expressed is called *Mendelian genetics*.

Genetics also determines your sex (as in maleness or femaleness), and your sex influences how certain traits are expressed. In this part, I explain what genetics is and what it's used for, how cells divide, and how traits are passed from parents to offspring.

Chapter 1

What Genetics Is and Why You Need to Know Some

Welcome to the complex and fascinating world of genetics. Genetics is all about physical traits and the DNA code that supplies the building plans for any organism. This chapter explains what the field of genetics is and what geneticists do. You get an introduction to the big picture and a glimpse at some of the details found in other chapters of this book.

What Is Genetics?

Genetics is the field of science that examines how traits are passed from one generation to the next. Simply put, genetics affects *everything* about *every* living thing on earth. An organism's *genes,* snippets of DNA that are the fundamental units of heredity, control how the organism looks, behaves, and reproduces. Because all biology depends on genes, understanding genetics as a foundation for all other life sciences, including agriculture and medicine, is critical.

From a historical point of view, genetics is still a young science. The principles that govern inheritance of traits by one generation from another were described (and promptly lost) less than 150 years ago. Around the turn of the 20th century, the laws of inheritance were rediscovered, an event that transformed biology forever. But even then, the importance of the star of the genetics show, DNA, wasn't really understood until the 1950s. Now, technology is helping geneticists push the envelope of knowledge every day.

Genetics is generally divided into four major subdivisions:

- ✔ **Classical, or Mendelian, genetics:** A discipline that describes how physical characteristics (traits) are passed along from one generation to another.

- ✔ **Molecular genetics:** The study of the chemical and physical structures of DNA, its close cousin RNA, and proteins. Molecular genetics also covers how genes do their jobs.

- ✔ **Population genetics:** A division of genetics that looks at the genetic makeup of larger groups.

- ✔ **Quantitative genetics:** A highly mathematical field that examines the statistical relationships between genes and the traits they encode.

In the academic world, many genetics courses begin with classical genetics and proceed through molecular genetics, with a nod to population, evolutionary, or quantitative genetics. This book follows the same path, because each division of knowledge builds on the one before it. That said, it's perfectly okay, and very easy, to jump around among disciplines. No matter how you take on reading this book, I provide lots of cross references to help you stay on track.

Classical genetics: Transmitting traits from generation to generation

At its heart, *classical genetics* is the genetics of individuals and their families. It focuses mostly on studying physical traits, or *phenotypes,* as a stand-in for the genes that control appearance.

Gregor Mendel, a humble monk and part-time scientist, founded the entire discipline of genetics. Mendel was a gardener with an insatiable curiosity to go along with his green thumb. His observations may have been simple, but his conclusions were jaw-droppingly elegant. This man had no access to technology, computers, or a pocket calculator, yet he determined, with keen accuracy, exactly how inheritance works.

Classical genetics is sometimes referred to as:

- ✔ **Mendelian genetics:** You start a new scientific discipline, and it gets named after you. Seems fair.

- ✔ **Transmission genetics:** This term refers to the fact that classical genetics describes how traits are passed on, or *transmitted,* by parents to their offspring.

No matter what you call it, classical genetics includes the study of cells and chromosomes (which I delve into in Chapter 2). Cell division is the machine that drives inheritance, but you don't have to understand combustion engines to drive a car, right? Likewise, you can dive straight into simple inheritance (see Chapter 3) and work up to more complicated forms of inheritance (in Chapter 4) without knowing anything whatsoever about cell division. (Mendel didn't know anything about chromosomes and cells when he figured this whole thing out, by the way.)

The genetics of sex and reproduction are also part of classical genetics. Various combinations of genes and chromosomes (strands of DNA) determine sex, as in maleness and femaleness. But the subject of sex gets even more complicated (and interesting): The environment plays a role in determining the sex of some organisms (like crocodiles and turtles), and other organisms can even change sex with a change of address. If I've piqued your interest, you can find out all the slightly kinky details in Chapter 5.

Classical genetics provides the framework for many subdisciplines. Genetic counseling (which I cover in Chapter 12) depends heavily on understanding patterns of inheritance to interpret people's medical histories from a genetics perspective. The study of chromosome disorders such as Down syndrome (see Chapter 15) relies on cell biology and an understanding of what happens during cell division. Forensics (see Chapter 18) also uses Mendelian genetics to determine paternity and to work out who's who with DNA fingerprinting.

Molecular genetics: DNA and the chemistry of genes

Classical genetics concentrates on studying outward appearances, but the study of actual genes falls under the heady title of *molecular genetics*. The area of operations for molecular genetics includes all the machinery that runs cells and manufactures the structures called for by the plans found in genes. The focus of molecular genetics includes the physical and chemical structures of the double helix, DNA, which I break down in all its glory in Chapter 6. The messages hidden in your DNA (your genes) constitute the building instructions for your appearance and everything else about you — from how your muscles function and how your eyes blink to your blood type, your susceptibility to particular diseases, and everything in between.

Your genes are expressed through a complex system of interactions that begins with copying DNA's messages into a somewhat temporary form called RNA (see Chapter 9). RNA carries the DNA message through the process of *translation* (covered in Chapter 10), which, in essence, is like taking a blueprint to a factory to guide the manufacturing process. Where your genes are concerned, the factory makes the proteins (from the RNA blueprint) that get folded in complex ways to make you.

The study of *gene expression* (how genes get turned on and off; flip to Chapter 11) and how the genetic code works at the levels of DNA and RNA are considered parts of molecular genetics. Research on the causes of cancer and the hunt for a cure (which I address in Chapter 14) focuses on the molecular side of things, because changes (referred to as *mutations*) occur at the chemical level of DNA (see Chapter 13 for coverage of mutations). Gene therapy (see Chapter 16), genetic engineering (see Chapter 19), and cloning (see Chapter 20) are all subdisciplines of molecular genetics.

Population genetics: Genetics of groups

Much to the chagrin of many undergrads, genetics is surprisingly mathematical. One area in which calculations are used to describe what goes on genetically is population genetics.

If you take Mendelian genetics and examine the inheritance patterns of many different individuals who have something in common, like geographic location, then you have population genetics. *Population genetics* is the study of the genetic diversity of a subset of a particular species (for details, jump to Chapter 17). In essence, it's a search for patterns that help describe the genetic signature of a particular group, such as the consequences of travel, isolation (from other populations), mating choices, geography, and behavior.

Population genetics helps scientists understand how the collective genetic diversity of a population influences the health of individuals within the population. For example, cheetahs are lanky cats; they're the speed demons of Africa. Population genetics has revealed that all cheetahs are very, very genetically similar; in fact, they're so similar that a skin graft from one cheetah would be accepted by any other cheetah. Because the genetic diversity of cheetahs is so low, conservation biologists fear that a disease could sweep through the population and kill off all the individuals of the species. It's possible that no animals would be resistant to the disease, and therefore, none would survive, leading to the extinction of this amazing predator.

Describing the genetics of populations from a mathematical standpoint is critical to forensics (see Chapter 18). To pinpoint the uniqueness of one DNA fingerprint, geneticists have to sample the genetic fingerprints of many individuals and decide how common or rare a particular pattern may be. Medicine also uses population genetics to determine how common particular mutations are and to develop new medicines to treat disease. For details on mutations, flip to Chapter 13; see Chapter 21 for information on genetics and the development of new medicines. Also, *evolutionary genetics,* or how traits change over time, is new to this edition; I cover the subject in Chapter 17.

Quantitative genetics: Getting a handle on heredity

Quantitative genetics examines traits that vary in subtle ways and relates those traits to the underlying genetics of an organism. A combination of whole suites of genes and environmental factors controls characteristics like retrieving ability in dogs, egg size or number in birds, and running speed in humans. Mathematical in nature, quantitative genetics takes a rather complex statistical approach to estimate how much variation in a particular trait is due to the environment and how much is actually genetic.

One application of quantitative genetics is determining how heritable a particular trait is. This measure allows scientists to make predictions about how offspring will turn out based on characteristics of the parent organisms. Heritability gives some indication of how much a characteristic (like seed production) can change when selective breeding (or, in evolutionary time, natural selection) is applied.

Living the Life of a Geneticist

Daily life for a geneticist can include working in the lab, teaching in the classroom, and interacting with patients and their families. In this section, you discover what a typical genetics lab is like and get a rundown of a variety of career paths in the genetics field.

Exploring a genetics lab

A genetics lab is a busy, noisy place. It's full of equipment and supplies and researchers toiling away at their workstations (called *lab benches,* even though the bench is really just a raised, flat surface that's conducive to working while standing up). Depending on the lab, you may see people looking very official in white lab coats or researchers dressed more casually in jeans and T-shirts. Every lab contains some or all of the following:

- ✔ Disposable gloves to protect workers from chemical exposure and to protect DNA and other materials from contamination.
- ✔ Pipettes (for measuring even the tiniest droplets of liquids with extreme accuracy), glassware (for liquid measurement and storage), and vials and tubes (for chemical reactions).
- ✔ Electronic balances for making super-precise measurements of mass.
- ✔ Chemicals and ultrapure water.

✔ A refrigerator (set at 40 degrees Fahrenheit), a freezer (at –4 degrees), and an ultracold freezer (at –112 degrees) for storing samples.

Repeated freezing and thawing causes DNA to break into tiny pieces, which destroys it. For that reason, freezers used in genetics labs aren't frost-free, because the temperature inside a frost-free freezer cycles up and down to melt any ice that forms.

✔ Centrifuges for separating substances from each other. Given that different substances have different densities, centrifuges spin at extremely high speeds to force materials to separate so that researchers can handle them individually.

✔ Incubators for growing bacteria under controlled conditions. Researchers often use bacteria for experimental tests of how genes work.

✔ Autoclaves for sterilizing glassware and other equipment using extreme heat and pressure to kill bacteria and viruses.

✔ Complex pieces of equipment such as thermocyclers (used for PCR; see Chapter 18) and DNA sequencers (see Chapter 8).

✔ Lab notebooks for recording every step of every reaction or experiment in nauseating detail. Geneticists must fully replicate (run over and over) every experiment to make sure the results are valid. The lab notebook is also a legal document that can be used in court cases, so precision and completeness are musts.

✔ Desktop computers packed with software for analyzing results and for connecting via the Internet to vast databases packed with genetic information (flip to the end of this chapter for the addresses of some useful Web sites).

Researchers in the lab use the various pieces of equipment and supplies from the preceding list to conduct experiments and run chemical reactions. Some of the common activities that occur in the genetics lab include

✔ Separating DNA from the rest of a cell's contents (see Chapter 6).

✔ Measuring the purity of a DNA sample and determining how much DNA (by weight) is present.

✔ Mixing chemicals that are used in reactions and experiments designed to analyze DNA samples.

✔ Growing special strains of bacteria and viruses to aid in examining short stretches of DNA (see Chapter 16).

✔ Using DNA sequencing (which I cover in Chapter 8) to learn the order of bases that compose a DNA strand (which I explain in Chapter 6).

✔ Setting up polymerase chain reactions, or PCR (see Chapter 18), a powerful process that allows scientists to analyze even very tiny amounts of DNA.

✔ Analyzing the results of DNA sequencing by comparing sequences from many different organisms (you can find this information in a massive, publicly available database — see the end of this chapter).

✔ Comparing DNA fingerprints from several individuals to identify perpetrators or to assign paternity (see Chapter 18).

✔ Holding weekly or daily meetings where everyone in the lab comes together to discuss results or plan new experiments.

Sorting through jobs in genetics

Whole teams of people contribute to the study of genetics. The following are just a few job descriptions for you to mull over if you're considering a career in genetics.

Lab tech

Lab technicians handle most of the day-to-day work in the lab. The tech mixes chemicals for everyone else in the lab to use in experiments. Techs usually prepare the right sorts of materials to grow bacteria (which are used as carriers for DNA; see Chapter 16), set up the bacterial cultures, and monitor their growth. Techs are also usually responsible for keeping all the necessary supplies straight and washing the glassware — not a glamorous job but a necessary one, because labs use tons of glass beakers and flasks that have to be cleaned.

When it comes to actual experiments, lab technicians are responsible for separating the DNA from the rest of the tissue around it and testing it for purity (to make sure no contaminants, like proteins, are present). Using a rather complicated machine with a strong laser, the tech can also measure exactly how much DNA is present. When a sufficiently pure sample of DNA is obtained, techs may analyze the DNA in greater detail (with PCR or sequencing reactions).

The educational background needed to be a lab tech varies with the amount of responsibility a particular position demands. Most techs have a minimum of a bachelor's degree in biology or some related field and need some background in microbiology to understand and carry out the techniques of handling bacteria safely and without contaminating cultures. And all techs must be good record-keepers, because every single activity in the lab must be documented in writing in the lab notebook.

Graduate student and post-doc

At most universities, genetics labs are full of *graduate students* working on either master's degrees or PhDs. In some labs, these students may be carrying out their own, independent research. On the other hand, many labs focus their work on a specific problem, like some specialized approach to studying cancer, and every student in that sort of lab works on some aspect of what his or her professor studies. Graduate students do a lot of the same things that lab techs do (see the preceding section), as well as design experiments, carry out those experiments, analyze the results, and then work to figure out what the results mean. Then, the graduate student writes a long document (called a *thesis* or *dissertation*) to describe what was done, what it means, and how it fits in with other people's research on the subject. While working in the lab, grad students take classes and are subjected to grueling exams (trust me on the grueling part).

All graduate students must hold a bachelor's degree. Performance on the standardized GRE (Graduate Record Exam) determines eligibility for admission to master's programs and may be used for selection for fellowships and awards.

If you're going to be staring down this test in the near future, you may want to get a leg up by checking out *The GRE Test For Dummies,* by Suzee Vlk, Michelle Rose Gilman, and Veronica Saydak (Wiley).

In general, it takes two or three years to earn a master's degree. A doctorate (denoted by *PhD*) usually requires anywhere from four to seven years of education beyond the bachelor's level.

After graduating with a PhD, a geneticist-in-training may need to get more experience before hitting the job market. Positions that provide such experience are collectively referred to as *post-docs* (post-doctoral fellows). A person holding a post-doc position is usually much more independent than a grad student when it comes to research. The post-doc often works to learn new techniques or to acquire a specialty before moving on to a position as a professor or a research scientist.

Research scientist

Research scientists work in private industries, designing experiments and directing the activities of lab techs. All sorts of industries employ research scientists, including

- ✔ Pharmaceutical companies, to conduct investigations on how drugs affect gene expression (see Chapter 11) and to develop new treatments such as gene therapy (see Chapter 16).
- ✔ Forensics labs, to analyze DNA found at crime scenes and to compare DNA fingerprints (see Chapter 18).
- ✔ Companies that analyze information generated by genome projects (human and others; see Chapter 11).
- ✔ Companies that support the work of other genetics labs by designing and marketing products used in research, such as kits used to run DNA fingerprints.

A research scientist usually holds a master's degree or a PhD. With only a bachelor's degree, several years of experience as a lab tech may suffice. Research scientists have to be able to design experiments and analyze results using statistics. Good record-keeping and strong communication skills (especially in writing) are musts. Most research scientists also have to be capable of managing and supervising people. In addition, financial responsibilities may include keeping up with expenditures, ordering equipment and supplies, and wrangling salaries of other personnel.

College or university professor

Professors do everything that research scientists do with the added responsibilities of teaching courses, writing proposals to get funds to support research, and writing papers on their research results for publication in reputable, peer-reviewed journals. Professors also supervise the lab techs, graduate students, and post-docs who work in their labs, which entails designing research projects and then ensuring that the projects are done correctly in the right amount of time (and under budget!).

Small schools may require a professor to teach as many as three courses every semester. Upper-tier institutions (think Big Ten or Ivy League) may require only one course of instruction per year. Genetics professors teach the basics as well as advanced and specialty courses like recombinant DNA (see Chapter 16) and population genetics (see Chapter 17).

To qualify for a professorship, universities require a minimum of a PhD, and most require additional post-doctoral experience. Job candidates must have already published research results to demonstrate the ability to do relevant research. Most universities also look for evidence that the professor-to-be will be successful at getting grants, which means the candidate must usually land a grant before getting a job.

Genetic counselor

Genetic counselors work with medical personnel to interpret the medical histories of patients and their families. The counselor usually works directly with the patient to assemble all the information into a family tree (see Chapter 12) and then looks for patterns to determine which traits may be hereditary. Counselors can also tell which diseases a patient is most likely to inherit. Genetic counselors are trained to conduct careful and thorough interviews to make sure that no information is missed or left out.

Genetic counselors usually hold a master's degree. Training includes many hours working with patients to hone interview and analysis skills (under the close supervision of experienced professionals, of course). The position requires excellent record-keeping skills and strict attention to detail. Genetic counselors also have to be good at interacting with all kinds of people, including research scientists and physicians. And the ability to communicate very well, both in writing and verbally, is a must.

The most essential skill of a genetic counselor is the ability to be nonjudgmental and nondirective. The counselor must be able to analyze a family history without bias or prejudice and inform the patient of his or her options without recommending any one course of action over another. Furthermore, the counselor must keep all information about his or her patients confidential, sharing information only with authorized personnel such as the person's own physician in order to protect the patient's privacy.

Great genetics Web sites to explore

The Internet is an unparalleled source of information about genetics. With just a few mouse clicks, you can find the latest discoveries and attend the best courses ever offered on the subject. Here's a quick sample.

- To see a great video that explains genetics and gives it a human face, check out "Cracking the Code of Life": www.pbs.org/wgbh/nova/genome/program.html.

- New discoveries are unveiled every day. To stay current, log on to www.sciencedaily.com/news/plants_animals/genetics/ and www.nature.com/ng/index.html.

- For students, http://learn.genetics.utah.edu/ can't be beat.

From the basics of heredity to virtual labs to cloning, it's all there in easy-to-grasp animations and language.

- Want to get all the details about genes and diseases? Start at www.ncbi.nlm.nih.gov/books/bv.fcgi?rid=gnd for the basics. You can find more advanced (and greatly detailed) information at Online Mendelian Inheritance in Man: www.ncbi.nlm.nih.gov/omim/.

- If you're interested in a career in genetics, the Genetics Society of America is ready to help: www.genetics-gsa.org/pages/careers_in_genetics.shtml.

Chapter 2

Basic Cell Biology

. . . .

In This Chapter

▶ Getting to know the cell

▶ Understanding chromosomes

▶ Exploring simple cell division

▶ Appreciating the complexities of meiosis

. . . .

Genetics and the study of how cells work are closely related. The process of passing genetic material from one generation to the next depends completely on how cells grow and divide. To reproduce, a simple organism such as bacteria or yeast simply copies its DNA (through a process called *replication,* which I cover in Chapter 7) and splits in two. But organisms that reproduce sexually go through a complicated dance that includes mixing and matching strands of DNA (a process called *recombination*) and then halving the amount of DNA for special sex cells, allowing completely new genetic combinations for their offspring. These amazing processes are part of what makes you unique. So come inside your cell — you need to be familiar with the processes of *mitosis* (cell division) and *meiosis* (the production of sex cells) to appreciate how genetics works.

Looking Around Your Cell

There are two basic kinds of organisms:

▶ **Prokaryotes:** Organisms whose cells lack a nucleus and therefore have DNA floating loosely in the liquid center of the cell

▶ **Eukaryotes:** Organisms that have a well-defined nucleus to house and protect the DNA

A *nucleus* is a compartment filled with DNA surrounded by a membrane.

The basic biologies of prokaryotes and eukaryotes are similar but not identical. Because all living things fall into these two groups, understanding the differences and similarities between cell types is important. In this section, I show you how to distinguish the two kinds of cells from each other, and you get a quick tour of the insides of cells — both with and without nuclei. Figure 2-1 shows you the structure of each type of cell.

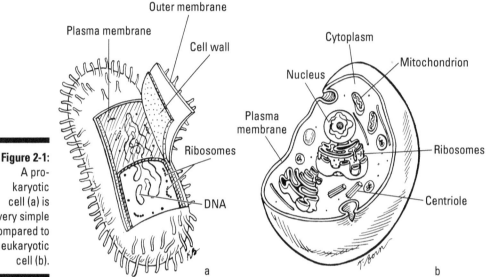

Figure 2-1:
A pro-
karyotic
cell (a) is
very simple
compared to
a eukaryotic
cell (b).

Cells without a nucleus

Scientists classify organisms composed of cells without nuclei as *prokaryotes,* which means "before nucleus." Prokaryotes are the most common forms of life on earth. You are, at this very moment, covered in and inhabited by millions of prokaryotic cells: bacteria. Much of your life and your body's processes depend on these arrangements; for example, the digestion going on in your intestines is partially powered by bacteria that break down the food you eat. Most of the bacteria in your body are completely harmless, but some species of bacteria can be vicious and deadly, causing rapidly transmitted diseases such as cholera.

All bacteria, regardless of temperament, are simple, one-celled, prokaryotic organisms. None has cell nuclei, and all are small cells with relatively small amounts of DNA (see Chapter 8 for more on the amounts of DNA different organisms possess).

The exterior of a prokaryotic cell is encapsulated by a *cell wall* that serves as the bacteria's only protection from the outside world. A *plasma membrane* (*membranes* are thin sheets or layers) regulates the exchange of nutrients, water, and gases that nourish the bacterial cell. DNA, usually in the form of a single, hoop-shaped piece, floats around inside the cell; segments of DNA like this one are called *chromosomes* (see the section "Examining the basics of chromosomes" later in the chapter). The liquid interior of the cell is called the *cytoplasm.* The cytoplasm provides a cushiony, watery home for the DNA and other cell machinery that carry out the business of living. Prokaryotes divide, and thus reproduce, by simple mitosis, which I cover in detail in the "Mitosis: Splitting Up" section later in the chapter.

Cells with a nucleus

Scientists classify organisms that have cells with nuclei as *eukaryotes,* which means "true nucleus." Eukaryotes range in complexity from simple, one-celled animals and plants to complex, multicellular organisms like you. Eukaryotic cells are fairly complicated and have numerous parts to keep track of (refer to Figure 2-1). Like prokaryotes, eukaryotic cells are held together by a *plasma membrane,* and sometimes a *cell wall* surrounds the membrane (plants, for example, have cell walls). But that's where the similarities end.

The most important feature of the eukaryotic cell is the *nucleus* — the membrane-surrounded compartment that houses the DNA that's divided into one or more chromosomes. The nucleus protects the DNA from damage during day-to-day living. Eukaryotic chromosomes are usually long, string-like segments of DNA instead of the hoop-shaped ones found in prokaryotes. Another hallmark of eukaryotes is the way the DNA is packaged: Eukaryotes usually have much larger amounts of DNA than prokaryotes, and to fit all that DNA into the tiny cell nucleus, it must be tightly wound around special proteins. (For all the details about DNA packaging for eukaryotes, flip to Chapter 6.)

Unlike prokaryotes, eukaryotes have all sorts of cell parts, called *organelles,* that help carry out the business of living. The organelles float around in the watery cytoplasm outside the nucleus. Two of the most important organelles are

- ✓ **Mitochondria:** The powerhouses of the eukaryotic cell, mitochondria pump out energy by converting glucose to ATP (adenosine triphosphate). ATP acts like a battery of sorts, storing energy until it's needed for day-to-day living. Both animals and plants have mitochondria.

- ✓ **Chloroplasts:** These organelles are unique to plants. They process the energy of sunlight into sugars that the plant mitochondria use to generate the energy that nourishes the living cells.

Eukaryotic cells are able to carry out behaviors that prokaryotes can't. For example, one-celled eukaryotes often have appendages, such as long tails (called *flagella*) or hair-like projections (called *cilia*), that work like hundreds of tiny paddles, helping them move around. Also, only eukaryotic cells are capable of ingesting fluids and particles for nutrition; prokaryotes must transport materials through their cell walls, a process that severely limits their dietary options.

In most multicellular eukaryotes, cells come in two basic varieties: body cells (called *somatic* cells) or sex cells. The two cell types have different functions and are produced in different ways.

Somatic cells

Somatic cells are produced by simple cell division called *mitosis* (see the section "Mitosis: Splitting Up" for details). Somatic cells of multicellular organisms like humans are differentiated into special cell types. Skin cells and muscle cells are both somatic cells, for instance, but if you were to examine your skin cells under a microscope and compare them with your muscle cells, you'd see that their structures are very different. The various cells that make up your body all have the same basic components (membrane, organelles, and so on), but the arrangements of the elements change from one cell type to the next so that they can carry out various jobs such as digestion (intestinal cells), energy storage (fat cells), or oxygen transport to your tissues (blood cells).

Sex cells

Sex cells are specialized cells used for reproduction. Only eukaryotic organisms engage in sexual reproduction, which I cover in detail at the end of this chapter in the section "Mommy, where did I come from?" *Sexual reproduction* combines genetic material from two organisms and requires special preparation in the form of a reduction in the amount of genetic material allocated to sex cells — a process called *meiosis* (see "Meiosis: Making Cells for Reproduction" later in the chapter for an explanation). In humans, the two types of sex cells are eggs and sperm.

Examining the basics of chromosomes

Chromosomes are threadlike strands composed of DNA. To pass genetic traits from one generation to the next, the chromosomes must be copied (see Chapter 7), and then the copies must be divvied up. Most prokaryotes have only one circular chromosome that, when copied, is passed on to the *daughter cells* (new cells created by cell division) during mitosis. Eukaryotes have more complex problems to solve (like divvying up half of the chromosomes to make sex cells), and their chromosomes behave differently during mitosis and meiosis. Additionally, various scientific terms describe the anatomy, shapes, number of copies, and situations of eukaryotic chromosomes. This section gets into the intricacies of chromosomes in eukaryotic cells because they're so complex.

Counting out chromosome numbers

Each eukaryotic organism has a specific number of chromosomes per cell — ranging from one to many. For example, humans have 46 total chromosomes. These chromosomes come in two varieties:

✔ **Sex chromosomes:** These chromosomes determine gender. Human cells contain two sex chromosomes. If you're female, you have two X chromosomes, and if you're male, you have an X and a Y chromosome. (To find out more about how sex is determined by the X and Y chromosomes, flip to Chapter 5.)

✔ **Autosomal chromosomes:** *Autosomal* simply refers to non-sex chromosomes. Sticking with the human example, if you do the math, you can see that humans have 44 autosomal chromosomes.

Ah, but there's more. In humans, chromosomes come in pairs. That means you have 22 pairs of uniquely shaped autosomal chromosomes plus 1 pair of sex chromosomes for a total of 23 chromosome pairs. Your autosomal chromosomes are identified by numbers — 1 through 22. So you have two chromosome 1s, two 2s, and so on. Figure 2-2 shows you how all human chromosomes are divided into pairs and numbered. (A *karyotype* like the one pictured in Figure 2-2 is one way chromosomes are examined; you discover more about karyotyping in Chapter 15.)

When chromosomes are sorted into pairs, the individual chromosomes in each pair are considered *homologous,* meaning that the paired chromosomes are identical to one another according to which genes they carry. In addition, your homologous chromosomes are identical in shape and size. These pairs of chromosomes are sometimes referred to as *homologs* for short.

Chromosome numbers can be a bit confusing. Humans are *diploid,* meaning we have two copies of each chromosome. Some organisms (like bees and wasps) have only one set of chromosomes (cells with one set of chromosomes are called *haploid*); others have three, four, or as many as sixteen copies of each chromosome! The number of chromosome sets held by a particular organism is called the *ploidy.* For more on chromosome numbers, see Chapter 15.

The total number of chromosomes doesn't tell you what the ploidy of an organism is. For that reason, the number of chromosomes an organism has is often listed as some multiple of *n.* A single set of chromosomes referred to by the *n* is the haploid number. Humans are *2n* = 46 (indicating that humans are diploid and their total number of chromosomes is 46). Human sex cells such as eggs or sperm are haploid (see "Mommy, where did I come from?" later in this chapter).

Geneticists believe that the homologous pairs of chromosomes in humans started as one set (that is, *haploid*), and the entire set was duplicated at some point in some distant ancestor, many millions of years ago.

Examining chromosome anatomy

Chromosomes are often depicted in stick-like forms, like those you see in Figure 2-3. Chromosomes don't look like sticks, though. In fact, most of the time they're loose and string-like. Chromosomes only take on this distinctive shape and form when cell division is about to take place (during metaphase of meiosis or mitosis). They're often drawn this way so that the special characteristics of eukaryotic chromosomes are easier to see. Figure 2-3 points out the important features of eukaryotic chromosomes.

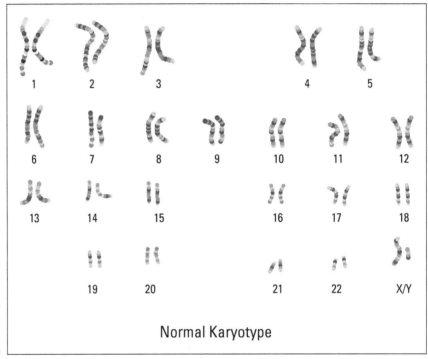

Normal Karyotype

The part of the chromosome that appears pinched (in Figure 2-3, located in the middle of the chromosomes) is called the *centromere*. The placement of the centromere (whether it's closer to the top, middle, or bottom of the chromosome; see Figure 2-4) is what gives each chromosome its unique shape. The ends of the chromosomes are called *telomeres*. Telomeres are made of densely packed DNA and serve to protect the DNA message that the chromosome carries. (Flip to Chapter 23 for more about telomeres and how they may affect the process of aging.)

The differences in shapes and sizes of chromosomes are easy to see, but the most important differences between chromosomes are hidden deep inside the DNA. Chromosomes carry *genes* — sections of DNA that make up the building plans for physical traits. The genes tell the body how, when, and where to make all the structures that are necessary for the processes of living (for more on how genes work, flip to Chapter 11). Each pair of homologous chromosomes carries the same — but not necessarily identical — genes. For example, both chromosomes of a particular homologous pair may contain the gene for hair color, but one can be a "brown hair" version of the gene — alternative versions of genes are called *alleles* (refer to Figure 2-3) — and the other can be a "blond hair" allele.

Any given gene can have one or more alleles. In Figure 2-3, one chromosome carries the allele *A* while its homolog carries the allele *a* (the relative size of an allele is very small; the alleles are large here so you can see them). The alleles code for the different physical traits *(phenotypes)* you see in animals and plants, like hair color or flower shape. You can find out more about how alleles affect phenotype in Chapter 3.

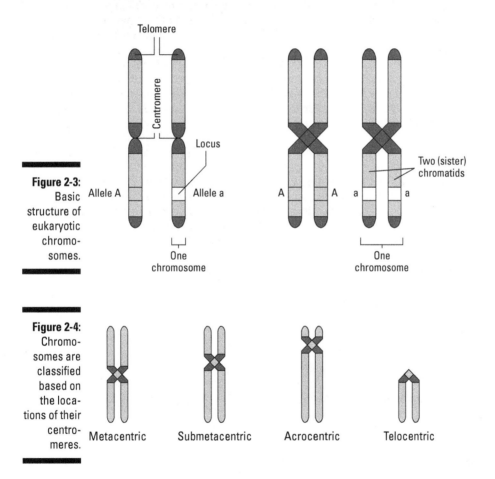

Figure 2-3: Basic structure of eukaryotic chromosomes.

Figure 2-4: Chromosomes are classified based on the locations of their centromeres.

Each point along the chromosome is called a *locus* (Latin for "place"). The plural of locus is *loci* (pronounced *low*-sigh). Most of the phenotypes that you see are produced by multiple genes (that is, genes occurring at different loci and often on different chromosomes) acting together. For instance, human eye color is determined by at least three genes that reside on two different chromosomes. You can find out more about how genes are arranged along chromosomes in Chapter 15.

Mitosis: Splitting Up

Most cells have simple lifestyles: They grow, divide, and eventually die. Figure 2-5 illustrates the basic life cycle of a typical somatic, or body, cell.

The *cell cycle* (the stages a cell goes through from one division to another) is tightly regulated; some cells divide all the time, and others never divide at all. Your body uses mitosis to provide new cells when you grow and to replace cells that wear out or become damaged from injury. Talk about multitasking — you're going through mitosis right now, while you read this book! Some cells divide only part of the time, when new cells are needed to handle certain jobs like fighting infection. Cancer cells, on the other hand, get carried away and divide too often. (In Chapter 14, you can find out how the cell cycle is regulated and what happens when it goes awry.)

The cell cycle includes *mitosis* — the process of reproducing the cell nucleus by division. The result of each round of the cell cycle is a simple cell division that creates two identical new cells from one original cell. During mitosis, all DNA present in the cell is copied (see Chapter 7), and when the original cell divides, a complete collection of all the chromosomes (in humans, 23 pairs) goes to each of the two resulting cells. Prokaryotes and some simple eukaryotic organisms use mitosis to reproduce themselves. (More complex eukaryotic organisms use *meiosis* for sexual reproduction, in which each of the two sex cells sends only one copy of each chromosome into the eggs or sperm. You can read all about that in the section "Meiosis: Making Cells for Reproduction" later in this chapter.)

Figure 2-5:
The cell cycle: mitosis, cell division, and all points in between.

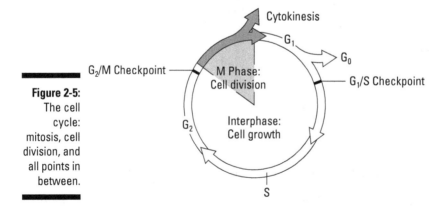

You should remember two important points about mitosis:

- ✔ **Mitosis produces two identical cells.** The new cells are identical to each other *and* to the cell that divided to create them.

- ✔ **Cells created by mitosis have exactly the same number of chromosomes as the original cell did.** If the original cell had 46 chromosomes, the new cells each have 46 chromosomes.

Mitosis is only one of the major phases in the cell cycle; the other is *interphase*. In the following sections, I guide you through the phases of the cell cycle and tell you exactly what happens during each one.

Step 1: Time to grow

Interphase is the part of the cell cycle during which the cell grows, copies its DNA, and prepares to divide. Interphase occurs in three stages: the G1 phase, the S phase, and the G2 phase.

G1 phase

When a cell begins life, such as the moment an egg is fertilized, the first thing that happens is the original cell starts to grow. This period of growth is called the *G1 phase* of interphase. Lots of things happen during G1: DNA supervises the work of the cell, *metabolism* (the exchange of oxygen and carbon dioxide) occurs, and cells breathe and "eat."

Some cells opt out of the cell cycle permanently, stop growing, and exit the process at G_0. Your brain cells, for example, have retired from the cell cycle. Mature red blood cells and muscle cells don't divide, either. In fact, human red blood cells have no nuclei and thus possess no DNA of their own.

If the cell in question plans to divide, though, it can't stay in G1 forever. Actively dividing cells go through the whole cell cycle every 24 hours or so. After a predetermined period of growth that lasts from a few minutes to several hours, the cell arrives at the first checkpoint (refer to Figure 2-5). When the cell passes the first checkpoint, there's no turning back.

Various proteins control when the cell moves from one phase of the cycle to the next. At the first checkpoint, proteins called *cyclins* and enzymes called *kinases* control the border between G1 and the next phase. Cyclins and kinases interact to cue up the various stages of the merry-go-round of cell division. Two particular chemicals, CDK (cyclin dependent kinase) and G1 cyclin, hook up to escort the cell over the border from G1 to S — the next phase.

S phase

S phase is the point at which the cell's DNA is replicated (here, *S* refers to *synthesis,* or copying, of the DNA). When the cell enters the S phase, activity around the chromosomes really steps up. All the chromosomes must be copied to make exact replicas that later are passed on to the newly formed daughter cells produced by cell division. DNA replication is a very complex process that gets full coverage in Chapter 7.

For now, all you need to know is that all the cell's chromosomes are copied during S, and the copies stay together as a unit (joined at the centromere; refer back to Figure 2-3) when the cell moves from S into G2 — the final step in interphase. The replicated chromosomes are called *sister chromatids* (refer to Figure 2-3), which are alike in every way. They carry the exact same copies of the exact same genes. During mitosis (or meiosis), the sister chromatids are divided up and sent to the daughter cells as part of the cell cycle.

G2 phase

The *G2 phase* leads up to cell division. It's the last phase before actual mitosis gets underway. G2, sometimes called *Gap 2,* gives the cell time to get bigger before splitting into two smaller cells. Another set of cyclins and CDK work together to push the cell through the second checkpoint located at the border between G2 and mitosis. (For details on the first checkpoint, jump back to the section "G1 phase.") As the cell grows, the chromosomes, now copied and hooked together as sister chromatids, stay together inside the cell nucleus. (The DNA is still "relaxed" at this point and hasn't yet taken on the fat, sausage-shaped appearance it assumes during mitosis.) After the cell crosses the G2/M checkpoint (refer to Figure 2-5), the business of mitosis formally gets underway.

Step 2: Divvying up the chromosomes

In the cell cycle, *mitosis* is the process of dividing up the newly copied chromosomes (that were created in interphase; see the preceding section) to make certain that the new cells each get a full set. Generally, mitosis is divided into four phases, which you can see in Figure 2-6 and read about in the following sections.

The phases of mitosis are a bit artificial, because the movement doesn't stop at each point; instead, the chromosomes cruise right from one phase to the next. But dividing the process into phases is useful for understanding how the chromosomes go from being all mixed together to neatly parting ways and getting into the proper, newly formed cells.

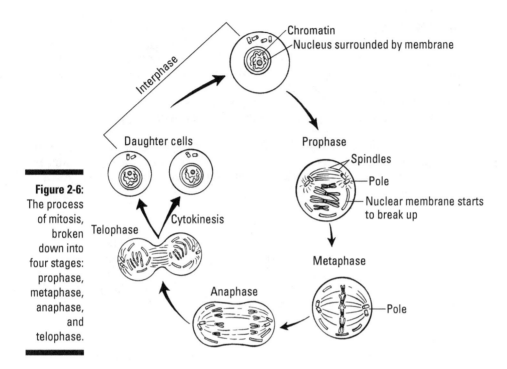

Figure 2-6:
The process
of mitosis,
broken
down into
four stages:
prophase,
metaphase,
anaphase,
and
telophase.

Prophase

During *prophase,* the chromosomes get very compact and condensed, taking
on the familiar sausage shape. During interphase (see the "Step 1: Time to
grow" section earlier in this chapter), the DNA that makes up the chromosomes is tightly wound around special proteins, sort of like string wrapped
around beads. The whole "necklace" is wound tightly on itself to compress
the enormous DNA molecules to sizes small enough to fit inside the cell
nucleus. But even when coiled during interphase, the chromosomes are still
so threadlike and tiny that they're essentially invisible. That changes during
prophase, when the chromosomes become so densely packed that you can
easily see them with an ordinary light microscope.

By the time they reach prophase, chromosomes have duplicated to form
sister chromatids (refer to Figure 2-3). Sister chromatids of each chromosome
are exact twin copies of each other. Each chromatid is actually a chromosome
in its own right, but thinking of chromosomes as chromatids may help you
keep all the players straight during the process of division.

As the chromosomes/chromatids condense, the cell nucleus starts breaking
up, allowing the chromosomes to move freely across the cell as the process
of cell division progresses.

Metaphase

Metaphase is the point when the chromosomes all line up in the center of the cell. After the nuclear membrane dissolves and prophase is complete, the chromosomes go from being a tangled mass to lining up in a more or less neat row in the center of the cell (refer to Figure 2-6). Threadlike strands called *spindles* grab each chromosome around its waist-like centromere. The spindles are attached to points on either side of the cell called *poles*.

Sometimes, scientists use geographic terms to describe the positions of chromosomes during metaphase: The chromosomes line up at the equator and are attached to the poles. This trick may help you better visualize the events of metaphase.

Anaphase

During *anaphase,* the sister chromatids are pulled apart, and the resulting halves migrate to opposite poles (refer to Figure 2-6). At this point, it's easy to see that the chromatids are actually chromosomes. Every sister chromatid gets split apart so that the cell that's about to be formed ends up with a full set of all the original cell's chromosomes.

Telophase

Finally, during *telophase,* nuclear membranes begin to form around the two sets of separated chromosomes (refer to Figure 2-6). The chromosomes begin to relax and take on their usual interphase form. The cell itself begins to divide as telophase comes to an end.

Step 3: The big divide

When mitosis is complete and new nuclei have formed, the cell divides into two smaller, identical cells. The division of one cell into two is called *cytokinesis* (*cyto* meaning "cell" and *kinesis* meaning "movement"). Technically, cytokinesis happens after metaphase is over and before interphase begins. Each new cell has a full set of chromosomes, just as the original cell did. All the organelles and cytoplasm present in the original cell are divided up to provide the new cell with all the machinery it needs for metabolism and growth. The new cells are now at interphase (specifically, the G1 stage) and are ready to begin the cell cycle again.

Meiosis: Making Cells for Reproduction

Meiosis is a cell division that includes reducing the chromosome number as preparation for sexual reproduction. Meiosis reduces the amount of DNA by half so that when fertilization occurs, each offspring gets a full set of chromosomes. As a result of meiosis, the cell goes from being diploid to being haploid. Or, to put it another way, the cell goes from being *2n* to being *n*. In humans, this means that the cells produced by meiosis (either eggs or sperm) have 23 chromosomes each — one copy of each of the homologous chromosomes. (See the section "Counting out chromosome numbers" earlier in this chapter for more information.)

Meiosis has many characteristics in common with mitosis. The stages go by similar names, and the chromosomes move around similarly, but the products of meiosis are completely different from those of mitosis. Whereas mitosis ends with two identical cells, meiosis produces *four* cells each with *half* the amount of DNA that the original cell contained. Furthermore, with meiosis, the homologous chromosomes go through a complex exchange of segments of DNA called *recombination.* Recombination is one of the most important aspects of meiosis and leads to genetic variation that allows each individual produced by sexual reproduction to be truly unique.

Meiosis goes through two rounds of division: meiosis I and the sequel, meiosis II. Figure 2-7 shows the progressing stages of both meiosis I and meiosis II. Unlike lots of movie sequels, the sequel in meiosis is really necessary. In both rounds of division, the chromosomes go through stages that resemble those in mitosis. However, the chromosomes undergo different actions in meiotic prophase, metaphase, anaphase, and telophase.

Students often get stuck on the phases of meiosis and miss its most important aspects: recombination and the division of the chromosomes. To prevent that sort of confusion, I don't break down meiosis by phases. Instead, I focus on the activities of the chromosomes themselves.

In meiosis I:

- The homologous pairs of chromosomes line up side by side and exchange parts. This is called *crossing-over* or *recombination,* and it occurs during prophase I.
- During metaphase I, the homologous chromosomes line up at the equator of the cell (called the *metaphase plate*), and homologs go to opposite poles during the first round of anaphase.
- The cell divides in telophase I, reducing the amount of genetic material by half, and enters a second round of division — meiosis II.

During meiosis II:

- The individual chromosomes (as sister chromatids) condense during prophase II and line up at the metaphase plates of both cells (metaphase II).
- The chromatids separate and go to opposite poles (anaphase II).
- The cells divide, resulting in a total of *four* daughter cells, each possessing *one* copy of each chromosome.

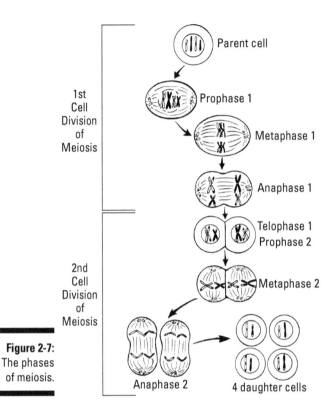

Figure 2-7:
The phases
of meiosis.

Meiosis part 1

Cells that undergo meiosis start in a phase similar to the interphase that precedes mitosis. The cells grow in a G1 phase, undergo DNA replication during S, and prepare for division during G2. (To review what happens in each of these phases, flip back to the section "Step 1: Time to grow.") When meiosis is about to begin, the chromosomes condense. By the time meiotic interphase is complete, the chromosomes have been copied and are hitched up as sister chromatids, just as they would be in mitosis. Next up are the phases of meiosis I, which I profile in the sections that follow.

Find your partner

During prophase I (labeled "I" because it's in the first round of meiosis), the homologous chromosomes find each other. These homologous chromosomes originally came from the mother and father of the individual whose cells are now undergoing meiosis. Thus, during meiosis, maternal and paternal chromosomes, as homologs, line up side by side. In Figure 2-2, you can see an entire set of 46 human chromosomes. Although the members of the pair seem identical, they're not. The homologous chromosomes have different combinations of alleles at the thousands of loci along each chromosome. (For more on alleles, jump to the section "Examining chromosome anatomy" earlier in this chapter.)

Recombining makes you unique

When the homologous chromosomes pair up in prophase I, the chromatids of the two homologs actually zip together, and the chromatids exchange parts of their arms. Enzymes cut the chromosomes into pieces and seal the newly combined strands back together in an action called *crossing-over.* When crossing-over is complete, the chromatids consist of part of their original DNA and part of their homolog's DNA. The loci don't get mixed up or turned around — the chromosome sequence stays in its original order. The only thing that's different is that the maternal and paternal chromosomes (as homologs) are now mixed together.

Figure 2-8 illustrates crossing-over in action. The figure shows one pair of homologous chromosomes and two loci. At both loci, the chromosomes have alternative forms of the genes. In other words, the alleles are different: Homolog one has *A* and *b,* and homolog two has *a* and *B.* When replication takes place, the sister chromatids are identical (because they're exact copies of each other). After crossing-over, the two sister chromatids have exchanged arms. Thus, each homolog has a sister chromatid that's different.

Partners divide

The recombined homologs line up at the metaphase equator of the cell (refer to Figure 2-7). The nuclear membrane begins to break down, and in a process similar to mitotic anaphase, spindle fibers grasp the homologous chromosomes by their centromeres and pull them to opposite sides of the cell.

At the end of the first phase of meiosis, the cell undergoes its first round of division (telophase 1, followed by cytokinesis 1). The newly divided cells each contain one set of chromosomes, the now partnerless homologs, still in the form of replicated sister chromatids.

When the homologs line up, maternal and paternal chromosomes pair up, but it's a tossup as to which side of the equator each one ends up on. Therefore, each pair of homologs divides independently of every other homologous pair. This is the basis of the principle of independent assortment, which I cover in Chapters 3 and 4.

Following telophase I, the cells enter an in-between round called *interkinesis* (which means "between movements"). The chromosomes relax and lose their fat, ready-for-metaphase appearance. Interkinesis is just a "resting" phase in preparation for the second round of meiosis.

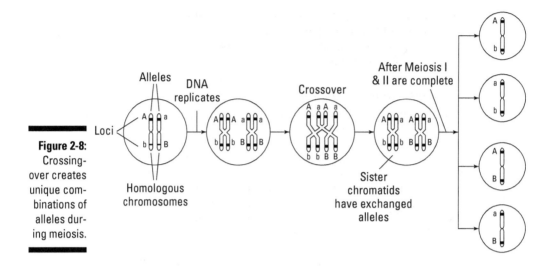

Figure 2-8:
Crossing-
over creates
unique com-
binations of
alleles dur-
ing meiosis.

Meiosis II: The sequel

Meiosis II is the second phase of cell division that produces the final product of meiosis: cells that contain only one copy of each chromosome. The
chromosomes condense once more to their now-familiar fat, sausage shapes.
Keep in mind that each cell has only a single set of chromosomes, which are
still in the form of sister chromatids.

During metaphase II, the chromosomes line up along the equator of the cells,
and spindle fibers attach at the centromeres. In anaphase II, the sister chromatids are pulled apart and move to opposite poles of their respective cell.
The nuclear membranes form around the now single chromosomes (telophase II). Finally, cell division takes place. At the end of the process, each of
the four cells contains one single set of chromosomes.

Mommy, where did I come from?

From gametogenesis, honey. Meiosis in humans (and in all animals that
reproduce sexually) produces cells called *gametes*. Gametes come in the form
of sperm (produced by males) or eggs (produced by females). When conditions are right, sperm and egg unite to create a new organism, which takes
the form of a *zygote*. Figure 2-9 shows the process of *gametogenesis* (the production of gametes) in humans.

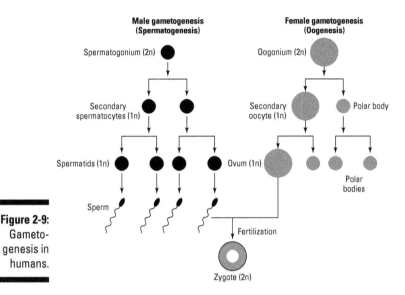

Figure 2-9:
Gameto-
genesis in
humans.

For human males, special cells in the male's sexual organs (testes) produce
spermatogonia. Spermatogonia are *2n* — they contain a full diploid set of
46 chromosomes (see the earlier section "Counting out chromosome numbers"). After meiosis I, each single spermatogonium has divided into two cells
called *secondary spermatocytes*. These spermatocytes contain only one copy
of each homolog (as sister chromatids). After one more division (meiosis II),
the *spermatids* that become sperm cells have one copy of each chromosome.
Thus, sperm cells are haploid and contain 23 chromosomes. Because males
have X and Y sex chromosomes, half their sperm (men produce literally millions) contain Xs and half contain Ys.

Human females produce eggs in much the same way that men produce
sperm. Egg cells, which are produced by the ovaries, start as diploid *oogonia*
(that is, *2n* = 46). The big difference between egg and sperm production is
that at the end of meiosis II, only one mature, haploid (23 chromosomes) sex
cell (as an egg) is produced instead of four (refer to Figure 2-9). The other
three cells produced are called *polar bodies;* the polar bodies aren't actual
egg cells and can't be fertilized to produce offspring.

Why does the female body produce one egg cell and three polar bodies? Egg
cells need large amounts of cytoplasm to nourish the zygote in the period
between fertilization and when the mother starts providing the growing
embryo with nutrients and energy through the placenta. The easiest way to
get enough cytoplasm into the egg when it needs it most is to put less cytoplasm into the other three cells produced in meiosis II.

Chapter 3

Visualize Peas: Discovering the Laws of Inheritance

. . . .

In This Chapter

▶ Appreciating the work of Gregor Mendel

▶ Understanding inheritance, dominance, and segregation of alleles

▶ Solving basic genetics problems using probability

. . . .

*A*ll the physical traits of any living thing originate in that organism's genes. Look at the leaves of a tree or the color of your own eyes. How tall are you? What color is your dog's or cat's fur? Can you curl or fold your tongue? Got hair on the backs of your fingers? All that and much more came from genes passed down from parent to offspring. Even if you don't know much about how genes work or even what genes actually are, you've probably already thought about how physical traits can be inherited. Just think of the first thing most people say when they see a newborn baby: Who does he or she look most like, mommy or daddy?

The *laws of inheritance* — how traits are transmitted from one generation to the next (including dominant-recessive inheritance, segregation of alleles into gametes, and independent assortment of traits) — were discovered less than 200 years ago. In the early 1850s, Gregor Mendel, an Austrian monk with a love of gardening, looked at the physical world around him and, by simply growing peas, categorized the patterns of genetic inheritance that are still recognized today. In this chapter, you discover how Mendel's peas changed the way scientists view the world. If you skipped Chapter 2, don't worry — Mendel didn't know anything about mitosis or meiosis when he formulated the laws of inheritance.

Mendel's discoveries have an enormous impact on your life. If you're interested in how genetics affects your health (Part III), reading this chapter and getting a handle on the laws of inheritance will help you.

Gardening with Gregor Mendel

For centuries before Mendel planted his first pea plant, scholars and scientists argued about how inheritance of physical traits worked. It was obvious that *something* was passed from parent to offspring, because diseases and personality traits seemed to run in families. And farmers knew that by breeding plants and animals with certain physical features that they valued, they could create varieties that produced desirable products, like higher yielding maize, stronger horses, or hardier dogs. But just how inheritance worked and exactly what was passed from parent to child remained a mystery.

Enter the star of our gardening show, Gregor Mendel. Mendel was, by nature, a curious person. As he wandered around the gardens of the monastery where he lived in the mid-19th century, he noticed that his pea plants looked different from one another in a number of ways. Some were tall and others short. Some had green seeds, and others had yellow seeds. Mendel wondered what caused the differences he observed and decided to conduct a series of simple experiments. He chose seven characteristics of pea plants for his experiments, as you can see in Table 3-1:

Table 3-1	**Seven Traits of Pea Plants Studied by Gregor Mendel**	
Trait	*Common Form*	*Uncommon Form*
Seed color	Yellow	Green
Seed shape	Round	Wrinkled
Seed coat color	Gray	White
Pod color	Green	Yellow
Pod shape	Inflated	Constricted
Plant height	Tall	Short
Flower position	Along the stem	At the tip of the stem

For ten years, Mendel patiently grew many varieties of peas with various flower colors, seed shapes, seed numbers, and so on. In a process called *crossing*, he mated parent plants to see what their offspring would look like. When he passed away in 1884, Mendel was unaware of the magnitude of his contribution to science. A full 34 years passed after publication of his work (in 1868) before anyone realized what this simple gardener had discovered. (For the full story on how Mendel's research was lost and found again, flip to Chapter 22.)

If you don't know much about plants, understanding how plants reproduce may help you appreciate what Mendel did. To mate plants, you need flowers and the dusty substance they produce called *pollen* (the plant equivalent of sperm). Flowers have structures called *ovaries* (see Figure 3-1); the ovaries are hidden inside the *pistil* and are connected to the outside world by the *stigma*. Pollen is produced by structures called *stamen*. Like those of animals, the ovaries of plants produce eggs that, when exposed to pollen (in a process called *pollination*), are fertilized to produce seeds. Under the right conditions, the seeds sprout to become plants in their own right. The plants growing from seeds are the offspring of the plant(s) that produced the eggs and the pollen. Fertilization can happen in one of two ways:

- ✔ **Out-crossing:** Two plants are crossed, and the pollen from one can be used to fertilize the eggs of another.

- ✔ **Self-pollination (or selfing):** Some flowers produce both flowers and pollen, in which case the flower may fertilize its own eggs. Not all plants can self-fertilize, but Mendel's peas could.

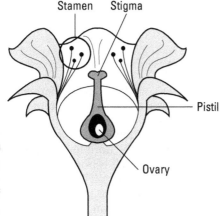

Stamen   Stigma

Pistil

Ovary

Figure 3-1: Reproductive parts of a flower.

Speaking the Language of Inheritance

You probably already know that genes are passed from parent to offspring and that somehow, genes are responsible for the physical traits (*phenotype*, such as hair color) you observe in yourself and the people and organisms around you. (For more on how genes do their jobs, you can flip ahead to Chapter 11.) The simplest possible definition of a *gene* is an inherited factor that determines some trait.

Genes come in different forms, called *alleles*. An individual's alleles determine the phenotype. The combinations of alleles of all the various genes that you possess make up your *genotype*. Genes occupy *loci* — specific locations along the strands of your DNA (*locus* is the singular form). Different traits (like hair texture and hair color) are determined by genes that occupy different loci, often on different chromosomes (see Chapter 2 for the basics of chromosomes). Take a look at Figure 3-2 to see how alleles are arranged in various loci along two pairs of generic chromosomes.

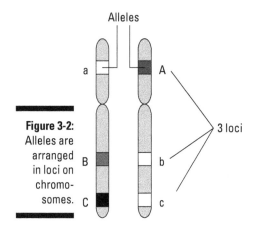

Figure 3-2:
Alleles are arranged in loci on chromosomes.

In humans (and many other organisms), alleles of particular genes come in pairs. If both alleles are identical in form, that locus is said to be *homozygous,* and the whole organism can be called a *homozygote* for that particular locus. If the two alleles aren't identical, then the individual is *heterozygous,* or a *heterozygote,* for that locus. Individuals can be both heterozygous and homozygous at different loci at the same time, which is how all the phenotypic variation you see in a single organism is produced. For example, your hair texture is controlled by one locus, your hair color is controlled by different loci, and your skin color by yet other loci. You can see how figuring out how complex sets of traits are inherited would be pretty difficult.

Simplifying Inheritance

When it comes to sorting out inheritance, it's easiest to start out with how one trait is transmitted from one generation to the next. This is the kind of inheritance, sometimes called *simple inheritance,* that Mendel started with when first studying his pea plants.

Mendel's choice of pea plants and the traits he chose to focus on had positive effects on his ability to uncover the laws of inheritance.

  ✔ **The original parent plants Mendel used in his experiments were true breeding.** When true breeders are allowed to self-fertilize, the exact same physical traits show up, unchanged, generation after generation.

True-breeding tall plants always produce tall plants, true-breeding short plants always produce short plants, and so on.

- ✔ **Mendel studied traits that had only two forms, or *phenotypes*, for each characteristic (like short or tall).** He deliberately chose traits that were either one type or another, like tall or short, or green-seeded or yellow-seeded. Studying traits that come in only two forms made the inheritance of traits much easier to sort out. (Chapter 4 covers traits that have more than two phenotypes.)

- ✔ **Mendel worked only on traits that showed an *autosomal dominant* form of inheritance — that is, the genes were located on autosomal (or non-sex) chromosomes.** (I discuss more complicated forms of inheritance in Chapters 4 and 5.)

Before his pea plants began producing pollen, Mendel opened the flower buds. He cut off either the pollen-producing part (the stamen) or the pollen-receiving part (the stigma) to prevent the plant from self-fertilizing. After the flower matured, he transferred pollen by hand — okay, not technically his hand; he used a tiny brush — from one plant (the "father") to another (the "mother"). Mendel then planted the seeds (the offspring) that resulted from this "mating" to see which physical traits each cross produced. The following sections explain the three laws of inheritance that Mendel discovered from his experiments.

Establishing dominance

For his experiments, Mendel crossed true-breeding plants that produced round seeds with true breeders that produced wrinkled seeds, crossed short true-breeders with tall true-breeders, and so on. Crosses of parent organisms that differ by only one trait, like seed shape or plant height, are called *monohybrid crosses.* Mendel patiently moved pollen from plant to plant, harvested and planted seeds, and observed the results after the offspring plants matured. His plants produced literally thousands of seeds, so his garden must have been quite a sight.

To describe Mendel's experiments and results, I refer to the parental generation with the letter *P*. I refer to the first offspring from a cross as *F1*. If F1 offspring are mated to each other (or allowed to self-fertilize), I call the next generation *F2* (see Figure 3-3 for the generation breakdown).

The results of Mendel's experiments were amazingly consistent. In every case when he mated true breeders of different phenotypes, all the F1 offspring had the same phenotype as one or the other parent plant. For example, when Mendel crossed a true-breeding tall parent with a true-breeding short parent, *all* the F1 offspring were tall. This result was surprising because until then, many people thought inheritance was a blending of the characteristics of the two parents — Mendel had expected his first generation offspring to be medium height.

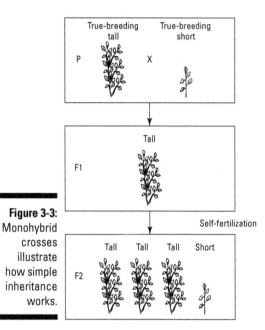

Figure 3-3:
Monohybrid
crosses
illustrate
how simple
inheritance
works.

If Mendel had just scratched his head and stopped there, he wouldn't have learned much. But he allowed the F1 offspring to self-fertilize, and something interesting happened: About 25 percent of the F2 offspring were short, and the rest, about 75 percent, were tall (refer to Figure 3-3).

From that F2 generation, when allowed to self-fertilize, his short plants were true breeders — all produced short progeny. His F2 tall plants produced both tall and short offspring. About one-third of his tall F2s bred true as tall. The rest produced tall and short offspring in a 3:1 ratio (that is, ¾ tall and ¼ short; refer to Figure 3-3).

After thousands of crosses, Mendel came to the accurate conclusion that the factors that determine seed shape, seed color, pod color, plant height, and so on are acting sets of two. He reached this understanding because *one* phenotype showed up in the F1 offspring, but *both* phenotypes were present among the F2 plants. The result in the F2 generation told him that whatever it was that controlled a particular trait (such as plant height) had been present but somehow hidden in the F1 offspring.

Mendel quickly figured out that certain traits seem to act like rulers, or dominate, other traits. *Dominance* means that one factor masks the presence of another. Round seed shape dominated wrinkled. Tall height dominated short. Yellow seed color dominated green. Mendel rightly determined the genetic principle of *dominance* by strictly observing phenotype in generation after generation and cross after cross. When true tall and short plants were crossed, each F1 offspring got one height-determining factor from each parent.

Because tall is *dominant* over short, all the F1 plants were tall. Mendel found that the only time *recessive* characters (traits that are masked by dominant traits) were expressed was when the two factors were alike, as when short plants self-fertilized.

Segregating alleles

Segregation is when things get separated from each other. In the genetic sense, what's separated are the two factors — the alleles of the gene — that determine phenotype. Figure 3-4 traces the segregation of the alleles for seed color through three generations. The shorthand for describing alleles is typically a capital letter for the dominant trait and the same letter in lowercase for the recessive trait. In this example, I use *Y* for the dominant allele that makes yellow seeds; *y* stands for the recessive allele that, when homozygous, makes seeds green.

The letters or symbols you use for various alleles and traits are arbitrary. Just make sure you're consistent in how you use letters and symbols, and don't get them mixed up.

In the segregation example featured in Figure 3-4, the parents (in the P generation) are homozygous. Each individual parent plant has a certain genotype — a combination of alleles — that determines its phenotype. Because pea plants are *diploid* (meaning they have two copies of each gene; see Chapter 2), the genotype of each plant is described using two letters. For example, a true-breeding yellow-seeded plant would have the genotype YY, and green-seeded plants are yy. The *gametes* (sex cells, as in pollen or eggs) produced by each plant bear only one allele. (Sex cells are *haploid;* see Chapter 2 for all the details on how meiosis produces haploid gametes.) Therefore, the true breeders can produce gametes of only one type — YY plants can only make Y gametes and yy plants can only produce y gametes. When a Y pollen and a y egg (or visa versa, y pollen and Y egg) get together, they make a Yy offspring — this is the heterozygous F1 generation.

The bottom line of the principle of segregation is this parsing out of the pairs of alleles into gametes. Each gamete gets one and only one allele for each locus; this is the result of homologous chromosomes parting company during the first round of meiosis (see Chapter 2 for more on how chromosomes split during meiosis). When the F1 generation self-fertilizes (to create the F2 generation), each plant produces two kinds of gametes: Half are Y, and the other half are y. Segregation makes four combinations of zygotes possible: YY, Yy, yY, or yy. (Yy and yY look redundant, but they're genetically significant because they represent different contributions [y or Y] from each parent.) Phenotypically, Yy, yY, and YY all look alike: yellow seeds. Only yy makes green seeds. The ratio of genotypes is 1:2:1 (¼ homozygous dominant: ½ heterozygous: ¼ homozygous recessive), and the ratio of phenotypes is 3 to 1 (dominant phenotype to recessive phenotype).

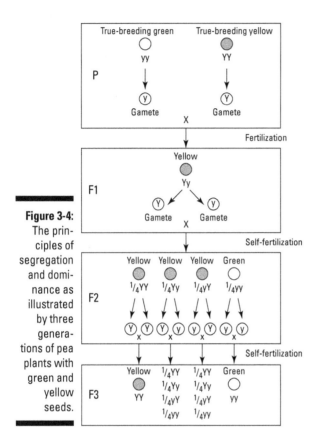

Figure 3-4: The principles of segregation and dominance as illustrated by three generations of pea plants with green and yellow seeds.

If allowed to self-fertilize in the F3 generation, yy parents make yy offspring, and YY parents produce only YY offspring. The Yy parents again make YY, Yy, and yy offspring in the same ratios observed in the F2: ¼ YY, ½ Yy, and ¼ yy.

Scientists now know that what Mendel saw acting in sets of two were genes. Single pairs of genes (that is, one locus) control each trait. That means that plant height is at one locus, seed color at a different locus, seed shape at a third locus, and so on.

Declaring independence

As Mendel learned more about how traits were passed from one generation to the next, he carried out experiments with plants that differed in two or more traits. He discovered that the traits behaved independently — that is, that the inheritance of plant height had no effect on the inheritance of seed color, for example.

REMEMBER

The independent inheritance of traits is called the *law of independent assortment* and is a consequence of meiosis. When homologous pairs of chromosomes separate, they do so randomly with respect to each other. The movement of each individual chromosome is independent with respect to every other chromosome. It's just like flipping a coin: As long as the coin isn't rigged, one coin flip has no effect on another — each flip is an independent event. Genetically, what this random separation amounts to is that alleles on different chromosomes are inherited independently.

Segregation and independent assortment are closely related principles. *Segregation* tells you that alleles at the same locus on pairs of chromosomes separate and that each offspring has the same chance of inheriting a particular allele from a parent. *Independent assortment* means that every offspring also has the same opportunity to inherit any allele at any other locus (but this rule has some exceptions; see Chapter 4).

Finding Unknown Alleles

Mendel crossed parent plants in many different combinations to work out the identity of the hidden factors (which we now know as genes) that produced the phenotypes he observed. One type of cross was especially informative. A *testcross* is when any individual with an unknown genotype is crossed with a true-breeding individual with the recessive phenotype (in other words, a homozygote).

Each cross provides different information about the genotypes of the individuals involved. For example, Mendel could take any plant with any phenotype and testcross it with a true-breeding recessive plant to find out which alleles the plant of unknown genotype carried. Here's how the testcross would work: A plant with the dominant phenotype, violet flowers, could be crossed with a true-breeding white flowered plant (ww). If the resulting offspring all had violet flowers, Mendel knew that the unknown genotype was homozygous dominant (WW). In Figure 3-5, you see the results of another testcross: A heterozygote (Ww) testcross yielded offspring of half white and half violet phenotypes.

Figure 3-5:
The results of testcrosses divulge unknown genotypes.

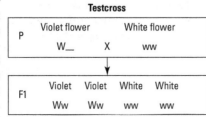

Applying Basic Probability to the Likelihood of Inheritance

Predicting the results of crosses is easy, because the rules of probability govern the likelihood of getting particular outcomes. The following are two important rules of probability that you should know:

- ✔ **Multiplication rule:** Used when the probabilities of events are independent of each other — that is, the result of one event doesn't influence the result of another. The combined probability of both events occurring is the product of the events, so you multiply the probabilities.

- ✔ **Addition rule:** Used when you want to know the probability of one event occurring as opposed to another, independent, event. Put another way, you use this rule when you want to know the probability of one *or* another event happening, but not necessarily both.

For more details about the laws of probability, check out the sidebar "Beating the odds with genetics."

Here's how you apply the addition and multiplication rules for monohybrid crosses (crosses of parent organisms that differ only by one trait). Suppose you have two pea plants. Both plants have violet flowers, and both are heterozygous (Ww). Each plant will produce two sorts of gametes, W and w, with equal probability — that is, half of the gametes will be W and half will be w for each plant. To determine the probability of a certain genotype resulting from the cross of these two plants, you use the multiplication rule and multiply probabilities. For example, what's the probability of getting a heterozygote (Ww) from this cross?

Because both plants are heterozygous (Ww), the probability of getting a W from plant one is ½, and the probability of getting a w from plant two is also ½. The word *and* tells you that you need to multiply the two probabilities to determine the probability of the two events happening together. So, ½ × ½ = ¼. But there's another way to get a heterozygote from this cross: Plant one could contribute the w, and plant two could contribute the W. The probability of this turn of events is exactly equal to the first scenario: ½ × ½ = ¼. Thus, you have two equally probable ways of getting a heterozygote: wW or Ww. The word *or* tells you that you must add the two probabilities together to get the total probability of getting a heterozygote: ¼ + ¼ = ½. Put another way, there's a 50 percent probability of getting heterozygote offspring when two heterozygotes are crossed.

Beating the odds with genetics

When you try to predict the outcome of a certain event, like a coin flip or the gender of an unborn child, you're using probability. For many events, the probability is either-or. For instance, a baby can be either male or female, and a coin can land either heads or tails. Both outcomes are considered equally likely (as long as the coin isn't rigged somehow). For many events, however, determining the likelihood of a certain outcome is more complicated. Deciding how to calculate the odds depends on what you want to know.

Take, for example, predicting the sex of several children born to a given couple. The probability of any baby being a boy is ½, or 50 percent. If the first baby is a boy, the probability of the second child being a boy is still 50 percent, because the events that determine sex are independent from one child to the next (see Chapter 2 for a rundown of how meiosis works to produce gametes for sex cells). That means the sex of one child has no effect on the sex of the next child. But if you want to know the probability of having two boys in a row, you multiply the probability

of each independent event together: ½ × ½ = ¼, or 25 percent. If you want to know the probability of having two boys *or* two girls, you add the probabilities of the events together: ¼ (the probability of having two boys) + ¼ (the probability of having two girls) = ½, or 50 percent.

Genetic counselors use probability to determine the likelihood that someone has inherited a given trait and the likelihood that a person will pass on a trait if he or she has it. For example, a man and woman are each carriers for a recessive disorder, such as cystic fibrosis. The counselor can predict the likelihood that the couple will have an affected child. Just as in Mendel's flower crosses, each parent can produce two kinds of gametes, affected or unaffected. The man produces half-affected and half-unaffected gametes, as does the woman. The probability that any child inherits an affected allele from the mom *and* an affected allele from the dad is ¼ (that's ½ × ½). The probability that a child will be affected *and* female is ⅛ (that's ¼ × ½). The probability that a child will be affected *or* a boy is ¾ (that's ¼ + ½).

Solving Simple Genetics Problems

Every genetics problem, from those on an exam to one that determines what coat color your dog's puppies may have, can be solved in the same manner. Here's a simple approach to any genetics problem:

1. **Determine how many traits you're dealing with.**

2. **Count the number of phenotypes.**

3. **Carefully read the problem to identify the question.** Do you need to calculate genetic or phenotypic ratios? Are you trying to determine something about the parents or the offspring?

4. **Look for words that mean *and* and *or* to help determine which probabilities to add and which to multiply.**

Deciphering a monohybrid cross

Imagine that you have your own garden full of the same variety of peas that Mendel studied. After reading this book, filled with enthusiasm for genetics, you rush out to examine your pea plants, having noticed that some plants are tall and others short. You know that last year you had one tall plant (which self-fertilized) and that this year's crop consists of the offspring of last year's one tall parent plant. After counting plants, you discover that 77 of your plants are tall, and 26 are short. What was the genotype of your original plant? What is the dominant allele?

You have two distinct phenotypes (tall and short) of one trait — plant height. You can choose any symbol or letter you please, but often, geneticists use a letter like *t* for short and then capitalize that letter for the other allele (here, *T* for tall).

One way to start solving the problem of short versus tall plants is to determine the ratio of one phenotype to the other. To calculate the ratios, add the number of offspring together: 77 + 26 = 103, and divide to determine the proportion of each phenotype: 77 ÷ 103 = 0.75, or 75 percent are tall. To verify your result, you can divide 26 by 103 to see that 25 percent of the offspring are short, and 75 percent plus 25 percent gives you 100 percent of your plants.

From this information alone, you've probably already realized (thanks to simple probability) that your original plant must have been heterozygous and that tall is dominant over short. As I explain in the "Segregating alleles" section earlier in this chapter, a heterozygous plant (Tt) produces two kinds of gametes (T or t) with equal probability (that is, half the time the gametes are T and the other half they're t). The probability of getting a homozygous dominant (TT) genotype is ½ × ½ = ¼ (that's the probability of getting T twice: T once *and* T a second time, like two coin flips in a row landing heads). The probability of getting a heterozygous dominant (T and t, *or* t and T) is ½ × ½ = ¼ (to get Tt) plus ½ × ½ = ¼ (tT). The total probability of a plant with the dominant phenotype (TT *or* Tt *or* tT) is ¼ + ¼ + ¼ = ¾. With 103 plants, you'd expect 77.25 (on average) of them to show the dominant phenotype — which is essentially what you observed.

Tackling a dihybrid cross

To become more comfortable with the process of solving simple genetics problems, you can tackle a problem that involves more than one trait: a *dihybrid cross*.

Here's the problem scenario. In bunnies, short hair is dominant. (If you're a rabbit breeder, please forgive my oversimplification.) Your roommate moves out and leaves behind two bunnies (you were feeding them anyway, and they're cute, so you don't mind). One morning you wake to find that your bunnies are now parents to a litter of babies.

- One is gray and has long fur.
- Two are black and have long fur.
- Two are gray and have short fur.
- Seven look just like the parents: black with short fur.

Besides the meaningful lesson about spaying and neutering pets, what can you discover about the genetics of coat color and hair length of your rabbits?

First, how many traits are you dealing with? I haven't told you anything about the gender of your baby bunnies, so it's safe to assume that sex doesn't have anything to do with the problem. (I take that back. Sex is the source of the problem — see Chapter 5 for more on the genetics of sex.) You're dealing with two traits: color of fur and length of fur. Each trait has two phenotypes: Fur can be black or gray, and length of fur can be long or short. In working through this problem, you're told upfront that short fur is a dominant trait, but you don't get any information about color.

The simplest method is to examine one trait at a time — in other words, look at the monohybrid crosses. (Jump back to the section "Deciphering a mono-hybrid cross" for a refresher.)

Both parents have short fur. How many of their offspring have short fur? Nine of twelve, and 9 ÷ 12 = ¾, or 75 percent. That means there are three short-haired bunnies to every one long-haired bunny.

Being identical in phenotype, the parents both have black coats. How many babies have black coats? Nine of twelve. There's that comfortingly familiar ratio again! The ratio of black to gray is 3 to 1.

From your knowledge of monohybrid crosses, you've probably guessed that the parent rabbits are heterozygous for coat color and, at the same time, are heterozygous for fur length. To be sure, you can calculate the probability of certain genotypes and corresponding phenotypes of offspring for two rabbits that are heterozygous at two loci (see Figure 3-6).

The phenotypic ratio observed in the rabbits' offspring (9:3:3:1; refer to Figure 3-6) is typical for the F2 generation in a dihybrid cross. The rarest phenotype is the one that's recessive for both traits; in this case, long hair and gray color are both recessive. The most common phenotype is the one that's dominant for both traits. The fact that seven of your twelve baby rabbits are black with short fur tells you that the probability of getting a particular allele for color and a particular allele for coat length is the product of two independent events. Coat color and hair length are coded by genes that are inherited independently — as you would expect under the principle of independent assortment.

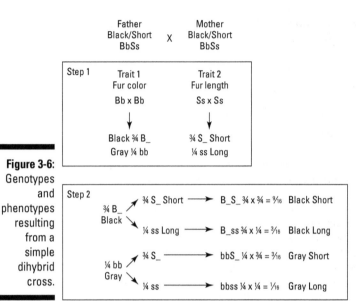

Figure 3-6:
Genotypes
and
phenotypes
resulting
from a
simple
dihybrid
cross.

Chapter 4

Law Enforcement: Mendel's Laws Applied to Complex Traits

Although nearly 150 years have elapsed since Gregor Mendel cultivated his pea plants (see Chapter 3), the observations he made and the conclusions he drew still accurately describe how genes are passed from parent to offspring. The basic laws of inheritance — dominance, segregation, and independent assortment — continue to stand the test of time.

However, inheritance isn't nearly as simple as Mendel's experiments suggest. Dominant alleles don't always dominate, and genes aren't always inherited independently. Some genes mask their appearances, and some alleles can kill. This chapter explains exactly how Mendel was right, and wrong, about the laws of inheritance and how they're enforced.

Dominant Alleles Rule . . . Sometimes

If Mendel had chosen a plant other than the pea plant for his experiments, he may have come to some very different conclusions. The traits that Mendel studied show *simple dominance* — when the dominant allele's *phenotype,* or physical trait (a yellow seed, for example), masks the presence of the recessive allele. The recessive phenotype (a green seed in this example) is only expressed when both alleles are recessive, which is written as *yy.* (Turn to Chapter 3 for the definitions of commonly used genetics terms such as *allele, recessive,* and *homozygote.*) But not all alleles behave neatly as dominant-recessive. Some alleles show incomplete dominance and therefore seem to display a blend of phenotypes from the parents. This section tells you how dominant alleles rule the roost — but only part of the time.

Wimping out with incomplete dominance

A trip to the grocery store can be a nice genetics lesson. Take eggplant, for example. Eggplant comes in various shades of (mostly) purple skin that are courtesy of a pair of alleles at a single locus interacting in different ways to express the phenotype — purple fruit color. Dark purple and white colors are both the result of homozygous alleles. Dark purple is homozygous for the dominant allele (PP), and white is homozygous for the recessive allele (pp). When crossed, dark purple and white eggplants yield light purple offspring — the intermediate phenotype. This intermediate color is the result of the allele for purple being incomplete in its dominance of the allele for white (which is actually the allele for no color).

With *incomplete dominance,* the alleles are inherited in exactly the same way they always are: One allele comes from each parent. The alleles still conform to the principles of segregation and independent assortment, but the way those alleles are expressed (the phenotype) is different. (You can find out about exceptions to the independent assortment rules in the section "Genes linked together" later in this chapter.)

Here's how the eggplant cross works: The parent plants are PP (for purple) and pp (for white). The F1 generation is all heterozygous (Pp), just as you'd expect from Mendel's experiments (see Chapter 3). If this were a case of simple dominance, all the Pp F1 generation would be dark purple. But in this case of incomplete dominance, the F1 generation comes out light purple (sometimes called violet). (The heterozygotes produce a less purple pigment, making the offspring lighter in color than homozygous purple plants.)

In the F2 (the result of crossing Pp with Pp), half the offspring have violet fruits (corresponding with the Pp genotype). One-quarter of the offspring are dark purple (PP) and one-quarter are white (pp) — these are the homozygous offspring. Rather than the 3:1 phenotypic ratio (three dark purple eggplants and one white eggplant) you'd expect to see with simple dominance, with incomplete dominance, you see a 1:2:1 ratio (one dark purple eggplant, two light purple eggplants, and one white eggplant) — the exact ratio of the underlying genotype (PP, Pp, Pp, pp).

Keeping it fair with codominance

When alleles share equally in the expression of their phenotypes, the inheritance pattern is considered *codominant.* Both alleles are expressed fully as phenotypes instead of experiencing some intermediate expression (like what's observed in incomplete dominance).

You can see a good example of codominance in human blood types. If you've ever donated blood (or received a transfusion), you know that your blood type is extremely important. If you receive the wrong blood type during a transfusion, you can have a fatal allergic reaction. Blood types are the result of proteins, called *antigens,* that your body produces on the surface of red blood cells. Antigens protect you from disease by recognizing invading cells (like bacteria) as foreign, and then binding to the cells and destroying them.

Your antigens determine your blood type. Several alleles code for blood antigens. Dominant alleles code two familiar blood types, A and B. When a person has both A and B alleles, the person's blood produces both antigens simultaneously and in equal amounts. Therefore, a person who has an AB genotype also has the AB phenotype.

The situation with ABO blood types gets more complicated by the presence of a third allele for type O in some people. The O allele is recessive, so ABO blood types show two sorts of inheritance:

✔ Codominance (for A and B)

✔ Dominant-recessive (A or B paired with the O allele)

Type O is only expressed in the homozygous state. For more information on multiple alleles, check out the section "More than two alleles" later in this chapter.

Dawdling with incomplete penetrance

Some dominant alleles don't express their influence consistently. When dominant alleles are present but fail to show up as a phenotype, the condition is termed *incompletely penetrant. Penetrance* is the probability that an individual having a dominant allele will show the associated phenotype. *Complete penetrance* means every person having the allele shows the phenotype. Most dominant alleles have 100 percent penetrance — that is, the phenotype is expressed in every individual possessing the allele. However, other alleles may show reduced, or incomplete, penetrance, meaning that individuals carrying the allele have a reduced probability of having the trait.

Penetrance of disease-causing alleles like those responsible for certain cancers or other hereditary disorders complicate matters in genetic testing (see Chapter 12 to find out more about genetic testing for disease). For example, one of the genes associated with breast cancer *(BRCA1)* is incompletely penetrant. Studies estimate that approximately 70 percent of women carrying the allele will be affected by breast cancer by age 70. Therefore, genetic tests indicating that someone carries the allele only point to increased risk, not a certainty of getting the disease, and indicate a need for affected women to be screened regularly for early signs of the disease, when treatment can be most effective.

Geneticists usually talk about penetrance in terms of a percentage. In this example, the breast cancer gene is 70 percent penetrant.

Regardless of penetrance, the degree to which an allele expresses the phenotype may differ from individual to individual; this variable strength of a trait is called *expressivity.* One trait with variable expressivity that shows up in humans is *polydactyly,* the condition of having more than ten fingers or toes. In persons with polydactyly, the expressivity of the trait is measured by the completeness of the extra digits — some people have tiny skin tags, and others have fully functional extra fingers or toes.

Alleles Causing Complications

The variety of forms that genes (as alleles) take accounts for the enormous diversity of physical traits you see in the world around you. For example, many alleles exist for eye color and hair color. In addition, several loci contribute to most phenotypes. Dealing with multiple loci and many alleles at each locus complicates inheritance patterns and makes them harder to understand. For many disorders, scientists don't fully understand the form of inheritance because variable expressivity and incomplete penetrance mask the patterns. Additionally, multiple alleles can interact as incompletely dominant, codominant, or dominant-recessive (see "Dominant Alleles Rule . . . Sometimes" earlier in this chapter for the whole story). This section explains how various alleles of a single gene can complicate inheritance patterns.

More than two alleles

When it came to his pea plant research, Mendel deliberately chose to study traits that came in only two flavors. For instance, his peas had only two flower color possibilities: white and purple. The allele for purple in the common pea plant is fully dominant, so it shows up as the same shade of purple in both heterozygous and homozygous plants. In addition to being fully dominant, purple is completely penetrant, so every single plant that inherits the gene for purple flowers has purple flowers.

If Mendel had been a rabbit breeder instead of a gardener, his would likely be a different story. He may not have earned the title "Father of Genetics," because the broad spectrum of rabbit coat colors would make most anyone simply throw up his hands.

To simplify matters, consider one gene for coat color in bunnies. The *C* gene has four alleles that control the amount of pigment produced in the hair shaft. These four alleles give you four rabbit color patterns to work with. The various rabbit color alleles are designated by the letter *c* with superscripts:

- ✔ **Brown (c⁺):** Brown rabbits are considered *wild-type,* which is generally considered the "normal" phenotype. Brown rabbits are brown all over.

- ✔ **Albino (c):** Rabbits homozygous for this color allele don't produce any pigment at all. Therefore, these white rabbits are considered *albino.* They have all-white coats, pink eyes, and pink skin.

- ✔ **Chinchilla (c^ch):** Chinchilla rabbits are solid gray (specifically, they have white hair with black tips).

- ✔ **Himalayan (c^h):** Himalayan rabbits are white but have dark hair on their feet, ears, and noses.

Wild-type is a bit of a problematic term in genetics. Generally, wild-type is considered the "normal" phenotype, and everything else is "mutant." *Mutant* is simply different, an alternative form that's not necessarily harmful. Wild-type tends to be the most common phenotype and is usually dominant over other alleles. You're bound to see wild-type used in genetics books to describe phenotypes such as eye color in fruit flies. Though rare, the mutant color forms occur in natural populations of animals. In the case of domestic rabbits, color forms other than brown are the product of breeding programs specifically designed to obtain certain coat colors.

Although a particular trait can be determined by a number of different alleles (as in the four allele possibilities for rabbit coat color), any particular animal carries only two alleles at a particular locus at one time.

The C gene in rabbits exhibits a dominance hierarchy common among genes with multiple alleles. Wild-type is completely dominant over the other three alleles, so any rabbit having the c⁺ allele will be brown. Chinchilla is incompletely dominant over Himalayan and albino. That means heterozygous chinchilla/Himalayan rabbits are gray with dark ears, noses, and tails. Heterozygous chinchilla/albinos are lighter than homozygous chinchillas. Albino is only expressed in animals that are homozygous (cc).

The color alleles in monohybrid crosses for rabbit color follow the same rules of segregation and independent assortment that apply to the pea plants that Mendel studied (see Chapter 3). The phenotypes for rabbit color are just more complex. For example, if you were to cross an albino rabbit (cc) with a homozygous chinchilla (c^ch c^ch), in the F2 generation (cc^ch mated with cc^ch) you'd get the expected 1:2:1 genotypic ratio (1 cc to 2 cc^ch to 1 c^ch c^ch); the phenotypes would show a corresponding 1:2:1 ratio (one albino, two light chinchilla, one full chinchilla).

A total of five genes actually control coat color in rabbits. The section "Genes in hiding" later in this chapter delves into how multiple genes interact to create fur color.

Lethal alleles

REMEMBER

Many alleles express unwanted traits (phenotypes) that indirectly cause suffering and death (such as the excessive production of mucus in the lungs of cystic fibrosis patients). Rarely, alleles may express the *lethal phenotype* — that is, death — immediately and thus are never expressed beyond the zygote. These alleles produce a 1:2 phenotypic ratio, because only heterozygotes and homozygous nonlethals survive to be counted.

The first lethal allele that scientists described was associated with yellow coat color in mice. Yellow mice are *always* heterozygous. When yellow mice are bred to other yellow mice, they produce yellow and non-yellow offspring in a 2:1 ratio, because all homozygous yellow mice die as embryos. Homozygous yellow has no real phenotype (beyond dead), because these animals never survive.

Lethal alleles are almost always recessive, and thus are expressed only in homozygotes. One notable exception is the gene that causes Huntington disease. Huntington disease (also known as Huntington chorea) is inherited as an autosomal dominant lethal disorder, meaning that persons with Huntington disease develop a progressive nerve disorder that causes involuntary muscle movement and loss of mental function. Huntington disease is expressed in adulthood and is always fatal. It has no cure; treatment is aimed at alleviating symptoms of the disease.

Making Life More Complicated

Many phenotypes are determined by the action of more than one gene at a time. Genes can hide the effects of each other, and sometimes one gene can control several phenotypes at once. This section looks at how genes make life more complicated (and more interesting).

When genes interact

If you don't mind returning to the produce section of your local grocery store (no more eggplants, I promise), you can observe the interaction of multiple genes to produce various colors of bell peppers. Two genes (R and C) interact to make these mild, sweet peppers appear red, brown, yellow, or green. You see four phenotypes as the result of two alleles at each locus.

Figure 4-1 shows the genetic breakdown of bell peppers. In the parental generation (P), you start with a homozygous dominant pepper (RRCC), which is red, crossed with a homozygous recessive (rrcc) green pepper. (This is a dihybrid cross — that is, one involving two genes — like the one I describe at the end of Chapter 3.) You can easily determine the expected genotypic ratios by considering each locus separately. For the F1 generation, that's really easy to do, because both loci are heterozygous (RrCc). Just like homozygous dominant peppers, fully heterozygous peppers are red. When the F1 peppers self-fertilize, the phenotypes of brown and yellow show up.

Brown pepper color is produced by the genotype R_cc. The blank means that the R locus must have at least one dominant allele present to produce color, but the other allele can be either dominant or recessive. Yellow is produced by the combination rrC_. To make yellow pigment, the C allele must be either heterozygous dominant or homozygous dominant with a recessive homozygous R allele. The F2 generation shows the familiar 9:3:3:1 dihybrid phenotypic ratio (just like the guinea pigs do in Chapter 3). The loci assort independently, just as you'd expect them to.

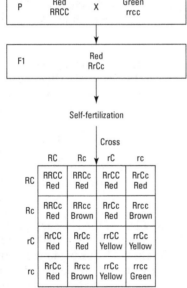

Figure 4-1: Genes interact to produce pigment in this dihybrid cross for pepper color.

P | Red RRCC | X | Green rrcc

F1 | Red RrCc

Self-fertilization

Cross

	RC	Rc	rC	rc
RC	RRCC Red	RRCc Red	RrCC Red	RrCc Red
Rc	RRCc Red	RRcc Brown	RrCc Red	Rrcc Brown
rC	RrCC Red	RrCc Red	rrCC Yellow	rrCc Yellow
rc	RrCc Red	Rrcc Brown	rrCc Yellow	rrcc Green

Conclusion: 9/16 Red 3/16 Brown 3/16 Yellow 1/16 Green

Genes in hiding

As the preceding section explains, in pepper color, the alleles of two genes interact to produce color. But sometimes, genes hide or mask the action of other genes altogether. This occurrence is called *epistasis*.

A good example of epistasis is the way in which color is determined in horses. Like that of dogs, cats, rabbits, and humans, hair color in horses is determined by numerous genes. At least seven loci determine color in horses. To simplify mastering epistasis, you tackle the actions of only three genes: W, E, and A (see Table 4-1 for a rundown of the genes and their effects). One locus (W) determines the presence or absence of color. Two loci (E and A) interact to determine the distribution of red and black hair — the most common hair colors in horses.

A horse that carries one dominant allele for W will be albino — no color pigments are produced, and the animal has white skin, white hair, and pink eyes. (Homozygous dominant for the white allele is lethal; therefore, no living horse possesses the WW genotype.) All horses that are some color other than white are homozygous recessive (ww). (If you're a horse breeder, you know that I'm really oversimplifying here. Please forgive me.) Therefore, the dominant allele W shows *dominant epistasis* because it masks the presence of other alleles that determine color.

If a horse isn't white (that is, not albino), then two main genes are likely determining its hair color: E and A. When the dominant allele E is present, the horse has black hair (it may not be black all over, but it's black somewhere). Black hair is expressed because the E locus controls the production of two pigments, red and black. EE and Ee horses produce both black and red pigments. Homozygous recessive (ee) horses are red; in fact, they're always red regardless of what's happening at the A locus. Thus, ee is *recessive epistatic,* which means that in the homozygous recessive individual, the locus masks the action of other loci. In this case, the production of black pigment is completely blocked.

When a horse has at least one dominant allele at the E locus, the A locus controls the amount of black produced. The A locus (also called *agouti,* which is a dark brown color) controls the production of black pigments. A horse with the dominant A allele produces black only on certain parts of its body (often on its mane, tail, and legs — a pattern referred to as *bay*). Horses that are aa are simply black. However, the homozygous recessive E locus (*ee*) masks the A locus entirely (regardless of genotype), blocking black color completely.

Table 4-1		Genetics of Hair Color in Horses	
Genotype	**Phenotype**	**Type of Epistasis**	**Effect**
WW__	Lethal	No epistasis	Death
Ww__	Albino	Dominant	Blocks all pigments
wwE_aa	Black	Recessive	Blocks red
wwE_A_	Bay or brown	No epistasis	Both red and black expressed
wwee__	Red	Recessive	Blocks black

This example of the genetics of horse hair color proves that the actions of genes can be complex. In this one example, you see a lethal allele (W) along with two other loci that can each mask the other under the right combination of alleles. This potential explains why it can be so difficult to determine how certain conditions are inherited. Epistasis can act along with reduced penetrance to create extremely elusive patterns of inheritance — patterns that often can only be worked out by examining the DNA itself. (I cover genetic testing in Chapter 12.)

Genes linked together

Roughly 30 years after Mendel's work was rediscovered in 1900 and verified by the scientific community (see Chapter 22 for the whole story), the British geneticist Ronald A. Fisher realized that Mendel had been exceptionally lucky — either that or he'd cheated. Of the many, many traits Mendel could have studied, he published his results on seven traits that conform to the laws of segregation and independent assortment, have two alleles, and show dominant-recessive inheritance patterns. Fisher asserted that Mendel must have published the part of his data he understood and left out the rest. (After Mendel died, all his papers were burned, so we'll never know the truth.) The rest would include all the parts that make inheritance messy, like epistasis and *linkage*.

Because of the way genes are situated along chromosomes, genes that are very close together spatially (that is, fewer than 50 million base pairs apart; see Chapter 6 for how DNA is measured in base pairs) are inherited together. When genes are so close together that they're inherited together (either all or part of the time), the genes are said to be *linked* (see Figure 4-2). The occurrence of linked genes means that not all genes are subject to independent assortment. To determine if genes are linked, geneticists carry out a process called *linkage analysis*.

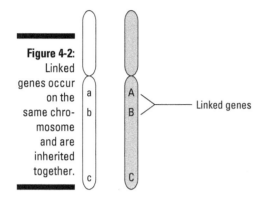

Figure 4-2: Linked genes occur on the same chromosome and are inherited together.

Linked genes

The process of linkage analysis is really a determination of how often *recombination* (the mixing of information, also called *crossing-over,* contained on the two homologous chromosomes; see Chapter 2) occurs between two or more genes. If genes are close enough together on the chromosome, they end up being linked more than 50 percent of the time. However, genes on the same chromosome can behave as if they were on different chromosomes, because during the first stage of meiosis (see Chapter 2), crossing-over occurs at many points along the two homologous chromosomes. If crossing-over splits two loci up more than 50 percent of the time, the genes on the same chromosome appear to assort independently, as if the genes were on different chromosomes altogether.

Generally, geneticists perform linkage analysis by examining dihybrid crosses (dihybrid means two loci; see Chapter 3) between a heterozygote and a homozygote. If you want to determine the linkage between two traits in fruit flies, for example, you choose an individual that's AaBb and cross it with one that's aabb. If the two loci, A and B, are assorting independently, you can expect to see the results shown in Figure 4-3. The heterozygous parent produces four types of gametes — AB, aB, Ab, and ab — with equal frequency. The homozygous parent can only make one sort of gamete — ab. Thus, in the F1 offspring, you see a 1:1:1:1 ratio.

But what if you see a completely unexpected ratio, like the one shown in Table 4-2? What does that mean? These results indicate that the traits are linked.

As you can see in Figure 4-4, the dihybrid parent makes four sorts of gametes. Even though the loci are on the same chromosome, the gametes don't occur in equal frequency. Most of the gametes show up just as they do on the chromosome, but crossover occurs between the two loci roughly 20 percent of the time, producing the two rarer sorts of gametes (each is produced about 10 percent of the time). Crossover occurs with roughly the same frequency in the homozygous parent, too, but because the alleles are the same, the results of those crossover events are invisible. Therefore, you can safely ignore that part of the problem.

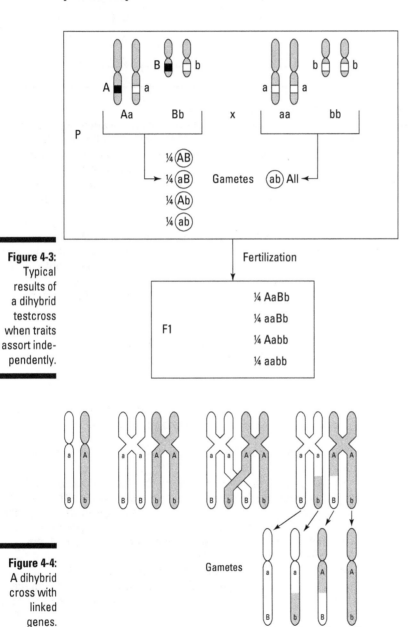

Figure 4-3:
Typical results of a dihybrid testcross when traits assort independently.

Figure 4-4:
A dihybrid cross with linked genes.

Table 4-2	Linked Traits in a Dihybrid Testcross	
Genotype	*Number of Offspring*	*Proportion*
Aabb	320	40%
aaBb	318	40%
AaBb	80	10%
aabb	76	10%

To calculate *map distance,* or the amount of crossover, between two loci, you divide the total number of recombinant offspring by the total number of offspring observed. The *recombinant offspring* are the ones that have a genotype different from the parental genotype. This calculation gives you a proportion: percent recombination. One map unit distance on a chromosome is equal to 1 percent recombination. Generally, one map unit is considered to be 1 million base pairs long.

As it turns out, genes for four of the traits Mendel studied were situated together on chromosomes. Two genes were on chromosome 1, and two were on chromosome 4; however, the genes were far enough apart that recombination was greater than 50 percent. Thus, all four traits appeared to assort independently, just as they would have if they'd been on four different chromosomes.

One gene with many phenotypes

Certain genes can control more than one phenotype. Genes that control multiple phenotypes are *pleiotropic.* Pleiotropy is very common; almost any major single gene disorder listed in the Online Mendelian Inheritance in Man database (www.ncbi.nlm.nih.gov/omim) shows pleiotropic effects.

Take, for example, phenylketonuria (PKU). This disease is inherited as a single gene defect and is autosomal recessive. When persons with the homozygous recessive phenotype consume substances containing phenylalanine, their bodies lack the proper biochemical pathway to break down the phenylalanine into tyrosine. As a result, phenylalanine accumulates in the body, preventing normal brain development. The primary phenotype of persons with PKU is mental retardation, but the impaired biochemical pathway affects other phenotypic traits as well. Thus, PKU patients also exhibit light hair color, unusual patterns of walking and sitting, skin problems, and seizures. All the phenotypic traits associated with PKU are associated with the single gene defect rather than the actions of more than one gene (see Chapter 12 for more details about PKU).

Uncovering More Exceptions to Mendel's Laws

As inheritance of genetic disorders is better studied, many exceptions to strict Mendelian inheritance rules arise. This section addresses four important exceptions.

Epigenetics

One of the biggest challenges to Mendel's laws comes from a phenomenon called *epigenetics*. The prefix *epi-* means "over" or "above." In epigenetics, organisms with identical alleles (including identical twins) may exhibit different phenotypes.

The difference in phenotypes doesn't come from the genes themselves but from elsewhere in the chemical structure of the DNA molecule (you can find out all about DNA's chemical and physical structure in Chapter 6). What happens is that tiny chemical tags, called *methyl groups,* are attached to the DNA. In essence, the tags act like the operating system in your computer that tells the programs how often to work, where, and when. In the case of epigenetics, the tags can shut genes down or turn genes on. Not only that, but the tags are inherited by the next generation as well.

Some epigenetic effects are normal and useful: They control how your various cells look and behave, like the differences between a heart muscle cell and a skin cell. However, other tags act like mutations and cause diseases like cancer (discover more about the role DNA plays in cancer in Chapter 14). Epigenetics is an exciting area of genetics research that will yield answers to how the genetic code in your DNA is affected by aging, your environment, and much more.

Genomic imprinting

Genomic imprinting is a special case of epigenetics. When traits are inherited on autosomal chromosomes, they're generally expressed equally in males and females. In some cases, the gender of the parent who contributes the particular allele may affect how the trait is expressed; this is called *genomic imprinting.*

Sheep breeders in Oklahoma discovered an amusing example of genomic imprinting. A ram named Solid Gold had unusually large hindquarters for his breed. Eventually, Solid Gold sired other sheep, which also had very large . . . butts. The breed was named Callipyge, which is Greek for *beautiful butt.* It turns out that six genes affect rump size in sheep. As breeders mated Callipyge sheep, it quickly became clear that the trait didn't obey Mendel's rules. Eventually, researchers determined that the big rump phenotype resulted only when the father passed on the trait. Callipyge ewes can't pass their big rumps on to their offspring.

The reasons behind genomic imprinting are still unclear. In the case of Callipyge sheep, scientists think there may be a mutation in a gene that regulates other genes, but why the expression of the gene is controlled by only paternal chromosomes remains a mystery. (Genomic imprinting is a big issue in cloning as well; see Chapter 20 for more on that topic.)

Anticipation

Sometimes, traits seem to grow stronger and gain more expressivity from one generation to the next. The strengthening of a trait as it's inherited is called *anticipation.* Schizophrenia is a disorder that's highly heritable and often shows a pattern of anticipation. It affects a person's mood and how she views herself and the world. Some patients experience vivid hallucinations and delusions that lead them to possess strongly held beliefs such as paranoia or grandeur. The age of onset of schizophrenic symptoms and the strength of the symptoms tend to increase from one generation to the next.

The reason behind anticipation in schizophrenia and other disorders, such as Huntington disease, may be that during replication (covered in Chapter 7), repeated sections of the DNA within the gene are easily duplicated by accident (see Chapter 13 for more on mutation by duplication). Thus, in successive generations, the gene actually gets longer. As the gene grows longer, its effects get stronger as well, leading to anticipation. In disorders affecting the brain, the mutation leads to malformed proteins (see Chapter 9 for how genes are translated into protein). The malformed proteins accumulate in the brain cells, eventually causing cells to die. Because the malformed proteins may get larger in successive generations, the effects show up when the person is young or they manifest themselves as a more severe form of the disease.

Environmental effects

Most traits show little evidence of environmental effect. However, the environment that some organisms live in controls the phenotype that some of its genes produce. For example, the gene that gives a Himalayan rabbit its characteristic phenotype of dark feet, ears, nose, and tail is a good example of a trait that varies in its expression based on the animal's environment. The pigment that produces dark fur in any animal results from the presence of an enzyme that the animal's body produces. But in this case, the enzyme's effect is deactivated at normal body temperature. Thus, the allele that produces pigment in the rabbit's fur is expressed only in the cooler parts of the body. That's why Himalayan rabbits are all white when they're born (they've been kept warm inside their mother's body) but get dark feet, ears, noses, and tails later in life. (Himalayans also change color seasonally and get lighter during the warmer months.)

Phenylketonuria (see "One gene with many phenotypes" earlier in this chapter) and other disorders of metabolism also depend on environmental factors — such as diet — for the expression of the trait.

Chapter 5

Differences Matter: The Genetics of Sex

In This Chapter

▶ How sex is determined in humans and other animals

▶ What sorts of disorders are associated with sex chromosomes

▶ How sex affects other traits

*S*ex is a term with many meanings. For geneticists, sex usually refers to two related concepts: the phenotype of sex (either male or female) and reproduction. It's hard to underestimate the importance of sex when it comes to genetics. Sex influences the inheritance of traits from one generation to the next and how those traits are expressed. Sexual reproduction allows organisms to create an amazing amount of genetic diversity via their offspring, which is handy because genetically diverse populations are more resilient in the face of disease and disaster. Many different individuals carrying many different alleles of the same genes increases the likelihood that some individuals will be resistant to disease and the effects of disaster and will pass that resistance on to their offspring. (For more on the importance of genetic diversity, flip to Chapter 17.)

In this chapter, you discover how chromosomes act to determine sex in humans and other organisms, how sex influences the expression of various nonsex (autosomal) traits, and what happens when too many or too few sex chromosomes are present.

X-rated: How You Got So Sexy

Presumably since the beginning of time, humans have been aware of the dissimilarities between the sexes. But it wasn't until 1905 that Nettie Stevens stared through a microscope long enough to discover the role of the Y chromosome in the grand scheme of things. Until Stevens came along, the much larger X chromosome was credited with creating all the celebrated differences between males and females.

From a genetics standpoint, the phenotypes of sex — male and female — depend on which type of gamete an individual produces. If an individual produces sperm (or has the potential to, when mature), it's considered male. If the individual can produce eggs, it's considered female. Some organisms are both male and female (that is, they're capable of producing viable eggs and sperm); this situation is referred to as *monoecy* (pronounced mo-*knee*-see, which means "one house"). Many plants, fish, and invertebrates (organisms lacking a bony spine like yours) are *monoecious* (mo-*knee*-shus).

Humans are *dioecious* (*di*-ee-shus; literally "two houses"), meaning that individuals have either functional male or female reproductive structures, but not both. Most of the species you're familiar with are dioecious: Mammals, insects, birds, reptiles, and many plants all have separate genders.

Organisms with separate genders get their sex phenotypes in various ways.

- ✔ Chromosomal sex determination occurs when the presence or absence of certain chromosomes control sex phenotype.
- ✔ Genetic sex determination occurs when particular genes control sex phenotype.
- ✔ The environment an organism develops in may determine its gender.

This section examines how chromosomes, genetics, and the environment determine whether an organism is male or female.

Sex determination in humans

In humans and most other mammals, males and females have the same number of chromosomes (humans have 46) in pairs (making humans *diploid*). Sex phenotype is determined by two sex chromosomes: X and Y. (Figure 5-1 shows the basic size and shape of these chromosomes.) Female humans have two X chromosomes, and male humans have one X and one Y. Check out the sidebar "The X (and Y) files" for how X and Y got their names. (Chromosomes have their stereotypical sausage shapes only during metaphase of mitosis or meiosis. Check out Chapter 2 for more details on mitosis and meiosis.)

The very important X

During metaphase, the X chromosome truly has an x-shape, with the centromere placed roughly in the middle (see Chapter 2 for more about chromosomes and their shapes). Genetically speaking, unlike the relatively puny Y chromosome, X is quite large. Of the 23 pairs of chromosomes ordered by size, X occupies the eighth place, weighing in at slightly over 150 million base pairs long. (See Chapter 6 for more about how DNA is measured in base pairs.)

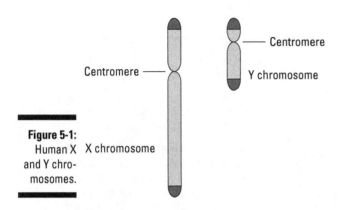

Figure 5-1:
Human X
and Y chro-
mosomes.

The X chromosome is home to between 900 and 1,200 genes and is incredibly important for normal human development. When no X is present, the zygote can't commence development. Table 5-1 lists a few of X's genes that are required for survival. Surprisingly, only one gene on X has a role in determining female phenotype; all the other genes that act to make females are on the autosomal (nonsex) chromosomes.

Table 5-1	Important Genes on the X Chromosome
Gene	*Function*
ALAS2	Directs formation of red blood cells
ATP7A	Regulates copper levels in the body
COL4A5	Required for normal kidney function
DMD	Controls muscle function and pathways between nerve cells
F8	Responsible for normal blood clotting

In all mammals (including humans), the developing embryo starts in what developmental biologists refer to as an *indifferent stage,* meaning the embryo has the potential to be either male or female. Here's how sex determination in mammals works: In roughly the fourth week of development, the embryo begins to develop a region near the kidneys called the *genital ridge.* Three genes (all on autosomes) kick in to convert the genital ridge tissue into tissue that can become sex organs. The tissue that's present by week seven in the embryo's development is called the *bipotential gonad* because it can become either testes or ovary tissue depending on which genes act next.

The X (and Y) files

Hermann Henking discovered the X chromosome while studying insects in the early 1890s. He wasn't quite sure what the lonely, unpaired structure did, but it seemed different from the rest of the chromosomes he was looking at. So rather than assign it a number (chromosomes are generally numbered according to size, largest to smallest), he called it X. In the early 1900s, Clarence McClung decided, rightly, that Henking's X was actually a chromosome, but he wasn't quite sure of its role. McClung started calling X the *accessory chromosome.* At the time, what we know as the Y chromosome carried the cumbersome moniker of *small ideochromosome.* The prefix *ideo-* means

"unknown" — in other words, McClung and other geneticists of the time had no idea what the little Y guy was for.

Edmund Wilson discovered XX-XY sex determination in insects in 1905 (independent of Nettie Stevens, who accomplished the same feat that year). Wilson seems to have had the honor of naming the Y chromosome. According to three genetics historians I consulted on the topic, Wilson first used the name Y in 1909. The Y designation was in no way romantic — it was just convenient shorthand. The new name caught on rapidly, and by 1914 or so, all geneticists were calling the two sex chromosomes X and Y.

If the embryo has at least one X and lacks a Y chromosome, two genes work together to give the embryo the female phenotype. The first gene, called *DAX1,* is on the X chromosome. The second gene, *WNT4,* is on chromosome 1. Together, these genes stimulate the development of ovary tissue. The ovary tissue excretes the hormone estrogen, which turns on other genes that control the development of the remaining female reproductive structures.

The not very significant Y

In comparison to X, the Y chromosome is scrawny, antisocial, and surprisingly expendable. Y contains between 70 and 300 genes along its 50-million base pair length and is generally considered the smallest and least gene-rich human chromosome. Most of Y doesn't seem to code for any genes at all; slightly over half the Y chromosome is junk DNA. Individuals with only one X and no Y can survive the condition (known as Turner syndrome; see the section "Sex-Determination Disorders in Humans" later in this chapter), demonstrating that Y supports no genes required for survival. Almost all the genes Y has are involved in male sex determination and sexual function.

Unlike the other chromosomes, most of Y doesn't recombine during meiosis (see Chapter 2 for details) because Y is so different from X — it has only small regions near the *telomeres* (the tips of chromosomes) that allow X and Y to pair during meiosis. Pairs of human chromosomes are considered *homologous,* meaning the members of each pair are identical in structure and shape and contain similar (although not identical) genetic information.

X and Y aren't homologous — they're different in size and shape and carry completely different sets of genes. Homologous autosomes can freely swap information during meiosis (a process referred to as *crossing-over*), but X and Y don't share enough information to allow crossing-over to occur. X and Y do pair up as if they were homologous so that the right number of chromosomes gets parsed out during meiosis.

Because Y doesn't recombine with other chromosomes, it's unusually good for tracing how men have traveled and settled around the world. The Y chromosome is even helping to clarify British history. For centuries, people have believed that Anglo-Saxons conquered Britain and more or less ran everyone else out. In a 2003 survey of over 1,700 British men, however, geneticists found evidence that different parts of the British Isles have differing paternal histories reflecting a complex and rich history of invasions, immigration, and intermarriage.

The most important of Y's genes is *SRY,* the Sex-determining Region Y gene, which was discovered in 1990. The *SRY* gene is what makes men. *SRY* codes for a mere 204 amino acids (flip to Chapter 10 for how the genetic code works to make proteins from amino acids). Unlike most genes (and most of Y, for that matter), *SRY* is junk-free — it contains no *introns* (sequences that interrupt the expressed part of genes; see Chapter 9 for a full description).

SRY's most important function is starting the development of testes. Embryos that have at least one Y chromosome differentiate into males when the *SRY* gene is turned on during week seven of development. *SRY* acts with at least one other gene (on chromosome 17) to stimulate the expression of the male phenotype in the form of testes. The testes themselves secrete testosterone, the hormone responsible for the expression of most traits belonging to males. (To find out how gene expression works, turn to Chapter 11.)

Sex determination in other organisms

In mammals, sex determination is directed by the presence of sex chromosomes that turn on the appropriate genes to make male or female phenotypes. In most other organisms, however, sex determination is highly variable. This section looks at how various arrangements of chromosomes, genes, and even temperature affect the determination of sex.

Insects

When geneticists first began studying chromosomes in the early 1900s, insects were the organisms of choice. Grasshopper, beetle, and especially fruit fly chromosomes were carefully stained and studied under microscopes (check out Chapter 15 for how geneticists study chromosomes). Much of what we now know about chromosomes in general and sex determination in particular comes from the work of these early geneticists.

In 1901, Clarence McClung determined that female grasshoppers had two X chromosomes, but males had only one (take a look at the sidebar "The X (and Y) files" for more about McClung's role in discovering the sex chromosomes). This arrangement, now known as XX-XO, with the O representing a lack of a chromosome, occurs in many insects. For these organisms, the number of X chromosomes in relation to the autosomal chromosomes determines maleness or femaleness. Two doses of X produce a female. One X produces a male.

In the XX-XO system, females (XX) are *homogametic,* which means that every gamete (in this case, eggs) that the individual produces has the same set of chromosomes composed of one of each autosome and one X. Males (XO) are *heterogametic;* their sperm can come in two different types. Half of a male's gametes have one set of autosomes and an X; the other half have one set of autosomes and no sex chromosome at all. This imbalance in the number of chromosomes is what determines sex for XX-XO organisms.

A similar situation occurs in fruit flies. Male fruit flies are XY, but the Y doesn't have any sex-determining genes on it. Instead, sex is determined by the number of X chromosomes compared to the number of sets of autosomes. The number of X chromosomes an individual has is divided by the number of sets of autosomes (sometimes referred to as the haploid number, *n*; see Chapter 2). This equation is the X to autosome (A) ratio, or X:A ratio. If the X:A ratio is ½ or less, the individual is male. For example, an XX fly with two sets of autosomes would yield a ratio of 1 (2 divided by 2) and would be female. An XY fly with two sets of autosomes would yield a ratio of ½ (1 divided by 2) and would be male.

Bees and wasps have no sex chromosomes at all. Their sex is determined by whether the individual is *diploid* (with paired chromosomes) or *haploid* (with a single set of chromosomes). Females develop from fertilized eggs and are diploid. Males develop from unfertilized eggs and are therefore haploid.

Birds

Like humans, birds have two sex chromosomes: Z and W. Female birds are ZW, and males are ZZ. Sex determination in birds isn't well understood; two genes, one on the Z and the other on the W, both seem to play roles in whether an individual becomes male or female. The Z-linked gene suggests that, like the XX-XO system in insects (see the preceding section), the number of Z chromosomes may help determine sex (but with reversed results from XX-XO). On the other hand, the W-linked gene suggests the existence of a "female-determining" gene. The chicken genome sequence (see Chapter 8 for the scoop) will provide critical information for geneticists to learn how sex is determined in birds. (Sex determination for some birdlike animals is even more complex; check out the hard-to-believe story of the platypus in Chapter 24.)

Nature's gender benders

Some organisms have *location-dependent* sex determination, meaning the organism becomes male or female depending on where it ends up. Take the slipper limpet, for example. Slipper limpets (otherwise known by their highly suggestive scientific name of *Crepidula fornicata*) have concave, unpaired shells and cling to rocks in shallow seawater environments. (Basically, they look like half of an oyster.) All young slipper limpets start out as male, but a male can become female as a result of his (soon to be her) circumstances. If a young slipper limpet settles on bare rock, it becomes female. If a male settles on top of another male, the one on the bottom becomes a female to accommodate the new circumstances. If a male is removed from the top of a pile and placed on bare rock, he becomes a she and awaits the arrival of a male. After an individual becomes female, she's stuck with the change and is a female from then on.

Some fish also change sex depending on their locations or their social situations. Blue-headed wrasse, large reef fish familiar to many scuba divers, change into females if a male is present. If no male is around, or if the local male disappears, large females change sex to become males. The fish's brain and nervous system control its ability to switch from one sex to another. An organ in the brain called the *hypothalamus* (you have one, too, by the way) regulates sex hormones and controls growth of the needed reproductive tissues.

To add to the list of the truly bizarre, a parasitic critter that lives inside certain fish has an unusual way of changing gender: cannibalism. When a male *Ichthyoxenus fushanensis,* which is a sort of parasitic pill bug (you may know the isopod as a roly-poly), eats a female (or vice versa), the diner changes sex — that is, he becomes a she. In the case of the isopod, the sex change is a form of hermaphroditism where the genders are expressed sequentially and in response to some change in the environment or diet.

Reptiles

Sex chromosomes determine the sex of most reptiles (like snakes and lizards). However, the sex of most turtles and all crocodiles and alligators is determined by the temperature the eggs experience during incubation. Female turtles and crocodilians dig nests and bury their eggs in the ground. Females usually choose nest sites in open areas likely to receive a lot of sunlight. Female turtles don't bother to guard their eggs; they lay 'em and forget 'em. Alligators and crocodiles, on the other hand, guard their nests (quite aggressively, as I can personally attest) but let the warmth of the sun do the work.

In turtles, lower temperatures (78–82 degrees Fahrenheit) produce all males. At temperatures over 86 degrees, all eggs become females. Intermediate temperatures produce both sexes. Male alligators, on the other hand, are produced only at intermediate temperatures (around 91 degrees). Cooler conditions (84–88 degrees) produce only females; really warm temperatures (95 degrees) produce all females also.

An enzyme called *aromatase* seems to be the key player in organisms with temperature-dependent sex determination. Aromatase converts testosterone into estrogen. When estrogen levels are high, the embryo becomes a female. When estrogen levels are low, the embryo becomes a male. Aromatase activity varies with temperature. In some turtles, for example, aromatase is essentially inactive at 77 degrees, and all eggs in that environment hatch as males. When temperatures around the eggs get to 86 degrees, aromatase activity increases dramatically, and all the eggs become females.

Sex-Determination Disorders in Humans

Homologous chromosomes line up and part company during the first phase of meiosis, which I explain in Chapter 2. The dividing up of chromosome pairs ensures that each gamete gets only one copy of each chromosome, and thus that zygotes (created from the fusion of gametes; see Chapter 2) have one pair of each chromosome without odd copies thrown in. But sometimes, mistakes occur. Xs or Ys can get left out, or extra copies can remain. These chromosomal delivery errors are caused by *nondisjunction,* which results when chromosomes fail to segregate normally during meiosis. (Chapter 15 has more information about nondisjunction and other chromosome disorders.)

Extra chromosomes can create all sorts of developmental problems. In organisms that have chromosomal sex determination, like humans, male organisms normally have only one X, giving them one copy of each gene on the X and allowing some genes on the X chromosome to act like dominant genes when, in fact, they're recessive (take a look ahead at "X-linked disorders" for more). Female organisms have to cope with two copies, or doses, of the X chromosome and its attendant genes. If both copies of a female's X were active, she'd get twice as much X-linked gene product as a male. (*X-linked* means any and all genes on the X chromosome.) The extra protein produced by two copies of the gene acting at once derails normal development. The solution to this problem is a process called *dosage compensation,* when the amount of gene product is equalized in both sexes.

Dosage compensation is achieved in one of two ways:

✔ The organism increases gene expression on the X to get a double dose for males. This is what happens in fruit flies, for example.

✔ The female inactivates essentially all the genes on one X to get a "half" dose of gene expression.

Both methods equalize the amount of gene product produced by each sex. In humans, dosage compensation is achieved by *X inactivation;* one X chromosome is permanently and irreversibly turned off in every cell of a female's body.

X inactivation in humans is controlled by a single gene, called *XIST* (for *X Inactive-Specific Transcript*), that lies on the X chromosome. When a female zygote starts to develop, it goes through many rounds of cell division. When the zygote gets to be a little over 16 cells in size, X inactivation takes place. The *XIST* gene gets turned on and goes through the normal process of transcription (covered in Chapter 9). The RNA (a close cousin of DNA; see Chapter 9 to learn more) produced when *XIST* is transcribed isn't translated into protein (see Chapter 10 for how translation works and what it does). Instead, the *XIST* transcript binds directly to one of the X chromosomes to inactivate its genes (much like RNA interference; see Chapter 11 for the details).

X inactivation causes the entire inactivated chromosome to change form; it becomes highly condensed and genetically inert. Highly condensed chromosomes are easy for geneticists to spot because they soak up a lot of dye (see Chapter 15 for how geneticists study chromosomes using dyes). Murray Barr was the first person to observe the highly condensed, inactivated X chromosomes in mammals. Therefore, these inactivated chromosomes are called *Barr bodies*.

You should remember two very important things about X inactivation:

- ✔ In humans, X inactivation is random. Only one X remains turned on, but which X remains on is completely up to chance.

- ✔ If more than two Xs are present, only one remains completely active.

The ultimate result of X inactivation is that the tissues that arise from each embryonic cell have a "different" X. Because females get one X from their father and the other from their mother, their Xs are likely to carry different alleles of the same genes. Therefore, their tissues may express different phenotypes depending on which X (Mom's or Dad's) remains active. This random expression of X chromosomes is best illustrated in cats.

Calico and tortoiseshell cats both have patchy-colored fur (often orange and black, but other combinations are possible). The genes that control these fur colors are on the X chromosomes. Male cats are usually all one color because they always have only one active X chromosome (and are XY). Females (XX), on the other hand, also have one active X chromosome, but the identity of the active X (maternal or paternal) varies over the cat's body. Therefore, calico females get a patchy distribution of color depending on which X is active (that is, as long as her parents had different alleles on their Xs). If you have a calico male cat, he possesses an extra X and has the genotype XXY. XXY cats have normal phenotypes. Unlike cats, humans with extra sex chromosomes have a variety of health problems, which I summarize later in this chapter.

Extra X's

Both males and females can have multiple X chromosomes, each with different genetic and phenotypic consequences. When females have extra X chromosomes, the condition is referred to as *Poly-X* (*poly* meaning "many"). Poly-X females tend to be taller than average and often have a thin build. Most Poly-X women develop normally and experience normal puberty, menstruation, and fertility. Rarely, XXX (referred to as *Triplo-X*) females have mental retardation; the severity of mental retardation and other health problems experienced by Poly-X females increases with the number of extra Xs. About one in every 1,000 girls is XXX.

Males with multiple X chromosomes are affected with *Klinefelter syndrome.* Roughly one in every 500 boys is XXY. Most often, males with Klinefelter are XXY, but some males have as many as four extra X chromosomes. Like females, males affected by Klinefelter undergo X inactivation so that only one X chromosome is active. However, the extra X genes act in the embryo before X inactivation takes place. These extra doses of X genes are responsible for the phenotype of Klinefelter. Generally, males with Klinefelter are taller than average and have impaired fertility (usually they're sterile). Men with Klinefelter often have reduced secondary sexual characteristics (such as less facial hair) and sometimes have some breast enlargement due to impaired production of testosterone.

For additional information and to find contacts in your area, contact Klinefelter Syndrome and Associates at 1-888-999-9428 (www.genetic.org) or the American Association for Klinefelter Syndrome Information and Support at 1-888-466-5747 (www.aaksis.org).

Extra Ys

Occasionally, human males have two or more Y chromosomes and one X chromosome. Most XYY men have a normal male phenotype, but they're often taller and, as children, grow a bit faster than their XY peers. Studies conducted during the 1960s and 1970s indicated that XYY men were more prone to criminal activity than XY men. Since then, findings have documented learning disabilities (XYY boys may start talking later than XY boys), but it seems that XYY males are no more likely to commit crimes than XY males.

One X and no Y

In some cases, individuals end up with one X chromosome. Such individuals have *Turner syndrome* and are female. Often, affected persons never undergo puberty and don't acquire secondary sex characteristics of adult women (namely, breast development and menstruation), and they tend to have short stature. In most other ways, girls and women with Turner syndrome are completely normal. Occasionally, however, they have kidney or heart defects. Turner syndrome (also referred to as *monosomy X,* meaning only one X is present) affects about one in 2,500 girls.

For additional information and to find contacts in your area, contact the Turner Syndrome Society of the United States at 1-800-365-9944 (or online at www.turner-syndrome-us.org) or the Turner Syndrome Society of Canada at 1-800-465-6744 (www.turnersyndrome.ca).

Found on Sex Chromosomes: Sex-linked Inheritance

Sex not only controls an organism's reproductive options; it also has a lot to do with which genes are expressed and how. *Sex-linked genes* are ones that are actually located on the sex chromosomes themselves. Some traits are truly X-linked (such as hemophilia) or Y-linked (such as hairy ears). Other traits are expressed differently in males and females even though the genes that control the traits are located on nonsex chromosomes. This section explains how sex influences (and sometimes controls) the phenotypes of various genetic conditions.

X-linked disorders

Genes on the X chromosome control X-linked traits. In 1910, Thomas H. Morgan discovered X-linked inheritance while studying fruit flies. Morgan's observations made him doubt the validity of Mendelian inheritance (see Chapter 3). His skepticism about Mendelian inheritance stemmed from the fact that he kept getting unexpected phenotypic ratios when he crossed red- and white-eyed flies. He thought the trait of white eyes was simply recessive, but when he crossed red-eyed females with white-eyed males, he got all red-eyed flies — the exact result you'd expect from a monohybrid cross. The F2 generation showed the expected 3:1 ratio, too.

But when Morgan crossed white-eyed females with red-eyed males, all the expected relationships fell apart. The F1 generation had a 1:1 ratio of white- to red-eyed flies. In the F2, the phenotypic ratio of white-eyed to red-eyed flies was also 1:1 — not at all what Mendel would have predicted. Morgan was flustered until he looked at which sex showed which phenotype.

In Morgan's F1 offspring from his white-eyed mothers and red-eyed fathers, all the sons were white-eyed (see Figure 5-2). Daughters of white-eyed females were red-eyed. In the F2, Morgan got equal numbers of white- and red-eyed males and females.

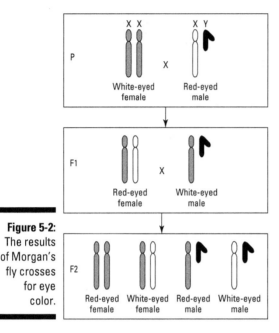

The results
of Morgan's
fly crosses
for eye
color.

Morgan was well aware of the work on sex chromosomes conducted by
Nettie Stevens and Edmund Wilson in 1905, and he knew that fruit flies have
XX-XY sex chromosomes. Morgan and his students examined the phenotypes
of 13 million fruit flies to confirm that the gene for eye color was located on
the X chromosome. (The next time you see a fruit fly in your kitchen, imagine
looking through a microscope long enough to examine 13 million flies!)

As it turns out, the gene for white eye color in fruit flies is recessive. The only
time it's expressed in females is when it's homozygous. Males, on the other
hand, show the trait when they have only one copy of the X-linked gene. For
all X-linked recessive traits, the gene acts like a dominant gene when it's in
the *hemizygous* (one copy) state. Any male inheriting the affected X chromosome shows the trait as if it were present in two copies (X-linked dominant
disorders also occur; see Chapter 12 for the details).

In humans, X-linked recessive disorders rarely show up in females. Instead,
X-linked recessive traits affect sons of women who are carriers. To see the
distribution of X-linked recessive disorders, check out the family tree for the
royal families of Europe in Chapter 12. Queen Victoria was apparently a carrier for the X-linked gene that causes hemophilia. None of Queen Victoria's
ancestors appears to have had hemophilia; geneticists think that the mutation originated with Queen Victoria herself (see Chapter 13 for more about
spontaneous mutations like these). Queen Victoria had one son with hemophilia, and two of her daughters were carriers.

Sex-limited traits

Sex-limited traits are inherited in the normal autosomal fashion but are never expressed in one sex, regardless of whether the gene is heterozygous or homozygous. Such traits are said to have 100 percent penetrance in one sex and zero penetrance in the other. (*Penetrance* is the probability that an individual having a dominant allele will show its effects; see Chapter 4 for more.) Traits such as color differences between male and female birds are sex-limited; both males and females inherit the genes for color, but the genes are expressed only in one sex (usually the male). In mammals, both males and females possess the genes necessary for milk production, but only females express these genes, which are controlled by hormone levels in the female's body (see Chapter 11 for more about how gene expression is controlled).

One trait in humans that's male-limited is precocious puberty. The corresponding gene, located on chromosome 2, causes boys to undergo the changes associated with teenage years, such as a deeper voice and beard and body hair growth, at very early ages (sometimes as young as 3 years of age). The allele responsible for precocious puberty acts as an autosomal dominant, expressed only in males. Females, regardless of genotype, never exhibit this kind of precocious puberty.

Sex-influenced traits

Sex-influenced traits are coded by genes on autosomes, but the phenotype depends on the sex of the individual carrying the affected gene. Sex-influenced traits come down to the issue of penetrance: The traits are more penetrant in males than females. Horns, hair, and other traits that make male organisms look different from females are usually sex-influenced traits.

In humans, male-pattern baldness is a sex-influenced trait. The gene credited with male hair loss is on chromosome 15. Baldness is autosomal dominant in men, and women only show the phenotype of hair loss when they're homozygous for the gene. The gene for male-pattern baldness has also been implicated in polycystic ovary disease in women. Women with polycystic ovary disease experience reduced fertility and other disorders of the reproductive system. The gene seems to act as an autosomal dominant for ovarian disease in women, much as it does for male-pattern baldness in men, so women with ovarian disease are usually heterozygous for the condition (and thus, not bald).

Y-linked traits

The Y chromosome carries few genes, and the genes it does carry are all related to male sex determination. Therefore, most of the Y-linked traits discovered so far have something to do with male sexual function and fertility. As you may expect, Y-linked traits are passed strictly from father to son. All Y-linked traits are expressed, because the Y is hemizygous (having one copy) and therefore has no other chromosome to offset gene expression. The amount of penetrance and expressivity that Y-linked traits show varies (see Chapter 4 for more details about penetrance and expressivity of autosomal dominant traits).

One trait that seems to be Y-linked but isn't related to sexual function is hairy ears. Men with hairy ears grow varying amounts of hair on their outer ears or from the ear canals. The trait appears to be incompletely penetrant, meaning not all sons of hairy-eared fathers show the trait. Hairy ears also show variable expressivity from very hairy to only a few stray hairs. Aren't you glad that geneticists have focused the powers of science at their disposal on making such important discoveries? Check out the section "The not very significant Y" earlier in this chapter for a rundown of other Y-linked genes in humans and other mammals.

Part II
DNA: The Genetic Material

In this part . . .

All life on earth depends on the essentially iconic double helix that holds all the genetic information of each and every individual. The physical and chemical makeup of DNA is responsible for DNA's massive storage capacity and controls how it's copied and how its message is passed on.

In this part, I explain how DNA is put together and how the messages are read and ultimately expressed as the traits of the organisms you see every day. The genetic code relies on DNA's close cousin, RNA, to carry the important messages of genes. The ultimate fate of DNA's messages is to create proteins, the building blocks of life. The following chapters tell you all about how DNA's blueprint is assembled from start to finish.

Chapter 6

DNA: The Basis of Life

· ·

In This Chapter
▶ Identifying the chemical components of DNA

▶ Understanding the structure of the double helix

▶ Looking at different DNA varieties

▶ Chronicling DNA's scientific history

· ·

*I*t's time to meet the star of the genetics show: *deoxyribonucleic acid,* otherwise known as DNA. If the title of this chapter hasn't impressed upon you the importance and magnitude of those three little letters, consider that DNA is also referred to as "*the* genetic material" or "*the* molecule of heredity." And you thought your title was impressive!

Every living thing on earth, from the smallest bacteria to the largest whale, uses DNA to store genetic information and transmits that info from one generation to the next; a copy of some (or all) of every creature's DNA is passed on to its offspring. The developing organism then uses DNA as a blueprint to make all its body parts. (Some non-living things use DNA to transmit information, too; see the nearby sidebar "DNA and the undead: The world of viruses" for details.)

To get an idea of how much information DNA stores, think about how complex your body is. You have hundreds of kinds of tissues that all perform different functions. It takes a lot of DNA to catalog all that. (See the section "Discovering DNA" later in this chapter to find out how scientists learned that DNA is the genetic material of all known life forms.)

The structure of DNA provides a simple way for the molecule to copy itself (see Chapter 7) and protects genetic messages from getting garbled (see Chapter 13). That structure is at the heart of forensic methods used to solve crimes, too (see Chapter 18). But before you can start exploring genetic information and applications of DNA, you need to have a handle on its chemical makeup and physical structure. In this chapter, I explore the essential makeup of DNA and the various sorts of DNA present in living things.

DNA and the undead: The world of viruses

Viruses contain DNA, but they aren't considered living things. To reproduce, a virus must attach itself to a living cell. As soon as the virus finds a host cell, the virus injects its DNA into the cell and forces that cell to reproduce the virus. A virus can't grow without stealing energy from a living cell, and it can't move from one organism to another on its own. Although viruses come in all sorts of fabulous shapes, they don't have all the components that cells do; in general, a virus is just DNA surrounded by a protein shell. So a virus isn't alive, but it's not quite dead either. Creepy, huh?

Deconstructing the Double Helix

If you're like most folks, when you think of DNA, you think of a double helix. But DNA isn't just a double helix; it's a *huge* molecule — so huge that it's called a *macromolecule*. It can even be seen with the naked eye! (Check out the nearby sidebar "Molecular madness: Extracting DNA at home" for an experiment you can do to see actual DNA.) If you were to lay out, end to end, all the DNA from just one of your cells, the line would be a little over 6 feet long! You have roughly 100,000,000,000,000 cells in your body (that's 100 trillion, if you don't feel like counting zeros). Put another way, laid out altogether, the DNA in your body would easily stretch to the sun and back — nearly 100 times!

You're probably wondering how a huge DNA molecule can fit into a teeny tiny cell so small that you can't see it with the naked eye. Here's how: DNA is tightly packed in a process called *supercoiling*. Much like a phone cord that's been twisted around and around on itself, supercoiling takes DNA and wraps it around proteins to form *nucleosomes*. Other proteins, called *histones,* hold the coils together. The nuclesomes and histones together form a structure similar to beads on a string. The whole "necklace" twists around itself so tightly that over 6 feet of DNA is compressed into only a few thousandths of an inch.

Although the idea of a DNA path to the sun works great for visualizing the size of the DNA molecule, an organism's DNA usually doesn't exist as one long piece. Rather, strands of DNA are divided into *chromosomes,* which are relatively short pieces. (I introduce chromosomes in Chapter 2 and discuss related disorders in Chapter 15.) In humans and all other *eukaryotes* (organisms whose cells have nuclei; see Chapter 2 for more), a full set of chromosomes is stored in the nucleus of each cell. That means that practically every cell contains a complete set of instructions to build the entire organism! The instructions are packaged as *genes.* A gene determines exactly how a specific trait will be expressed. Genes and how they work are topics I discuss in detail in Chapter 11.

Molecular madness: Extracting DNA at home

Using this simple recipe, you can see DNA right in the comfort of your own home! You need a strawberry, salt, water, two clear jars or juice glasses, a sandwich bag, a measuring cup, a white coffee filter, clear liquid soap, and rubbing alcohol. (Other foods such as onions, bananas, kiwis, and tomatoes also work well if strawberries are unavailable.) After you've gathered these ingredients, follow these steps:

1. **Put slightly less than ⅜ cup of water into the measuring cup. Add ¼ teaspoon of salt and enough clear liquid soap to make ⅜ cup of liquid altogether. Stir gently until the salt dissolves into the solution.**

   The salt provides sodium ions needed for the chemical reaction that allows you to see the DNA in Step 6. The soap causes the cell walls to burst, freeing the DNA inside.

2. **Remove the stem from the strawberry, place the strawberry into the sandwich bag, and seal the bag. Mash the strawberry thoroughly until completely pulverized (I roll a juice glass repeatedly over my strawberry to pulverize it). Make sure you don't puncture the bag.**

3. **Add 2 teaspoons of the liquid soap-salt solution to the bag with the strawberry, and then reseal the bag. Mix gently by** compressing the bag or rocking the bag back and forth for at least 45 seconds to one minute.

4. **Pour the strawberry mixture through the coffee filter into a clean jar. Let the mixture drain into the jar for 10 minutes.**

   Straining gets rid of most of the cellular debris (a fancy word for gunk) and leaves behind the DNA in the clean solution.

5. **While the strawberry mixture is draining, pour ¼ cup of rubbing alcohol into a clean jar and put the jar in the freezer. After 10 minutes have elapsed, discard the coffee filter and pulverized strawberry remnants. Put the jar with the cold alcohol on a flat surface where it will be undisturbed, and pour the strained strawberry liquid into the alcohol.**

6. **Let the jar sit for at least 5 minutes, and then check out the result of your DNA experiment. The cloudy substance that forms in the alcohol layer is the DNA from the strawberry. The cold alcohol helps strip the water molecules from the outside of the DNA molecule, causing the molecule to collapse on itself and "fall out" of the solution.**

 Cells with nuclei are found only in eukaryotes; however, not every eukaryotic cell has a nucleus. For example, humans are eukaryotes, but human red blood cells don't have nuclei. For more on cells, flip to Chapter 2.

 The tutorial offered at www.umass.edu/molvis/tutorials/dna/ provides an excellent complement to the information on the structure of DNA I cover in this section. You can access incredible, interactive views of precisely how DNA is put together to form the double helix. A click-and-drag feature allows you to turn the molecule in any direction to better understand the structure of the genetic material, to highlight different parts of the molecule, and to see exactly how all the parts fit together.

Chemical ingredients of DNA

DNA is a remarkably durable molecule; it can be stored in ice or in a fossilized bone for thousands of years. DNA can even stay in one piece for as long as 100,000 years under the right conditions. This durability is why scientists can recover DNA from 14,000-year-old mammoths and learn that the mammoth is most closely related to today's Asian elephants. (Scientists have recovered ancient DNA from an amazing variety of organisms — check out the sidebar "Still around after all these years: Durable DNA" for more.) The root of DNA's extreme durability lies in its chemical and structural makeup.

CASE STUDY

Still around after all these years: Durable DNA

When an organism dies, it starts to decay and its DNA starts to break down (for DNA, this means breaking into smaller and smaller pieces). But if a dead organism dries out or freezes shortly after death, decay slows down or even stops. Because of this kind of interference with decay, scientists have been able to recover DNA from animals and humans that roamed the earth as many as 100,000 years ago. This recovered DNA tells scientists a lot about life and the conditions of the world long ago. But even this very durable molecule has its limits — about a million years or so.

In 1991, hikers in the Italian Alps discovered a human body frozen in a glacier. As the glacier melted, the retreating ice left behind a secret concealed for over 5,000 years: an ancient human. The Ice Man, renamed Otzi, has yielded amazing insight into what life was like in northern Italy thousands of years ago. Scientists have recovered DNA from this lonely shepherd, his clothing, and even the food in his stomach. Apparently, red deer and ibex meat were part of his last meal. His food was dusted with pollen from nearby trees, so even the forest he walked through can be identified!

By analyzing Otzi's mitochondrial (mt) DNA, which he inherited from his mother (see the "Mitochondrial DNA" section later in this chapter), scientists discovered that he wasn't related to any modern European population studied so far. A team of investigators from Australia, led by the late Thomas Loy, examined blood found on Otzi's clothing and possessions. Like modern forensic scientists, Loy's team determined that four different people's DNA fingerprints were present, in addition to Otzi's own (to find out how DNA fingerprints are used to solve modern crimes, check out Chapter 18). The team found blood from two different people on Otzi's arrow, a third person's blood on his knife, and a fourth person's blood on his clothing. These findings led people to speculate that he was involved in a fight shortly before he died.

Otzi isn't the only ancient human whose DNA scientists are analyzing. Neandertals were humans that roamed the earth up to about 30,000 years ago (give or take several centuries). Using 38,000-year-old mtDNA, researchers have discovered that Neandertals had a substantially different mtDNA profile than modern humans, suggesting that while modern humans and Neandertals lived at the same time, they probably didn't interbreed (or if they did, none of the descendants survived to be represented in human populations now). In addition, Neandertals were lactose-intolerant; they lacked the gene that codes for the enzyme that breaks down lactose (a sugar present in milk). Neandertals probably were able to speak much as we do — they carried a version of the gene associated with human speech.

Chemically, DNA is really simple. It's made of three components: nitrogen-rich bases, deoxyribose sugars, and phosphates. The three components, which I explain in the following sections, combine to form a *nucleotide* (see the section "Assembling the double helix: The structure of DNA" later in this chapter). Thousands of nucleotides come together in pairs to form a single molecule of DNA.

Covering the bases

Each DNA molecule contains thousands of copies of four specific nitrogen-rich bases:

- ✔ Adenine (A)
- ✔ Guanine (G)
- ✔ Cytosine (C)
- ✔ Thymine (T)

As you can see in Figure 6-1, the bases are comprised of carbon (C), hydrogen (H), nitrogen (N), and oxygen (O) atoms.

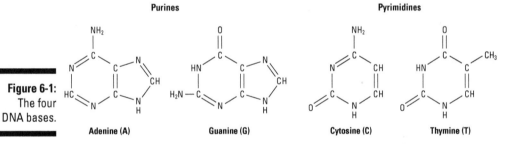

Figure 6-1: The four DNA bases.

The four bases come in two flavors:

- ✔ **Purines:** The two purine bases in DNA are adenine and guanine. If you were a chemist, you'd know that the word *purine* means a compound composed of two rings (check out adenine's and guanine's structures in Figure 6-1). If you're like me (not a chemist), you're likely still familiar with one common purine: caffeine.

- ✔ **Pyrimidines:** The two pyrimidine bases in DNA are cytosine and thymine. The term *pyrimidine* refers to chemicals that have a single six-sided ring structure (see cytosine's and thymine's structures in Figure 6-1).

Because they're rings, all four bases are flat molecules. And as flat molecules, they're able to stack up in DNA much like a stack of coins. The stacking arrangement accomplishes two things: It makes the molecule both compact and very strong.

It's been my experience that students and other folks get confused by spatial concepts where DNA is concerned. To see the chemical structures more easily, DNA is often drawn as if it were a flattened ladder. But in its true state, DNA isn't flat — it's three-dimensional. Because DNA is arranged in strands, it's also linear. One way to think about this structure is to look at a phone cord (that is, if you can find a phone that isn't cordless). A phone cord spirals in three dimensions, yet it's linear (rope-like) in form. That's sort of the shape DNA has, too.

The bases carry the information of DNA, but they can't bond together by themselves. Two more ingredients are needed: a special kind of sugar and a phosphate.

Adding a spoonful of sugar and a little phosphate

To make a complete nucleotide (thousands of which combine to make one DNA molecule), the bases must attach to deoxyribose and a phosphate molecule. *Deoxyribose* is ribose sugar that has lost one of its oxygen atoms. When your body breaks down *adenosine triphosphate* (ATP), the molecule your body uses to power your cells, ribose is released with a phosphate molecule still attached to it. Ribose loses an oxygen atom to become deoxyribose (see Figure 6-2) and holds onto its phosphate molecule, which is needed to transform a lone base into a nucleotide.

Figure 6-2:
The chemical structure of ribose and deoxyribose.

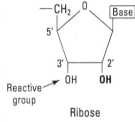

Ribose is the precursor for deoxyribose and is the chemical basis for RNA (see Chapter 9). The only difference between ribose and deoxyribose sugars is the presence or absence of an oxygen atom at the 2' site.

Chemical structures are numbered so you can keep track of where atoms, branches, chains, and rings appear. On ribose sugars, numbers are followed by an apostrophe (') to indicate the designation "prime." The addition of "prime" prevents confusion with numbered sites on other molecules that bond with ribose.

Deoxy- means that an oxygen atom is missing from the sugar molecule and defines the *D* in DNA. As an added touch, some authors write "2-" before the "deoxy-" to indicate which site lacks the oxygen — the number 2 site, in this case. The OH group at the 3' site of both ribose and deoxyribose is a *reactive group*. That means the oxygen atom at that site is free to interact chemically with other molecules.

Assembling the double helix: The structure of DNA

Nucleotides are the true building blocks of DNA. In Figure 6-3, you see the three components of a single nucleotide: one deoxyribose sugar, one phosphate, and one of the four bases. (Flip back to "Chemical ingredients of DNA" for the details of these components.) To make a complete DNA molecule, single nucleotides join to make chains that come together as matched pairs and form long double strands. This section walks you through the assembly process. To make the structure of DNA easier to understand, I start with how a single strand is put together.

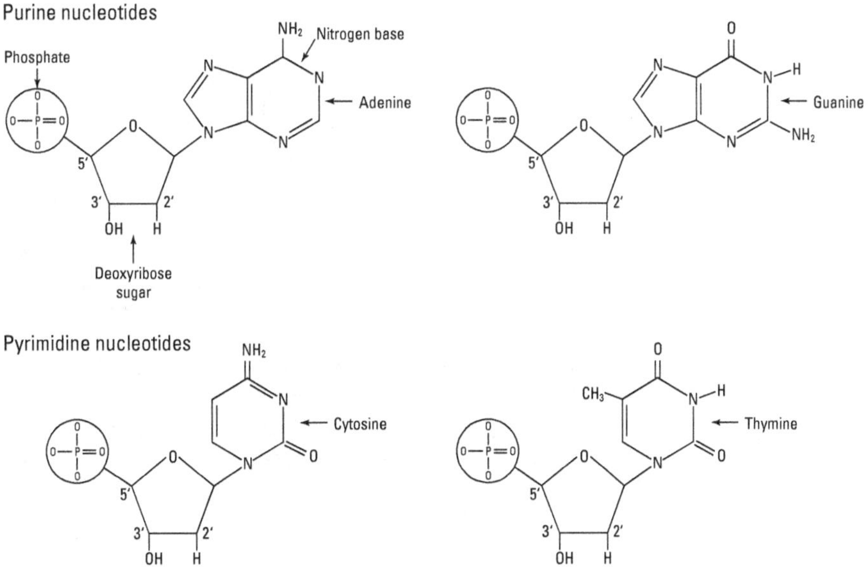

Purine nucleotides

Phosphate

Nitrogen base

← Adenine

← Guanine

Deoxyribose sugar

Figure 6-3: Chemical structures of the four nucleotides present in DNA.

Pyrimidine nucleotides

← Cytosine

← Thymine

DNA normally exists as a double-stranded molecule. In living things, new DNA strands are *always* put together using a preexisting strand as a pattern (see Chapter 7).

Starting with one: Weaving a single strand

Hundreds of thousands of nucleotides link together to form a strand of DNA, but they don't hook up haphazardly. Nucleotides are a bit like coins in that they have two "sides" — a phosphate side and a sugar side. Nucleotides can only make a connection by joining phosphates to sugars. The bases wind up parallel to each other (stacked like coins), and the sugars and phosphates run perpendicular to the stack of bases. A long strand of nucleotides put together in this way is called a *polynucleotide* strand (*poly* meaning "many"). In Figure 6-4, you can see how the nucleotides join together; a single strand would comprise one-half of the two-sided molecule (the chain of sugars, phosphates, and one of the pair of bases).

Because of the way the chemical structures are numbered, DNA has numbered "ends." The phosphate end is referred to as the 5' (5-prime) end, and the sugar end is referred to as the 3' (3-prime) end. (If you missed the discussion of how the chemical structure of deoxyribose is numbered, check out the earlier section "Adding a spoonful of sugar and a little phosphate.") The bonds between a phosphate and two sugar molecules in a nucleotide strand are collectively called a *phosphodiester bond.* This is a fancy way of saying that two sugars are linked together by a phosphate in between.

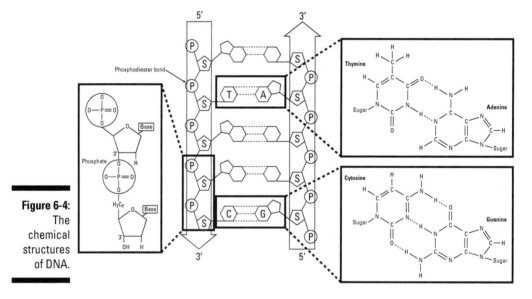

Figure 6-4:
The chemical structures of DNA.

After they're formed, strands of DNA don't enjoy being single; they're always looking for a match. The arrangement in which strands of DNA match up is very, very important. A number of rules dictate how two lonely strands of DNA find their perfect matches and eventually form the star of the show, the molecule you've been waiting for — the double helix.

Doubling up: Adding the second strand

A complete DNA molecule has

- ✔ Two side-by-side polynucleotide strands twisted together
- ✔ Bases attached in pairs in the center of the molecule
- ✔ Sugars and phosphates on the outside, forming a backbone

If you were to untwist a DNA double helix and lay it flat, it would look a lot like a ladder (refer to Figure 6-4). The bases are attached to each other in the center to make the rungs, and the sugars are joined together by phosphates to form the sides of the ladder. It sounds pretty straightforward, but this ladder arrangement has some special characteristics.

If you were to separate the ladder into two polynucleotide strands, you'd see that the strands are oriented in opposite directions (shown with arrows in Figure 6-4). The locations of the sugar and the phosphate give nucleotides heads and tails, two distinct ends. (If you skipped that part, it's in the earlier section "Starting with one: Weaving a single strand.") The heads-tails (or in this case, 5'-3') orientation applies here. This head-to-tail arrangement is called *antiparallel,* which is a fancy way of saying that something is parallel and running in opposite directions. Part of the reason the strands must be oriented this way is to guarantee that the dimensions of the DNA molecule are even along its entire length. If the strands were put together in a parallel arrangement, the angles between the atoms would be all wrong, and the strands wouldn't fit together.

The molecule is guaranteed to be the same size all over because the matching bases *complement* each other, making whole pieces that are all the same size. Adenine complements thymine, and guanine complements cytosine. The bases *always* match up in this complementary fashion. Therefore, in every DNA molecule, the amount of one base is equal to the amount of its complementary base. This condition is known as *Chargaff's rules* (see the "Obeying Chargaff's rules" section later in the chapter for more on the discovery of these rules).

Why can't the bases match up in other ways? First, purines are larger than pyrimidines (see "Covering the bases" earlier in the chapter). So matching like with like would introduce irregularities in the molecule's shape. Irregularities are bad because they can cause mistakes when the molecule is copied (see Chapter 13).

An important result of the bases' complementary pairing is the way in which the strands bond to each other. Hydrogen bonds form between the base pairs. The number of bonds between the base pairs differs; G-C (guanine-cytosine) pairs have three bonds, and A-T (adenine-thymine) pairs have only two. Figure 6-4 illustrates the structure of the untwisted double helix — specifically, the bonds between base pairs. Every DNA molecule has hundreds of thousands of base pairs, and each base pair has multiple bonds, so the rungs of the ladder are very strongly bonded together.

When inside a cell, the two strands of DNA gently twist around each other like a spiral staircase (or a strand of licorice, or the stripes on a candy cane . . . anybody else have a sweet tooth?). The antiparallel arrangement of the two strands is what causes the twist. Because the strands run in opposite directions, they pull the sides of the molecule in opposite directions, causing the whole thing to twist around itself.

Most naturally occurring DNA spirals clockwise, as you can see in Figure 6-5. A full twist (or complete turn) occurs every ten base pairs or so, with the bases safely protected on the inside of the helix. The helical form is one way that the information that DNA carries is protected from damage that can result in mutation.

The helical form creates two grooves on the outside of the molecule (see Figure 6-5). The major groove actually lets the bases peep out a little, which is important when it's time to read the information DNA contains (see Chapter 10).

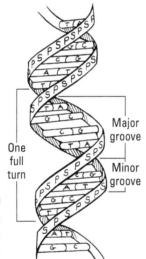

One
full
turn

Major
groove

Minor
groove

Figure 6-5:
The DNA
double helix.

Because base pairs in DNA are stacked on top of each other, chemical interactions make the center of the molecule repel water. Molecules that repel water are called *hydrophobic* (Greek for "afraid of water"). The outside of the DNA molecule is just the opposite; it attracts water. The result is that the inside of the helix remains safe and dry while the outside is encased in a "shell" of water.

Here are a few additional details about DNA that you need to know:

- ✔ **A DNA strand is measured by the number of base pairs it has.**

- ✔ **The sequence of bases in DNA isn't random.** The genetic information in DNA is carried in the order of the base pairs. In fact, the genes are encoded in the base sequences. Chapter 10 explains how the sequences are read and decoded.

- ✔ **DNA uses a preexisting DNA strand as a pattern or template in the assembly process.** DNA doesn't just form on its own. The process of making a new strand of DNA using a preexisting strand is called *replication.* I cover replication in detail in Chapter 7.

Examining Different Varieties of DNA

All DNA has the same four bases, obeys the same base pairing rules, and has the same double helix structure. No matter where it's found or what function it's carrying out, DNA is DNA. That said, different sets of DNA exist within a single organism. These sets carry out different genetic functions. In this section, I explain where the various DNAs are found and describe what they do.

Nuclear DNA

Nuclear DNA is DNA in cell nuclei, and it's responsible for the majority of functions that cells carry out. Nuclear DNA carries codes for *phenotype,* the physical traits of an organism (for a review of genetics terms, see Chapter 3). Nuclear DNA is packaged into chromosomes and passed from parent to offspring (see Chapter 2). When scientists talk about sequencing the human genome, they mean human nuclear DNA. (A *genome* is a full set of genetic instructions; see Chapter 11 for more about the human genome.) The nuclear genome of humans is comprised of the DNA from all 24 chromosomes (22 autosomes plus one X and one Y; see Chapter 2 for chromosome lingo).

Mitochondrial DNA

Animals, plants, and fungi all have *mitochondria* (for a review of cell parts, turn to Chapter 2). These powerhouses of the cell come with their own DNA, which is quite different in form (and inheritance) from nuclear DNA (see the preceding section). Each *mitochondrion* (the singular word for *mitochondria*) has many molecules of mitochondrial DNA — *mtDNA,* for short.

Mighty mitochondria

Mitochondrial DNA (mtDNA) bears a strong resemblance to a bacterial DNA. The striking similarities between mitochrondria and a certain bacteria called *Rickettsia* have led scientists to believe that mitochrondria originated from *Rickettsia*. *Rickettsia* causes typhus, a flu-like disease transmitted by flea bites (the flea first bites an infected rat or mouse and then bites a person). As for the similarities, neither *Rickettsia* nor mitochondria can live outside a cellular home, both have circular DNA, and both share similar DNA sequences (see Chapter 8 for how DNA sequences are compared between organisms). Instead of being parasitic like *Rickettsia,* however, mitochondria are considered *endosymbiotic,* meaning they must be inside a cell to work *(endo-)* and they provide something good to the cell *(-symbiotic).* In this case, the something good is energy.

Because mtDNA is passed only from mother to child (see the earlier section "Mitochondrial DNA" for an explanation), scientists have compared mtDNA from people all over the world to investigate the origins of modern humans. These comparisons have led some scientists to believe that all modern humans have one particular female ancestor in common, a woman who lived on the African continent about 200,000 years ago. This hypothetical woman has been called "Mitochondrial Eve," but she wasn't the only woman of her time. There were many women, but apparently, none of their descendants survived, making Eve what scientists refer to as our "most recent common ancestor," or MRCA. Some evidence suggests that all humans are descended from a rather small population of about 100,000 individuals, meaning that all people on earth have common ancestry.

Whereas human nuclear DNA is linear, mtDNA is circular (hoop-shaped). Human mtDNA is very short (slightly less than 17,000 base pairs) and has 37 genes, which account for almost the entire mtDNA molecule. These genes control cellular metabolism — the processing of energy inside the cell.

Half of your nuclear DNA came from your mom, and the other half came from your dad (see Chapter 2 for the scoop on how meiosis divides up chromosomes). But *all* your mtDNA came from your mom. All your mom's mtDNA came from her mom, and so on. All mtDNA is passed from mother to child in the cytoplasm of the egg cell (go to Chapter 2 for cell review).

Sperm cells have essentially no cytoplasm and thus, virtually no mitochondria. Special chemicals in the egg destroy the few mitochondria that sperm do possess.

Chloroplast DNA

Plants have three sets of DNA: nuclear in the form of chromosomes, mitochondrial, and *chloroplast DNA* (cpDNA). Chloroplasts are organelles found only in plants, and they're where *photosynthesis* (the conversion of light to chemical energy) occurs. To complicate matters, plants have mitochondria (and thus mtDNA) in their chloroplasts. Like mitochondria, chloroplasts probably originated from bacteria (see the sidebar "Mighty mitochondria").

Chloroplast DNA molecules are circular and fairly large (120,000–160,000 base pairs) but only have about 120 genes. Most of those genes supply information used to carry out photosynthesis. Inheritance of cpDNA can be either maternal or paternal, and cpDNA, along with mtDNA, is transmitted to offspring in the cytoplasm of the seed.

Digging into the History of DNA

Back when Mendel was poking around his pea pods in the early 1860s (see Chapter 3), neither he nor anybody else knew about DNA. DNA was discovered in 1868, but its importance as *the* genetic material wasn't appreciated until nearly a century later. This section gives you a rundown on how DNA and its role in inheritance was revealed.

Discovering DNA

In 1868, a Swiss medical student named Johann Friedrich Miescher isolated DNA for the first time. Miescher was working with white blood cells that he obtained from the pus drained out of surgical wounds (yes, this man was dedicated to his work). Eventually, Miescher established that the substance he called *nuclein* was rich in phosphorus and was acidic. Thus, one of his students renamed the substance *nucleic acid,* a name DNA still carries today. Like Mendel's findings on the inheritance of various plant traits, Miescher's work wasn't recognized for its importance until long after his death, and it took 84 years for DNA to be recognized as *the* genetic material. Until the early 1950s, everyone was sure that protein had to be the genetic material because, with only four bases, DNA seemed too simple.

In 1928, Frederick Griffith recognized that bacteria could acquire something — he wasn't quite sure what — from each other to transform harmless bacteria into deadly bacteria (see Chapter 22 for the whole story). A team of scientists led by Oswald Avery followed up on Griffith's experiments and determined that the "transforming principle" was DNA. Even though Avery's results were solid, scientists of the time were skeptical about the significance of DNA's role in inheritance. It took another elegant set of experiments using a virus that infected bacteria to convince the scientific community that DNA was the real deal.

Alfred Chase and Martha Hershey worked with a virus called a *bacteriophage* (which means "eats bacteria," even though the virus actually ruptures the bacteria rather than eats it). Bacteriophages grab onto the bacteria's cell wall and inject something into the bacteria. At the time of Hershey and Chase's experiment, the injected substance was unidentified. The bacteriophage produces its offspring inside the cell and then bursts the cell wall open to free the viral "offspring." Offspring carry the same traits as the original attacking bacteriophage, so it was certain that whatever got injected must be the genetic material, given that most of the bacteriophage stays stuck on the outside of the cell. Hershey and Chase attached radioactive chemicals to track different parts of the bacteriophage; for example, they used sulfur to track protein, because proteins contain sulfur, and DNA was marked with phosphorus (because of the sugar-phosphate backbone). Hershey and Chase reasoned that offspring bacteriophages would get marked with one or the other, depending on which — DNA or protein — turned out to be the genetic material. The results showed that the viruses injected only DNA into the bacterial cell to infect it. All the protein stayed stuck on the outside of the bacterial cell. They published their findings in 1952, when Hershey was merely 24 years old!

Obeying Chargaff's rules

Long before Hershey and Chase published their pivotal findings, Erwin Chargaff read Oswald Avery's paper on DNA as the transforming principle (see Chapter 22) and immediately changed the focus of his entire research program. Unlike many scientists of his day, Chargaff recognized that DNA was the genetic material.

Chargaff focused his research on learning as much as he could about the chemical components of DNA. Using DNA from a wide variety of organisms, he discovered that all DNA had something in common: When DNA was broken into its component bases, the amount of guanine fluctuated wildly from one organism to another, but the amount of guanine always equaled the amount of cytosine. Likewise, in every organism he studied, the amount of adenine equaled the amount of thymine. Published in 1949, these findings are so consistent that they're called *Chargaff's rules*. Unfortunately, Chargaff was unable to realize the meaning of his own work. He knew that the ratios said something important about the structure of DNA, but he couldn't figure out what that something was. It took a pair of young scientists named Watson and Crick — Chargaff called them "two pitchmen in search of a helix" — to make the breakthrough.

Hard feelings and the helix: Franklin, Wilkins, Watson, and Crick

If you don't know the name Rosalind Franklin, you should. Her data on the shape of the DNA molecule revealed its structure as a double helix. Watson and Crick get all the credit for identifying the double helix, but Franklin did much of the work. While researching the structure of DNA at King's College,

London, in the early 1950s, Franklin bounced X-rays off the molecule to produce incredibly sharp, detailed photos of it. Franklin's photos show a DNA molecule from the end, not the side, so it's difficult to envision the side view of the double helix you normally see. Yet Franklin knew she was looking at a helix.

Meanwhile, James Watson, a 23-year-old postdoctoral fellow at Cambridge, England, was working with a 38-year-old graduate student named Francis Crick. Together, they were building an enormous model of metal sticks and wooden balls, trying to figure out the structure of the same molecule Franklin had photographed.

Franklin was supposed to be collaborating with Maurice Wilkins, another scientist in her research group, but she and Wilkins despised each other (because of a switch in research projects in which Franklin was instructed to take over Wilkins's project without his knowledge). As their antagonism grew, so did Wilkins's friendship with Watson. What happened next is the stuff of science infamy. Just a few weeks before Franklin was ready to publish her findings, Wilkins showed Franklin's photographs of the DNA molecule to Watson — without her knowledge or permission! By giving Watson access to Franklin's data, Wilkins gave Watson and Crick the scoop on the competition.

Watson and Crick cracked the mystery of DNA structure using Chargaff's rules (see the section "Obeying Chargaff's rules" for details) and Franklin's measurements of the molecule. They deduced that the structure revealed by Franklin's photo, hastily drawn from memory by Watson, had to be a double helix, and Chargaff's rules pointed to bases in pairs. The rest of the structure came together like a big puzzle, and they rushed to publish their discovery in 1953. Franklin's paper, complete with the critical photos of the DNA molecule, was published in the same issue of the journal *Nature*.

In 1962, Watson, Crick, and Wilkins were honored with the Nobel Prize. Franklin wasn't properly credited for her part in their discovery but couldn't protest because she had died of ovarian cancer in 1957. It's quite possible that Franklin's cancer was the result of long-term exposure to X-rays during her scientific career. In a sense, Franklin sacrificed her life for science.

Chapter 7

Replication: Copying Your DNA

....

....

*E*verything in genetics relies on *replication* — the process of copying DNA accurately, quickly, and efficiently. Replication is part of reproduction (producing eggs and sperm), development (making all the cells needed by a growing embryo), and maintaining normal life (replacing skin, blood, and muscle cells).

Before meiosis can occur (see Chapter 2), the entire genome must be replicated so that a potential parent can make the eggs or sperm necessary for creating offspring. After fertilization occurs, the growing embryo must have the right genetic instructions in every cell to make all the tissues needed for life. As life outside the womb goes on, almost every cell in your body needs a copy of the entire genome to ensure that the genes that carry out the business of living are present and ready for action. For example, because you're constantly replacing your skin cells and white blood cells, your DNA is being replicated right now so that your cells have the genes they need to work properly.

This chapter explains all the details of the fantastic molecular photocopier that allows DNA — the stuff of life — to do its job. First, you tackle the basics of how DNA's structure provides a pattern for copying itself. Then, you find out about all the enzymes — those helpful protein workhorses — that do the labor of opening up the double-stranded DNA and assembling the building blocks of DNA into a new strand. Finally, you see how the copying process works, from beginning (origins) to ends (telomeres).

Unzipped: Creating the Pattern for More DNA

DNA is the ideal material for carrying genetic information because it

- ✔ Stores vast amounts of complex information *(genotype)* that can be "translated" into physical characteristics *(phenotype)*

- ✔ Can be copied quickly and accurately

- ✔ Is passed down from one generation to the next (in other words, it's *heritable*)

When James D. Watson and Francis Crick proposed the double helix as the structure of DNA (see Chapter 6 for coverage of DNA), they ended their 1953 paper with a pithy sentence about replication. That one little sentence paved the way for their next major publication, which hypothesized how replication may work. It's no accident that Watson and Crick won the Nobel Prize; their genius was uncanny and amazingly accurate. Without their discovery of the double helix, they never could've figured out replication, because the trick that DNA pulls off during replication depends entirely on how DNA is put together in the first place.

If you skipped Chapter 6, which focuses on how DNA is put together, you may want to skim over that material now. The main points about DNA you need to know to understand replication are:

- ✔ DNA is double-stranded.

- ✔ The nucleotide building blocks of DNA always match up in a complementary fashion — A (adenosine) with T (thymine) and C (cytosine) with G (guanine).

- ✔ DNA strands run antiparallel (that is, in opposite directions) to each other.

If you were to unzip a DNA molecule by breaking all the hydrogen bonds between the bases, you'd have two strands, and each would provide the pattern to create the other. During replication, special helper chemicals called *enzymes* bring matching (complementary) nucleotide building blocks to pair with the bases on each strand. The result is two exact copies built on the *templates* that the unzipped original strands provide.

Figure 7-1 shows how the original double-stranded DNA supplies a template to make copies of itself. This mode of replication is called *semiconservative*. No, this isn't how DNA may vote in the next election! In this case, semiconservative means that only half the molecule is "conserved," or left in its original state. (*Conservative,* in the genetic sense, means keeping something protected in its original state.)

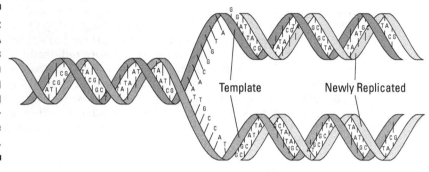

Figure 7-1: DNA provides its own pattern for copying itself using semiconservative replication.

Template   Newly Replicated

At Columbia University in 1957, J. Herbert Taylor, Philip Woods, and Walter Hughes used the cell cycle to determine how DNA is copied (see Chapter 2 for a review of mitosis and the cell cycle). They came up with two possibilities: conservative or semiconservative replication.

Figure 7-2 shows how conservative replication may work. For both conservative and semiconservative replication, the original, double-stranded molecule comes apart and provides the template for building new strands. The result of semiconservative replication is two complete, double-stranded molecules, each composed of half "new" and half "old" DNA (which is what you see in Figure 7-1). Following conservative replication, the complete, double-stranded copies are composed of all "new" DNA, and the templates come back together to make one molecule composed of "old" DNA (as you can see in Figure 7-2).

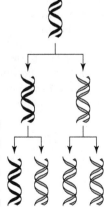

Figure 7-2: Conservative replication.

To sort out replication, Taylor and his colleagues exposed the tips of a plant's roots to water that contained a radioactive chemical. This chemical was a form of the nucleotide building block *thymine,* which is found in DNA. Before cells in the root tips divided, their chromosomes incorporated the radioactive thymine as part of newly replicated DNA. In the first step of the experiment, Taylor and his team let the root tips grow for eight hours. That was just long enough for the DNA of the cells in the growing tips to replicate. The researchers collected some cells after this first step to see whether one or both sister chromatids of each chromosome were radioactive. Then, for the second step, they put the root tips in water with no radioactive chemical in it. After the cells started dividing, Taylor and his team examined the replicated chromosomes while they were in *metaphase* (when the replicated chromosomes, called *sister chromatids,* are all lined up together in the center of the cell, before they're pulled apart to opposite ends of the soon-to-divide cell; see Chapter 2).

The radioactivity allowed Taylor and his team to trace the fate of the template strands after replication was completed and determine whether the strands stayed together with their copies (semiconservative) or not (conservative). They examined the results of both steps of the experiment to ensure that their conclusions were accurate.

If replication was semiconservative, Taylor, Woods, and Hughes expected to find that one sister chromatid of the replicated chromosome would be radioactive and the other would be radiation-free — and that's what they got. Figure 7-3 shows how their results ended up as they did. The shaded chromosomes represent the ones containing the radioactive thymine. After one round of replication in the presence of the radioactive thymine (Step 1 in Figure 7-3), the entire chromosome appears radioactive.

If Taylor and his team could have seen the DNA molecules themselves (as you do figuratively here), they would have known that one strand of each double-stranded molecule contained radioactive thymine and the other did not (the radioactive strands are depicted with a thicker line). After one round of replication without access to the radioactive thymine (Step 2 in Figure 7-3), one sister chromatid was radioactive, and the other was not. That's because each strand from Step 1 provided a template for semiconservative replication: The radioactive strand provided one template, and the nonradioactive strand provided the other. After replication was completed, the templates remained paired with the new strands. This experiment showed conclusively that DNA replication is truly semiconservative — each replicated molecule of DNA is half "new" and half "old."

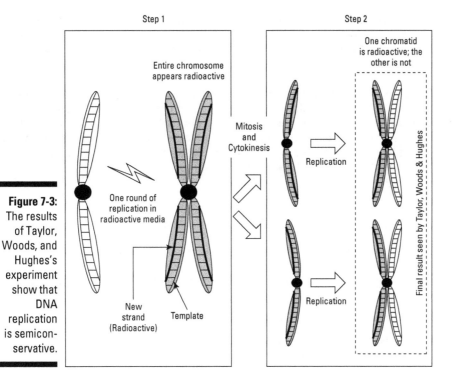

Figure 7-3:
The results
of Taylor,
Woods, and
Hughes's
experiment
show that
DNA
replication
is semicon-
servative.

How DNA Copies Itself

Replication occurs during interphase of each cell cycle, just before prophase
in both mitosis and meiosis. If you skipped over Chapter 2, you may want
to take a quick glance at it to get an idea of when replication occurs with
respect to the life of a cell.

The process of replication follows a very specific order:

1. The helix is opened up to expose single strands of DNA.

2. Nucleotides are strung together to make new partner strands for the two
   original strands.

DNA replication was first studied in bacteria, which are *prokaryotic* (lacking
cell nuclei). All nonbacterial life forms (including humans) are *eukaryotes*
(composed of cells with nuclei). Prokaryotic and eukaryotic DNA replication
differ in a few ways. Basically, bacteria use slightly different versions of the

same enzymes that eukaryotic cells use, and most of those enzymes have similar names. If you understand prokaryotic replication, which I explain in this section, you have enough background to understand the details of eukaryotic replication, too.

Most eukaryotic DNA is linear, whereas most bacterial DNA (and your mitochondrial DNA) is circular. The shape of the chromosome (an endless loop versus a string) doesn't affect the process of replication at all. However, the shape means that circular DNAs have special problems to solve when replicating their hoop-shaped chromosomes. See the section "How Circular DNAs Replicate" later in this chapter to find out more.

Meeting the replication crew

For successful replication, several players must be present:

- ✔ **Template DNA,** a double-stranded molecule that provides a pattern to copy
- ✔ **Nucleotides,** the building blocks necessary to make new DNA
- ✔ **Enzymes and various proteins** that do the unzipping and assembly work of replication, called *DNA synthesis*

Template DNA

In addition to the material earlier in this chapter detailing how the template DNA is replicated semiconservatively (see "Unzipped: Creating the Pattern for More DNA"), it's vitally important for you to understand all the meanings of the term *template*.

- ✔ Every organism's DNA exists in the form of chromosomes. Therefore, the chromosomes undergoing replication and the template DNA uses during replication are one and the same.
- ✔ Both strands of each double-stranded original molecule are copied, and therefore, each of the two strands serves as a template (that is, a pattern) for replication.

The bases of the template DNA provide critical information needed for replication. Each new base of the newly replicated strand must be *complementary* (that is, an exact match; see Chapter 6 for more about the complementary nature of DNA) to the base opposite it on the template strand. Together, template and replicated DNA (like you see in Figure 7-1) make two identical copies of the original, double-stranded molecule.

Nucleotides

DNA is made up of thousands of nucleotides linked together in paired strands. (If you want more details about the chemical and physical constructions of DNA, flip to Chapter 6.) The nucleotide building blocks of DNA that come together during replication start in the form of *deoxyribonucleoside triphosphates,* or *dNTPs,* which are made up of

- ✔ A sugar (deoxyribose)
- ✔ One of four bases (adenine, guanine, thymine, or cytosine)
- ✔ Three phosphates

Figure 7-4 shows a dNTP being incorporated into a double-stranded DNA molecule. The dNTPs used in replication are very similar in chemical structure to the ones in double-stranded DNA (you can refer to Figure 6-3 in Chapter 6 to compare a nucleotide to the dNTP in Figure 7-4). The key difference is the number of phosphate groups — each dNTP has three phosphates, and each nucleotide has one.

Take a look at the blowup of the dNTP in Figure 7-4. The three phosphate groups (the "tri-" part of the name) are at the top end (usually referred to as the 5-prime, or 5') of the molecule. At the bottom left of the molecule, also known as the 3-prime (3') spot, is a little tail made of an oxygen atom attached to a hydrogen atom (collectively called an *OH group* or a *reactive group*). The oxygen atom in the OH tail is present to allow a nucleotide in an existing DNA strand to hook up with a dNTP; multiple connections like this one eventually produce the long chain of DNA. (For details on the numbered points of a molecule, such as 5' or 3', see Chapter 6.)

When DNA is being replicated, the OH tail on the 3' end of the last nucleotide in the chain reacts with the phosphates of a newly arrived dNTP (as shown in the right-hand part of Figure 7-4). Two of the dNTP's three phosphates get chopped off, and the remaining phosphate forms a phosphodiester bond with the previously incorporated nucleotide (see Chapter 6 for all the details about phosphodiester bonds). Hydrogen bonds form between the base of the template strand and the complementary base of the dNTP (see Chapter 6 for more on the bonds that form between bases). This reaction — losing two phosphates to form a phosphodiester bond and hydrogen bonding — converts the dNTP into a nucleotide. (The only real difference between dNTP and the nucleotide it becomes is the number of phosphates each carries.) Remember, the template DNA must be single-stranded for these reactions to occur (see "Splitting the helix" later in this chapter).

Each dNTP incorporated during replication must be complementary to the base it's hooked up with on the template strand.

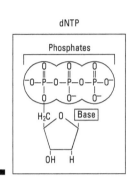

Figure 7-4:
Connecting the chemical building blocks (nucleotides as dNTPs) during DNA synthesis.

A nucleotide is a deoxyribose sugar, a base, and a phosphate joined together as a unit. A nucleotide is a nucleotide regardless of whether it's part of a whole DNA molecule or not. A dNTP is also a nucleotide, just a special sort: a nucleotide triphosphate.

Enzymes

Replication can't occur without the help of a huge suite of enzymes. *Enzymes* are chemicals that cause reactions. Generally, enzymes come in two flavors: those that put things together and those that take things apart. Both types are used during replication.

Although you can't always tell the function of an enzyme (building or destroying) by its name, you can always identify enzymes because they end in *-ase*. The *-ase* suffix usually follows a reference to what the enzyme acts on. For example, the enzyme helicase acts on the helix of DNA to make it single-stranded (helix + ase = helicase).

So many enzymes are used in replication that it's hard to keep up with them all. However, the main players and their roles are:

- ✔ **Helicase:** Opens up the double helix
- ✔ **Gyrase:** Prevents the helix from forming knots

✓ **Primase:** Lays down a short piece of RNA (a primer) to get replication started (see Chapter 8 for more on RNA)

✓ **DNA polymerase:** Adds dNTPs to build the new strand of DNA

✓ **Ligase:** Seals the gaps between newly replicated pieces of DNA

✓ **Telomerase:** Replicates the ends of chromosomes (the telomeres) — a very special job

Prokaryotes have 5 forms of DNA polymerase, and eukaryotes have at least 13 forms. In prokaryotes, DNA polymerase III is the enzyme that performs replication. DNA polymerase I removes RNA primers and replaces them with DNA. DNA polymerases II, IV, and V all work to repair damaged DNA and carry out proofreading activities. Eukaryotes use a whole different set of DNA polymerases. (For more details on eukaryotic DNA replication, see the section "Replication in Eukaryotes" later in the chapter.)

Splitting the helix

DNA replication starts at very specific spots, called *origins,* along the double-stranded template molecule. Bacterial chromosomes are so short (only about 4 million base pairs; see Chapter 11) that only one origin for replication is needed. Copying bigger genomes would take far too long if each chromosome had only one origin, so to make the process of copying very rapid, human chromosomes each have thousands of origins. (See the section "Replication in Eukaryotes" later in this chapter for more details on how human DNA is replicated.)

Special proteins called *initiators* move along the double-stranded template DNA until they encounter a group of bases that are in a specific order. These bases represent the origin for replication; think of them as a road sign with the message: "Start replication here." The initiator proteins latch onto the template at the origin by looping the helix around themselves like looping a string around your finger. The initiator proteins then make a very small opening in the double helix.

Helicase (the enzyme that opens up the double helix) finds this opening and starts breaking the hydrogen bonds between the complementary template strands to expose a few hundred bases and split the helix open even wider. DNA has such a strong tendency to form double-strands that if another protein didn't come along to hold the single strands exposed by helicase apart, they'd snap right back together again. These proteins, called *single-stranded-binding* (SSB) proteins, prop the two strands apart so replication can occur. Figure 7-5 shows the whole process of replication. For now, focus on the part that shows how helicase breaks the strands apart as it moves along the double helix and how the strands are kept separated and untwisted.

If you've had any experience with yarn or fishing line, you know that if string gets twisted together and you try to pull the strands apart, a knot forms. This same problem occurs when opening up the double helix of DNA. When helicase starts pulling the two strands apart, the opening of the helix sends extra turns along the intact helix. To prevent DNA from ending up a knotty mess, an enzyme called *gyrase* comes along to relieve the tension. Exactly how gyrase does this is unclear, but some researchers think that gyrase actually snips the DNA apart temporarily to let the twisted parts relax and then seals the molecule back together again.

Priming the pump

When helicase opens up the molecule, a Y forms at the opening. This Y is called a *replication fork*. You can see a replication fork in Figure 7-5, where the helicase has split the DNA helix apart. For every opening in the double-stranded molecule, two forks form on opposite sides of the opening. DNA replication is very particular in that it can only proceed in one direction: 5-prime to 3-prime (5' → 3'). In Figure 7-5, the top strand runs 3' → 5' from left to right, and the bottom strand runs 5' → 3' (that is, the template strands are *antiparallel;* see Chapter 6 for more about the importance of the antiparallel arrangement of DNA strands).

Replication must proceed antiparallel to the template, running 5' to 3'. Therefore, replication on the top strand runs right to left; on the bottom strand, replication runs left to right.

After helicase splits the molecule open (as I explain in the preceding section), two naked strands of template DNA are left. Replication can't start on the naked template strands because it hasn't started yet. (That sounds a bit like Yogi Berra saying "It ain't over 'til it's over," doesn't it?) All funny business aside, nucleotides can only form chains if a nucleotide is already present with a free reactive tail on which to attach the incoming dNTP. DNA solves the problem of starting replication by inserting *primers,* little complementary starter strands made of RNA (refer to Figure 7-5).

Primase, the enzyme that manufactures the RNA primers for replication, lays down primers at each replication fork so that DNA synthesis can proceed from 5' → 3' on both strands. The RNA primers made by primase are only about 10 or 12 nucleotides long. They're complementary to the single strands of DNA and end with the same sort of OH tail found on a nucleotide of DNA. (To find out more about RNA, flip to Chapter 8.) DNA uses the primers' free OH tails to add nucleotides in the form of dNTPs (see "Nucleotides" earlier in this chapter); the primers are later snipped out and replaced with DNA (see "Joining all the pieces" later in this chapter).

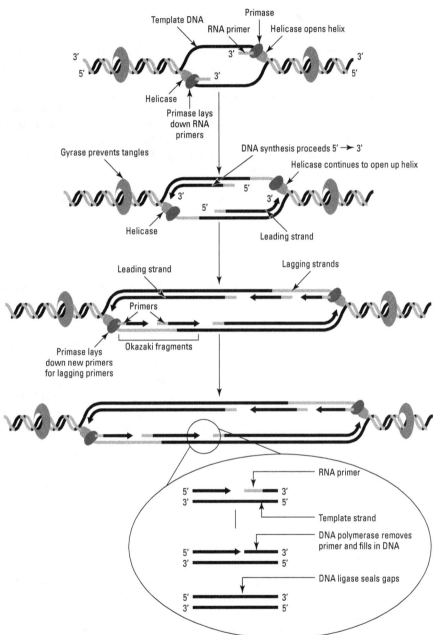

Figure 7-5:
The process of replication.

Leading and lagging

As soon as the primers are in place, actual replication can get underway. *DNA polymerase* is the enzyme that does all the work of replication. At the OH tail of each primer, DNA polymerase tacks on dNTPs by snipping off two phosphates and forming phosphodiester bonds (see Chapter 6). Meanwhile, helicase opens up the helix ahead of the growing chain to expose more template strand. From Figure 7-5, it's easy to see that replication can just zoom along this way — but only on one strand (in this case, the top strand in Figure 7-5). The replicated strands keep growing continuously 5' → 3' as helicase makes the template available.

At the same time, on the opposite strand, new primers have to be added to take advantage of the newly available template. The new primers are necessary because a naked strand (the bottom one in Figure 7-5) lacking the necessary free nucleotide for chain-building is created by the ongoing splitting of the helix.

Thus, the interaction of opening the helix and synthesizing DNA 5' → 3' on one strand while laying down new primers on the other leads to the formation of *leading* and *lagging strands*.

- **Leading strands:** The strands formed in one bout of uninterrupted DNA synthesis (you can see a leading strand in Figure 7-6). Leading strands follow the lead, so to speak, of helicase.

- **Lagging strands:** The strands that are begun over and over as new primers are laid down. Synthesis of the lagging strands stops when they reach the 5' end of a primer elsewhere on the strand. Lagging strands "lag behind" leading strands in the sense of frequent starting and stopping versus continuous replication. (Replication happens so rapidly that there's no difference in the amount of time it takes to replicate leading and lagging strands.) The short pieces of DNA formed by lagging DNA synthesis have a special name: *Okazaki fragments,* named for the scientist, Reiji Okazaki, who discovered them.

Joining all the pieces

After the template strands are replicated, the newly synthesized strands have to be modified to be complete and whole:

- The RNA primers must be removed and replaced with DNA.

- The Okazaki fragments formed by lagging DNA synthesis must be joined together.

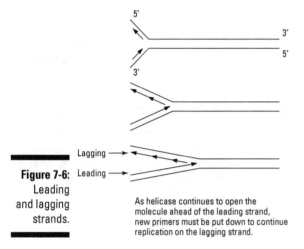

Figure 7-6:
Leading and lagging strands.

As helicase continues to open the molecule ahead of the leading strand, new primers must be put down to continue replication on the lagging strand.

A special kind of DNA polymerase moves along the newly synthesized strands seeking out the RNA primers. When DNA polymerase encounters the short bits of RNA, it snips them out and replaces them with DNA. (Refer to Figure 7-5 for an illustration of this process.) The snipping out and replacing of RNA primers proceeds in the usual 5' → 3' direction of replication and follows the same procedures as normal DNA synthesis (adding dNTPs and forming phosphodiester bonds).

After the primers are removed and replaced, one phosphodiester bond is missing between the Okazaki fragments. *Ligase* is the enzyme that seals these little gaps (*ligate* means to join things together). Ligase has the special ability to form phosphodiester bonds without adding a new nucleotide.

Proofreading replication

Despite its complexity, replication is unbelievably fast. In humans, replication speeds along at about 2,000 bases a minute. Bacterial replication is even faster at about 1,000 bases per *second!* Working at that speed, it's really no surprise that DNA polymerase makes mistakes — about one in every 100,000 bases is incorrect. Fortunately, DNA polymerase can use the backspace key!

DNA polymerase constantly checks its work though a process called *proofreading* — the same way I proofread my work as I wrote this book. DNA polymerase looks over its shoulder, so to speak, and keeps track of how well the newly added bases fit with the template strand. If an incorrect base is added, DNA polymerase backs up and cuts the incorrect base out. The snipping process is called *exonuclease activity,* and the correction process requires DNA polymerase to move 3' → 5' instead of the usual 5' → 3' direction. DNA proofreading eliminates most of the mistakes made by DNA polymerase, and the result is nearly error-free DNA synthesis. Generally, replication (after proofreading) has an astonishingly low error rate of one in 10 million base pairs.

If DNA polymerase misses an incorrect base, special enzymes come along after replication is complete to carry out another process, called *mismatch repair* (much like my editors checked my proofreading). The mismatch repair enzymes detect the bulges that occur along the helix when noncomplementary bases are paired up, and the enzymes snip the incorrect base out of the newly synthesized strand. These enzymes replace the incorrect base with the correct one and, like ligase, seal up the gaps to finish the repair job.

Replication is a complicated process that uses a dizzying array of enzymes. The key points to remember are:

- Replication always starts at an origin.

- Replication can only occur when template DNA is single-stranded.

- RNA primers must be put down before replication can proceed.

- Replication always moves 5' → 3'.

- Newly synthesized strands are exact complementary matches to template ("old") strands.

Replication in Eukaryotes

Although replication in prokaryotes and eukaryotes is very similar, you need to know about four differences:

- For each of their chromosomes, eukaryotes have many, many origins for replication. Prokaryotes generally have one origin per circular chromosome.

- The enzymes that prokaryotes and eukaryotes use for replication are similar but not identical. Compared to prokaryotes, eukaryotes have many more DNA polymerases, and these DNA polymerases carry out other functions besides replication.

- Linear chromosomes, found in eukaryotes, require special enzymes to replicate the *telomeres* — the ends of chromosomes.

- Eukaryotic chromosomes are tightly wound around special proteins in order to package large amounts of DNA into very small cell nuclei.

Pulling up short: Telomeres

When linear chromosomes replicate, the ends of the chromosomes, called *telomeres,* present special challenges. These challenges are handled in different ways depending on what kind of cell division is taking place (that is, mitosis versus meiosis).

At the completion of replication for cells in mitosis, a short part of the telomere tips is left single-stranded and unreplicated. A special enzyme comes along and snips off this unreplicated part of the telomere. Losing this bit of DNA at the end of the chromosome isn't as big a deal as it may seem, because telomeres, in addition to being the ends of chromosomes, are long strings of *junk DNA.* Junk DNA doesn't contain genes but may have other important functions (see Chapter 11 for the details).

For telomeres, being junk DNA is good because when telomeres get snipped off, the chromosomes aren't damaged too much and the genes still work just fine — up to a point. After many rounds of replication, all the junk DNA at the ends of the chromosomes is snipped off (essentially, the chromosomes run out of junk DNA), and actual genes themselves are affected. Therefore, when the chromosomes of a mitotic cell (like a skin cell, for example) get too short, the cell dies through a process called *apoptosis.* (I cover apoptosis in detail in Chapter 14.) Paradoxically, cell death through apoptosis is a good thing because it protects you from the ravages of mutations, which can cause cancer.

If the cell is being divided as part of meiosis, telomere snipping is not okay. The telomeres must be replicated completely so that perfectly complete, full-size chromosomes are passed on to offspring. An enzyme called *telomerase* takes care of replicating the ends of the chromosomes. Figure 7-7 gives you an idea of how telomerase replicates telomeres. Primase lays down a primer at the very tip of the chromosome as part of the normal replication process. DNA synthesis proceeds from 5' → 3' as usual, and then, a DNA polymerase comes along and snips out the RNA primer from 5' → 3'. Without telomerase, the process stops, leaving a tail of unreplicated, single-stranded DNA flapping around (this is what happens during mitosis).

Telomerase easily detects the unreplicated telomere because telomeres have long sections of guanines, or Gs. Telomerase contains a section of cytosine-rich RNA, allowing the enzyme to bind to the unreplicated, guanine-rich telomere. Telomerase then uses its own RNA to extend the unreplicated DNA template by about 15 nucleotides. Scientists suspect that the single-stranded template then folds back on itself to provide a free OH tail to replicate the rest of the telomere in the absence of a primer (see "Priming the pump" earlier in this chapter).

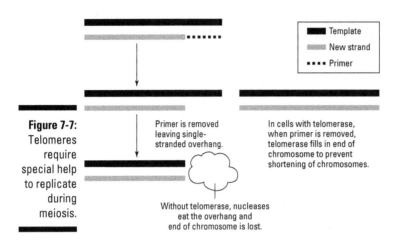

Legend:
- Template
- New strand
- Primer

Figure 7-7: Telomeres require special help to replicate during meiosis.

Primer is removed leaving single-stranded overhang.

Without telomerase, nucleases eat the overhang and end of chromosome is lost.

In cells with telomerase, when primer is removed, telomerase fills in end of chromosome to prevent shortening of chromosomes.

Finishing the job

Your DNA (and that of all eukaryotes) is tightly wound around special structures called *nucleosomes* (not to be confused with nucleotides) so that the enormous molecule fits neatly into the cell nucleus. (See Chapter 6 for the details on just how big a molecule of DNA really is.) Like replication, packaging DNA is a very rapid process. It happens so quickly that scientists aren't exactly sure how DNA gets unwrapped from the nucleosomes to replicate and then gets wrapped around the nucleosomes again.

In the packaging stage, DNA is normally twisted tightly around hundreds of thousands of nucleosomes, much like string wrapped around beads. The whole "necklace" gets wound very tightly around itself in a process called *supercoiling*. Supercoiling is what allows the 3.5 billion base pairs of DNA that make up your 46 chromosomes to fit inside the microscopic nuclei of your cells. Altogether, about 150 base pairs of DNA are wrapped around each nucleosome and secured in place with a little protein called a *histone*. In Figure 7-8, you can see the nucleosomes, histones, and supercoiled "necklace."

DNA is packaged in this manner both before and after replication. Because only 30 or 40 base pairs of DNA are exposed between nucleosomes, the DNA must be removed from the nucleosomes in order to replicate. If it isn't removed from the nuclesomes, the enzymes used in replication aren't able to access the entire molecule.

As helicase opens up the DNA molecule during replication, an unidentified enzyme strips off the nucleosome beads at the same time. As soon as the DNA is replicated, the DNA (both old and new) is immediately wrapped around waiting nucleosomes. Studies show that the old nucleosomes (from before replication) are reused along with newly assembled nucleosomes to package the freshly replicated DNA molecule.

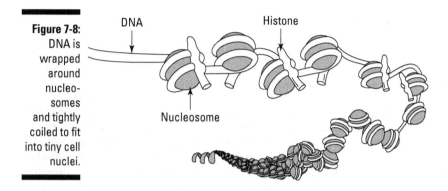

Figure 7-8:
DNA is wrapped around nucleo-somes and tightly coiled to fit into tiny cell nuclei.

DNA

Histone

Nucleosome

How Circular DNAs Replicate

Circular DNAs are replicated in three different ways, as shown in Figure 7-9. Different organisms take different approaches to solve the problem of replicating hoop-shaped chromosomes. Theta replication is used by most bacteria, including *E. coli*. Viruses use rolling circle replication to rapidly manufacture vast numbers of copies of their genomes. Finally, human mitochondrial DNA and the chloroplast DNA of plants both use D-loop replication.

Theta

Theta replication refers to the shape the chromosome takes on during the replication process. After the helix splits apart, a bubble forms, giving the chromosome a shape reminiscent of the Greek letter theta (Θ; see Figure 7-9). Bacterial chromosomes have only one origin of replication (see "Splitting the helix"), so after helicase opens the double helix, replication proceeds in both directions simultaneously, rapidly copying the entire molecule. As I describe in the section "Leading and lagging," leading and lagging strands form, and ligase seals the gaps in the newly synthesized DNA to complete the strands. Ultimately, theta replication produces two intact, double-stranded molecules.

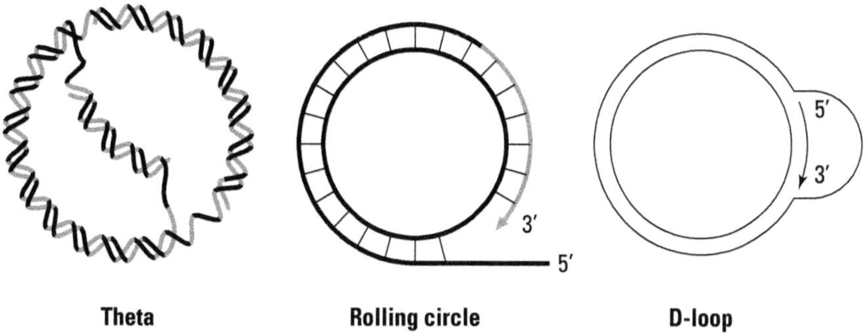

Figure 7-9:
Circular DNA can be replicated in one of three ways.

3′

5′

5′

3′

Theta   **Rolling circle**   **D-loop**

Rolling circle

Rolling circle replication creates an odd situation. No primer is needed because the double-stranded template is broken at the origin to provide a free OH tail to start replication. As replication proceeds, the inner strand is copied continuously as a leading strand (refer to Figure 7-9). Meanwhile, the broken strand is stripped off. As soon as enough of the broken strand is freed, a primer is laid down so replication can occur as the broken strand is stripped away from its complement. Thus, rolling circle replication is continuous on one strand and lagging on the other. As soon as replication is completed for one copy of the genome, the new copies are used as templates for additional rounds of replication. Viral genomes are often very small (only a few thousand base pairs), so rolling circle replication is an extremely rapid process that produces hundreds of thousands of copies of viral DNA in only a few minutes.

D-loop

Like rolling circle replication, *D-loop replication* creates a displaced, single strand (refer to Figure 7-9). Helicase opens the double-stranded molecule, and an RNA primer is laid down, displacing one strand. Replication then proceeds around the circle, pushing the displaced strand off as it goes. The intact, single strand is released and used as a template to synthesize a complementary strand.

Chapter 8

Sequencing Your DNA

* *

In This Chapter

▷ Discovering the genomes of other species

▷ Appreciating the contributions of the Human Genome Project

▷ Sequencing DNA to determine the order of the bases

* *

*I*magine owning a library of 22,000 books. I don't mean just any books; this collection contains unimaginable knowledge, such as solutions to diseases that have plagued humankind for centuries, basic building instructions for just about every creature on earth, and even the explanation of how thoughts are formed inside your brain. This fabulous library has only one problem — it's written in a mysterious language, a code made up of only four letters that are repeated in arcane patterns. The very secrets of life on earth have been contained within this library since the dawn of time, but no one could read the books — until now.

The 22,000 books are the genes that carry the information that make you. The library storing these books is the human genome. Sequencing *genomes* (that is, all the DNA in one set of chromosomes of an organism), both human genomes and those of other organisms, means discovering the order of the four bases (C, G, A, and T) that make up DNA. The order of the bases in DNA is incredibly important because it's the key to DNA's language, and understanding the language is the first step in reading the books of the library. Most of your genes are identical to those in other species, so sequencing the DNA of other organisms, such as fruit flies, roundworms, chickens, and even yeast, supplies scientists with a lot of information about the human genome and how human genes function.

Trying on a Few Genomes

Humans are incredibly complex organisms, but when it comes to genetics, they're not at the top of the heap. Many complex organisms have vastly larger genomes than humans do. Genomes are usually measured in the number of base pairs they contain (flip to Chapter 6 for more about how DNA is put together in base pairs). Table 8-1 lists the genome sizes and estimated number of genes for various organisms (for some genomes, like grasshoppers, the numbers of genes are still unknown). Human genome size runs a distant fifth behind salamanders, amoebas, and grasshoppers. It's humbling, but true — a single-celled amoeba has a gigantic genome of over 670 billion base pairs. If genome size and complexity were related (and they obviously aren't), you'd expect the amoeba to have a small genome compared to more complex organisms. On the flip side, it doesn't take a lot of DNA to have a big impact on the world. For example, the HIV virus, which causes AIDS, is a mere 9,700 bases long and is responsible for the deaths of over 25 million people worldwide. With only nine genes, HIV isn't very complex, but it's still very dangerous.

Even organisms that are very similar have vastly different genome sizes. Fruit flies have roughly 180 million base pairs of DNA. Compare that to the grasshopper genome, which weighs in at a whopping 180 *billion* base pairs. But fruit flies and grasshoppers aren't *that* different. So if it isn't organism complexity, what causes the differences in genome size among organisms?

Table 8-1	Genome Sizes of Various Organisms	
Species	*Number of Base Pairs*	*Number of Genes*
HIV virus	9,700	9
E. coli	4,600,000	3,200
Yeast	12,000,000	6,532
Flu bacteria	19,000,000	1,700
Roundworm	103,000,000	20,158
Mustard weed	120,000,000	27,379
Fruit fly	180,000,000	14,422
Chicken	1,000,000,000	15,926
Mouse	3,400,000,000	22,974
Corn	2,500,000,000	50,000–60,000
Human	3,000,000,000	22,258
Grasshopper	180,000,000,000	unknown
Amoeba dubia	670,000,000,000	unknown
Salamander	765,000,000,000	unknown

Part of what accounts for the variation in genome size from one organism to the next is number of chromosomes. Particularly in plants, the number of chromosome sets (called *ploidy;* see Chapter 15) explains why some plant species have very large genome sizes. For example, wheat is *hexaploid* (six copies of each chromosome) and has a gigantic genome of 16 billion base pairs. Rice, on the other hand, is *diploid* (two copies of each chromosome) and has a mere 430 million base pairs.

Chromosome number doesn't tell the whole story, however. The number of genes within a genome doesn't reveal how big the genome is. Arguably, mice are somewhat more complex than corn, but they have at least 27,000 fewer genes! On top of that, the mouse genome is larger than the corn genome by about a million base pairs. What the human genome has that the mustard weed genome may lack is lots of repetition.

DNA sequences fall into two major categories:

- ✔ Unique sequences found in genes (I cover genes in Chapter 11)
- ✔ Repetitive sequences that make up noncoding DNA

The presence of repetitive sequences of DNA in some organisms seems to best explain genome size — that is, large genomes have many repeated sequences that smaller genomes lack. Repetitive sequences vary from 150 to 300 base pairs in length and are repeated thousands and thousands of times. These big chunks of sequences don't code for proteins, though. Because, at least initially, all this repetitive DNA didn't seem to do anything, it was dubbed *junk DNA*.

Junk DNA has suffered a bum rap. For years, it was touted as a genetic loser, just along for the ride, doing nothing except getting passed on from one generation to the next. But no more. At long last, so-called junk DNA is getting proper respect. Scientists realized quite some time ago that a lot of DNA besides genes gets transcribed into RNA (see Chapter 9 for more on the transcription process). But after being transcribed, this noncoding "junk" didn't appear to be translated into protein (see Chapter 10 for more on the translation process). New evidence suggests that repeated sequences control transcription. A recent study identified 200,000 transcription start sites within repetitive DNA in the human and mouse genomes, suggesting that "junk" DNA may turn out to be the most important part of the genome, controlling everything from how organisms develop as embryos to what color your eyes are.

Sequencing Your Way to the Human Genome

One of the ways scientists figure out what functions various kinds of sequences carry out is by comparing genomes of different organisms. To make these comparisons, the projects I describe in this section use the methods I explain in the section "Sequencing: Reading the Language of DNA" later in this chapter. The results of these comparisons tell us a lot about ourselves and the world around us.

The DNA of all organisms holds a vast amount of information. Amazingly, most cell functions work the same, regardless of which animal the cell comes from. Yeast, elephants, and humans all replicate DNA in the same way, using almost identical genes. Because nature uses the same genetic machinery over and over, finding out about the DNA sequences in other organisms tells us a lot about the human genome (and it's far easier to experiment with yeast and roundworms than with humans). Table 8-2 is a timeline of the major milestones of DNA sequencing projects so far. In this section, you find out about several of these projects, including the granddaddy of them all, the Human Genome Project.

Table 8-2	Major Milestones in DNA Sequencing
Year	*Event*
1985	Human Genome Project is proposed.
1990	Human Genome Project officially begins.
1992	First map of all genes in the entire human genome is published.
1995	First sequence of an entire living organism — *Haemophilus influenzae,* a flu bacteria — is completed.
1997	Genome of *Escherichia coli,* the most common intestinal bacteria, is completed.
1999	First human chromosome, chromosome 22, is completely sequenced. Human Genome Project passes the 1 billion base pairs milestone.
2000	Fruit fly genome is completed. First entire plant genome — *Arabidopsis thaliana,* the common mustard plant — is sequenced.
2001	First working "draft" of the entire human genome is published.
2002	Mouse genome is completed.
2004	Chicken genome is completed, as is the *euchromatin* (gene-containing) sequence of the human genome.
2006	Cancer Genome Atlas project launched.
2008	First high-resolution map of genetic variation among humans is published.

The yeast genome

Brewer's yeast (scientific name *Saccharomyces cerevisiae*) was the first eukaryotic genome to be fully sequenced. (*Eukaryotes* have cells with nuclei; see Chapter 2.) Yeast has an established track record as one of the most useful organisms known to humankind. It's responsible for making bread rise and for the fermentation that results in beer and wine. It's also a favorite organism for genetic study. Much of what we know about the eukaryotic cell cycle (see Chapter 2) came from yeast research. Yeast has provided information about how genes are inherited together (called linkage; see Chapter 4) and how genes are turned on and off (see Chapter 10). Because many human genes have yeast counterparts, yeast is extremely valuable for finding out how our own genes work.

Yeast has roughly 6,000 genes and 16 chromosomes. Altogether, about 70 percent of the yeast genome consists of actual genes. Yeast genes work in neighborhoods to carry out their functions; genes that are physically close together on chromosomes are more likely to work together than those that are far apart. The discovery of gene networks in yeast may help researchers better understand what causes complex diseases such as Alzheimer's disease, diabetes, and lupus in humans. Disorders such as these aren't typically inherited in simple Mendelian fashion (see Chapter 3) and are likely to be controlled by many genes working together.

The sequencing of the yeast genome was quite a feat. Over 600 researchers in 100 laboratories across the world participated in the project. The technology used at the time was much slower than what's available to researchers now (see the sidebar "Open access and the Human Genome Project" for details). Despite the technological disadvantage, the sequence that this phenomenal team of scientists produced was extremely accurate — especially when compared to the human genome (see "The Human Genome Project" section later in this chapter).

The elegant roundworm genome

The genome of the lowly roundworm, more properly referred to by its full name *Caenorhabditis elegans,* was the first genome of a multicellular organism to be fully sequenced. Weighing in at roughly 97 million base pairs, the roundworm boasts nearly 20,000 genes — only a few thousand fewer than the human genome — on just six chromosomes. Like humans, roundworms have lots of junk DNA; only 25 percent of the roundworm genome is made up of genes.

Roundworms are a fabulous species to study because they reproduce sexually and have organ systems, such as digestive and nervous systems, similar to those in much more complex organisms. Additionally, roundworms have a sense of taste, can detect odors, and react to light and temperature, so they're ideal for studying all sorts of processes, including behavior. Full-grown roundworms have exactly 959 cells and are transparent, so figuring out how their cells work was relatively easy. Scientists determined the exact function of each of the 959 roundworm cells! Although roundworms live in soil, these microscopic organisms have contributed to our understanding of many human diseases.

One of the ways to discover what a gene does is to stop it from functioning and observe the effect. In 2003, a group of researchers fed roundworms a particular kind of RNA that temporarily puts gene function on hold (see Chapter 10 for how this effect on gene function works). By briefly turning genes off, the scientists were able to determine the functions of roughly 16,000 of the round-worms' genes. Another study using the same technique identified how fat storage and obesity are controlled in roundworms. Given that an amazing 70 percent of proteins that humans produce have roundworm counterparts, these gene function studies have obvious implications for human medicine.

The chicken genome

Chickens don't get enough respect. The study of chicken biology has revealed much about how organisms develop from embryos to adults. For example, a study of how a chicken's wings and legs are formed in the egg greatly enhanced a study of human limb formation. Chickens have contributed to our understanding of diseases such as muscular dystrophy and epilepsy, and chicken eggs are the principal ingredient used to produce vaccinations to fight human disease epidemics. So when the chicken genome was sequenced in 2004, there should have been a lot of crowing about the underappreciated chicken.

The chicken genome is really different from mouse and human genomes. It's much smaller (about a third as big as the human genome), with fewer chromosomes (39 compared to our 46) and a similar number of genes (23,000 or so). Roughly 60 percent of chicken genes have human counterparts. Unlike mammals, some chicken chromosomes are tiny (only about 5 million base pairs). These micro-chromosomes are unique because they have a very high content of guanine and cytosine (see Chapter 6 for more about the bases that make up DNA) and very few repetitive sequences.

Not surprisingly, chickens have lots of genes that code for *keratin* — the stuff that makes their feathers (and your hair). The big surprise regarding the completed chicken genome was that chickens have lots of genes for sense of smell. Until recently, scientists thought that most birds have a really poor sense of smell. Now, they realize that sense of taste is what birds lack. The chicken genome also revealed that a particular gene previously known only to exist in humans is also present in chickens. This gene, called *interleukin 26,* is important in immune responses and may allow researchers to better understand how to fight disease. One disease they're particularly interested in is avian flu which is often deadly to humans but doesn't make birds sick. Ultimately, comparing the chicken and human genomes may allow scientists to understand how and why diseases like the "bird flu" move so easily between chickens and humans.

The Human Genome Project

In 2001, the triumphant publication of the human genome sequence was heralded as one of the great feats of modern science. The sequence was considered a draft, and indeed, it was a really *rough* draft. The 2001 sequence was woefully incomplete (it represented only about 60 percent of the total human genome) and was full of errors that limited its utility. In 2004, the *euchromatic* (or gene-containing) sequence had only a few gaps, and most of the errors had been corrected. By 2008, new technologies allowed comparisons between individual humans, laying the foundation for a better understanding of how genes vary to create the endless phenotypes you see around you.

The Human Genome Project (HGP) is akin to some of the greatest adventures of all time — it's not unlike putting a person on the moon. However, unlike the great technological achievements of space exploration, which cost tens of billions of dollars and require technology that becomes obsolete or wears out, the HGP carries a mere $3 billion price tag and has unlimited utility. When first proposed in 1985, the HGP was considered completely impossible. At that time, sequencing technology was slow, requiring several days to generate only a few hundred base pairs of data (see the sidebar "Open access and the Human Genome Project" to find out how this process was sped up). James Watson, one of the discoverers of DNA structure way back in the 1950s (see Chapter 6), was one of the first to push the project (in 1988) from idea to reality during his tenure as director of the National Institutes of Health. When the project got off the ground in 1990, a global team of scientists from 20 institutions participated. (The 2001 human genome sequence paper had a staggering 273 authors.)

The enormous benefits of the HGP remain underappreciated. Most genetic applications wouldn't exist without the HGP. Here are just a few:

- Development of bioinformatics, an entirely new field focused on advancing technological capability to generate genetic data, catalog results, and compare genomes (flip to Chapter 23 for more).
- Development of drugs and gene therapy (see Chapter 16).
- Diagnosis and treatment of genetic disorders (which I cover in Chapter 12).
- Forensics applications, such as identification of criminals and determination of identity after mass disasters (flip to Chapter 18).
- Generation of thousands of jobs and economic benefits of over $25 billion in one year alone (2001).
- Identification of bacteria and viruses to allow for targeted treatment of disease. Some antibiotics, for example, target some strains of bacteria better than others. Genetic identification of bacteria is quick and inexpensive, allowing physicians to rapidly identify and prescribe the right antibiotic.
- Knowledge of which genes control what functions and how those genes are turned on and off (see Chapter 11).
- Understanding of the causes of cancer (which I cover in Chapter 14).

Listing and explaining all the HGP's discoveries would fill this book and then some. As you can see in Table 8-2, all other genome projects — mouse, fruit fly, yeast, roundworm, mustard weed, and so on — were started as a result of the HGP.

As the HGP progressed, the gene count in the human genome steadily declined. Originally, researchers thought that humans had as many as 100,000 genes. But as new and more accurate information has become available over the years, they've determined that the human genome has only about 22,000 genes. Genes are often relatively small, from a base-pair standpoint (roughly 3,000 base pairs), meaning that less than 2 percent of your DNA actually codes for some protein. The number of genes on different chromosomes varies enormously, from nearly 3,000 genes on chromosome 1 (the largest) to 231 genes on the Y chromosome (the smallest).

The Human Genome Project has revealed the surprisingly dynamic and still changing nature of the human genome. One of the surprising discoveries of the HGP is that the human genome is still "growing." Genes get duplicated and then gain new functions, a process that has produced as many as 1,100 new genes. Likewise, genes lose function and "die." Thanks to this death process, 37 genes in the human genome that were once functional now exist as *pseudogenes,* which have the sequence structure of normal genes but no longer code for proteins (see Chapter 11 for more about genes).

Of the human genes that researchers have identified, they only understand what about half of them do. Comparisons with genomes of other organisms help identify what genes do, because most of the proteins that human genes produce have counterparts in other organisms. Thus, humans share many genes in common with even the simplest organisms, such as bacteria and worms. Over 99 percent of your DNA is identical to that of any other human on earth, and as much as 98 percent of your DNA is identical to the sequences found in the mouse genome. Perhaps the greatest take-home message of the HGP is how alike all life on earth really is.

Sequencing: Reading the Language of DNA

The chemical nature of DNA (which I cover in Chapter 6) and the replication process (which you can discover in Chapter 7) are essential to DNA sequencing. DNA sequencing also makes use of a reaction that's similar to the polymerase chain reaction (PCR) used in forensics; if you want more details about PCR, check out Chapter 18.

Identifying the players in DNA sequencing

New technologies are rapidly changing the way DNA sequencing is done (see the sidebar "Open access and the Human Genome Project" for more info). The old tried-and-true approach I describe here, called the Sanger method (after inventor Frederick Sanger), still provides the basis for many of the new methods.

The key ingredients for DNA sequencing are:

- **DNA:** From a single individual of the organism to be sequenced.

- **Primers:** Several thousand copies of short sequences of DNA that are complementary to the part of the DNA to be sequenced.

- **dNTPs:** Many As, Gs, Cs, and Ts, put together with sugars and phosphates as *nucleotides,* the normal building blocks of DNA.

- **ddNTPs:** Many As, Gs, Cs, and Ts as nucleotides that each lack an oxygen atom at the 3' spot.

- **Taq polymerase:** The enzyme that puts the DNA molecule together (see Chapter 18 for more details on Taq).

The use of ddNTPs is the key to how sequencing works. Take a careful look at Figure 8-1. On the left is a generic dNTP, the basic building block of DNA used during replication (if you don't remember all the details, flip to Chapter 6 for more on dNTPs). The molecule on the right is ddNTP *(dideoxyribonucleoside triphosphate).* The ddNTP is identical to the dNTP in every way except that it has no oxygen atom at the 3' spot. No oxygen means no reaction, because the phosphate group of the next nucleotide can't form a phosphodiester bond (see Chapter 6) without that extra oxygen atom to aid the reaction. The next nucleotide can't hook up to ddNTP at the end of the chain, and the replication process stops. So how does *stopping* the reaction help the sequencing process? The idea is to create thousands of short pieces of DNA that give the identity of each and every base along the sequence.

The result of a typical sequencing reaction is a thousand fragments representing a thousand bases of the template strand. The shortest fragment is made up of a primer and one ddNTP representing the complement of the first base of the template. The next shortest fragment is made up of the primer, one nucleotide (from a dNTP), and a ddNTP — and so on, with the largest fragment being a thousand bases long.

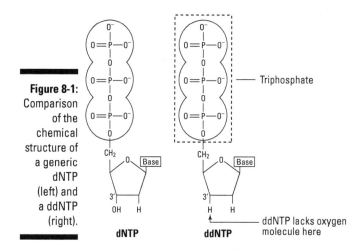

Figure 8-1: Comparison of the chemical structure of a generic dNTP (left) and a ddNTP (right).

Triphosphate

ddNTP lacks oxygen molecule here

dNTP

ddNTP

Finding the message in sequencing results

To see the results of the sequencing reaction, scientists put the DNA fragments through a process called *electrophoresis*. Electrophoresis is the movement of charged particles (in this case, DNA) under the influence of electricity. The purpose of electrophoresis is to sort the fragments of DNA by size, from smallest to largest. The smallest fragment gives the first base in the sequence, the second-smallest fragment gives the second base, and so on, until the largest fragment gives the last base in the sequence. This arrangement of fragments allows researchers to read the sequence in its proper order.

A computer-driven machine called a *sequencer* uses a laser to see the colored dyes of the ddNTPs at the end of each fragment. The laser shines into the gel and reads the color of each fragment as it passes by. Fragments pass the laser in order of size, from smallest to largest. Each dye color signals a different letter: As show up green, Ts are red, Cs are blue, and Gs are yellow. The computer automatically translates the colors into letters and stores all the information for later analysis.

The resulting picture is a series of peaks, like you see in Figure 8-2. Each peak represents a different base. The sequence indicated by the peaks is the *complement* of the template strand (see Chapter 6 for more on the complementary nature of DNA). When you know the complement of the template, you know the template sequence itself. You can then mine this information for the location of genes (see Chapter 10) and compare it to the sequences of other organisms, such as those listed in Table 8-1.

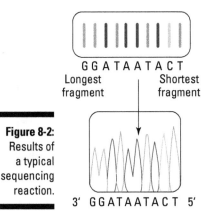

G G A T A A T A C T

Longest fragment

Shortest fragment

Figure 8-2:
Results of
a typical
sequencing
reaction.

3' G G A T A A T A C T 5'

Open access and the Human Genome Project

Prior to the Human Genome Project (HGP), sequencing was a very difficult and time-consuming enterprise. Getting a 1,000-base long sequence required about three days of work and used radioactive chemicals instead of dyes. Sequences were read by hand and had to be run over and over again to fill in gaps and correct mistakes. Every single sequence had to be entered into the computer by hand — imagine typing thousands of As, Gs, Ts, and Cs! It would have taken centuries to sequence the human genome using the old methods. The sheer magnitude of the HGP required faster and easier techniques.

Numerous companies, government labs, and universities searched for solutions to make sequencing faster, better, and cheaper. When the HGP began, one automated sequencer machine produced 1,500 sequences (of 1,000 base pairs each) in about 24 hours. Many laboratories worked together using automated sequencers running 24 hours a day to power through the entire human genome. Still, it took about 15 years to complete the HGP!

New technologies are leaving the once-grand HGP in the dust, as sequencing entire genomes is faster and cheaper than ever. For example, a microbe genome that required 3 months of work in 1995 was entirely sequenced in just 4 hours in 2006. Using high-throughput sequencing, it takes a staff of four people about one month to decode an entire human's genome at a cost of $50,000 (as compared to the original HGP, which came in at roughly $500 million). These new technologies are paving the way for personalized medicine, rapid detection of disease, gene therapy, and much more.

Chapter 9

RNA: DNA's Close Cousin

DNA is the stuff of life. Practically every organism on earth relies on DNA to store genetic information and transmit it from one generation to the next. The road from *genotype* (building plans) to *phenotype* (physical traits) begins with *transcription* — making a special kind of copy of DNA. DNA is so precious and vital to *eukaryotes* (organisms made up of cells with nuclei) that it's kept packaged in the cell nucleus, like a rare document that's copied but never removed from storage. Because it can't leave the safety of the nucleus, DNA directs all the cell's activity by delegating responsibility to another chemical, RNA. RNA carries messages out of the cell nucleus into the cytoplasm (visit Chapter 2 for more about navigating the cell) to direct the production of proteins during *translation,* a process you find out more about in Chapter 10.

You Already Know a Lot about RNA

If you read Chapter 6, in which I cover DNA at length, you already know a lot about *ribonucleic acid,* or RNA. From a chemical standpoint, RNA is very simple. It's composed of

✔ Ribose sugar (instead of deoxyribose, which is found in DNA)

✔ Four nucleotide bases (three you know from DNA — adenine, guanine, and cytosine — plus an unfamiliar one called *uracil*)

✔ Phosphate (the same phosphate found in DNA)

RNA has three major characteristics that make it different from DNA:

- ✔ RNA is very unstable and decomposes rapidly.
- ✔ RNA contains uracil in place of thymine.
- ✔ RNA is almost always single-stranded.

Using a slightly different sugar

Both RNA and DNA use a *ribose* sugar as a main element of their chemical structures. The ribose sugar used in DNA is deoxyribose (find out more about this sugar in Chapter 6). RNA, on the other hand, uses unmodified ribose. Take a careful look at Figure 9-1. You can see that three spots on ribose are marked with numbers. (On ribose sugars, numbers are followed by an apostrophe ['] to indicate the designation "prime;" see Chapter 6 for more information.) Ribose and deoxyribose both have an oxygen (O) atom and a hydrogen (H) atom (an OH group) at their 3' sites.

OH groups are also called *reactive groups* because oxygen atoms are very aggressive from a chemical standpoint (so aggressive that some chemists say they "attack" incoming atoms). The 3' OH tail is required for phosphodiester bonds to form between nucleotides in both ribose and deoxyribose atoms, thanks to their aggressive oxygen atoms. (For the scoop on how phosphodiester bonds form during replication, see Chapter 7.)

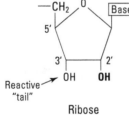
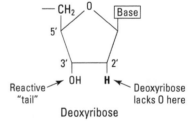

Figure 9-1: The ribose sugar is part of RNA.

The difference between the two molecules is an oxygen atom at the 2' spot: absent (with deoxyribose) or present (with ribose). This one oxygen atom has a huge hand in the differing purposes and roles of DNA and RNA:

- ✔ **DNA:** DNA must be protected from decomposition. The absence of one oxygen atom is part of the key to extending DNA's longevity. When the 2' oxygen is missing, as in deoxyribose, the sugar molecule is less likely to get involved in chemical reactions (because oxygen is chemically aggressive); by being aloof, DNA avoids being broken down.

✔ **RNA:** RNA easily decomposes because its reactive 2' OH tail introduces RNA into chemical interactions that break up the molecule.
Unlike DNA, RNA is a short-term tool the cell uses to send messages
and manufacture proteins as part of gene expression (which I cover in
Chapter 10). Messenger RNAs (mRNAs) carry out the actions of genes.
Put simply, to turn a gene "on," mRNAs have to be made, and to turn a
gene "off," the mRNAs that turned it "on" have to be removed. So the 2'
OH tail is a built-in mechanism that allows RNA to be decomposed, or
removed, rapidly and easily when the message is no longer needed and
the gene needs to be turned "off" (see Chapter 11 for more on turning
genes off and on).

Meeting a new base: Uracil

RNA is composed of four nucleotide bases. Three of the four bases may be
quite familiar to you because they're also part of DNA: adenine (A), guanine
(G), and cytosine (C). The fourth base, uracil (U), is found only in RNA. (In
DNA, the fourth base is thymine. See Chapter 6 for details.) RNA's bases are
pictured in Figure 9-2.

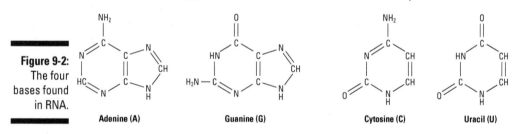

Figure 9-2:
The four
bases found
in RNA.

Uracil may be new to you, but it's actually the precursor of DNA's thymine.
When your body produces nucleotides, uracil is hooked up with a ribose and
three phosphates to form a ribonucleoside triphosphate (rNTP). (Check out
Figure 9-5 later in the chapter to see an rNTP.) If DNA is being replicated, or
copied (see Chapter 7 for the details on DNA's copying process), deoxyribonucleotide triphosphates (dNTPs) of thymine — not uracil — are needed,
meaning that a few things have to happen:

✔ The 2' oxygen must be removed from ribose to make deoxyribose.

✔ A chemical group must be added to uracil's ring structure (all the bases
are rings; see Chapter 6 for details on how these rings stack up). Folic
acid, otherwise known as vitamin B9, helps add a carbon and three
hydrogen atoms (CH_3, referred to as a *methyl group*) to uracil to convert
it to thymine.

Uracil carries genetic information in the same way thymine does, as part of sequences of bases. (In fact, the genetic code that's translated into protein is written using uracil; see Chapter 10 for more on the genetic code.)

The complementary base pairing rules that apply to DNA (see Chapter 6) also apply to RNA: purines with pyrimidines (that is, G with C and A with U). So why are there two versions of essentially the same base (uracil and thymine)?

- ✔ Thymine protects the DNA molecule better than uracil can because that little methyl group (CH_3) helps make DNA less obvious to chemicals called *nucleases* that chew up both DNA and RNA. Nucleases are *enzymes* (chemicals that cause reactions to occur) that act on nucleic acids (see Chapter 6 for why DNA and RNA are called nucleic acids). Your body uses nucleases to attack unwanted RNA and DNA molecules (such as viruses and bacteria), but if methyl groups are present, nucleases can't bond as easily with the nucleic acid to break its chains. (The methyl group also makes DNA hydrophobic; see Chapter 6 for why DNA is afraid of water.)

- ✔ Uracil is a very friendly base; it easily bonds with the other three bases to form pairs. Uracil's amorous nature is great for RNA, which needs to form all sorts of interesting turns, twists, and knots to do its job (see the next section, "Stranded!"). DNA's message is too important to trust to such an easygoing base as uracil; strict base pairing rules must be followed to protect DNA's message from mutation (see Chapter 13 for more on how base pair rules protect DNA's message from getting garbled). Thymine, as uracil's less friendly near-twin, only bonds with adenine, making it perfectly suited to protect DNA's message.

Stranded!

RNA is almost always single-stranded, and DNA is always double-stranded. The double-stranded nature of DNA helps protect its message and provides a simple way for the molecule to be copied during replication. Like DNA, RNA loves to hook up with complementary bases. But RNA is a bit narcissistic; it likes to form bonds with itself (see Figure 9-3), creating what's called a *secondary structure*. The primary structure of RNA is the single-stranded molecule; when the molecule bonds with itself and gets all twisted and folded up, the result is the secondary structure.

Three major types of RNA carry out the business of expressing DNA's message (Chapter 23 covers other RNAs). Although all three RNAs function as a team during translation (which I cover in Chapter 10), the individual types carry out very specific functions.

 ✔ **mRNA:** Carries out the actions of genes

 ✔ **tRNA:** Carries amino acids around during translation (see Chapter 10 for more on translation)

 ✔ **rRNA:** Puts amino acids together in chains (see Chapter 10 for more on rRNA's role during translation)

Primary Structure

Figure 9-3:
Single-
stranded
RNAs form
interesting
shapes in
order to
carry out
various
functions.

5′ AUGCGGCUACGUAACGAGCUUAGCGCGUAUACCGAAAGGGUAGAAC 3′

Complementary regions bond to form secondary structure

Transcription: Copying DNA's Message into RNA's Language

A *transcript* is a record of something, not an exact copy. In genetics, *transcription* is the process of recording part of the DNA message in a related, but different, language — the language of RNA. (To review differences between DNA and RNA, jump back to "You Already Know a Lot about RNA," earlier in this chapter.) Transcription is necessary because DNA is too valuable to be moved or tampered with. The DNA molecule is *the* plan, and any error that's introduced into the plan (as a mutation, which I address in Chapter 13) causes lots of problems. If part or all of the DNA molecule were lost, the cell would die (flip to Chapter 14 for more on cell death). Transcription keeps DNA safe by letting a temporary RNA copy take the risk of leaving the cell nucleus and going out into the cytoplasm.

Messenger RNAs (mRNAs) are the specific type of RNA responsible for carrying DNA's message from the cell nucleus into the cytoplasm (check out Chapter 2 for a review of cell parts).

With *transcription,* the DNA inside the nucleus goes through a process similar to *replication* (see Chapter 7) to get the message out as RNA. When DNA is replicated, the result is another DNA molecule that's exactly like the original in every way. But in transcription, many mRNAs are created because, instead of transcribing the entire DNA molecule, only messages of genes are transcribed into mRNA. Transcription has several steps:

1. Enzymes identify the right part of the DNA molecule to transcribe (see the upcoming section "Getting ready to transcribe").

2. The DNA molecule is opened up to make the message accessible (see "Initiation").

3. Enzymes build the mRNA strand (see "Elongation").

4. The DNA molecule snaps shut to release the newly synthesized mRNA (see "Termination").

Getting ready to transcribe

In preparing to transcribe DNA into mRNA, three things need to be completed:

✔ Locate the proper gene sequence within the billions of bases that make up DNA.

✔ Determine which of the two strands of DNA to transcribe.

✔ Gather up the nucleotides of RNA and the enzymes needed to carry out transcription.

Locating the gene

Your chromosomes are made up of roughly 3 billion base pairs of DNA and contain roughly 22,000 genes (see Chapter 8). But only about 1 percent of your DNA gets transcribed into mRNA. Genes, the sequences that do get transcribed, vary in size. The average gene is only about 3,000 base pairs long, but the human genome also has some gigantic genes — for example, the gene that's implicated in a particular form of muscular dystrophy (Duchenne) is a whopping 2.5 million base pairs.

Before a gene of any size can be transcribed, it must be located. The cue that says "start transcription here" is written right into the DNA in regions called *promoters.* (The promoter also controls how often the process takes place; see the "Initiation" section later in the chapter.) The sequence that indicates where to stop transcribing is called a *terminator.* The gene, the promoter, and the terminator together are called the *transcription unit* (see Figure 9-4).

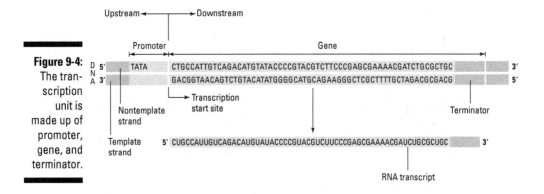

Figure 9-4:
The tran-
scription
unit is
made up of
promoter,
gene, and
terminator.

The promoter sequences tell the enzymes of transcription where to start work and are located within 30 or so base pairs of the genes they control. Each gene has its own promoter. In eukaryotes, the beginning sequence of the promoter is always the same, and it's called the *TATA box* because the sequence of the bases is TATAAA. The presence of TATA tells the transcription-starting enzyme that the gene to transcribe is about 30 base pairs away. Sequences like TATA that are the same in many (if not all) organisms are called *consensus sequences,* indicating that the sequences agree or mean the same thing every-where they appear.

Locating the right strand

By now you've (hopefully) picked up on the fact that DNA is double-stranded. Those double strands aren't identical, though; they're complementary, mean-ing that the sequence of bases matches up, but it doesn't spell the same words of the genetic code (see Chapter 10 for genetic code info). The genetic code of DNA works like this: Bases of genes are read in three base sets, like words. For example, three adenines in a row (AAA) are transcribed into mRNA as three uracils (UUU). During translation, UUU tells the ribosome to use an amino acid called phenylalanine as part of the protein it's making. If the complementary DNA, TTT, were transcribed, you'd wind up with an mRNA saying AAA, which specifies lysine. A protein containing lysine will function differently than one containing phenylalanine.

Because complements don't spell the same genetic words, you can get two dif-ferent messages depending on which strand of DNA is transcribed into mRNA. Therefore, genes can only be read from *one* of the two strands of the double-stranded DNA molecule — but which one? The TATA box (the promoter; see the preceding "Locating the gene" section) not only indicates where a gene is but also tells which strand holds the gene's information. TATA boxes indicate that a gene is about 30 bases away going in the 3' direction (sometimes referred to as *downstream*). Genes along the DNA molecule run in both direc-tions, but any given gene is transcribed only in the 3' direction. Because only one strand is transcribed, the two strands are designated in one of two ways:

- ✓ **Template:** This strand provides the pattern for transcription.

- ✓ **Nontemplate:** This strand is the original message that's actually being transcribed.

TATA is on the nontemplate strand and indicates that the other (complementary) strand is to be used as the template for transcription. Look back at Figure 9-4 and compare the template to the RNA transcript — they're complementary. Now compare the mRNA transcript to the nontemplate strand. The only difference between the two is that uracil appears in place of thymine. The RNA is the transcript of the nontemplate strand.

Gathering building blocks and enzymes

In addition to template DNA (see the preceding section), the following ingredients are needed for successful transcription:

- ✓ **Ribonucleotides,** the building blocks of RNA

- ✓ **Enzymes and other proteins,** to assemble the growing RNA strand in the process of *RNA synthesis*

The building blocks of RNA are nearly identical to those used in DNA synthesis, which I explain in Chapter 7. The differences, of course, are that for RNA, ribose is used in place of deoxyribose, and uracil replaces thymine. Otherwise, the rNTPs (ribonucleoside triphosphates; see Figure 9-5) look very much like the dNTPs you're hopefully already familiar with.

In a process similar to replication, transcription requires the services of various enzymes to:

- ✓ Find the promoter (see the earlier "Locating the gene" section)

- ✓ Open up the DNA molecule (see the later "Initiation" section)

- ✓ Assemble the growing strand of RNA (see the later "Elongation" section)

Unlike replication, though, transcription has fewer enzymes to keep track of. The main player is RNA polymerase. Like DNA polymerase (which you can meet in Chapter 7), *RNA polymerase* recognizes each base on the template and adds the appropriate complementary base to the growing RNA strand, substituting uracil where DNA polymerase would supply thymine. RNA polymerase hooks up with a large group of enzymes — called a *holoenzyme* — to carry out this process. The individual enzymes making up the holoenzyme vary between prokaryotes and eukaryotes, but their functions remain the same: to recognize and latch onto the promoter and to call RNA polymerase over to join the party.

Eukaryotes have three kinds of RNA polymerase, which vary only in which genes they transcribe.

✔ RNA polymerase I takes care of long rRNA molecules.

✔ RNA polymerase II carries out the synthesis of most mRNA and some tiny, specialized types of RNA molecules that are used in RNA editing after transcription is over (see "Post-transcription Processing" later in this chapter).

✔ RNA polymerase III transcribes tRNA genes and other small RNAs used in RNA editing.

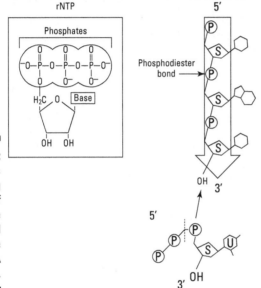

Figure 9-5:
The basic building blocks of RNA and the chemical structure of an RNA strand.

Initiation

Initiation includes finding the gene and opening up the DNA molecule so that the enzymes can get to work. The process of initiation is pretty simple:

1. **The holoenzyme (group of enzymes that hook up with RNA polymerase) finds the promoter.**

   The promoter of each gene controls how often transcription makes an mRNA transcript to carry out the gene's action. RNA polymerase can't bind to a gene that isn't scheduled for transcription. In eukaryotes, *enhancers,* which are sequences sometimes distantly located from the transcription unit, also control how often a particular gene is transcribed. To find out more about how genes are turned on, flip to Chapter 11.

2. **RNA polymerase opens up the double-stranded DNA molecule to expose a very short section of the template strand.**

When the promoter "boots up" to initiate transcription, the holoenzyme complex binds to the promoter site and signals RNA polymerase. RNA polymerase binds to the template at the start site for transcription. RNA polymerase can't "see" past the sugar-phosphate backbone of DNA, so transcription can't occur if the molecule isn't first opened up to expose single strands. RNA polymerase melts the hydrogen bonds between the double-stranded DNA molecule and opens up a short stretch of the helix to expose the template. The opening created by RNA polymerase when it wedges its way between the two strands of the helix is called the *transcription bubble* (see Figure 9-6).

3. **RNA polymerase strings together rNTPs to form mRNA (or one of the other types of RNA, such as tRNA or rRNA).**

RNA polymerase doesn't need a primer to begin synthesis of a new mRNA molecule (unlike DNA replication; see Chapter 7 for details). RNA polymerase simply reads the first base of the transcription unit and lays down the appropriate complementary rNTP. This first rNTP doesn't lose its three phosphate molecules because no phosphodiester bond is formed at the 5' side. Those two extra phosphates remain until the mRNA is edited later in the transcription process (see "Post-transcription Processing" later in this chapter).

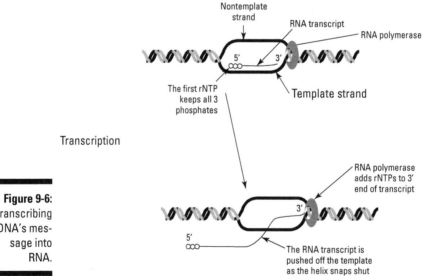

Transcription

Figure 9-6: Transcribing DNA's message into RNA.

Elongation

After RNA polymerase puts down the first rNTP, it continues opening the DNA helix and synthesizing mRNA by adding rNTPs until the entire transcriptional unit is transcribed. The transcription bubble (the opening between DNA strands) itself is very small; only about 20 bases of DNA are exposed at a time. So as RNA polymerase moves down the transcription unit, only the part of the template that's actively being transcribed is exposed. The helix snaps shut as RNA polymerase steams ahead to push the newly synthesized mRNA molecule off the template (refer to Figure 9-6). An enzyme like gyrase (see Chapter 7) probably works to keep the DNA molecule from getting knotted up during the opening, transcribing, and closing process (but scientists aren't certain at this point).

The transcriptional units of genes contain sequences that aren't translated into protein. However, these sequences may control how genes are expressed (see Chapter 11 to find out more). As you may expect, geneticists have come up with terms for the parts that are translated and those that aren't:

- ✔ **Introns:** Noncoding sequences that get their name from their *in*tervening presence. Genes often have many introns that fall between the parts of the gene that code for phenotype.
- ✔ **Exons:** Coding sequences that get their name from their *ex*pressed nature.

The entire gene — introns and exons — is transcribed (refer to Figure 9-6). After transcription has terminated, part of the editing process is the removal of introns. I cover the process of snipping out introns and splicing together exons in the section "Editing the message," later in this chapter.

Prokaryotes don't have introns because prokaryotic genes are all coding, or exon. Only eukaryotes have genes interrupted by intron sequences. Almost all eukaryotic genes have at least one intron; the maximum number of introns in any one gene is 200. Scientists continue to explore the function of introns, which in part control how different mRNAs are edited.

Termination

When RNA polymerase encounters the terminator (as a sequence in the DNA, not the scary, gun-toting movie character), it transcribes the terminator sequence and then stops transcription. What happens next varies depending on the organism.

✔ In prokaryotic cells, some terminator sequences have a series of bases that are complementary and cause the mRNA to fold back on itself. The folding stops RNA polymerase from moving forward and pulls the mRNA off the template.

✔ In eukaryotic cells, a special protein called a *termination factor* aids RNA in finding the right stopping place.

In any event, after RNA polymerase stops adding rNTPs, the mRNA gets detached from the template. The holoenzyme and RNA polymerase let go of the template, and the double-stranded DNA molecule snaps back into its natural helix shape.

Post-transcription Processing

Before mRNA can venture out of the cell nucleus and into the cytoplasm for translation, it needs a few modifications. And I just happen to cover them in the following sections.

Adding cap and tail

The "naked" mRNA that's produced by transcription needs to get dressed before translation:

✔ A 5' cap is added.

✔ A long tail of adenine bases is tacked on.

RNA polymerase starts the process of transcription by using an unmodified rNTP (see the section "Initiation" earlier in this chapter). But a 5' cap needs to be added to the mRNA to allow the ribosome to recognize it during translation (see Chapter 10 for more on translation). The first part of adding the cap is the removal of one of the three phosphates from the leading end of the mRNA strand. A guanine, in the form of a ribonucleotide, is then attached to the lead base of the mRNA. (Figure 9-7 illustrates the process of cap and tail attachment to the mRNA.) Several groups composed of a carbon atom with three hydrogen atoms (CH_3, called a *methyl group*) attach at various sites — on the guanine and on the first and second nucleotides of the mRNA. Like the methyl groups that protect the thymine-bearing DNA molecule, the methyl groups at the 5' end of the mRNA protect it from decomposition and allow the ribosome to recognize the mRNA as ready for translation.

In eukaryotes, a long string of adenines is added to the 3' end of the mRNA to further protect the mRNA from natural nuclease activity long enough to get translated (see Figure 9-7). This string is called the *poly-A tail*. RNA molecules are easily degraded and destroyed because of their temporary natures. Like memos, RNA molecules are linked to a specific task, and when the task is over, the memo is discarded. But the message has to last long enough to be read, sometimes more than once, before it hits the shredder (in this case, nucleases do the shredding instead of guilty business executives). The length of the poly-A tail determines how long the message lasts and how many times it can be translated by the ribosomes before nucleases eat the tail and destroy the message.

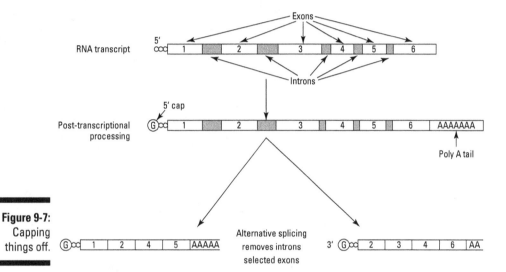

Figure 9-7:
Capping
things off.

Editing the message

The final step in preparing mRNA for translation is twofold: removing the noncoding intron sequences and stringing the exons together without interruptions between them. Several specialized types of RNA work to find the start and end points of introns, pull the exons together, and snip out the extra RNA (that is, the intron).

While it's still in the nucleus, a complex of proteins and small RNA molecules called a *spliceosome* inspects the newly manufactured mRNA. The spliceosome is like a roaming workshop that recognizes introns and works to remove them from between exons. The spliceosome recognizes consensus sequences that mark the beginnings and endings of introns (look back at the "Locating the gene" section to review consensus sequences). The spliceosome grabs each end of the intron and pulls the ends toward each other to form a loop. This movement has the effect of bringing the beginning of one exon close to the end of the preceding one. The spliceosome then snips out the intron and hooks the exons together in a process called *splicing*. Splicing creates a phosphodiester bond between the two exon sequences, which seals them together as one strand of mRNA.

Introns can be spliced out leaving all the exons in their original order, or introns *and* exons can be spliced out to create a new sequence of exons (refer to Figure 9-6 for a couple of examples). The splicing of introns and exons is called *alternative splicing* and results in the possibility for one gene to be expressed in different ways. Thanks to alternative splicing, the 22,000 or so genes in humans are able to produce around 90,000 different proteins. New evidence suggests that practically all multi-exon genes (which make up roughly 86 percent of the human genome) can be sliced and diced in multiple ways, thanks to alternative splicing.

One of the secrets to the genetic flexibility of alternative splicing is sequences called *Alu elements*. Alu elements are fairly short sequences that show up all over the human genome (see Chapter 8 for how scientists are exploring the human genome) — your DNA may have as many as 1 million copies of Alu. Alu can be spliced into or out of genes (sometimes more than once) to create alternative forms of mRNA from the same original gene sequence. This sequence turns out to act as an exon and is considered a reason to scrap the term "junk DNA" altogether. The enormous versatility of RNA editing has lead some scientists to think of RNA as "the" genetic material instead of DNA (see Chapter 23).

After the introns are spliced and all the exons are strung together, the mRNA molecule is complete and ready for action. It migrates out of the cell nucleus, encounters an army of ribosomes, and goes through the process of translation — the final step in converting the genetic message from DNA to protein.

Chapter 10

Translating the Genetic Code

*F*rom building instructions to implementation, the message that DNA carries follows a predictable path. First, DNA provides the template for transcription of the message into RNA. Then, RNA (in the form of messenger RNA) moves out of the cell nucleus and into the cytoplasm to provide the building plans for *proteins*. Every living thing is made of proteins, which are long chains of amino acids called *polypeptides* that are folded into complex shapes and hooked together in intricate ways.

All the physical characteristics (that is, the *phenotypes*) of your body are made up of thousands of different proteins. Of course, your body is also composed of other things, too, like water, minerals, and fats. But proteins supply the framework to organize all those other building blocks, and proteins carry out all your necessary bodily functions, like digestion, respiration, and elimination.

In this chapter, I explain how RNA provides the blueprint for manufacturing proteins, the final step in the transformation from *genotype* (genetic information) to phenotype. Before you dive into the translation process, you need to know a few things about the genetic code — the information that mRNA carries — and how the code is read. If you skipped over Chapter 8, you may want to go back and review its material on RNA before moving on.

Discovering the Good in a Degenerate

When Watson and Crick (along with Rosalind Franklin; see Chapter 6 for the full scoop) discovered that DNA is made up of two strands composed of four bases, the big question they faced was: How can only four bases contain enough information to encode complex phenotypes?

Complex phenotypes (such as your bone structure, eye color, and ability to digest spicy food) are the result of combinations of proteins. The genetic code (that is, DNA transcribed as RNA; see Chapter 9) provides the instructions to make these proteins (via translation; see "Meeting the Translating Team" later in this chapter). Proteins are made up of amino acids strung together in various combinations to create chains called polypeptides (which is a fancy way of saying "protein"). Polypeptide chains can vary from 50 to 1,000 amino acids in length. Because there are 20 different amino acids, and because chains are often more than 100 amino acids in length, the variety of combinations is enormous. For example, a polypeptide that's only 5 amino acids long has 3,200,000 combinations!

After experiments showed that DNA was truly the genetic material (see Chapter 6), skeptics continued to point to the simplicity of the four bases in RNA and argued that a code of four bases wouldn't work to encode complex peptides. Reading the genetic code one base at a time — U, C, A, and G — would mean that there simply weren't enough bases to make 20 amino acids. So it was obvious to scientists that the code must be made up of multiple bases read together. A two-base code didn't work because it only produced 16 combinations — too few to account for 20 amino acids. A three-base code (referred to as a *triplet code*) looked like overkill, because a *codon,* which is a combination of three nucleotides in a row, that chooses from four bases at each position produces 64 possible combinations. Skeptics argued that a triplet code contains too much redundancy — after all, there are only 20 amino acids.

As it turns out, the genetic code is *degenerate,* which is a fancy way of saying "too much information." Normally, degenerate means something to the effect of "bad and getting worse" (it's usually used to describe some people — I won't name names). In the genetic sense, the degeneracy of the triplet code means that the code is highly flexible and tolerates some mistakes — which is a good thing.

Several features of the genetic code are important to keep in mind. The code is

- **Triplet,** meaning that bases are read three at a time in codons.

- **Degenerate,** meaning that 18 of the 20 amino acids are specified by two or more codons (see the next section, "Considering the combinations").

- **Orderly,** meaning that each codon is read in only one way and in only one direction, just as English is read left to right (see "Framed! Reading the code" later in this chapter).

- **Nearly universal,** meaning that just about every organism on earth interprets the language of the code in exactly the same way (see "Not quite universal" for exceptions).

Considering the combinations

Only 61 of the 64 codons are used to specify the 20 amino acids found in proteins. The three codons that don't code for any amino acid simply spell "stop," telling the ribosome to cease the translation process (see "Termination" later in this chapter). In contrast, the one codon that tells the ribosome that an mRNA is ripe for translating — the "start" codon — codes for an amino acid, *methionine*. (The "start" amino acid comes in a special form; see "Initiation" later in this chapter.) In Figure 10-1, you can see the entire code with all the alternative spellings for the 20 amino acids. (See "Meeting the Translating Team" later in this chapter for more details about amino acids.)

First Letter	Second Letter				Third Letter
	U	C	A	G	
U	phenylalanine	serine	tyrosine	cysteine	U
	phenylalanine	serine	tyrosine	cysteine	C
	leucine	serine	STOP	STOP	A
	leucine	serine	STOP	tryptophan	G
C	leucine	proline	histidine	arginine	U
	leucine	proline	histidine	arginine	C
	leucine	proline	glutamine	arginine	A
	leucine	proline	glutamine	arginine	G
A	isoleucine	threonine	asparagine	serine	U
	isoleucine	threonine	asparagine	serine	C
	isoleucine	threonine	lysine	arginine	A
	methionine & START	threonine	lysine	arginine	G
G	valine	alanine	aspartate	glycine	U
	valine	alanine	aspartate	glycine	C
	valine	alanine	glutamate	glycine	A
	valine	alanine	glutamate	glycine	G

Figure 10-1: The 64 codons of the genetic code, as written by mRNA.

For many of the amino acids, the alternative spellings differ only by one base — the third base of the codon. For example, four of the six spellings for leucine start with the bases CU. This flexibility at the third position of the codon is called a *wobble*. The third base of the mRNA can vary, or wobble, without changing the meaning of the codon (and thus the amino acid it codes for). The wobble is possible because of the way *tRNAs (transfer RNAs)* and mRNAs pair up during the process of translation. The first two bases of the code on the mRNA and the partner tRNA (which is carrying the amino acid specified by the codon) must be exact matches. However, the third base of the tRNA can break the base-pairing rules, allowing bonds with mRNA bases other than the usual complements. This rule violation, or wobble, allows different spellings to code for the same amino acid. However, some codons, like one of the three stop codons (spelled UGA), have only one meaning; wobbles in this stop codon change the meaning from stop to either cysteine (spelled UGU or UGC) or tryptophan (UGG).

Framed! Reading the code

Besides its combination possibilities, another important feature of the genetic code is the way in which the codons are read. Each codon is separate, with no overlapping. And the code doesn't have any punctuation — it's read straight through without pauses.

The codons of the genetic code run sequentially, as you can see in Figure 10-2. Each codon is read only once using a *reading frame,* a series of sequential, non-overlapping codons. The start codon defines the position of the reading frame. In the mRNA in Figure 10-2, the sequence AUG, which spells methionine, is a start codon. After the start codon, the bases are read three at a time without a break until the stop codon is reached. (Mutations often disrupt the reading frame by inserting or removing one base; see Chapter 13 for more details.)

Figure 10-2:
The genetic code is non-overlapping and uses a reading frame.

Nucleotide sequence

A U G C G A G U C U U G C A G . . .

Nonoverlapping code

A U G | C G A | G U C | U U G | C A G | . . .
   1   2   3   4   5

Not quite universal

The meaning of the genetic code is nearly universal. That means nearly every organism on earth uses the same spellings in the triplet code. Mitochondrial DNA spells a few words differently from nuclear DNA, which may explain (or at least relate back to) mitochondria's unusual origins (see Chapter 6). Plants, bacteria, and a few microorganisms also use unusual spellings for one or more amino acids. Otherwise, the way the code is read — influenced by its degenerate nature, with wobbles, without punctuation, and using a specific reading frame — is the same. As scientists tackle DNA sequencing for various creatures (see Chapter 8), more unusual spellings are likely to pop up.

Meeting the Translating Team

Translation is the process of converting information from one language into another. In this case, the genetic language of nucleic acid is translated into the language of protein. Translation takes place in the cytoplasm of cells. After messenger RNAs (mRNAs) are created through transcription and move into the cytoplasm, the protein production process begins (see Chapter 9 for the lowdown on mRNA). The players involved in protein production include

- ✔ **Ribosome:** The big protein-making factory that reads mRNA's message and carries out the message's instructions. Ribosomes are made up of *ribosomal RNA* (rRNA) and are capable of constructing any sort of protein.

- ✔ **The genetic code:** The message carried by mRNA (see "Discovering the Good in a Degenerate" earlier in this chapter for more on the genetic code).

- ✔ **Amino acids:** Complex chemical compounds containing nitrogen and carbon; 20 amino acids strung together in thousands of unique combinations are used to construct proteins.

- ✔ **Transfer RNA (tRNA):** Runs a courier service to provide amino-acid building blocks to the working ribosome; each tRNA summoned by the ribosome grabs the amino acid that the codon specifies.

Taking the Translation Trip

Translation proceeds in a series of predictable steps:

1. A ribosome recognizes an mRNA and latches onto its 5' cap (see Chapter 8 for an explanation of how and why mRNAs get caps). The ribosome slurps up the mRNA and carefully scrutinizes it, looking for codons that form the words of the genetic code, beginning with the start codon.

2. tRNAs supply the amino acids dictated by each codon when the ribosome reads the instructions. The ribosome assembles the polypeptide chain with the help of various enzymes and other proteins.

3. The ribosome continues to assemble the polypeptide chain until it reaches the stop codon. The completed polypeptide chain is released.

After it's released from the ribosome, the polypeptide chain is modified and folded to become a mature protein.

Initiation

Preparation for translation consists of two major events:

- ✔ The tRNA molecules must be hooked up with the right amino acids in a process called *charging.*

- ✔ The ribosome, which comes in two pieces, must assemble itself at the start codon of the mRNA.

Charge! tRNA hooks up with a nice amino acid

Transfer RNA (tRNA) molecules are small, specialized RNAs produced by transcription. However, unlike mRNAs, tRNAs are never translated into protein; tRNA's whole function is ferrying amino acids to the ribosomes for assembly into polypeptides. tRNAs are uniquely shaped to carry out their job. In Figure 10-3, you see two depictions of tRNA. The illustration on the left shows you tRNA's true form. The illustration on the right is a simplified version that makes tRNA's parts easier to identify. The cloverleaf shape is one of the keys to the way tRNA works. tRNA gets its unusual configuration because many of the bases in its sequence are complements; the strand folds, and the complementary bases form bonds, resulting in the loops and arms of a typical tRNA.

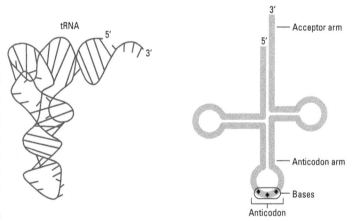

Figure 10-3: tRNA has a unique shape that helps it ferry amino acids to the ribosomes.

The two key elements of tRNA are

- ✔ **Anticodon:** A three-base sequence on one loop of each tRNA; the anticodon is complementary to one of the codons spelled by mRNA.

- ✔ **Acceptor arm:** The single-stranded tail of the tRNA; where the amino acid corresponding to the codon is attached to the tRNA.

REMEMBER

The codon of mRNA specifies the amino acid used during translation. The anti-codon of the tRNA is complementary to the codon of mRNA and specifies which amino acid each tRNA is built to carry.

Like a battery, tRNAs must be charged in order to work. tRNAs get charged with the help of a special group of enzymes called *aminoacyl-tRNA synthetases.* Twenty synthetases exist, one for each amino acid specified by the codons of mRNA. Take a look at the illustration on the right in Figure 10-3, the schematic of tRNA. The aminoacyl-tRNA synthetases recognize sequences of bases in the anticodon of the tRNA that announce which amino acid that particular tRNA is built to carry. When the aminoacyl-tRNA synthetase encounters the tRNA molecule that matches its amino acid, the synthetase binds the amino acid to the tRNA at the acceptor arm — this is the charging part. Figure 10-4 shows the connection of amino acid and tRNA. The synthetases proofread to make sure that each amino acid is on the appropriate tRNA. This proofreading ensures that errors in tRNA charging are very rare and prevents errors in translation later on. With the amino acid attached to it, the tRNA is charged and ready to make the trip to the ribosome.

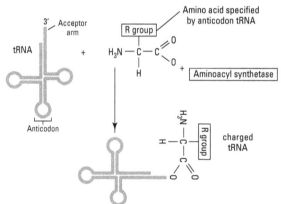

Figure 10-4:
tRNA
charging.

Putting the ribosome together

Ribosomes come in two parts called *subunits* (see Figure 10-5), and ribosomal subunits come in two sizes: large and small. The two subunits float around (sometimes together and sometimes as separate pieces) in the cytoplasm until translation begins. Unlike tRNAs, which match specific codons, ribosomes are completely flexible and can work with any mRNA they encounter. Because of their versatility, ribosomes are sometimes called "the workbench of the cell."

When fully assembled, each ribosome has two sites and one slot:

✔ **A-site (acceptor site):** Where tRNA molecules insert their anticodon arms to match up with the codon of the mRNA molecule.

✔ **P-site (peptidyl site):** Where amino acids get hooked together using peptide bonds.

✔ **Exit slot:** Where tRNAs are released from the ribosome after their amino acids become part of the growing polypeptide chain.

Before translation can begin, the smaller of the two ribosome subunits attaches to the 5' cap of the mRNA with the help of proteins called *initiation factors.* The small subunit then scoots along the mRNA until it hits the start codon (AUG). The P-site on the small ribosome subunit lines up with the start codon, and the small subunit is joined by the tRNA carrying methionine (UAC), the amino acid that matches the start codon. The "start" tRNA totes a special version of methionine called *fMet* (short for *N-formylmethionine*). Only the tRNA for fMet can attach to the ribosome at the P-site without first going through the A-site. The tRNA uses its anticodon, which is complementary to the codon of the mRNA, to hook up to the mRNA. The large ribosome subunit joins with the small subunit to begin the process of hooking together all the amino acids specified by the mRNA (refer to Figure 10-5).

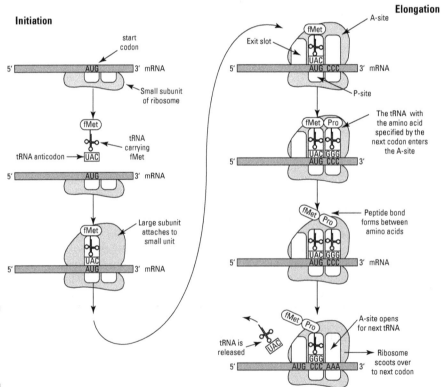

Figure 10-5:
Initiation and elongation.

Elongation

When the initiation process is complete, translation proceeds in several steps called *elongation,* which you can follow in Figure 10-5.

1. The ribosome calls for the tRNA carrying the amino acid specified by the codon residing in the A-site. The appropriate charged tRNA inserts its anticodon arm into the A-site.

2. Enzymes bond the two amino acids attached to the acceptor arms of the tRNAs in the P- and A-sites.

3. As soon as the two amino acids are linked together, the ribosome scoots over to the next codon of the mRNA. The tRNA that was formerly in the P-site now enters the exit site, and because it's no longer charged with an amino acid, the empty tRNA is released from the ribosome. The A-site is left empty, and the P-site is occupied by a tRNA holding its own amino acid and the amino acid of the preceding tRNA. The process of moving from one codon to the next is called *translocation* (not to be confused with the chromosomal translocations I describe in Chapter 15, where pieces of whole chromosomes are inappropriately swapped).

The ribosome continues to scoot along the mRNA in a 5' to 3' direction. The growing polypeptide chain is always attached to the tRNA that's sitting in the P-site, and the A-site is opened up repeatedly to accept the next charged tRNA. The process comes to a stop when the ribosome encounters one of the three stop codons. (For more on stop codons, see "Considering the combinations" earlier in this chapter.)

Termination

No tRNAs match the stop codon, so when the ribosome reads "stop," no more tRNAs enter the A-site (see Figure 10-6). At this point, a tRNA sits in the P-site with the newly constructed polypeptide chain attached to it by the tRNA's own amino acid. Special proteins called *release factors* move in and bind to the ribosome; one of the release factors recognizes the stop codon and sparks the reaction that cleaves the polypeptide chain from the last tRNA. After the polypeptide is released, the ribosome comes apart, releasing the final tRNA from the P-site. The ribosomal subunits are then free to find another mRNA to begin the translation process anew. Transfer RNAs are recharged with fresh amino acids and can be used over and over. Once freed, polypeptide chains assume their unique shapes and sometimes hook up with other polypeptides to carry out their jobs as fully functioning proteins (see the "Proteins Are Precious Polypeptides" section later in the chapter).

Messenger RNAs may be translated more than once and, in fact, may be translated by more than one ribosome at a time. As soon as the start codon emerges from the ribosome after the initiation of translation, another ribosome may recognize the mRNA's 5' cap, latch on, and start translating. Thus, many polypeptide chains can be manufactured very rapidly.

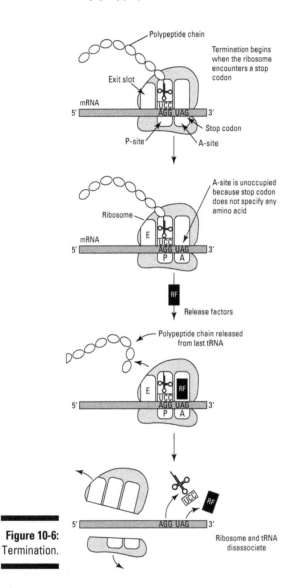

Figure 10-6:
Termination.

Challenging the dogma

In other disciplines (say, physics), laws abound to describe the goings-on of the world. The law of gravity, for example, tolerates no violators. But genetics doesn't have laws because scientists keep acquiring new information. One exception is the *Central Dogma of Genetics*. A *dogma* isn't law; rather, it's more or less universally accepted opinion about how the world works. In this case, the Central Dogma of Genetics (coined by our old friend Francis Crick, of DNA-discovery fame; see Chapter 6) posited that the trip from genotype to phenotype is a one-way information highway.

Genetics seems to be a subject full of exceptions, and the Central Dogma is no ... exception. Reverse transcription (that is, transmitting RNA's message back into DNA) does occur in some cases like viruses such as HIV, the virus that causes AIDS. RNA may also undergo replication (much as DNA does; see Chapter 7) transmitting information from RNA to RNA. Some evidence has even shown that DNA can be translated directly into protein without RNA at all (at least under laboratory conditions). In addition, there have been many new discoveries about the powerful roles that RNA has outside of translation. It turns out that many non-coding RNAs exist — that is, RNAs that don't code for proteins but play important roles in how genes are expressed (gene expression is the topic of Chapter 11).

Another idea that nearly attained the status of law was the *one gene–one polypeptide hypothesis. Polypeptides,* more familiarly known as proteins, are the products of gene messages. Back in the early 1940s, long before DNA was known to be the genetic material, two scientists, George Beadle and Edward Tatum, determined that genes code for proteins. Through a complex set of experiments, Beadle and Tatum discovered that each protein chain manufactured during translation is the product of only one gene's message. We now know that many different mRNA combinations are possible from a single gene. Each mRNA acts alone to make one polypeptide. Even here, there can be exceptions — some organisms may use a single codon to signal two different amino acids.

Proteins Are Precious Polypeptides

Besides water, the most common substance in your cells is protein. Proteins carry out the business of life. The key to a protein's function is its shape; completed proteins can be made of one or more polypeptide chains that are folded and hooked together. The way proteins fit and fold together depends on which amino acids are present in the polypeptide chains.

Recognizing radical groups

Every amino acid in a polypeptide chain shares several features, which you can see in Figure 10-7:

✔ A positively charged amino group (NH₂) attached to a central carbon atom

✔ A negatively charged carboxyl group (COOH) attached to the central carbon atom opposite the amino group

✔ A unique combination of atoms that form branches and rings, called *radical groups,* that differentiate the 20 amino acids specified by the genetic code

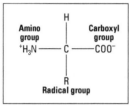

Radical groups

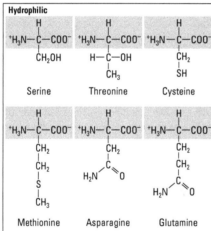

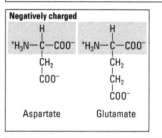

Figure 10-7: The 20 amino acids used to construct proteins.

Amino acid radical groups come in four flavors: water-loving (hydrophilic), water-hating (hydrophobic), negatively charged (bases), and positively charged (acids). When their amino acids are part of a polypeptide chain, radical groups of adjacent amino acids alternate sides along the chain (refer to Figure 10-7). Because of their differing affinities (those four flavors), the radical groups either repel or attract neighboring groups. This reaction leads to folding and gives each protein its shape.

Giving the protein its shape

Proteins are folded into complex and often beautiful shapes, as you can see in Figure 10-8. These arrangements are partly the result of spontaneous attractions between radical groups (see the preceding section for details) and partly the result of certain regions of polypeptide chains that naturally form spirals (also called *helices,* not to be confused with DNA's double helix in Chapter 6). The spirals may weave back and forth to form sheets. These spirals and sheets are referred to as a *secondary structure* (the simple, unfolded polypeptide chain is the *primary structure*).

Proteins are often modified after translation and may get hooked up with various other chemical groups and metals (such as iron). In a process similar to the post-transcription modification of mRNA, proteins may also be sliced and spliced. Some protein modifications result in natural folds, twists, and turns, but sometimes the protein needs help forming its correct conformation. That's what chaperones are for.

Chaperones are molecules that mold the protein into shape. Chaperones push and pull the protein chains until the appropriate radical groups are close enough to one another to form chemical bonds. This sort of folding is called a *tertiary structure.*

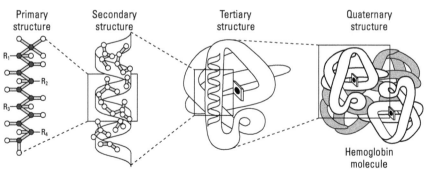

Primary structure   Secondary structure   Tertiary structure   Quaternary structure

Hemoglobin molecule

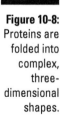

Figure 10-8: Proteins are folded into complex, three-dimensional shapes.

When two or more polypeptide chains are hooked to make a single protein, they're said to have a fourth degree, or *quaternary structure.* For example, the hemoglobin protein that carries oxygen in your blood is a well-studied protein with a quaternary structure. Two pairs of polypeptide chains form a single hemoglobin protein. The chains, two called *alpha-globin chains* and two called *beta-globin chains,* each form helices, which you can see in Figure 10-8, that wind around and fold back on themselves into tertiary structures. Associated with the tertiary structures are iron-rich *heme* groups that have a strong affinity for oxygen. For more on how good proteins go bad, flip to Chapters 11 and 13.

Chapter 11

Gene Expression:
What a Cute Pair of Genes

In This Chapter

▷ Confining gene activities to the right places

▷ Scheduling genes to do certain jobs

▷ Controlling genes before and after transcription

*E*very cell in your body (with very few exceptions) carries the entire set of genetic instructions that make, well, everything about you. Your eye cells contain the genes for growing hair. Your nerve cells contain the genes that turn on cell division — yet your nerve cells don't divide (under normal conditions; see Chapter 14 for what happens when things go wrong). Genes that are supposed to be active in certain cells are turned on only when needed and then turned off again, like turning off the light in a room when you leave.

So why, then, aren't your eyeballs hairy? It boils down to gene expression. *Gene expression* is how genes make their products at the right time and in the right place. This chapter examines how your genes work and what controls them.

Getting Your Genes Under Control

Gene expression occurs throughout an organism's life, starting at the very beginning. When an organism develops — first as a *zygote* (the fertilized egg) and later as an embryo and fetus — genes turn on to regulate the process. At first, all the cells are exactly alike, but that characteristic quickly changes. (Cells that have the ability to turn into any kind of tissue are *totipotent;* see Chapter 20 for more on totipotency.) Cells get instructions from their DNA to turn into certain kinds of tissues, such as skin, heart, and bone. After the tissue type is decided, certain genes in each cell become active, and others get permanently turned off. That's because gene expression is highly *tissue-specific,* meaning certain genes are active only in certain tissues or at particular stages of development.

In part, the tissue-specific nature of gene expression is because of location — genes in cells respond to cues from the cells around them. Other than location, some genes respond to cues from the environment; other genes are set up to come on and then turn off at a certain stage of development. Take the genes that code for hemoglobin, for example.

Your *genome* (your complete set of genetic information) contains a large group of genes that all code for various components that make up the big protein, called *hemoglobin,* that carries oxygen in your blood. Hemoglobin is a complex structure comprised of two different types of proteins that are folded and joined together in pairs. During your development, nine different hemoglobin genes interacted at different times to make three kinds of hemoglobin. Changing conditions make it necessary for you to have three different sorts of hemoglobin at different stages of your life.

When you were still an embryo, your hemoglobin was composed mostly of epsilon-hemoglobin (Greek letters are used to identify the various types of hemoglobin). After about three months of development, the epsilon-hemoglobin gene was turned off in favor of two fetal hemoglobin genes (alpha and gamma). (*Fetal hemoglobin* is comprised of two proteins — two alphas and two gammas — folded and joined together as one functional piece.) When you were born, the gene producing the gamma-hemoglobin was shut off, and the beta-hemoglobin gene, which works for the rest of your life, kicked in.

Heat and light

Organisms have to respond quickly to changing conditions in order to survive. When external conditions turn on genes, it's called *induction.* Responses to heat and light are two types of induction that scientists understand particularly well.

When an organism is exposed to high temperatures, a suite of genes immediately kicks into action to produce *heat-shock proteins.* Heat has the nasty effect of mangling proteins so that they're unable to function properly, referred to as *denaturing.* Heat-shock proteins are produced by roughly 20 different genes and act to prevent other proteins from becoming denatured. Heat-shock proteins can also repair protein damage and refold proteins to bring them back to life. Heat-shock responses are best studied in fruit flies, but humans have a large number of heat-shock genes, too. These genes protect you from the effects of stress and pollutants.

Your daily rhythms of sleeping and waking are controlled, in part, by light. Even cancer may have a connection to light. When you're exposed to light during nighttime, your normal production of melatonin (a hormone that regulates sleep, among other things) is disrupted. In turn, a gene called *period* (so named because it controls circadian rhythms) is inactivated. Altered activity by the period gene is linked to breast cancer as well as depressed immune function. The increased incidence of breast cancer in women working the night shift was so dramatic that the researchers deemed night-shift work as a probable carcinogen.

The genes controlling the production of all these hemoglobins are on two chromosomes, 11 and 16 (see Figure 11-1). The genes on both chromosomes are turned on in order, starting at the 5' end of the group for embryonic hemoglobin (see Chapter 6 for how DNA is set up with numbered ends). Adult hemoglobin is produced by the last set of genes on the 3' end.

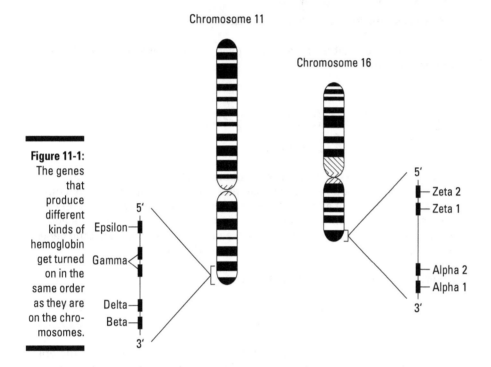

Figure 11-1: The genes that produce different kinds of hemoglobin get turned on in the same order as they are on the chromosomes.

Transcriptional Control of Gene Expression

Most gene control in eukaryotes, like you and me, occurs during transcription. I cover the basic transcription process in Chapter 9; this section covers how and when transcription is carried out to control when genes are and aren't expressed.

When a gene is "on," it's being transcribed. When the gene is "off," transcription is suspended. The only way that proteins (the stuff phenotype is made of; see Chapter 10) can be produced during translation is through the work of messenger RNA (mRNA). Transcription produces the mRNAs used in translation; therefore, when transcription is happening, translation is in motion, and gene expression is on. When transcription is stopped, gene expression is shut down, too. The timing of transcription can be controlled by a number of factors, including

✔ DNA accessibility

✔ Regulation from other genes

✔ Signals sent to genes from other cells by way of hormones

DNA must unwind a bit from its tight coils in order to be available for transcription to occur.

Tightly wound: The effect of DNA packaging

The default state of your genes is off, not on. Starting in the off position makes sense when you remember that almost every cell in your body contains a complete set of all your genes. You just can't have every gene in every cell flipped on and running amok all the time; you want specific genes acting only in the tissues where their actions are needed. Therefore, keeping genes turned off is every bit as important as turning them on.

Genes are kept in the off position in two ways:

✔ **Tight packaging:** DNA packaging is a highly effective mechanism to make sure that most genes are off most of the time because it prevents transcription from occurring by preventing transcription factors from getting access to the genes. DNA is an enormous molecule, and the only way it can be scrunched down small enough to fit into your cell's nuclei is by being tightly wound round and round itself in supercoils. First, the DNA is wrapped around special proteins called histones. Then, the DNA and the histones, which together look a bit like beads on a string, are wrapped around and around themselves to form the dense DNA known as *chromatin*. When DNA is wrapped up this way, it can't be transcribed, because transcription factors can't bind to the DNA to find the template strand and copy it. This is the heart of epigenetics (see Chapter 4).

✔ **Repressors:** *Repressors* are proteins that prevent transcription by binding to the same DNA sites that transcription activators would normally use or by interfering with the activities of the group of enzymes that kick off transcription (called the holoenzyme complex; see Chapter 9). In either case, DNA is prevented from unwinding, and the genes are kept turned off.

But genes can't stay off forever. Certain sections of DNA come prepackaged for unwinding, allowing the genes in those areas to be turned on more easily whenever they're needed.

To find out which genes are prepackaged for unwrapping, researchers exposed DNA to an enzyme called *DNase I,* which actually digests DNA. DNase I isn't a part of normal transcription; instead, it provides a signal to geneticists that a region of packaged DNA is less tightly wound than regions around it. Geneticists added DNase I to DNA to see which parts of the genome were sensitive to being degraded by the enzyme's activity. The sections of DNA left behind in these experiments contained genes that were always turned off in the tissue type the cell belonged to. The parts that were digested weren't tightly wound and thus harbored the genes that could be turned on when needed.

To turn genes on, the DNA must be removed from its packaging. To unwrap DNA from the nucleosomes, specific proteins must bind to the DNA to unwind it. Lots of proteins — including transcription factors, collectively known as *chromatin-remodeling complexes* — carry out the job of unwinding DNA depending on the needs of the organism. Most of these proteins attach to a region near the gene to be activated and push the histones aside to free up the DNA for transcription. As soon as the DNA is available, transcription factors, which in some types of cells are always lurking around, latch on and immediately get to work. As I explain in Chapter 9, transcription gets started when a group of enzymes called the *holoenzyme complex* binds to the promoter sequence of the DNA. Promoter sequences are part of the genes they control and are found a few bases away. *Transcription activator proteins* are part of the mix. These proteins help get all the right components in place at the gene at the right moment. Transcription activators also have the ability to shove histones out of the way to make the DNA template available for transcription.

Genes controlling genes

Four types of genes micromanage the activities of other genes. In this section, I divide these genes up into two groups based on how they relate to one another.

Micromanaging transcription

Three types of genes act as regulatory agents to turn transcription up *(enhancers),* turn it down *(silencers),* or drown out the effects of enhancing or silencing elements *(insulators).*

- ✔ **Enhancers:** This type of gene sequence turns on transcription and speeds it up, making transcription happen faster and more often. Enhancers can be upstream, downstream, or even smack in the middle of the transcription unit. Furthermore, enhancers have the unique ability to control genes that are distantly located (like thousands of bases away) from the enhancer's position. Nonetheless, enhancers are very tissue-specific in their activities — they only influence genes that are normally activated in that particular cell type.

Researchers are still working to get a handle on how enhancers do their jobs. Like the proteins that turn transcription on, enhancers seem to have the ability to rearrange nucleosomes and pave the way for transcription to occur. The enhancer teams up with transcription factors to form a complex called the *enhanceosome*. The enhanceosome attracts chromatin-remodeling proteins to the team along with RNA polymerase to allow the enhancer to supervise transcription directly.

✔ **Silencers:** These are gene sequences that hook up with repressor proteins to slow or stop transcription. Like enhancers, silencers can be many thousands of bases away from the genes they control. Silencers work to keep the DNA tightly packaged and unavailable for transcription.

✔ **Insulators:** Sometimes called *boundary elements,* these sequences have a slightly different job. Insulators work to protect some genes from the effects of silencers and enhancers, confining the activity of those sequences to the right sets of genes. Usually, this protection means that the insulator must be positioned between the enhancer (or silencer) and the genes that are off limits to the enhancer's (or silencer's) activities.

Given that enhancers and silencers are often far away from the genes they control, you may be wondering how they're able to do their jobs. Most geneticists think that the DNA must loop around to allow enhancers and silencers to come in close proximity to the genes they influence. Figure 11-2 illustrates this looping action. The promoter region begins with the TATA box and extends to the beginning of the gene itself. Enhancers interact with the promoter region to regulate transcription.

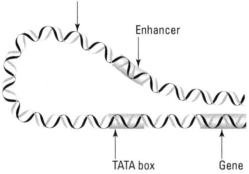

Figure 11-2: Enhancers loop around to turn on genes under their control.

Jumping genes: Transposable elements

Some genes like to travel. They hop around from place to place, inserting themselves into a variety of locations, causing mutations in genes, and changing the ways other genes do business. These wanderers are called *transposable elements* (TEs), and they're quite common — 50 percent of your DNA is made up of transposable elements, also known as *jumping genes.*

Barbara McClintock discovered TEs in 1948. She called them *controlling elements* because they control gene expression of other genes. McClintock was studying the genetics of corn when she realized that genes with a habit of frequently changing location were controlling kernel color. In her research, these genes showed up first on one chromosome, but in another individual, the genes mapped to a completely different chromosome. (You can find out more about Dr. McClintock in Chapter 22.)

It appears that TEs travel at will, showing up whenever and wherever they please. How they pull off this trick isn't completely clear, because TEs have several options when it comes to travel. They take advantage of breaks in DNA, but not just any break will do — the break must include little overhanging bits of single-stranded DNA (see Figure 11-3). Some TEs replicate themselves to hop into the broken spots. Others, which go by the special name *retrotransposons,* make use of RNA to do the job.

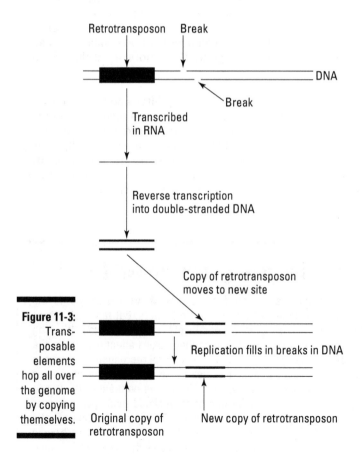

Figure 11-3: Transposable elements hop all over the genome by copying themselves.

Retrotransposons are transcribed just like all other DNA: An RNA transcript is produced. But then the RNA transcript is transcribed again by a special enzyme to make a double-stranded DNA copy of the RNA transcript. Because the result is a DNA copy made from an RNA transcript, the process used by retrotransposons is called *reverse transcription*. The DNA copy is then inserted into a break, and the newly copied retrotransposon makes itself comfortable.

Hormones turn genes on

Hormones are complex chemicals that control gene expression. They're secreted by a wide range of tissues in the brain, gonads (organs or glands, such as ovaries and testes, that produce reproductive cells), and other glands throughout the body. Hormones circulate in the bloodstream and can affect tissues far away from the hormones' production sites. In this way, they can affect genes in many different tissues simultaneously. Essentially, hormones act like a master switch for gene regulation all over the body. Take a look at the sidebar "Hormones make your genes go wild" for more about the effects hormones have on your body.

Some hormones are such large molecules that they often can't cross into the cells directly. These large hormone molecules rely on receptor proteins inside the cell to transmit their messages for them in a process called *signal transduction*. Other hormones, like steroids, are fat-soluble and small, so they easily pass directly into the cell to hook up with receptor proteins. Receptor proteins (and hormones small enough to enter the cell on their own) form a complex that moves into the cell nucleus to act as a transcription factor to turn specific genes on.

Hormones make your genes go wild

Dioxins are long-lived chemicals that are released into the environment through incineration of waste, coal-burning power plants, paper manufacturing, and metal smelting operations, to name a few. It turns out that dioxin can mimic estrogens and turn on genes all by itself. That's scary because it means that dioxin can cause cancer and birth defects.

Dioxin is a chemical with an unfortunate affinity for fat. Animals store dioxin in their fat cells, so most of the dioxins you're exposed to come in the food you eat. Meats and dairy products are the worst offenders, but fatty fish sometimes contain elevated levels, too. It's long been known that dioxins affect estrogens, the hormones that control reproduction in women and, to some degree, men, too. The good news is that dioxin levels are on the decline. Dioxin emissions have declined by 90 percent over the last 18 years. Unfortunately, dioxin that's already present in the environment breaks down slowly, so it's likely to persist for some time to come.

A swing and a miss: The genetic effects of anabolic steroids

Anabolic-androgenic steroids are in the news a lot these days. These steroids are synthetic forms of testosterone, the hormone that controls male sex determination (see Chapter 5). The anabolic aspect refers to chemicals that increase muscle mass; the androgenic aspect refers to chemicals that control gonad functions such as sex drive and, in the case of men, sperm production. High-profile athletes, including some famous baseball players, may have abused one or more of these drugs in an effort to improve performance. Reports also suggest that use of anabolic steroids is common among young athletes in high school and college.

Hormones like testosterone control gene expression. Research suggests that testosterone exerts its anabolic effects by depressing the activity of a tumor suppressor gene that produces the protein p27. When p27 is depressed in muscle tissue, the tissue's cells can divide more rapidly, resulting in the bulky physique prized by some athletes. Anabolic steroids apparently also accelerate the effects of the gene that causes male pattern baldness (see Chapter 5); thus, men carrying that allele and taking anabolic steroids become permanently bald faster and at a younger age than normal.

Defects in tumor-suppressor genes such as p27 are widely associated with cancer. Not only that, but some cancers depend on hormones to provide signals that tumor cells respond to (by multiplying). At least one study suggests that anabolic steroids are actually carcinogenic, meaning that their chemicals cause mutations that lead to cancer. Because illegally obtained steroids may also contain additional unwanted and potentially carcinogenic chemicals, mutagenic chemicals may be introduced into the body while simultaneously depressing the activity of a tumor-suppressor gene. It doesn't take a genius to realize that this is dangerous. Cancers associated with anabolic-androgenic steroid abuse include liver cancer, testicular cancer, leukemia, and prostate cancer.

The genes that react to hormone signals are controlled by DNA sequences called *hormone response elements* (HREs). HREs sit close to the genes they regulate and bind with the hormone-receptor complex. Several HREs can influence the same gene — in fact, the more HREs present, the faster transcription takes place in that particular gene.

Retroactive Control: Things That Happen after Transcription

After genes are transcribed into mRNA, their actions can still be controlled by events that occur later.

Interfering RNAs knock out genes

The world of RNAi (RNA interference; see "Shut up! mRNA silencing") is creating quite a splash in the understanding of how gene expression is controlled. The breakthrough moment came when two geneticists, Andrew Fire and Craig Mello, realized that by introducing certain double-stranded RNA molecules into roundworms, they could shut off genes at will. It turns out that scientists can put the RNAi into roundworm food and knock out gene function not only in the worm that eats the concoction but also in its offspring!

Since this discovery in 2003, geneticists have identified naturally occurring interfering RNAs in all sorts of organisms. The most well-known RNAi tend to be very short (only about 20 or so bases long) and hook up with special proteins, called *argonautes,* to regulate genes (mostly by silencing them). The argonaute proteins

actually do the work, guided to the right target by the RNAi. RNAi finds its complementary mRNA (the product of the gene to be regulated), and the argonaute breaks down the mRNA, rendering it nonfunctional. New RNAi's are being discovered all the time, and their full importance in regulating genes is only just being realized. Longer, noncoding RNAs (over 200 bases long) are also produced during transcription; scientists are hard at work determining what functions those have.

The most promising applications for RNAi are in gene therapy (jump to Chapter 16 for that discussion). Using synthetic RNAi, geneticists have knocked out genes in all sorts of organisms, including chickens and mice. Work is also underway to knock out the function of genes in viruses and cancer cells.

Nip and tuck: RNA splicing

As you discover in Chapter 9, genes have sections called *exons* that actually code for protein products. Often, in between the exons are *introns,* interruptions of noncoding DNA that may or may not do anything. When genes are transcribed, the whole thing is copied into mRNA. The mRNA transcript has to be edited — meaning the introns are removed — in preparation for translation. When multiple introns are present in the unedited transcript, various combinations of exons can result from the editing process. Exons can be edited out, too, yielding new proteins when translation rolls around. This creative editing process allows genes to be expressed in new ways; one gene can code for more than one protein. This genetic flexibility is credited for the massive numbers of proteins you produce relative to the number of genes you have (see Chapter 9 for more on the potential of gene editing).

One gene in which genetic flexibility is very apparent is *DSCAM.* Named for the human disorder it's associated with — Down Syndrome Cell Adhesion Molecule — DSCAM may play a role in causing the mental disabilities that accompany Down syndrome. In fruit flies, DSCAM is a large gene with 115 exons and at least 100 splicing sites. Altogether, DSCAM is capable of coding for a whopping 30,016 different proteins. However, protein production from DSCAM is tightly regulated; some of its products only show up during early stages of fly development. The human version of DSCAM is less showy in that it makes only a few proteins, but other genes in the human genome are likely to be as productive at making proteins as DSCAM of fruit flies, making this a "fruitful" avenue of research. Humans have very few genes relative to the number of proteins we have in our bodies. Genes like DSCAM may help geneticists understand how a few genes can work to produce many proteins.

With scientists wise to the nip and tuck game played by mRNA, the next step in deciphering this sort of gene regulation is figuring out how the trick is done and what controls it. Researchers know that a complex of proteins called a *spliceosome* carries out much of the work in cutting and pasting genes together. How the spliceosome's activities are regulated is another matter altogether. Knowing how it all works will come in handy though, because some forms of cancer, most notably pancreatic cancer, can result from alternative splicing run amok.

Shut up! mRNA silencing

After transcription produces mRNA, genes may be regulated through *mRNA silencing*. mRNA silencing is basically interfering with the mRNA somehow so that it doesn't get translated. Scientists don't fully understand exactly how organisms like you and me use mRNA silencing, called *RNAi* (for *RNA interference*), to regulate genes. Geneticists know that most organisms use RNAi to stymie translation of unwanted mRNAs and that double-stranded RNA provides the signal for the initiation of RNAi, but the details are still a mystery. The discovery of RNAi has produced a revolution in the study of gene expression; see the sidebar "Interfering RNAs knock out genes" for more.

RNA silencing isn't just used to regulate the genes of an organism; sometimes it's used to protect an organism from the genes of viruses. When the organism's defenses detect a double-stranded virus RNA, an enzyme called *dicer* is produced. Dicer chops the double-stranded RNA into short bits (about 20 or 25 bases long). These short strands of RNA, now called *small interfering RNAs* (siRNAs), are then used as weapons against remaining viral RNAs. The siRNAs turn traitor, first pairing up with RNA-protein complexes produced by the host and then guiding those complexes to intact viral RNA. The viral RNAs are then summarily destroyed and degraded.

mRNA expiration dates

After mRNAs are sliced, diced, capped, and tailed (see Chapter 9 for how mRNA gets dressed up), they're transported to the cell's cytoplasm. From that moment onward, mRNA is on a path to destruction because enzymes in the cytoplasm routinely chew up mRNAs as soon as they arrive. Thus, mRNAs have a relatively short lifespan, the length of which (and therefore the number of times mRNA can be translated into protein) is controlled by a number of factors. But the mRNA's poly-A tail (the long string of adenines tacked on to the 3' end) seems to be one of the most important features in controlling how long mRNA lasts. Key aspects of the poly-A tail include:

- **Tail length:** The longer the tail, the more rounds of translation an mRNA can support. If a gene needs to be shut off rapidly, the poly-A tail is usually pretty short. With a short tail, when transcription comes to a halt, all the mRNA in the cytoplasm is quickly used up without replacement, thus halting protein production, too.

- **Untranslated sequences before the tail:** Many mRNAs with very short lives have sequences right before the poly-A tail that, even though they aren't translated, shorten the mRNA's lifespan.

Hormones present in the cell may also affect how quickly mRNAs disappear. In any event, the variation in mRNA expiration dates is enormous. Some mRNAs last a few minutes, meaning those genes are tightly regulated; other mRNAs hang around for months at a time.

Gene Control Lost in Translation

Translation of mRNA into amino acids is a critical step in gene expression. (Flip to Chapter 10 for a review of the players and process of translation.) But sometimes genes are regulated during or even after translation.

Modifying where translation occurs

One way gene regulation is enforced is by hemming in mRNAs in certain parts of the cytoplasm. That way, proteins produced by translation are found only in certain parts of the cell, limiting their utility. Embryos use this strategy to direct their own development. Proteins are produced on different sides of the egg to create the front and back, so to speak, of the embryo.

Modifying when translation occurs

Just because an mRNA gets to the cytoplasm doesn't mean it automatically gets translated. Some gene expression is limited by certain conditions that block translation from occurring. For example, an unfertilized egg contains lots of mRNAs supplied by the female. Translation actually occurs in the unfertilized egg, but it's slow and selective. All that changes when a sperm comes along and fertilizes the egg: Preexisting mRNAs are slurped up by waiting ribosomes, which are signaled by the process of fertilization. New proteins are then rapidly produced from the maternal mRNAs.

Controlling gene expression by controlling translation occurs in one of two ways:

- ✔ The machinery that carries out translation, such as the initiator proteins that interact with ribosomes, is modified to increase or decrease how effectively translation occurs.
- ✔ mRNA carries a message that controls when and how it gets translated.

All mRNAs carry short sequences on their 5' ends that aren't translated, and these sequences can carry messages about the timing of translation. The untranslated sequences are recognized with the help of translation initiation factors that help assemble the ribosome at the start codon of the mRNA. Some cells produce mRNAs but delay translation until certain conditions are met. Some cells respond to levels of chemicals that the cell's exposed to. For example, the protein that binds to iron in the blood is created by translation only when iron is available, even though the mRNAs are being produced all the time. In other cases, the condition of the organism sends the message that controls the timing of translation. For example, insulin, the hormone that regulates blood sugar levels, controls translation, but when insulin's absent, the translation factors lock up the needed mRNAs and block translation from occurring. When insulin arrives on the scene, the translation factors release the mRNAs, and translation rolls on, unimpeded.

Modifying the protein shape

The proteins produced by translation are the ultimate form of gene expression. Protein function, and thus gene expression, can be modified in two ways: by changing the protein's shape or by adding components to the protein. The products of translation, the amino acid chains, can be folded in various ways to affect their functions (see Chapter 9 for how amino acid chains are folded). Various components — carbohydrate chains, phosphates, and metals such as iron — can be added to the chain, also changing its function. Occasionally, the folding of proteins can go horribly wrong; for an explanation of one of the scariest products of this type of error, mad cow disease, check out the sidebar "Proteins gone wrong."

Proteins gone wrong

Cruetzfeldt-Jakob disease (CJD) is a frightening disorder of the brain. Sufferers first experience memory loss and anxiety, and they ultimately develop tremors and lose intellectual function. CJD is the human form of what's popularly known as *mad cow disease*. The pathogen isn't a bacteria, virus, or parasite — it's an infectious protein called a *prion*. One of the scariest aspects of prions is that they seem to be able to replicate on their own by hijacking normal proteins and refolding them.

The gene that codes for the prion protein is found in many different organisms, including humans. After it's mutated (and what the unmutated version does isn't really clear), the protein produced by the gene folds into an unusual, flattened sheet. After one prion protein is acquired, that prion can hijack the normal products of unmutated prion genes, turning them into misfolded monsters, too. Prion proteins gum up the brain of the affected organism and eventually have fatal results. As if this outcome weren't frightening enough, it seems that prions can jump from one species to another.

Scientists are fairly certain that some of the cows originally infected by mad cow disease contracted it by eating feed contaminated by sheep meat. The deceased sheep were infected with a prion that causes yet another icky disease called *scrapie,* which destroys the brains of infected animals. Scientists believe that when humans consume beef products from cows affected by mad cow disease, the prions in the meat can migrate through the human body and continue doing their dirty work.

Part III
Genetics and Your Health

The 5th Wave   By Rich Tennant

"You can do all the DNA testing you want Pinocchio, but I still feel this is your baby."

In this part . . .

Genetics affects your everyday life. Viruses, bacteria, parasites, and hereditary diseases all have their roots in DNA. That's why as soon as scientists uncovered the chemical nature of DNA, the race was on to read the code directly.

Genetic information is used to track, diagnose, and treat genetic diseases. The chapters in this part help you unravel the mysterious connections between DNA and your health. I explain how genetic counselors read your family tree to help you better understand your family medical history. I cover the ways in which mutations alter genes and the consequences of those changes. And because serious problems arise when chromosomes aren't doled out in the usual way — leading to too many or too few — I explain what the numbers mean. Finally, I share some exciting information about how genetics may someday reshape medical treatments in the form of gene therapies.

Chapter 12

Genetic Counseling

*I*f you're thinking of starting a family or adding to your brood, you may be wondering what your little ones will look like. Will they get your eyes or your dad's hairline? If you know your family's medical history, you may also have significant worries about diseases such as cystic fibrosis, Tay-Sachs, or sickle cell anemia. You may worry about your own health, too, as you contemplate news stories dealing with cancer, heart disease, and diabetes, for example. All these concerns revolve around genetics and the inheritance of a predisposition for a particular disease or the inheritance of the disorder itself.

Genetic counselors are specially and rigorously trained to help people learn about the genetic aspects of their family medical histories. This chapter explains the process of genetic counseling, including how counselors generate family trees and estimate probability of inheritance and how genetic testing is done when genetic disorders are anticipated.

Getting to Know Genetic Counselors

Like it or not, you have a family. You have a mother and a father, grandparents, and perhaps children of your own. You may not think of them, but you also have hundreds of ancestors — people you've never met — whose genes you carry and may pass down to descendants in the centuries to come.

Genetic counselors help people like you and me examine our families' genetic histories and uncover inherited conditions. They work with medical personnel like physicians and nurses to interpret medical histories of patients and their families. Although they aren't trained as geneticists, they usually hold a master's degree in genetic counseling and have an extensive background in genetics (and can solve genetics problems in a snap; see

Chapters 3 through 5 for some examples) so that they can spot patterns that signal an inherited disorder. (For more on genetic counselors and other career paths in genetics, see Chapter 1.)

Genetics counselors perform a number of functions, including

- ✔ Constructing and interpreting family trees, sometimes called *pedigrees,* to assess the likelihood that various inherited conditions will be (or have been) passed on to a particular generation.
- ✔ Counseling families about options for diagnosis and treatment of genetic conditions.

Physicians most commonly refer the following types of people or patients to genetic counselors:

- ✔ Couples who are concerned about exposure to substances known to cause birth defects (such as radiation, viruses, drugs, and chemicals)
- ✔ Couples who have experienced more than one miscarriage or stillbirth or who have problems with infertility
- ✔ Parents of a child who shows symptoms of a genetic disorder
- ✔ People with a family history of a particular disorder, such as cystic fibrosis, who are planning a family
- ✔ People with a family history of inherited diseases like Parkinson disease or certain cancers such as breast, ovarian, or colon cancer who may be considering genetic testing to determine their risk of getting the disease
- ✔ Women over 35 who are pregnant or planning a pregnancy
- ✔ Women who have had an abnormal screening test, such as an ultrasound, during a pregnancy

I cover many of the scientific reasons for the inheritance of genetic disorders elsewhere in this book. Mutations within genes are the root cause of many genetic disorders (including cystic fibrosis, Tay-Sachs disease, and sickle cell anemia), and I cover mutation in detail in Chapter 13. I discuss the causes and genetic mechanics of cancer in Chapter 14. I explain chromosomal disorders such as Down syndrome, trisomy 13, and fragile X syndrome in Chapter 15. Finally, I cover gene therapy treatments for inherited disorders in Chapter 16.

Building and Analyzing a Family Tree

Often the first step in genetic counseling is drawing a family tree. The tree usually starts with the person for whom the tree is initiated; this person is called the *proband.* The proband can be a newly diagnosed child, a woman planning a pregnancy, or an otherwise healthy person who's curious about risk for inherited disease. Often, the proband is simply the person who meets with the genetic counselor and provides the information used to plot out the family tree. The proband's position in the family tree is always indicated by an arrow, and he or she may or may not be affected by an inherited disorder.

Genetic counselors use a variety of symbols on family trees to indicate personal traits and characteristics. For instance, certain symbols convey sex, gene carriers, whether the person is deceased, and whether the person's family history is unknown. The manner in which symbols are connected show relationships among people, such as which offspring belong to which parents, whether someone is adopted, and whether someone is a twin. Check out Figure 12-1 for a detailed key to the symbols typically used in pedigree analysis.

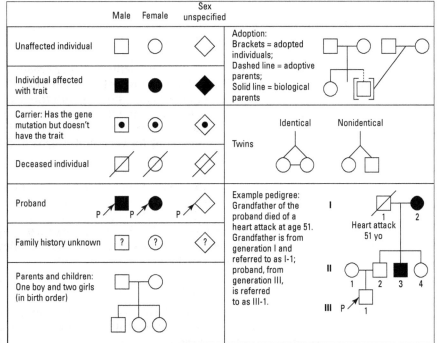

Figure 12-1: Symbols commonly used in pedigree analysis.

In a typical pedigree, the age or date of birth of each person is noted on the tree. If deceased, the person's age at the time of death and the cause of death are listed. Some genetic traits are more common in certain regions of the world, so it's useful to include all kinds of other details about family history on the pedigree, such as what countries people immigrated from or how they're related. Every member of the family should be listed, along with any medical information known about that person, including the age at which certain medical disorders occurred. In the example in Figure 12-1, the grandfather of the proband died of a heart attack at age 51. Including this information creates a record of all disorders with the relation to the family tree so that the counselor is more likely to detect every inherited disease present in the family. (Medical information doesn't appear in Figure 12-1, but it's normally a part of a tree.)

Medical problems often listed on pedigrees include

- ✔ Alcoholism or drug addiction
- ✔ Asthma
- ✔ Birth defects, miscarriages, or stillbirths
- ✔ Cancer
- ✔ Heart disease, high blood pressure, or stroke
- ✔ Kidney disease
- ✔ Mental illness or mental retardation

Human couples have only a few children relative to other creatures, and humans start producing offspring after a rather long childhood. Geneticists rarely see neat offspring ratios (such as four siblings with three affected and one unaffected) in humans that correspond to those observed in animals (take a look at Chapters 3 and 4 for more on common offspring ratios). Therefore, genetic counselors must look for very subtle signs to detect particular patterns of inheritance in humans.

When the genetic counselor knows what kind of disorder or trait is involved, he or she can determine the likelihood a particular person will possess the trait or pass it on to his or her children. (Sometimes, the disorder is unidentified, such as when a person has a family history of "heart trouble" but doesn't have a precise diagnosis.) Genetic counselors use the following terms to describe the individuals in a pedigree:

- ✔ **Affected:** Any person having a given disorder.
- ✔ **Heterozygote:** Any person possessing one copy of the mutated gene coding for a disorder (an allele; see Chapter 2 for details). An unaffected heterozygote is called a *carrier*.
- ✔ **Homozygote:** Any person possessing two copies of the allele for a disorder. This person can also be described as *homozygous*.

The particular way in which most human genetic disorders are passed down to later generations — the *mode of inheritance* — is well established. After a genetic counselor determines which family members are affected or are likely to be carriers, it's relatively easy to determine the probability of another person being a carrier or inheriting the disorder.

In the following sections, I explore the modes of inheritance for human genetic disorders, how genetic counselors map these modes, and how you (and your counselor) can figure out the probability of passing these traits on to offspring. For additional background on each of these modes of inheritance and the subject of inheritance in general, see Chapters 3 through 5.

Autosomal dominant traits

A *dominant* trait or disorder is one that's expressed (or manifested) in anyone who inherits the mutation for the trait. *Autosomal dominant* means that the gene is carried on a chromosome other than a sex chromosome (meaning not on an X or a Y; see Chapter 3 for more details). In human pedigrees, autosomal dominant traits have some typical characteristics:

 ✔ Affected children are born to an affected parent.

 ✔ Both males and females are affected with equal frequency.

 ✔ If neither parent is affected, usually no child is affected.

 ✔ The trait doesn't skip generations.

Figure 12-2 shows the pedigree of a family with an autosomal dominant trait. In the figure, affected persons are shaded, and you can clearly see how only affected parents have affected children. The trait can be passed to a child from either the mother or the father. Generally, affected parents have a 50-percent chance of passing an autosomal dominant trait or disorder on to each child.

Some common autosomal dominant disorders are

 ✔ Achondroplasia, a form of dwarfism

 ✔ Huntington disease, a progressive and fatal disease affecting the brain and nervous system

 ✔ Marfan syndrome, a disorder affecting the skeletal system, heart, and eyes

 ✔ Polydactyly, or extra fingers and toes

The normal pattern of autosomal dominant inheritance has three exceptions:

 ✔ **Reduced penetrance:** *Penetrance* is the percentage of individuals having a particular gene (genotype) that actually display the physical characteristics dictated by the gene (or express the gene as phenotype, scientifically speaking; see Chapter 3 for a full rundown of genetics terms). Many autosomal dominant traits have complete penetrance, meaning that every person inheriting the gene shows the trait. But some traits have *reduced penetrance,* meaning only a certain percentage of individuals inheriting the gene show the phenotype.

When an autosomal dominant disorder shows reduced penetrance, the phenotype skips generations. Check out Chapter 3 for more details on reduced penetrance.

✔ **New mutations:** In the case of new mutations that are autosomal dominant, the trait appears for the first time in a particular generation and can appear in every generation thereafter. You can flip to Chapter 13 to find out more details about mutations — how they occur and how they're passed on.

✔ **Variable expressivity:** Expressivity is the degree to which a trait is expressed. Some conditions may be undiagnosed in earlier generations because the condition is so mild, it goes undetected. Turn to Chapter 4 to find out more about expressivity.

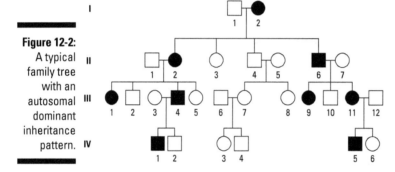

Figure 12-2: A typical family tree with an autosomal dominant inheritance pattern.

Autosomal recessive traits

Recessive disorders are expressed only when an individual inherits two identically altered (or mutated) copies of the gene that causes the disorder. It's then said that the individual is *homozygous* for that gene (see Chapter 3 for more details on inheritance). Like autosomal dominant disorders, autosomal recessive disorders are coded in genes found on chromosomes other than sex chromosomes. In pedigrees, such as the one in Figure 12-3, autosomal recessive disorders typically have the following characteristics:

✔ Affected children are born to unaffected parents.

✔ Both males and females are affected equally.

✔ Children born to parents who share common ancestry (such as ethnic or religious background) are more likely to be affected than those of parents with different backgrounds.

✔ The disorder or trait skips one or more generations, or is present only in a single generation (siblings).

The probability of inheriting an autosomal recessive disorder varies depending on which alleles parents carry (see Chapter 3 for all the details on how the odds of inheritance are calculated):

- ✔ **When both parents are carriers,** every child born to the couple has a 25 percent chance of being affected.

- ✔ **When one parent is a carrier and the other isn't,** every child has a 50 percent chance of being a carrier. No child will be affected.

- ✔ **When one parent is a carrier and the other is affected,** each child has a 50 percent chance of being affected. All unaffected children from the union will be carriers.

- ✔ **When one parent is affected and the other is unaffected (and not a carrier),** all children born to the couple will be carriers. No children will be affected.

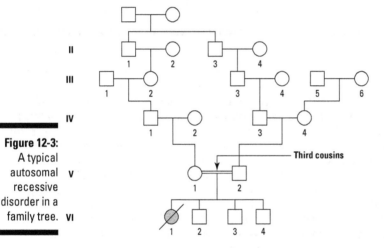

Figure 12-3: A typical autosomal recessive disorder in a family tree.

Cystic fibrosis (CF) is an autosomal recessive disorder that causes severe lung and digestive problems in affected persons. As with all autosomal recessive disorders, if both members of a couple are carriers for cystic fibrosis, they have a 25 percent chance of having an affected child with each pregnancy they have. That's because both the man and the woman are heterozygous for the allele that codes for cystic fibrosis, and each has a 50 percent probability of contributing the CF allele. You calculate the probability of *both* members of the couple contributing CF alleles in one fertilization event by multiplying the probability of each event happening independently. The probability the father contributes his CF allele is 50 percent, or 0.5; the probability the mother contributes her CF allele is also 50 percent, or 0.5. The probability that both contribute their allele is $0.5 \times 0.5 = 0.25$, or 25 percent. For more details on how to calculate probabilities of inheritance, flip to Chapters 3 and 4.

Genetic disorders in small populations

The Pennsylvania Amish don't have electricity in their homes, don't drive cars, and don't use e-mail or cellphones. They live simply in the modern world as a religious way of life. Because Amish people marry within their faith, certain genetic disorders are common. Amish families come by horse and buggy to the Clinic for Special Children in Strasburg, Pennsylvania, for genetic testing. By partnering with an ultra–high-tech company, the clinic provides rapid, inexpensive genetic testing. Among the clinic's findings is the fact that the Old Order Amish of southeastern Pennsylvania suffer from a devastating form of sudden infant death syndrome (SIDS). Altogether, the Belleville Amish community has mourned the loss of over 21 babies (one family lost six infants to the disorder). Researchers at the Translational Genomics Research Institute in Phoenix, Arizona, were able to locate the mutated gene that causes the SIDS using microarray technology (see Chapter 23). Sadly, no treatment yet exists for this type of SIDS, but gene therapy (which I cover in Chapter 16) may offer hope for small populations such as the Amish.

Some autosomal recessive disorders are more common among people of certain religious or ethnic groups, because people belonging to those groups tend to marry within the group. After many generations, everyone within the group shares common ancestry. When cousins or other close relatives marry, such relationships are referred to as *consanguineous* (meaning "same blood"). Generally, people who are more distantly related than fourth cousins aren't considered "related," but in fact, those persons still share alleles from a common ancestor. When populations are founded by rather small groups of people, those groups often have higher rates of particular genetic disorders than the general population; for more details, take a look at the sidebar "Genetic disorders in small populations." In these cases, autosomal recessive disorders may no longer skip generations, because so many persons are heterozygous and thus carriers of the disorder.

X-linked recessive traits

Males are XY and therefore have only one copy of the X chromosome; they don't have a second X to offset the expression of a mutant allele on the affected X. Thus, similar to autosomal dominant disorders, X-linked recessive disorders express the trait fully in males, even though they're not homozygous. Females rarely show X-linked recessive disorders, because being homozygous for the disorder is very rare. In pedigrees, X-linked recessive disorders have the following characteristics:

    ✔ Affected sons are born to unaffected mothers.

    ✔ Far more males than females are affected.

    ✔ The trait is *never* passed from father to son.

    ✔ The disorder skips one or more generations.

Unaffected parents can have unaffected daughters and one or more affected sons. Women who are carriers frequently have brothers with the disease, but if families are small, a carrier may have no affected immediate family members. Sons of affected fathers are never affected, but daughters of affected fathers are always carriers, because daughters must inherit one of their X chromosomes from their fathers. In this case, that X chromosome will always carry the allele for the disorder. The pedigree in Figure 12-4 is a classic example of a well-researched family possessing many carriers for the X-linked disorder hemophilia, a devastating disorder that prevents normal clotting of the blood. For more on the royal families whose history is pictured in Figure 12-4, see the sidebar "A royal pain in the genes."

The probability of inheritance of X-linked disorders depends on gender. Female carriers have a 50 percent likelihood of passing the gene on to each child. Males determine the gender of their offspring, making the chance of any particular child being a boy 50 percent. Therefore, the likelihood of a carrier mom having an affected son is 25 percent (chance of having a son = 0.5; chance of a son inheriting the affected X = 0.5; therefore, $0.5 \times 0.5 = 0.25$, or 25 percent).

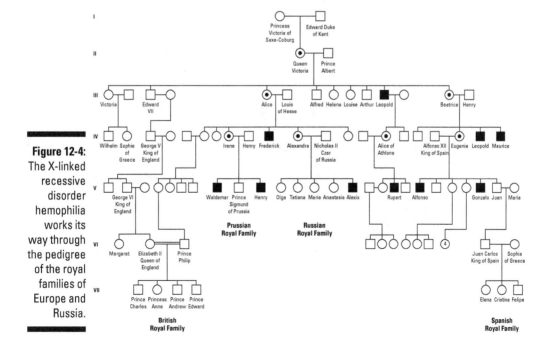

Figure 12-4:
The X-linked recessive disorder hemophilia works its way through the pedigree of the royal families of Europe and Russia.

A royal pain in the genes

You can find one of the most famous examples of an X-linked family pedigree in the royal families of Europe and Russia, which you can see in Figure 12-4. Queen Victoria of England had one son affected with hemophilia. It's not clear whom Queen Victoria inherited the allele from; she may have been the victim of spontaneous gene mutation. In any event, two of her daughters were carriers, and she had one affected son, Leopold. Queen Victoria's granddaughter Alexandra was also a carrier. Alexandra married Nicholas Romanov, who became czar of Russia, and together they had five children: four daughters and one son. The son, Alexis, suffered from hemophilia.

The role Alexis's disease played in his family's ultimate fate is debatable. Clearly, however, one of the men who influenced the downfall of Russia's royal family was linked to the family as Alexis's "doctor." Gregory Rasputin was a self-proclaimed faith healer; in photographs, he appears wild-eyed and deeply intense. He's generally perceived to have been a fraud, but at the time, he had a reputation for miraculous

healings, including helping little Alexis recover from a bleeding crisis. Despite Rasputin's talent for healing, Alexis didn't live to see adulthood. Shortly after the Russian Revolution broke out, the entire Russian royal family was murdered. (Rasputin himself had been murdered some two years earlier.)

In a bizarre final twist to the Romanov tale, a road repair crew discovered the family's bodies in 1979. Oddly, two of the family members were missing. Eleven people were supposedly killed by firing squad on the night of July 16, 1918: the Russian royal family (Alexandra, Nicholas, and their five children) along with three servants and the family doctor. However, the bodies of Alexis and his little sister, Anastasia, have never been found. Using DNA fingerprinting, researchers confirmed the identities of Alexandra and her children by matching their mitochondrial DNA to that of one of Queen Victoria's living descendants, Prince Philip of England. (To find out more about the forensic uses of DNA, flip to Chapter 18.)

X-linked dominant traits

Like autosomal dominant disorders, X-linked dominant traits don't skip generations. Every person who inherits the allele expresses the disorder. The family tree in Figure 12-5 shows many of the hallmarks of X-linked dominant disorders:

- ✔ Affected mothers have both affected sons and daughters.
- ✔ Both males and females are affected.
- ✔ All daughters of affected fathers are affected.
- ✔ The trait doesn't skip generations.

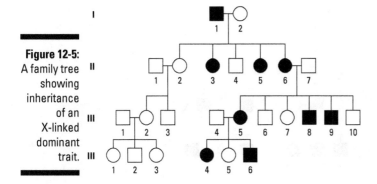

Figure 12-5:
A family tree
showing
inheritance
of an
X-linked
dominant
trait.

X-linked dominant traits show up more often in females than males because females can inherit an affected X from either parent. In addition, some disorders are lethal in males who are *hemizygous* (having only one copy of the chromosome, not two; see Chapter 5). Affected females have a 50 percent chance of having an affected child of either sex. Males never pass their affected X to sons; therefore, sons of affected fathers and unaffected mothers have *no* chance of being affected, in contrast to daughters, who are always affected. The probability of an affected man having an affected child is 50 percent (that is, equal to the likelihood of having a daughter).

Y-linked traits

The Y chromosome is passed strictly from father to son. By definition, Y-chromosome traits are considered hemizygous. Y-chromosome traits are expressed as if they were dominant because there's only one copy of the allele per male, with no other allele to offset the effect of the gene. Y-linked traits are easy to recognize when seen in a pedigree, such as Figure 12-6, because they have the following characteristics:

- ✔ Affected men pass the trait to all their sons.
- ✔ No women are ever affected.
- ✔ The trait doesn't skip generations.

Because the Y chromosome is tiny and has relatively few genes, Y-linked traits are very rare. Most of the genes involved control male-only traits such as sperm production and testis formation. If you're female and your dad has hairy ears, you can relax — hairy ears is also considered a Y-linked trait.

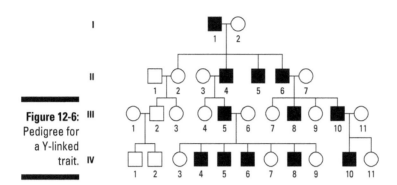

Figure 12-6:
Pedigree for
a Y-linked
trait.

Genetic Testing for Advance Notice

With the advent of many new technologies (some of which grew out of the Human Genome Project, which I explain in Chapter 8), genetic testing is easier and cheaper than ever. Genetic testing and genetic counseling often go hand in hand. The genetic counselor works to identify which disorders occur in the family, and testing then examines the DNA directly to determine whether the disorder-causing gene is present. Your physician may refer you or a family member for genetic testing for a variety of reasons, particularly if you

✔ Are a healthy person concerned about certain heritable disorders in your ethnic background or family such as breast cancer or Huntington disease

✔ Are a healthy person with a family history of a recessive disorder, and you're thinking about having a child

✔ Are a pregnant woman over 35

✔ Are an affected person and need to confirm a diagnosis

✔ Have an infant who's at risk (because his or her parents are known or suspected carriers)

General testing

Every person the world over carries one or more alleles that cause genetic disease. Most of us never know which alleles or how many we carry. If you have a family member who's affected with a rare genetic disorder, particularly an autosomal dominant disorder with incomplete penetrance or delayed onset, you may be vitally concerned about which allele(s) you carry. Persons currently unaffected with certain disorders can seek genetic testing to learn if they're carriers. Most tests involve a blood sample, but some are done with a simple cheek swab to capture a few skin cells. You can find more about genetic testing for inherited disorders in Chapter 13 and about testing for inherited forms of cancer in Chapter 14. Genetic testing has many ethical implications, as I cover in Chapter 21.

Prenatal testing

Prenatal diagnosis is commonly used for unborn children of women over 35, because such women are much more likely than younger women to have children with chromosomal disorders (see Chapter 15). Prenatal testing is designed to allow time for couples to make decisions about treatments to be administered either during pregnancy or after delivery of an affected infant.

Chorionic villus sampling and amniocentesis

For definitive diagnosis of a genetic disorder, testing requires tissue of the affected person. Two common prenatal tests used to obtain fetal tissue for testing are *chorionic villus sampling* (CVS) and *amniocentesis*. Both tests require ultrasound to guide the instruments used to obtain the samples (see the following section for more info on ultrasound).

- **CVS** is usually done late in the first trimester of pregnancy (weeks 10 to 12). A catheter is inserted vaginally and guided to the outer layer of the placenta, called the *chorion*. Gentle suction is used to collect a small sample of chorionic tissue. The placental tissue arises from the fetus, not the mother, so the collected cells give an accurate picture of the fetus's chromosome number and genetic profile. The advantages of CVS are that it can be done earlier than most other prenatal genetic tests; it's extremely accurate; and because a relatively large sample is obtained, results are rapidly produced. CVS is associated with a slightly higher rate of miscarriage.

- **Amniocentesis** is usually done early in the second trimester of pregnancy (weeks 15 and beyond). Amniocentesis is used to obtain a sample of the amniotic fluid that surrounds the growing fetus, because amniotic fluid contains fetal cells (skin cells that have sloughed off) that can be examined for prenatal testing. The fluid is drawn directly from the uterus using a needle inserted through the abdomen. Because fetal cells in the fluid are at a very low concentration, the cells must be grown in a lab to provide enough tissue for testing, making results slow to come (about one to two weeks). But the results are accurate, and complications following the procedure (such as miscarriage) are rare.

Ultrasound

Ultrasound technology allows physicians to examine a growing fetus visually, along with its spinal cord, brain, and all its organs. Ultrasound can be done much earlier in a woman's pregnancy than CVS or amniocentesis.

Ultrasound directs extremely high frequency sound waves through the mother's abdominal wall. The sound waves bounce off the fetus and return to a receiver that then converts the sound wave "picture" into a visual image. New ultrasound technologies include powerful computers that put together a three-dimensional image, giving amazingly crisp pictures of facial features and body parts. Ultrasound is generally used to screen for genetic disorders associated with physical features or deformities. Ultrasound can be used at any time during pregnancy and is completely non-invasive, with little or no risk to mother or baby.

Newborn screening

Some genetic disorders are highly treatable using dietary restrictions. Therefore, all newborns in the United States are tested for two common, highly treatable genetic disorders: *phenylketonuria* and *galactosemia*. Both of these disorders are autosomal recessive.

- **Phenylketonuria** causes mental retardation due to the buildup of *phenylalanine* (an amino acid that's part of a normal diet) in the brain of affected persons. A diet low in phenylalanine allows such persons to live symptom-free lives. (This disorder and the potential to control it are the reasons certain diet colas contain warning labels regarding phenylalanine content.) Phenylketonuria occurs once in every 10,000 to 20,000 births.

- **Galactosemia** is a disorder similar to phenylketonuria that results from an inability to break down one of the products of lactose (milk sugar). A lactose-free diet allows affected persons to live symptom-free lives. If untreated, galactosemia results in brain damage, kidney and liver failure, and often death. Galactosemia occurs once in every 45,000 births.

Testing for these two disorders isn't actually genetic testing; rather, the tests are designed to look for the presence of abnormal amounts of either phenylalanine or galactose — the phenotypes of the disorders. As technologies advance, these tests may be replaced with direct DNA examination by gene chips (which you can read more about in Chapter 23).

Chapter 13

Mutation and Inherited Diseases: Things You Can't Change

....

In This Chapter

▶ Considering the different types and causes of mutation

▶ Realizing the consequences of and repairs for mutation

▶ Looking at some common inherited diseases

....

Despite what you may think, mutation is good thing. *Mutation,* which is simply genetic change, is responsible for all phenotypic variation. Variation in flower colors and plant height, the flavor of different varieties of apples, the differences among dog breeds, you name it — the natural process that created all those different phenotypes is mutation. Mutation occurs all the time, spontaneously and pretty much randomly.

But like many good things, mutation can also be bad. It can disrupt normal gene activity and cause disease such as cancer (flip to Chapter 14 for details) and birth defects (see Chapter 15). In this chapter, you discover what causes mutations, how DNA can repair itself in the face of mutation, and what the consequences are when repair attempts fail.

Sorting Out Types of Mutations

Mutations fall into two major categories, and the distinction between the two is important to keep in mind:

> ✔ **Somatic mutations:** Mutations in body cells that don't make eggs or sperm. Mutations that occur in the somatic cells aren't *heritable* — that is, the changes can't be passed from parent to offspring — but they do affect the person with the mutation.

✔ **Germ-cell mutations:** Mutations in the sex cells (germ cells like eggs and sperm; see Chapter 2 for the scoop on cell types) that lead to embryo formation. Unlike somatic mutations, germ-cell mutations often don't affect the parent. Instead, they affect the offspring of the person with the mutation and are heritable from then on.

Some disorders have elements of both somatic and germ-cell (heritable) mutations. Many cancers that run in families arise as a result of somatic mutations in persons who are already susceptible to the disease because of mutations they inherited from one or both parents. (You can find out more about heritable cancers in Chapter 14.)

Both somatic and germ-cell mutations usually come about, in a general sense, because of

✔ **Substitutions of one base for another:** Substitutions are sometimes called *point mutations.* Usually, only one mistaken base is involved, although sometimes both the base and its complement are changed (for a review of the chemistry of DNA, turn to Chapter 6). This type of mutation breaks down further into two categories:

  • **Transition mutation:** When a purine base is substituted for the other purine, or one pyrimidine is substituted for the other pyrimidine. Transition mutations are the most common form of substitution errors.

  • **Transversion mutation:** When a purine replaces a pyrimidine (or vice versa).

✔ **Insertions and deletions of one or more bases:** When an extra base is added to a strand, the error is called an *insertion.* Dropping a base is considered a *deletion.* Insertions and deletions are the most common forms of mutation. When the change happens within a gene, both insertions and deletions lead to a change in the way the genetic code is read during translation (flip to Chapter 10 for a translation review). Translation involves reading the genetic code in three-letter batches, so when one or two bases are added or deleted, the reading frame is shifted. This *frameshift mutation* results in a completely different interpretation of what the code says and produces an entirely different amino acid strand. As you can imagine, these effects have disastrous consequences, because the expected gene product isn't produced. If three bases are added or deleted, the reading frame isn't affected. The result of a three-base insertion or deletion, called an *in-frame mutation,* is that one amino acid is either added (insertion) or lost (deletion). In-frame mutations can be just as bad as frameshift mutations. I cover the consequences of these sorts of mutations in the section "Facing the Consequences of Mutation" later in this chapter.

What Causes Mutation?

Mutations can occur for a whole suite of reasons. In general, though, the causes of mutations are either random or because of exposure to outside agents such as chemicals or radiation. In the sections that follow, I delve into each of these causes.

Spontaneous mutations

Spontaneous mutation occurs randomly and without any urging from some external cause. It's a natural, normal occurrence. Because the vast majority of your DNA doesn't code for anything, most spontaneous mutation goes unnoticed (check out Chapter 8 for more details about your noncoding "junk" DNA). But when mutation occurs within a gene, the function of the gene can be changed or disrupted. Those changes can then result in unwanted side effects (such as cancer, which I address in Chapter 14).

Scientists are all about counting, sorting, and quantifying, and it's no different with mutations. Spontaneous mutations are measured in the following ways:

- ✔ **Frequency:** Mutations are sometimes measured by the frequency of occurrence. *Frequency* is the number of times some event occurs within a group of individuals. When you hear that one in some number of persons has a particular disease-causing allele, the number is a frequency. For example, one study estimates that the X-linked disease hemophilia has a frequency of 13 cases for every 100,000 males.

- ✔ **Rate:** Another way of looking at mutations is in the framework of a *rate,* like the number of mutations occurring per round of cell division, or the number of mutations per gamete or per generation. Mutation rates appear to vary a lot from organism to organism. Even within a species, mutation rates vary depending on which part of the genome you're examining. Some convincing studies show that mutation rate even varies by sex and that mutation rates are higher in males than females (check out the sidebar "Dad's age matters, too" for more on this topic). Regardless of how it's viewed, spontaneous mutation occurs at a steady but very low rate (like around one per million gametes).

Most spontaneous mutations occur because of mistakes made during replication (all the details of how DNA replicates itself are in Chapter 7). Here are the three main sources of error that can happen during replication:

✔ Mismatched bases are overlooked during proofreading.

✔ Strand slip-ups lead to deletions or insertions.

✔ Spontaneous but natural chemical changes cause bases to be misread during replication, resulting in substitutions or deletions.

Mismatches during replication

Usually, *DNA polymerase* catches and fixes mistakes made during replication. DNA polymerase has the job of reading the template, adding the appropriate complementary base to the new strand, and then proofreading the new base before moving to the next base on the template. DNA polymerase can snip out erroneous bases and replace them, but occasionally, a wrong base escapes detection. Such an error is possible because noncomplementary bases can form hydrogen bonds through what's called *wobble pairing*. As you can see in Figure 13-1, wobble pairing can occur

✔ **Between thymine and guanine** without any modifications to either base (because these noncomplementary bases can sometimes form bonds in odd spots).

✔ **Between cytosine and adenine** only when adenine acquires an additional hydrogen atom (called *protonation*).

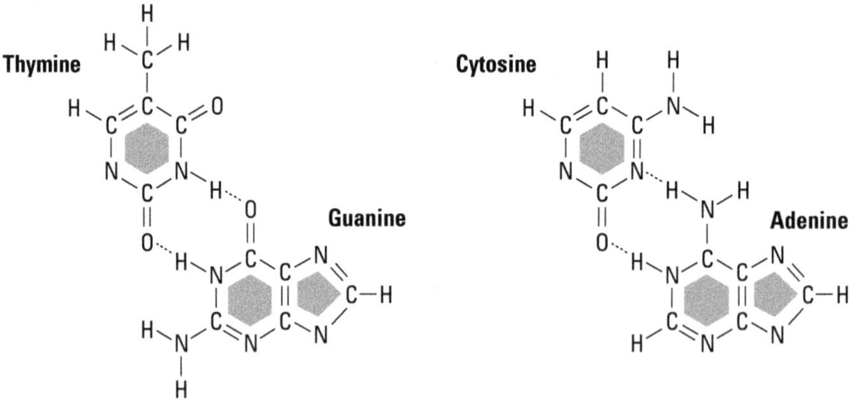

Figure 13-1: Wobble base pairing allows mismatched bases to form bonds.

If DNA repair crews don't catch the error and fix it (see the section "Evaluating Options for DNA Repair" later in this chapter), and the mismatched base remains in place, the mistake is perpetuated after the next round of replication, apparent in Figure 13-2. The mistaken base is read as part of the template strand, and its complement is added to the newly replicated strand opposite. Thus, the mutation is permanently added to the structure of the DNA in question.

Dad's age matters, too

The relationship between maternal age and an increased incidence of chromosome problems, particularly Down syndrome, is very well-known. *Nondisjunction events* — the failure of chromosomes to separate normally during meiosis — in developing eggs are thought to be a consequence of aging in women. Very few similar genetic problems appear to arise in men, who, unlike women, produce new *gametes* (reproductive cells) in the form of sperm throughout their lifetime. However, older men are susceptible to germ-cell mutations that can cause heritable disorders in their children.

The reason that older men are more susceptible to spontaneous germ-cell mutations is

the same reason that they're less likely to have nondisjunctions — males produce sperm throughout their life. This continued sperm production means that a 50-year-old man's germ cells have replicated over 800 times. As DNA ages, replication gets less accurate, and repair mechanisms become faulty. Thus, older fathers have an increased risk (although it's still only slight) of fathering children with genetic disorders. *Achondroplasia* (an autosomal dominant form of dwarfism that's typified by shortened limbs and an enlarged head), *Marfan syndrome* (a disorder of skeletal and muscle tissue that causes heart and eye problems) and *progeria* (a disease that causes rapid aging in children) are all associated with older fathers.

Figure 13-2:
A mismatched base pair creates a permanent change in the DNA with one round of replication.

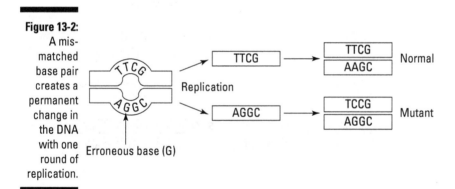

Erroneous base (G)

Strand slip-ups

During replication, both strands of DNA are copied more or less at the same time. Occasionally, a portion of one strand (either the template or the newly synthesized strand) can form a loop in a process called *strand slippage*. In Figure 13-3, you can see that strand slippage in the new strand results in an insertion, and slippage in the template strand results in a deletion.

Strand slippage is associated with repeating bases. When one base is repeated more than five times in a row (AAAAAA, for example), or when any number of bases are repeated over and over (such as AGTAGTAGT), strand slippage during replication is far more likely to occur. In some cases, the mistakes produce lots of variation in noncoding DNA, and the variation is useful for determining individual identity; this is the basis for DNA fingerprinting (see Chapter 18 for that discussion). When repeat sequences occur within genes, the addition of new repeats can lead to a stronger effect of the gene. This strengthening effect, called *anticipation,* occurs in genetic disorders such as Huntington disease. (You can find out more about anticipation in Chapter 4.)

Another problem that repeated bases generate is unequal crossing-over. During meiosis, homologous chromosomes are supposed to align exactly so that exchanges of information are equal and don't disrupt genes (turn to Chapter 2 for a meiosis review). Unequal crossing-over occurs when the exchange between chromosomes results in the swapping of uneven amounts of material. Repeated sequences cause unequal crossovers because so many similar bases match. The identical bases can align in multiple, matching ways that result in mismatches elsewhere along the chromosome. Unequal crossover events lead to large-scale chromosome changes (like those I describe in Chapter 15). Chromosomes in cells affected by cancer are also vulnerable to crossing-over errors (see Chapter 14 for details).

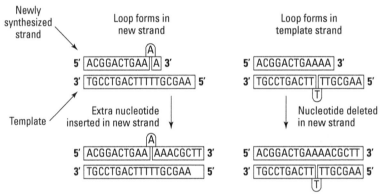

Figure 13-3: Strand slippage causes loops to form during replication, resulting in deletions or insertions.

Spontaneous chemical changes

DNA can undergo spontaneous changes in its chemistry that result in both deletions and substitutions. DNA naturally loses purine bases at times in a process called *apurination.* Most often, a purine is lost when the bond between adenine and the sugar, deoxyribose, is broken. (See Chapter 6 for a reminder of what a nucleotide looks like.) When a purine is lost, replication treats the spot occupied by the orphaned sugar as if it never contained a base at all, resulting in a deletion.

Deamination is another chemical change that occurs naturally in DNA. It's what happens when an amino group (composed of a nitrogen atom and two hydrogens — NH_2) is lost from a base. Figure 13-4 shows the before and after stages of deamination. When cytosine loses its amino group, it's converted to uracil. Uracil normally isn't found in DNA at all because it's a component of RNA. If uracil appears in a DNA strand, replication replaces the uracil with a thymine, creating a substitution error. Until it's snipped out and replaced during repair (see "Evaluating Options for DNA Repair" later in this chapter), uracil acts as a template during replication and pairs with adenine. Ultimately, what was a C-G pair transitions into an A-T pair instead.

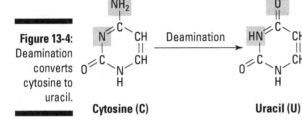

Figure 13-4:
Deamination converts cytosine to uracil.

Induced mutations

Induced mutations result from exposure to some outside agent such as chemicals or radiation. It probably comes as no surprise to you to find out that many chemicals can cause DNA to mutate. *Carcinogens* (chemicals that cause cancers) aren't uncommon; the chemicals in cigarette smoke are probably the biggest offenders. In addition to chemicals that cause mutations, sources of radiation, from X-rays to sunlight, are also mutagenic. A *mutagen* is any factor that causes an increase in mutation rate. Mutagens may or may not have phenotypic effects — it depends on what part of the DNA is affected. The following sections cover two major categories of mutagens: chemicals and radiation. Each causes different damage to DNA.

Chemical mutagens

The ability of chemicals to cause permanent changes in the DNA of organisms was discovered by Charlotte Auerbach in the 1940s (see the sidebar "The chemistry of mutation" for the full story). There are many types of mutagenic chemicals; the following sections address four of the most common.

Base analogs

Base analogs are chemicals that are structurally very similar to the bases normally found in DNA. Base analogs can get incorporated into DNA during replication because of their structural similarity to normal bases. One base analog, 5-bromouracil, is almost identical to the base thymine. Most often, 5-bromouracil (also known as 5BU), which is pictured in Figure 13-5, gets incorporated as a substitute for thymine and, as such, is paired with adenine. The problem arises when DNA replicates again with 5-bromouracil as part of the template strand; 5BU is mistaken for a cytosine and gets mispaired with guanine. The series of events looks like this: 5-bromouracil is incorporated where thymine used to be, so T-A becomes 5BU-A. After one round of replication, the pair is 5BU-G, because 5BU is prone to chemical changes that make it a mimic of cytosine, the base normally paired with guanine. After a second round of replication, the pair ends up as C-G, because 5BU isn't found in normal DNA. Thus, an A-T ends up as a C-G pair.

Another class of base analog chemicals that foul up normal base pairing is *deaminators*. Deamination is a normal process that causes spontaneous mutation; however, problems arise because deamination can get speeded up when cells are exposed to chemicals that selectively knock out amino groups converting cytosines to uracils.

Figure 13-5:
Base analogs, such as 5-bromouracil, are very similar to normal bases.

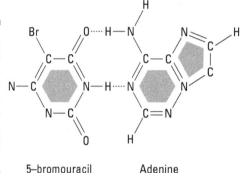

5–bromouracil   Adenine

Alkylating agents

Like base analogs, *alkylating agents* induce mispairings between bases. Alkylating agents, such as the chemical weapon mustard gas, add chemical groups to the existing bases that make up DNA. As a consequence, the altered bases pair with the wrong complement, thus introducing the mutation. Surprisingly, alkylating agents are often used to fight cancer as part of chemotherapy; therapeutic versions of alkylating agents may inhibit cancer growth by interfering with the replication of DNA in rapidly dividing cancer cells.

Free radicals

Some forms of oxygen, called *free radicals,* are unusually reactive, meaning they react readily with other chemicals. These oxygens can damage DNA directly (by causing strand breaks) or can convert bases into new unwanted chemicals that, like most other chemical mutagens, then cause mispairing during replication. Free radicals of oxygen occur normally in your body as a product of metabolism, but most of the time, they don't cause any problems. Certain activities — such as cigarette smoking and high exposure to radiation, pollution, and weed killers — increase the number of free radicals in your system to dangerous levels.

Intercalating agents

Many different kinds of chemicals wedge themselves between the stacks of bases that form the double helix itself, disrupting the shape of the double helix. Chemicals with flat ring structures, such as dyes, are prone to fitting themselves between bases in a process called *intercalation*. Figure 13-6 shows intercalating agents at work. Intercalating agents create bulges in the double helix that often result in insertions or deletions during replication, which in turn cause frameshift mutations.

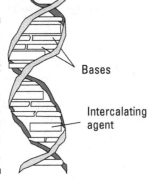

Figure 13-6:
Intercalating agents fit between the stacks of bases to disfigure the double helix.

Bases

Intercalating agent

Radiation

Radiation damages DNA in a couple of different ways. First, radiation can break the strands of the double helix by knocking out bonds between sugars and phosphates (see Chapter 6 for a review of how the strands are put together). If only one strand is broken, the damage is easily repaired. But when two strands are broken, large parts of the chromosome can be lost; these kinds of losses can affect cancer cells (see Chapter 14) and cause birth defects (see Chapter 15).

Second, radiation causes mutation through the formation of *dimers*. Dimers (*di-* meaning "two"; *mer* meaning "thing") are unwanted bonds between two bases stacked on top of each other (on the same side of the helix, rather than on opposite sides). They're most often formed when two thymines in a DNA sequence bind together, which you can see in Figure 13-7.

Thymine dimers can be repaired, but if damage is extensive, the cell dies (see Chapter 14 for how cells are programmed to die). When dimers aren't repaired, the machinery of DNA replication assumes that two thymines are present and puts in two adenines. Unfortunately, cytosine and thymine can also form dimers, so the default repair strategy sometimes introduces a mutation instead.

The chemistry of mutation

If ever anyone had an excuse to give up, it was Charlotte Auerbach. Born in Germany in 1899, Auerbach was part of a lively and highly educated Jewish family. In spite of her deep interest in biology, she became a teacher, convinced that higher education would be closed to her because of her religious heritage. As anti-Jewish sentiment in Germany grew, Auerbach lost her teaching job in 1933 when every Jewish secondary-school teacher in the country was fired. As a result, she emigrated to Britain, where she earned her PhD in genetics in 1935. Charlotte Auerbach didn't enjoy the respect her degree and abilities deserved. She was treated as a lab technician and instructed to clean the cages of experimental animals. All that changed when she met Herman Muller in 1938. Like Auerbach, Muller was interested in how genes work; his approach to the problem was to induce mutations using radiation and then examine the effects produced by the defective genes. Inspired by Muller, Auerbach began work on chemical mutagens. She focused her efforts on mustard gas, a horrifically effective chemical weapon used extensively during World War I. Her research involved heating liquid mustard gas and exposing fruit flies to the fumes. It's a wonder her experiments didn't kill her.

What Charlotte's experiments did do was show that mustard gas is an alkylating agent, a mutagen that causes substitution mutations. Shortly after the end of World War II, and after persevering through burns caused by hot mustard gas, Auerbach published her findings. At last, she received the recognition and respect her work warranted. Charlotte Auerbach went on to have a long and highly successful career in genetics. She stopped working only after old age robbed her of her sight. She died in Edinburgh, Scotland, in 1994 at the age of 95.

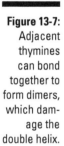

Figure 13-7: Adjacent thymines can bond together to form dimers, which damage the double helix.

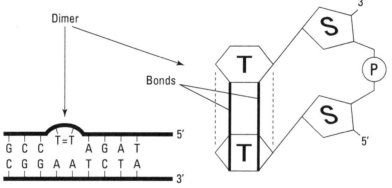

Facing the Consequences of Mutation

When a gene mutates and that mutation is passed along to the next generation, the new, mutated version of the gene is considered a new allele. *Alleles* are simply alternative forms of genes. For most genes, many alleles exist. The effects of mutations that create new alleles are compared with the mutations' physical *(phenotypic)* effects. If a mutation has no effect, it's considered *silent*. Most silent mutations result from the redundancy of the genetic code. The code is redundant in the sense that multiple combinations of bases have identical meanings (see Chapter 9 for more about the redundancy of genetic code).

Sometimes, mutations cause a completely different amino acid to be put in during translation. Mutations that actually alter the code are called *missense mutations*. A *nonsense mutation* occurs when a message to stop translation (called a *stop codon*) is introduced into the middle of the sequence. The introduction of the stop codon usually means the gene stops functioning altogether.

Mutations are often divided into two types:

- ✔ **Neutral:** When the amino acid produced from the mutated gene still creates a fully functional, normal protein (via translation; see Chapter 9).

- ✔ **Functional change:** When a new protein is created representing a change in function of the gene. A *gain-of-function mutation* creates an entirely new trait or phenotype. Sometimes, the new trait is harmless, like a new eye color. In other cases, the gain is decidedly harmful and usually autosomal dominant (flip to Chapter 12 for more on autosomal dominant traits) because the gene is producing a new protein that actually does something (the gain-of-function part). Even though there's only one copy of the new allele, its effect is noticeable and thus considered dominant over the original, unmutated allele.

  If a mutation causes the gene to stop functioning altogether or vastly alters normal function, it's considered a *loss-of-function mutation.* All nonsense mutations are loss-of-function mutations, but not all loss-of-function mutations are the result of nonsense mutations. The usefulness of the protein made from a particular gene can be lost, even when no stop codon has been added prematurely. Insertions and deletions are often loss-of-function mutations because they cause frameshifts (Chapter 9 explains how the genetic code is read in frames). Frameshifts cause an entirely new set of amino acids to be put together from the new set of instructions. Most of the time, these new proteins are useless and nonfunctional. Loss-of-function mutations are usually recessive because the normal, unmutated allele is still producing product — usually enough to compensate for the mutated allele. Loss-of-function mutations are only detected when a person is homozygous for the mutation and is making no functional gene product at all.

Evaluating Options for DNA Repair

Mutations in your DNA can be repaired in four major ways:

- **Mismatch repair:** Incorrect bases are found, removed, and replaced with the correct, complementary base. Most of the time, DNA polymerase, the enzyme that helps make new DNA, immediately detects mismatched bases put in by mistake during replication. DNA polymerase can back up and correct the error without missing a beat. But if a mismatched base gets put in some other way (through strand slip-ups, for example), a set of enzymes that are constantly scrutinizing the double strand to detect bulges or constrictions signals a mismatched base pair. The mismatch repair enzymes can detect any differences between the template and the newly synthesized strand, so they clip out the wrong base and, using the template strand as a guide, insert the correct base.

- **Direct repair:** Bases that are modified in some way (like when oxidation converts a base to some new form) are converted back to their original states. Direct repair enzymes look for bases that have been converted to some new chemical, usually by the addition of some unwanted group of atoms. Instead of using a cut-and-paste mechanism, the enzymes clip off the atoms that don't belong, converting the base back to its original form.

- **Base-excision repair:** Base-excisions and nucleotide-excisions (check out the next bullet) work in much the same way. *Base-excisions* occur when an unwanted base (such as uracil; see the section "Spontaneous chemical changes" earlier in this chapter) is found. Specialized enzymes recognize the damage, and the base is snipped out and replaced with the correct one.

- **Nucleotide-excision repair:** *Nucleotide-excision* means that the entire nucleotide (and sometimes several surrounding nucleotides as well) gets removed all at once. When intercalating agents or dimers distort the double helix, nucleotide-excision repair mechanisms step in to snip part of the strand, remove the damage, and synthesize fresh DNA to replace the damaged section.

  As with base excision, specialized enzymes recognize the damaged section of the DNA. The damaged section is removed, and newly synthesized DNA is laid down to replace it. In nucleotide-excision, the double helix is opened up, much like it is during replication (which I cover in Chapter 7). The sugar-phosphate backbone of the damaged strand is broken in two places to allow removal of that entire portion of the strand. DNA polymerase synthesizes a new section, and DNA ligase seals the breaks in the strand to complete the repair process.

Examining Common Inherited Diseases

Even though mutation is a common occurrence, most inherited diseases are comfortingly rare. Inherited disorders are often recessive and show up only when an individual is homozygous for the trait. Inherited diseases aren't non-existent, though. The following sections provide details on three relatively common inherited diseases. You can find out more about inheritance patterns in Chapter 12.

Cystic fibrosis

The most common inherited disorder among Caucasians in the United States is cystic fibrosis (CF). This autosomal recessive disorder occurs in roughly one in every 3,000 births (*autosomal recessive* means the gene isn't on a sex chromosome and a person must have two copies of the allele to get the disease; see Chapter 3). The mutations (there can be many) that cause CF occur in a gene located on chromosome 7. Persons affected with CF produce thick, sticky mucus in their lungs, intestines, and pancreas.

The gene implicated in CF, called the *cystic fibrosis transmembrane conductance regulator gene* (or *CFTR* for short), normally controls the passage of salt across cell membranes. Water naturally moves to areas where salt is more concentrated, so the movement of salt from one place to another has an effect on how much water is present in parts of the body. In persons with CF, the removal of salt from the body (via sweat) is abnormally high. As a result, the lungs, pancreas, and digestive system can't retain enough water to dilute the mucus normally found in those systems, so the buildup of thick mucus blocks breathing passages and makes waste elimination difficult, causing severe breathing and digestive difficulties and a high susceptibility to respiratory illnesses.

CF is diagnosed in two ways:

- ✔ Persons who may be carriers for the mutated allele can undergo genetic testing.
- ✔ Children possibly affected by the disease are diagnosed by a "sweat test." Their sweat is tested for salt content, and abnormally high amounts of salt indicate that the child has the disease.

CF is a target of gene therapy (see Chapter 16), but it resists a cure. Most afflicted persons must endure a lifetime of treatment that includes having someone pound on their chests so that they can remove the mucus from their lungs by coughing. The prognosis for CF has improved dramatically, yet most persons affected by the disease don't live far beyond their 30s.

For additional information on cystic fibrosis and to find contacts in your area, contact the Cystic Fibrosis Foundation at 800-344-4823 (www.cff.org) or the Canadian Cystic Fibrosis Foundation at 800-378-2233 (www.cystic fibrosis.ca).

Sickle cell anemia

Sickle cell anemia is the most common genetic disorder among African Americans in the United States — roughly one in every 400 births is affected by this autosomal recessive disorder. The mutation responsible for sickle cell is found on chromosome 11, the gene responsible for making one part of the protein complex that composes hemoglobin (check out Chapter 9 for how complex proteins are formed). In the case of sickle cell, one base is mutated from adenine to thymine (a *transversion*). The mistake changes one amino acid added during translation from glutamic acid to valine, producing a protein that folds improperly and can't carry oxygen effectively.

The red blood cells of persons affected by sickle cell take on the disease's characteristic crescent shape when oxygen levels in the body are lower than usual (often as the result of aerobic exercise). The sickling event has the side effect of causing blood clots to form in the smaller blood vessels (capillaries) throughout the body. Clot formation is extremely painful and also causes damage to tissues that are sensitive to oxygen deprivation. Persons with sickle cell are vulnerable to kidney failure, yet with good medical care, most affected persons live into middle adulthood (40 to 50 years of age).

For more information on sickle cell anemia, contact the American Sickle Cell Anemia Association at 216-229-8600 (www.ascaa.org).

Tay-Sachs disease

An autosomal recessive disorder, Tay-Sachs disease is a progressive, fatal disease of the nervous system and is unusually common among persons of *Ashkenazi* (Eastern European) Jewish ancestry. One in every 30 to 40 persons of Jewish ancestry is a carrier of Tay-Sachs disease. French Canadians and persons of Cajun (south Louisiana) descent are also often carriers of the mutated allele.

The mutation that causes Tay-Sachs disease is found in the gene that codes for the enzyme hexosaminidase A *(HEXA)*. Normally, your body breaks down a class of fats called *gangliosides*. When *HEXA* is mutated, the normal metabolism of gangliosides stops and the fats build up in the brain, causing damage. Children inheriting two copies of the affected allele are normal at birth, but as the fats build up in their brain over time, these children become blind, deaf, mentally impaired, and ultimately paralyzed. Most children with Tay-Sachs disease don't survive beyond the age of 4. Unlike some metabolic disorders, such as phenylketonuria (see Chapter 12), changes in diet don't prevent the buildup of the unwanted chemical in the body.

For more information on Tay-Sachs disease, contact the National Tay-Sachs & Allied Diseases Association at 800-906-8723 (www.ntsad.org).

Chapter 15

Chromosome Disorders: It's All a Numbers Game

In This Chapter

▶ Examining chromosomes to figure out numbers and sets

▶ Understanding how things go wrong with chromosomes

*T*he study of chromosomes is, in part, the study of cells. Geneticists who specialize in *cytogenetics,* the genetics of the cell, often examine chromosomes as the cell divides because that's when the chromosomes are easiest to see. Cell division is one of the most important activities that cells undergo; it's required for normal life, and a special sort of cell division prepares sex cells for the job of reproduction. Chromosomes are copied and divvied up during cell division, and getting the right number of chromosomes in each cell as it divides is critical. Most chromosome disorders (such as Down syndrome) occur because of mistakes during *meiosis* (the cell division that makes sex cells; see Chapter 2).

This chapter helps you understand how and why chromosome disorders occur. You find out some of the ways geneticists study the chromosome content of cells. Knowing chromosome numbers allows scientists to decode the mysteries of inheritance, especially when the number of chromosomes (called *ploidy*) gets complicated. Counting chromosomes also allows doctors to determine the origin of physical abnormalities caused by the presence of too many or too few chromosomes.

If you skipped over Chapter 2, you may want to flip back to it before reading this chapter to get a handle on the basics of chromosomes and how cells divide.

What Chromosomes Reveal

One way a geneticist counts chromosomes is with the aid of microscopes and special dyes to see the chromosomes during *metaphase* — the one time in the cell cycle when the chromosomes take on a fat, easy-to-see, sausage shape. (Jump to Chapter 2 to review the cell cycle.) Here's how the process of examining chromosomes works:

1. A sample of cells is obtained. Almost any sort of dividing cell works as a sample, including root cells from plants, blood cells, or skin cells.

2. The cells are *cultured* — given the proper nutrients and conditions for growth — to stimulate cell division.

3. Some cells are removed from the culture and treated to stop mitosis during metaphase.

4. Dyes are added to make the chromosomes easy to see.

5. The cells are inspected under a microscope. The chromosomes are sorted, examined for obvious abnormalities, and counted.

This process of chromosome examination is called *karyotyping*. A karyotype reveals exactly how many chromosomes are present in a cell, along with some details about the chromosomes' structure. Scientists can only see these details by staining the chromosomes with special dyes.

When examining a karyotype, a geneticist looks at each individual chromosome. Every chromosome has a typical size and shape; the location of the centromere and the length of the chromosome arms (the parts on either side of the centromere) are what define each chromosome's physical appearance (refer to Chapter 2 to see what some chromosomes look like up close). The two types of chromosome arms are the

✔ *p* **arm:** The shorter of the two arms (from the word *petite*, French for "small")

✔ *q* **arm:** The longer arm (because *q* follows *p* alphabetically)

In some disorders, one of the chromosome arms is misplaced or missing. Therefore, geneticists often refer to the chromosome number along with the letter *p* or *q* to communicate which part of the chromosome is affected.

Counting Up Chromosomes

Ploidy sounds like some bizarre, extraterrestrial, science-fiction creature, but the word actually refers to the number of chromosomes a particular organism has. Two sorts of "ploidys" are commonly bandied about in genetics:

✔ **Aneuploid** refers to an imbalance in the number of chromosomes. Situations involving aneuploidy are often given the suffix *-somy* to communicate whether chromosomes are missing *(monosomy)* or extra *(trisomy)*.

✔ **Euploid** refers to the number of *sets* of chromosomes an organism has. Thus, *diploid* tells you that the organism in question has two sets of chromosomes (often written as *2n,* with *n* being the haploid number of chromosomes in the set; see Chapter 2 for more on how chromosomes are counted up). When an organism is euploid, its total number of chromosomes is an exact multiple of its haploid number *(n).*

Aneuploidy: Extra or missing chromosomes

Shortly after Thomas Hunt Morgan discovered that certain traits are linked to the X chromosome (see Chapter 5 for the full story), his student Calvin Bridges discovered that chromosomes don't always play by the rules. The laws of Mendelian inheritance depend on the segregation of chromosomes — an event that takes place during the first phase of meiosis (see Chapter 2 for meiosis coverage). But sometimes chromosomes don't segregate; two or more copies of the same chromosome are sent to one *gamete* (sperm or egg), leaving another gamete without a copy of one chromosome. Through his study of fruit flies, Bridges discovered the phenomenon of *nondisjunction,* the failure of chromosomes to segregate properly. Figure 15-1 shows nondisjunction at various stages of meiotic division. (For more on how Morgan and Bridges made their discoveries, check out the sidebar "Flies!")

While studying eye color in flies (flip to Chapter 5 for more about this X-linked trait), Bridges crossed white-eyed female flies with red-eyed males. He expected to get all white-eyed sons and all red-eyed daughters from this sort of monohybrid cross (Chapter 3 explains monohybrid crosses). But every so often, he got red-eyed sons and white-eyed daughters. Bridges already knew that females get two copies of the X chromosome and males get only one, and that eye color is linked with X. He also knew that eye color is a recessive trait; the only way females could have white eyes is to have two copies of X that both have the allele for white. So how could the odd combinations of sex and eye color that Bridges saw occur?

Bridges realized that the X chromosomes of some of his female parent flies must not be obeying the rules of segregation. During the first round of meiosis, the homologous pairs of chromosomes should separate. If that doesn't happen, some eggs get two copies of the mother's X chromosome (see Figure 15-1). In Bridges's research, both copies of the mother's X carried the allele for white eyes. When a red-eyed male fertilized a two-X egg, two results were possible, as you can see in Figure 15-2. An XXX zygote resulted in a red-eyed daughter (which usually died). An XXY zygote turned out to be a white-eyed female (check out Chapter 5 for how sex is determined in fruit flies). Fertilized eggs that had no X chromosome resulted in a red-eyed male (with genotype X). Eggs that didn't get an X chromosome and receive a Y from the father were never viable at all.

Many human chromosomal disorders arise from a sort of nondisjunction similar to that of fruit flies. For more information on these disorders, take a look at the section "Exploring Chromosome Variations" later in this chapter.

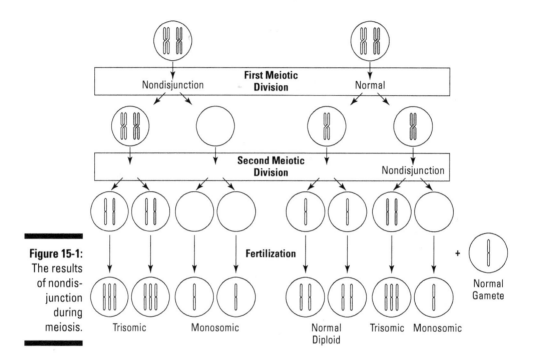

Figure 15-1:
The results of nondisjunction during meiosis.

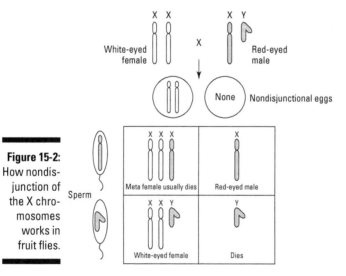

Figure 15-2:
How nondisjunction of the X chromosomes works in fruit flies.

Flies!

Some of the greatest scientific discoveries have been made in the humblest of settings. Take Thomas Hunt Morgan's laboratory, affectionately known as the Fly Room. A mere 368 square feet, it was crammed with eight students, their desks, hundreds of glass milk bottles full of fruit flies, and large bunches of bananas hung from the ceiling as food for the fruit flies. The room reeked of rotting bananas, literally buzzed with escapee flies, and had more than its fair share of cockroaches. Yet from 1910 to 1930, this cramped setting was home to some of the most important scientific discoveries of its time — discoveries that still apply to the understanding of genetics today.

Calvin Bridges and Alfred Sturtevant were both undergraduates at Columbia University in New York City in 1909. After hearing a lecture presented by Morgan, both Bridges and Sturtevant landed desk space in the Fly Room. Gregor Mendel's work had only just been rediscovered, so it was an exciting time for genetics. Fruit flies made perfect study organisms to test all the latest ideas, so the men of the Fly Room (collaborator Nettie Stevens was at the Carnegie Institution) spent hours discussing the latest publications and their own research findings. After one such discussion, Sturtevant rushed home to work up his latest idea: a map of the genes on the X chromosome. Sturtevant created his chromosome map — still accurate to this day — when he was just 20 and still an undergraduate. Bridges, at the ripe old age of 24, went on to discover nondisjunction of fly chromosomes — definitive proof that Morgan's theory of chromosomal inheritance was correct.

Euploidy: Sets of chromosomes

Every species has a typical number of chromosomes revealed by its karyotype. For example, humans have 46 total chromosomes (humans are diploid, $2n$, and $n = 23$). Your dog, if you have one, is also diploid and has 78 total chromosomes, while house cats have $2n = 38$. Chromosome number isn't very consistent, even among closely related organisms. For example, despite their similar appearance, two species of Asian deer are both diploid but have very different chromosome numbers: One species has 23 chromosomes, and the other has 6.

Many organisms have more than two sets of chromosomes (a single set of chromosomes referred to by the n is the haploid number) and are therefore considered *polyploid*. Polyploidy is rare in animals but not unheard of. Plants, on the other hand, are frequently polyploid. The reason that polyploidy is rare is sexual reproduction. Most animals reproduce sexually, meaning each individual produces eggs or sperm that unite to form zygotes that grow into offspring. An equal number of chromosomes must be allotted to each gamete for fertilization and normal life processes to occur. When an individual, such as a plant, is polyploid (particularly odd numbers like $3n$), most of its gametes wind up with an unusual number of chromosomes. This imbalance in the number of chromosomes results, functionally, in sterility (see the sidebar "Stubborn chromosomes" for more details).

Stubborn chromosomes

Horses are diploid and have 64 chromosomes. Donkeys, which are also diploid, are closely related to horses but have only 62 chromosomes. When a horse mates with a donkey, the result is a mule. These horse-donkey hybrids are larger versions of horses and have big ears and a famously stubborn disposition. Mules are usually sterile because the ploidies of horses and mules (or of donkeys and mules) are a poor match. Genetically, mules have 32 horse chromosomes and 31 donkey chromosomes, giving them a total of 63 chromosomes altogether and the odd chromosome number of $2n = 63$ — that's diploid but not euploid. When meiosis takes place, the homologous chromosomes should pair up and then segregate. During meiosis in mules, however, chromosomes often come together in groups of three, five, or six. As a result, mule gametes don't get a full complement of chromosomes and aren't viable to be fertilized. So how can any mule be a parent?

That's what the owners of a mule named Krause must have wondered in 1984 when she unexpectedly produced a foal — named Blue Moon because of the rarity of mule parenthood. Krause cohabitated with a male donkey, but genetic analysis revealed that Blue Moon had a mule genotype: 63 chromosomes that were half horse and half donkey. Apparently, when Krause's cells underwent meiosis, her horse chromosomes all segregated together. This is an outrageously improbable outcome — on the order of one in 4 billion! Even more amazingly, Krause had a second foal with the same horse-donkey genotype, meaning she produced a second egg with all horse chromosomes.

The only other way a mule can be a "parent" is via cloning, which I cover in Chapter 20. Idaho Gem, the first mule clone, was born in 2003.

Plants sometimes get around the problem of polyploidy (and its corresponding sterility) through a process called *apomixis.* Part of meiosis, apomixis results in an egg with a full complement of chromosomes. Eggs produced via apomixis can form seeds without being fertilized and therefore can produce new plants from seed. Dandelions, those hardy, persistent weeds known to all gardeners, reproduce using apomixis. Dandelions have $n = 8$ chromosomes that can come in sets of two ($2n = 16$), three ($3n = 24$), or four ($4n = 32$).

Many commercial plants are polyploid because plant breeders discovered that polyploids often are much larger than their wild counterparts. Wild strawberries, for instance, are diploid, tiny, and very tart. The large, sweet strawberries you buy in the grocery store are actually octaploid, meaning they have eight sets of chromosomes (that is, they're $8n$). Cotton is tetraploid ($4n$), and coffee can have as many as eight sets of chromosomes, while bananas are often triploid ($3n$). Many of these polyploids came about naturally and, after being discovered by plant breeders, were cultivated from cuttings (and other nonsexual plant propagation methods).

Not all polyploids are sterile. Those that result from crosses of two different species (called *hybridization*) are often fertile. The chromosomes of hybrids may have less trouble sorting themselves out during meiosis, allowing for normal gamete formation to take place. One famous animal example of a rarely fertile hybrid is a horse-donkey cross that results in a mule. Take a look at the "Stubborn chromosomes" sidebar for more information.

Exploring Chromosome Variations

Chromosomal abnormalities, in the form of aneuploidy (see the earlier section "Aneuploidy: Extra or missing chromosomes"), are very common among humans. Roughly 8 percent of all conceptions are aneuploid, and it's estimated that up to half of all miscarriages happen because of some form of chromosome disorder. Sex chromosome disorders are the most commonly observed type of aneuploidy in humans (flip to Chapter 5 for more on sex chromosomes) because X-chromosome inactivation allows individuals with more than two X chromosomes to compensate for the extra "doses" and survive the condition.

Four common categories of aneuploidy crop up in humans:

- **Nullisomy:** Occurs when a chromosome is missing altogether. Generally, embryos that are nullisomic don't survive to be born.

- **Monosomy:** Occurs when one chromosome lacks its homolog.

- **Trisomy:** Occurs when one extra copy of a chromosome is present.

- **Tetrasomy:** Occurs when four total copies of a chromosome are present. Tetrasomy is extremely rare.

Most chromosome conditions are referred to by category of aneuploidy followed by the number of the affected chromosome. For example, trisomy 13 means that three copies of chromosome 13 are present.

When chromosomes go missing

Monosomy (when one chromosome lacks its homolog) in humans is very rare. The majority of embryos with monosomies don't survive to be born. For liveborn infants, the only autosomal monosomy reported in humans is monosomy 21. Signs and symptoms of monosomy 21 are similar to those of Down syndrome (covered later in this section). Infants with monosomy 21 often have numerous birth defects and rarely survive for longer than a few days or weeks. The other monosomy commonly seen in children is monosomy of the X chromosome. Children with this condition are always female and usually lead normal lives. For more on monosomy X (also known as Turner syndrome), see Chapter 5. Monosomy 21 is the result of nondisjunction during meiosis (see the section "Aneuploidy: Extra or missing chromosomes" earlier in this chapter).

Many monosomies are partial losses of chromosomes, meaning that part (or all) of the missing chromosome is attached to another chromosome. Movements of parts of chromosomes to other, nonhomologous chromosomes are the result of *translocations.* I cover translocations in more detail in the section "Translocations" later in this chapter.

Finally, monosomies can occur in cells because of mistakes that occur during cell division (mitosis). Many of these monosomies are associated with chemical exposure and various sorts of cancers. Chapter 14 covers cell monosomies and cancer in detail.

When too many chromosomes are left in

Trisomies (when one extra copy of a chromosome is present) are the most common sorts of chromosomal abnormalities in humans. The most common trisomy is Down syndrome, or trisomy 21. Other, less common trisomies include trisomy 18 (Edward syndrome), trisomy 13 (Patau syndrome), and trisomy 8. All these trisomies are usually the result of nondisjunction during meiosis.

Down syndrome

Trisomy of chromosome 21, commonly called *Down syndrome,* affects between 1 in 600 to 1 in 800 infants. People with Down syndrome have some rather stereotyped physical characteristics, including distinct facial features, altered body shape, and short stature. Individuals with Down syndrome usually have mental retardation and often have heart defects. Nevertheless, they often lead fulfilling and active lives well into adulthood.

One of the most striking features of Down syndrome (and trisomies in general) is the precipitous increase in the number of Down syndrome babies born to mothers over 35 (see Figure 15-3). Women between 18 and 25 have a very low risk of having a baby with trisomy 21 (roughly 1 in 2,000). The risk increases slightly but steadily for women between 25 and 35 (about 1 in 900 for women 30 years old) and then jumps dramatically. By the time a woman is 40, the probability of having a child with Down syndrome is 1 in 100, and by the age of 50, the probability of conceiving a Down syndrome child is 1 in 12. Why does the risk of Down syndrome increase in the children of older women?

The majority of Down syndrome cases seem to arise from nondisjunction during meiosis. The reason behind this failure of chromosomes to segregate normally in older women is unclear. In females, meiosis actually begins in the fetus (flip to Chapter 2 for a review of gametogenesis in humans). All developing eggs go through the first round of prophase, including recombination. Meiosis in future egg cells then stops in a stage called *diplotene,* the stage of crossing-over, where homologous chromosomes are hooked together and are in the process of exchanging parts of their DNA. Meiosis doesn't start back up again until a particular developing egg is going through the process of ovulation. At that point, the egg completes the first round of meiosis and then halts again. When sperm and egg unite, the nucleus of the egg cell finishes meiosis just before the nuclei of the sperm and egg fuse to complete the process of fertilization. (In human males, meiosis begins in puberty, is ongoing, and continues without the pauses that occur in females.)

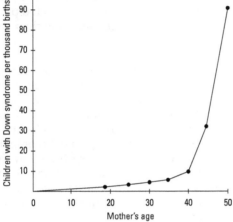

Figure 15-3: Risk of a Down syndrome pregnancy as a function of maternal age.

Roughly 75 percent of the nondisjunctions responsible for Down syndrome occur during the first phase of meiosis. Oddly, most of the chromosomes that fail to segregate seem also to have failed to undergo crossing-over, suggesting that the events leading up to nondisjunction begin early in life. Scientists have proposed a number of explanations for the cause of nondisjunction and its associated lack of crossing-over, but they haven't reached an agreement about what actually happens in the cell to prevent the chromosomes from segregating properly.

Every pregnancy is an independent genetic event. So although age is a factor in calculating risk of trisomy 21, Down syndrome with previous pregnancies doesn't necessarily increase a woman's risk of having another child affected by the disorder.

Some environmental factors have been implicated in Down syndrome that may increase the risk for women younger than 30. Scientists think that women who smoke while on oral contraceptives (birth control pills) may have a higher risk of decreased blood flow to their ovaries. When egg cells are starved for oxygen, they're less likely to develop normally, and nondisjunction may be more likely to occur.

Familial Down syndrome

A second form of Down syndrome, *familial Down syndrome,* is unrelated to maternal age. This disorder occurs as a result of the fusion of chromosome 21 to another autosome (often chromosome 14). This fusion is usually the result of a *translocation* — what happens when nonhomologous chromosomes exchange parts. In this case, the exchange involves the long arm of chromosome 21 and the short arm of chromosome 14. This sort of translocation is called a *Robertsonian translocation.* The leftover parts of chromosomes 14 and 21 also fuse together but are usually lost to cell division and aren't inherited. When a Robertsonian translocation occurs, affected persons can end up with several sorts of chromosome combinations in their gametes, as shown in Figure 15-4.

For familial Down syndrome, a translocation carrier has one normal copy of chromosome 21, one normal copy of chromosome 14, and one fused translocation chromosome. Carriers aren't affected by Down syndrome because their fused chromosome acts as a second copy of the normal chromosome. When a carrier's cells undergo meiosis, some of their gametes have one translocated chromosome or get the normal complement that includes one copy of each chromosome. Fertilizations of gametes with a translocated chromosome and a normal chromosome 21 produce the phenotype of Down syndrome. Roughly 10 percent of the liveborn children of carriers have trisomy 21. Carriers have a greater chance than normal of miscarriage because of monosomy (of either 21 or 14) and trisomy 14.

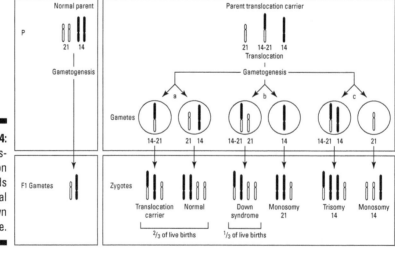

Figure 15-4: A translocation that leads to familial Down syndrome.

Other trisomies

Trisomy 18, also called *Edward syndrome,* also results from nondisjunction. About 1 in 6,000 newborns has trisomy 18, making it the second most common trisomy in humans. The disorder is characterized by severe birth defects including severe heart defects and brain abnormalities. Other defects associated with trisomy 18 include a small jaw relative to the face, clenched fingers, rigid muscles, and foot defects. Most affected infants with trisomy 18 don't live past their first birthdays. Like trisomy 21, the chance of having a baby with trisomy 18 is higher in women who become pregnant when they're older than 35.

The third most common trisomy in humans is *trisomy 13,* or *Patau syndrome.* About 1 in 12,000 live births is affected by trisomy 13; many embryos with this condition miscarry early in pregnancy. Babies born with trisomy 13 have a very short life expectancy — most die before the age of 6 months. However, some may survive until 2 or 3 years of age; records show that two children with Patau syndrome lived well into childhood (one died at 11 and the other at 19). Babies affected by trisomy 13 have extremely severe brain defects along with many facial structure defects. Absent or very small eyes and other defects of the eye, cleft lips, cleft palates, heart defects, and *polydactyly* (extra fingers and toes) are common among these children.

Another type of trisomy, *trisomy 8,* occurs very rarely (1 in 25,000 to 50,000 births). Children born with trisomy 8 have a normal life expectancy but often are affected by mental retardation and physical defects such as contracted fingers and toes.

Other things that go awry with chromosomes

In addition to monosomies and trisomies, numerous other chromosomal disorders can occur in humans. Whole sets of chromosomes can be added, or chromosomes can be broken or rearranged. This section covers some of these other sorts of chromosome disorders.

Polyploidy

Polyploidy, the occurrence of more than two sets of chromosomes, is extremely rare in humans. Two reported conditions of polyploidy are *triploid* (three full chromosome sets) and *tetraploid* (four sets). Most polyploid pregnancies result in miscarriage or stillbirth. All liveborn infants with triploidy have severe, untreatable birth defects, and most don't survive longer than a few days.

Mosaicism

Mosaicism is a form of aneuploidy that creates patches of cells with variable numbers of chromosomes. Early in embryo development, a nondisjunction similar to the one shown in Figure 15-1 can create two cells that are aneuploid (most often one cell is trisomic, with one extra chromosome copy, and the other is monosomic, with a chromosome missing its homolog). A cell can also lose a chromosome, leading to a monosomy without an accompanying trisomy. All the cells that descend from the aneuploid cells created during mitosis are also aneuploid. The magnitude of the effects of mosaicism depends on when the error occurs: If the error happens very early, most of the individual's cells are affected.

Most mosaicisms are lethal except when the mosaic cell line is confined to the placenta. Many embryos with placenta mosaics develop normally and suffer no ill effects. Sex chromosome mosaics are the most common in humans; XO-XXX and XO-XXY are common mosaic genotypes. Trisomy 21 also appears as a mosaic with normal diploid cells. Often, individuals with mosaicism are affected in the same ways as persons who are entirely aneuploid.

Fragile X syndrome

Many chromosomes have *fragile sites* — parts of the chromosome that show breaks when the cells are exposed to certain drugs or chemicals. Eighty such fragile sites are common to all humans, but other sites appear because of rare mutations. One such site, fragile X on the X chromosome, is associated with the most common inherited form of mental retardation.

Fragile X syndrome results from a mutation in a gene called *FMR1* (for Fragile Mental Retardation gene 1). Like many X-linked mutations, fragile X syndrome is recessive. Therefore, women are usually mutation carriers, and men are most often affected by the disorder. Males with fragile X syndrome usually have some form of mental retardation that can vary in severity from mild behavioral or learning disabilities all the way to severe intellectual disabilities and autism. Men and boys with fragile X syndrome often have prominent ears and long faces with large jaws.

Fragile X often shows *genetic anticipation* — that is, the disorder gets more severe from one generation to the next. Within *FMR1* is a series of three bases that are repeated over and over (see Chapter 6 for details about how DNA is put together). When the DNA is replicated (or copied; see Chapter 7), repeats can easily be added by mistake, making the repeat sequence longer. In persons with fragile X syndrome, the three bases can be repeated hundreds of times (instead of the normal 5 to 40). As the gene gets longer, the effects of the mutation become more severe, with subsequent offspring suffering stronger effects of the disorder. You can find out more about anticipation in Chapter 4.

Rearrangements

Large-scale chromosome changes are called *chromosomal rearrangements.*
Four kinds of chromosomal rearrangements, shown in Figure 15-5, are possible:

- ✔ **Duplication:** Large parts of the chromosome are copied more than once, making the chromosome substantially longer.

- ✔ **Inversion:** A section of the chromosome gets turned around, reversing the sequence of genes.

- ✔ **Deletion:** Large parts of the chromosome are lost.

- ✔ **Translocation:** Parts are exchanged between nonhomologous chromosomes.

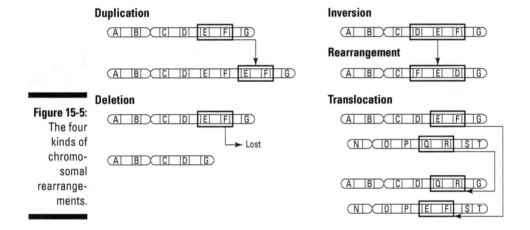

Figure 15-5:
The four
kinds of
chromo-
somal
rearrange-
ments.

All chromosomal rearrangements are mutations. Normally, mutations are very small changes within the DNA (that often have very big impacts). Mutations that involve only a few bases can't be detected by staining the chromosomes and examining the karyotype (see "What Chromosomes Reveal" for more on karyotypes). However, large-scale chromosomal changes can be diagnosed from the karyotype because they involve huge sections of the DNA. In humans, deletions and duplications are common causes of mental retardation and physical defects.

Duplications

Duplications (in this case, large, unwanted copies of portions of the chromo-some) most often arise from unequal crossing-over (see "Deletions" later in this chapter). Most disorders arising from duplications are considered partial trisomies because large portions of one chromosome are usually present in triplicate.

Duplication of part of chromosome 15 is implicated in one form of autism. Autistic persons typically have severe speech impairment, don't readily interact with or respond to other persons, and exhibit ritualized and repetitive behaviors. Mental retardation may or may not be present. Persons with autism are difficult to assess because of their impaired ability to communicate. Other chromosomal rearrangements, including large-scale deletions and translocations, have also been identified in cases of autism.

Inversions

If a chromosome break occurs, sometimes DNA repair mechanisms (explained in Chapter 13) can repair the strands. If two breaks occur, part of the chromosome may be reversed before the breaks are repaired. When a large part of the chromosome is reversed and the order of the genes is changed, the event is called an *inversion*. When inversions involve the centromere, they're called *pericentric;* inversions that don't include the centromere are called *paracentric*.

Hemophilia type A may be caused, in some cases, by an inversion within the X chromosome. Patients with hemophilia have impaired blood clot formation; as a result, they bruise easily and bleed freely from even very small cuts. Mild injuries can result in extremely severe blood loss. Like most X-linked disorders, hemophilia is more common in males than females. In this case, two genes coding for the clotting factors are interrupted by the inversion, rendering both genes nonfunctional.

Deletions

Deletion, or loss, of a large section of a chromosome usually occurs in one of two ways:

- ✔ The chromosome breaks during interphase of the cell cycle (see Chapter 2 for cell cycle details), and the broken piece is lost when the cell divides.
- ✔ Parts of chromosomes are lost because of unequal crossing-over during meiosis.

Normally, when chromosomes start meiosis, they evenly align end to end with no overhanging parts. If chromosomes align incorrectly, crossing-over can create a deletion in one chromosome and an insertion of extra DNA in the other, as shown in Figure 15-6. Unequal crossover events are more likely to occur where many repeats are present in the DNA sequence (see Chapter 8 for more on DNA sequences).

Cri-du-chat syndrome is a deletion disorder caused by the loss of the short arm of chromosome 5 (varying amounts of chromosome 5 can be lost, up to 60 percent of the arm). *Cri-du-chat* is French for "cry of the cat" and refers to the characteristic, high-pitched cry that infants affected by the syndrome make. Cri-du-chat syndrome is an autosomal dominant condition; affected persons are almost always heterozygous for the mutation. Children with cri-du-chat syndrome have unusually small heads, round faces, wide-set eyes, and intellectual disabilities. Cri-du-chat syndrome is one of the more common chromosomal deletions and occurs in about 1 in 20,000 births. Most persons with cri-du-chat syndrome don't survive into adulthood. Because the majority of these deletions are new mutations, affected persons usually have no family history of cri-du-chat syndrome.

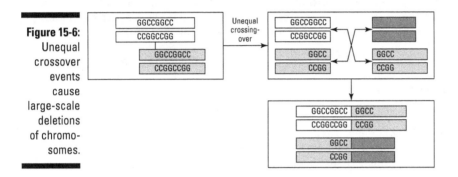

Figure 15-6: Unequal crossover events cause large-scale deletions of chromosomes.

Deletion of part of the long arm of chromosome 15 results in *Prader-Willi syndrome*. This particular deletion is always in the father's chromosome, and the tendency to pass on the deletion appears to be heritable. Women with pregnancies affected by Prader-Willi syndrome usually notice that their babies start moving in the womb later and move less than unaffected babies. Affected infants are less active and have decreased muscle tone, which sometimes causes breathing problems. These infants have trouble feeding and usually don't grow at a normal rate. Children with Prader-Willi syndrome can have mental retardation, but their intellectual disabilities usually aren't very severe. Feeding problems early in life often give way to obesity later on, but persons with Prader-Willi syndrome almost always have small stature. Like cri-du-chat syndrome, Prader-Willi syndrome is often the result of spontaneous mutation (see Chapter 12 for more on genetic disorders).

Translocations

Translocations involve the exchange of large portions of chromosomes. They occur between nonhomologous chromosomes and come in two types:

- ✔ **Reciprocal translocation:** An equal (balanced) exchange in which each chromosome winds up with part of the other. This is the most common form of translocation.

- ✔ **Nonreciprocal translocation:** An uneven exchange in which one chromosome gains a section but the other chromosome does not, resulting in a deletion.

Like inversions, translocations can result from broken chromosomes that get mismatched before the repair process is complete. When two chromosomes are broken, they can exchange pieces (reciprocal or balanced translocation), gain pieces (nonreciprocal translocation), or lose pieces (deletion). When the breaks interrupt one or more genes, those genes are rendered nonfunctional.

One disorder in humans that sometimes involves a balanced translocation event is bipolar disorder. Bipolar disorder may result when chromosomes 9 and 11 exchange parts, interrupting a gene on chromosome 11. This gene, called *DIBD1* (for Disrupted in Bipolar Disorder gene 1) has also been implicated in other psychiatric disorders such as schizophrenia.

Chromosomes 11 and 22 are often involved in balanced translocation events that cause birth defects (such as cleft palate, heart defects, and mental retardation) and a hereditary form of breast cancer. Chromosome 11 seems particularly prone to breakage in an area that has many repeated sequences (where two bases, A and T, are repeated many times sequentially). Most repeated sequences like this one are considered junk DNA (see Chapter 8 for an explanation of junk DNA). Because both chromosome 11 and chromosome 22 contain similar repeat sequences, the repeats may allow crossover events to occur by mistake, resulting in a reciprocal translocation.

In many cases, a translocation event occurs spontaneously in one parent, who then passes the disrupted chromosomes on to his or her offspring, resulting in partial trisomies and partial deletions. In these cases, the carrier parents may be unaffected by the disorder.

Part IV
Genetics and Your World

The 5th Wave
By Rich Tennant

In this part . . .

The technology surrounding genetics can seem bewildering, so this part aims to make understanding all the complexity less daunting.

I summarize how you can trace human history using genetics and how human activities affect the genetics of populations of animals and plants around the world. If you've ever marveled at the crime-solving power of forensics, you get all the details of DNA's contributions to the war on crime here. With the same technology used in forensics, humans can move genes from one organism to another for all sorts of reasons; I explain the perils and progress in genetic engineering and cloning in this part. And finally, because genetics knowledge opens up a lot of choices, I cover the ups and downs of ethics and genetics.

Chapter 17

Tracing Human History and the Future of the Planet

*1*t's impossible to overestimate the influence of genetics on our planet. Every living thing depends on DNA for its life, and all living things, including humans, share DNA sequences. The amazing similarities between your DNA and the DNA of other living things suggest that all living things trace their history back to a single source. In a very real sense, all creatures great and small are related somehow.

You can examine the genetic underpinnings of life in all sorts of ways. One powerful method for understanding the patterns hidden in your DNA is to compare the DNA of many individuals as a group. This specialty, called *population genetics,* is a powerful tool. Geneticists use this tool to study not only human populations but also animal populations to understand how to protect endangered species, for example. By comparing DNA sequences of various species, scientists also infer how natural selection acts to create evolutionary change. In this chapter, you find out how scientists analyze genetics of populations and species to understand where we came from and where we're going.

Genetic Variation Is Everywhere

The next time you find yourself channel surfing on the TV, pause a moment on one of the channels devoted to science or animals. The diversity of life on earth is truly amazing. In fact, scientists still haven't discovered all the species living on our planet; the vast rain forests of South America, the deep-sea vents of the ocean, and even volcanoes hold undiscovered species.

The interconnectedness of all living things, from a scientific perspective, can't be overstated. The sum total of all the life on earth is referred to as *biodiversity*. Biodiversity is self-sustaining and is life itself. Together, the living things of this planet provide oxygen for you (and everything else) to breathe, carbon dioxide to keep plants alive and regulate the temperature and weather, rainwater for you and your food supply, nutrient cycling to nourish every single creature on earth, and countless other functions.

Biodiversity provides so many essential functions for human life that these services have been valued at $33 trillion a year (yes, that's trillion with a "t"). (In case you're wondering, researchers manage to put dollar values on functions that the earth performs naturally, like rainfall, oxygen production, nutrient cycles, soil formation, and pollination, to name a few.)

Underlying the world's biodiversity is *genetic variation*. When you look around at the people you know, you see enormous variation in height, hair and eye color, skin tone, body shape — you name it. That phenotypic (physical) variation implies that each person differs genetically, too. Likewise, the individuals in all populations of other sexually reproducing organisms vary in phenotype and genotype as well. Scientists describe the genetic variation in *populations* (defined as groups of interbreeding organisms that exist together in both time and space) in two ways:

- ✔ **Allele frequencies:** How often do various alleles (alternate versions of a particular section of DNA) show up in a population?

- ✔ **Genotype frequencies:** What proportion of a population has a certain genotype?

Allele frequencies and genotype frequencies are both ways of measuring the contents of the gene pool. The *gene pool* refers to all the possible alleles of all the various genes that, collectively, all the individuals of any particular species have. Genes get passed around in the form of alleles that are carried from parent to child as the result of sexual reproduction. (Of course, genes can be passed around without sex — viruses leave their genes all over the place. See Chapter 14 for one way in which viruses leave their genetic legacies.)

Allele frequencies

Alleles are various versions of a particular section of DNA (like alleles for eye color; flip to Chapter 3 for a review of terms used in genetics). Most genes have many different alleles. Geneticists use DNA sequencing (which I explain in Chapter 8) to examine genes and determine how many alleles may exist. To count alleles, they examine the DNA of many different individuals and look for differences among base pairs — the As, Gs, Ts, and Cs — that comprise DNA. For the purposes of population genetics, scientists also look for individual differences in *junk DNA* (DNA that doesn't appear to code for phenotype;

see Chapter 18 for more about how noncoding DNA is used to provide DNA fingerprints).

Some alleles are very common, and others are rare. To identify and describe patterns of commonness and rarity, population geneticists calculate allele frequencies. What geneticists want to know is what proportion of a population has a particular allele. This information can be vitally important for human health. For example, geneticists have discovered that some people carry an allele that makes them immune to HIV infection, the virus that causes AIDS.

An allele's frequency — how often the allele shows up in a population — is pretty easy to calculate: Simply divide the number of copies of a particular allele by the number of copies of all the alleles represented in the population for that particular gene.

If you know the number of *homozygotes* (individuals having two identical copies of a particular allele) and *heterozygotes* (individuals having two different alleles of a gene), you can set the problem up using these two equations: $p + q = 1$ or $q = 1 - p$. In a two-allele system, a lowercase letter p is usually used to represent one allele frequency, and q is used for the other. Always, $p + q$ must equal 1 (or 100 percent). For example, say you want to know the frequency for the dominant allele (R) for round peas in a population of plants like the ones Mendel studied (see Chapter 3 for all the details about Mendel's experiments). You know that there are 60 RR plants, 50 Rr plants, and 20 rr plants. To determine the allele frequency for R (referred to as p), you multiply the number of RR plants by 2 (because each plant has two R alleles) and add that value to the number of Rr plants: $60 \times 2 = 120 + 50 = 170$. Divide the sum, 170, by two times the total plants in the population (because each plant as two alleles), or $2(60 + 50 + 20) = 260$. The result is 0.55, meaning that 55 percent of the population of peas have the allele R. To get the frequency of r (that is, q), simply subtract 0.55 from 1.

The situation gets pretty complicated, mathematically speaking, when several alleles are present, but the take-home message of allele frequency is still the same: All allele frequencies are the proportion of the population carrying at least one copy of the allele. And all the allele frequencies in a given population must add to 1 (which can be expressed as 100 percent, if you prefer).

Genotype frequencies

Most organisms have two copies of every gene (that is, they're *diploid*). Because the two copies don't necessarily have to be identical, individuals can be either heterozygous or homozygous for any given gene. Like alleles, genotypes can vary in frequency. Genotypic frequencies tell you what proportion of individuals in a population are homozygous and, by extension, what proportion are heterozygous. Depending on how many alleles are present in a population, many different genotypes can exist. Regardless, the sum total of all the genotype frequencies for a particular locus (location on a particular chromosome; see Chapter 2 for details) must equal 1 (or 100 percent if you work in percentage instead of proportion).

To calculate a genotypic frequency, you need to know the total number of individuals who have a particular genotype. For example, suppose you're dealing with a population of 100 individuals; 25 individuals are homozygous recessive (aa), and 30 are heterozygous (Aa). The frequency of the three genotypes (assuming there are only two alleles, A and a) is shown in the following, where the total population is represented by *N*.

$$\text{Frequency of } AA = \frac{\text{Number of } AA \text{ individuals}}{N}$$

$$\text{Frequency of } Aa = \frac{\text{Number of } Aa \text{ individuals}}{N}$$

$$\text{Frequency of } aa = \frac{\text{Number of } aa \text{ individuals}}{N}$$

Allele frequency and genotype frequency are very closely related concepts because genotypes are derived from combinations of alleles. It's easy to see from Mendelian inheritance (see Chapter 3) and pedigree analysis (see Chapter 12) that if an allele is very common, homozygosity is going to be high. It turns out that the relationship between allele frequency and homozygosity is quite predictable. Most of the time, you can use allele frequencies to estimate genotypic frequencies using a genetic relationship called the *Hardy-Weinberg law* of population genetics, which I explain in the next section.

Breaking Down the Hardy-Weinberg Law of Population Genetics

Godfrey Hardy and Wilheim Weinberg never met, yet their names are forever linked in the annals of genetics. In 1908, both men, completely independent of each other, came up with the equation that describes how genotypic frequencies are related to allele frequencies. Their set of simple and elegant equations accurately describes the genetics of populations for most organisms. What Hardy and Weinberg realized was that in a two-allele system, all things being equal, homozygosity and heterozygosity balance out. Figure 17-1 shows how the *Hardy-Weinberg equilibrium,* as this genetic balancing act is known, looks in a graph.

Relating alleles to genotypes

An *equilibrium* occurs when something is in a state of balance. Genetically, an equilibrium means that certain values remain unchanged over the course of time. The Hardy-Weinberg law says that allele and genotype frequencies will remain unchanged, generation after generation, as long as certain conditions are met. In order for a population's genetics to follow Hardy-Weinberg's relationships:

✔ **The organism must reproduce sexually and be diploid.** Sex provides the opportunity to achieve different combinations of alleles, and the whole affair (pardon the pun) depends on having alleles in pairs (but many alleles can be used; you're not limited to two at a time).

✔ **The allele frequencies must be the same in both sexes.** If alleles depend entirely on maleness or femaleness, the relationships don't fall into place, because not all offspring have an equal chance to inherit the alleles — alleles on the Y chromosome (see Chapter 5) violate Hardy-Weinberg rules.

✔ **The loci must segregate independently.** Independent segregation of loci is the heart of Mendelian genetics, and Hardy-Weinberg is directly derived from Mendel's laws.

✔ **Mating must be random with respect to genotype.** Matings between individuals have to be random, meaning that organisms don't sort themselves out based on the genotype in question.

Figure 17-1:
The Hardy-Weinberg graph describes the relationship between allele and genotype frequencies.

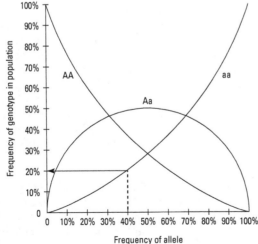

Hardy-Weinberg makes other assumptions about the populations it describes, but the relationship is pretty tolerant of violations of those expectations. Not so with the four aforementioned conditions. When one of the four major assumptions of Hardy-Weinberg isn't met, the relationship between allele frequency and genotype frequency usually starts to fall apart.

The Hardy-Weinberg equilibrium relationship is often illustrated graphically, and the Hardy-Weinberg graph is fairly easy to interpret. On the left side of the graph in Figure 17-1 is the genotypic frequency (as a percentage of the total population going from 0 at the bottom to 100 percent at the top). Across the bottom of the graph is the frequency of the recessive allele, a (going 0 to 100 percent, left to right). To find the relationship between genotype frequency and allele frequency according to Hardy-Weinberg, just follow a straight line up from the bottom and then read the value off the left side of the graph. For example, if you want to know what proportion of the population is homozygous aa when the allele frequency of a is 40 percent, start at the 40 percent mark along the bottom of the graph and follow a path straight up (shown in Figure 17-1 with a dashed line) until you get to the line marked aa (which describes the genotype frequency for aa). Take a horizontal path (indicated by the arrow) to the left and read the genotypic frequency. In this example, 20 percent of the population is expected to be aa when 40 percent of the population carries the a allele.

It makes sense that when the allele a is rare, aa homozygotes are rare, too. As allele a becomes more common, the frequency of homozygotes slowly increases. The frequency of the homozygous dominant genotype, AA, behaves the same way but as a mirror image of aa (the genotype frequency for aa) because of the relationship of the alleles A to a in terms of their own frequency: $p + q$ must equal 1. If p is large, q must be small and vice versa.

Check out the humped line in the middle of Figure 17-1. This is the frequency of heterozygotes, Aa. The highest proportion of the population that can be heterozygous is 50 percent. You may guess that's the case just by playing around with monohybrid crosses like those I describe in Chapter 3. No matter what combination of matings you try (AA with aa, Aa with Aa, Aa with aa, and so on), the largest proportion of Aa offspring you can ever get is 50 percent. Thus, when 50 percent of the population is heterozygous, the Hardy-Weinberg equilibrium predicts that 25 percent of the population will be homozygous for the A allele, and 25 percent will be homozygous for the a allele. This situation occurs only when p is equal to q — in other words, p equals q equals 50 percent.

Many loci obey the rules of the Hardy-Weinberg law in spite of the fact that the assumptions required for the relationship aren't met. One of the major assumptions that's often violated among humans is random mating. People tend to marry each other based on their similarities, such as religious background, skin color, and ethnic characteristics. For example, people of similar socioeconomic background tend to marry each other more often than chance would predict. Nevertheless, many human genes are still in Hardy-Weinberg equilibrium. That's because matings may be dependent on some characteristics but are still independent with respect to the genes. The gene that confers immunity to HIV is a good example of a locus in humans that obeys the Hardy-Weinberg law despite the fact that its frequency was shaped by a deadly disease.

Violating the law

Populations can wind up out of Hardy-Weinberg equilibrium in several ways. One of the most common departures from Hardy-Weinberg occurs as a result of *inbreeding*. Put simply, inbreeding happens when closely related individuals mate and produce offspring. Purebred dog owners are often faced with this problem because certain male dogs sire many puppies, and a generation or two later, descendents of the same male are mated to each other. (In fact, selective inbreeding is what created the various dog breeds to begin with.)

Inbreeding tends to foul up Hardy-Weinberg because some alleles start to show up more and more often than others. In addition, homozygotes get more common, meaning fewer and fewer heterozygotes are produced. Ultimately, the appearance of recessive phenotypes becomes more likely. For example, the appearance of hereditary problems in some breeds of animals, such as deafness among Dalmatian dogs, is a result of generations of inbreeding.

The high incidence of particular genetic disorders among certain groups of people, such as Amish communities (see Chapter 12), is also a result of inbreeding. Even if people in a group aren't all that closely related anymore, if a small number of people started the group, everyone in the group is related somehow. (Relatedness shows up genetically even within large human populations; take a look at the section "Mapping the Gene Pool" in this chapter to find out how.)

Loss of heterozygosity is thought to signal a population in peril. Populations with low levels of heterozygosity are more vulnerable to disease and stress, and that vulnerability increases the probability of extinction. Much of what's known about loss of heterozygosity and resulting problems with health of individuals — a situation ironically called *inbreeding depression* — comes from observations of captive animals, like those in zoos. Many animals in zoos are descended from captive populations, populations that had very few founders to begin with. For example, all captive snow leopards are reportedly descended from a mere seven animals.

Not just captive animals are at risk. As habitats for animals become more and more altered by human activity, natural populations get chopped up, isolated, and dwindle in size. Conservation geneticists, like yours truly, work to understand how human activities affect natural populations of birds and animals. See the sidebar "Genetics and the modern ark" for more about how zoos and conservation geneticists work to protect animals from inbreeding depression and rescue species from extinction.

CASE STUDY

Genetics and the modern ark

As human populations grow and expand, natural populations of plants and animals start getting squeezed out of the picture. One of the greatest challenges of modern biology is figuring out a way to secure the fate of worldwide biodiversity. Preserving biodiversity often takes two routes: establishment of protected areas and captive breeding.

Protected areas such as parks set aside areas of land or sea to protect all the creatures (animals and plants) that reside within its borders. Some of the finest examples of such efforts are found among America's national parks. But although protecting special areas helps preserve biodiversity, these islands of biodiversity also allow populations to become isolated. With isolation, smaller populations start to inbreed, resulting in genetic disease and vulnerability to extinction. Sometimes, it's necessary for conservation geneticists to step in and lend a hand to rescue these isolation populations from genetic peril. For example, greater prairie chickens were common in the Midwest at one time. By 1990, their populations were tiny and isolated. Isolation contributed to inbreeding, causing their eggs to fail to hatch. In order

to help rebuild a healthy population, biologists brought in more birds from populations elsewhere to increase genetic diversity. The strategy worked — the prairie chickens' eggs now hatch with healthy chicks that are hoped to bring the population back from the brink of extinction.

Captive breeding efforts by zoos, wildlife parks, and botanical gardens are also credited with preserving species. Twenty-five animal species that are completely extinct in the wild still survive in zoos thanks to captive breeding programs. Most programs are designed to provide not only insurance against extinction but also breeding stock for eventual reintroduction into the wild. Unfortunately, zoo populations often descend from very small founder populations, causing considerable problems with inbreeding. Inbreeding leads to fertility problems and the death of offspring shortly after birth. In the last 20 years, zoos and similar facilities have worked to combat inbreeding by keeping track of pedigrees (like the ones that appear in Chapter 12) and swapping animals around to minimize sexual contact between related animals.

Mapping the Gene Pool

When the exchange of alleles, or *gene flow,* between groups is limited, populations take on unique genetic signatures. In general, unique alleles are created through mutations (see Chapter 13). If groups of organisms are geographically separated and rarely exchange mates, mutant alleles become common within populations. What this amounts to is that some alleles are found in only certain groups, giving each group a unique genetic identity. (After some time, these alleles usually conform to a Hardy-Weinberg equilibrium within each population; see the section "Breaking Down the Hardy-Weinberg Law of Population Genetics" for details.) Geneticists identify genetic signatures of unique alleles by looking for distinct patterns within genes and certain sections of junk DNA (see Chapter 18 for how junk DNA conceals genetic information).

Mutant alleles that show up outside the population they're usually associated with suggest that one or more individuals have moved or dispersed between populations. Geneticists use these genetic hints to trace the movements of animals, plants, and even people around the world. In the sections that follow, I cover some of the latest efforts to do just that.

One big happy family

With the contributions of the Human Genome Project (covered in Chapter 11), human population geneticists have a treasure trove of information to sift through. Using new technologies, researchers are learning more than ever before about what makes various human populations distinct. One such effort is the HapMap Project. Hap stands for *haplotype,* which is another way of saying an inventory of human alleles. The alleles being studied for the HapMap aren't necessarily alleles from specific genes; many are alleles within the junk DNA. The HapMap takes advantage of single base pair changes, called SNPs (see Chapter 18), in the DNA; SNPs are the results of thousands of substitution mutations. Most of these tiny changes have no effect on phenotype, but collectively they vary enough from one population to another to allow geneticists to discern each population's genetic signature.

After geneticists understand how much diversity exists among haplotypes, they work to create genetic maps that relate SNP alleles to geographic locations. Essentially, all humans tend to divide up genetically into the three continents of Africa, Asia, and Europe. This isn't too surprising — humans have been in North and South America for only 10,000 years or so. When the genetic uniqueness of the Old World's people was described, geneticists examined populations in North America and other immigrant populations to see if genetics could predict where people came from. For example, genetic analyses of a group of immigrants in Los Angeles accurately determined which continent these people originally lived on. Some geneticists believe that the genetic maps can be even more specific and may point people to countries, and maybe even cities, where their ancestors once lived. The ultimate goal of the HapMap Project is to link haplotypes to populations along with information about the environment, family histories, and medical conditions to development tailor-made treatments for diseases.

Because humans love to travel, geneticists have also compared rates of movements between men and women. Common wisdom suggests that, historically, men tended to move around more than women did (think Christopher

Columbus or Leif Ericson). However, DNA evidence suggests that men aren't as prone to wander as previously believed. Geneticists compared mitochondrial DNA (passed from mother to child) with Y chromosome DNA (passed from father to son). It seems that women have migrated from one continent to another eight times more frequently than males. The tradition of women leaving their own families to join their husbands may have contributed to the pattern, but another possible explanation exists: A pattern of *polygyny,* men fathering children by more than one woman. So, back to that bit about men wandering. . . .

Uncovering the secret social lives of animals

Gene flow can have an enormous impact on threatened and endangered species. For example, scientists in Scandinavia were studying an isolated population of gray wolves not long ago. Genetically, the population was very inbred; all the animals descended from the same pair of wolves. Heterozygosity was low and, as a consequence, so were birth rates. When the population suddenly started to grow, the scientists were shocked. Apparently, a male wolf migrated over 500 miles to join the pack and father wolf pups. Just one animal brought enough new genes to rescue the population from extinction.

Mating patterns of animals often provide biologists with surprises. Because humans like to form monogamous pairs, scientists have compared birds to humankind by pointing to our apparently similar mating habits. As it turns out, birds aren't so monogamous after all. In most species of perching birds (the group that includes pigeons and sparrows, to name two widespread types), 20 percent of all offspring are fathered by some male other than the one with whom the female spends all her time. By spreading paternity among several males, a female bird makes sure that her offspring are genetically diverse. And genetic diversity is incredibly important to help fend off stress and disease.

Genetics reveals that some birds are really frisky. For example, fairy wrens — tiny, brilliant-blue songbirds — live in Australia in big groups; one female is attended by several males who help her raise her young. But none of the males attending the nest actually fathers any of the kids — female fairy wrens slip off to mate with males in distant territories. Other birds form family groups. Florida scrub jays — beautiful aquamarine natives of central Florida — stay home and help mom and dad raise younger brothers and sisters. Eventually, older kids inherit their parents' territory. Another Australian species, white-winged choughs, put a whole different twist on gathering a labor force for raising their kids. Chough (pronounced *chuff*) families kidnap their neighbors' kids and put them to work raising offspring.

It turns out that humans aren't the only ones who live in close association with their parents, brothers, or sisters for their entire lives. Some species of whales live in groups called *pods.* Every pod represents one family: moms, sisters, brothers, aunts, and cousins, but not dads. Different pods meet up to find mates — as in the son/brother of one pod may mate with the daughter/sister of another pod. Males father offspring in different pods but stay with their own families for their entire lives. Sadly, geneticists learned about whale family structures and mating habits by taking meat from whales that had been killed by people. Like so many of the world's creatures, whales are killed by hunters. Hopefully, though, the information that scientists gather when whales are harvested will contribute to their conservation, allowing the planet's amazing biodiversity to persist for generations to come.

Changing Forms over Time: The Genetics of Evolution

Evolution, or how organisms change over time, is a foundational principle of biology. When Charles Darwin put forth his observations about natural selection, the genetic basis for inheritance was unknown. Now, with powerful tools like DNA sequencing (which appears in Chapter 8), scientists are documenting evolutionary change in real time, as well as uncovering how species share ancestors from long ago.

When genetic variation arises (from mutation, which I talk about in Chapter 13), new alleles are created. Then, *natural selection* acts to make particular genetic variants more common by way of improved survival and reproductive success for some individuals over others. In this section, you discover how genetics and evolution are inextricably tied together.

Genetic variation is key

All evolutionary change occurs because genetic variation arises through mutation. Without genetic variation, evolution can't take place. While many mutations are decidedly bad (I discuss those in Chapter 13), some mutations confer an advantage, such as resistance to disease.

No matter how a mutation arises or what consequences it causes, the change must be heritable, or passed from parent to offspring, to drive evolution.

Until recently, it wasn't possible to examine heritable variation directly. Instead, phenotypic variation was used as an indicator of how much genetic variation might exist. With the help of DNA sequencing, scientists have come to realize that genetic variation is vastly more complex than anyone ever imagined.

Heritable genetic variation alone doesn't mean that evolution will occur, however. The final piece in the evolutionary puzzle is natural selection. Put simply, natural selection occurs when conditions favor individuals carrying particular traits. By favor, it's meant that those individuals reproduce and survive better than other individuals carrying a different set of traits. This success is sometimes referred to as *fitness,* which is the degree of reproductive success associated with a particular genotype. When an organism has high fitness, its genes are being passed on successfully to the next generation. Through its effects on fitness, natural selection produces *adaptations,* or sets of traits that are important for survival. The white fur of polar bears, which allow them to blend into the snowy landscape of Arctic regions, is an example of an adaptation.

Where new species come from

Probably since the dawn of time (or at least the dawn of humankind, anyhow), humans have been classifying and naming the creatures around them. The formalized species naming system, what scientists call *taxonomic classification,* has long relied on physical differences and similarities between organisms as a means of sorting things out. For example, elephants from Asia and elephants from Africa are obviously both elephants, but they're so different in their physical characteristics, among other things, that they're considered separate species. Over the past 50 years or so, the way in which species are classified has changed as scientists have gained more genetic information about various organisms.

One way of classifying species is the *biological species concept,* which bases its classification on reproductive compatibility. Organisms that can successfully reproduce together are considered to be of the same species, and those that can't reproduce together are a different species. This definition leaves a lot to be desired, because many closely related organisms can interbreed yet are clearly different enough to be separate species.

Another method of classification, one that works a bit better, says that species are groups of organisms that maintain unique identities — genetically, physically, and geographically — over time and space. A good example of this definition of species is dogs and wolves. Both dogs and wolves are in the same pigeonhole, so to speak — they're both in the genus *Canis.* (Sharing a genus name tells you that organisms are quite similar and very closely related.) But their species names are different. Dogs are always *Canis familiaris,* but there are many species of wolves, all beginning with *Canis* but ending with a variety of species names to accurately describe how different they are from each other (such as gray wolves, *Canis lupus,* and red wolves, *Canis rufus*). Genetically, dogs and wolves are very distinct, but they aren't so different that they can't interbreed. Dogs and wolves occasionally mate and produce offspring, but left to their own devices, they don't interbreed.

When populations of organisms become reproductively isolated from each other (that is, they no longer interbreed), each population begins to evolve independently. Different mutations arise, and with natural selection, the passage of time leads to the accumulation of different adaptations. In this way, after many generations, populations may become different species.

Growing the evolutionary tree

One of the basic concepts behind evolution is that organisms have similarities because they're related by descent from a common ancestor. Genetics and DNA sequencing techniques have allowed scientists to study these evolutionary relationships, or *phylogenies,* among organisms. For example, the DNA sequence of a particular gene may be compared across many organisms. If the gene is very similar or unchanged from one species to another, the species would be considered more closely related (in an evolutionary sense) than species that have accumulated many mutational changes in the same gene.

One way to represent the evolutionary relationships is with a tree diagram. In a similar fashion to the pedigrees used to study genetics in family relationships (flip to Chapter 12 for pedigree analysis), evolutionary trees like the one in Figure 17-2 illustrate the family relationships among species. The trunk of an evolutionary tree represents the common ancestor from which all other organisms in the tree descended. The branches of the tree show the evolutionary connections between species. In general, shorter branches indicate that species are more closely related.

Chapter 20

Cloning: You're One of a Kind

In This Chapter

▶ Defining cloning

▶ Understanding how cloning works

▶ Looking at some common clone abnormalities

▶ Sorting out the arguments for and against cloning

*I*t sounds like science fiction: Harvest your genetic information, implant that information into an egg cell, and after nine months, welcome a new baby into the world. A new baby with a difference — it's a clone.

Depending on your point of view, cloning organisms may sound like a nightmare or a dream come true. Whatever your opinion, cloning is most definitely not science fiction; decisions about experimental cloning are being made right now, every day. This chapter covers cloning: what it is, how it's done, and what its impact is from a biological point of view. You get to know the problems inherent in clones, along with the arguments for and against cloning (not just of humans — of animals and plants, too). Get ready for an interesting story, and remember, it ain't fiction!

Send in the Clones

A *clone* is simply an identical copy. When geneticists talk about cloning, they're most often talking about copying some part of the DNA (usually a gene). Geneticists clone DNA in the lab every day — the technology is simple, routine, and unremarkable. Cloning genes is a vital part of

✔ DNA sequencing (see Chapter 8)

✔ The study of gene functions (see Chapter 11)

✔ The creation of recombinant organisms (see Chapter 16)

✔ The development of gene therapy (see Chapter 16)

Another meaning of the word *cloning* is to make a copy of an entire organism as a reproductive strategy. When referring to a whole creature as opposed to DNA, a clone is an organism that's created via asexual reproduction, meaning that offspring are produced without the parent having sex first. Cloning occurs naturally all the time in bacteria, plants, insects, fish, and lizards. For example, one type of asexual reproduction is *parthenogenesis,* which occurs when a female makes eggs that develop into offspring without being fertilized by a male (for some of you female readers, I'm sure this sounds very appealing). So if reproduction by cloning is a natural, normal biological process, what's the big deal with cloning organisms using technology?

Cloning Animals: Like No Udder

Cloning animals hit the news big time in 1997 with the birth of Dolly, an unremarkable looking Finn Dorset lamb. Named after the well-endowed country singer Dolly Parton, Dolly the sheep was a clone of one of her mother's udder cells. (If you didn't grow up on a farm, *udders* are the part of the animal that produces milk — in other words, breasts. Hence the name of everyone's favorite clone.) I use the term "mother" rather loosely when it comes to Dolly; the cells came from one animal, the egg was derived from a second animal, and yet a third female was the birth mom.

Dolly's name was intended as a bit of a joke, but the fact that an animal had been cloned meant many people weren't laughing. Images of a future filled with mass-produced human beings began to fill the minds of many. Clones aren't unique individuals and, in cases like Dolly's, are produced via technology. Therefore, human rights advocates and religious leaders often object to cloning on moral or ethical grounds (see "Arguments against cloning" later in this chapter).

Despite her ordinary appearance, Dolly was unique in that no other mammal had been reproduced successfully via cloning using a somatic (body) cell (see the section "Discovering why Dolly is really something to bah about" later in the chapter). But Dolly wasn't the first organism to be cloned.

Cloning before Dolly: Working with sex cells

Experimental cloning started in the 1950s. In 1952, researchers transplanted the nucleus from a frog embryo into a frog egg. This and subsequent experiments were designed not to clone frogs but to discover the basis of *totipotent cells.* Totipotent cells are capable of becoming any sort of cell and are the basis for all multicellular organisms. Totipotency lies at the heart of developmental genetics.

For most organisms, after an egg is fertilized, the zygote begins developing by cell division, which I walk you through in Chapter 2. Division proceeds through 2, 4, 8, and 16 cells. After the zygote reaches the 16-cell stage, the cells wind up in a hollow ball arrangement called a *blastocyst.* Figure 20-1 shows the stages of development from 2 cells to blastocyst.

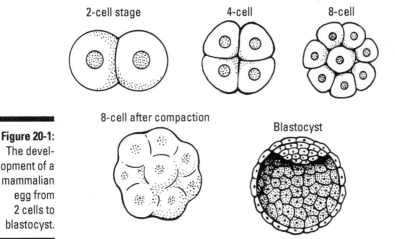

2-cell stage   4-cell   8-cell

8-cell after compaction

Blastocyst

Figure 20-1:
The development of a mammalian egg from 2 cells to blastocyst.

Zygote development in mammals is unique because the cells don't all divide at the same time or in the same order. Instead of proceeding neatly from 2 to 4 to 8, the cells often wind up in odd numbers. Mammal zygotes have a unique stage of development, called *compaction,* when the cells go from being separate little balls into a single, multicellular unit (refer to Figure 20-1). Compaction occurs after the third round of cell division. After compaction, the cells divide again (up to roughly 16), the inner cell mass forms (this will become the fetus), and fluid accumulates in the center of the ball of cells to form the blastocyst.

After a few more divisions, the cells rearrange into a three-layered ball called a *gastrula.* The innermost layer of the gastrula is *endoderm* (literally "inner skin"), the middle is *mesoderm* ("middle skin"), and the outermost is *ectoderm* ("outer skin"). Each layer is composed of a batch of cells, so from the gastrula stage onward, what cells turn into depends on which layer they start out in. In other words, the cells are no longer totipotent; they have specific functions.

So why is totipotency important? The entire body plan of an organism is coded in its DNA. Practically every cell gets a copy of the entire body plan (in the cell nucleus; see Chapter 6 for more on DNA and cells). Despite having access to the entire genome, however, eye cells produce only eye cells, not blood cells or muscle cells. All cells arise from totipotent cells but end up *nullipotent* — able to produce only cells like themselves. Totipotent cells hold the key to gene expression and what turns genes on and off (which I cover in detail in Chapter 11). Understanding what controls totipotency also has broad implications for curing diseases such as cancer (see Chapter 14), treating spinal cord injuries using totipotent stem cells (see Chapter 23), and curing inherited disorders (see Chapter 15).

Discovering why Dolly is really something to bah about

The scientific breakthrough that Dolly the sheep signifies isn't cloning. The real breakthrough is that Dolly started off as a nullipotent cell nucleus. For many years, scientists couldn't be certain that loss of totipotency didn't involve some change at the genetic level. In other words, researchers wondered if the DNA itself got altered during the process of going from totipotent to nullipotent. Dolly convincingly demonstrated that nuclear DNA is nuclear DNA regardless of what sort of cell it comes from. (See Chapter 6 for more about nuclear DNA.) Theoretically, *any* cell nucleus is capable of returning to totipotency. That may turn out to be very good news.

The promise of *therapeutic cloning* is that someday doctors will be able to harvest your cells, use your DNA to make totipotent cells, and then use those cells to cure your life-threatening disease or restore your damaged spinal cord to full working order. However, creating totipotent cells from nullipotent cells to treat injury or disease is difficult and triggers significant ethical debates (see "Fighting the Clone Wars" later in this chapter), so realizing the potential of therapeutic cloning may be a very long way off. Meanwhile, *reproductive cloning* — the process of creating offspring asexually — is already causing quite a stir. For a taste of some of the excitement, see the sidebar "Aclone in the universe?"

Aclone in the universe?

When a human clone was reportedly born in December 2002, the news wasn't wholly unexpected. A company called Clonaid made the announcement and, purportedly, the clone; the company claimed that one cloned child had been born and numerous clone babies were on the way. The question is: On their way from where? As it turns out, Clonaid was founded by a group called the Raelians. While being entertained by sexy robots on board an alien spacecraft, Rael, the group's founder, reportedly learned that all humans are descended from clones created 25,000 years ago by space aliens.

But Clonaid's claims (all of them, including the sexy robot thing) are unsubstantiated. Shortly after the initial announcement of cloning success, Clonaid was invited to submit samples for genetic testing to support its claim. Ultimately, Clonaid refused genetic tests as an infringement on the right to privacy by the cloned child's parents. There's no word on how many parents the cloned child may have (with the egg mother, womb mother, and cell donor, it could be as many as three different people!). At the time of this writing, Clonaid continues to tout human cloning services for which it reportedly charges $200,000. Among other interesting tidbits, its Web site says that the company found living cells in a body that was dead for over four months, giving a whole new meaning to the "living dead."

Creating Clones

Despite the fact that rats, mice, goats, cows, horses, pigs, and cats have all been cloned, cloning isn't easy or routine. Cloning efficiency (the number of live offspring per cloning attempt) is generally very low. Dolly, for example, was the only live offspring out of 277 tries. All sorts of other biological problems also arise from cloning, but to understand them, you first need to understand how clones are created. (I return to the subject of challenges and problems in the "Confronting Problems with Clones" section later in the chapter.)

Making twins

One simple way to make a clone is to take advantage of the natural process of twinning. Identical twins normally arise from a single fertilized egg, called a *zygote* (see the "Cloning before Dolly: Working with sex cells" section earlier in the chapter). The zygote goes through a few rounds of cell division, and then the cells separate into two groups, each going on to form one offspring.

Artificial twinning is relatively simple and was first done successfully (in sheep) in 1979. A single fertilized egg was used, meaning that the offspring was the result of sexual reproduction. Zygotes from normally fertilized (sexually produced) eggs were harvested from ewes (female sheep). The zygote was allowed to divide up to the 16-cell stage (see the "Cloning before Dolly: Working with sex cells" section earlier in the chapter). The 16 cells were then divided into two groups, which went right on dividing, and after they were implanted into the reproductive tract of the ewe, they resulted in twins. The twins were genetically identical to each other because they were produced from the same fertilized egg.

In cows, about 25 percent of artificial embryo splits result in twin births; 75 percent result in only one calf. Nonetheless, the procedure is successful enough to increase the number of calves by about 50 percent over conventional fertilizations. This sort of cloning is relatively routine in agricultural settings and has received surprisingly little attention in the debate over cloning. The fact that the clones arise from a fertilized egg may have dampened the furor somewhat.

Using a somatic cell nucleus to make a clone

Somatic cells are body cells. Typically, body cells are *nullipotent,* meaning they only make more of the same kind of cell by mitosis (see Chapter 2 for all the details on mitosis). For example, your bone cells only make more bone cells, your blood cells only make more blood cells, and so on. Most somatic cells have nuclei that contain all the information needed to make an entire organism — in the case of cloning, a clone of the cell's owner (sometimes referred to as a *donor*).

Harvesting the donor cell

The choice of cell type used for cloning isn't trivial. The cells must grow well *in vitro* (literally "in glass," as in a test tube), and those from the female reproductive tract (mammary, uterine, and ovarian cells) seem to work best. Sorry, guys, but so far, very few clones are male.

Because body cells are often in the process of dividing (mitosis), the donor's cell must be treated to stop cell division and leave the cell in the G0 stage of mitosis (see Chapter 2). In this state, the chromosomes are "relaxed," and the DNA isn't undergoing replication. After the cell is made inactive, the nucleus of the donor cell and all the chromosomes inside it are harvested. This harvest is usually accomplished by gently drawing the cell nucleus out with a needle attached to a syringe-like tool called a *pipette.* The process of removing a cell nucleus is called *enucleation,* and the resulting cell is *enucleated* (that is, lacking a nucleus).

Harvesting the egg cell

To complete the process of making a clone using the somatic cell method, another cell is needed — this time, an egg cell. Egg cells are generally the largest cells in the body. In fact, a mature mammalian egg cell is visible to the naked eye; it's about the size of a very small speck of dust, like what you might see floating in the air when a shaft of sunlight pierces an otherwise dark room.

To harvest an egg cell, the female animal (here, called the *egg mother*) is treated with a hormone to stimulate ovulation. When the egg mother produces eggs, she first makes an *oocyte,* or immature egg (see Chapter 2 for a full rundown of egg production as part of gametogenesis). At the oocyte stage, the egg has completed the first round of meiosis (meiosis I) but isn't ready to be fertilized. The oocyte is harvested, and all the chromosomes are removed (oocytes don't really have nuclei to contain chromosomes) using the same method used for the somatic cell, leaving only the cytoplasm behind (take a peek at Figure 20-2). Also remaining in the oocyte's cytoplasm are mitochondria, which each contain a copy of the egg mother's mitochondrial DNA (see Chapter 6). After the clone is formed, the egg mother's mitochondrial DNA and the donor cell's nuclear DNA may interact and have unexpected consequences (see "Confronting Problems with Clones" later in this chapter).

As it turns out, some egg cells are really versatile. Rabbit egg cells have been used to clone cats, for example. Generally, though, staying within a species works best — that is, cat egg cells work best with cat somatic cell nuclei. See the sidebar "Clone, Spot, clone!" for more about cloned kitties.

Putting it all together

With both the donor cell and the egg cell in hand, the nucleus from the donor cell is injected into the enucleated oocyte (see Figure 20-2). The donor nucleus is fused with the oocyte using a brief electrical shock. This little jump-start plays the part of fertilization: The oocyte starts dividing and begins developing into an embryo. After cell division is well established, the dividing cells are implanted into a female (the birth or gestation mother) for the remainder of the pregnancy. Dolly the sheep clone was born after 148 days of gestation, which is about 5 days longer than average for a Finn Dorset sheep.

Clone, Spot, clone!

Yes, folks, it's possible to clone your kitty or duplicate your doggie. That was the promise of a company called Genetic Savings and Clone, which offered tissue preservation services and cloning. The first cloned cat, named CC for Copy Cat, was produced by researchers at Texas A&M University in 2002 (the ultimate revenge for all those Aggie jokes, I guess). The work, funded by billionaire John Sperling, was originally meant for canine cloning. Sperling wanted to clone his own beloved dog, Missy, who died in 2002. Like most cloning efforts, success rates are low; only one in 87 attempts produce a live kitten. But as it turns out, that old phrase "copy cat" has a deeper meaning — cats are a lot easier to clone than dogs for a number of reasons. Dogs' reproductive biology isn't very amenable to the forced ovulation required for oocyte harvesting. Unfortunately, demand for cloned pets wasn't sufficient to keep Genetic Savings and Clone in business; they folded in 2006.

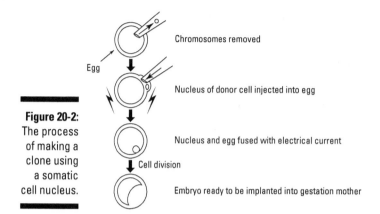

Chromosomes removed

Egg

Nucleus of donor cell injected into egg

Nucleus and egg fused with electrical current

Cell division

Embryo ready to be implanted into gestation mother

Figure 20-2:
The process
of making a
clone using
a somatic
cell nucleus.

Confronting Problems with Clones

At birth, Dolly seemed normal in every way. She grew to adulthood, was mated to a ram, and gave birth to her own lambs (a total of six over her lifetime). However, Dolly lived only 6 years; normally, Finn Dorsets live 11 or 12 years. Dolly became ill with a lung disease and was euthanized to relieve her suffering. The first hint that Dolly wasn't completely normal was arthritis. She developed painful inflammation in her joints when she was only 4 years old. Arthritis isn't unusual in sheep, but it usually only occurs in very old animals.

As it turns out, a number of abnormalities are common among clones. Clones suffer from a variety of physical ailments, including heart malformations, high blood pressure, kidney defects, impaired immunity to diseases, liver disorders, malformed body parts, diabetes, and obesity. The following sections examine the most common physical problems clones face.

Faster aging

Before somatic cells divide during mitosis, the DNA in each cell must replicate (see Chapter 7 for replication information). Each chromosome is copied except for the chromosomes' ends, called *telomeres,* which aren't fully replicated. As a result, telomeres shorten as the cell goes through repeated rounds of mitosis. Shortening of telomeres is associated with aging because it happens over time (see the sidebar "Your aging DNA" for more). Telomere shortening may mean problems for clones created through somatic nucleus transfer because, in essence, such clones start out with "aged" DNA.

Dolly the cloned sheep had abnormally short telomeres, giving rise to the worry that perhaps all clones may suffer from degenerative diseases because of premature aging. Research with other clones has provided conflicting results. Some clones, like Dolly, have shortened telomeres. Surprisingly, some clones seem to have reversed the effects of aging; specifically, their telomeres are repaired and end up longer than those of the donor. What this reversal suggests is that embryonic cells have *telomerase,* the enzyme that builds new telomeres using an RNA template during DNA replication (see Chapter 7 for more about telomerase and its role in replication). In the end, the possibility of premature aging in clones is a real one, but not all clones seem to be susceptible to it.

Your aging DNA

As you get older, your body changes: You get wrinkles, your parts start to sag, and your hair goes gray. Eventually, the chromosomes in some of your cells get so short that they can no longer function properly, and the cells die. This progressive cell death is thought to cause the unwelcome signs of aging you're familiar with. In fact, the shortening of telomeres in most animals is so predictable that it can be used to determine how old an animal is.

All your cells have the genes to make telomerase (see Chapter 7). But telomerase genes are turned on only in certain kinds of cells: germ cells (those that make eggs and sperm), bone marrow cells, skin cells, hair follicle cells, and the cells that line the intestinal walls (in other words, cells that divide a lot). Cancer cells also have telomerase activity, a fact that allows the unregulated growth of tumors that's sometimes fatal (see Chapter 14 for more on genetics and cancer).

In experiments, mice without a functioning telomerase gene age faster than normal mice.

This finding led some researchers to believe that telomerase may be used (eventually) to reverse or prevent aging in humans. Recently, however, research shows that telomere length is only part of the story. Telomeres interact with proteins that cover them and act as caps. When those protein caps are missing, the cell cycle gets disrupted and may stop altogether, causing premature cell death. Finally, stress may play a significant role in how fast telomeres shorten. A study of mothers with chronically ill children showed that signs of aging were accelerated in the moms of ill children compared to moms of the same age with healthy children. The stressed moms had shortened telomeres and, from a cellular point of view, were up to 10 years older than their actual ages. Although telomerase may someday be part of treating stress and aging, research indicates that the best bet against aging may be lowering stress levels the old-fashioned way: rest and relaxation.

Bigger offspring

Clones tend to be physically large; at birth, they have higher than average weight and larger than normal body size. Many clones, such as cows and sheep, must be delivered by cesarean section because they're too large to be born naturally. In part, the large birth size of clones is due to the fact that they stay in the womb longer than usual. Dolly the cloned sheep, for example, was born about five days after her birth mother's "due date." Offspring not born shortly after the normal due date (in humans, about two weeks late) are at great risk for stillbirth and complications, such as difficulty breathing. Clones tend to have very large *placentas* (the organ that links fetus to mother for oxygen and nutrition), which may contribute to their larger size, but the exact reason for the longer gestation periods is unclear.

The problem with oversize clones is so pervasive that it's been dubbed *large offspring syndrome,* or LOS. Many offspring, including humans, produced using *in vitro fertilization* (so-called "test-tube babies") also suffer from LOS, suggesting that it's not necessarily a problem associated with cloning. Instead, LOS seems to result from manipulation of the embryo. These manipulations cause changes in the way genes for growth are expressed (see Chapter 11 for more about gene expression).

Genomic imprinting occurs when genes are expressed based on which parent they come from. (For more on genomic imprinting, jump to the sidebar "It takes two to make a baby.") In the case of LOS, what seems to happen is that the genes derived from the most recent male ancestor tell the fetus to grow faster and bigger than normal. Normally, genomic imprinting affects fewer than 1,000 genes (out of 22,000 or so total genes in humans; see Chapter 8). How these "paternal" genes get turned on is anybody's guess, but the interaction of sperm with egg during fertilization is likely part of the answer. The end result of LOS is large offspring that often suffer from a variety of birth defects and are at risk for certain kinds of cancer. Estimates of LOS in human children born by *in vitro* fertilization are about 5 percent. (Normally, LOS occurs in less than 1 percent of children produced through natural fertilization.)

It takes two to make a baby

Needing a mom and a dad to make a baby sounds like common sense, but the wonders of genetic engineering suggest otherwise (after all, Dolly had three mothers and no father). Maternal and paternal DNA *are* required for successful reproduction — at least by mammals — because of genomic imprinting.

Genomic imprinting was first discovered in studies with mice. Researchers created mouse embryos with DNA from either female or male mice, but not both. Embryos with only paternal or maternal DNA didn't develop normally, indicating that both male and female DNA are required for successful development. In other studies, mice were engineered to have certain genes (see Chapter 19 for more on transgenic animals). The expression of the genes in offspring of the transgenic mice depended on which parents transmitted the genes. All offspring inherited the genes, but the genes were expressed only when the fathers transmitted them. Likewise, certain genes were expressed only when transmitted by the mothers. Thus, the growth and development of offspring is regulated by genes turned on simply because they come from mom or dad. Those genes then act in concert to regulate normal development of the embryo.

Developmental disasters

The percentage of cloning attempts that result in live births is extremely low. Generally, scientists must carry out hundreds of cell transfers to produce one offspring. Most clones perish immediately because they never implant into the gestation mother's uterus. Of the embryos that do implant and begin development, more than half die before birth. In many cases, the placenta is malformed, preventing the growing fetus from obtaining proper nutrition and oxygen.

In most cloning attempts, two females are involved. The egg comes from one female and gets implanted into another female for gestation. Therefore, another cause of early death may be that the gestation mother rejects the clone as foreign. In these cases, the gestation mother's immune system doesn't recognize the embryo as her own (because it's not) and secretes antibodies to destroy it. *Antibodies* are chemicals that the body produces to interact with bacteria, viruses, and foreign tissues to fight disease.

Some of the problems suffered by clones may result from the mismatch between mitochondrial and nuclear DNA. When an oocyte is harvested from a female different from the somatic cell (see the earlier section "Using a somatic cell nucleus to make a clone"), the egg contains roughly 100,000 copies of the egg mother's mitochondrial DNA. Unless the donor cell comes from the egg mother's sister, the somatic cell nucleus comes from a cell with a different mitochondrial genome. This mismatch means that the clone isn't a true clone — its DNA differs slightly from the donor. Cloned mice with mismatched mitochondrial and nuclear DNA tend to have decreased growth rates compared to cloned mice with matched mitochondrial and nuclear genomes.

The type of donor cell used also makes a difference in the clone's health. When introduced into the oocyte, the donor cell nucleus gets "reprogrammed" somehow to go from nullipotent to totipotent. Some cell nuclei seem to be better at resetting to totipotent than others. Almost all clones whose genomes don't get reprogrammed perish.

Effects of the environment

Clones are *never* truly exact copies of the donor organism, because genes interact with the environment in unique ways to form phenotypes, or physical qualities. If you've ever known a set of identical twins, you know that twins are very different from each other. *Monozygotic* (a fancy term for "identical" that literally means "one egg") twins have different fingerprints, develop at different rates, have different preferences, and die at different times. Being genetically identical doesn't mean they're truly, 100 percent identical.

The environment's role in development is perhaps best illustrated by experiments using plants. Suppose shoots from a single plant are rooted and grown at different locations. In essence, the plants are clones of the parent plant. If genetic control were perfect, we'd expect identical plants to perform in identical ways, regardless of environmental conditions. However, the plants in our experiment grow at very different rates depending on their location. In other words, identical plants perform differently under different conditions. Likewise, genetically identical mice raised under exactly the same conditions don't respond in identical ways to exactly the same doses of medications.

All organisms respond to their environment in unique and unpredictable ways. From the very beginning, animals experience unique conditions inside the womb. Hormonal exposure during pregnancy can have profound effects on developing organisms. For example, female piglets sandwiched between brothers while in the womb are more aggressive as adults than females that were situated between sisters. This is because male piglets secrete testosterone — a hormone that increases aggressive behavior.

Attempts to replicate organisms exactly are doomed to failure. Genetics doesn't control destiny, because genes aren't expressed in predictable ways. Persons carrying mutations for certain diseases don't have a 100-percent probability of developing those diseases (see Chapter 13). Likewise, clones don't express their genes in precisely the same way as the donor organism. Add the differences in mitochondrial DNA, *in utero* conditions (clones usually develop in a different womb), and time periods to the huge differences already present, and the only conclusion is that no clone will ever experience the world in precisely the same way as the donor organism did.

Fighting the Clone Wars

The arguments for and against cloning are numerous. In the sections that follow, I review some of the main points in both the pro and con corners. As you read, understand that these aren't *my* opinions and arguments; I only summarize what others have argued before me. I try to be balanced and fair, because before you can responsibly take a position on cloning, you need to know both sides of this controversial topic. And for more information on ethical considerations in genetics, see Chapter 21.

Arguments for cloning

Like every other scientific discovery, cloning can be used to do a lot of good. Cloning for medical and therapeutic purposes gives enormous hope that paralyzed persons will walk again and that people suffering from previously incurable conditions such as muscular dystrophy and diabetes will be cured. Cloning has provided scientists with some important answers about how genetics works. Prior to these discoveries, the changes that occur from embryo to adult were believed to cause permanent changes to the organism's DNA. Now we know that's not true. Because all DNA has the potential to return to totipotence, doctors have the unparalleled opportunity to correct genetic defects and provide treatment for devastating progressive diseases.

Another plus in the pro-cloning camp is that cloning may provide genetically matched organisms that will streamline research into the causes and treatments of diseases such as cancer. Because matched comparisons are scientifically more powerful, fewer animals are needed to conduct experiments. Such changes are an important advance over current research methods and will improve conditions for experimental animals.

Advancing knowledge of genetics can provide dramatic benefits not only to humans but also to the planet as a whole. Cloning may represent the last hope for some rare and endangered species. When only a few individuals remain, cloning may provide additional individuals to allow the population to survive. Given that the earth is experiencing its largest wave of species extinctions since ancient times, cloning may be a very significant advance for conservation biology.

Arguments against cloning

Although cloning represents an enormous opportunity, it's an opportunity fraught with danger. For the first time in history, humans possess the technology to create genetically modified organisms. That capability extends not just to animals and plants but to humans as well. Furthermore, the genetic diversity that gives the natural world its rich texture is endangered by a unique threat — that of creating organisms that are genetically identical.

As I discuss in Chapter 17, genetic diversity is extremely important to establishing and maintaining the health and well-being of populations of organisms. Research shows that genetically diverse populations are more resilient to environmental stress and are better at resisting disease. Thus, creating populations of genetically similar organisms exposes all organisms to greater threats of disease. Lack of genetic diversity in populations of other organisms may ultimately expose humans to threats as well. For example, genetically identical crops could all fall prey to the same disease and, consequently, seriously endanger food supplies (this isn't as farfetched as it sounds). In fact, efforts to archive genetically diverse strains of plants are already underway lest unique genetic characteristics, like disease resistance, are lost.

Furthermore, cloning is fraught with problems for which no good alternatives exist. For now, all cloning requires oocytes from female organisms. Those oocytes are obtained by first treating females with large doses of fertility drugs to stimulate ovulation. Such drugs stress the female's system enormously and increase the rate of cell turnover in her ovaries. Some studies indicate that the drugs used for stimulating ovulation expose females to increased risk of ovarian cancer. And the risk doesn't end there. When eggs are produced, they must be surgically removed under anesthesia. Regardless of the precautions, the female organism can and does experience pain. Animals can't give or withhold consent, so they're subjected to these procedures whether they like it or not.

After eggs are harvested and donor cells are fused with them, development of an embryo begins. The vast majority of cloning attempts, regardless of their ultimate purpose, result in death of the embryo. Granted, these embryos have no nerve cells and no consciousness that scientists know of, but nevertheless, living organisms are produced with little or no hope of survival.

If clones are successfully created, their quality of life may be poor. Clones suffer from a myriad of disorders for which causes are unknown. They may age prematurely and are likely at risk for disorders that are yet unrecognized consequences of the methods used in the cloning process. Like the experimental animals used for egg production, cloned animals can't withhold their consent and withdraw from study.

The most contentious issue posed by cloning technology is the production of human clones. As with animals, most cloned human embryos would have no hope of survival. Women must consent to painful and potentially dangerous procedures to produce eggs, and some women must consent to carry the developing child and risk the emotional trauma of miscarriage or stillbirth. From an emotional standpoint, children created this way would be genetically identical to some other person, whether that person is living or dead. The pressure to be like someone else would undoubtedly be enormous. Further, because of the genetic similarities to some other individual, parents may have unrealistic expectations of their cloned offspring. Do individual humans have a right to genetic uniqueness? It's a difficult question, but it's one we need to answer soon, before human cloning becomes true reality.

Evolution and Behavior

GREG KRUKONIS • TRACY BARR •
TARA RODDEN ROBINSON

BIO 130
Henry Ford Community College

—Wiley Custom Learning Solutions—

Brief Contents

Taken from: *Genetics for Dummies*, Second Edition by Tara Rodden Robinson

Chapter 21

Giving Ethical Considerations Their Due

*T*he field of genetics grows and changes constantly. If you follow the news, you're likely to hear about several new discoveries every week. When it comes to genetics, the amount of information is bewildering, and the possibilities are endless. If you've already read many of the chapters in this book, you have a taste of the many choices and debates created by the burgeoning technology surrounding our genes.

With such a fast-growing and far-reaching field as genetics, ethical questions and issues arise around every corner and are interconnected with the applications and procedures. Throughout this book, I highlight this interconnectedness. I cover animal welfare issues (in the context of cloning) in Chapter 20. Conservation of the environment and endangered species is a key part of the discussion of population genetics in Chapter 17. Chapter 19 touches on the potential dangers — to the environment and to humans — of genetic engineering. Genetic counseling, including some of the issues surrounding prenatal testing, is the subject of Chapter 12. And in Chapter 16 I discuss gene therapy as an experimental form of treatment.

But I couldn't end the discussion of genetics and your world without some final comments on the ethical issues that genetic advances raise. In this chapter, you find out how genetics has been misunderstood, misinterpreted, and misused to cause people harm based on their racial, ethnic, or socioeconomic status. The rapidly growing field of genetics is contributing to ideas about how modern humans can mold the future of their offspring, so this chapter dispels the myth of the designer baby. You discover how information you give out and receive can be used for and against you. Finally, you gain a better understanding of the next generation of studies based on the Human Genome Project and the ethical issues that mapping human genetic diversity will bring up.

Profiling Genetic Racism

One of the biggest hot button issues of all time has to be *eugenics*. In a nutshell, eugenics is the idea that humans should practice selective reproduction in an effort to "improve" the species. If you read Chapter 19, which explains how organisms can be genetically engineered, you probably already have some idea of what eugenics in the modern age may entail (transgenic, made-to-order babies, perhaps?). Historically, the most blatant examples of eugenics are genocidal activities the world over. (Perhaps the most infamous example occurred in Nazi Germany during the 1930s and 1940s.)

The story of eugenics begins with the otherwise laudable Francis Galton, who coined the term in 1883. (Galton is best remembered for his contribution to law enforcement: He invented the process used to identify persons by their fingerprints. Check out Chapter 18 for more on the genetic version of fingerprinting.) In direct and vocal opposition to the U.S. Constitution, Galton was quite sure that all men were *not* created equal (I emphasize here that he was particularly fixated on men; women were of no consequence in his day). Instead, Galton believed that some men were quite superior to others. To this end, he attempted to prove that "genius" is inherited. The view that superior intelligence is heritable is still widely held despite abundant evidence to the contrary. For example, twin studies conducted as far back as the 1930s show that genetically identical persons are not intellectually identical.

Galton, who was one of Charles Darwin's cousins, gave eugenics its name, but his ideas weren't unique or revolutionary. During the early 20th century, as understanding of Mendelian genetics (see Chapter 3) gathered steam, many people viewed eugenics as a highly admirable field of study. Charles Davenport was one such person. Davenport holds the dubious distinction of being the father of the American eugenics movement (one of his eugenics texts is subtitled "The science of human improvement by better breeding"). The basis of Davenport's idea is that "degenerate" people shouldn't reproduce. This notion arose from something called *degeneracy theory,* which posits that "unfit" humans acquire certain undesirable traits because of "bad environments" and then pass on these traits genetically. To these eugenicists, unfit included "shiftlessness," "feeblemindedness," and poverty, among other things.

While the British, including Galton, advocated perpetuating good breeding (along with wealth and privilege), many American eugenicists focused their attention on preventing *cacogenics,* which is the erosion of genetic quality. Therefore, they advocated forcibly sterilizing people judged undesirable or merely inconvenient. Shockingly, the forcible sterilization laws of this era have never been overturned, and until the 1970s, it was still common practice to sterilize mentally ill persons without their consent — an estimated 60,000 people in the United States suffered this atrocity. Some societies have taken this sick idea a step further and *murdered* the "unfit" in an effort to remove them and their genes permanently.

Sadly, violent forms of eugenics, such as genocide, rape, and forced sterilization, are still advocated and practiced all over the world. But not all forms of eugenics are as easy to recognize as these extreme examples. To some degree, eugenics lies at the heart of most of the other ethical quandaries I address in this chapter. In addition, it only requires a little imagination to see how gene therapy (Chapter 16), gene transfer (Chapter 19), or DNA fingerprinting (Chapter 18) can be abused to advance the cause of eugenics.

Ordering Up Designer Babies

One of the more contentious issues with a root in eugenics stems from a combination of prenatal diagnosis and the fantasy of the perfect child to create a truly extreme makeover — designer babies. In theory, a designer baby may be made-to-order according to a parent's desire for a particular sex, hair and eye color, and maybe even athletic ability.

The myth of designer babies

The term *designer baby* gets tossed around quite a bit these days. In essence, the term is associated with genetically made-to-order offspring. As of this writing, neither the technology nor sufficient knowledge of the human genome exists to make the designer baby a reality.

The fantasy of the designer baby, like cloning (see Chapter 20), rests on the fallacy of *biological determinism* (which, by the way, is what eugenics bases some of its lies on, too; jump back to "Profiling Genetic Racism" to find out about eugenics). Biological determinism assumes that genes are expressed in precise, repeatable ways — in other words, genetics is identity is genetics. However, this assumption isn't true. Gene expression is highly dependent on environment, among other things (see Chapter 10 for more details about how gene expression works).

Furthermore, the *in vitro* fertilization process that plays a role in current-day applications of the science in question (see the next section) is a very dicey and difficult process at best — just ask any couple who's gone through it in an effort to get pregnant. *In vitro* procedures are extremely expensive, invasive, and painful, and women must take large quantities of strong and potentially dangerous fertility medications to produce a sufficient number of eggs. And in the end, the majority of fertilizations don't result in pregnancies.

The reality of the science: Prenatal diagnosis

So where does the myth of designer babies come from? Using procedures similar to those leading up to cloning (covered in Chapter 20), *preimplantation genetic diagnosis,* or PGD, is performed before a fertilized egg implants in the womb. Although it's true that PGD opens the remote possibility of creating transgenic humans using the same technology used to create transgenic animals (see Chapter 19 for details), the likelihood of PGD becoming commonplace is extremely remote.

The process of PGD is technologically complicated. First, unfertilized eggs are harvested from a female donor. *In vitro fertilization* (the process to produce the so-called test-tube baby) is performed, and then the fertilized eggs are tested for specific gene mutations or other genetic variations. In a few rare cases, desperate parents have created embryos this way specifically to look for genetic compatibility with preexisting offspring — the plan being to conceive a sibling who can provide stem cells or bone marrow to save the life of a living sibling suffering from an otherwise untreatable disease. Saving the lives of living children is undoubtedly a laudable goal; the problem arises with what's done with the fertilized eggs that don't meet the desired criteria (if, for example, they don't have the desired tissue match). Even if inserted into the mother's uterus, the vast majority of these fertilized eggs would never implant and thus would not survive. Although lack of implantation is also true when conception occurs naturally, it's still a very tough call to decide the fate of extra embryos. Options include donation to other couples, donation for research purposes, or destruction.

PGD and other forms of prenatal diagnosis allow parents the choice to prevent, alleviate, or reduce suffering (their own or someone else's). But like deciding the fate of extra embryos, this is very deep and muddied water. Without getting too philosophical, suffering is a highly personal experience; that is, what constitutes suffering to one person may look relatively okay to someone else. One example of relative suffering that comes up a lot is hereditary deafness. If a deaf couple chooses prenatal diagnosis, what's the most desirable outcome? On one hand, a deaf child shares the worldview of his or her parents. On the other hand, a hearing child fits into the world of nondeaf people more easily. By now, you see how complex the issues surrounding prenatal diagnosis are. It seems clear that right answers, if there are any, will be very hard to come by.

Who Knows? Getting Informed Consent

Informed consent is a sticky ethical and legal issue. Basically, the idea is that a person can only truly make a decision about having a procedure when he or she is fully apprised of all the facts, risks, and benefits. Informed consent can only be given by the person receiving the procedure or by that person's legal guardian. Generally, guardianship is established in cases where the recipient of the procedure is too young to make decisions for him or herself or is mentally incapacitated in some way; presumably, guardians have the best interests of their wards at heart.

Three major issues exist in the debate over informed consent:

- ✔ Genetic testing can be carried out on embryos, the deceased, and samples obtained from anyone during the simplest of medical procedures.

- ✔ Experimental genetic treatments (that is, gene therapies; see Chapter 16) have, by their very nature, unpredictable outcomes, making risk difficult to quantify to prospective participants.

- ✔ After tissue samples are obtained and genetic profiling is done, information storage and privacy assurance could be problematic.

Placing restrictions on genetic testing

Genetic testing in the forms of DNA fingerprinting, SNP analysis (see Chapter 18), and gene sequencing (see Chapter 11), among others, is now routine, fast, and relatively cheap. The testing can glean massive amounts of information — from an individual's sex to his or her racial and ethnic makeup — from even a very tiny sample of tissue. The procedure can also detect the presence of mutations for inherited disorders. But given that your DNA has so much personal information stored in it, shouldn't you have complete control over whether you're tested? The answer to this question is becoming more and more contentious as the definitions of, and limits to, informed consent are explored. The rights of persons both living and dead are at stake.

For example, the descendents of Thomas Jefferson consented to genetic testing in 1998 to settle a long-standing controversy about Jefferson's relationship with one of his slaves, Sally Hemings (see Chapter 18 for the full story). In the Jefferson case, the matter was more than just academic curiosity because the right to burial in the family cemetery at Monticello was at stake.

The issue of informed consent, or lack thereof, is complicated by the ability to store tissue for long periods of time. In some cases, patients or their guardians gave informed consent for certain tests but didn't include tests that hadn't yet been developed. Some institutions routinely practice long-term tissue storage, making informed consent a frequent point of contention. For example, a children's hospital in Britain was taken to task over storage of organs that were obtained during autopsies but weren't returned for internment with the rest of the body. Parents of the affected deceased gave consent for the autopsies but not for the retention of tissues.

Biologists also use stored tissue to create *cell-lines,* living tissues that grow in culture tubes for research purposes. The original cell donors are often dead, usually from the disease under study. Cell-lines aren't that hard to make and maintain (if you know what you're doing), but the creation of cell-lines raises the question of whether the original donor has ownership rights to cells descended from his or her tissue. Cell-lines sometimes result in patents for lucrative treatments; should donors or their heirs get a royalty? (A court decision in California said no.)

Moreover, some cell-lines are developed using unfertilized human eggs, creating another ethical quandary. One type of stem cell research fuses an egg (that has had its nucleus removed) with an adult somatic cell in an attempt to create a stem cell-line that's matched with the somatic cell donor's tissue. This sort of research requires huge numbers of human eggs. In a controversial move, the New York Stem Cell Foundation's ethics committee voted to allow women to be paid for their eggs. Though limiting payments to compensation for "time and burden," the decision increases worries about both placing egg donors' health at risk and the commercialization of human body parts.

Practicing safe genetic treatment

If you've ever had to sign a consent for treatment form, you know it can be a sobering experience. Almost all such forms include some phrase that communicates the possibility of death. With a gulp, most of us sign off and hope for the best. For routine procedures and treatments, our faith is usually repaid with survival. Experimental treatments are harder to gauge, though, and fully informing someone about possible outcomes is very difficult.

The 1999 case of Jesse Gelsinger (covered in Chapter 16) brought the problem of informed consent and experimental treatment into a glaring, harsh light. Jesse died after receiving an experimental treatment for a hereditary disorder that, by itself, wasn't likely to kill him. His treatment took place as part of a clinical trial designed to assess the effects of a particular therapy in relatively healthy patients and to work out any difficulties before initiating treatments on patients for whom the disease would, without a doubt, be fatal (in this case, infants homozygous for the allele). What researchers knew about all the possible outcomes and what the Gelsinger family was told before treatment began is debatable.

Almost every article on gene therapy published since the Gelsinger case makes mention of it. In fact, most researchers in the field divide the development of gene therapies into two categories: before and after Gelsinger. Sadly, Gelsinger's death probably contributed very little to the broader understanding of gene therapy. Instead, the impacts of the Gelsinger case are that clinical trials are now harder to initiate, criteria for patient inclusion and exclusion are heightened, and disclosure and reporting requirements are far more stringent. These changes are basically a double-edged sword: New regulations protect patients' rights and simultaneously decrease the likelihood that researchers will develop treatments to help those who desperately need them. Like so many ethical issues, a safe and effective solution may prove elusive.

Keeping it private

Another issue in the informed consent debate relates to privacy. When genetic tests are conducted, the data recorded often includes detailed medical histories and other personal information, all of which aids researchers or physicians in the interpretation of the genetic data obtained. So far, so good. But what happens to all that information? Who sees it? Where's it stored? And for how long?

Privacy is a big deal, particularly in American culture. Laws exist to protect one's private medical information, financial status, and juvenile criminal records (if any). Individuals are protected from unwarranted searches and surveillance, and they have the right to exclude unwanted persons from their private property. Genetic information is likely to fall under existing medical privacy laws, but there's one twist: Genetic information contains an element of the future, not just the past.

When you carry a mutation for susceptibility to breast cancer, you have a greater likelihood of developing breast cancer than someone who doesn't have the allele (see Chapter 14). A breast cancer allele doesn't guarantee you'll develop the cancer, though; it just increases the probability. If you were to be tested for the breast cancer allele and found to have it, that information would become part of your medical record. Besides your doctor and appropriate medical personnel, who might learn about your condition? Your insurance company, that's who. So far, situations like this haven't presented a big problem because few people have had genetic tests. Many genetic tests are often expensive and aren't part of routine healthcare, but as technology advances and gets cheaper (like microarrays; see Chapter 23), genetic testing is likely to become more common. And that shift may be both a blessing and a curse.

As a patient, knowing that you have a genetic mutation is a really good thing, because the condition may be treatable, or an early detection screening may help you prevent more serious complications. For example, cancers that are caught early have far better prognoses than those diagnosed in later stages. However, knowing about a genetic mutation may give insurance companies the chance to issue or cancel policies, thus unfairly limiting your access to healthcare or employment. Sadly, at least one employer has been caught attempting to test workers for genetic predispositions to certain injuries (in this case, carpal tunnel syndrome, a repetitive stress injury to the hands and arms) without the employees' knowledge — clearly, a violation of informed consent.

Genetic privacy issues also feed into the controversies surrounding the Human Genome Project and efforts to characterize human population genetics. Critics fear that if certain mutations or health problems are genetically linked to groups of people, discrimination and bias will result. Fortunately, lawmakers are taking steps to protect you and your genetic privacy. In 2008, former U.S. President George W. Bush signed the Genetic Information Nondiscrimination Act (GINA), which prohibits both health insurance companies and employers from discriminating against someone based on information from genetic testing. In addition, most state legislatures have enacted similar laws.

Genetic Property Rights

According to U.S. law, a patent gives the patent owner exclusive rights to manufacture and sell his or her invention for a certain length of time (usually 20 years). That may not sound like a big deal, but what makes patents scary is that companies are patenting *genes* — DNA sequences that hold the instructions for life. And it's not just any genes, either. They're patenting *your* genes.

Patents are granted to *inventors,* but the people (or companies) holding gene patents didn't invent the genes that naturally occur in living organisms. According to most legal experts, genes are "unpatentable products of nature." Yet so far, American and European patenting authorities have viewed genes in the same legal light as manmade chemicals. Generally, patent-holding companies sequence the genes and convert them to another form called cDNA (*c* means complementary; see Chapter 16 for coverage of translation). Then they seek a patent on the cDNA rather than the gene itself. Another approach to the patenting process is that the company discovers a gene (or a disease-causing version of it) and then invents products such as diagnostic tests that have something to do with the gene.

Just how a company can own and exercise exclusive rights over your genes is a little hard to understand. An example of how gene patenting works comes from the invention of the process of PCR (see Chapter 22 for the whole tale). The process uses an enzyme that's produced by a very special sort of bacteria. The gene that codes for that enzyme (called *Taq polymerase*) is easily moved into other bacteria, such as *E. coli,* using recombinant DNA techniques (explained in Chapter 16). This means that *E. coli* can produce the enzyme that can then be used to run PCR. But if any other geneticist uses that gene to make Taq polymerase, a royalty must be paid to the company that patented it. Not surprisingly, this company is now the biggest manufacturer of Taq in the world, raking in profits in the billions of dollars.

Here are examples of how ugly the gene-patenting game can get:

- ✔ In 2001, an American company got a European patent for *BRCA1,* one of the breast cancer genes (see Chapter 14 for a full description of this mutation). A mutation in this gene can lead to cancer, and presumably, no one would want to purchase a case of breast cancer. So why patent it? Because the company holding the patent can charge large sums to test people to determine whether they carry the mutation.

- ✔ A large drug company holds a patent on a gene test that can determine whether the company's product will work for certain persons. The company refuses to actually develop the test or let anyone else have a crack at it because doing so may reduce sales of the medication in question.

- ✔ Companies patent disease-causing bacteria and viral genes for the same reasons — to block diagnosis and treatment — until a hefty licensing fee has been paid.

Such use of genetic patents impedes both research to combat disease and access to healthcare. Because of these kinds of manipulations, gene patents are beginning to meet with strong and vocal opposition.

Gene-patenting policies may endanger your health in other ways as well.

- ✔ When commercial outfits get genetic information, they treat it as their personal property. Therefore, they don't always report gene sequences and experiment results in the appropriate scientific literature (thus avoiding review and verification by experts in the field). To market their products, these companies must go through the regulatory process mandated by the government to ensure consumer safety, but that regulatory review process has suffered noticeable shortcomings of late — particularly when products are allowed to pass muster while some conflict of interest is at work (think stock options, as was the case in shake-ups at the U.S. National Institutes of Health in 2005).

- ✔ Sadly, universities have gotten in on the act. In one instance, the search for the genes responsible for autism was held up because several universities refused to share information with, of all people, the parents of autistic children. Each university wanted to be the first to (you guessed it) patent the "autism gene." As a result, an independent foundation was established to create a public repository for genetic information about autism, because such actions are a direct assault on the openness of the scientific research itself.

The days of gene patents may be numbered, however. In 2009, cancer patient Genae Girard, along with four other patients, genetics researchers, and others, filed suit against a company that owns the patent on two genes associated with breast cancer risk. If their challenge is successful, restrictions on testing and other sorts of research could be lifted, paving the way to more open exchange of knowledge and lowering the costs of testing.

Part V
The Part of Tens

"So, Bateson—how's the work in genetics and plant hybridization coming?"

In this part . . .

Genetics is equal parts great history and amazing future. The discoveries of the past depended on the genius of many individuals. Likewise, the marvels of the future will be shaped by teams of researchers and entrepreneurs.

This part exposes you to genetics' past and allows you to glimpse its future as well. I introduce you to the ten most important people and events that shaped what genetics is today, and I explain the next big things (or ten of them, at least) on the genetics horizon. Finally, I shake things up with ten hard-to-believe (and all true!) genetics stories.

Chapter 22

Ten Defining Events in Genetics

Many milestones define the history of genetics. This chapter focuses on nine that I don't cover in other chapters of the book and one that I do (the Human Genome Project is so important that I cover it in Chapter 8 and here, too). The events listed here appear roughly in order of historical occurrence.

The Publication of Darwin's "The Origin of Species"

Earthquakes have aftershocks — little mini-earthquakes that rattle around after the main quake. Events in history sometimes cause aftershocks, too. The publication of one man's life's work is such an event. From the moment it hit the shelves in 1856, Charles Darwin's *The Origin of Species* was deeply controversial (and still is).

The basis of evolution is elegantly simple: Individual organisms vary in their ability to survive and reproduce. For example, a sudden cold snap occurs, and most individuals of a certain bird species die because they can't tolerate the rapid drop in temperature. But individuals of the same species that can tolerate the unexpected freeze survive and reproduce. As long as the ability to deal with rapid temperature drops is heritable, the trait is passed to future generations, and more and more individuals inherit it. When groups of individuals are isolated from each other, they wind up being subjected to different sorts of events (such as weather patterns). After many, many years, stepwise changes in the kinds of traits that individuals inherit based on events like a sudden freeze accumulate to the point that populations with common ancestors become separate species.

Darwin concluded that all life on earth is related by inheritance in this fashion and thus has a common origin. Darwin arrived at his conclusions after years of studying plants and animals all over the world. What he lacked was a convincing explanation for how individuals inherit advantageous traits. Yet the explanation was literally at his fingertips. Gregor Mendel figured out the laws of inheritance at about the same time that Darwin was working on his book (see Chapter 3). Apparently, Darwin failed to read Mendel's paper — he scrawled notes on the papers immediately preceding and following Mendel's paper but left Mendel's unmarked. Darwin's copious notes show no evidence that he was even aware of Mendel's work.

Even without knowledge of how inheritance works, Darwin accurately summarized three principles that are confirmed by genetics:

- **Variation is random and unpredictable.** Studies of mutation confirm this principle (see Chapter 13).

- **Variation is *heritable* (it can be passed on from one generation to the next).** Mendel's own research — and thousands of studies over the past century — confirms heritability. With DNA fingerprinting, heritable genetic variation can be traced directly from parent to offspring (see Chapter 18 for how paternity tests use heritable genetic markers to determine which male fathered which child).

- **Variation changes in frequency over the course of time.** The Hardy-Weinberg principle formalized this concept in the form of population genetics in the early 1900s (see Chapter 17). Since the 1970s, genetic studies using DNA sequencing (along with other methods) have confirmed that genetic variation within populations changes because of mutation, accidents, and geographic isolation, to name only a few causes.

Regardless of how you view it, the publication of Darwin's *The Origin of Species* is pivotal in the history of genetics. If no genetic variation existed, all life on earth would be precisely identical. Variation gives the world its rich texture and complexity, and it's what makes you wonderfully unique.

The Rediscovery of Mendel's Work

In 1866, Gregor Mendel wrote a summary of the results of his gardening experiments with peas (which I detail in Chapter 3). His work was published in the scientific journal *Versuche Pflanzen Hybriden,* where it gathered dust for nearly 40 years. Although Mendel wasn't big on self-promotion, he sent copies of his paper to two well-known scientists of his time. One copy remains missing; the other was found in what amounts to an unopened envelope — the pages were never cut. (Old printing practices resulted in pages being folded together; the only way to read the paper was to cut the pages apart.) Thus, despite the fact that his findings were published and distributed (though limitedly), his peers didn't grasp the magnitude of Mendel's discovery.

Mendel's work went unnoticed until three botanists — Hugo de Vries, Erich von Tschermak, and Carl Correns — all reinvented Mendel's wheel, so to speak. These three men conducted experiments that were very similar to Mendel's. Their conclusions were identical — all three "discovered" the laws of heredity. De Vries found Mendel's work referenced in a paper published in 1881. (De Vries coined the term *mutation,* by the way.) The author of the 1881 paper, a man by the unfortunate name of Focke, summarized Mendel's findings but didn't have a clue as to their significance. De Vries correctly interpreted Mendel's work and cited it in his own paper, which was published in 1900. Shortly thereafter, Tschermak and Correns also discovered Mendel's publication through de Vries's published works and indicated that their own independent findings confirmed Mendel's conclusions as well.

William Bateson is perhaps the great hero of this story. He was already incredibly influential by the time he read de Vries's paper citing Mendel, and unlike many around him, he recognized that Mendel's laws of inheritance were revolutionary and absolutely correct. Bateson became an ardent voice spreading the word. He coined the terms *genetics, allele* (shortened from the original *allelomorph*), *homozygote,* and *heterozygote*. Bateson was also responsible for the discovery of linkage (see Chapter 4), which was experimentally confirmed later by Morgan and Bridges.

The Transforming Principle

Frederick Griffith wasn't working to discover DNA. The year was 1928, and the memory of the deadly flu epidemic of 1918 was still fresh in everyone's mind. Griffith was studying pneumonia in an effort to prevent future epidemics. He was particularly interested in why some strains of bacteria cause illness and other seemingly identical strains do not. To get to the bottom of the issue, he conducted a series of experiments using two strains of the same species of bacteria, *Streptococcus pneumonia.* The two strains looked very different when grown in a Petri dish, because one grew a smooth carpet and the other a lumpy one (he called it "rough"). When Griffith injected smooth bacteria into mice, they died; rough bacteria, on the other hand, were harmless.

To figure out why one strain of bacteria was deadly and the other wasn't, Griffith conducted a series of experiments. He injected some mice with heat-killed smooth bacteria (which turned out to be harmless) and others with heat-killed smooth in combination with living rough bacteria. This combo proved deadly to the mice. Griffith quickly figured out that something in the smooth bacteria *transformed* rough bacteria into a killer. But what? For lack of anything better, he called the responsible factor the *transforming principle* (which now sounds like a good title for a diet book).

Oswald Avery, Maclyn McCarty, and Colin MacLeod teamed up in the 1940s to discover that Griffith's transforming principle was actually DNA. This trio made the discovery by a dogged process of elimination. They showed that fats and proteins don't do the trick; only the DNA of smooth bacteria provides live rough bacteria with the needed ingredient to get nasty. Their results were published in 1944, and like Mendel's work nearly a century before, their findings were largely rejected.

It wasn't until Erwin Chargaff came along that the transforming principle started to get the appreciation it deserved. Chargaff was so impressed that he changed his entire research focus to DNA. Chargaff eventually determined the ratios of bases in DNA that helped lead to Watson and Crick's momentous discovery of DNA's double helix structure (flip to Chapter 6 for all the details).

The Discovery of Jumping Genes

By all accounts, Barbara McClintock was both brilliant and a little odd; a friend once described her as "not fooled or foolable." McClintock was unorthodox in both her research and her outlook as she lived and worked alone for most of her life. Her career began in the early 1930s and took her into a man's world — very few women worked in the sciences in her day.

In 1931, McClintock collaborated with another woman, Harriet Creighton, to demonstrate that genes are located on chromosomes. This fact sounds so self-evident now, but back then, it was a revolutionary idea. Creighton and McClintock showed that corn chromosomes recombine during meiosis (see Chapter 2 for the scoop on meiosis). By tracking the inheritance of various traits, they figured out which genes were getting moved during translocation events (see Chapter 15). *Translocations* hook up chunks of chromosomes in places where they don't belong. Chromosomes with translocations look very different from normal chromosomes, making it easy to track their inheritance. By linking physical traits to certain parts of one odd-looking chromosome, Creighton and McClintock demonstrated that crossover events between chromosomes move genes from one chromosome to another.

McClintock's contribution to genetics goes beyond locating genes on chromosomes, though. She also discovered traveling bits of DNA, sometimes known as jumping genes (see Chapter 11 for more). In 1948, McClintock, working independently, published her results demonstrating that certain genes of corn could hop around from one chromosome to another *without* translocation. Her announcement triggered little reaction at first. It's not that people thought McClintock was wrong; she was just so far ahead of the curve that her fellow geneticists couldn't comprehend her findings. Alfred Sturtevant (who was responsible for the discovery of gene mapping) once said, "I didn't understand one word she said, but if she says it is so, it must be so!"

It took nearly 40 years before the genetics world caught up with Barbara McClintock and awarded her the Nobel Prize in Physiology or Medicine in 1983. By then, jumping genes had been discovered in many organisms (including humans). Feisty to the end, this grand dame of genetics passed away in 1992 at the age of 90.

The Birth of DNA Sequencing

So many events in the history of genetics lay a foundation for other events to follow. Federick Sanger's invention of chain-reaction DNA sequencing (which I cover in Chapter 8) is one of those foundational events. In 1980, Sanger shared his second Nobel Prize (in Chemistry) with Walter Gilbert for their work on DNA. Sanger had already earned a Nobel Prize in Chemistry in 1958 for his pioneering work on the structure of the protein insulin. (*Insulin* is produced by your pancreas and regulates blood sugar; its absence results in diabetes.)

Sanger figured out the entire process used for DNA sequencing. Every single genetics project that has anything to do with DNA uses Sanger's method. *Chain-reaction sequencing,* as Sanger's method is called, uses the same mechanics as replication in your cells (see Chapter 7 for a rundown of replication). Sanger figured out that he could control the DNA building process by snipping off one oxygen molecule from the building blocks of DNA. The resulting method allowed identification of every base, in order, along a DNA strand, sparking a revolution in the understanding of how your genes work. This process is responsible for the Human Genome Project, DNA fingerprinting (see Chapter 18), genetic engineering (see Chapter 19), and gene therapy (see Chapter 16).

The Invention of PCR

In 1985, while driving along a California highway in the middle of the night, Kary Mullis had a brainstorm about how to carry out DNA replication in a tube (see Chapter 7 for the scoop on replication). His idea led to the invention of *polymerase chain reaction* (PCR), a pivotal point in the history of genetics.

I detail the entire process of how PCR is used in DNA fingerprinting in Chapter 18. In essence, PCR acts like a copier for DNA. Even the tiniest snippet of DNA can be copied. This concept is important because, so far, technology isn't sophisticated enough to examine one DNA molecule at a time. Scientists need many copies of the same molecule before enough is present for them to detect and study. Without PCR, large amounts of DNA are needed to generate a DNA fingerprint, but at many crime scenes, only tiny amounts of DNA are present. PCR is the powerful tool that every crime lab in the country now uses to detect the DNA left behind at crime scenes and to generate DNA fingerprints.

Mullis's bright idea turned into a billion dollar industry. Although he reportedly was paid a paltry $10,000 for his invention, he received the Nobel Prize for Chemistry in 1993 (a sort of consolation prize).

The Development of Recombinant DNA Technology

In 1970, Hamilton O. Smith discovered *restriction enzymes,* which act as chemical cleavers to chop DNA into pieces at very specific sequences. As part of other research, Smith put bacteria and a bacteria-attacking virus together. The bacteria didn't go down without a fight — instead, it produced an enzyme that chopped the viral DNA into pieces, effectively destroying the invading virus altogether. Smith determined that the enzyme, now known as *HindII* (named for the bacteria *Haemophilus influenzae Rd*), cuts DNA every time it finds certain bases all in a row and cuts between the same two bases every time.

This fortuitous (and completely accidental!) discovery was just what was needed to spark a revolution in the study of DNA. Some restriction enzymes make offset cuts in DNA, leaving single-stranded ends. The single-strand bits of DNA allow geneticists to "cut-and-paste" pieces of DNA together in novel ways, forming the entire basis of what's now known as *recombinant DNA technology.*

Gene therapy (see Chapter 16), the creation of genetically engineered organisms (see Chapter 19), and practically every other advance in the field of genetics these days all depend on the ability to cut DNA into pieces without disabling the genes and then to put the genes into new places — a feat made possible thanks to restriction enzymes.

Today, researchers use thousands of restriction enzymes to help map genes on chromosomes, determine the function of genes, and manipulate DNA for diagnosis and treatment of disease. Smith shared the Nobel Prize in Physiology or Medicine in 1978 with two other geneticists, Dan Nathans and Werner Arber, for their joint contributions to the discovery of restriction enzymes.

The Invention of DNA Fingerprinting

Sir Alec Jeffreys has put thousands of wrongdoers behind bars. Almost single-handedly, he's also set hundreds of innocent people free from prison. Not bad for a guy who spends most of his time in the genetics lab.

Jeffreys invented DNA fingerprinting in 1985. By examining the patterns made by human DNA after it was diced up by restriction enzymes, Jeffreys realized that every person's DNA produces a slightly different number of various sized fragments (which number in the thousands).

Jeffreys's invention has seen a number of refinements since its inception. PCR and the use of STRs (*short tandem repeats;* see Chapter 18) have replaced the use of restriction enzymes. Modern methods of DNA fingerprinting are highly repeatable and extremely accurate, meaning that a DNA fingerprint can be stored much like a fingerprint impression from your fingertip. More than 100 laboratories in the United States alone now make use of the methods that Jeffreys pioneered. The information that these labs generate is housed in a huge database hosted by the FBI, granting any police department quick access to data that can help match criminals to crimes.

In 1994, Queen Elizabeth II knighted Jeffreys for his contributions to law enforcement and his accomplishments in genetics.

The Explanation of Developmental Genetics

As I explain in Chapter 8, every cell in your body has a full set of genetic instructions to make all of you. The master plan of how an entire organism is built from genetic instructions remained a mystery until 1980, when Christiane Nüsslein-Volhard and Eric Wieschaus identified the genes that control the whole body plan during fly development.

Fruit flies and other insects are constructed of interlocking pieces, or segments. A group of genes (collectively called *segmentation genes*) tells the cells which body segments go where. These genes, along with others, give directions like top and bottom and front and back, as well as the order of body regions in between. Nüsslein-Volhard and Wieschaus made their discovery by mutating genes and looking for the effects of the "broken" genes. When segmentation genes get mutated, the fly ends up lacking whole sections of important body parts or certain pairs of organs.

A different set of genes (called *homeotic genes*) controls the placement of all the fly's organs and appendages, such as wings, legs, eyes, and so on. One such gene is *eyeless*. Contrary to what would seem logical, *eyeless* actually codes for normal eye development. Using the same recombinant DNA techniques made possible by restriction enzymes (see the section "The Development of Recombinant DNA Technology" earlier in the chapter), Nüsslein-Volhard and Wieschaus moved *eyeless* to different chromosomes where it could be turned on in cells in which it was normally turned off. The resulting flies grew eyes in all sorts of strange locations — on their wings, legs, butts, you name it. This research showed that, working together, segmentation and homeotic genes put all the parts in all the right places. Humans have versions of these genes, too; your body-plan genes were discovered by comparing fruit fly genes to human DNA (see Chapter 8 for how the genomes of organisms affect you).

The Work of Francis Collins and the Human Genome Project

In 1989, Francis Collins and Lap-Chee Tsui identified the single gene responsible for cystic fibrosis. The very next year, the Human Genome Project (HGP) officially got underway. A double-doctor (that is, a doc with an MD and PhD), Collins later replaced James Watson as the head of the National Human Genome Research Institute in the United States and supervised the race to sequence the entire human genome from start to finish. In 2009, Collins became the director of the U.S. National Institutes of Health.

Collins is one of the true heroes of modern genetics. He kept the HGP ahead of schedule and under budget. He continues to champion the right to free access to all the HGP data, making him a courageous opponent of gene patents and other practices that restrict access to discovery and healthcare, and he's a staunch defender of genetic privacy (see Chapter 21 for more on these subjects). Although the human genome is still bits and pieces away from being completely sequenced, the project wouldn't have been a success without the tireless work of Collins, who's still an active gene hunter. His lab is now searching out the genes responsible for adult-onset diabetes.

Chapter 23

Ten Hot Issues in Genetics

In This Chapter

▶ Tracking potential advances in medicine and aging

▶ Continuing research on stem cells and antibiotic resistance

▶ Identifying the DNA bar codes of living things

Genetics is a field that grows and changes with every passing day. The hottest journals in the field *(Nature* and *Science)* are full of new discoveries each and every week. This chapter shines the spotlight on ten of the hottest topics and next big things in this ever-changing scientific landscape.

Personalized Medicine

The fourth biggest cause of death in the United States is adverse reactions to medications. Up to 100,000 people die each year from something that's meant to help them. Why? The tool scientists use to answer that question is *pharmacogenomics,* the analysis of the human genome and heredity to determine how drugs work in individual people. The idea is that the reason certain people have adverse reactions to certain drugs and others don't lies somewhere in their DNA. If researchers could develop a simple test to detect these DNA differences, doctors would never prescribe the wrong drugs in the first place. (Oddly, this idea sometimes doesn't go over well with drug companies; for more on the connection between the two, check out Chapter 21.) The overarching goal of personalized medicine is a new brand of care that can be designed to fit the unique genetic makeup of each individual patient.

That's the good news. The bad news is that nobody knows how many genes are involved in diseases, and many genes can cause the *same* disease. Not only that, but *epigenetics* (flip to Chapter 4 to find out more about epigenetics) further complicates matters by turning genes on and off in unexpected ways. All this adds up to more confusion and fewer genetics-based treatments, meaning that the promises of personalized medicine may wind up being slow, or impossible, to realize.

Stem Cell Research

Stem cells may hold the key to curing brain and spinal cord injuries. They may be part of the cure for cancer. These little wonders may be *the* magic bullet to solving all sorts of medical problems, but they're at the center of controversies so big that their potential remains untested.

Stem cells are hot research topics because they're totipotent. *Totipotence* means that stem cells can turn into any kind of tissue, from brain to muscle to bone, just to name a few. Not too surprisingly, stem cells are what undifferentiated embryos are made of; that is, a fertilized egg, shortly after it starts dividing, is composed entirely of stem cells. At a certain point during development, all the cells get their assignments, and totipotence is long gone (except for DNA, which retains surprising flexibility — DNA's totipotence is what allows cloning to work; see Chapter 20).

You've probably guessed (or already knew) that the source of stem cells for research is embryonic tissue — and therein lies the rub. As of this writing, researchers haven't found a way to harvest stem cells without sacrificing the embryo in the process. They can collect stem cells from adults (from various places, including blood), but adult stem cells lack some of the totipotent potential of embryonic cells and are present in very low numbers, which makes using adult stem cells problematic. Nonetheless, adult stem cells may work better than embryonic ones for therapeutic purposes, because researchers can harvest them from a patient, modify them, and return them to the patient, eliminating the chance of tissue rejection. (For the lowdown on gene therapy, see Chapter 16.) A potential compromise may be collecting the cells from an umbilical cord after a child is born; these cells are even better than adult stem cells. Stem cells in one form or another may yet find their way into modern medicine, but for now, moral and ethical opposition to the use of embryonic cells stymies stem cell research because most of it depends on the use of embryonic tissues.

Aging Genes

Aging is not for the timid. Skin sags, hair turns gray, joints hurt. Sounds like fun, doesn't it? The effects may be obvious, but the process of *senescence* (the fancy term for aging) is still quite a mystery. Scientists know that the ends of your chromosomes (called *telomeres*) sometimes get shorter as you get older (see Chapter 7), but they aren't sure that those changes are what make old folks old. What is known is that when telomeres get too short, cells die, and cell death is clearly part of the aging process.

The enzyme that can prevent telomeres from shortening, *telomerase* (see Chapter 7), seems an obvious target for anti-aging research. Cells that have active telomerase don't die because of shortened telomeres. For instance, cancer cells often have active telomerase when normal cells don't; telomerase activity contributes to the unwanted longevity that cancer cells enjoy (flip to Chapter 14 for the details). If geneticists can get a handle on telomerase — turning it on where it's wanted without causing cancer — aging may become controllable.

In addition, geneticists have discovered that old cells perk up when put in the company of younger cells. This finding indicates that cells have plenty of capacity to regenerate themselves — they just need a little incentive. Another recent study suggests that calorie restriction in a person's diet also helps defer the effects of aging. Researchers found that when mice were put on a calorie-restricted diet, a gene kicked in to slow programmed cell death (called *apoptosis;* see Chapter 14).

New information on how to prevent aging is in high demand. If keeping young turns out to be as simple as spending time with younger people and eating less, aging may be a lot more fun than it seems.

Proteomics

Genomics, the study of whole genomes, will soon have to make room for the next big thing: *proteomics,* the study of all the proteins an organism makes. Proteins do all the work in your body. They carry out all the functions that genes encode, so when a gene mutation occurs, the protein is what winds up being altered (or goes missing altogether). Given the link between genes and proteins, the study of proteins may end up telling researchers more about genes than the genes themselves!

Proteins are three-dimensional (see Chapter 9 for an explanation). Proteins not only get folded into complex shapes but also get hooked up with other proteins and decorated with other elements such as metals. (See Chapter 9 for more on how proteins are modified from plain amino acid chains to get gussied up to do their jobs.) Currently, scientists can't just look at a protein and tell what its function is. If it's possible to decode them, though, proteins may be a big deal in the fields of medical drugs and treatments, because medications act upon the proteins in your system.

Cataloging all the proteins in your proteome hasn't been easy, because researchers have to sample every tissue to find them all. Nonetheless, the rewards of discovering new drugs and treatments for previously untreatable diseases may make the effort worthwhile. Like personalized medicine, however, proteomics hasn't made a big splash in clinical settings just yet — complexities and technological setbacks have slowed progress.

Bioinformatics

You live in the information age, with practically everything you need at your fingertips. But where genetics is concerned, it's the information overflow age — thousands and thousands of DNA sequences, gobs of proteins, tons of data. It's hard to know where to start or how to sort through the mountains of chatter to get to the real messages. Never fear! *Bioinformatics For Dummies* is here! (I'm not kidding. It's a real *For Dummies* title. For specifics, check out www.dummies.com.)

Bioinformatics is the process of using a computer to sort through massive biological databases. Anyone with an Internet connection can access these databases with the click of a mouse (surf to www.ncbi.nlm.nih.gov to reach the National Center for Biotechnology Information). Hop online and you can search all the results of the entire Human Genome Project, check out the latest gene maps, and look up anything about any disease that has a genetic basis.

Not only that, but bioinformatics gives you ready access to powerful analytical tools — the kind the pros use. Gene hunters use these tools to compare human DNA sequences with those in other animals (see Chapter 8 for a rundown of critters whose DNA has been sequenced). As one of the next big things in genetics, bioinformatics provides the tools to catalog, keep track of, and analyze all the data generated by geneticists the world over. This data is then used for all the applications I cover in this book — from genetic counseling to cloning and beyond.

Gene Chips

Technology is at the heart of modern genetics, and one of the most useful developments in genetic technology is the *gene chip.* Also known as *microarrays,* gene chips allow researchers to quickly determine which genes are at work (that is, being expressed) in a given cell (see Chapter 11 for a full rundown on how your genes do their jobs).

Gene expression depends on messenger RNA (mRNA), which is produced through transcription (see Chapter 9). The mRNAs get tidied up and sent out into the cell cytoplasm to be translated into proteins (see Chapter 10 for how translation works to make proteins). The various mRNAs in each cell tell how many and exactly which of the thousands of genes are at work at any given moment. In addition, the number of copies of each mRNA conveys an index of the strength of gene expression (see Chapter 11 for more on gene expression). The more copies of a particular mRNA, the stronger the action of the gene that produced it.

Gene chips are grids composed of bits of DNA that are complementary to the mRNAs the geneticist expects to find in a cell (I explain the method used to detect the mRNAs in the first place in Chapter 16). It works like this: The bits of DNA are attached to a glass slide. All the mRNAs from a cell are passed over the gene chip, and the mRNAs bind to their DNA complements on the slide. Geneticists measure how many copies of a given mRNA attach themselves to any given spot on the slide to determine which genes are active and what their strength is.

Gene chips are relatively inexpensive to make and can each test hundreds of different mRNAs, making them a valuable tool for gene discovery and mapping. Scientists are also using microarrays to screen thousands of genes rapidly to pick up on mutations that cause diseases, as well as chromosome abnormalities (like those I describe in Chapter 15). One way they perform this screening is by comparing mRNAs from normal cells to those from diseased cells (such as cancer). By comparing the genes that are turned on or off in the two cell types, geneticists can determine what's gone wrong and how the disease may be treated.

Evolution of Antibiotic Resistance

Unfortunately, not all "next big things" are good. Antibiotics are used to fight diseases caused by bacteria. When penicillin (a common antibiotic) was developed, it was a wonder drug that saved thousands and thousands of lives. However, many antibiotics are nearly useless now because of the evolution of *antibiotic resistance*.

Bacteria don't have sex, but they still pass their genes around. They achieve this feat by passing around little circular bits of DNA called *plasmids.* Almost any species of bacteria can pass its plasmids on to any other species. Thus, when bacteria that are resistant to a particular antibiotic run into bacteria that aren't resistant, the exchange of plasmids endows the formerly susceptible bacteria with antibiotic resistance. Antibacterial soaps and the overprescribing of antibiotics make the situation worse by killing off all the nonresistant bacteria, leaving only the resistant kind behind.

Antibiotic-resistant bacteria are showing up not only in hospitals but also in natural environments. Farmers pump their animals full of antibiotics in an effort to keep them free from disease. Thus, antibiotic-resistant bacteria abound in farm sewage, and eventually, the runoff ends up in lakes, streams, and rivers that provide drinking water for humans. Many of those bacteria cause human diseases, and because they start off as antibiotic-resistant bacteria, treating illnesses that they cause is difficult. Meanwhile, scientists work to develop new, more powerful antibiotics in an effort to stay one step ahead of the bacteria.

Genetics of Infectious Disease

I'm guessing that you're too young to remember the flu epidemic of 1918 (I certainly am!). My aunt, who was a schoolteacher in 1918, told me that half the students at her tiny, rural Louisiana school died, along with the school's other teacher. All told, 20 million people worldwide died of the flu in that horrific epidemic. The virus was so deadly that people caught it in the morning and died the same day!

A frightening descendent of the virus that caused the 1918 pandemic is still around. Swine flu turned into a global pandemic in June 2009, affecting thousands of people around the world. Fortunately, this new virus, known as *H1N1,* is not as severe as its predecessor, causing only acute illness in most cases.

Influenza viruses frequently start out as bird diseases (usually carried in the guts of domestic poultry) that move from birds to a new host. Flu viruses pull off this transformation by picking up new genes from the DNA of their hosts or from other viruses. This means that the flu viruses are constantly evolving, changing their surface proteins to allow invasion into new hosts (like pigs and humans) and new organ systems (like airways and lungs).

The 2009 swine flu possesses genes from two different pig flu viruses (that is, viruses that cause influenza in the pigs themselves). Pigs are unusual in that they can contract flu from humans, birds, and one another. After they're infected, pig cells are capable of simultaneously hosting multiple viruses, which allows the viruses to acquire new genes very easily. It's not clear how this swine flu made the jump to humans, though, because pig-to-person transmission is very rare.

Bioterrorism

After September 11, 2001, terrorism moved to the forefront of many people's mind. Hot on the heels of the disaster in New York City was another threat in the form of anthrax-laced letters. (Anthrax is a deadly disease caused by a soil bacterium.) Opening junk mail in the United States went from merely annoying to potentially threatening.

Anthrax and other infectious organisms are potential weapons that can be used by terrorists — a form of warfare called *bioterror.* Suddenly, the researchers working on anthrax genetics — people who had toiled away in underfunded obscurity — were national treasures. U.S. government spending on efforts to counter the bioterror threat shot up. Since 2001, the United

States has spent roughly $50 billion on biodefense, including studies of infectious disease and measures aimed at protecting public health. As a result of these expenditures, scientists are also able to quickly identify the pathogens behind disease outbreaks unrelated to bioterror. For example, researchers identified a new species of Ebola (which causes a nearly always fatal form of hemorrhagic fever) during a 2008 outbreak in Uganda.

Critics have argued that the push for anti-bioterror research means that many important and more immediate problems go unsolved. Furthermore, the bad guys may not even have the technology needed to make the sophisticated biological weapons that big money is spent to counter. Meanwhile, new regulations make research harder to conduct. Scientists can no longer easily exchange biological samples, meaning that the experts can't always get the research materials they need to do their work.

DNA Bar Coding

You're probably familiar with the black and white codes on the packaging of everything you purchase, from peanuts to computers. The computer bar code allows stores to track inventory and pricing of every item they carry. One of the hottest topics in genetics is how the genetic code may be used in a similar way to identify and track living things.

The idea is pretty simple: Using genes in mitochondrial DNA (which you can read about in Chapter 6), scientists look for sequences unique to particular species. After they determine that a sequence reliably identifies a given species of animal, the "bar code" is registered in a database. So far, nearly 65,000 species have been matched with a DNA bar code.

Though the idea behind DNA bar coding is simple, the genetics behind it are amazingly complex. Because practically all organisms carry identical DNA sequences (you and a banana, for example, share over 90 percent of your DNA in common), finding sequences that match up with one, and only one, species has been difficult. For this reason, many researchers criticize the idea. In addition, closely related species rarely interbreed, but they do so often enough that genetic lines are too blurry to make bar coding them reliable. Nonetheless, DNA bar coding has tremendous potential. For example, some genetic sleuthing in 2009 showed that almost half of the New York City sushi restaurants sampled had mislabeled their fish and were even serving up endangered species such as bluefin tuna. Such information may eventually be used to protect fisheries from being overexploited and to protect consumers from being mislead.

Glossary

adenine: Purine base found in DNA and RNA.

allele: Alternative form of a gene.

amino acid: Unit composed of an amino group, a carboxyl group, and a radical group; amino acids link together in chains to form polypeptides.

anaphase: Stage of cell division in mitosis when replicated chromosomes (as chromatids) separate. In meiosis, homologous chromosomes separate during anaphase I, and replicated chromosomes (as chromatids) separate during anaphase II.

aneuploidy: Increase or decrease in the number of chromosomes; a deviation from an exact multiple of the haploid number of chromosomes.

anticipation: Increasing severity or decreasing age of onset of a genetic trait or disorder with successive generations.

anticodon: The three nucleotides in a tRNA (transfer RNA) complementary to a corresponding codon of mRNA.

antiparallel: Parallel but running in opposite directions; orientation of two complementary strands of DNA.

apoptosis: Normal process of regulated cell death.

autosome: A nonsex chromosome.

backcross: Cross between an individual with an F1 genotype and an individual with one of the parental (P) genotypes.

bacteriophage: Virus that infects bacterial cells.

base: One of the three components of a nucleotide. DNA and RNA have four bases.

cell cycle: Repeated process of cell growth, DNA replication, mitosis, and cytokinesis.

centromere: Region at the center of a chromosome that appears pinched during metaphase; where spindle fibers attach during mitosis and meiosis.

chromatid: One half of a replicated chromosome.

chromosome: Linear or circular strand of DNA that contains genes.

codominance: When heterozygotes express both alleles equally.

codon: Combination of three nucleotides in an mRNA that correspond to an amino acid.

complementary: Specific matching of base pairs in DNA or RNA.

consanguineous: Mating by related individuals.

crossing-over: Equal exchange of DNA between homologous chromosomes during meiosis.

cytokinesis: Cell division.

cytosine: A pyrimidine base found in DNA and RNA.

ddNTP: Dideoxyribonucleotide; identical to dNTP but lacking an oxygen at the 3' site. Used in DNA sequencing.

deamination: When a base loses an amino group.

degenerate: Property of the genetic code whereby some amino acids are encoded by more than one codon.

deletion: Mutation resulting in the loss of one or more nucleotides from a DNA sequence.

denaturation: Melting bonds between DNA strands, thereby separating the double helix into single strands.

depurination: When a nucleotide loses a purine base.

dihybrid cross: Cross between two individuals who differ at two traits or loci.

diploid: Possessing two copies of each chromosome.

DNA: Deoxyribonucleic acid; the molecule that carries genetic information.

dNTP: Deoxyribonucleotide; the basic building block of DNA used during DNA replication consisting of a deoxyribose sugar, three phosphate molecules, and one of four nitrogenous bases.

dominant: An allele or phenotype that completely masks another allele or phenotype. The phenotype exhibited by both homozygotes and heterozygotes carrying a dominant allele.

epigenetics: Changes in gene expression and phenotype caused by characteristics of DNA outside the genetic code itself.

epistasis: Gene interaction in which one gene hides the action of another.

eukaryote: Organism with a complex cell structure and a cell nucleus.

euploid: Organism possessing an exact multiple of the haploid number of chromosomes.

exon: Coding part of a gene.

expressivity: Variation in the strength of traits.

F1 generation: First generation offspring of a specific cross.

F2 generation: Offspring of the F1 generation.

gamete: Reproductive cell; sperm or egg cell.

gene: Fundamental unit of heredity. A specific section of DNA within a chromosome.

genome: A particular organism's full set of chromosomes.

genotype: The genetic makeup of an individual. The allele(s) possessed at a given locus.

guanine: Purine base found in DNA and RNA.

gyrase: Enzyme that acts during DNA replication to prevent tangles from forming in the DNA strand.

haploid: Possessing one copy of each chromosome.

helicase: Enzyme that acts during DNA replication to open the double helix.

heterozygote: Individual with two different alleles of a given gene or locus.

homologous chromosomes: Two chromosomes that are identical in shape and structure and carry the same genes. Diploid organisms inherit one homologous chromosome from each parent.

homozygote: Individual with two identical alleles of a given gene or locus.

insertion: Mutation resulting in the addition of one or more nucleotides to a DNA sequence.

interphase: Period of cell growth between divisions.

intron: Noncoding part of a gene. Intervening sequences that interrupt exons.

ligase: Enzyme that acts during replication to seal gaps created by lagging strand DNA synthesis.

linkage: Inheriting genes located close together on chromosomes as a unit.

locus: A specific location on a chromosome.

meiosis: Cell division in sexually reproducing organisms that reduces amount of genetic information by half.

metaphase: Stage of cell division when chromosomes align along the equator of the dividing cell.

mitosis: Simple cell division without a reduction in chromosome number.

nucleotide: Building block of DNA; composed of a deoxyribose sugar, a phosphate, and one of four nitrogenous bases.

P generation: Parental generation in a genetic cross.

penetrance: Percentage of individuals with a particular genotype that express the trait.

phenotype: Physical characteristics of an individual.

polypeptide: Chain of amino acids that form a protein.

prokaryote: Organism with a simple cell structure and no cell nucleus.

prophase: Stage of cell division when chromosomes contract and become visible and nuclear membrane begins to break down. In meiosis, crossing-over takes place during prophase.

purine: Compound composed of two rings.

pyrimidine: Chemicals that have a single, six-sided ring structure.

recessive: A phenotype or allele exhibited only by homozygotes.

replication: Process of making an exact copy of a DNA molecule.

RNA: Ribonucleic acid; the single-stranded molecule that transfers information carried by DNA to the protein-manufacturing part of the cell.

telomere: Tip of a chromosome.

telophase: Stage of cell division when chromosomes relax and the nuclear membrane re-forms.

thymine: Pyrimidine base found in DNA but not RNA.

totipotent: A cell that can develop into any type of cell.

uracil: Pyrimidine base found in RNA but not DNA.

zygote: Fertilized egg resulting from the fusion of a sperm and egg cell.

Index

Notes

Notes

Notes

Notes

Notes

Notes

Notes

Notes

Notes

Notes

Notes

Notes

Notes

Notes

Notes

Notes

CPSIA information can be obtained
at www.ICGtesting.com
Printed in the USA
FSHW020103090120
65807FS

9 781118 895467